International Marketing

D0764455

Book Activation Key

011   WT3ABS

This key activates your online textbook.
Scratch off gray area above to see your book activation key. If the key is
already visible, then it has been used and is no longer valid. Contact us at
www.atomicdog.com or **800-310-5661 x6** to order your online textbook.

International Marketing

Managing Worldwide Operations in a Changing International Environment

Dana-Nicoleta Lascu

University of Richmond

Cincinnati, Ohio
www.atomicdog.com

Copyright © 2003 by Atomic Dog Publishing. All rights reserved.

Library of Congress Control Number: 2002108526

ISBN 1-931442-59-2

No part of this publication may be reproduced, stored in a retrieval system, or transmitted, in any form
or by any means, electronic, mechanical, photocopying, recording, or otherwise, without the prior
written permission of the publisher.

Printed in the United States of America by Atomic Dog Publishing,
1203 Main Street, Third Floor, Cincinnati, OH 45202

10 9 8 7 6 5 4 3 2

Dedication

This book is dedicated to the memory of Valeria and Isidor Lupse, who fostered an imaginative environment, who taught me that anything was possible, and who shielded me from fear (during the invasion of Czechoslovakia, they told me that all the airplanes overhead were going to America, the land of the new world); to the memory of Daniel Suguru, my close friend and one of the first victims of AIDS; to Aloys Nyabutsitsi and his family, who lost their lives for being proud members of the Watutsi tribe; and to Ofra Haza and Umm Kulthoum, the divas of music who inspired the world to unite through song.

Brief Contents

Preface xv
About the Author xvii

Part 1

Introduction to International Marketing   1

1 Scope, Concepts, and Drivers of International Marketing   3

Part 2

The International Marketing Environment   17

2 An Overview of the International Marketing Environment   19

3 International Trade: Barriers and Facilitators   43

4 Regional Economic and Political Integration   67

5 Cultural Influences on International Marketing   85

Part 3

International Marketing Strategy Decisions   111

6 International Marketing Research: Practices and Challenges   113

7 International Marketing Segmentation, Targeting, and Positioning   145

8 The International Marketing Plan and Entry Mode Selection   163

Part 4

Managing the International Marketing Mix   179

9 Products and Services: Branding Decisions in International Markets   181

10 International Product and Service Strategies   199

11 Managing International Distribution Operations and Logistics   219

12 International Retailing   231

13 The International Promotional Mix and Advertising Strategies   251

14 International Publicity, Public Relations, and Sales Promotion Strategies   271

15 International Personal Selling and Personnel Management   283

16 International Pricing Strategy   297

Part 5

International Marketing Strategy: Implementation   313

17 Organizing and Controlling International Marketing Operations and Developing an International Marketing Plan   315

Appendix   325
Glossary   379
Index   397

vii

Contents

Preface   xv
About the Author   xvii

Part 1

Introduction to International Marketing   1

Chapter 1

**Scope, Concepts, and Drivers
of International Marketing   3**

Learning Objectives   4
1-1 The Importance of International Marketing   5
1-2 Levels of International Marketing Involvement   5
1-3 The EPRG Framework and International
    Marketing Concepts   6
    1-3a Ethnocentric Orientation   6
    1-3b Polycentric Orientation   7
    1-3c Regiocentric Orientation   7
    1-3d Geocentric Orientation   8
1-4 Drivers of International Expansion   8
    1-4a Drivers in the Business Environment   9
    1-4b Firm-Specific Drivers   12
1-5 Obstacles to Internationalization   13
    1-5a Self-Reference Criterion   13
    1-5b Government Barriers   14
    1-5c International Competition   14
Chapter Summary   15
Discussion Questions   16

Part 2

The International Marketing Environment   17

Chapter 2

**An Overview of the International
Marketing Environment   19**

Learning Objectives   20
2-1 The Economic Environment
    of International Marketing   21
    2-1a The World Economy   21
    2-1b The Economic Development Disparity   21
2-2 Perspectives on Economic Development   22
    2-2a The Rostow Modernization Model   22
    2-2b The Marxist-Leninist Model of Economic
        Development   23
    2-2c Development Philosophies and the Developing
        World   24
2-3 Levels of Economic Development   26
    2-3a The Importance of Emerging Markets   27
2-4 The Political Environment of International
    Marketing   28
    2-4a Political Risk: An Overview   29
    2-4b Nationalism   31
    2-4c Political Risks and Risk Management
        in International Marketing   32
2-5 The International Legal Environment   35
    2-5a Legal Systems   35
    2-5b Jurisdiction   36
    2-5c Intellectual Property Rights Protection   37
    2-5d Home-Country Legislation Affecting
        Multinational Firms Operating Overseas   40
Chapter Summary   41
Discussion Questions   42

Chapter 3

International Trade: Barriers and Facilitators 43

Learning Objectives 44
3-1 Arguments for Protectionism 45
   3-1a Protection of Markets with Excess Productive
      Capacity 46
   3-1b Employment Protection and Protection of Markets
      with Excess Labor 46
   3-1c Infant Industry Arguments and Arguments
      Related to the Industrialization
      of Developing Countries 46
   3-1d Natural Resources Conservation and Protection
      of the Environment 46
   3-1e Protection of Consumers 47
   3-1f National Defense Interests 47
3-2 Tools of Government Protectionism:
    Tariff and Nontariff Barriers 47
   3-2a Tariffs 47
   3-2b Nontariff Barriers 48
3-3 Facilitators of International Trade 54
   3-3a International Trade and Economic
      Development Organizations 54
   3-3b Government Organizations 60
   3-3c Other Institutions and Procedures Facilitating
      International Trade 62
Chapter Summary 65
Discussion Questions 66

Chapter 4

Regional Economic and Political Integration 67

Learning Objectives 68
4-1 Determinants of Economic and Political
    Integration 69
   4-1a A Common Culture 69
   4-1b A History of Common Economic
      and Political Dominance 69
   4-1c Regional Proximity 69
   4-1d Economic Considerations 70
   4-1e Political Considerations 70
4-2 Levels of Regional Economic
    and/or Political Integration
    and Examples of Integration Successes 71
   4-2a Bilateral Agreements and Multilateral Forums
      and Agreements 71
   4-2b Free Trade Agreements 73
   4-2c Customs Unions 76
   4-2d Common Markets 76
   4-2e Monetary Union 78
   4-2f Political Union 80
Chapter Summary 84
Discussion Questions 84

Chapter 5

Cultural Influences on International Marketing 85

Learning Objectives 86
5-1 Culture Defined 87
5-2 Elements of Culture 88
   5-2a Language 88
   5-2b Religion 92
   5-2c Cultural Values 95
   5-2d Cultural Norms: Imperatives, Exclusives,
      and Adiaphoras 96
   5-2e National/Regional Character 98
5-3 Cultural Variability 103
   5-3a The Hofstede Dimensions 103
5-4 Cultural Change and Marketing 105
5-5 The Self-Reference Criterion and Ethnocentrism 106
5-6 The Global Consumer Culture 108
Chapter Summary 109
Discussion Questions 110

Part 3

International Marketing Strategy Decisions 111

Chapter 6

**International Marketing Research:
Practices and Challenges 113**

Learning Objectives 114
6-1 The Need for International Marketing Research 115
6-2 Defining International Marketing Research 115
6-3 The Scope of International Marketing Research 116
   6-3a Research of Industry, Market Characteristics,
      and Market Trends 116
   6-3b Buyer Behavior Research 116
   6-3c Product Research 117
   6-3d Distribution Research 119
   6-3e Promotion Research 121
   6-3f Pricing Research 122
6-4 The International Marketing Research Process 123
   6-4a Defining the Research Problem and Research
      Objectives 123
   6-4b Developing the Research Plan 124
   6-4c Deciding on Information Sources 124
   6-4d Determining Research Approaches 131
   6-4e Designing the Data Collection Instrument 137
   6-4f Deciding on the Sampling Plan 139
   6-4g Collecting, Analyzing, and Interpreting
      the Information 139
6-5 Decision Support Systems for Global Marketing 140
   6-5a Sales Forecasting 141
Chapter Summary 143
Discussion Questions 144

Chapter 7

International Marketing Segmentation, Targeting, and Positioning 145

Learning Objectives 146
7-1 The Rationale for Target Marketing 147
7-2 International Market Segmentation 147
  7-2a Requirements for International Segmentation 147
  7-2b Macro-Segmentation: Country Attractiveness Analysis 149
  7-2c Micro-Segmentation: Focusing on the Target Consumer 152
7-3 Targeting International Consumers 156
  7-3a Target Market Decisions: Country Screening and Selection 156
  7-3b Target Market Decisions: The Target Market Strategy 157
7-4 Positioning the Brand 159
  7-4a Attribute/Benefit Positioning 159
  7-4b Price/Quality Positioning 160
  7-4c Use or Applications Positioning 160
  7-4d Product User Positioning 160
  7-4e Product Class Positioning 161
  7-4f Competitor Positioning 161
Chapter Summary 161
Discussion Questions 162

Chapter 8

The International Marketing Plan and Entry Mode Selection 163

Learning Objectives 164
8-1 Developing an International Marketing Strategy 165
8-2 Developing an International Marketing Plan 165
8-3 Deciding on the International Entry Mode 168
  8-3a Indirect Exporting 168
  8-3b Direct Exporting 169
  8-3c Licensing 169
  8-3d Franchising 170
  8-3e Joint Ventures 172
  8-3f Consortia 175
  8-3g Wholly Owned Subsidiaries 175
  8-3h Branch Offices 176
  8-3i Strategic Alliances 176
Chapter Summary 177
Discussion Questions 178

Part 4

Managing the International Marketing Mix 179

Chapter 9

Products and Services: Branding Decisions in International Markets 181

Learning Objectives 182
9-1 Standardization Versus Adaptation 183
  9-1a Global Standardization 183
  9-1b Regional Standardization 185
  9-1c Global Localization 186
  9-1d Mandatory Adaptation 188
  9-1e Local, Nonmandatory Adaptation 188
9-2 Private-Label (Retailer) Brands 188
9-3 Global Branding and Country-of-Origin Information 189
  9-3a Product-Country and Service-Country Stereotypes 190
  9-3b Country of Origin and Ethnocentrism 192
9-4 The Service Side: Tariff and Nontariff Barriers to Entry 193
9-5 Products, Services, and Culture 193
9-6 Protecting Brand Names 194
  9-6a Identifying Types of Counterfeiting 195
  9-6b Combating Counterfeiting 196
Chapter Summary 197
Discussion Questions 198

Chapter 10

International Product and Service Strategies 199

Learning Objectives 200
10-1 The International Product Life Cycle (IPLC) 201
  10-1a The Product Introduction Stage 202
  10-1b The Growth Stage 202
  10-1c The Maturity Stage 202
  10-1d The Decline Stage 203
10-2 Managing the International Product and Service Mix 203
  10-2a Length 204
  10-2b Width 204
  10-2c Depth 204
10-3 New Product Development 204
  10-3a Generating New Product Ideas 206
  10-3b Screening New Product Ideas 208
  10-3c Developing and Evaluating Concepts 209
  10-3d Performing a Product Business Analysis 209
  10-3e Designing and Developing the Product 209
  10-3f Test Marketing 210
  10-3g Launching the Product Internationally 212

10-4 Degree of Product/Service Newness 213
10-5 Product Diffusion 215
    10-5a Product Factors 215
    10-5b Country (Market) Factors 215
    10-5c Consumer Adopters 216
Chapter Summary 217
Discussion Questions 218

Chapter 11

**Managing International Distribution Operations
and Logistics 219**

Learning Objectives 220
11-1 Issues Related to International Distribution 221
    11-1a Using Established Channels 221
    11-1b Building Own Channels 221
11-2 Middlemen Involved in International
        Distribution 221
    11-2a Home-Country Middlemen 222
    11-2b Foreign-Country Middlemen 224
    11-2c Alternative International Distribution
            Structures 224
11-3 Facilitators of International Distribution
        and Logistics 224
    11-3a Distribution Centers 225
    11-3b Transportation Firms 225
    11-3c Home-Country and Foreign-Country Freight
            Forwarders and Customs Brokers 225
    11-3d Government Agencies 225
    11-3e Nongovernmental Organizations 226
    11-3f Other Service Providers 227
    11-3g Logistics Alliances 227
11-4 Challenges to International Distribution
        and Logistics 227
    11-4a Challenges to Distribution in Developing
            Countries 227
    11-4b Parallel Imports 227
Chapter Summary 230
Discussion Questions 230

Chapter 12

International Retailing 231

Learning Objectives 232
12-1 International Expansion of Retailers 233
12-2 International Retailing Defined 234
12-3 Retail Formats: Variations in Different Markets 234
    12-3a General Merchandise Retailing 234
    12-3b Food Retailers 241
    12-3c Nonstore Retailing 244

12-4 Issues in International Retailing 247
    12-4a Legislation and Regulation 247
    12-4b Taxation and Cross-Border Shopping 248
    12-4c Variation in Retail Practices: A Consumer
            Perspective 248
    12-4d Variation in Retail Practice: Salespeople
            and Management 249
Chapter Summary 250
Discussion Questions 250

Chapter 13

**The International Promotional Mix
and Advertising Strategies 251**

Learning Objectives 252
13-1 The International Promotional Mix 253
13-2 The International Communication Process 253
13-3 Advertising 256
    13-3a The Media Infrastructure 256
    13-3b The Advertising Infrastructure 264
    13-3c The Advertising Strategy 266
Chapter Summary 269
Discussion Questions 269

Chapter 14

**International Publicity, Public Relations,
and Sales Promotion Strategies 271**

Learning Objectives 272
14-1 Publicity and Public Relations 273
    14-1a Publicity 273
    14-1b Public Relations 274
14-2 Consumer Sales Promotion 276
    14-2a Adaptation of Sales Promotion 276
    14-2b The Online Venue for Sales Promotion 278
    14-2c Legal and Ethical Issues in Consumer
            Sales Promotion 278
    14-2d The Future of Consumer Sales Promotion 279
14-3 International Trade Promotion (Trade Shows
        and Exhibitions) 279
Chapter Summary 281
Discussion Questions 281

Chapter 15

**International Personal Selling
and Personnel Management 283**

Learning Objectives 284
15-1 International Presence and Personnel Issues 285
    15-1a Expatriates 285
    15-1b Host-Country Nationals (Locals) 287
    15-1c A Recent Alternative: Long-Distance
            International Selling 287

15-2 Managing International Employees 288
   15-2a Managing Relationships 288
   15-2b Understanding the International Buyer-Seller
      Relationship 288
   15-2c Understanding Cultural Values and the
      Relationship between Buyer and Seller 289
15-3 Successfully Managing Expatriates 290
   15-3a Recruiting Expatriates 290
   15-3b Attenuating Culture Shock 291
   15-3c Training for International Assignments 292
   15-3d Motivating Expatriates 292
   15-3e Obstacles to the International Sales Mission 294
   15-3f Repatriation Issues 294
Chapter Summary 295
Discussion Questions 296

Chapter 16

International Pricing Strategy 297

Learning Objectives 298
16-1 Pricing Decisions and Internal Challenges
    of Multinational Firms 299
   16-1a Production Facilities 299
   16-1b Ability to Keep Track of Costs 299
16-2 Environment-Related Challenges and Pricing
    Decisions 299
   16-2a The Competitive Environment 300
   16-2b The Political and Legal Environment 302
   16-2c The Economic and Financial Environment 303
16-3 International Pricing Decisions 308
   16-3a Price Setting 308
   16-3b Aggressive Export Pricing 308
   16-3c Standardized Pricing Versus Local Pricing 309
   16-3d Penetration Pricing and Skimming
      Strategies 310
Chapter Summary 310
Discussion Questions 311

Part 5

**International Marketing Strategy:
Implementation 313**

Chapter 17

**Organizing and Controlling International
Marketing Operations and Developing
an International Marketing Plan 315**

Learning Objectives 316
17-1 Organizing for International Marketing
    Operations 317
   17-1a Factors in the Firm's Environment 317
   17-1b Factors within the Firm 317

17-2 Examining International Organizational Designs 318
   17-2a The International Division Structure 318
   17-2b The Worldwide Regional Division Structure 318
   17-2c The Product Division Structure 318
   17-2d The Matrix Structure 319
17-3 Controlling International Marketing Operations 319
   17-3a Formal Controls 320
   17-3b Informal Controls 321
17-4 Devising the International Marketing Plan 321
   17-4a Company and Country Background 322
   17-4b Environmental Analysis 322
   17-4c International Marketing Mix Decisions 322
   17-4d Establishing Methods for Control
      of the International Operation 322
Chapter Summary 324
Discussion Questions 324

Appendix 325
A: Munich Re 327
B: Bavarian Motor Works: Diversifying a
    Prestige Brand 333
C: Campina, Naturally 341
D: Royal Philips Electronics 349
E. Hilton Sorrento Palace: Changing
    Targeting Strategies 355
F: AvtoVAZ: Maintaining Local Competitive
    Advantage 361
G: Disneyland Resort Paris: Reinventing the Mouse
    for the European Market 367
H: Siemens: International Entry Modes and the
    Siemens Umbrella Brand 373

Glossary **379**
Index **397**

Preface

Preface

International marketing represents my area of didactic concentration and reflects my research positioning in the marketing academic spectrum. In the process of teaching an international marketing course for more than a decade, I attempted to find the ideal textbook for my students, one that challenged them and interested them the most. Although I could not settle on one text, the early 1990s offered an opportunity: None of the available textbooks addressed the rapid changes in the political, legal, and financial environment. Most made no mention of the transformation of Central and Eastern Europe, the GATT Uruguay Round, and the formation of the European Monetary Union. At that point, I wrote the missing chapters, using them as handouts in class. That effort marked the incipient stage of the current textbook: It germinated the thought that writing an international textbook might be something of long-term interest.

International Marketing: Managing Worldwide Operations in a Changing International Environment reflects my teaching philosophy: creating vivid, memorable examples that help students retain international marketing theory and facts. I have spent time with local students and students from the United States in different countries and acted, in turn, as a student of their impressions and reactions. I use in the text the more memorable aspects of these experiences—those that had the most resonance in my international marketing class—to ensure that the notions explained in the text come to life for university-level students. I also share my own perspectives as a product of different cultures who has experienced and observed marketing on four continents, and both as an expatriate and as a local who has functioned under a free-market system and under a repressive, anti-consumerist command economy. These experiences are further supplemented with material collected in my recent research and other fieldwork and with materials obtained from various international sources: newspapers and magazines (*The Financial Times, Le Monde, The Economist, The International Herald Tribune, Wall Street Journal Europe and Asia, Frankfurter Allgemeine, Süddeutsche Zeitung, Die Zeit, L'Express, Le Point, Jeune Afrique,* and local and international fashion magazines); government and non-governmental organizations' publications (World Bank, United Nations Development Program, among others); as well as publications aimed at expatriates (*Delegates' World, Le Monde Diplomatique*).

The text adopts strategic, applications-oriented approaches to country- and region-specific environments. These are also illustrated with interviews conducted for the textbook and for the case studies in the instructor's manual with international and local (national) marketing managers and with marketing theorists who uphold different international marketing philosophies. And interviews with consumers are used to illustrate a number of consumer behavior issues in the chapters.

Online and in Print

International Marketing: Managing Worldwide Operations in a Changing International Environment is available online as well as in print. The online chapters demonstrate how the interactive media components of the text enhance presentation and understanding. For example,

- Animated illustrations help to clarify concepts.

- Clickable glossary terms provide immediate definitions of key concepts.

- The search function allows you to quickly locate discussions of specific topics throughout the text.

You may choose to use just the online version of the text, or both the online and print versions together. This gives you the flexibility to choose which combination of resources works best for you. To assist those who use the online and print versions together, the primary heads and subheads in each chapter are numbered the same. For example, the first primary head in Chapter 1 is labeled 1-1, the second primary head in this chapter is labeled 1-2, and so on. The subheads build from the designation of their corresponding primary head: 1-1a, 1-1b, etc. This numbering system is designed to make moving between the online and print versions as seamless as possible.

Finally, next to a number of figures in the print version of the text, you will see an interactive figure icon like the one on the left. The icon indicates that this figure in the online version of the text is interactive in a way that applies, illustrates, or reinforces the concept.

Acknowledgments

I would like to express my gratitude for all the support I have received in building this textbook. My thanks go to the team at Atomic Dog Publishing for all their support and guidance in the process of accomplishing this project. Steve Scoble and Kendra Leonard were instrumental in the materialization of the text; without their support through each stage of the project, this book could not have become a reality. I would also like to thank Charles Hutchinson, Nicky Hardy, and Victoria Putman for their dedicated work and for sharing their talent on this project. I would like to thank my international marketing students throughout the years and my current students and student assistants[1] for their valuable feedback; Mrs. Sandra Blanchard for all her support and dedication during the creation of this text; my colleague and former chairman, Harold Babb, and my dean, Karen Newman, and former dean, Randolph New, for their support throughout the text development process. My thanks go to my husband, Bram Opstelten, for his extensive input on all the chapters and for his support throughout the years that this text took to develop (I could not have done it without him), and to Michael and Daniel for forcing me to be aware of children's programming and products in all the countries where we have traveled. I would also like to thank my parents, Lucia and Damian Lascu, for the formidable international experiences that this book is based on and for creating and facilitating the foundations for this text.

[1]Tiffany Allen, Joanna Applegate, Anne Carson Crumley, Kristin DeYonker, Jessica DiTommaso, Franklin Fowler, Andrea Fuller, Ryan Ganley, Christianne Goldman, Catherine Hopkins, Kimberly Hribar, Elizabeth Manera, Paula Munafo, Lisa Myers, Pascal Ontijd, George Papalexandratos, Akshay Patil, Leslie Ramich, Taylor Roberts, Kerrie Robinson, Teri Schrettenbruner, Brian Stroop, Amber Summers, Brian Thoms, Maria Vornovitsky, Elise Woodling, and Sean Wygovsky.

About the Author

Dana-Nicoleta Lascu

University of Richmond

Dana-Nicoleta Lascu is associate professor of marketing and chair of the marketing department at the University of Richmond, in Richmond, Virginia. She has a Ph.D. in marketing from the University of South Carolina, a Master of International Management with concentrations in marketing and finance from the American Graduate School of International Management (Thunderbird), and a B.A. in English and French from the University of Arizona. She has taught international marketing at the University of Richmond for more than a decade and has published her research in international marketing in journals such as *International Marketing Review, International Business Review, European Journal of Marketing, Journal of Euromarketing, Journal of International Consumer Marketing, Journal of Teaching in International Business,* and *Multinational Business Review.* She has organized a number of international conferences and published related proceedings (among them, the 1996 World Business Congress, in Bermuda, and the Sixth Conference on Marketing and Development, 1997, in Romania) and has participated as track chair, session chair, or conference co-chair in numerous other national and international conferences. She is on the editorial board of a number of international marketing journals.

Dana Lascu worked previously as a simultaneous and consecutive translator (in English, French, and Romanian) for the Romanian government (the Central Committee of the Youth Union and the Ministry of Foreign Trade) and for the United Nations, Kigali, Rwanda, where she translated documents for the 1982 Round Table for International Aid. She also worked in international training in the United States, teaching managerial skills to civil servants from developing countries and developing related training proposals.

Part 1

Introduction to International Marketing

Chapter 1
Scope, Concepts, and Drivers
of International Marketing

Scope, Concepts, and Drivers of International Marketing

Key Terms

domestic marketing
drivers in the business
   environment
driver of internationalization
ethnocentric orientation
export marketing
firm-specific drivers
geocentric orientation

global marketing
international marketing
multinational marketing
obstacles to internationalization
polycentric orientation
regiocentric orientation
self-reference criterion

Outline

Learning Objectives
1-1 The Importance of
   International Marketing
1-2 Levels of International
   Marketing Involvement
1-3 The EPRG Framework and
   International Marketing
   Concepts
   1-3a Ethnocentric Orientation
   1-3b Polycentric Orientation
   1-3c Regiocentric Orientation
   1-3d Geocentric Orientation
1-4 Drivers of International
   Expansion
   *1-4a Drivers in the Business
     Environment*
   1-4b Firm-Specific Drivers
1-5 Obstacles to
   Internationalization
   1-5a Self-Reference Criterion
   1-5b Government Barriers
   1-5c International Competition
Chapter Summary
Discussion Questions

Learning Objectives

Learning Objectives

By the end of this chapter, you should be able to:

- Define international marketing and identify the different levels of international involvement
- Describe the different company orientations and philosophies toward international marketing

- Identify environmental and firm-specific drivers that direct firms toward international markets
- Identify obstacles preventing firms from engaging in successful international ventures

More than ever before, firms are looking for success beyond their national borders, partnering with foreign firms, or entering new markets on their own. In the past, internationalization was an option for large firms that had the necessary resources to enter and develop new markets. Today, small and medium-size businesses have access to international markets and can benefit from new venues—e.g., the Internet—and new markets—e.g., emerging markets worldwide—for selling their products.

Companies can look at international markets as a possible venue for distributing overproduction. Alternatively, they can look at the international market as a source of limitless opportunity—Federal Express, when assessing its growth opportunities, states: "International, sky is the limit."[1]

Federal Express has traditionally pursued markets only in industrialized countries. In many developing countries (in Sub-Saharan Africa, for example), its competitor, DHL, was the first to enter the market, securing business from the national government, to the expatriate community, to local and international businesses operating there. When Federal Express decided these markets had potential, it had to spend large amounts of money to promote its services in these developing countries and to gain access there. Similarly, Pepsi set up a strategic alliance with government agencies in Central and Eastern Europe in the late 1960s, at a time when Coca-Cola did not consider communist countries in Europe as an attractive investment venue. As a first mover into this market, Pepsi was able to secure exclusive access and effectively blocked Coca-Cola's access for decades. In the 1990s, when these markets opened their doors to foreign investment, Coca-Cola had to spend huge amounts of money to overtake Pepsi's lead in these markets, with limited success.

This chapter will introduce the different internationalization philosophies of international firms and address the drivers (environmental and firm-specific) of and obstacles to international expansion.

---

1. FedEx Corporation Presents, internal presentation.

1-1 The Importance of International Marketing

The United States constitutes one of the most important world markets, providing and consuming a high percentage of worldwide products and services. With time, it has become evident, however, that this percentage is getting smaller: less than 25 percent. For companies to achieve their full potential and to effectively compete with foreign companies in the same league, it is crucial that they expand into international markets to take advantage of global market opportunities, to keep pace with competition, and to maximize the potential of their product mix.

Throughout history, companies have achieved worldwide dominance in spite of the smaller size of their country of origin and their home country's limited market; it should be noted, however, that an international presence was essential for their success. Successful global companies from the Netherlands, a smaller country in Western Europe, have become giants of industry worldwide. Among them are Philips (electronics), Royal Ahold (retail), Royal Dutch/Shell (petrol; Netherlands/United Kingdom), and Unilever (consumer products; Netherlands/United Kingdom). Japanese firms dominate many industries; among them are Mitsui and Mitsubishi (electronics, banking, import-export, among others), Dentsu (advertising), Sony and Panasonic (electronics), Ito Yokado (retail)—and the list continues.

International companies such as General Motors, Mitsubishi, Microsoft, and Exxon earn profits greater than the Gross Domestic Product of many developing countries; and their total market value is several times the size of their profits. Even successful small businesses can attribute their survival and/or success to international markets. Companies, in order to achieve their potential, must constantly monitor the international environment for opportunities. Recently, privatization in countries where government monopolies have dominated for decades has made it possible for multinationals to compete for local airline, railway, and telecommunications industries. In the future, postal services might constitute the new competitive territory of international companies.

1-2 Levels of International Marketing Involvement

All companies are affected by elements of the international marketing environment. In terms of international marketing involvement, however, companies have different degrees of commitment. A company engaging in **domestic marketing** has the least commitment to international marketing. This company is focusing solely on domestic consumers and on the home-country environment. The home-country environment, however, is affected by developments in the international environment; furthermore, the local company is directly affected by local competition, which could come from global companies.

At the next level, **export marketing,** a firm could be involved in exporting, indirectly, through orders from international clients, or directly: The company actively seeks international clients. For both export marketers and domestic marketers, the international market constitutes an extension of the domestic market, and is not given special consideration. Such firms have an ethnocentric philosophy to internationalization, as will be shown in section 1-3a, "Ethnocentric Orientation."

International marketing activities require a substantial focus on international consumers in a particular country or countries (when more countries are involved, international marketing is often referred to as **multinational marketing**). International marketing is thus defined as the processes involved in the creation, production, distribution, promotion, and pricing of products, services,

Domestic marketing Marketing that is focused solely on domestic consumers and on the home-country environment.

Export marketing Involvement in international marketing limited to the exporting function; although the firm actively seeks international clients, it considers the international market an extension of the domestic market and does not give it special consideration.

International marketing The processes involved in the creation, production, distribution, promotion, and pricing of products, services, ideas, and experiences for international markets; these processes require a substantial focus on international consumers in a particular country or countries.

Multinational marketing Marketing in different countries without coordinating across operations.

ideas, and experiences for international markets. The international company is present in different countries with sales offices and subsidiaries, or is an active partner in strategic alliances with local companies. It is important to note that, in this case, international activities are not coordinated across the different countries, nor across different regions. An international company, according to this definition, has a polycentric or regiocentric philosophy to internationalization, as will be seen in sections 1-3b, "Polycentric Orientation," and 1-3c, "Regiocentric Orientation."

Global marketing International marketing activities that do not have a country or region focus and that are possible due to the emergence of global consumer segments and efficient global allocation of company talent and resources.

Global marketing involves marketing activities across different countries without focusing primarily on national or regional segmentation. Global marketing is possible due to the emergence of global consumer segments, and due to efficient global allocation of company talent and resources. A company engaging in global marketing has a geocentric philosophy to internationalization.

It should be noted, however, that the terms defined in the preceding paragraphs are often used interchangeably by nonbusiness and business alike—even by international managers. "International," "global," and "multinational" are used to refer to any company crossing borders, without particular reference to the global strategy used. The descriptions of the levels of international marketing involvement should primarily guide one to understand when distinctions are made. A superior approach to distinguishing between companies' international orientation and philosophy is the EPRG Framework.

1-3 The EPRG Framework and International Marketing Concepts

Management's orientation toward the internationalization of the firm's operations affects each of the functional areas of the firm, and, as such, has a direct impact on the marketing functions within the firm. Management's philosophy on international involvement affects decisions such as the firm's response to global threats and opportunities and related resource allocation. Companies' philosophies on international involvement can be described, based on the EPRG Framework, as ethnocentric, polycentric, regiocentric, and geocentric.[2]

1-3a Ethnocentric Orientation

Ethnocentric orientation Company strategies consistent with the belief that domestic strategies, techniques, and personnel are superior to foreign ones and therefore provide the most effective framework for the company's overseas involvement; companies adopting this perspective view international operations and customers as secondary to domestic operations and customers.

Eli Lilly is an ethnocentric firm.[3] Top management at Eli Lilly places most of the emphasis on product research and development, in an effort to bring to the marketplace high-performance pharmaceutical products. Firms with an **ethnocentric orientation** are guided by a *domestic market extension concept:* In general, top management of firms with an ethnocentric orientation consider that domestic strategies, techniques, and personnel are superior to foreign ones, and therefore provide the most effective framework for the company's overseas involvement; consequently, international operations and customers are considered secondary to domestic operations and customers.[4] Ethnocentric firms are likely to be highly centralized, and consider that the purpose of their international operations is to identify markets that could absorb surplus domestic production; alternatively,

---

2. Howard Perlmutter, "The Tortuous Evolution of the Multinational Corporation," *Columbia Journal of World Business,* January–February 1969.

3. Thomas W. Malnight, "Globalization of an Ethnocentric Firm: An Evolutionary Perspective," *Strategic Management Journal,* Vol. 16, No. 2, February 1995, pp. 119–142.

4. David J. Lemak and Wiboon Arunthanes, "Global Business Strategy: A Contingency Approach," *Multinational Business Review,* Vol. 5, No. 1, Spring 1997, pp. 26–37.

international operations could represent a cash cow that generates revenue and necessitates only minimal attention and investment. Consequently, plans for international markets are developed primarily in-house, by an international division, and are similar to those for the domestic market.[5] Firms in the tobacco industry,[6] as well as firms at the forefront of technology, tend to have an ethnocentric marketing orientation.

It should be mentioned that, often, ethnocentric firms approach globalization by internationalizing at the level of the function, rather than the firm; for example, the marketing department may have a geocentric strategy even if top management has an ethnocentric orientation.[7]

1-3b Polycentric Orientation

Firms with a **polycentric orientation** are guided by a *multidomestic market concept.* Managers of polycentric firms are very much aware of the importance of individual international markets to the success of their business and are likely to establish individual businesses, typically wholly owned subsidiaries or marketing subsidiaries, in each of the countries where they operate. The assumption the company makes is that each market is unique and needs to be addressed individually. Consequently, the company is fully decentralized and engages in minimal coordination with the headquarters.

Each subsidiary has its own marketing plans and objectives and operates autonomously as an independent profit center on an individual country basis to achieve its goals; all marketing activities are performed in each country independently of the company headquarters.[8] To address local consumer needs, marketing research is conducted independently in each overseas market, and products are fully adapted to meet these needs, or even separate product lines are developed to meet the needs of the individual markets.

In the process of developing individual strategies for each market, the company does not coordinate activities across the different countries and cannot benefit from economies of scale that such coordination would allow. Furthermore, numerous functions are duplicated, and, ultimately, final product costs are higher to the end consumer. For decades, Ford used a polycentric strategy in meeting the needs of budget-conscious consumers by developing a Ford Escort automobile for the United Kingdom that looked different from the one sold in the United States or Southeast Asia.[9] Currently, the automobile addressing the needs of the budget-conscious consumer, the Ford Focus, looks identical in each market: Ford has adopted a geocentric approach to product development.

1-3c Regiocentric Orientation

Firms with a regiocentric or a geocentric orientation are guided by a *global marketing concept.* Companies adopting a **regiocentric orientation** view world regions as distinct markets that share economic, political, and/or cultural traits such that they would be viable candidates for a regionwide marketing approach. A regiocentric orientation is now possible due to the success of regional economic and political integration that allows for implementing a uniform marketing strategy in the entire region. Member countries of the European Union, for example,

Polycentric orientation
Company strategies predicated on the assumption that each country's market is unique and should be addressed individually, with a country-specific marketing mix.

Regiocentric orientation
Company strategies that view world regions as distinct markets that share economic, political, and/or cultural traits that will respond to a regionwide marketing approach.

---

5. Ibid.

6. Ibid.

7. Malnight, "Globalization of an Ethnocentric Firm," pp. 119–142.

8. Lemak and Arunthanes, "Global Business Strategy," pp. 26–37.

9. Ibid.

are candidates for Pan-European marketing strategies, whereas signatory countries of the North American Free Trade Agreement lend themselves to a successful marketing strategy aimed at the North American market. PepsiCo appears to have a regiocentric orientation: Its divisions are organized based on location, with regional offices coordinating all local marketing activities. For example, Pepsi's East European operations are coordinated by its Vienna (Austria) office, which devises the company's regional objectives and oversees the implementation of the company's marketing strategy in the region.

1-3d Geocentric Orientation

Geocentric orientation
Company strategies that are consistent with the belief that the entire world, without national and regional distinctions, constitutes a potential market with identifiable, homogeneous segments that need to be addressed differentially.

Firms in which top management adopts a **geocentric orientation** perceive the entire world—without national and regional distinctions—as a potential market with identifiable, homogeneous segments that need to be addressed differentially, with tailored marketing strategies, regardless of geographic location or nationality. Coordinated management policies are designed to reflect the full integration among worldwide operations.

The objective of a geocentric company is most often to achieve a position as a low-cost manufacturer and marketer of its product line; such a firm achieves a strategic competitive advantage by developing manufacturing processes that add more value per unit cost to the final product than its rivals.[10] McDonald's has been successful as a result of its geocentric philosophy. The company uses local products to ultimately offer a similar service to consumers from Mexico City to Mumbay. In Europe, McDonald's is using Polish potatoes, which do not lend themselves to a thin, McDonald's cut, but which are touted to be the best in the region. It also uses local beef from the European regions not affected/threatened by livestock disease. In India or Pakistan, for example, McDonald's serves lamb or vegetarian burgers. Throughout the world, it provides a uniform service that offers, in addition to the fast food it is known for, clean restrooms, air conditioning, and service with a smile—even in markets where a smile is a rare occurrence in a service encounter.

1-4 Drivers of International Expansion

Few companies operate in an isolated, country-specific environment, and even fewer can effectively avoid international involvement. Local firms manufacturing for local consumers are dependent on equipment, parts, and/or raw materials originating abroad. They sell to clients and final consumers who have had exposure to international trade practices and to international products. A complete isolation from international influence is possible only a closed environment, in countries such as North Korea, where, for different reasons, consumers are shielded from international influence.

Drivers in the business environment   Elements in the business environment, such as competition, technology, and labor costs, causing the firm to become involved internationally.

Firm-specific drivers   Elements specific to the firm, such as product life cycle, causing the firm to become involved internationally.

Companies most often cannot avoid involvement in international marketing; increasingly, companies cannot afford to avoid involvement in international marketing. Avoiding international expansion could mean losing market share to competitors and missing numerous opportunities created by changes in the international environment. **Drivers in the business environment** and **firm-specific drivers,** addressed in sections 1-4a, "Drivers in the Business Environment," and 1-4b, "Firm-Specific Drivers," as well as Figure 1-1, help international companies benefit from such opportunities.

---

10. Ibid.

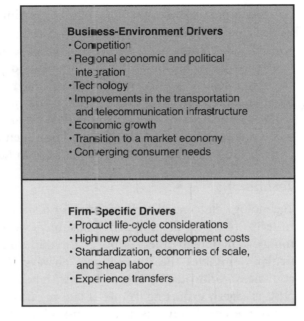

Figure 1-1
International marketing drivers.

1-4a Drivers in the Business Environment

Competition

Competitive pressure is frequently a **driver of internationalization.** McCann Erickson, a leading advertising agency, follows one of its longtime clients, Coca-Cola, in every country where the company is present around the globe; McCann Erickson has been handling the Coca-Cola account in 89 countries since 1942.[11] That often means that McCann Erickson loses money in countries where its accounts are limited, but, where, nevertheless, it chooses to be present to serve the advertising needs of Coke. If McCann Erickson chose not to serve its client in a market, Coca-Cola might resort to the services of a competitor, and, based on the company experience with the competitor, Coca-Cola might replace McCann Erickson with the competing advertising firm.

Driver of internationalization
A driver in the environment—such as competition, technology, or labor costs—or within the firm—such as product life cycle—that causes the firm to go international.

Regional Economic and Political Integration

In addition to cultural similarities—language and religion, for example—economic and political integration play an important part in facilitating international trade. Regional agreements such as the North American Free Trade Agreement (NAFTA), the Southern Cone Common Market (MERCOSUR), and the politically and economically integrated European Union ("Fortress Europe") are examples of successful attempts at lowering or eliminating barriers between member countries and promoting trade within the perimeter of each common market.[12] The benefits of integration benefit companies from nonmember states as well. It permits subsidiaries incorporated in the respective markets to benefit from free trade within the region, and allows firms outside the integrated regions to conduct business within the common market without the impediments typically posed by crossing national borders—customs paperwork, separate tariffs for each country, etc.

---

11. Hillary Chura, "Coke Brands IPG as Global Ad Strategist," *Advertising Age,* Vol. 71, No. 50, December 4, 2000, p. 50.

12. Regional economic and political integration will be addressed at length in Chapter 4.

A company from the United States exporting products to multiple countries in the European Union, for example, will cross borders only once: The company will do the customs paperwork and pay the required customs duties only once, instead of applying for an import license and paying customs duties in every country where it exports products. A subsidiary of a company from the United States incorporated in any country of the European Union is a corporate citizen of the European Union. Consequently, the subsidiary does not have to pay duties when it crosses borders of European Union member states, nor foreign exchange costs, because all transactions are conducted in Euros.

Technology

Technology has created opportunities for firms involved in international business. In terms of media development, consumers worldwide are exposed to programming originating in other countries. Programming from the United States in particular dominates the international airways: *Baywatch* has been followed by audiences worldwide, CNN is popular with business people around the world, and NBC is eagerly exporting its mix of late-night comedy and news magazines to the rest of the world. Advertising also crosses borders, exposing consumers to brands from other countries. The Web and the Internet have revolutionized the way many companies conduct business, offering, for example, small businesses instant and unlimited international exposure—something that brick-and-mortar stores and traditional manufacturers have taken years to achieve.

Improvements in the Transportation and Telecommunication Infrastructure

Closely linked to technology are the leaps in the area of transportation and, particularly, in the technology infrastructure. In the recent past, a Mercedes Benz service station in Bujumbura, Burundi (Sub-Saharan East Africa), attempting to contact the company factory in Stuttgart, Germany, to order a part, would tie up an English- or German-speaking employee for most of the day for this purpose. The employee would book the telephone call with the operator early in the morning and would typically be contacted by the afternoon; the call would be facilitated by an operator in Brussels, Belgium (all calls to Burundi went via cable from Belgium to its former colonies in East Africa), who would link the factory to the service station. The quality of the connection would often be problematic, necessitating a second request for a telephone connection. An alternative would have been placing the request via telex (faxing was not an option, nor was the use of e-mail).

Today, a telephone connection to Burundi would be done via satellite, at a significantly lower cost than previously, when it was handled via cable. The communication would be crisp and clear, especially if a cellular phone is used; analog telephones are still problematic. Teleconferencing is also becoming common in international business transactions. Also, faxing and e-mailing constitute viable options for written communication between the service station and the German factory.

Transportation has been greatly improved in the past two decades. The introduction of containers for international inter-modal (ship, truck, train) shipping greatly facilitates the transportation of physical goods. For passenger transport, efficient and rapid air travel has become more affordable, allowing for frequent interaction between expatriate or local employees and employees from the company headquarters.

Economic Growth

Economic growth constitutes a very important driver of internationalization. Economic development in general, and increased buying power—attributed to the emergence of a strong middle class in large markets, such as those of Brazil and India, for example—have created markets of high potential for international brands. Economic growth has also opened markets that have been previously closed or that have limited international competition: A case in point is China, where consumers are no longer restricted with regard to their consumption and physical movement. Emerging economies are more open to foreign trade and no longer severely limit international firms operating in these markets, invoking that, by doing so, they are within their rights according to the General Agreement for Tariffs and Trade, because they are protecting fledgling local industries.

Transition to a Market Economy

The transition of the former Eastern Bloc countries to a market economy has led to rapid economic development in many countries in the region and has created important new markets for international brands. Another important outcome of the transition to a market economy has been the deregulation and privatization of former government monopolies; under the former Communist regimes, all industry was run by inefficient state enterprises. Opportunities exist for product manufacturers, such as Altria (formerly Philip Morris), Whirlpool, Unilever, Procter & Gamble, Colgate-Palmolive, and other lesser known companies, to purchase or partner with local companies operating at a loss producing low-quality goods and to turn them around into successful enterprises selling global brands to local consumers. Similarly, service providers, from Accenture to Pizza Hut, are entering these markets, engaging in the highest level of commitment: foreign direct investment.

Currently, international companies, joint ventures between multinationals and local companies, private local businesses, as well as some remnants of the former system—state-owned enterprises—compete for local consumers in the transition economies of Central and Eastern Europe. At the same time, satellite television and the Internet expose these consumers to programming, to information, and to advertising for international brands, shaping consumer desires and brand preferences. Companies that have, over time, ignored these markets due to the obstacles they posed (limiting operations, limiting their access to hard currency, and restricting repatriation of profits) are now embracing the many opportunities unleashed by transition.

Converging Consumer Needs

Exposure to global brands in one's home country and, while traveling abroad, to media advertising these brands has created demand for many global products. Consumers worldwide are loyal to international brands such as Nike sneakers, Levi's jeans, Coca-Cola, Heineken beer, and Ralph Lauren shirts. Uniform consumer segments are emerging worldwide: Generation X consumers in the United States and in Southeast Asia are loyal to the same soft-drink brands, wear the same brands of clothing, listen to the same music, have the same idols, see the same television shows, and watch MTV for entertainment.

During their international travels, consumers purchase brands and services available in their own home country, which they are familiar with. Most often, these offerings are successful international products and services. Alternatively, consumers who have traveled abroad bring with them product experiences and demand brands that may not be available in the home-country market. This would generate pull demand, whereby consumers request the product from the retailers, who subsequently convey the information up the distribution chain to wholesalers, who would then order the product.

Firms facing similar consumers demanding in unison the same products have a relatively easy task in addressing the needs of these consumers, using a similar marketing strategy throughout the region. Entry in such uniform markets is facilitated by selling the same product regardless of market, and by the use of the same advertising campaign to address Generation X in the United States, France, Malaysia, and El Salvador.

1-4b Firm-Specific Drivers

Product Life-Cycle Considerations

A main driver behind international expansion is a firm's attempt to prolong the product life cycle. Products that are in late maturity, or even in the decline stage, can change their position on the global product life-cycle stage by going into markets where the product is in high demand. To illustrate this point, the cigarette industry is in either the late maturity stage or in the decline stage in many industrialized countries. By entering emerging markets where cigarettes are in the growth stage and consumers have increasing purchase power, such as China, Central and Eastern Europe, the cigarette industry is in fact prolonging its products' life cycle.

High New Product Development Costs

The concept herein is related to the product life cycle. Companies often spend long periods of time and significant amounts of money to develop new products. Nike, on the average, spends close to a year to develop, test, and manufacture new product designs that then last on the shelves in the United States for only six months. Despite the size and the purchase power of the U.S. market, it is unlikely that Nike would fully recover its product development costs and make a profit as well if it limits its sales to this country. This is especially true for companies at the forefront of technology (manufacturers of high tech equipment and electronics, pharmaceutical firms, and others), which need to tap large markets for long periods to recoup costs and to make a profit as well; hence, for these companies, going international is not a choice—it is a precondition for survival.

Standardization, Economies of Scale, and Cheap Labor

During the maturity stage of the product life cycle, the core product is likely to achieve a standard in a particular industry: Competitors—typically an oligopoly—respond to consumer needs by offering products whose components are interchangeable and which converge toward the brand experiencing the greatest consumer franchise (demand). Standards, for example, have been established in the personal computer industry (the IBM standard) and the videocassette recorder industry (the VHS standard). During the maturity stage, firms also increasingly compete on price: Typically, they attempt to lower the product manufacturing costs by achieving economies of scale in production. In addition, firms at maturity also move manufacturing operations and facilities abroad, to developing countries, in an attempt to take advantage of significantly lower labor costs.

Experience Transfers

International firms benefit from lessons they learn in the different parts of the world. Colgate-Palmolive, for example, developed its successful Axion paste for washing dishes for its Latin American market after noting that women washed dishes by hand, dunking their hands in a small tub with a few slivers of soap. The same product was then offered to consumers in Central and Eastern Europe after noting that they washed dishes using a similar method—and the product was a hit. Service providers such as Pizza Hut found that they were more successful with consumers in general, but especially with younger generations of consumers in Central and Eastern Europe, if they played pop music, on the rather loud side. As a result, they started entering new markets by partnering with radio stations and discos.

Such experience transfers are not limited to product or service providers. As will be seen in Chapter 12, "International Retailing," the new Tesco Extra hypermarket (superstore) in the city of Newcastle, United Kingdom, is based on a Tesco hypermarket first introduced by the same U.K. retailer in Hungary.[13]

1-5 Obstacles to Internationalization

Companies attempting to establish and maintain an international presence are likely to encounter **obstacles to internationalization** both from within the company and from outside. Such obstacles can be financial in nature: The company might not have the finances to expand beyond national frontiers. Others are psychological: Fear of an unknown international environment or of local business practices may keep the company from international engagement. These two types of barriers, however, could equally affect the company's local expansion efforts: Companies may not have the finances to expand beyond a small regional market, or they fear going into new markets where consumers may not be familiar with their products and hence may not respond to their marketing strategy.

Some obstacles are encountered only by firms in their process of internationalization—obstacles that they are unlikely to encounter in other expansion efforts. They are the self-reference criterion, government barriers, and international competition (see Figure 1-2).

1-5a Self-Reference Criterion

Of crucial importance to international operations is the ability of the firm, and especially of its marketing program, to adapt to the local business environment in order to serve the needs of local consumers and to address the requirements of local government, industry, and channels of distribution. An impediment to adaptation is the **self-reference criterion**, defined as individuals' conscious and unconscious reference to their own national culture, to home-country norms, values, as well as to their knowledge and experience, in the process of making decisions in the host country.

Obstacles to internationalization Impediments that the firm may encounter in the process of internationalizing.

Self-reference criterion Individuals' conscious and unconscious reference to their own national culture, to home-country norms and values, and to their knowledge and experience in the process of making decisions in the host country.

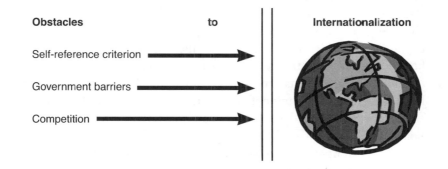

Obstacles	to	Internationalization
Self-reference criterion	⟶	
Government barriers	⟶	
Competition	⟶	

Figure 1-2
Obstacles to internationalization.

---

13. Alexandra Jardine, "Retailers Go on International Shopping Trip," *Marketing*, January 20, 2000, p. 15.

Chapter 5, "Cultural Influences on International Marketing," illustrates a number of situations in which self reference can lead to a breakdown in communication between parties from different cultures. For example, an employee of a large multinational company from the United States conducting business in Japan who has been trained by career counselors in the U.S. that looking one's counterpart in the eyes conveys directness and honesty is likely to be perceived as abrasive and challenging. Similarly, if the same employee proceeds directly to transacting the business deal in Latin America or Southern Europe (instead of first interacting in a social setting in order to establish rapport), he/she would be perceived as arrogant, interested only in the bottom line, rather than in a long-term working relationship.

A first step to minimizing the impact of the self-reference criterion is selecting appropriate personnel for international assignments. Such employees are sensitive to others and have experience working in different environments. Second, it would be important to train expatriates to focus on and be sensitive to the local culture, rather than limit their personal interactions to own-country nationals or to expatriates from countries with cultures that are similar to one's own. In fact, an organization-level general orientation that instills and demonstrates sensitivity to international environments and openly spurns value judgments and national stereotyping should be instilled at the firm level.

1-5b Government Barriers

Local governments, especially governments in developing countries, keep a tight control over international market entrants, permitting or denying access to international firms based on criteria that are deemed important for national industry and/or security considerations at a particular point in time. Among formal methods used by national governments to restrict or impede entrance of international firms in the local market are tariffs and barriers such as import quotas, or policies of restricting import license awards, foreign exchange restrictions, and local content requirements, among others. Member countries of the World Trade Organization, signatories of the General Agreement on Tariffs and Trade, or members of regional economic integration agreements such as NAFTA and the European Union find it very difficult to use tariffs as a means of restricting international expansion of companies in the countries' territories. Increasingly, they are using nontariff barriers, such as cumbersome procedures for import paperwork processing, delays in granting licenses, or preference given to local service providers and product manufacturing for all contracting work.

1-5c International Competition

Although competition can be a driver of internationalization, competitors can also erect barriers to new entrants in a market. They often do so by employing strategies such as blocking channels of distribution, binding retailers into exclusive agreements, slashing prices temporarily to prevent product adoption, or engaging in an advertising blitz that could hurt a company's initial sales in a market and cause it to retrench. With heavy competition from new and lesser brands in Asia, Central and Eastern Europe, and North Africa and the Middle East, Marlboro has created a strong defensive strategy for its cigarettes: It slashed prices by as much as a third, and advertised heavily anywhere it was legal, especially on billboards in the center of different capital cities and towns in the provinces.

As an example, sales of Marlboro in South-Eastern Europe were hurt by various local competitors and, in particular, by a successful international brand, Assos, from Greece. Assos was rapidly gaining a leading position in a number of markets in the region when Marlboro went on the offensive, limiting Assos's market share to a point where the company was forced to abandon many of its markets. Marlboro effectively put in question the international expansion of many new European and Asian brands, as well as new brands from the United States (it decimated, for instance, sales of new brands of American cigarettes created specifically for the Russian market).

Chapter Summary

- **Define international marketing and identify the different levels of international involvement**

  A firm can elect to engage in different levels of international expansion. A domestic firm will focus on the domestic market and ignore international possibilities. At the next level, firms can export their products overseas, taking advantage of international opportunities to increase their sales and profits. Firms involved in international marketing are serving international consumers and are present in different countries (but do not coordinate between-countries activities under a regional office or subsidiary) with sales offices, subsidiaries, or in partnership with local or other international firms. Global marketing involves coordination of all marketing activities within a particular region or worldwide.

- **Describe the different company orientations and philosophies toward international marketing**

  Depending on the type of industry or service they are in and depending on the extent to which a company has an international focus, companies adopt different orientations and philosophies toward internationalization. Ethnocentric companies consider domestic strategies, techniques, and personnel as superior to foreign ones; these strategies then provide the framework for the company's overseas operations, which are secondary to domestic operations. Companies with a polycentric orientation focus on different international markets without coordinating between international activities. Companies with a regiocentric orientation coordinate their operations regionally, whereas companies with a geocentric orientation coordinate their marketing and management policies worldwide, fully integrating their operations and addressing uniform segments worldwide.

- **Identify environmental and firm-specific drivers that direct firms toward international markets**

  A number of elements in the business environment direct the firm to explore international opportunities. One such element is competitive pressure, the need to serve clients regardless of market attractiveness, preventing them from switching to the service of a competitor. Opportunities in the environment, such as worldwide economic growth and new emerging markets, regional economic and political integration and the removal of trade barriers, improvements in the transportation and telecommunication infrastructure, and advancement in technology worldwide also prompt international firms to pursue international markets. The advent of technology and media influence, economic prosperity, and consumer travel are creating uniform segments of consumers with similar preferences that international firms could serve effectively with standardized strategies. Firms facing decreasing sales attributed to a mature home market can extend the life cycle of their products by going international: Cigarette companies are in a late maturity stage in the United States but, most likely, in late growth stage worldwide. During the maturity stage, as products start competing on price, companies benefit from going international to take advantage of cheaper and yet competent labor and new markets.

- **Identify obstacles preventing firms from engaging in successful international ventures**

  Obstacles to international marketing are the self-reference criterion—conscious and unconscious reference to one's national culture, to home-country norms, values, as well as to one's knowledge and experience, in the process of making decisions in the host country. Additional obstacles can be the local and national governments of the host country, which could impose entry barriers or prevent the company from repatriating profits, and competitive barriers to entry.

Discussion Questions

Discussion Questions

1. Discuss the differences between firm internationalization philosophies.

2. Try to work backward from a company's web page and attempt to infer its internationalization philosophy. Look at the Procter & Gamble (www.pg.com) web pages describing the company's international involvement and its international product mix. What orientation do you believe this company has and why?

3. What are the drivers in the international business environment that lead a firm to engage in international operations? What are some of the firm-specific drivers leading to internationalization?

4. What is the "self-reference criterion"?

5. How can governments and competitors prevent a firm from entering a particular market?

The International Marketing Environment

Chapter 2
An Overview of the
International Marketing
Environment

Chapter 3
International Trade:
Barriers and Facilitators

Chapter 4
Regional Economic
and Political Integration

Chapter 5
Cultural Influences
on International Marketing

An Overview of the International Marketing Environment

Key Terms

antitrust laws	expropriation	Overseas Private Investment
arbitration	feudalism	Corporation (OPIC)
big emerging markets	Foreign Corrupt Practices Act	patent
bourgeoisie	high mass consumption	political risk
capitalism	home-country laws	primitive society
code law	host-country laws	Rostow modernization model
common law	imperialism	slavery-based society
communism	intellectual property rights	socialism
confiscation	international laws	take-off
copyright	Islamic law	Trade-Related Aspects
corruption laws	jurisdiction	of Intellectual Property
creeping expropriation	Marxist-Leninist development	Rights (TRIPS)
developed countries	model	trade secrets
developing countries	mediation	trademark
domestication	monopolistic capitalism	traditional society
drive to maturity	nationalism	transitional society
emerging markets	nationalization	

Outline

Learning Objectives
2-1 The Economic Environment
  of International Marketing
  2-1a The World Economy
  2-1b The Economic
    Development Disparity
2-2 Perspectives on Economic
  Development
  2-2a The Rostow
    Modernization Model
  2-2b The Marxist-Leninist
    Model of Economic
    Development
  2-2c Development Philosophies
    and the Developing World
2-3 Levels of Economic
  Development
  2-3a The Importance
    of Emerging Markets
2-4 The Political Environment
  of International Marketing
  2-4a Political Risk:
    An Overview
  2-4b Nationalism
  2-4c Political Risks and
    Risk Management in
    International Marketing
2-5 The International Legal
  Environment
  2-5a Legal Systems
  2-5b Jurisdiction
  2-5c Intellectual Property
    Rights Protection
  2-5d Home-Country
    Legislation Affecting
    Multinational Firms
    Operating Overseas
Chapter Summary
Discussion Questions

Learning Objectives

Learning Objectives

By the end of this chapter, you should be able to:

- Provide an overview of the world economic environment and examine different perspectives on economic development
- Address differences between countries of different levels of economic development and discuss the importance of emerging markets
- Examine the indicators of political risk and address international firm approaches to political risk management
- Describe how international law, home-country law, and host-country law affect international firm operations and address issues related to jurisdiction
- Discuss different legal systems, intellectual property laws, and national laws with extra-territorial impact that affect the international firm

The transition economies that first opened their markets to multinational firms and privatized national industries experienced the greatest degree of growth and were most successful in developing national industrial sectors that competed effectively with the international firms. Yet, despite the clear, positive impact on economic development, successful multinationals face extensive criticism from developing countries in Africa and Asia: Their presence in these countries and their market dominance are often likened to a form of neo-colonialism—industrial colonialism.

Countries where multiple tribes have co-existed for decades without any conflict, where the president and his army have led effectively, spreading the wealth to the population and attracting in the country foreign direct investment, fall victim to a civil war. Multinational firms leave their assets open to plundering and promptly ship their expatriates to safety. This scenario is played over and over in the world: Multinational companies in Chad, Rwanda, Burundi, the former Zaire, Sierra Leone, Bosnia and Herzegovina, and Croatia have all experienced losses. Multinational companies are also victims of corporate terrorism, which is on the increase worldwide.

Some companies operate in environments where everything is forbidden unless expressly allowed. Other companies operate in environments where everything is perceived as allowed unless expressly forbidden. Companies operating in legally ambiguous environments face ethical and legal challenges from host-country national governments, para-national institutions, and the home-country government that they have to address effectively in order to survive in international markets.

This chapter will focus on elements in the environment of international marketing. We will examine the impact of the economic, political, and legal environment on the international marketing operations of the firm.

2-1 The Economic Environment of International Marketing

2-1a The World Economy

It is common today to hear that, when the United States sneezes, Europe and Japan catch a cold. This is an understatement. When the United States is experiencing a downturn in the economy, reverberations echo throughout the world: Central and South American countries need to be rescued by the International Monetary Fund; all the Asian economies flounder; banks in developing countries default on their debt. The United States is equally affected by the world economy. The Asian crisis of the late 1990s sent stock markets tumbling in the United States and in the rest of the world. In the Internet Age, countries are becoming more and more connected by trade, by capital markets, by the flow of technology and ideas across national borders, and by psychology: Rather than rising and falling separately, national economies increasingly respond to the same forces.[1] Interdependence has become the leading principle of globalization.

In sectoral examples, an excess of steel in the world markets, attributed to overproduction in Russia, led to restructuring of the industry elsewhere in the world, leaving only a few players in the world steel oligopoly. And underproduction of oil attributed to Organization of the Petroleum Exporting Countries (OPEC) (www.opec.org) controls has historically led to inflation worldwide. On the positive side, the boom in technology stocks in 1999 has led to much—albeit short-lived—prosperity in many developed countries, as well as in countries that stress technical training, and software design, in particular, such as India. Never in the history of mankind has there been such a degree of interdependence.

The international economy has indeed become one single unit. Major companies simply cannot afford a local, home-country focus: The market share game is played on a world scale. A one-world commercial future is close to being a reality: Whereas 60 countries (excluding Eastern Europe and countries with fewer than one million people) have a GNP of less than US$10 billion, 135 multinational firms have revenues in excess of that amount, in a world where multinationals are breaking down barriers that have withstood armies, missionaries, crusaders, and politicians.[2]

2-1b The Economic Development Disparity

In the current economic environment, firms from industrialized countries and their representative governments dominate the world economy, allocating resources worldwide based on market potential, rather than on local population needs, creating a growing gap between the have countries and have-not countries. Developing countries, on the other hand, control resources (raw materials, labor) that multinationals need, control access to local consumers, and frequently pose barriers to international business operations in an attempt to lessen the development gap. It is important, under this environment, to understand the existing dynamics between countries at different levels of economic and market development and the philosophies underlying those dynamics.

---

1. Michael J. Mandel, "In a One-World Economy, a Slump Sinks All Boats," *Business Week,* Industrial Technology Edition, No. 3738, June 25, 2001, pp. 38–39.

2. Russell W. Belk, "Hyperreality and Globalization: Culture in the Age of Ronald McDonald," *Journal of International Consumer Marketing,* Vol. 8, No. 3/4, 1996, pp. 23–37; and Leslie Sklair, "Competing Models of Globalization: Theoretical Frameworks and Research Agendas," working paper, London School of Economics and Political Science, University of London, London, United Kingdom.

Rostow modernization model
An economic development model attributed to Rostow, according to which each stage of economic advance is a function of productivity, economic exchange, technological improvements, and income.

Marxist-Leninist development model   A development model attributed to Karl Marx and Vladimir Lenin which maps the development of society from an agrarian, traditional society to a society characterized by shared ownership of the means and outcomes of production and an equitable resource allocation; advancement from one stage to another is based on class struggle and transfer of ownership from one class to another and, ultimately, to the state.

Traditional society   A stage in economic development defined by Rostow as one in which the economy is dominated by agriculture and relatively few exchange transactions occur.

Transitional society   A stage in the economic development process described by Rostow as characterized by increased productivity in agriculture and by the emergence of modern manufacturing.

Take-off   A stage in economic development described by Rostow as one in which economic growth becomes the norm and improvements in production lead to the emergence of leading sectors.

Drive to maturity   A stage in economic development, described by Rostow, as characterized by the technological and entrepreneurial skill to produce anything society chooses to produce.

High mass consumption
A stage in economic development, described by Rostow, as characterized by leading sectors shifting toward durable goods.

2-2 Perspectives on Economic Development

Two models of economic development have gained acceptance in the world: a Western model, best articulated by **Rostow,** and the **Marxist-Leninist** model, which still constitutes a dominant development philosophy in some developing countries. It must be noted that the fall of communism in Europe and the recent structural changes in China and Vietnam have reduced considerably the areas dominated by the Marxist-Leninist philosophy on economic development.

2-2a The Rostow Modernization Model[3]

According to the Rostow model, each stage is a function of productivity, economic exchange, technological improvements, and income. Economic growth requires advancing from one stage to another. The modernization stages are

- Traditional society
- Transitional society
- Take-off
- The drive to maturity
- High mass consumption

Traditional Society

Countries in the **traditional society** stage are characterized by an economic structure that is dominated by agriculture. Minimal productivity occurs, and only a few exchange transactions take place. Economic change and technological improvements are not sufficient to sustain any growth in per capita output, which is low.

Transitional Society (Pre-Conditions for Take-Off)

The **transitional society** stage is characterized by increased productivity in agriculture, and modern manufacturing begins to emerge. In manufacturing, low productivity remains the norm.

Take-Off

During **take-off,** growth becomes the norm and improvements in production lead to the emergence of leading sectors. Income rises across the board, and a new class of entrepreneurs emerges.

The Drive to Maturity

In the **drive-to-maturity** stage, modern technology is fully adopted in all economic activity, and new leading sectors emerge. The economy demonstrates the technological and entrepreneurial skill to produce anything it chooses to. The economy looks beyond the country's border for development.

High Mass Consumption

In the age of **high mass consumption,** leading sectors shift toward durable goods. A surge occurs in per capita income and increased allocation to social welfare programs. The masses can afford goods beyond food, clothing, and shelter.

---

3. See Walt W. Rostow, *The Stages of Economic Growth: A Non-Communist Manifesto,* London and New York: Cambridge University Press, 1960; ———, "The Concept of a National Market and Its Economic Growth Implications," in *Marketing and Economic Development,* edited by P. D. Bennett, 1965, Chicago: American Marketing Association, pp. 11–20; and ———, *The Stages of Economic Growth,* Second Edition, 1971, London: Cambridge University Press.

2-2b The Marxist-Leninist Model of Economic Development

The Marxist-Leninist model and its dialectic materialism theories approach economic development philosophy similarly in the first stage. The subsequent stages are depicted as a class struggle ending in revolution, which is needed for advancement to the next stage. Advancement is a function of the control of means of production, of production outcomes, of resource allocation, and the development of a mindset devoid of materialist needs.

The stages in this model are

- The primitive society
- The slavery-based society
- Feudalism
- The capitalist society
- The socialist society
- Communism

The Primitive Society

Countries in the **primitive society** stage are similar to those in traditional society. There is joint, tribal ownership of the means of production, which are minimal, primitive, and centered on agricultural tasks, for the use of all the members of the commune within the tribe. Much of the agriculture is slash-and-burn, with the tribes moving in the quest for new territory. All tribal members in this egalitarian society work for the common welfare of the tribe.

The Slavery-Based Society

The **slavery-based society** emerges as a result of tribes taking over other tribes and enslaving their population. Slaves are now property of the conquering tribe. Under the Roman, Mesopotamian, and Egyptian rule, slaves toiled in agriculture and built infrastructures, such as access roads and irrigation systems. Tribal territory ownership is established as a first step toward establishing private property. Trading agricultural goods and tools between tribes is becoming common.

Feudalism

Under the feudal society known as **feudalism,** feudal lords own armies, land, and the dwellers of the land. Land is primarily in the hands of the feudal family; production is still primarily agricultural. Guilds are emerging as a production unit, manufacturing goods and training future manufacturers under apprenticeships. Trading is common and widespread, and exchange is now primarily based on gold as currency.

The Capitalist Society

The capitalist society is represented by two stages. The first stage is characterized by an emerging **bourgeoisie** (developed from the guild class) as a ruling class, alongside with the aristocracy (the former feudal family). The bourgeoisie creates lucrative means of production, and it achieves high productivity at the expense of exploited workers. Production shifts gradually from the agrarian sector to the industrial sector.

The second stage of **capitalism** is multinational **imperialism.** Imperialist capitalism is characterized by a capital that loses its national identity by crossing borders; in fact, the export of capital, hence international trade, is a central mechanism of imperialism. The international firm is a double parasite exploiting

Primitive society   The first stage of economic and political development, characterized, according to Marxist-Leninist theory, by the joint tribal ownership of primitive means of production centered on agricultural tasks.

Slavery-based society   A stage of economic and political development, which, according to Marxist-Leninist theory, emerges as a result of tribes' dominance over other tribes: Dominant tribes claim ownership of conquered tribes and their property.

Feudalism   A stage in economic and political development, which, according to Marxist-Leninist theory, is characterized by the dominance of feudal lords, who own the land and its dwellers.

Bourgeoisie   A dominant social class, which, according to Marxist-Leninist theory, establishes lucrative means of production and achieves high productivity at the expense of exploited workers.

Capitalism   A stage of economic and political development, which, according to Marxist-Leninist theory, is characterized, in its early stages, by an emerging bourgeoisie, the shift of production from the agrarian sector to the industrial sector, and, in its later stages, by imperialism, where capital loses its national identity by crossing borders and establishing monopolies.

Imperialism   A stage of economic and political development, in which, according to Marxist-Leninist theory, capital loses its national identity by crossing borders.

Monopolistic capitalism
A stage of economic and political development, in which, according to Marxist-Leninist theory, multinational companies establish monopolies and expand internationally with the goal of subjugating developing countries.

its own working class, as well as workers in less-developed countries. Multinational firms represent the modality for national domination of developing countries, and for the domination and subjugation of workers and peasants worldwide. The creation of international monopolies (**monopolistic capitalism**) represents the most advanced stage of capitalist dominance.

The Socialist Society

The socialist society is also composed of two stages. The first stage is a transition stage that leads to the disappearance of private property—which is replaced by collective, state property. Countries in this stage typically are formally known as People's Republics.

Socialism   A transition stage of economic and political development, characterized, according to Marxist-Leninist theory, by the disappearance of private property and its replacement with collective, state property.

    Socialism in its more advanced stage takes the form of the multilaterally developed socialist society. Socialist Republics, as countries in this stage are referred to, are characterized by state ownership of all the means of production. The state also controls the modes of production, allocating resources to industry, agriculture, education, and healthcare based on societal needs. With the exception of some remnants of capitalism, such as private property limited to one's dwelling, and philosophies that need to be erased at the next stage—materialism, for example—the state has in place most mechanisms necessary for the transition to communism.

The Communist Society

Communism   A stage in economic and political development, which, according to Marxist-Leninist theory, is characterized by state and cooperative ownership of all means of production and property.

No country has ever claimed to have reached the communist stage. Under **communism**, all means of production and private property are under state ownership and/or cooperative ownership. The state is in charge of allocation of resources to sectors as needed and to individuals (goods and services) according to their needs. Communism develops "the new man," one for whom work is a need and who will work according to his ability. There is no need for private property, and there is no materialism in society.

    In the early stages of communism, Lenin argued that foreign capital is important in the development process as a source of advanced technology; his solution was a leasing system whereby foreign firms would participate in particular projects and regions in communist countries for a limited amount of time.[4] In practice, this concept was soon countered by the implications of the Cold War and by Stalin's theory of two parallel markets (capitalist and socialist), which stressed internal integration among socialist countries for mutual economic development; according to this theory, capitalist markets were inherently weak, and socialist countries needed to isolate themselves from the capitalist world.[5]

    The Rostow model and the Marxist-Leninist model are comparable, up to a point. In Figure 2-1, the models work in parallel up to the level of the drive-to-maturity stage in the Rostow model and the capitalist stage in the Marxist-Leninist model.

2-2c Development Philosophies and the Developing World

Although there are claims that Marxism is vanquished as an economic system, it is certainly not extinct as a development philosophy. In the context of the global triumph of the market system, Marxist-Leninist theory stands as a competing alternative for developing nations seeking to avoid domination by advanced market

---

4. Barkley Rosser, Jr., and Marina V. Rosser, "Islamic and Neo-Confucian Perspectives on the New Traditional Economy," *Eastern Economic Journal*, Vol. 24, No. 2, Spring 1998, pp. 217–227.

5. Roger Hayter and Sun Sheng Han, "Reflections on China's Open Policy Towards Foreign Direct Investment, *Regional Studies*, Vol. 32, No. 1, February 1998, pp. 1–16.

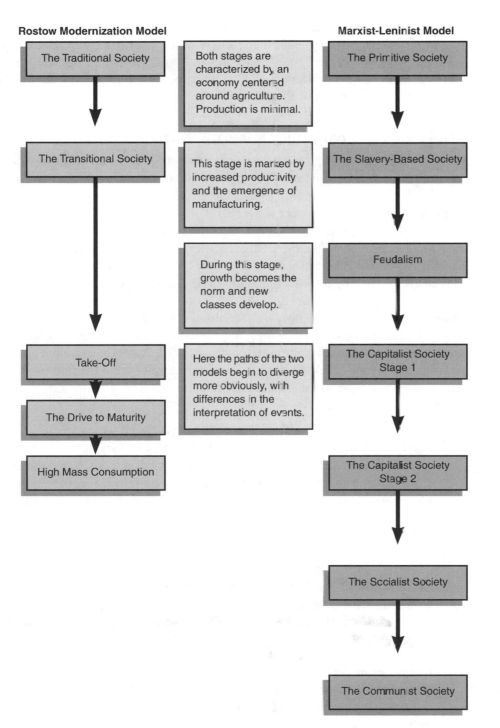

Rostow Modernization Model

The Traditional Society

The Transitional Society

Take-Off

The Drive to Maturity

High Mass Consumption

Both stages are characterized by an economy centered around agriculture. Production is minimal.

This stage is marked by increased productivity and the emergence of manufacturing.

During this stage, growth becomes the norm and new classes develop.

Here the paths of the two models begin to diverge more obviously, with differences in the interpretation of events.

Marxist-Leninist Model

The Primitive Society

The Slavery-Based Society

Feudalism

The Capitalist Society Stage 1

The Capitalist Society Stage 2

The Socialist Society

The Communist Society

Figure 2-1
A comparison of the Rostow and the Marxist-Leninist models.

capitalist economies: The collective orientation of more traditional developing countries competes, thus, with market-oriented capitalism, fueling anticolonial and anti-imperialist sentiments.[6] Socialist ideas of sharing wealth, leveling inequality, eliminating homelessness, and providing basic needs such as health, food, education, and shelter to all citizens appeal to many in the poor, developing countries that were long suppressed and exploited by colonial and imperialist powers; at the heart of this philosophy are issues of equitable distribution of national income, improvement in the welfare of the masses, and economic justice.[7]

---

6. Rosser and Rosser, "Islamic and Neo-Confucian Perspectives," pp. 217–227.

7. Ali Farazmand, "Development and Comparative Public Administration: Past, Present, and Future," *Public Administration Quarterly*, Vol. 20, No. 3, Fall 1996, pp. 343–364.

In an attempt to counter these philosophies, Western financial- and institutional-strengthening assistance to developing countries grew dramatically to strengthen their political and ruling elites and the regimes they operated and to eliminate some of the hardships such as absolute poverty, hunger, and disasters the masses suffered; the result of this effort is mixed.[8]

2-3 Levels of Economic Development

There are many competing classifications of countries from an economic development perspective. Historically, the informal and frequently used classification in the West has referred to highly industrialized, developed countries as the First World, to socialist countries as the Second World, and to developing countries as the Third Word. Of this classification, only the term "the Third World" has been used widely, and it is still being used, even after the fall of communism. A United Nations (www.un.org) classification contrasts LLDCs (least-developed countries, and the lowest-income countries) and LDCs (less-developed countries, and lower-income countries) to developed countries. Yet other classifications bring in other dimensions, such as NICs (newly industrialized countries), in reference to Taiwan, Singapore, South Korea, and Hong Kong (known in the 1980s and 1990s as the *Asian Tigers,* and **emerging markets** (such as Brazil, Argentina, Chile, Peru, and the transitional economies of Central and Eastern Europe). For the purpose of this textbook, we will refer to three categories of countries, based on the classification used by the World Bank (www.worldbank.org):

- **Developed countries**—These highly industrialized countries have well-developed industrial and service sectors. In this category fall newly industrialized countries, as well as countries that have had a developed status for many years. Although these countries present great potential because they have consumers with the highest per capita income, they also present challenges to international firms because their markets are in the maturity stage, consumers have established preferences, and competition is intense. The World Bank refers to the countries in this category as high-income countries, with a GNP per capita of US$9,266 and above.
- **Countries with emerging markets**—Countries considered emerging markets are both developing rapidly and have great potential. They are countries in Latin America, such as Argentina, Brazil, Uruguay, Paraguay, Chile, Peru, Bolivia, to name a few; countries in Asia, such as China, with its immense market, and India, with its substantial middle class; and the transition economies of Central and Eastern Europe, which are rapidly privatizing state-owned industries and adopting market reforms. Important in this category are **big emerging markets (BEMs)**, which present the greatest potential for international trade and expansion. The World Bank refers to the countries in this category as middle-income countries, with a GNP per capita of US$766 to US$9,265.
- **Developing countries**—Countries in this category are primarily agrarian, have low per capita income levels, and are located in different regions in Asia and in Sub-Saharan Africa. Developing countries are often neglected or under-served by large multinationals and consequently present great potential as niche markets. Even the countries with the lowest

Emerging markets Countries that are developing rapidly and have great economic potential; the World Bank characterizes them as middle-income countries, with a GNP per capita of US$766 to US$9,265.

Developed countries Highly industrialized countries with well-developed service sectors, mature markets, and intense competition; they are characterized by the World Bank as high-income, with a GNP per capita of US$9,266 and above.

Big emerging markets (BEMs) Large markets characterized by rapid economic development and high potential; big emerging markets set the pace for the economy in their geographic region.

Developing countries Countries that are primarily agrarian, often neglected or under-served by large multinationals, and characterized by the World Bank as low-income countries, with a GNP per capita of less than US$755.

---

8. Ibid.

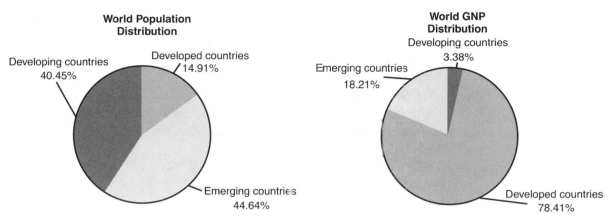

Figure 2-2
An illustration of economic disparity: Population and Gross National Product statistics for developed, emerging, and developing countries.

Adapted from World Development Indicators, Washington, D.C.: World Bank, 2000.

per capita income have a stratum of society that can afford global products. Furthermore, because they are primary recipients of international development aid, they present important opportunities for firms operating in the areas of infrastructure development and industrial sector development, and for related consultancies. The World Bank refers to the countries in this category as low-income countries, with a GNP per capita of less than US$755. Throughout the textbook, there are examples of marketing challenges and opportunities in emerging markets and in developing countries.

The discrepancy between the countries in the three categories is evident: With regard to the GNP distribution worldwide, developed, highly industrialized countries account for close to 80 percent of the world's gross national product, whereas they account for less than 15 percent of the population (see Figure 2-2).

2-3a The Importance of Emerging Markets

Countries with emerging markets present great potential to international firms. Their attractiveness lies primarily in their rate of economic growth—7 percent per year, for the past decade, compared to 2.3 percent for Western Europe and North America.[9] Countries that have been identified as emerging markets by *The Economist* in its regular reports on emerging markets are the following:

- In Asia: China, India, Indonesia, Malaysia, the Philippines, Singapore, South Korea, Thailand
- In Africa and the Middle East: Israel, South Africa
- In Europe: The Czech Republic, Greece, Poland, Portugal, Russia, Turkey
- In Latin America: Argentina, Brazil, Chile, Mexico, Venezuela

Other countries are likely prospects for the emerging market category, based on their economic policies and performance in the past decade. Among them are Slovenia, Slovakia, Croatia, Romania, Bulgaria, the Ukraine, Latvia, Estonia, Lithuania, and Belarus in Central and Eastern Europe; and Colombia, Paraguay, Peru, and Uruguay in Latin America. These countries are rapidly privatizing their economies and adopting the economic reforms necessary to create a stable, growing economy.

---

9. Robert Lloyd George, *The Handbook of Emerging Markets: A Country-By-Country Guide to the World's Fastest Growing Economies,* Chicago, Illinois: Probus Publications, 1994.

Countries with emerging markets that are expected to have a successful economic future share a number of traits:[10]

- High political stability
- A sound currency
- A low level of inflation
- Privatization policies that reduce government deficit, create first-time share owners who vote for pro-business conservative policies, and diminish the power of trade unions
- Policies that facilitate repatriation of dividends and capital
- Policies that are in line with international accounting standards
- Open disclosure of directors' interests
- Policies that stress regular reporting of earnings and sales figures
- A sound and comprehensive system of corporate law
- A liquid and well-traded securities market reflecting fair prices
- A high savings rate
- Strong government support for internationalization
- A people characterized by integrity, a strong work ethic, and respect for the law

Of interest to multinationals are what the United States Department of Commerce refers to as big emerging markets (BEMs). These markets share all the traits of emerging markets and present the most potential because they are large, have large populations, and, consequently, set the pace for the economy in the region. Among these countries are China and India (both with a population exceeding one billion), South Korea, Argentina, Brazil, Mexico, South Africa, Poland, and Turkey.

2-4 The Political Environment of International Marketing

Companies contemplating any international involvement must have an in-depth knowledge of the political environment in the countries where they are doing business. This is especially important for companies that are involved in foreign direct investment—companies that undertake the greatest level of risk. Whenever there are discussions of **political risk**, they typically involve the host country—the country of international operations. It should be noted, however, that the international company is also affected by political developments in its home country— the country where the parent company is headquartered. A United States-based company planning to enter Cuba in the late 1990s, when the Clinton administration appeared to relax anti-Cuba restrictions, had many more prospects then than it had immediately thereafter, when the Bush administration attempted to enforce the embargo.

At the basis of international law lies the concept of sovereignty— self-determination and independence from external interference in internal affairs, and complete authority over all nationals living in the country and beyond its borders (individuals and corporations). All countries in the world are sovereign, and yet all must curtail sovereignty in order to co-exist in the world of nations and defend their national interests. Countries, by permitting international trade and by entering into international agreements, limit their sovereignty. When countries perceive that international firms, governments, or organizations have

Political risk The risk associated with actions of local, regional, and/or parastatal governing bodies affecting the international company, and with the overall economic and political stability within a particular country.

10. Adapted from Lloyd George, *The Handbook of Emerging Markets,* 1994.

infringed upon their right to self-determination, they can invoke national sovereignty and take actions that erect barriers to trade, or even jeopardize the presence of international companies within their borders.

Ideally, a multinational firm will encounter an environment in both the host and home country that is politically stable and pro-trade. This is not the case for most firms all of the time: The government they have established relationships with could collapse overnight, and its replacement could have ties with a competitor—or it could be against foreign business altogether (as was the case of Iran during the Islamic Revolution and of Cuba and Eastern Europe after the communist takeover). The stable environment where the business has operated for decades is suddenly at the center of a civil war that nobody had foreseen: In the case of Rwanda and Burundi, many international businesses were forced to leave their inventory and buildings behind when the genocide began. A protectionist measure of one government could launch a series of retaliations both by the government and by the populace: When the United States instituted measures against European protectionism by increasing duties on nonessential European exports (cheese, perfume, soap, accessories), it had not expected the retaliations of Europeans against icons of U.S. business, such as McDonald's and Coca-Cola.

2-4a Political Risk: An Overview

Evaluating Political Risk

A company has several resources at its disposal to evaluate country risk: The State Department, the Department of Commerce, and other governmental and nongovernmental agencies provide data on country political risk that is current and continuously updated to reflect new developments in each country around the world. Some examples of useful publications providing periodic information on country risk are

- Business periodicals such as *The Economist* and *The Wall Street Journal*—particularly the European and Asian editions
- Commercial sources, such as the Economist Intelligence Unit, Ltd., Chase (particularly its guide for exporters), and RUNDT's World Business Intelligence. RUNDT's (S. J. Rundt & Associates, Inc.), for example, provides information on political developments, on currency, and on the regulatory environment; it provides insurance data and trade information, as well as a country risk rating on a scale from 1 to 10, and risk perception and collection experience for the previous four months.

Political Risk Signals

A number of country risk elements should be monitored on a regular basis to keep track of developments that might ultimately affect the international company. These elements are illustrated in Figure 2-3.

Economic Performance

A poor economic performance and forecast are likely to lead to greater levels of unrest in the country. Of particular concern are high inflationary rates and high unemployment rates, both of which could lead to political instability.

General business performance is also important. Commercial payment terms and collection experience indicate the availability of hard currency reserves and access to hard currency. Default on loans is likely to be a threat to companies

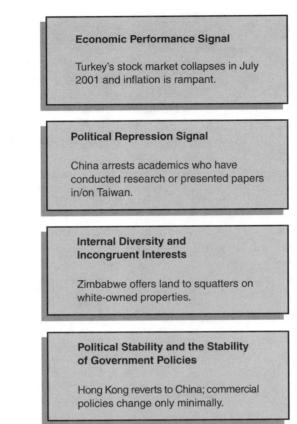

Figure 2-3
Country risk elements.

contemplating to enter the market. Finally, an increase in regulatory restrictions on investment, capital, or trade flows should be closely monitored.[11]

Political Repression

Repression of certain ethnic groups is a signal of potential political instability. The repression of the Albanian minority in the former Yugoslavia resulted in war in the region, as did the repression of the Tutsi minority by the Hutu in East Africa. Other areas are also ripe for conflict: The repression of gypsies and Muslims in Central and Eastern Europe could present a problem in the future.

General repression by the elite—especially if the elite's position is not considered legitimate[12]—is always a signal of political instability. Personality cults in particular are problematic because they bring about widespread antipathy.

Internal Diversity and Incongruent Interests

Even if no political repression exists within a country, ethnic diversity and incongruent interests lead to a history of distrust and conflict (open or simmering) in the population. In Nigeria, the Ibo, Yoruba, and Hausa tribes have had a history of conflict, even though today, the country is relatively calm. Romania has a large minority of Hungarians who are actively advocating secession and annexation of the region where Hungarians represent the dominant population to Hungary. In more developed countries, substantial ethnic conflict still exists, not just between the established ethnicities—as in the case of Belgium, where the Flemish (Dutch)

---

11. Richard B. Loth, "How to Evaluate Country Risk," *Credit and Financial Management*, Vol. 88, No. 6, June 1986, p. 27.

12. Ilan Alon and Matthew A. Martin, "A Normative Model of Macro Political Risk Assessment," *Multinational Business Review*, Vol. 6, No. 2, Fall 1998, pp. 10–19.

and Wallonians (French) often find themselves in opposition—but also between the new immigrants and long-established nationals—as in the case of Germany, where Turkish immigrants have been targets of hate crime.

Political Stability and the Stability of Government Policies

Although presidents and governments change every few years, with a few exceptions, national government policies do not necessarily change radically, nor does the level of political risk. On average, Italy has had a new government for every year since World War II, and yet its commercial policies have remained unchanged. Germany has had pro-business conservatives at its helm, followed by a government with a more socialist bent, with no substantial impact on international business. Former communists have succeeded democratic presidents in Central and Eastern Europe without any substantial change in the countries' pro-business attitudes. Hong Kong has become an integral part of China, and, to date, this has created more opportunities than threats for international business.

Yet political change can be a cause for concern for international firms. Companies that have operated in countries that have had decades of stability and prosperity under a one-party rule can be affected instantly by political turmoil. Although transition from a one-party rule can be peaceful, as in the case of Mexico, when Vicente Fox took over as president from Ernesto Zedillo and the PRI (the Institutional Revolutionary Party, the ruling party for more than seventy years), this is usually the exception. In the case of Central and Eastern Europe, such a change presented opportunities, but also created regional instability, particularly in Serbia, Bosnia-Herzegovina, Croatia, and other regions. In addition to a change in the ruling party, companies should look for other signals that announce political instability: Tamil separatists in Sri Lanka, political riots in Indonesia, squatters in Zimbabwe, Rwandan refugees in Uganda—all spell trouble for the companies operating in the respective countries.

2-4b Nationalism

The expression of fierce nationalist sentiment, or **nationalism,** in a country where the company is operating could constitute a cause for concern to the international company. The expression of nationalist feelings, such as pride in a country's history and accomplishments, is common in most countries.

Nationalist sentiment may signal attempts at separation from or isolation of a particular segment of society, which could lead to political instability in the country; this is the case of the Tamil separatist movement in Sri Lanka, which has led to economic chaos in the country. Particularly problematic for international business are expressions of antiforeigner sentiment and/or antiforeign business bias. Shared beliefs that engaging in international business represents selling one's country raise questions about the future environment in the respective country. In the United States, in the 1980s, the "buy American" slogans echoing especially in the automobile and textile industries presented great concern to European and Asian business and private investors. Of special concern to international marketing managers is *consumer ethnocentrism*—the belief that buying foreign goods will put local companies out of business and is, consequently, morally wrong.[13] Countries where such beliefs predominate are more likely to erect barriers to international trade.

Nationalism An expression of fierce nationalist sentiment in a country where a company is operating, which poses an implicit threat to the company and its operations.

---

13. Terence A. Shimp and Subhash Sharma, "Consumer Ethnocentrism: Construction and Validation of the CETSCALE," *Journal of Marketing Research*, Vol. 24, No. 3 (August) 1987, pp. 280–289.

2-4c Political Risks and Risk Management in International Marketing

Nationalism and claims to national sovereignty can lead to protectionist measures on the part of the host-country government, while political instability can lead to the failure of the economy. All can harm the operations of the company in the respective country, from hurting its sales and overall prospects in the market to a complete loss of company assets. In the sections "Risks Related to Government Trade Policies," "Risks Related to Government Economic Policy," "Risks Related to Labor and Action Groups," and "Risks Related to Terrorism," following examples of risks a company can experience in international markets are examples of risk management for each category of risk.

Risks Related to Government Trade Policies

The host-country government can erect trade barriers, imposing tariffs and non-tariff barriers on international business, such as exchange-rate controls, voluntary export restraints and other types of quotas, and export/import license requirements. The company could also find itself falling victim to a trade war, where the host country and home country are reciprocally restricting the flow of goods. Or the company's home-country government can impose embargoes and sanctions on the host country, which could force the company to exit the market. All these issues are addressed at length in Chapter 3, "International Trade: Barriers and Facilitators."

Risks Related to Government Economic Policy

Local governments can use taxes as a means to control foreign investment: During downturns in the local economy, governments find that taxing foreign companies provides a source of valuable revenue. Under more extreme conditions, especially if accompanied by a radical change in the political leadership, change can lead to the (mainly involuntary) transfer of the firm's assets to local (national) ownership. Companies face the following types of risks:

- Confiscation
- Expropriation
- Creeping expropriation
- Nationalization
- Domestication

Confiscation

Confiscation The foreign government seizure of company assets and/or investors' assets without any compensation.

Confiscation refers to the seizing of company assets and/or investors' assets without any compensation. In the 1940s and 1950s, most private companies operating in Central and Eastern Europe had their assets confiscated. More recently, all U.S. firms operating in Iran were confiscated when Shah Reza Pahlavi was dethroned. As a result of the confiscation of U.S. multinationals' assets in Iran after the Islamic Revolution, the United States imposed an embargo on trade with Iran.

Expropriation

Expropriation The foreign government seizure of company assets with partial reimbursement, usually not at market value.

Expropriation involves some reimbursement for company assets, usually not at their market value. When Fidel Castro ascended to power in Cuba and a totalitarian regime was instituted, the assets of U.S. multinationals and U.S. citizens were seized. The Castro government offered payment that was deemed inappropriate, and, as a result, the United States imposed an embargo on trade with Cuba that is currently still in effect.

Creeping Expropriation

Creeping expropriation refers to a condition characterized as "difficult bureaucracies, unreliable judicial systems, shifting regulations, and corrupt operating environments."[14] Although not explicit, government actions discourage foreign investment, especially investment in nonessential sectors. This strategy typically uses additional barriers that are imposed on international trade.

Nationalization

Nationalization involves a takeover by the local government with the aim of creating a government-run industry. International law regards nationalization as legitimate as long as it is in the public interest and it offers fair compensation to the international company and to its investors. In 1997, the Korean government decided to nationalize the automobile company Kia Motors by converting the state-run Koreas Development bank's debt into an equity stake in the company.[15] In the aftermath of the Asian crisis, governments began nationalizing ailing banks across the region: In Indonesia, the government controls nearly all of the country's biggest banks and has taken over around 75 percent of all bank assets; whereas in Japan, as a result of nationalization, the government, instead of markets, now plays a larger role in determining the flow of capital.[16]

Domestication

Domestication occurs when the local government requires a gradual transfer of ownership and management to locals. This transfer is usually completed over time, through consecutive government decrees aimed at reducing the presence of multinationals in nonessential local sectors (such as the consumer goods sector).

Companies can protect themselves against political instability by understanding the structure of the government, the political parties, and the ideologies of the ruling party, as well as the competing ideologies of the opposition. As a first step, companies must make every attempt to be exemplary corporate citizens in every country where they operate. A solid reputation for product quality and community involvement can create a general environment that is favorable toward a company's local operations.

A company also can minimize its risk by partnering with local companies, creating local expertise in product manufacturing and management, and/or using local suppliers. McDonald's, for example, is frequently stressing the use of local ingredients in all of its offerings. Similarly, companies that produce products deemed essential for local development, such as industrial products, high technology products, or pharmaceutical products, are less vulnerable to changes in government policies than companies that manufacture goods that are considered nonessential, such as consumer goods.

Companies can obtain insurance coverage against nationalization from private insurance sources. For example, companies such as Global Risk Advisors insure against confiscation, expropriation, and nationalization, in addition to providing insurance against war risk, localized or subnational conflicts, kidnapping, ransom, and extortion, property terrorism, and currency inconvertibility, among

Creeping expropriation A situation characterized by bureaucratic red tape and corruption, an unreliable judicial system, and shifting regulations, where foreign government actions discourage foreign investment, especially investment in nonessential sectors.

Nationalization The takeover of company assets by a foreign government with the aim of creating a government-run industry.

Domestication The process initiated by a foreign government leading to the gradual transfer of ownership and management to locals.

14. Richard Karp, "Risk's Rewards," *Barron's*, Vol. 79, No. 16, April 1999, p. 16.

15. Sohn Young-Ju, "Saving Kia," *Business Korea*, Vol. 15, No. 1, January 1998, p. 15.

16. Henny Sender, "Reflation Is No Panacea," *Far Eastern Economic Review*, Vol. 161, No. 48, November 26, 1998, p. 93.

Overseas Private Investment Corporation (OPIC)
U.S. government corporation that provides loans, guarantees, and insurance to U.S. corporations investing in countries that present high political risk.

others.[17] The U.S. government, through the **Overseas Private Investment Corporation,** or **OPIC** (http://www.opic.gov), also offers policies that insure companies against expropriation, nationalization, or confiscation by foreign governments. OPIC insures U.S. investments in emerging markets and developing countries against expropriation and political violence, such as revolution and war.

Risks Related to Labor and Action Groups

In many countries, labor unions are very powerful and can readily influence national policies. For example, layoffs by foreign companies can bring about negative feelings that are likely to affect the company in the long term. Boycotts initiated by action groups can also negatively affect the company. Esso (Exxon) recently was the victim of a "Boycott Esso" campaign aimed at the United States' environmental policies. These actions are not usually sanctioned by the national government, but they are, nevertheless, legal.

Companies have some control over the actions of labor and action groups. Although they cannot control market demand and derived demand for labor, companies can provide severance packages that are fair, as well as invest in the services of job placement businesses in an effort to seek placement for the employees who have been terminated. To avoid negative public sentiment, companies must be politically neutral and keep a distance from local politics. Too close an association with a regime could elicit a negative attitude toward the company and its products. Pepsi, unfairly, is perceived as the drink that greased the hands of the former communist elite in Central and Eastern Europe, whereas Coke is associated with the new, free society. It is important for a firm to be perceived as a good citizen of the country where it operates, as a company that has created opportunities for locals and that continues to serve their interests.

Risks Related to Terrorism

International terrorist attacks against multinational interests culminated with the September 11, 2001, attack on the World Trade Center in New York City. In recent years, terrorist attacks have been steadily increasing in frequency. Organizations or businesses with a United States connection alone were hit 206 times in 2000, up from 169 in 1999; internationally, private-sector facilities were attacked 384 times, up from 276 in 1999, while only 17 government facilities and 13 military facilities were similarly hit around the globe. Terrorism was most lethal in Asia in the year 2000, with 281 of the 405 international victims perishing there. Africa had the second highest total, with 73 dead.[18]

The events of September 2001 have exponentially altered the trend of those statistics. In a choreographed operation, terrorists hijacked four planes that took off within minutes of each other, took control, and crashed into each of the World Trade Center twin towers and the Pentagon. Experts evaluated these attacks as the culmination of a twenty-year trend toward assaults aimed to kill many people in technically complex operations.[19] A blow to the financial nerve center of capitalism,[20] the September 11 events disrupted financial operations worldwide, dis-

---

17. Karp, "Risk's Rewards," p. 16.

18. Michael Gips, "Businesses Bearing Brunt of Terrorism," *Security Management,* Vol. 45, No. 8, August 2001, p. 18.

19. Joseph Kahn, "A Trend Toward Attacks That Emphasize Deaths," *The New York Times,* September 12, 2001, p. A18.

20. Steve Lohr, "Financial District Vows to Rise from the Ashes," *The New York Times,* September 14, 2001, p. A6.

placed hundreds of businesses in the area and beyond, and, for the first time ever, stopped all travel in U.S. airspace. An "attack on the world's … superpower, undertaken as a consequence of specific American alliances and actions,"[21] these actions are representative of corporate terrorism with the greatest of scopes.

Companies have some control, however, in reducing their likelihood of becoming victims of terrorism by training employees in terrorism avoidance, such as briefing personnel on what to expect when entering high-risk areas and offering training for eluding roadblocks and avoiding hazardous encounters.[22] Companies can also purchase insurance against terrorist acts from private insurance companies. For example, Cigna International's International Specialty Products & Services offers insurance products that cover kidnapping, detention (kidnapping without asking for ransom), hijacking, evacuation, business interruption and extra expenses, product recall expenses, and expenses arising from child abduction (such as hiring private investigators or posting rewards for information).[23]

2-5 The International Legal Environment

International marketing is affected by three bodies of law:

- **International laws**—A body of rules and regulations that countries agree to abide by. International law addresses agreements among countries with regard to trade, protection of property, and other issues in the political and economic sphere. International law agreements, although not enforceable, can be appropriately addressed by international law bodies.
- **Host-country laws**—Laws of the different countries where the company operates. The legal system in the host country could differ substantially from that of the company's home country.
- **Home-country laws**—Laws of the company's home country. Home-country laws follow the company all over the world.

U.S. companies must abide by all three types of law. For example, they must abide by international trade laws and agreements, such as World Trade Organization (WTO) trade regulations; they must abide by host-country laws governing every aspect of the company's operations; and they must abide by home-country laws, such as antitrust regulations and corrupt practices regulations.

2-5a Legal Systems

Three legal systems are predominant: common law, code law, and Islamic law.

Common Law

Common law is based on prior court rulings (legal precedent). It has its roots in English common law, on which U.S. law is based. This system of law is shared by many of the countries formerly colonized by Great Britain.

Code (Civil) Law

Code law—or civil law—refers to comprehensive written laws that specify what constitutes legal behavior. Code law has its roots in Roman law. This system of law is shared by most of the countries in the world, including most of Europe, Latin America, China, Taiwan, Japan, and South Korea.

International laws Rules and regulations that countries agree to abide by, addressing agreements among countries with regard to trade, protection of property, and other issues in the political and economic sphere.

Host-country laws Local laws; laws of the different countries where a company operates.

Home-country laws Laws of a company's home country that follow the international company all over the world.

Common law Laws that are based on prior court rulings (legal precedents).

Code law Comprehensive written laws that specify what constitutes legal behavior.

---

21. Susan Sontag, "The Talk of the Town, Tuesday, and After," *The New Yorker,* September 24, 2001, p. 32.

22. *Best's Review,* "Counter-Terrorism Driver Training May Thwart Executive Kidnapping," Vol. 98, No. 2, June 1997, p. 95.

23. Ibid.

Socialist countries still dealing with the legacy of communism are now converging on adopting civil law. Under the socialist system, countries of the Former Soviet Union and the Eastern Bloc had a system of laws that allowed a large degree of flexibility in enforcement. All the nomenklatura (high-ranking communist party officials and their offspring) were largely exempt from enforcement, with some exceptions. For the commoner, however, unsubstantiated blame activities deemed illegal—listening to Western radio stations, harboring a Western visitor—could place the individual in prison indefinitely. Such corruption appears to persist in this part of the world, where performance in the legal system is contingent on the firm's networks.

Islamic Law

Islamic law A system of law based on the interpretation of the Koran, Islam's holy book, and on interpretations of the practices and sayings of the prophet Muhammad.

Islamic law (sha'ria) is a system of law based on the interpretation of the Koran, Islam's holy book, and on interpretations of the practices and sayings of the prophet Muhammad. Islamic law establishes rules for business practices that can affect firm operations. For example, it requires the sexes to be separate; in practice, this means that women cannot interact in any environment with men with whom they are not related. It bans the consumption of products such as pork and alcohol, it does not allow banks to offer or charge interest, and it requires Muslims to pray five times a day and to fast in the month of Ramadan.

All of these factors have an impact on firms' local operations wherever Islamic law constitutes the basis of the legal system—in North Africa and the Middle East, and in Pakistan and Malaysia, among others. For example, business activities must be organized daily around prayer time. During Ramadan, business performance is generally low; in fact, many international businesses rely on the foreign, non-Muslim, workforce to carry out the firm's operations during this month.

2-5b Jurisdiction

With different legal systems worldwide, and with international laws, home-country laws, and host-country laws that govern all aspects of doing business internationally, it is important to establish **jurisdiction** in international legal disputes. No automatic supranational jurisdiction is assigned to an international court, unless the dispute takes place between companies and/or countries in the European Union; in this case, jurisdiction lies with the European Court of Justice (www.europa.eu.int). Legal disputes that arise between governments are usually handled by the International Court of Justice (www.icj-cij.org) in the Hague, within the United Nations system. International commercial law is usually handled in the home or host country of the company, or even in a third country, depending on where lies the jurisdiction for the matter under litigation. Because jurisdiction is often difficult to determine, it is advisable that each contract specifies the venue for handling the dispute and the procedure—a venue that is agreeable to all the parties involved.

Jurisdiction The country and/or legal body where a particular dispute should be adjudicated, according to the country's law, or according to the legal body's principles, respectively.

The contract should also specify whether the dispute settlement process will involve procedures other than litigation, which is often too costly and leads to negative perceptions in the international business community of the companies involved. Such procedures may be as follows:

Mediation Nonbinding procedure for conflict resolution involving an independent third party.

- **Mediation**—A nonbinding procedure that involves an independent third party. The disadvantage of mediation is that any decision of the mediator is nonbinding. The perspective of a neutral third party, however, could provide better insights into how the issue is perceived by the larger business community; moreover, not accepting the terms of mediation could signal to firms outside the conflict that the firm seen as being at fault might not be a reliable future partner.

- **Arbitration**—A procedure that involves an independent third party; the outcome of arbitration is a binding decision. Agreeing to arbitration does not necessarily mean that the companies found to be at fault will adhere to the decisions; if they do not, however, their reputation in the international business community is likely to suffer. Arbitration is often preferred to litigation. It is a much faster procedure that is likely to cost the company much less than a lawsuit.

2-5c Intellectual Property Rights Protection

Violation of **intellectual property rights** is the most significant threat to the competitiveness of companies involved in international business.[24] Intellectual property is the result of ideas and creativity transformed into products, services, and experiences that are protected for a specified period of time from unauthorized commercialization. Companies from developed countries manufacturing brand name products are the primary victims of intellectual property rights infringement and are leading the fight against violations. Losses attributed to the violation of intellectual property rights are estimated to be $60 billion a year, and its primary victims are the most innovative, fastest-growing industries such as software (with estimated annual losses at $11.4 billion), pharmaceuticals (with estimated losses at $1 billion), and entertainment (with estimated annual losses at $8 to $10 billion and expected to rise due to Internet piracy).[25]

Intellectual property protection takes on different forms:

- Protection of the rights of the inventor or of the firm employing the inventor to use and sell the invention for a specified period of time—this type of intellectual property is known as a **patent.** In many countries around the world, multinationals are racing to local patent offices to apply for patents to protect and enforce their technology; in Korea, for example, local memory chip and electronics firms are embroiled in patent disputes, fending off lawsuits initiated by multinational firms such as IBM and NEC, and the stakes are high: Losers will not only suffer financial setbacks in the form of paying royalties, but will also suffer the stigma of being labeled copycats.[26] This situation will ultimately be rectified by the World Trade Organization, which will institute uniform patent rules that all members are expected to follow.
- Protection of the rights to an original work of art (literature, music, film, design, and other works), allowing the owner the right to reproduce, sell, perform, or film the work—this is known as **copyright.** National and international associations are actively fighting copyright infringement. In the United States, such an organization is the International Intellectual Property Alliance, or IIPA (www.iipa.com). The IIPA is formed in conjunction with the Association of American Publishers, the Business Software Alliance, the Interactive Digital Software Association, the Motion Picture

Arbitration Binding procedure for conflict resolution involving an independent third party; a faster and less costly procedure than a lawsuit.

Intellectual property rights Laws protecting the rights of the inventor or of the firm employing the inventor to use and sell an invention for a specified period of time.

Patent Protection of the rights of the inventor or of the firm employing the inventor to use and sell an invention for a specified period of time.

Copyright The rights to an original work of art (literature, music, film, design, and other works), enabling the owner to reproduce, sell, perform, or film the work.

---

24. Ilkka A. Ronkainen and Jose-Luis Guerrero-Cusumano, "Correlates of Intellectual Property Violation," *Multinational Business Review,* Vol. 9, No. 1, Spring 2001, pp. 59–65.

25. Ibid.

26. Business Korea, "Copycats Beware," Vol. 18, No. 3, March 2001, pp. 44–45.

Association of America, the National Music Publishers' Association, and the Recording Industry Association of America; recently, the IIPA filed petitions with the Office of the U.S. Trade Representative to investigate copyright infringement in the CD and CD-ROM markets in Brazil, Costa Rica, Guatemala, Russia, and Uruguay.[27]

- Protection of a brand name, mark, symbol, motto, or slogan that identifies a particular manufacturer's brand and distinguishes it from the competitors' brands in the same product category—this is known as **trademark.** Trademark infringement occurs at many levels, from directly copying the product, as in the case of counterfeit Rolex watches and Gucci and Fendi purses selling for $30 in the streets of New York City, Hong Kong, and Paris and in many bazaars in developing countries. Brand name counterfeiting involves using the brand name, but not the product design, as in the case of Oleg Cassini and Christian Dior plain Egyptian cotton t-shirts selling in the streets of Cairo. Design copying, which is legal, involves using a popular design without the trademark, as in shirts with a crocodile or polo player that do not have the respective Lacoste and Ralph Lauren names, and Peugeot watches that look just like the Rolex oyster.
- Protection of know-how, formulas, and special blends that are not registered, and thus not protected by law—these are shared with licensees, franchisers, or other partners and are known as **trade secrets.**

Trademark   A brand name, mark, symbol, motto, or slogan that identifies a particular manufacturer's brand and distinguishes it from the competitors' brands in the same product category.

Trade secrets   Intellectual property such as know-how, formulas, special blends, and other elements that are not registered, and are thus not protected by law.

Factors Influencing Intellectual Property Rights Violations

The degree of intellectual property rights violation is influenced by a number of market factors,[28] such as

- Lack of appropriate legislation (e.g., for software)
- Lax enforcement, especially for local firms
- Unavailability of the authentic products, or when available, their high price provides justification for both the violators and the respective governments to allow the practice

and cultural factors, such as

- Values that perceive imitation as a high form of flattery
- A culture characterized by interpersonal distrust and feelings of not getting a fair deal
- A culture characterized by an emphasis on acquisition of material wealth at the expense of caring for others; in this instance in particular, the focus of acquisition are status brands consumed and/or displayed publicly, rather than privately
- Beliefs that technology is in the common domain and that use of others' intellectual property is appropriate

Involvement in regional trade agreements and other trade organizations is also sought to diminish the likelihood that a country would tolerate violation of intellectual property rights. In fact, intellectual property rights used to be largely a domestic issue, with individual countries deciding on their own levels of legal protection and enforcement; today, countries that join the World Trade Organization,

---

27. Heather R. Goldstein, David M. Lange, Andrew E. Roth, and James D. Lawrence, "International Intellectual Property Alliance Points USTR Toward Brazil, Costa Rica, Guatemala, Russia, Uruguay," *Intellectual Property & Technology Law Journal,* Vol. 12, No. 11, November 2000, p. 27.

28. See Ronkainen and Guerrero-Cusumano, "Correlates of Intellectual Property Violation," pp. 59–65.

or WTO (www.wto.org), must also sign on to the **Trade-Related Aspects of Intellectual Property Rights (TRIPS)** agreement, an international agreement that sets out minimum standards for the legal protection of intellectual property.[29]

Multinationals seeking TRIPS's protection around the world still depend on each country's patent office to grant those rights and their judicial, customs, and police services to enforce them (in Europe, regionwide patents can be obtained). TRIPS offers rules describing the protection these systems must provide, including extending intellectual property rights to include computer programs, integrated circuits, plant varieties, and pharmaceuticals, which were unprotected in most developing countries until this agreement. According to TRIPS, patents can be granted for any new technological process or product, and the protection lasts 20 years from the date of application.[30]

In addition to TRIPS, and working in conjunction with the World Trade Organization, international conventions have been gaining strength. Among these conventions are the Berne Convention for copyrighted works, under the auspices of the World Intellectual Property Organization;[31] the Paris Convention for the protection of industrial property; and the Madrid Arrangement, which established the Bureau for the International Registration of Trademarks.

Helping these organizations and conventions are, in particular, national governments of developed countries, which are protecting their multinationals. In the United States, the Patent and Trademark Office has an annual budget of $1 billion; a staff of more than 3,000 highly trained scientists, engineers, and legal experts; more than 600 judges to preside over patent disputes; and a vast customs service to clamp down on counterfeiting.[32] To protect intellectual property rights in the Internet Age, the United States government passed the Digital Millennium Copyright Act.

Developing countries frequently argue that intellectual property protection is yet another arm that is used in placing them at an economic disadvantage. From their point of view, patents and copyrights impose great cost on consumers in developing countries. In recent examples, AIDS activists and the government in South Africa argued that patents were killing the country's millions of HIV-infected patients who could not afford the drug. Mexican peasants were enraged that a U.S. company received the exclusive right to market enola beans in the United States because they have been growing the bean for generations, and the protection is restricting their ability to export the drug north of the border.[33] Activists argue that intellectual property protection allows Western multinationals to set up monopolies; to drive out local competing brands; to divert research and development away from the needs of developing countries; and to drive up prices while preventing poor people from getting life-saving drugs, interfering with age-old farming practices, and allowing foreign "pirates" to raid local resources, such as medicinal plants, without getting permission or paying compensation.[34]

Trade-Related Aspects of Intellectual-Property Rights (TRIPS)   An international agreement, under the World Trade Organization, that sets out minimum standards for the legal protection of intellectual property. (See www.wto.org.)

29. *The Economist,* "Special: The Right to Good Ideas Patents and the Poor," Vol. 359, No. 8227 June 23, 2001, pp. 21–23.

30. Ibid.

31. Ronkainen and Guerrero-Cusumano, "Correlates of Intellectual Property Violation," pp. 59–65.

32. *The Economist,* "Special: The Right to Good Ideas Patents and the Poor," pp. 21–23.

33. Ibid.

34. Ibid.

2-5d Home-Country Legislation Affecting Multinational Firms Operating Overseas

Antitrust Laws

Antitrust laws Laws designed to prevent anticompetitive activities, such as the creation of monopolies and cartels.

Antitrust laws of home and host countries are designed to prevent domestic anticompetitive activities, such as the creation of monopolies and cartels. The United States was among the first to impose its antitrust laws on firms in the United States and on U.S. firms operating abroad. Increasingly, governments of other countries are enacting and enforcing antitrust legislation that affects multinationals worldwide. In fact, antitrust enforcement in the United States often appears to be more lenient than in other developed countries. For example, the European Commission vetoed mergers between competitors after the U.S. gave these mergers a green light—as in the case of the General Electric failed takeover attempt of Honeywell and the MCI Worldcom and Sprint proposed merger.[35]

The United States allows certain types of collusion in the case of small and medium-size firms that might not have the resources to embark on a successful export program. The U.S. Congress passed the Export Trading Company Act in the 1980s to encourage firms to join forces in exporting by exempting them from antitrust laws.

Corruption Laws

Corruption laws Laws designed to prevent multinational corporations from using unethical means to obtain competitive advantage in a particular market.

Corruption laws of home and host countries are designed to prevent multinational corporations from using unethical means to obtain competitive advantage in a particular market. The World Bank surveyed 3,600 companies in 69 countries and found that 40 percent of firms paid bribes; this figure in industrial countries was 15 percent, and in the former Soviet Union, it increased to 60 percent. Similarly, the European Bank for Reconstruction and Development (EBRD), which encourages investments in the former Eastern Bloc, has called Eastern Europe's bribe-seeking a deterrent to foreign investment.[36]

Foreign Corrupt Practices Act (FCPA) Legislation that makes it illegal for companies and their representatives to bribe government officials and other politicians or candidates to political office, either directly or through third parties.

The U.S. **Foreign Corrupt Practices Act (FCPA)** makes it illegal for companies and their representatives to bribe government officials and other politicians or candidates to political office. The Act also prohibits payment to third parties when the company has good reason to assume that part of that payment is being used for bribery purposes. U.S. multinational companies take such laws very seriously—some even address their commitment to reject bribery and other corruption in their mission statement (Caterpillar does so, for example)—even though forbidding these practices places U.S. firms at a disadvantage. In a number of high-profile cases, investigators found that illegal payments were made by firms operating in Canada, Colombia, Cook Islands, the Dominican Republic, Egypt, Germany, Iraq, Israel, Jamaica, Mexico, Niger, Nigeria, and Trinidad and Tobago; these payments ranged from $22,000 to $9.9 million and represented percentages of up to 20 percent of the business obtained. Seventeen companies have been charged under the FCPA, with fines ranging from $10,000 to $21.8 million.[37]

---

35. Edmund L. Andrews and Paul Meller, "EU Vetoes GE's Plan to Acquire Honeywell," *International Herald Tribune*, Frankfurt, July 4, 2001, pp. 1, 5.

36. Jack G. Kaikati, George M. Sullivan, John M. Virgo, T. R. Carr, and Katherine S. Virgo, "The Price of International Business Morality: Twenty Years Under the Foreign Corrupt Practices Act," *Journal of Business Ethics*, Vol. 26, No. 3, August 2000, pp. 213–222.

37. Ibid.

Chapter Summary

- **Provide an overview of the world economic environment and examine different perspectives on economic development**

Countries are becoming more and more interconnected by trade, and developments in one region have immediate repercussions in the rest of the world. There are two primary views on the economic development process: The Rostow model portrays economic development as a function of productivity, exchange, technology, and income; whereas the Marxist-Leninist model portrays development as a function of the control on the means of production, of production outcomes, resource allocation, and the development of a mindset devoid of materialist needs. These two models follow a parallel route from the traditional society to the industrialized society stage—the latter characterized by modern technology and international business expansion (and known as the drive to maturity in the Rostow framework and capitalism in the Marxist-Leninist framework). They diverge on subsequent stages: Rostow's model refers to the high-mass-consumption stage as one where a surge occurs in per capita income and increased allocation to social welfare programs; whereas the Marxist-Leninist model has as next stages socialism and communism, both characterized by state and collective ownership and the elimination of private property in a new, egalitarian society. Although the Marxist-Leninist model in practice has suffered a powerful defeat due to the collapse of communism in Central and Eastern Europe, it still has some appeal in developing countries arguing against market-oriented capitalism, fueling anticolonial, anticapitalist sentiment, while advocating a collective societal orientation.

- **Address differences between countries of different levels of economic development and discuss the importance of emerging markets**

Countries belong to different development categories. Developed countries are highly industrialized, have well-developed industrial and service sectors, and present great potential, with a GNP per capita of $9,266; they also present a challenge because their markets are in the maturity stage, consumers have established preferences, and competition is intense. Countries with emerging markets are developing rapidly and have great potential, as they privatize state-owned industries and adopt market reforms; of these countries, big emerging markets (BEMs) present the greatest potential for international trade and expansion. These countries are middle-income countries, with a GNP per capita of US$766 to US$9,265. Developing countries are primarily agrarian, have a low GNP per capita (less than $755), and are located in different regions in Asia and in Sub-Saharan Africa; they

tend to be neglected or under-served by large multinationals and thus present great potential as niche markets.

- **Examine the indicators of political risk and address international firm approaches to political risk management**

Several indicators signal political risk: economic performance, political repression, the existence of multiple groups with incongruent interests, rampant nationalism, and political instability. Some of the risks that companies can experience in foreign markets involve some level of dispossession, such as nationalization, expropriation, confiscation; risks related to action groups and labor; as well as corporate terrorism, which is on the increase. Firms can reduce risk by being good corporate citizens, by partnering with local firms, and by purchasing risk insurance.

- **Describe how international law, home-country law, and host-country law affect international firm operations and address issues related to jurisdiction**

International companies are subject to multiple sets of laws: laws of the host country, laws of the home country—such as anticompetitiveness (antitrust) laws and corruption laws—and international laws, which could be laws of a regional governance body, such as the European Union, or laws of an international body, such as the World Trade Organization. Under this complex scenario, jurisdiction often becomes a problem; it is advisable that firms entering into agreements agree upon jurisdiction and on the procedure needed for conflict resolution.

- **Discuss different legal systems, intellectual property laws, and national laws with extra-territorial impact that affect the international firm**

The three primary types of legal systems are common law (based on prior court rulings, with roots in English common law); code law, or civil law, which draws upon comprehensive written laws that specify what constitutes legal behavior (with roots in Roman law); and Islamic law, a system of law based on the interpretation of Islam's holy book and the practices and sayings of the prophet Muhammad.

One issue facing multinationals today is the violation of intellectual property rights, which constitutes a great threat to firms' competitiveness. Protection of patents, copyrights, trademarks, and trade secrets is difficult to enforce due to lax attitudes attributed to cultural values and to economic and political motivations of national governments. This type of protection might have better prospects now that more countries have become members of the World Trade Organization and are signatories of the Trade-Related Aspects of Intellectual Property Rights (TRIPS) agreement.

Discussion Questions

Discussion Questions

1. Compare the Rostow and the Marxist-Leninist models of economic development. How do you explain the two models in light of developments over the past decade in Central and Eastern Europe?

2. Why do developing countries continue to embrace the Marxist-Leninist model of economic development?

3. Describe indicators of political risk. Examine current events and identify some of the political risks that multinational companies could face in the world today.

4. Discuss two home-country laws that affect U.S. businesses operating internationally.

5. What are some examples of violations of international property rights? Give some examples of counterfeiting.

Chapter

3

International Trade: Barriers and Facilitators

Key Terms

African Development Bank
antidumping
Asian Development Bank
automatic import license
blocked currency
boycott
countervailing duty actions
currency and capital flow
    controls
differential exchange rate
embargo
employment protection
European Bank for
    Reconstruction and
    Development
foreign exchange permit
foreign trade zones
General Agreement on Tariffs
    and Trade (GATT)
Group of Eight (G8)

import quota
infant industry argument
Inter-American Development
    Bank
International Monetary Fund
    (IMF)
local content requirement
maquiladora
Ministry of Foreign Affairs
Ministry of Trade
Most-Favored-Nation Status
nonautomatic import license
nontariff barriers
off-shore assembly plants
orderly market arrangements
paratariff measures
price controls
protection of markets
    with excess labor

protection of markets with
    excess productive capacity
protectionism
sanctions
special economic zones
standards as barriers to trade
tariffs
United Nations organizations
United States Agency
    for International
    Development (USAID)
United States Department
    of Commerce
United States State
    Department
voluntary export restraints
voluntary import expansion
World Bank
World Trade Organization
    (WTO)

Outline

Learning Objectives
3-1 Arguments for
    Protectionism
    3-1a Protection of Markets
        with Excess Productive
        Capacity
    3-1b Employment Protection
        and Protection of Markets
        with Excess Labor
    3-1c Infant Industry Arguments
        and Arguments Related
        to the Industrialization
        of Developing Countries
    3-1d Natural Resources
        Conservation and
        Protection of the
        Environment
    3-1e Protection of Consumers
    3-1f National Defense Interests
3-2 Tools of Government
    Protectionism: Tariff and
    Nontariff Barriers
    3-2a Tariffs
    3-2b Nontariff Barriers
3-3 Facilitators of International
    Trade
    3-3a International Trade and
        Economic Development
        Organizations
    3-3b Government
        Organizations
    3-3c Other Institutions and
        Procedures Facilitating
        International Trade
Chapter Summary
Discussion Questions

Learning Objectives

Learning Objectives

By the end of this chapter, you should be able to:

- Identify different trade barriers imposed on international trade and arguments used by governments to erect and maintain these barriers
- Provide an overview of key international organizations facilitating international trade directly or by promoting economic development

- Identify government efforts involved in promoting economic development and trade
- Describe other trade facilitators, such as foreign trade zones, off-shore assembly plants and special economic zones, and the Most-Favored-Nation Status

Businesses must face numerous barriers when entering international markets. Barriers to entry can be imposed by local and international competition, by the local channel structure, and by logistics and other firms offering marketing support. Factors in the economic, political, financial, and legal environment also can create barriers for businesses attempting to expand internationally—as was seen in Chapter 2, "An Overview of the International Marketing Environment." Even protectionist tendencies within a regionally integrated area could impose barriers to entry. For example, one of the first nicknames that the European Union acquired in the late 1980s was "Fortress Europe," for its potential to restrict access to this large, integrated market to companies from its member countries; that has not held true so far—but the possibility for it still remains. This chapter focuses on government-initiated protectionist strategies, such as tariff and nontariff barriers.

The reduction in trade barriers constitutes a main concern of multinationals and their representative governments. In addition to participating in numerous regional treaties, governments have joined forces to create forums for discussion of trade issues and mechanisms for the reduction of trade restrictions. One such organization, the World Trade Organization, has had a significant positive impact on trade, reigning in protectionist strategies of important players in the world of trade, such as China, and opening formerly closed markets to international companies. Nevertheless, despite its accomplishments, this organization has met substantial opposition recently from groups that perceive globalization as the promotion of corporate interests to the detriment of the individual, of developing countries, and of the environment. This chapter focuses on facilitators to international trade, and addresses the opposition to trade expansion by environmentalists and developing countries. Chapter 4, "Regional Economic and Political Integration," addresses regional economic and political integration as yet another mechanism used to eliminate trade barriers.

Protection of local markets from foreign companies constitutes an important mandate for national and local governments alike. Many political careers have been built and defended on market protection rhetoric. "We will not sell our country" has been a slogan of countries resisting foreign economic and political dominance in the past. Today, it is a slogan used against multinationals that are rapidly expanding, taking over emerging markets, and bringing with them a consumption culture perceived to go against local culture and traditions. These multinationals also are seen as eliminating small local producers and service providers, bankrupting formerly productive factories, and replacing abundant local labor with more efficient advanced technology, increasing local unemployment and disrupting political stability.

Some of the arguments for **protectionism** are indeed valid. The **infant industry argument** is aimed at protecting an emerging national industry from powerful international competitors, which could easily squeeze out a newcomer to the business merely with its brand name resonance and with pricing strategies that a new industry could not possibly sustain in the long term. The argument stressing the industrialization of developing countries also is valid for similar reasons. The national defense argument is regarded as justified in international trade forums and is widely accepted as a reasonable argument for protectionism.

> **Protectionism** All actions by national and local governments aimed at protecting local markets from foreign competitors.
>
> **Infant industry argument** A protectionist strategy aimed at protecting a national industry in its infancy from powerful international competitors.

There is also the argument for environmental protection and/or protection of natural resources and the need for maintaining standards to the benefit of all humankind; this line of arguments is also soundly reasoned. The problem with this defense of protectionism arises when the standards imposed are, in fact, simple protectionist arms that require foreign competition to go through excessive and unwarranted bureaucratic exercise, or when these requirements are imposed on international firms but not on local firms—or not to the same degree.

In general, it is believed that consumers pay the final price for the cost of strategies of protectionism. Arguments for protectionism ignore the economic advantages of free trade and the importance of adopting open market mechanisms for optimal long-term market performance. In fact, history has amply demonstrated that a government's right and authority to pick and choose winners among industries and firms could be corrupted and distorted by local influential firms, power-seeking politicians, and favor-seeking lobby groups.[1] Politicians, particularly in the United States, favor trade barriers and vote for imposing them because such strategies appeal directly to the concerns of their constituencies regarding the possibility of losing their jobs. What these politicians do not consider is the subsequent retaliatory action of other governments which will negatively affect the domestic economy, the higher consumer prices attributed to the tax imposed to subsidize the domestic industry, and higher prices attributed to the reduction in competition in the local market.[2]

3-1 Arguments for Protectionism

Sections 3-1 through 3-1f describe arguments most often advanced to justify the imposition of tariff and nontariff trade barriers.

---

1. Victor V. Cordell and Erin Breland, "Conflicting Competition Policies in a Globalized Business Environment: Prospects for Cooperation and Convergence," *Competitiveness Review,* Vol. 10, No. 1, 2000, pp. 104–122.

2. Ibid.

3-1a Protection of Markets with Excess Productive Capacity

Markets that have excess productive capacity have committed significant resources to the production facilities. In the case of Central and Eastern Europe, for example, the standard for production during the central planning years under communism was represented by mammoth factories employing hundreds of thousands of workers, each charged with minuscule repetitive tasks under an elaborate division-of-labor program. The goal of such programs was both to ensure productivity and to assure a place of work to every individual, qualified or not. Such factories had, in addition to the workers, structures with directors and paradirectors, all served by several secretaries whose specializations varied from typing to answering telephones, to making coffee, to taking care of the director's family's personal shopping.

After the fall of communism, the new factory owners (often foreign) quickly realized that they needed only a fraction of the workers for optimal production and proceeded to fire the rest, leading to regional unrest. Currently, remaining factories are protected from foreign buyouts and are managed locally. Often they are state-owned enterprises. National governments protect them from foreign investors. They also protect these enterprises by limiting the entrance of competing products, such as superior steel and higher-performance tractors, by arguing that such restrictions are instituted to **protect a market with excess productive capacity.**

3-1b Employment Protection and Protection of Markets with Excess Labor

Under the scenario presented in section 3-1a, the markets of Central and Eastern Europe—especially those in the countries of the Former Soviet Union—are now experiencing high levels of excess labor and underemployment, all of which lead to flares of social unrest. As a result, local politicians actively lobby against granting import licenses for products competing with locally produced goods that are established in the market. Arguments invoking **employment protection** are used to ensure that competing multinationals do not import products manufactured elsewhere that might drive local manufacturers out of business and create local unemployment. The argument also is used against multinationals that might purchase local plants and fire most of the redundant workers to create acceptable levels of profitability. A related argument, invoking the **protection of markets with excess labor,** is also used to prevent more efficient multinationals from taking over local businesses and streamlining local operations.

3-1c Infant Industry Arguments and Arguments Related to the Industrialization of Developing Countries

The infant industry arguments and arguments related to the industrialization of developing countries are considered valid: Developing countries need to protect their markets from competitors from countries with an established industrial base. Foreign competitors would be able to offer higher quality products at lower costs and would undoubtedly undercut local manufacturers attempting to break into the market. Foreign competition would present the greatest challenge to local industries in their infancy.

3-1d Natural Resources Conservation and Protection of the Environment

The resource conservation argument is considered to be valid in international trade organization forums, especially in light of worldwide shortages of raw mate-

Protection of markets with excess productive capacity
A protectionist measure used to prevent foreign buyouts, invoking the protection of local labor.

Employment protection
Protection of local employment by not granting import licenses for products competing with similar, locally produced, goods.

Protection of markets with excess labor   The erection of barriers to imports of products competing with local offerings in an effort to protect local jobs rials. Similarly, a balance sometimes has to be struck between free trade and legitimate arguments such as those centering on environmental protection, but governments still need to find a way of agreeing when curbs on trade can be an acceptable way to pursue a greater good.[3]

The problem with these two arguments arises when they are used arbitrarily, with a clear bias against international firms, either imposing the standards only on foreign firms or requiring them to meet higher standards than local firms.

3-1e Protection of Consumers

Protection of consumers is an often-echoed argument that ultimately favors local, over international, business. Standards that are rigidly applied against foreign businesses, quality controls that necessitate layers of costly bureaucracy, and arbitrary product origin requirements, among others, are invoked as a basis for this argument. Politicians in the European Union have argued that they were protecting consumers by imposing standards on imported beef: Listening to the unified voices of their constituencies and attempting to protect the local beef industry against the high-quality, cheap, corn-fed U.S. beef, the European Union banned its import, invoking the use of growth hormones in the United States. With cattle in many countries of the European Union plagued by mad-cow and/or hoof-and-mouth disease, the primary option available to European consumers is expensive Argentine beef. This is an unequivocal demonstration that consumer-protection-gone-too-far is not necessarily in the interest of the consumer.

3-1f National Defense Interests

The national defense argument is also perceived as valid, and it is often invoked in international trade forums. Publications that attempt to destabilize the government, armament, and other similar products are often under an import ban. More recently, the national defense argument has been advocated by developing countries and/or by countries that attempt to control and restrict access of their population to Western influence. Such nations may perceive a threat in the unrestricted imports of information-based services through electronic channels; countries such as China, Singapore, and Saudi Arabia impose restrictions on and even ban ownership of satellite dishes, whereas other nations are attempting to control citizen access on the World Wide Web (WWW).[4]

3-2 Tools of Government Protectionism: Tariff and Nontariff Barriers

3-2a Tariffs

Tariffs are any type of tax imposed on goods entering a particular country. Tariffs are imposed to

Tariffs Taxes imposed on goods entering a country.

- Discourage imports of particular goods, such as consumer goods, which often are not considered essential in developing countries
- Penalize countries that are not politically aligned with the importing country, or countries that are imposing tariffs or nontariff restrictions on goods from the importing country
- Generate revenues for the importing country

---

3. *The Economist*, "Leaders: Storm Over Globalization," Vol. 353, No. 8_47, November 27, 1999, pp. 15–16.

4. Christopher H. Lovelock and George S. Yip, "Developing Global Strategies for Service Businesses," *California Management Review*, Vol. 38, No. 2, Winter 1996, pp. 64–86.

In general, tariffs that are assessed by the United States are relatively low, less than 10 percent. Some developing countries set tariffs higher than 100 percent for products that compete with an infant industry. For example, countries attempting to develop their own automobile industry are likely to impose very high tariffs to all automobiles imported into the country.

3-2b Nontariff Barriers

Nontariff barriers include all measures, other than traditional tariffs, that are used to distort international trade flows; they raise prices of both imports and import-competing goods and favor domestic over foreign supply sources by causing importers to charge higher prices and to restrict import volumes.[5]

In the past twenty years, in an attempt to keep markets closed without going against the General Agreement on Tariffs and Trade (GATT) and the World Trade Organization (see Chapter 4), governments have created new nontariff barriers, such as orderly market arrangements, voluntary import expansion, and voluntary export restraints, which limit market access for foreign businesses. These nontariff barriers have been erected by many countries, but most are imposed by the United States, members of the European Union, and by other industrialized countries on exporting countries such as Japan, South Korea,[6] and developing countries.[7] Other, more traditional, nontariff barriers include quotas, currency controls, and standards—such as environmental, quality, performance, and health standards, all of which are expensive to provide and to evaluate. Boycotts, embargoes, and sanctions are the most severe barriers to trade that are imposed usually to punish a company or a national government.

Nontariff barriers are constantly evolving: They are in a continuous process of refinement, aimed at avoiding scrutiny from the World Trade Organization or other trade organizations. Although the most frequently encountered nontariff barriers are described here, it is important to note that new variants of the barriers described are continuously emerging in the global trade arena.

Import Quotas and Orderly Market Arrangements

Import quotas specify a maximum quantity (unit limit) or a value (usually specified in the national currency) of a product that may be imported during a specified period. Quotas are administered either on a global first-come, first-served basis or on a bilateral basis to restrict shipments from a specific supply source—such as the Multifiber Arrangement.[8]

The Multifiber Arrangement was initiated as a temporary measure in 1974 (but lasted 21 years!). Its articulated goals were to expand trade, to reduce barriers to trade, and to initiate a progressive liberalization of world trade in textile products, while ensuring the orderly and equitable development of this trade and avoiding disruptive effects in individual markets and on individual lines of production in both importing and exporting countries.[9] In reality, this was an **orderly market arrangement,** an intricate process of establishing quotas in the textile and

Nontariff barriers All measures, other than traditional tariffs, used to distort trade flows, used to increase prices of imports, and thus favor domestic over foreign products.

Import quota The maximum quantity (unit limit) or value of a product that may be imported during a specified period.

Orderly market arrangements Protectionist measures involving intricate processes for establishing quotas in the textile and apparel industries.

---

5. Don P. Clark, "Are Poorer Developing Countries the Targets of U.S. Protectionist Actions?" *Economic Development and Cultural Change,* Vol. 47, No. 1, October 1998, pp. 193–207.

6. Cordell and Breland, "Conflicting Competition Policies in a Globalized Business Environment," pp. 104–122.

7. Clark, "Are Poorer Developing Countries the Targets of U.S. Protectionist Actions?" pp. 193–207.

8. Ibid.

9. Richard Hughes, "The Uruguay Round: New Approach for the Textiles and Clothing Sector," *International Trade Forum,* No. 4, 1995, pp. 4–11.

apparel industries, initiated by the United States and Europe, whose textile operations were moving to Asia to take advantage of cheaper labor. The Multifiber Arrangement was nullified under the Uruguay Round of the General Agreement on Tariffs and Trade in 1995 but has since been replaced by very similar nontariff barriers.

Nonautomatic Import Licenses

Nonautomatic import licenses are issued on a discretionary basis and are used to restrict imports of a given product. Licensing requirements can restrict the volume of imports, as do quotas, or they can be used to impose on the exporter or importer specific conditions that will result in fewer imports.[10] It should be mentioned that the World Trade Organization presently requires member countries to ensure transparency of the import-license granting process; they are asked to do so by publicizing information concerning administration of restrictions, by listing information regarding the licenses granted over the most recent period, and, where practicable, by providing additional import statistics of the products concerned.[11]

Nonautomatic import license
A license issued on a discretionary basis to restrict imports of a given product and/or from a particular country.

Automatic Import Licenses

Automatic import licenses are granted freely to importing companies. Automatic licenses are used by the importing country's government for the purpose of import surveillance: The licenses have the potential to discourage import surges, they place additional administrative and financial burdens on the importer, and they may also raise costs by delaying product shipments.[12]

Automatic import license
A license granted freely to importing companies but may be used by government for the purpose of import surveillance, thus discouraging import surges, imposing administrative and financial burdens on importers, and delaying shipment.

Voluntary Import Expansion (VIE)

Under a **voluntary import expansion** (VIE), a country agrees to open its markets to imports. Voluntary import expansions increase foreign access to a domestic market, while increasing competition and reducing prices. Voluntary import expansions are not voluntary at all: A country agrees to import products as a result of pressure from another country. An example of voluntary import expansion is Japan's decision to avert U.S.-imposed trade sanctions by importing U.S. semiconductors.[13]

Voluntary import expansion
A government's response to protectionist threats from another country whereby it agrees to open markets to imports and/or to increase foreign access to a domestic market to avoid more severe protectionist action.

Voluntary Export Restraints (VER)

Voluntary export restraints (VERs) are self-imposed quotas and constitute a barrier to trade often used in the 1980s to protect local industries. The United States, for example, used voluntary export restraints to protect local steel and automobile industries. Voluntary export restraints are agreed upon by the importing country and the exporting country. A country that is subject to voluntary export restraints limits the quantity of products it exports to another, primarily because it attempts, by doing so, to avoid more severe, future mandatory import restrictions. Voluntary export quotas are still used today even though they have been banned by the Uruguay Round of the General Agreement on Tariffs and Trade (and now by the

Voluntary export restraints
A government's self-imposed export quotas to a particular country that are established to avoid more severe protectionist action by the respective importing country.

10. Clark, "Are Poorer Developing Countries the Targets of U.S. Protectionist Actions?" pp. 193–207.

11. Richard Brechter, "The WTO at a Glance," *The China Business Review*, Vol. 24, No. 3, May/June 1997, pp. 16–17.

12. Clark, "Are Poorer Developing Countries the Targets of U.S. Protectionist Actions?" pp. 193–207.

13. Theresa M. Greaney, "Import Now! An Analysis of Market-Share Voluntary Import Expansions (VIEs)," *Journal of International Economics*, Vol. 40, No. 1/2, February 1996, pp. 149–170.

World Trade Organization) since 1999. The United States is imposing them informally, for example, for Japanese steel imports; this protection mechanism has been used since 1969 in the long history of trade protection of the U.S. steel industry.[14]

Price Controls: Increasing Prices of Imports

Price controls have a direct effect on a product mix aimed at a particular market. Increasing the price of imports to match minimum prices of domestic offerings is one such strategy that is frequently used for both products and for retailers. For example, Japan uses such controls to ensure that locally produced rice is not at a disadvantage relative to rice imports from the United States, which are of equally high quality but are sold at much lower prices. In this instance, the prices of imports are held artificially high so that local consumers would not discriminate in favor of U.S. competitors. Similarly, Wal-Mart and other discounters and category specialists (see Chapter 12, "International Retailing") in the European Union are constantly scrutinized and often pressured by local authorities to raise prices; EU governments charge that these international retailers price products below cost to drive out smaller competitors.

Price Controls: Antidumping and Countervailing Duty Actions

Antidumping and **countervailing duty actions** were designed to counter unfair competition, such as predatory pricing. Dumping refers to selling below fair value to undermine competitors' charging the market price and/or to get rid of excess inventory—with the same outcome, of undermining competition. When used as price controls, antidumping measures involve initiating investigations to determine whether imports are sold below fair value, imposing duties to offset dumping, as well as adopting other measures to counter the effects of dumping. Countervailing measures include investigations to determine whether imports are sold below fair prices as a result of foreign subsidies; such determination is usually followed by duties that are imposed to offset this practice and measures taken to offset effects of subsidies.[15]

To the detriment of international trade, such measures have become protectionist tools that are used to intimidate importers and restrict trade. The European Union has been under scrutiny recently for excessive use of antidumping investigations. Such investigations probing into antidumping activity and countervailing duty investigations are focused on a specific product from a particular supply source, and thus they are frequently referred to as "made-to-measure" protectionist devices.[16]

Price Controls: Paratariff Measures

Paratariff measures are charges that increase the costs of imports in a manner similar to tariffs. Such measures include allowing an initial number of product units to enter the country duty-free and charging tariffs to subsequent shipments in excess of this quota; they also include advance import deposits, additional import charges, seasonal tariffs, and customs charges. The United States uses many of these paratariff measures to discourage shipment of certain agricultural products from developing countries.[17]

Price controls Strategies requiring a product to sell for a particular price in the local market; price control strategies are typically used to increase the prices of imports to match the minimum prices of local competition.

Antidumping Legislation designed to counter unfair price competition; lengthy antidumping investigations can also serve as an impediment to trade.

Countervailing duty actions Investigations initiated to determine whether imports are sold below fair prices as a result of foreign subsidies and the subsequent establishment of measures to offset subsidies.

Paratariff measures Additional, nontariff fees that increase the costs of imports in a manner similar to tariffs.

---

14. Jae W. Chung, "Effects of U.S. Trade Remedy Law Enforcement Under Uncertainty: The Case of Steel," *Southern Economic Journal,* Vol. 65, No. 1, July 1998, pp. 151–159.

15. Clark, "Are Poorer Developing Countries the Targets of U.S. Protectionist Actions?" pp. 193–207.

16. Ibid.

17. Ibid.

Standards

Standards as barriers to trade are frequently used as barriers to imports, primarily imposed by highly industrialized countries. Problematic are standards that are especially strict, such as those imposed by the European Union against hormone-fed U.S. beef and bio-engineered corn and soybeans on safety grounds. Standards that discriminate against foreign firms in particular, or that simply create more bureaucratic hurdles for importing firms, act as nontariff barriers to trade.

On the positive side, excessive standards could and often do help local and international industry alike, by deterring gray markets. For example, the United States has very strict environmental and manufacturing standards for automobiles. Importing an automobile that is not specifically designed according to U.S. specifications is very costly: One has to use expensive automobile conversion services and obtain the appropriate Department of Transportation authorization to use the vehicle.

Local Content Requirements and Foreign Ownership: Percentage Requirements

Governments of many emerging market economies mandate that a certain percentage of the products imported are locally produced: They mandate a **local content requirement.** This requirement can often be met by manipulating and/or assembling the product on the territory of the importing country—usually in a foreign trade zone. China, for example, has always presented a challenge to importing firms. Multinational firms often join with Chinese partners and agents to either package or manufacture enough of the product to have it qualify based on local content requirements; firms often do tricky calculations on local services and part values to meet such local content edicts.[18]

In addition to the traditional local content requirements, there are other forms of favoring local contribution and labor. For example, governments often impose regulations to protect local carriers for passenger and freight transportation. An example would be restricting foreign airlines' landing rights or ability to pick up passengers at an intermediate stop ("third freedom" rights); this requirement favors national airlines operating on international routes.[19]

Foreign ownership restrictions also are widely used. Some ownership restrictions refer to the percentage ownership in a business—for example, requiring 51 percent or more of a joint venture to be owned by a national firm. Other restrictions are even more stringent and discriminatory in favor of nationals. The history of Indonesia's automobile industry is a case in point. Initially, the industry was in the hands of Indonesians from the military ranks or senior officials; as the "New Order" was instituted, the industry went into the hands of the ruling Suharto family and of the large Chinese conglomerates, creating a powerful lobbyist that was able to ban imports of motor vehicles until 1993, when the ban was replaced by tariffs in the range of 175 to 275 percent.[20]

It should be mentioned that service industries in particular are subjected to regulations that invoke foreign ownership restrictions. Creative strategies that employ an ambiguous legal environment are used to block entry of international service providers or to place them at a disadvantage relative to local competitors.

Standards as barriers to trade
Trade barriers imposing performance, environmental, or other requirements that are primarily aimed at imports.

Local content requirement
A protectionist measure requiring that a certain percentage of the products imported are locally produced.

---

18. Jack Robertson, "Foreign Exporters Learn to Deal with China's Local-Content Rules," *Ebn,* Issue 1258, April 16, 2001, p. 43.

19. Lovelock and Yip, "Developing Global Strategies for Service Businesses," pp. 64–86.

20. Yumiko Okamoto and Fredrik Sjoholm, "Productivity in the Indonesian Automotive Industry," *ASEAN Economic Bulletin,* Vol. 17, No. 1, April 2000, pp. 60–73.

Boycott

Boycott   An action calling for a ban on consumption of all goods associated with a particular company and/or country.

A **boycott** is usually initiated as the result of an action group calling for a ban on consumption of all goods associated with a particular company and/or country. Often, boycotts target a company that is representative, or even synonymous, with its country of origin. For example, when the uprising in the West Bank and Gaza erupted, Coke sales in neighboring Egypt and Jordan were hit by local boycott calls.[21] McDonald's restaurants were the target of French protesters, who were against tariffs imposed by the United States on European Union countries. Exxon-owned Esso has been the target of a high-profile boycott campaign by groups angered at its support of the U.S. government's rejection of the Kyoto climate change pact.[22]

Embargoes and Sanctions

Embargo   The prohibition of all business deals with the country that is the target of the embargo, endorsed or initiated by the company's home country.

Sanctions   Punitive trade restrictions applied by a country or a group of countries against another country for noncompliance.

Embargoes and **sanctions** are imposed by a country (or a number of countries) against another country. An embargo prohibits all business deals with the country that is the target of the embargo, often affecting businesses from third countries that do business with both the country (or countries) imposing the embargo and the country under embargo. The embargo could be limited to a particular product and/or to particular circumstances. For example, "smart sanctions" have been imposed by the United States and the United Kingdom on Iraq's oil exports, modifying the oil embargo against Iraq to allow for use of oil revenues aimed at humanitarian purposes. Liberia is presently experiencing an arms embargo imposed by the United Nations Security Council as a punishment for its support of Sierra Leone's Revolutionary United Front.

The United States has imposed, for decades, a full embargo against Cuba. The embargo covers any commercial and noncommercial relationship with Cuba, and it even prohibits visits to the country by U.S. citizens, with some exceptions. Furthermore, multinational companies from other countries doing business in the United States are prohibited, under the embargo, from engaging in any business deals with Cuba. Unfortunately for the United States, this strategy does not appear to reach its goal—punishing Fidel Castro, Cuba's president since the onset of the embargo, and his communist regime, by derailing its economy. On the contrary, Cuba is reaching out to the world by transforming itself into a hub for information technology, one where U.S. companies may be at a disadvantage relative to competition in the future.[23]

Finally, a form of nonretaliatory embargo exists: It is imposed when imports into a country that has established quotas for a particular product exceed those quotas.

Currency and Capital Flow Controls

Currency and capital flow controls   All protectionist activities involving the control of capital and hard currency flows in and out of a particular country.

Strategies involving **currency and capital flow controls** are used in economies that are under tight government control and/or that are experiencing hard-currency shortages. In the case of capital flow, countries use arguments of self-determination to ensure that regions in the country are uniformly developed or that there would not be a capital flight from the country. Such strategies affect international businesses in that they restrict market-dictated activity in the name of protectionism.

---

21. Peter Lagerquist, Charmaine Seitz, and Harry Maurer, "Where Coke Is It–If the Trucks Get Through," *Business Week*, Industrial/Technology Edition, No. 3743, July 30, 2001, p. 4EU2.

22. James Curtis, "Body Shop Plans to Scale Down Its Political Activity," *Marketing*, July 26, 2001, p. 3.

23. Davis P. Goodman, "Getting Over the Slump," *World Trade*, Vol. 14, No. 7, July 2001, p. 8.

Governments use currency flow restrictions primarily to influence the stability of the national currency. Such restrictions, however, directly affect the flow of imports into the country, by giving priority to desirable goods and restricting the import of less desirable goods and services. Among the currency controls used by governments are the following:

- Blocked currency
- Differential exchange rates
- Foreign exchange permits

Blocked Currency

A country using a **blocked currency** strategy does not allow importers to exchange local currency for the seller's currency. This strategy can be used as a political weapon, to create obstacles for international business attempting to enter the country. More often, however, the strategy is used because the country is experiencing acute balance-of-payments difficulties. Firms fortunately have at their disposal countertrade strategies to address this type of barrier. Under a typical scenario, the exporter sells goods in exchange for local currency and uses the proceeds to purchase local goods for sale abroad; U.S. companies in the past often bought goods from Mexico and from Eastern Europe with local currency to address this barrier.[24]

Another method that firms can use to bypass blocked exchange rates entails using unofficial (and, from the perspective of the importing country, illegal) exchange offices. Such offices exist both abroad and in the importing country; however, they offer unfavorable exchange rates and expose the company to the risk of government action against it.

Differential Exchange Rates

Two types of **differential exchange rates** can be used. The first, which is government imposed, refers to a strategy the government uses to promote imports of desirable and necessary goods, such as armament and petrol, and to discourage imports of less desirable and necessary goods, such as consumer goods and services, entertainment, and the like. Offering a less favorable exchange rate for international products and services reflects a government strategy that ultimately increases the cost of this second category of products to the final consumer and discourages its purchase.

A second type of differential exchange rate is favorable to the international firm importing products into this market. In this situation, a difference exists between the black market exchange rate and the official government exchange rate, with the black market rate being higher than the government rate. The rate difference is a reflection of economic distortion: A high black market exchange rate can signal a likely depreciation of the local currency, or foreign exchange rationing by the government, or both. A large difference between the government and the free exchange rate can also be interpreted as a tax on exports and a subsidy on imports, stimulating the diversion of resources from the official to the black market sector.[25]

Blocked currency A strategy that does not allow importers to exchange local currency for the seller's currency or a currency that the seller is willing to accept as payment (hard currency).

Differential exchange rate The rate imposed by the local government to promote imports of desirable and necessary goods; it also can be the difference between the black market exchange rate and the official government rate.

---

24. Kwabena Anyane-Ntow and Santhi Harvey, "A Countertrade Primer," *Management Accounting*, Vol. 76, No. 10, April 1995, pp. 47–50.

25. Martha de Melo, Cevdet Denizer, Alan Gelb, and Stoyan Tenev, "Circumstance and Choice: The Role of Initial Conditions and Policies in Transition Economies," *The World Bank Economic Review*, Vol. 15, No. 1, 2001, pp. 1–31.

Foreign Exchange Permits

Foreign exchange permit
A permit that is generally provided by a country's Central Bank in conjunction with the Department of Trade (Ministry of Foreign Trade) and that gives priority to imports of goods considered to be in the national interest.

Countries attempting to control foreign exchange often require the use of **foreign exchange permits.** Such permits are typically provided by the Central Bank. They also give priority to imports of goods that are in the national interest and delay access to foreign exchange for products that are not deemed essential. An exchange permit can also stipulate differential exchange rates. Most countries that experience a shortage of hard currency require foreign exchange permits. China and countries in Sub-Saharan Africa currently require such permits. In the past, Latin American and Eastern European countries relied heavily on the use of foreign exchange permits for imports.

3-3 Facilitators of International Trade

Several important international and local institutions play an active role in promoting international trade and have a considerable impact on the development of international trade and marketing operations. International trade and development organizations and governmental organizations alike are working individually and jointly to increase the flow of goods, to open access to products and services, and to minimize costs to companies and final consumers by limiting or eliminating the layers of bureaucratic interference in the firms' international operations. Sections 3-3a through 3-3c address some of the most prominent international trade and development organizations. They also address the role of national governments in promoting the international involvement of local business and in opening local markets to foreign investment—particularly foreign direct investment. It should be mentioned, however, that equally important strides have been made to date by trade agreements. The levels of economic and political integration such agreements have achieved permit free movement of labor and capital and open or nearly open access to markets by firms operating in the region; the topic of regional economic and political integration will be addressed in Chapter 4.

3-3a International Trade and Economic Development Organizations

This chapter provides an overview of the most important trade and economic development organizations worldwide in terms of their overall impact on companies and markets. It must be noted, however, that, in addition to these organizations, other entities provide similar, but typically more targeted, input into the international trade process. They do so directly, by facilitating trade, or indirectly, by developing national infrastructures essential to the flow of goods and communication. For example, the Belgian government and the Dutch government have specific structures that operate individually and jointly, with other international development organizations, to help former colonies in East Africa and Asia, respectively. The French Ministry of Cooperation has a similar mission.

This discussion centers primarily on the World Trade Organization and the G8, organizations that have made significant inroads with regard to the liberalization of trade in the recent decade, facilitating the marketing of goods and services in markets previously deemed inaccessible and reducing barriers to trade worldwide. It also focuses on the two Bretton Woods organizations, which have provided support for development and trade in the free world for five decades—the World Bank and the International Monetary Fund.

The World Trade Organization (WTO) (www.wto.org) and the General Agreement on Tariffs and Trade (GATT)

The **General Agreement on Tariffs and Trade (GATT)** was signed by 123 nations agreeing to promote trade and eliminate trade barriers. Under the agreement, the signatory countries committed to open their markets to international business and to use the GATT forum to resolve trade disputes. In practice, however, trade disputes took too long to be resolved, and GATT had no enforcement power. GATT's Uruguay Round, which took place between 1986 and 1994, and was subsequently finalized at Marrakech in 1995, has substantially changed international trade regulation, replacing the original GATT regulations with a newly empowered **World Trade Organization (WTO),** which currently has 142 member countries from a world total of 187. The WTO is forever changing the way countries regulate international business on their own territory and beyond. The organization's most important trait is that membership is predicated on full implementation and adherence to all GATT agreements.

World Trade Organization candidate countries often must radically change their trade practices and, implicitly, their internal economic structures, to gain membership. For example, China has attempted for fifteen years to gain membership in the World Trade Organization. Its impediments to access were attributed primarily due to its trade restrictions (attributed to concerns about the impact of open markets on its economy) and its demands to be allowed to subsidize agricultural output at the rate of developing countries; to gain access to the WTO, China had to lower tariffs on imports such as automobiles and new technologies and to make it easier for foreign companies to establish certain types of businesses in the country.[26]

The WTO is run by member governments, and its decisions are made either by governments' trade ministers (the organization's highest authority), who meet every two years, or by official representatives, who meet regularly in Geneva, Switzerland, the organization's headquarters; routine issues are addressed by councils, committees, working parties, and negotiating groups.[27] Ministerial meetings have met with substantial opposition in the last few years. For example, the 1999 ministerial meeting faced 50,000 protesters in Seattle; this may explain why subsequent meetings were organized in locations such as Doha, Qatar, where the government bans activities of all organizations that are critical of any other Arab government or of institutions that the respective governments are members of.[28] It is significant that opposition groups see in globalization the promotion of corporate interests to the detriment of the individual, of developing countries, and of the environment.

WTO's main functions are

- Providing assistance to developing and transition economies.
- Offering specialized help for export promotion, through the International Trade Center.
- Promoting regional trade agreements.
- Promoting cooperation in global economic policy-making.

General Agreement on Tariffs and Trade (GATT) The international trade agreement promoting trade and eliminating trade barriers, opening markets to international business, and creating a forum for resolving trade disputes; GATT issues are now addressed by the World Trade Organization. (See www.wto.org.)

World Trade Organization (WTO) The largest and most influential international trade organization whose primary goal is ensure the free flow of trade; WTO's agreements (negotiated and signed by member countries, ratified in their parliaments) represent trade rules and regulations and act as contracts guaranteeing countries' trade rights and binding governments to trade policies. (See www.wto.org.)

26. Elizabeth Olson, "Beijing Clears Major WTO Obstacles," *International Herald Tribune,* Frankfurt. July 4, 2001, p. 9.

27. www.wto.org

28. Michael Maiello, "Hoisted by Qatar?" *Forbes,* May 14, 2001, p. 60.

- Reviewing members' trade policies.
- Engaging in routine notification when members introduce new trade measures or alter old ones.[29]

WTO agreements cover goods, services, and intellectual property and address issues such as[30]

- Reducing tariff and nontariff trade barriers on specific categories of goods and services. In this regard, WTO has made important strides in the area of manufactured goods, as well as in the area of information technology. It is still working on eliminating barriers in the area of agriculture, where GATT allowed, until recently, government subsidies and permitted import quotas.
- Opening service markets to international business. The General Agreement on Trade in Services (GATS) has established rules for specific sectors, outlining principles that require countries to offer access to their markets. GATS initially covered banking, securities, and insurance.
- Regulating the protection and enforcement of intellectual property rights for trademarks, patents, and copyrights—under the Agreement on Trade-Related Aspects of Intellectual Property Rights (TRIPS).
- Dealing with antidumping activities.
- Addressing subsidies and trade restrictions designed to safeguard domestic industries such as technical regulations and standards, import licensing, rules of origin, and other measures that impede international trade.
- Settling disputes. Member states cannot ignore any of the dispute resolution decisions handled by the Dispute Settlement Body—as they previously have, under GATT. Examples of disputes handled by the DSB are Venezuela's complaint against the United States over discrimination in gasoline imports (requiring higher standards for imports than for locally produced gasoline).
- Reviewing regularly individual countries' trade policies to ensure compliance with the WTO and transparency.

Group of Eight (G8)

Group of Eight (G8) A group of the eight most industrialized countries: Canada, France, Germany, Italy, Japan, the United Kingdom, the United States, and Russia; the group addresses issues such as biotechnology and food safety, economic development, arms control and nonproliferation, organized crime, drug trafficking, terrorism, environmental issues, digital opportunities, microeconomic issues, and trade. (See www.g7.utoronto.ca.)

Members of the **Group of Eight (G8)** most industrialized countries are Canada, France, Germany, Italy, Japan, Russia, the United Kingdom, and the United States. The Group began as the G7, excluding Russia, during the 1970s economic crisis, as a forum for addressing economic and financial issues. The organization's yearly meetings involve heads of state, government ministers, and directors of central banks. The G8 currently addresses issues such as biotechnology and food safety, economic development, disarmament, arms control and nonproliferation, organized crime, drug trafficking, terrorism, environmental issues, digital opportunities issues, microeconomic issues, and trade.

Russia, the group's most recent member (formally since 1998), first participated in the organization's meetings in 1991. Russia's economy, however, is the size of that of Denmark,[31] and its inclusion in the G8 is often questioned. Ultimately, most of the economic deliberations are done in the G7 format, without including Russia, primarily through the regular meetings of the G7 finance ministers. Moreover, because Russia is not a member of the World Trade Organization (WTO), it

---

29. www.wto.org

30. For a comprehensive overview of the WTO, see the Web site at www.wto.org.

31. Barry D. Wood, "Economic Summits from Rambouillet to Cologne," *Europe*, No. 387, June 1999, pp. 18–22.

does not participate in deliberations concerning this organization. For example, Russia did not participate in the G7 discussions within the framework of the WTO ministerial meeting in Doha, Qatar, which addressed, among others, market access of and technical assistance to developing countries.

The G8 has met with substantial criticism on a number of sectoral problems that it was unable to adequately address. Among its missteps and shortcomings are the following: a failed $24 billion aid program in 1992 to turn Russia into a market economy; the Group's inability to foresee the Mexican crisis in 1994 and the Asian meltdown in 1997; its failure to devise ways to make Japan's economy grow or Europe's to produce jobs and faster growth, and to adequately respond to globalization and the challenge of emerging markets.[32] The G8 has also been criticized for its failure to challenge China on its human rights record. Among the G8 successes are the unity developed within the group on a variety of issues. The group has addressed successfully topics ranging from debt to nuclear power control—at the very least by providing a credible forum for discussion of these issues; of particular note is the 1989 G7 Paris meeting that created the European Bank for Reconstruction and Development to help Eastern Europe in its process of transition to a market economy.[33]

The International Monetary Fund (IMF) (www.imf.org) and the World Bank (www.worldbank.org)

The **International Monetary Fund (IMF)** and the **World Bank** were created at the United Nations Monetary and Financial Conference, as a result of the Bretton Woods Agreement in 1944, to address the need of global economic development, stability, and rebuilding after the Second World War and the 1930s Great Depression. Both the International Monetary Fund and the World Bank are specialized agencies of the United Nations; membership in the World Bank requires membership in the IMF.

The goal of the IMF was to establish an innovative monetary system and an institution charged with monitoring it. The IMF is based on the proposals put forth by Harry Dexter White in the United States and John Maynard Keynes in the United Kingdom. At its foundation lies a system that would encourage the unrestricted conversion of one currency to another by establishing a clear and unequivocal value for each currency.[34] Currently, the organization, whose mission has significantly expanded since its debut, is located in Washington, D.C. The IMF comprises more than 180 member countries who are free to join the organization—as such, they are obligated to adhere to its charter of rights and obligations—or to leave the organization (as Cuba, Indonesia, and Poland have done in the past).[35]

The IMF directly links members' voting power to the amount they contribute to the institution; as such, the United States has more than 265,000 votes (18 percent of the total).[36] The organization's international civil servants are international experts and nationals of the different member countries and operate under a Managing Director, who is typically a European. Currently, Horst Köhler (from Germany), who follows Michel Camdessus (France), occupies this position.

International Monetary Fund (IMF) Traditionally the lender of last resort; the IMF also has assumed the position of mediator between debtors and creditors, imposing stabilization programs; debt-reduction guidelines; ceilings for bank credit, budget deficit, borrowing, and international reserves; and development programs for borrowing countries. (See www.imf.org.)

World Bank The World Bank Group, headquartered in Washington, D.C., that is one of the largest sources of funds for development assistance aimed at the poorest countries worldwide. (See www.worldbank.org.)

---

32. Ibid.

33. Ibid.

34. www.imf.org

35. Ibid.

36. Ibid.

Traditionally, the IMF has played the role of lender of last resort; more recently, however, it has also assumed the position of mediator between debtors and creditors. Through its stabilization programs, the IMF imposes debt reduction guidelines; ceilings for bank credit, budget deficit, borrowing, and international reserves; and particular development programs that the borrowing countries have to follow. In the recent past, the IMF offered countries in Central and Eastern Europe loans for restructuring their economies. Its most recent bailout activities focused on Brazil, Argentina, and Turkey. The bailout of Argentina with an $8 billion package has a unique twist: Disbursement of $3 billion of the funds may hinge on a reschedule of Argentina's public debt. Brazil received a $15 billion line of credit (this follows a $41 billion rescue package that Brazil received in 1998), contingent on its strengthening fiscal and monetary policies, and implementing a structural reform agenda.[37] These actions were necessary because these two important emerging markets were unable to attract foreign direct investment from developed countries such as the United States, Japan, and Europe, which were themselves going through a period of slow growth or recession.[38]

The IMF also offers training and technical assistance for monetary and financial strategists from borrowing countries through its field offices and publishes statistical information based on accurate data that member countries provide as a requirement for membership.

The World Bank is the largest international bank that sponsors economic development projects. The World Bank, headquartered in Washington, D.C., employs international specialists in economics, finance, and sectoral development. In addition, it has field offices in developing countries, overseeing projects in the area of industry, health, poultry and dairy production, among others. While, in the past, the World Bank's focus was in the area of industrial and infrastructure development, its current priorities lie primarily in the areas of health (it provided a $500 million umbrella loan for programs to combat HIV/AIDS in Sub-Saharan Africa) and information technology (in 2000, the World Bank awarded $1.5 billion in contracts to IT companies).[39]

Both the IMF and the World Bank have met with their share of criticism. The IMF has been criticized for imposing unduly rapid or overly detailed structural adjustment programs; consequently, countries are unlikely to feel a sense of ownership of programs that stretch their capacity for implementation and, as a result, may lack the political will needed to carry them out.[40] The World Bank has been criticized for lending primarily to countries with access to private international capital; according to the Bank's own analysis, the countries that could make best use of its resources receive a comparatively small share.[41]

Nevertheless, the accomplishments of the World Bank and the IMF and their impact on economic development and trade cannot be ignored. They have been instrumental in fostering economic and political stability in developing countries. They have protected banks from developed countries by preventing firms in volatile regions from defaulting on their debt. They have helped create viable

---

37. Joseph Kahn, "I.M.F. Ready for Brazil and Argentina Rescues," *The New York Times,* August 4, 2001, p. A4.

38. Ibid.

39. Erin Butler, "New Directions for Investment in Developing Countries," *World Trade,* Vol. 16, No. 6, June 2001, pp. 24–28.

40. Flemming Larsen, "The IMF's Dialogue with Nongovernmental Organizations," *Finance & Development,* Vol. 38, No. 1, March 2001, pp. 54–56.

41. *The Economist,* "Reforming the Sisters: If America's New Administration Would Like a Challenge, It Can Try Changing the IMF and World Bank," Vol. 358, No. 8209, February 17, 2001, pp. 23–24.

industrial, agricultural, and infrastructure projects. Also, they have contributed substantially to the training and development of local expertise in different sectors. Furthermore, the two agencies provide reliable statistics in areas related to finance, economic development, trade, population trends, and national policies, among others.

Other Development Banks

A number of development banks with a regional focus also are instrumental in advancing economic development and in providing support for business and trade. Among the development banks are the following:[42]

- The **African Development Bank** (www.afdb.org), headquartered in Abidjan, Ivory Coast, has as a primary goal poverty reduction. It provides support and expertise in areas such as agriculture, human resources, and health services, and it emphasizes small businesses as its target recipients.
- The **Asian Development Bank** (www.adb.org), headquartered in Manila, the Philippines, focuses on the private sector. The bank sponsors projects aimed at increasing access to technology and improving the functioning of government. Together with the World Bank and the IMF, the Asian Development Bank was instrumental in Asia's recovery from the 1990s' financial crisis.
- The **European Bank for Reconstruction and Development** (www.ebrd.com), headquartered in London, United Kingdom, has as main goals reforming and strengthening markets in the transition economies of Central and Eastern Europe. Among others it has played an important role in the development of legal and institutional frameworks, in reducing barriers to foreign investment, and in strengthening the countries' financial markets and their private sector.
- The **Inter-American Development Bank** (www.iadb.org), headquartered in Washington, D.C., has as primary clients companies that do not ordinarily deal with the large development banks. Like the other banks, the IADB funds private sector projects, but it also has as priorities modernizing the government, strengthening institutions, and overcoming the "digital divide."

United Nations Organizations

A number of United Nations (www.un.org) bodies promote the economic and financial welfare of developing countries; in particular, these organizations focus on developing the industrial, communication, and transportation infrastructure of developing countries. The impact of such development on fostering trade and foreign direct investment in these markets is substantial. Among the United Nations agencies involved in economic development are the United Nations Development Program (UNDP), headquartered in New York. The UNDP assists, coordinates, finances, and supervises various projects, ranging from institutional strengthening and support to building factories, to developing methane gas extraction facilities, to financing the building of bridges and highways or telecommunications networks. In its efforts, the UNDP, primarily a human development organization, is assisted by other specialized **United Nations organizations—** about 16 in number. Among them and directly involved in economic development and the development of international trade are

African Development Bank A bank, headquartered in Abidjan, Ivory Coast, that has as a primary goal poverty reduction in Africa, providing support and expertise in agriculture, human resources, and health services, with an emphasis on small business. (See www.afdb.org.)

Asian Development Bank A bank, headquartered in Manila, the Philippines, that focuses on the private sector in Asia, sponsoring projects aimed at increasing access to technology and improving the functioning of government in the region. (See www.adb.org.)

European Bank for Reconstruction and Development A bank headquartered in London, United Kingdom, which has as main goals reforming and strengthening markets in the transition economies of Central and Eastern Europe. (See www.ebrd.com.)

Inter-American Development Bank A bank headquartered in Washington, D.C., aiding companies in the Americas that do not ordinarily deal with the large development banks; this bank is involved in funding private sector projects, modernizing governments, strengthening institutions, and eliminating technology barriers. (See www.iadb.org.)

United Nations organizations The totality of United Nations bodies created to maintain international peace and security; to develop relations among nations; to achieve international cooperation in solving international economic, social, cultural, or humanitarian problems; and to encourage respect for human rights and fundamental freedoms using the venues offered by the different UN organizations. (See www.un.org.)

---

42. See Butler, "New Directions for Investment," pp. 24–28, for a more detailed account on each of these development banks.

- The United Nations Industrial Development Organization (UNIDO), headquartered in Vienna, Austria, which offers or subcontracts expertise in industrial project design and implementation, often providing turn-key factories to countries in need.
- The United Nations Conference on Trade and Development (UNCTAD), headquartered in Geneva, Switzerland, assists developing countries in developing international trade relations and promotes the integration of trade, environment, and development.
- The Regional Economic Commission for Africa; for Asia and the Pacific; for Europe, North America, and the Commonwealth of Independent States (CIS); for Latin America and the Caribbean; and for Western Asia is the regional arm of the United Nations. It offers support for the economic and social development of its member States, fosters regional integration, and promotes international cooperation for regional development.
- The Food and Agriculture Organization (FAO), headquartered in Rome, Italy, which offers expertise in agricultural projects.

The United Nations agencies also provide statistical data on developing countries, with a focus on different industry sectors, health, and agriculture.

3-3b Government Organizations

Promoting international trade constitutes one of the more important tasks of the national and local government of most countries. Most of the international marketing literature explores the different strategies used by government to protect local industry, trade, and service providers from international competition; such publications often ignore efforts of local and national government bodies in increasing exports and in promoting foreign direct investment locally. This discussion details the involvement of the United States' federal, state, and local governments in promoting international trade. It should be mentioned that most developed countries have similar institutions to those described herein, and offer similar support to local businesses attempting to market their products internationally and to international businesses entering the local market.

Regardless of the level of country economic development, most international trade issues are addressed by the national Department of Commerce, known as the **Ministry of Trade** or, more specifically, the Ministry of Foreign Trade. Frequently, the Ministry of Trade works in tandem with the State Department, known as the **Ministry of Foreign Affairs,** promoting the respective country's foreign policy.

United States Agencies: Federal and State Government

Many United States federal, state, and local government agencies promote the interests of United States businesses abroad, encouraging their international involvement in the form of export promotion or by providing foreign direct investment support. They also actively encourage foreign direct investment in the United States. Among the United States agencies supporting activities of international business are the United States Agency for International Development and United States Department of Commerce.

United States Agency for International Development (USAID)

The **United States Agency for International Development (USAID)** is an independent agency of the federal government. Similarly to the United Nations Development Program and other development organizations, USAID engages in

Ministry of Trade The international institutional equivalent of the Department of Commerce; it coordinates a country's international trade relations.

Ministry of Foreign Affairs The international institutional equivalent of the State Department; it coordinates a country's involvement in international relations.

United States Agency for International Development (USAID) An independent agency of the federal government that supports the economic development of and trade with developing countries aligned politically with the United States. (See www.usaid.gov.)

economic development-related operations. Unlike the development organizations previously discussed, USAID is an arm of the **United States State Department,** supporting the economic development of and trade with developing countries aligned politically with the United States. USAID's origins are traced to the Marshall Plan of reconstruction in Europe after World War II, and it was created to advance U.S. foreign policy in developing countries by supporting economic growth and agricultural development, global health, conflict prevention, and developmental relief. In doing so, USAID gives priority to U.S. contracting firms; it has working relationships with more than 3,500 U.S. companies.[43]

United States Department of Commerce

The **United States Department of Commerce** engages in many activities that promote trade. It offers export assistance and counseling to businesses involved in international trade, it provides country information and the assistance of country specialists, and it helps bring buyers and sellers together through trade shows and other trade-related events. Its International Trade Administration district offices are located in the United States and in key international markets; their mission is to promote trade interests of U.S. business abroad. The Department of Commerce also regulates trade by issuing export licenses and by offering food, health, and safety inspections and certification.

An important arm of the Department of Commerce is the Export-Import Bank of the United States (the Ex-Im Bank). The Bank, created in 1934, works with city and state governments to offer export counseling and financial assistance to companies doing business in or planning to do business in international markets. Examples of Ex-Im's financial assistance are export credit insurance, guaranteed loans, pre-export financing to small- and medium-size exporters, grants for feasibility studies and project planning for projects in developing countries, and technical assistance grants, among others. The Ex-Im Bank also makes loans to foreign purchasers who purchase U.S. goods and services.[44]

State and Local Government Agencies

Examples of government agencies actively supporting international trade are the state economic development offices. Most of the fifty U.S. states have a department whose goal is to promote local firms internationally; this is typically the Department of Economic Development. States further international trade interests of local companies by setting up representative offices abroad, in key markets, such as the European Union and Japan. They often also target big emerging markets, such as those of China, Brazil, and India—countries with a large and increasingly prosperous middle class—as well as wealthier developing countries, such as oil exporting countries (for instance, Saudi Arabia, the United Arab Emirates, and Venezuela).

Among the trade services that state governments provide—often free of charge—are export counseling, full or partial sponsoring of trade promotion (primarily trade shows), and dissemination of market information.

State and local governments also actively attempt to attract international business. For example, the state of South Carolina and the town of Greenville were able to draw substantial investments from noteworthy international firms such as BMW, Michelin, and Fuji. As a result of foreign direct investment in the state,

United States State Department
The foreign affairs arm of the United States government, in charge of promoting relations with other governments. (See www.state.gov.)

United States Department of Commerce   The U.S. governmental agency that oversees and promotes trade, offering export assistance and counseling to U.S. businesses involved in international trade, providing country information and country specialists, and bringing buyers and sellers together.

---

43. www.usaid.gov

44. See www.exim.gov for information about Ex-Im Bank.

South Carolina has been able to add numerous new jobs. In fact, the foreign-owned firms alone added 20,600 new jobs in the 1990s—most with higher-than-average salaries.[45]

3-3c Other Institutions and Procedures Facilitating International Trade

Foreign Trade Zones (FTZs)

Foreign trade zones Tax-free areas in a country that are not considered part of the respective country in terms of import regulations and restrictions.

A **foreign trade zone** or free trade zone (FTZ) is a tax-free area in a particular country that is not considered part of the respective country in terms of import regulations and restrictions. Products can be shipped to a free trade zone, undergo additional manufacturing processes, and then be shipped further to the target market. Such products are not assessed any duties and cannot be subjected to tariffs or quotas unless they enter the territory of the host country of the free trade zone. A foreign trade zone is a site within a particular country that is considered to be an international area; merchandise in the FTZ, both foreign and domestic, is outside the jurisdiction of the host country's customs services.[46]

Initiated by governments, foreign trade zones stimulate domestic and international commerce. In the United States, the Foreign Trade Zone Act of 1934 allows for the creation of foreign trade zones for the purpose of stimulating U.S. domestic and international commerce by allowing firms to decrease tariff-related costs through their trade operations in the foreign trade zones.[47] FTZs are usually located in or near a port of entry and are usually operated as a public utility by a public entity such as the Port of Portland, the Indianapolis Airport Authority, or the Crowfield Corporate Center in Charleston, South Carolina.[48]

FTZs are regulated by the U.S. Foreign Trade Zones Board, which is part of the U.S. Department of Commerce, and by U.S. Customs, as part of the U.S. Temporary Entry System—designed to encourage the export of goods with foreign content and the re-export of foreign goods and to reduce the costs of using foreign goods.[49]

Foreign trade zones offer advantages to both the host country and to international firms operating in the foreign trade zone. In the host country, the foreign trade zone benefits

- Domestic manufacturers, distributors, and suppliers by creating demand for their services, products, and raw materials. FTZ activities may involve manipulation, such as product inspecting, labeling, repairing, and sorting; small- and large-scale manufacturing, including manufacturing, assembling, and processing; warehousing; exhibiting; and distributing to domestic and foreign markets.[50] Such operations also create jobs in the FTZ country.

---

45. Ryan Lizza, "Silent Partner," *The New Republic*, Vol. 222, No. 2, January 10, 2000, pp. 22–25.

46. George F. Hanks and Lucinda Van Alst, "Foreign Trade Zones," *Management Accounting*, Vol. 80, No. 7, January 1999, pp. 20–23.

47. Lynette Knowles Mathur and Ike Mathur, "The Effectiveness of the Foreign-Trade Zone as an Export Promotion Program: Policy Issues and Alternatives," *Journal of Macromarketing*, Vol. 17, No. 2, Fall 1997, pp. 20–31.

48. Hanks and Van Alst, "Foreign Trade Zones," pp. 20–23.

49. Knowles Mathur and Mathur, "The Effectiveness of the Foreign-Trade Zone as an Export Promotion Program," pp. 20–31.

50. Ibid.

- The country's trade balance. Re-exports from the country where the foreign trade zone is located add to the total number of exports from that country, thereby increasing its trade balance.

The international firm operating in the foreign trade zone benefits from the following:

- Foreign goods that enter the foreign trade zone are exempt from the usual customs duties, tariffs, and other import controls, as long as the goods do not enter the country.
- For firms that ultimately export to the country where the FTZ is located, the FTZ provides flexibility by lowering and/or deferring tariffs for goods that are subject to tariffs. There are no time limitations for the foreign goods' presence in the foreign trade zone. Thus, goods that are assessed tariffs on the imported components are placed in storage in the FTZ and are imported into the country only when demand for the product is high or when import quota opportunities open up.
- Rather than bringing the equipment directly into the country and paying duties immediately, equipment can be brought into the FTZ, shown to customers, and the payment of duties can be delayed until the goods are sold; this is especially beneficial for high-value items.[51]
- A free trade zone is also a location that is used for breaking bulk. Components that are purchased from a foreign supplier to be used in a just-in-time manufacturing environment can be shipped into the FTZ in bulk to optimize quantity discounts and shipping costs. When these components are in the zone, they are repackaged into smaller quantities for shipment to the manufacturing plants; this helps the company postpone the payment of duties until the items are shipped to the plant rather than when they arrive into the country.[52]
- A free trade zone lowers prices for goods sold in the importing country: Unassembled goods are cheaper to transport, and duties are assessed at lower rates for unassembled, than for assembled, goods. Furthermore, duties can be avoided for goods that have been damaged in transportation.
- A free trade zone also helps when an importing country imposes local content regulations on products from abroad: Local content is provided through the manipulation processes taking place in the FTZ.
- FTZs are usually bonded and must be secured and enclosed, which make them safer than most ports of entry, thus decreasing insurance costs for companies using them. In the United States, for example, unauthorized removal of goods from an FTZ is a federal offense.[53]
- Products that are manipulated in a foreign trade zone may be labeled as manufactured in the FTZ host country. A favorable attitude toward the respective country and its products (that is, a favorable country-of-origin effect) would greatly benefit the companies selling the product.

Foreign trade zones can range from no more than an assigned building close to a river port or a floor in a building adjacent to the local airport, to a gigantic operation with fully integrated multi-modal access. An example of the latter is the Jebel Ali Free Zone of Dubai—one of the largest foreign trade zones in the world.

---

51. Hanks and Van Alst, "Foreign Trade Zones," pp. 20–23.

52. Ibid.

53. Ibid.

The Jebel Ali Free Zone houses operations of more than 1,200 companies from 72 countries, offering state-of-the-art transport and communications facilities in its 100-square-kilometer site. More than 100 U.S. companies have manufacturing, maintenance, or transshipment operations there, including AlliedSignal, DHL, Federal Express, General Motors, Johnson & Johnson, Microsoft, and Union Carbide—and all are allowed 100 percent foreign ownership of operations, 100 percent repatriation of capital and profits, a 15-year corporate tax holiday, and a full exemption from personal income taxes.[54] In return for access to 1.5 billion consumers in the region (from countries surrounding the Persian Gulf and Red Sea), companies incur four up-front costs: a license ($954), registration as a Free Zone Establishment ($2,725), lease of space (prebuilt space and land start at $32,686 a year), and telecom hookup ($381).[55]

Other Types of Customs-Privileged Facilities

Off-shore assembly plants Plants located in customs-privileged bonded areas in countries with low labor costs, where products are manipulated and re-exported.

Worldwide, there are variations on the foreign trade zone. They are similar to the foreign trade zone in that they have some type of customs-privileged facilities that may be restricted to a region, to a plant (when such a plant is used for product assembly purposes, it is known as an **off-shore assembly plant),** or to a bonded warehouse. **Special economic zones** in China and **maquiladoras** in Mexico are examples of customs-privileged facilities that typically exist in countries with low-cost labor. Under most arrangements, products are brought into an in-bond area, manipulated (processed, repackaged, assembled), and then re-exported to the country where the products originated. Low import tariffs are only assessed at this point, and only on the value-added processing that took place in the special economic zone. Some limits are typically placed on products that are imported into the special economic zone country to encourage re-exporting.

Special economic zones Customs-privileged manufacturing facilities in China where multinational companies can take advantage of low-cost labor.

Maquiladora Customs-privileged contract manufacturing facilities in Mexico that take advantage of low-cost labor.

Most-Favored-Nation Status Favored trade status granted by Congress for imported products from selected countries, which are not party to a preferential trade agreement with the United States.

Most-Favored-Nation (MFN) Status

An important trade policy tool that is used by the United States is the **Most-Favored-Nation Status.** This status grants preferential tax treatment on imported products from selected countries that are not part of a trade agreement with the United States. Granting of the MFN clause has been linked to U.S. foreign policy. Receiving the MFN clause is predicated on countries' human rights records (as in the case of China in the 1990s), or as a reward for alignment with U.S. interests (as in the case of Romania before the fall of communism, when the country opposed Soviet interference in the internal affairs of Warsaw Pact member countries).

---

54. Josh Martin, "Dubai: A Model FTZ," *Management Review,* Vol. 87, No. 11, December 1998, p. 25.

55. Ibid.

Chapter Summary

Chapter Summary

- **Identify different trade barriers imposed on international trade and arguments used by governments to erect and maintain these barriers**

  Governments impose barriers to international trade to protect national industries and nationals (consumers, employees). Arguments for protectionism include protection of markets with excess productive capacity, employment protection, protection of infant industries, protection of national resources and the environment, protection of consumers, and national defense. Governments can impose tariffs on foreign business, or nontariff barriers, such as import quotas, required import licenses, voluntary imports, or voluntary export restraints. They also can impose price controls, such as simply increasing the prices of imports, filing antidumping and countervailing duty actions to delay imports, or imposing additional tariffs (paratariffs) to shipments that exceed quotas. Alternatively, they can impose currency and capital flow controls, by blocking local currency exchange, by charging differential exchange rates, and by restricting the number of foreign exchange permits issued. Standards are also used to restrict imports, as are local content requirements. Finally, boycotts, embargoes, and sanctions restrict international trade by blocking all trade to the targeted areas.

- **Provide an overview of key international organizations facilitating international trade directly or by promoting economic development**

  Among the organizations that are most active in and have the greatest impact on promoting international trade are the World Trade Organization, which provides trade assistance and development assistance to developing countries, promotes trade agreements, and reviews member countries' trade policies to ensure that they conform to the organization's trade requirements; the Group of Eight, which is a forum of the most developed countries in the world and addresses economic and financial issues, with trade as a main focus; the International Monetary Fund and the World Bank, two specialized United Nations agencies that address the need of global economic development, imposing restructuring standards on aid recipients; other development banks; and the different United Nations organizations that promote the economic and financial welfare of developing countries, as well as their participation in international trade.

- **Identify government efforts involved in promoting economic development and trade**

  National and local governments are active in promoting international trade and development through a number of agencies and departments. Among them are the United States Agency for International Development, which supports the economic development of and trade with developing countries that are politically aligned with the United States; the Department of Commerce, which engages in activities from promoting export assistance to organizing trade shows and events, to providing financial assistance to international business; and various state and local government agencies whose primary mission is to promote international trade involvement of local business.

- **Describe other trade facilitators, such as foreign trade zones, off-shore assembly plants and special economic zones, and the Most-Favored-Nation Status**

  Foreign trade zones are tax-free areas in a country that are not considered part of that country from the import regulations' perspective and where products undergo additional manufacturing and are further shipped to other destination countries. They create employment in the host country, and they lower or defer import duties for the manufacturing firm. Off-shore assembly plants and special economic zones are customs-privileged facilities in countries with low-cost labor where products are manipulated and then re-exported. The Most-Favored-Nation Status, conferred by Congress in the U.S., offers preferential trade status to countries that are not part of a trade agreement with the U.S.

Discussion Questions

Discussion Questions

1. Discuss the different arguments used by countries invoking the protection of national industry and consumers.

2. Look up recent articles regarding China's trade restrictions. Which of these arguments does it appear to advocate?

3. What are the different financial controls imposed on international trade, i.e., price controls and currency controls?

4. Describe the mission and accomplishments of the World Trade Organization.

5. How do international organizations overlap in their efforts to promote trade and economic development?

6. What are the U.S. equivalents of the Ministry of Foreign Trade and the Ministry of Foreign Affairs? How do they promote trade?

Regional Economic and Political Integration

Key Terms

Andean Common Market (AnCom)
Arab Maghreb Union (AMU)
ASEAN Free Trade Area (AFTA)
Asia-Pacific Economic Cooperation (APEC)
Association of Southeast Asian Nations (ASEAN)
bilateral agreement
Central American Common Market (CACM)
Central European Free Trade Agreement (CEFTA)
common market
Common Market for Eastern and Southern Africa (COMESA)
Commonwealth of Independent States (CIS)
Council of Ministers
Council of Mutual Economic Assistance (CMEA)
Council of Nations
customs union

Economic Community of West African States (ECOWAS)
Euroland
European Atomic Energy Community
European Central Bank
European Coal and Steel Community
European Commission
European Council
European Court of Justice
European Exchange Rate Mechanism (ERM)
European Free Trade Association (EFTA)
European Monetary Union (EMU)
European Parliament
European Union
free trade agreement
Free Trade Area of the Americas (FTAA)
Latin American Free Trade Association (LAFTA)

Latin American Integration Association (LAIA)
Maastricht Treaty
monetary union
multilateral forums and agreements
North American Free Trade Agreement (NAFTA)
North Atlantic Treaty Organization (NATO)
Organization for Economic Co-operation and Development (OECD)
Organization of the Petroleum Exporting Countries (OPEC)
political union
South African Customs Union (SACU)
Southern African Development Community (SADC)
Southern Cone Common Market (MERCOSUR)
West African Economic and Monetary Union (WAEMU)

Outline

Learning Objectives
4-1 Determinants of Economic and Political Integration
    4-1a A Common Culture
    4-1b A History of Common Economic and Political Dominance
    4-1c Regional Proximity
    4-1d Economic Considerations
    4-1e Political Considerations
4-2 Levels of Regional Economic and/or Political Integration and Examples of Integration Successes
    4-2a Bilateral Agreements and Multilateral Forums and Agreements
    4-2b Free Trade Agreements
    4-2c Customs Unions
    4-2d Common Markets
    4-2e Monetary Union
    4-2f Political Union
Chapter Summary
Discussion Questions

Learning Objectives

Learning Objectives

By the end of this chapter, you should be able to:

- Provide an overview of the determinants of regional economic and political integration
- Examine the different levels of economic and political integration and identify, within each world region,

economic and political agreements that have met with success

- Examine the functions of the different policy and governance bodies of the European Union

Not too long ago, shipping goods in Europe was a complicated process: Waiting in lines at the border, filling out paperwork, going through customs, and paying duties were all part of the border-crossing process. Today, much of Europe has customs offices only at airports or ports, and there, no companies from the European Union are subjected to customs processing and duties. Removal of restrictions in the European Union is not limited to the movement of goods; it covers movement of all capital and labor.

Countries in Europe that are not members of the European Union aspire to become part of the European Union and benefit from the many advantages of integration. Countries in the rest of the world are actively building similar regions aimed at removing trade and other barriers. Many countries hope to jointly create a world economic area where all countries can benefit from the free movement of goods.

Chapter 3, "International Trade: Barriers and Facilitators," examined the many initiatives undertaken within the framework of the World Trade Organization (WTO) to reduce trade barriers and to promote unimpeded economic cooperation worldwide. A parallel effort aimed at economic, as well as political, integration is also attempted regionally, with various degrees of success. This chapter describes the determinants of regional economic and political integration, the different forms of integration, and, for each type of regional integration, it offers examples of successful agreements in all regions of the world.

4-1 Determinants of Economic and Political Integration

Numerous factors prompt countries to favor trade with other countries (neighboring countries in particular). Sharing a culture, a common language, a common history, or even common borders may lead countries to join forces in an effort to eliminate barriers to trade. The factors described in sections 4-1a through 4-1e compel countries to lower barriers and to expand trade with each other for mutual benefit.

4-1a A Common Culture

Regardless of whether a common culture was fostered by a former colonial power, people in neighboring countries often share a language, as well as other cultural elements, such as traditions, norms, and religion. As will be addressed in Chapter 5, "Cultural Influences on International Marketing," many areas in the world are characterized by cultural similarity. For example, in North Africa and the Middle East, the preponderant language is Arabic, and the environment of business, as well as everyday life, is structured in accordance with Islamic law. Similarly, Latin America shares Spanish as the dominant language, and Catholicism as its religion; as such, individuals in the region share rituals, traditions, and personal values.

The commonality of language and other elements of culture facilitate interaction between neighboring countries and promote cooperation: In an economic relationship in which culture does not constitute a barrier to communication, individuals are more likely to understand their counterparts and their position.

4-1b A History of Common Economic and Political Dominance

A history of dominance by one nation in a region often leads to shared cultural elements among the different peoples in that region, as well as to similar economic and political structures. Russia's economic, political, and cultural dominance in the Former Soviet Union has resulted, for example, in the use of the Russian language from the Baltics (Estonia, Lithuania, and Latvia) and the Ukraine, to the Asian republics of the former federation, such as Turkmenistan and Azerbaijan. The countries also shared economic and marketing structures, many of which continue to survive—for example, state-owned enterprises and large, nationwide distributors. In other examples, countries in East Africa formerly colonized by Belgium share a common second language (French), as well as extensive economic and political ties with the former colonist; and former colonies of the British Empire form the Commonwealth of Nations, a body that meets periodically to address issues of common concern and that recognizes the British Monarchy as its symbolic leader.

From a marketer's point of view, such similarities facilitate a standardized approach to the market. From the countries' perspective, regional economic integration is facilitated by the similarity of economic structures established by the former colonial power and the shared language and culture.

4-1c Regional Proximity

Regional proximity is an important facilitator of economic cooperation. Although countries do not need to have a common border to engage in cooperative agreements, access that is facilitated by direct and effective transportation and communication systems greatly increases the likelihood that the economic relationship will survive over time. In the case of the **European Union** (www.europa.eu.int), the member countries are quite dissimilar culturally; however, their regional proximity and the highly developed transportation infrastructure within the region, as

European Union An economic union consisting of most of the Western European countries; it is the only agreement that has achieved full economic integration and is now pursuing political integration. (See www.europa.eu.int.)

well as economic similarity between the different countries, have all greatly contributed to the success of regional economic and political integration.

4-1d Economic Considerations

It has been amply demonstrated that countries characterized by a similar level of economic development are more likely to be successful in establishing and maintaining regional economic integration mechanisms than countries of different levels of economic development. In the latter case, it is typical that the larger, more developed economies are likely to further their interests at the expense of countries that lag behind on economic development. In effect, countries of similar development levels are more likely to create a successful common market that assures preferential treatment for goods manufactured in the region, while also securing a substantial local consumer market. As countries prosper further as a result of this proven mechanism, the regional market then opens to firms from outside its boundaries, benefiting international enterprise regardless of national origin.

As mentioned in section 4-1c, the European Union is not characterized by a shared regional culture. The Union is successful primarily due to economic commonalities shared by member countries. Among others, they are

- A highly developed industrial base and overall productivity, translating into a high Gross Domestic Product (GDP) per capita
- An extensive transportation and telecommunications infrastructure, which is indispensable in trading relationships
- Prosperous consumers who can afford to purchase the goods and services of local firms

It should be emphasized, however, that the member countries have developed at different levels, and, often, constituents of the wealthier countries (such as Germany and the Netherlands) have deplored having to adopt policies that would benefit the lesser developed countries in the Union. Furthermore, the member countries of the European Union and of other forms of regional economic integration often differ with regard to the economic and trade policies they advocate. For example, the Netherlands and Germany stress the importance of market mechanisms and interfere only minimally in the regulation of business, whereas France is more likely to intervene. France often stresses social welfare at the expense of market development, and is often plagued by union activity that frequently paralyzes different sectors of the economy (the post office and the national airline industry constitute relatively recent examples). Similarly, in the case of the Southern Cone Common Market (MERCOSUR), the member countries disagree with the candidate members on the common external tariffs they should impose on international business entering the region.

4-1e Political Considerations

One of the more important obstacles to regional economic and political integration is the threat of losing national identity and sovereignty as part of the larger regional structure. Countries have many icons of national identity that generations have fought for centuries to maintain; such icons range from the form of government (republic, monarchy, and/or loose federation) to currency, language, and traditions. In the process of engaging in regional political and economic integration, member countries must choose, to a certain extent, to relinquish important aspects of their sovereignty and identity. For members of the European

Union, such decisions have ranged, among others, from minor issues, such as the number of hours that civil servants have for a lunch break (in Spain, it is argued that it is the individual's right to have more than one hour), to completely doing away with the French franc, the German deutsche mark, and the Italian lira in favor of the common currency—the Euro.

A principal consideration in accepting to relinquish part of national identity constitutes the importance of the regional group as a whole to the advancement of national priorities. A successful regional economic and political integration is one that promises a more substantial and more rapid economic development for member countries than they would otherwise experience in isolation from the country group, and one that equitably addresses and protects regional, as well as national, economic and political interests. In the case of the European Union, considerations of national sovereignty and national priorities take second place to joint interests in the creation of a viable, large market—"Fortress Europe"—which provides a credible balance to large economic and political powers, such as those of the United States, Japan, China, and Russia, among others. The Southern Cone Common Market (MERCOSUR) accomplishes similar goals for the otherwise smaller South American member countries.

4-2 Levels of Regional Economic and/or Political Integration and Examples of Integration Successes

Typically, member countries go through different stages of regional economic and political integration. Although most member countries start at the industry-specific bilateral or multilateral agreement level, theoretically at least, more complex regional agreements could jump to a more advanced stage, such as a common market, while simultaneously setting up a framework for a free trade agreement and customs union. Most commonly, however, member countries could target a more advanced framework, as their name might indicate (e.g., Southern Cone Common Market), but go through the different steps nevertheless (the Southern Cone Common Market is currently attempting to advance from the free trade association/agreement stage to the customs union stage). Sections 4-2a through 4-2f present the different levels of economic and/or political integration agreements, from the more basic to the more advanced, along with current and past examples within each category.

4-2a Bilateral Agreements and Multilateral Forums and Agreements

Numerous examples of bilateral and multilateral agreements exist. Some are industry specific, others involve some or all products exchanged between countries. In fact, most member countries of the more complex regional economic and political forms of integration engaged, as a first step, in some type of regional cooperation. Governments could enter into agreements that are limited to a particular industry; the agreements could involve the development of an industry sector, such as participating in the development of a hydroelectric plant in an area that would serve neighboring countries, or it could entail lowering or eliminating tariffs on certain goods that are traded between the member countries, such as coal and steel. The European Union had its earliest attempts at economic integration in the form of the **European Coal and Steel Community,** established in the late 1950s, and the subsequent structure, the **European Atomic Energy Community.**

European Coal and Steel Community An agreement that represents an early attempt at tariff reduction between members of the European Union.

European Atomic Energy Community A precursor to the European Union, it addressed issues related to the use and control of atomic energy.

Bilateral agreement   Regional trade cooperation between two countries aimed at reducing or eliminating trade barriers for all or for selected products.

Multilateral forums and agreements   Agreements that involve multiple countries, have an informal structure, and/or do not necessarily have regional integration as their goal.

Organization of the Petroleum Exporting Countries (OPEC) Industry-specific (oil) multilateral agreement aimed at managing the output and price of oil. (See www.opec.com.)

North Atlantic Treaty Organization (NATO) A military agreement between countries that were, initially, not part of the Soviet Bloc. (See www.nato.int.)

Organization for Economic Co-operation and Development (OECD)   An economic multilateral agreement. (See www.oecdobserver.org.)

Asia-Pacific Economic Cooperation (APEC)   A trade group including all major economies of the Asia-Pacific region, it is a forum for economic cooperation and has as its goal the gradual reduction of barriers to trade and investment between member countries. (See www.apecsec.org.sg.)

Commonwealth of Independent States (CIS)   A political agreement between the twelve non-Baltic countries of the former Soviet Union. (See www.cis.minsk.by.)

What differentiates these agreements from the formal regional integration formats is that either they are limited to two countries (**bilateral agreements**), or, if they involve multiple countries (**multilateral forums and agreements**), the agreements have a less formal structure and/or do not aim at regional integration. Examples of bilateral agreements are infinite, and they are often the foundation for the more formal regional integration attempts. Multilateral agreements that primarily provide a forum for regional cooperation endeavors are numerous. Some are industry specific, such as the **Organization of the Petroleum Exporting Countries (OPEC).** Some are military in nature, such as the **North Atlantic Treaty Organization (NATO).** Others have an economic focus—for example, the **Organization for Economic Co-operation and Development (OECD).**

A noteworthy economic organization is the **Asia-Pacific Economic Cooperation**, or **APEC** (www.apecsec.org.sg). APEC was established to mitigate the economic block and trade protection trend prevailing in the 1970s and 1980s; it was established in 1989 at a ministerial meeting in Canberra, Australia, with the mission to create an open economic alliance in the Asia-Pacific region.[1] This trade group includes all the major economies of the region (the United States and Canada are member countries), accounting for 42 percent of global trade.[2] APEC provides a forum for economic cooperation and the gradual reduction of barriers to trade and investment between member countries. Although the group does not attempt to forge an institutional integration that would be required under a free trade association or a more advanced regional economic and political integration format, APEC has nevertheless been instrumental in fostering free trade. Most of its advances so far have been made in the area of computers and the Internet: APEC members agreed upon a moratorium on customs duties over the Internet, on safeguards against software piracy, and on eliminating tariffs on computers and semiconductors.[3] APEC also represents a forum for member countries to address issues critical to trade; for example, before its ascension to the WTO, China used the APEC forum to announce a number of important reductions in protectionism.[4]

An example of a political agreement—which we place in this category because of its failure to achieve a substantial level of regional integration—is the **Commonwealth of Independent States (CIS).** The twelve non-Baltic successors to the Union of the Soviet Socialist Republics (the Soviet Union) formed the Commonwealth of Independent States. This organization has never had any noteworthy economic content; and, even politically, the CIS became fractured in the second half of the 1990s with the GUUAM grouping (Georgia, Ukraine, Uzbekistan, Azerbaijan, and Moldova) operating explicitly as a counter to Russian hegemony.[5] The Union of Four (Russia, Belarus, Kazakhstan, and the Kyrgyz Republic) considered creating a customs union, with Russia's tariff as the putative common external tariff, but, apart from steps toward a bilateral agreement between Belarus and Russia aimed at creating an economic union, nothing has come to fruition.[6] Finally, the Central Asian states of the Former Soviet Union have drawn up numerous plans for regional cooperation—they must cooperate on nontrade matters such as the

1. *Business Korea*, "The History of APEC," April 2000, Vol. 17, No. 4, pp. 54–55.

2. Ibid.

3. Laura D'andrea Tyson, "The Message from Asia: Trade Locally, Think Globally," *Business Week*, December 4, 2000, Issue 3710, p. 28.

4. Ibid.

5. Richard Pomfret, "Reintegration of Formerly Centrally Planned Economies Into the Global Trading System," *ASEAN Economic Bulletin*, April 2001, Vol. 18, No. 1, pp. 35–47.

6. Ibid.

desiccation of the Aral Sea—but the establishment of a Central Asian Economic Community has had little impact to date.[7]

4-2b Free Trade Agreements

A **free trade agreement** takes place between two or more countries and involves a reduction in, or even elimination of, customs duties and other trade barriers on all goods and services traded between the member countries. Countries are free to charge their own tariffs to all entities external to the free trade market. The following are present and past examples of free trade agreements:

- European Free Trade Association
- Central European Free Trade Agreement
- Association of Southeast Asian Nations
- ASEAN Free Trade Area
- North American Free Trade Agreement
- Free Trade Area of the Americas
- Southern African Development Community
- Arab Maghreb Union

The European Free Trade Association (EFTA) (www.efta.int)

The current member countries of the **European Free Trade Association (EFTA)** are Iceland, Liechtenstein, Norway, and Switzerland; previously, Sweden, Austria, and Finland were also members but have since joined the European Union. EFTA has constituted for decades another example of successful regional economic integration in Europe—in addition to the European Union.

In 1993, EU and EFTA created the European Economic Area, representing the world's largest single market with 380 million consumers. Since then, however, the European Union has created new regulations with the Maastricht, Amsterdam, and Nice treaties, and has created new powers of authority in areas such as environmental and labor market policies.[8] Norway is the only EFTA country to participate in the Schengen agreement on the elimination of border controls, in the EU common foreign and security policy; none of the EFTA countries have joined the European Monetary Union.[9]

At present, politicians in the EFTA countries want to be at least unofficially part of the EU but believe that public opinion at home is against further EU integration. The EU, on the other hand, does not appear to be interested in new negotiations that would offer EFTA members a greater involvement in the EU. The focus of the EU is eastern expansion (with Central European Free Trade Agreement, or CEFTA, members joining shortly), and the members are faced with the following constraints:[10]

- Numerous complexities related to the different stages and phases of eastward enlargement
- Possibilities of looser associated memberships
- Special rights of nonmembers
- Periods of transition to membership and special arrangements

Free trade agreement
An agreement whose goal is the reduction in, or even elimination of, customs duties and other trade barriers on all goods and services traded between member countries.

European Free Trade Association (EFTA)   A free trade agreement between Iceland, Liechtenstein, Norway, and Switzerland; previously, Sweden, Austria, and Finland were also members, but they have since joined the European Union. (See www.efta.int.)

---

7. Ibid.

8. Robert von Lucius, "Nordic Neighbors Feel Snubbed," *Frankfurter Allgemeine Zeitung*, July 6, 2001. No. 154, p. 3.

9. Ibid.

10. For a discussion of the current conflict between the EU and EFTA, see Lucius, "Nordic Neighbors Feel Snubbed," p. 3.

In general, the perception of European Union members is that EFTA, especially Norway and Iceland, would like to have more impact on the decision-making process within the EU, in particular on legal decisions (where nonmembers have no influence at all), and share in the benefits of the single European market, but are not prepared to share in the costs and other obligations of membership.[11]

In spite of the national vote against joining the European Union, Switzerland is engaging in bilateral negotiations, securing agreements that would help it join: It has negotiated issues in the area of the collection of statistics, the environment, agricultural production and customs fraud, cross-border security, youth, and education, among others; all negotiations must be ratified further by the national parliaments of the EU countries.[12]

The Central European Free Trade Agreement (CEFTA) (www.cefta.org)

Member countries of the **Central European Free Trade Agreement** (**CEFTA**) are Hungary, the Czech Republic, Slovakia, and Poland; they are the most developed of the former Soviet Bloc countries, and all are likely to join the European Union this decade. At present, the member countries are attempting to reduce all duties and nontariff barriers on goods trading between them and are adopting many of the policies that will facilitate their adherence to the European Union; for example, they are, among others, pegging their respective currencies on the Euro and adopting the European Union regulations on product origins.

The Association of Southeast Asian Nations (ASEAN) (www.asean.or.id) and the ASEAN Free Trade Area (AFTA)

The **Association of Southeast Asian Nations** (**ASEAN**) is the primary and most successful example of regional economic integration in Asia. Member countries are attempting to reduce tariffs and to create an environment that promotes mutual involvement in industrial development in the region. The goal of ASEAN is ultimately to create a free trade area where tariff and nontariff barriers are eliminated, and to provide a substantial market of more than 330 million consumers to companies in the region. Members of ASEAN are Brunei, Cambodia, Indonesia, Laos, Malaysia, Myanmar, the Philippines, Singapore, Thailand, and Vietnam, which have signed the **ASEAN Free Trade Area** (**AFTA**).

ASEAN countries are pursuing free trade agreements with countries such as Japan,[13] and even laying the groundwork for the formalization of currency swap agreements with Japan, South Korea, and China, whereby countries agree to give each other money to bolster foreign exchange reserves in the event of a currency crisis.[14]

The North American Free Trade Agreement (NAFTA) (www.nafta-customs.org)

Signatory countries of the **North American Free Trade Agreement** (**NAFTA**) are the United States, Canada, and Mexico. The goal of the 1994 treaty is to eliminate

---

Central European Free Trade Agreement (CEFTA) An economic alliance between the most developed of former Soviet Bloc countries attempting to reduce all duties and nontariff barriers on goods; member countries are adopting policies that will facilitate their adherence to the European Union. (See www.cefta.org.)

Association of Southeast Asian Nations (ASEAN) A successful example of integration in Asia, creating an environment that promotes mutual involvement in industrial development in the region and a free trade area composed of Brunei, Cambodia, Indonesia, Laos, Malaysia, Myanmar, the Philippines, Singapore, Thailand, and Vietnam. (See www.asean.or.id.)

ASEAN Free Trade Area (AFTA) A free trade agreement signed by members of the Association of Southeast Asian Nations (ASEAN). (See www.asean.or.id.)

North American Free Trade Agreement (NAFTA) An agreement between the United States, Canada, and Mexico, aiming to eliminate tariff and nontariff barriers between the countries. (See www.nafta-customs.org.)

---

11. Ibid.

12. Edward Taylor, "EU and Switzerland Resume Talks on Bilateral Accords," *Wall Street Journal Europe,* July 6–7, 2001, p. 2.

13. *World Trade,* "Asia/Pacific Rim: Japan, ASEAN Set Up Free Trade Agreement Study Group," July 2001, Vol. 14, No. 7, p. 18.

14. Neil Saker, "The Foundations of Stability," *Far Eastern Economic Review,* May 24, 2001, Vol. 164, No. 20, p. 55.

all tariff and nontariff barriers, such as import licenses and quotas, between the member countries and to offer free access to companies from member countries to a single market of almost 400 million consumers. As with other free trade agreements, member countries charge their own duties and other tariffs to companies from nonmember countries entering the respective markets. One of the more important decisions for NAFTA involves the rules of origin: To benefit from a duty-free status, goods must have a 60 percent North American content.

NAFTA has initially generated great fears in the United States. It was described by a former presidential candidate and NAFTA opponent as the "giant sucking sound" that would move all jobs South of the U.S. border. Indeed, U.S. workers have experienced some level of job loss that can be directly attributed to NAFTA, in the lumber and textile industries, for example. However, it also can be argued that NAFTA created jobs in the U.S. For example, in terms of trade flow, NAFTA has fared very well: U.S. merchandise exports to Mexico have increased by 170 percent, and Mexican exports to the U.S. have increased by 241 percent since 1993.[15] NAFTA has brought substantial foreign direct investment to Mexico ($85 billion[16]), creating stability in the country, and lessening its dependence on the United States.

In spite of its free-market rhetoric, however, the United States has engaged in protectionist activity that hampers free trade among member countries; for example, recently, the U.S. Congress, pressured by domestic truck drivers, voted to keep Mexican truckers out of most of the U.S.[17]

The Free Trade Area of the Americas (FTAA)

The **Free Trade Area of the Americas (FTAA)** is an ambitious plan to create a market of about 800 million people and an annual production worth $11 trillion in the Americas.[18] The organization has the ambitious goal to create a free trade association by 2005, but its progress is greatly impeded by protectionist fears voiced in the United States, reminiscent of the unfounded dismal NAFTA predictions.[19] Member countries are the 34 democratic nations of North, Central, and South America.

The Southern African Development Community (SADC)

The **Southern African Development Community (SADC)** is a free trade organization that promotes economic cooperation among a coalition of 14 of Africa's more affluent and developed nations. The organization is designed to foster increased economic and governmental stability through the use of collective peacekeeping forces and should be credited for the recent relative stability of the region.[20]

Its member countries are Angola, Botswana, the Democratic Republic of Congo (DRC), Lesotho, Madagascar, Malawi, Mozambique, Namibia, Seychelles, the Republic of South Africa (RSA), Swaziland, Tanzania, Zambia, and Zimbabwe.

Free Trade Area of the Americas (FTAA) A plan to create a free trade association by 2005 that would comprise all member countries of the thirty-four democratic nations of North, Central, and South America. (See www.ftaa-alca.org.)

Southern African Development Community (SADC) A free trade organization that promotes economic cooperation among a coalition of fourteen of Africa's more affluent and developed nations, designed to foster increased economic and governmental stability through the use of collective peace-keeping forces.

15. Charles J. Whalen, Paul Magnusson, and Geri Smith, "NAFTA's Scorecard: So Far, So Good," *Business Week,* July 9, 2001, Issue 3740, pp. 54–56.

16. Ibid.

17. *Business Week,* "No Time for Protectionism," July 23, 2001, Issue 3742, p. 98.

18. Ernesto Zedillo, Former President of Mexico, "Commentary," *Forbes,* July 23, 2001, p. 49.

19. Ibid.

20. Ryan Fahey, "Congo Tensions: The SADC's Shortcomings," *Harvard International Review,* Spring 1999, Vol. 21, No. 2, pp. 14–16.

The Arab Maghreb Union (AMU)

Arab Maghreb Union (AMU)
An attempt, in the early 1980s, at creating a free trade area in the Southern Mediterranean area; it was not successful due to conflict.

Better known as the Union du Maghreb Arab (UMA), the **Arab Maghreb Union (AMU)** has had less success than most of the examples of regional economic and political integration associations mentioned here. Members in the AMU (Algeria, Libya, Mauritania, Morocco, and Tunisia) pledged to form a powerful economic bloc and a free trade area in the Southern Mediterranean region in the early 1980s. The organization has not operated since its inception in 1989, however, due to border disputes between Morocco and Algeria. It should be noted, however, that, within the group, bilateral talks have taken place between Morocco and Tunisia on issues of trade, investment, fishing, and tourism.[21]

4-2c Customs Unions

Customs union A market composed of member countries imposing identical import duties and sharing import regulations.

A **customs union** is a free trade association that may have either eliminated or greatly reduced all tariffs and other trade restrictions for member countries, and that has adopted common external tariffs on products imported from outside the free trade area. Although the Andean Common Market and the Southern Cone Common Market aspire to become a common market, at present they are only customs unions; they are, however, in the process of agreeing upon common external tariffs.

South African Customs Union (SACU)

South African Customs Union (SACU) A custom market that includes Botswana, Swaziland, Lesotho, and Namibia. The group's main trading partner is South Africa, and member countries have partially or entirely tied their currencies to the South African rand.

Member countries of the **South African Customs Union (SACU)** are Botswana, Swaziland, Lesotho, and Namibia. The group's main trading partner is South Africa, and member countries have partially or entirely tied their currencies to the South African rand.

4-2d Common Markets

Common market A market composed of member countries, characterized by the unrestricted movement of goods, labor, and capital.

Member countries to a **common market** agreement eliminate all tariff and non-tariff barriers to trade, adopt common external tariffs, and allow for the free movement of capital and labor within the common market. Although only the European Union has achieved (and surpassed) the common market stage, a number of other forms of economic integration are aiming to achieve this stage—among them, the Andean Common Market and the Southern Cone Common Market.

Maastricht Treaty The treaty credited with establishing the European Union, eliminating all tariffs; establishing common external tariffs; allowing for the free movement of capital and labor within its territory; and setting regulations involving common trade policies, common agricultural and industrial policies, and common monetary and fiscal policies between member countries. (See www.europa.eu.int.)

In Europe, member countries agreed, at the Treaty of Rome, to establish the European Economic Community (EEC), eliminating all internal tariffs and duties, establishing common external tariffs, and allowing for the free movement of capital and labor within its territory. At this point, member countries also set in place regulations and bodies that would ultimately form the basis for a monetary and political union—an event that was to take place in 1992, on the occasion of the **Maastricht Treaty,** commonly known as the eagerly anticipated "Europe 1992." Such regulations involved common trade policies, common agricultural and industrial policies, and common monetary and fiscal policies.

European Exchange Rate Mechanism (ERM) A precursor of the Euro, a float that included the Euro, the then-theoretical currency of the European Union; the float allowed for variability in each currency.

As an example of common monetary policies and precursors to a monetary union, member countries agreed to create a common float that would include the embryonic Euro, the then-theoretical currency of Europe. The float was known as the **European Exchange Rate Mechanism (ERM).** The ERM was also known as the "snake," as it changed its shape based on the fluctuation of the different cur-

---

21. *Barclays Economic Review,* "International Economy: Africa," Third Quarter 1999, pp. 29–31.

rencies. According to the ERM, a currency could fluctuate only up to 2.5 percent of its value in either direction; when this value was consistently surpassed, the mechanism would adjust the currency upward or downward, respectively, creating a snake-like structure. A float that performed well was an important prerequisite to the success of a monetary union; this, as we will see in section 4-2e, "Monetary Union," was not the case in 1992, the date established for the creation of the monetary union.

Other examples of regional economic integration aiming to establish a common market are as follows:

- Latin American Integration Association
- Andean Community
- Southern Cone Common Market
- Central American Common Market
- Common Market for Eastern and Southern Africa

The Latin American Integration Association (LAIA)

The **Latin American Integration Association (LAIA)** was created in 1980 to replace the **Latin American Free Trade Association (LAFTA)**. LAFTA was an attempt by member countries to establish a free trade association. Its demise was attributed to the disparity in the level of development of member countries, and to the protectionist policies of countries with enormous foreign debt experiencing high inflation, currency devaluation, and economic crises. LAFTA is important in that it constituted a first step in an ambitious plan to create a common market that comprises all of Latin America, under the umbrella of the Latin American Integration Association.

The Latin American Integration Association member countries are Argentina, Bolivia, Brazil, Chile, Colombia, Ecuador, Mexico, Paraguay, Peru, Uruguay, and Venezuela. Under LAIA, member countries are encouraged to establish bilateral and multilateral agreements aimed at reducing tariff and nontariff barriers. LAIA offers differential treatment to countries of different levels of development to avoid preferential treatment of the larger countries (blamed for the failure of LAFTA). Member countries are at present members of two successful common markets—the Andean Common Market (AnCom) and the Southern Cone Common Market (MERCOSUR).

The Andean Community (AnCom)

The **Andean Common Market (AnCom),** known previously as the Andean Pact, was established in the 1970s and renamed as the Andean Community in 1996. In addition to eliminating trade restrictions (tariff and nontariff) within the Andean region, AnCom also provides for uniform external tariffs and rules for foreign investment. Its member countries are Bolivia, Colombia, Ecuador, Panama, Peru, and Venezuela. Peru left AnCom in 1997 but remains a participant, although it does not take part in AnCom's external tariffs.[22]

One of AnCom's accomplishments is that member countries have agreed on levels of external tariffs covering 95 percent of products, whereby raw materials and basic industrial feedstuffs pay a 5 percent duty, intermediate manufacturers pay a 10 or 15 percent duty, and finished goods are taxed at 20 percent.[23]

Latin American Integration Association (LAIA) Latin America's largest trade agreement striving to establish bilateral and multilateral agreements aimed at reducing tariff and nontariff barriers.

Latin American Free Trade Association (LAFTA) An attempt by Latin American countries to establish a free trade association; its demise is attributed to the economic disparity between member countries and to protectionist policies.

Andean Common Market (AnCom) A trade group of the Andean countries that aspires to become a common market; it is currently in the process of agreeing upon common external tariffs. (See www.comunidadandina.org.)

---

22. Lara L. Sowinski, "Latin America: The Land of No Borders," *World Trade,* July 2000, Vol. 13, No. 7, pp. 44–47.

23. Ibid.

The Southern Cone Common Market (MERCOSUR)

Southern Cone Common Market (MERCOSUR) A free trade agreement in South America that has met with considerable success; MERCOSUR is presently in the process of becoming a viable customs union. (See www.mercosur.org.)

The **Southern Cone Common Market (MERCOSUR)** is among the most successful common markets. Initially, it started as a bilateral agreement between Brazil and Argentina aimed at eliminating trade restrictions between the two countries. MERCOSUR now comprises two additional member countries—Paraguay and Uruguay. Two other members, Chile and Bolivia, have a pending status. Although Chile and Bolivia have both qualified for membership, the two countries continue to disagree with the other members on the common tariffs (Chile insists on a much lower external tariff than the agreement provides for) to be charged to companies from nonmember countries and consequently retain an associate status.

Initially, MERCOSUR was expected to look north, at NAFTA, for trade and cooperation accords; surprisingly, it has opted to first approach the European Union in an ambitious agreement that would phase out all trade barriers by 2005.[24]

The Central American Common Market (CACM)

Central American Common Market (CACM) An economic agreement between Central American countries; this agreement includes plans for forming a regional economic union similar to the European Union, and to advance regional and international trade.

The economic agreement between Belize, Costa Rica, the Dominican Republic, El Salvador, Guatemala, Honduras, Nicaragua, and Panama, known as the **Central American Common Market (CACM),** includes plans for forming a regional economic union similar to the European Union, and to advance regional and international trade. The plan also encompasses political, cultural, and environmental measures.[25]

The Common Market for Eastern and Southern Africa (COMESA)

Common Market for Eastern and Southern Africa (COMESA) An agreement between twenty member countries aimed at achieving economic integration; COMESA is currently eliminating all tariff and nontariff barriers to trade and is in the process of adopting common external tariffs. (See www.comesa.int.)

The **Common Market for Eastern and Southern Africa (COMESA)** plans full economic integration, allowing for the free movement of labor and capital by 2004, the free movement of people by 2014, and a currency union by 2025; it is, however, clear that the organization faces substantial political and economic obstacles given the political and economic instability in the region.[26] Specifically, the difficulties facing member countries include a poor compliance with tariff reductions and concerns over customs revenue losses; further complicating the matter is the fact that, despite diplomatic pressure, South Africa is not a member.[27] COMESA has 20 member countries: Angola, Burundi, Comoros, Democratic Republic of Congo, Djibouti, Egypt, Eritrea, Ethiopia, Kenya, Madagascar, Malawi, Mauritius, Namibia, Rwanda, Seychelles, Sudan, Swaziland, Uganda, Zambia, and Zimbabwe.

4-2e Monetary Union

Monetary union A form of economic integration characterized by the establishment of a common central bank enacting monetary policy for the group.

The establishment of a **monetary union** involves the creation of a unified central bank and the use of a single currency. The following are examples of successful monetary unions:

- European Monetary Union
- West African Economic and Monetary Union
- Economic Community of West African States

---

24. Ibid.

25. Ibid.

26. *Country Monitor,* "Comesa's Free-Trade Area," November 6, 2000, Vol. 8, No. 43, p. 4.

27. *Barclays Economic Review,* "International Economy," pp. 29–31.

It should be noted, however, that successful monetary unions do not necessarily mean successful economic integration and the elimination of trade restrictions.

The European Monetary Union (Euroland) (www.europa.eu.int)

The 1992 Maastricht Treaty had as a purpose to provide for the **European Monetary Union (EMU)** and to create the European Central Bank, a single currency, and fixed exchange rates. The creation of a monetary union was, however, hindered in 1992 by an exceptionally strong German mark, boosted particularly by the financing of reconstruction for Eastern Germany (the former East Germany) and the high interest rates it offered to foreign investors. This, coupled with a recession taking place in Europe, led to a crisis that caused the British pound and the Spanish peseta to lose their value overnight and to float out of the European Exchange Rate Mechanism. To member countries, at the time, it appeared that the German Central Bank was likely to dominate the European body, and, for a while, the Euro lost popular support, especially in Britain. At present, members of the European Union are implicitly members of the European Monetary Union, with an active European Central Bank, with a joint monetary policy and the Euro as the common currency.

Currently, countries that are full members of the European Monetary Union are Austria, Belgium, Finland, France, Germany, Ireland, Italy, Luxembourg, the Netherlands, Portugal, and Spain—the countries that joined in the first wave the European Economic and Monetary Union. These countries are often referred to as **Euroland.**

The West African Economic and Monetary Union (WAEMU)

The **West African Economic and Monetary Union (WAEMU)** is one of the first attempts at economic integration in Africa. Although successful as a monetary union that has adopted a single currency—the CFA franc—trade is quite modest within the WAEMU.[28] WAEMU member countries are Benin, Burkina Faso, Ivory Coast, Guinea-Bissau, Mali, Niger, Senegal, and Togo.

The Economic Community of West African States (ECOWAS)

The purpose of the **Economic Community of West African States (ECOWAS)** is to achieve complete economic integration. At present, ECOWAS member countries are also attempting to address impediments to the integration process that are attributed to civil unrest, to regional conflict, to a lag in economic development compared to other market groups in the world, and to the domination of the group by Nigeria.

ECOWAS's plans, however, are ambitious. Six of the fifteen members—Gambia, Ghana, Guinea, Liberia, Nigeria, and Sierra Leone—have set up a monetary union and have committed to adopting a common currency by 2003 and to merge with the WAEMU by 2004. In this regard, they have pledged to meet stringent convergence criteria, such as 5 percent inflation, a maximum budget deficit-to-GDP ratio of 4 percent, and central bank financing of the budget deficit limited to 10 percent of the previous year's tax revenue, among others.[29] ECOWAS

European Monetary Union (EMU) A union composed of the members of the European Union who adhere to the joint monetary policy enacted by the European Central Bank and who have adopted the Euro as the single currency. (See www.europa.eu.int.)

Euroland The nickname of the European Monetary Union. (See www.europa.eu.int.)

West African Economic and Monetary Union (WAEMU) One of the first attempts at economic integration in Africa. Although it is successful as a monetary union that has adopted a single currency, trade is quite modest within the WAEMU. (See www.dakarcom.com/EconReports/econ_waemu.htm.)

Economic Community of West African States (ECOWAS) A free trade agreement that strives to achieve economic integration in West Africa; domination by Nigeria, civil unrest, and regional conflict have served as impediments in the group's success. (See www.ecowas.int.)

---

28. Jacqueline Irving, "Point/Counterpoint: The Pros and Cons of Expanded Monetary Union in West Africa," *Finance & Development*, March, 2001, Vol. 38, No. 1, pp. 24–28.

29. Ibid.

member countries are Benin, Burkina Faso, Cape Verde, Ivory Coast, Gambia, Ghana, Guinea, Guinea-Bissau, Liberia, Mali, Niger, Nigeria, Senegal, Sierra Leone, and Togo.

4-2f Political Union

Political union The highest level of regional integration; it assumes a viable economic integration and involves the establishment of viable common governing bodies, legislative bodies, and enforcement powers.

Council of Mutual Economic Assistance (CMEA) A trade agreement between the countries of the Soviet Bloc that disintegrated after the fall of communism. CMEA was an economic body similar in nature to a free trade area, and approached what would be considered a political union.

European Council The highest policy-making body of the European Union. (See www.europa.eu.int.)

European Parliament The Parliament of the European Union, composed of members elected every five years by direct universal suffrage; seats in the Parliament are allocated among member states based on their population. (See www.europa.eu.int.)

Council of Nations The constitutional council of the European Union consisting of representatives from parliaments of EU member states. (See www.europa.eu.int.)

Council of Ministers The decision-making body (the legislature) of the European Union, composed of one minister from each member country.

A political union represents the highest level of integration; it assumes a viable economic integration and involves the establishment of viable common governing bodies, legislative bodies, and enforcement powers. Although there are many examples of political unions, the European Union (www.europa.eu.int) is the only example to date of successful voluntary political integration. In other examples, the countries of the former Soviet Bloc were members of the **Council of Mutual Economic Assistance (CMEA),** an economic body similar in nature to a free trade area, as well as members of the Warsaw Pact, a political/military body aimed at countering the North Atlantic Treaty Organization (NATO); under this format, member countries of CMEA also approached what would be considered a political union. CMEA did not survive beyond the fall of communism. An example of nonvoluntary integration is also the Commonwealth of Independent States, discussed in section 4-2a, "Bilateral Agreements and Multilateral Forums and Agreements."

The European Union, an entity composed of fifteen member states, is well on its way to becoming a political union. In this regard, it has agreed on a common foreign policy, a common security policy that includes defense agreements, a common legal system, and a common enforcement system that works across borders for mutual purposes. As such, it has set in place a number of governmental bodies, as shown in Figure 4-1.

The **European Council,** in which heads of government meet, is the highest policy-making body of the European Union.

The **European Parliament,** located in Strasbourg, France (see Figure 4-2), is a body of 546 members elected every five years by direct universal suffrage. Seats are allocated among member states based on their population.

The Parliament debates the policies and legislation in the European Union. In the past, it was mainly a consultative body that passed on most of the proposed legislation with a simple-majority voting. More recently, however, it has experienced extensive debate and lobbying from member countries on key international business issues. In one example, the Parliament killed a measure that would have made it easier to mount corporate takeovers; the vote is attributed to a string of hostile takeovers, such as Vodafone, the British mobile telephone company taking over its German rival, Mannesmann.[30]

The **Council of Nations** consists of representatives from parliaments of member states, and it acts as a constitutional council. It has the power to overrule the Court of Justice.

The **Council of Ministers**, the decision-making body (the legislature) of the European Union, is composed of one minister from each member country. The Council of Ministers passes laws based on proposals of the European Commission. Different ministers from each country, depending on the issue debated, meet at various locations to vote on directives advanced by the Commission. For example, EU energy ministers have met in Stockholm to vote on EU electricity and natural gas directives: The plans would allow businesses and households to choose their electricity and natural gas suppliers.[31]

---

30. Paul Meller, "EU Parliament Rejects Bill to Ease Takeovers," *International Herald Tribune*, Frankfurt, July 5, 2001, pp. 1, 10.

31. *Wall Street Journal Europe*, "EU Energy Chief Expects Power Deal by the End of the Year," July 6–7, 2001, p. 3.

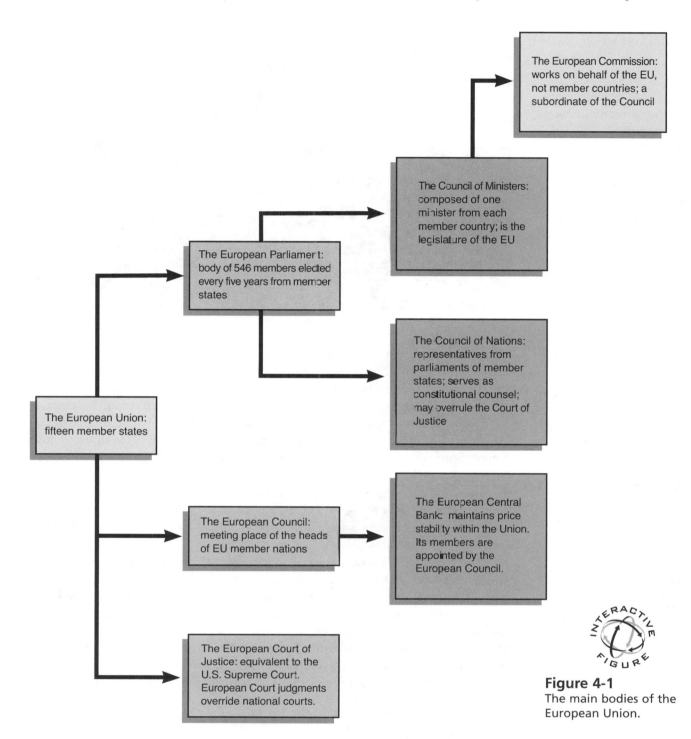

Figure 4-1
The main bodies of the European Union.

The **European Commission** is subordinated to the Council, as a civil service. The Commission consists of a president and commissioners who are appointed for a four-year term and are in charge of initiating and supervising the execution of laws and policies. This executive body of the European Union is located in Brussels, Belgium. It is important to note that the European Commission acts only on behalf and in the interest of the European Union, and not that of individual member states. It answers to the European Parliament.

Many of the European Commission rulings affect international business worldwide: A company that wants to do business in Europe must abide by the

European Commission
The body of the European Union in charge of initiating and supervising the execution of laws and policies.
(See www.europa.eu.int.)

Figure 4-2
The members of Parliament meet once a month in the European Parliament building in Strasbourg, France. This building ended the fight between Strasbourg and Bruxelles (Belgium) and the debate on the primary location of the European Parliament; it should be noted, however, that the work of the European Parliament is also conducted in Bruxelles and Luxembourg.

European Central Bank
The bank of the European Union charged with enacting monetary policy for the twelve countries that share a common currency, the Euro. (See www.europa.eu.int.)

European Court of Justice
The Supreme Court–equivalent of the European Union. (See www.europa.eu.int.)

Commission's ruling.[32] In a recent example, the European Commission blocked General Electric's $42 billion takeover of Honeywell International, due to the danger that GE could use Honeywell's strength in avionics equipment to expand its competitive strength in aircraft engines; the Commission rejected the merger of MCI Worldcom and Sprint on the grounds that the company would be able to dictate prices for Internet access in Europe, and blocked a merger between two British travel agencies invoking the threat of collective dominance.[33] In another example, the European Commission raided nine mobile-service providers in Britain and Germany, including giants Deutsche Telekom AG, the Vodafone Group PLC, and France Telecom SA, looking for evidence of price fixing in setting roaming tariffs; in such cases, if collusion is found, providers could face fines and cease-and-desist orders.[34]

The **European Central Bank** is charged with enacting monetary policy for the twelve countries that share a common currency, the Euro. Its goal is to maintain price stability within the European Monetary Union. The members of the European Central Bank board are appointed by the European Council by a simple majority vote. The equivalent of the Federal Reserve Bank for the United States, the European Central Bank tends to be much more conservative, and does not typically yield to individual countries' demands to reduce interest rates in an attempt to boost the economy during a downturn. Since its debut, the Euro has lost its value relative to the U.S. dollar.

The **European Court of Justice** is the European Union's equivalent of the U.S. Supreme Court. The Court's decisions are final, binding to member countries, and cannot be appealed in national courts. Also, European Court judgments overrule those of national courts.

32. Brian M. Carney, "Mario Monti, Central Planner: Does the European Union's Competition Commissioner Really Believe in Competition?" *Wall Street Journal Europe*, July 6–7, 2001, p. 6.

33. Edmund L. Andrews and Paul Meller, "EU Vetoes GE's Plan to Acquire Honeywell," *International Herald Tribune*, Frankfurt, July 4, 2001, pp. 1, 5.

34. Philip Shishkin, William Boston, and Almar LaTour, "Nine Mobile Firms Are Raided in Probe of Roaming Tariffs: EU Antitrust Officials Look for Evidence of Collusion in Germany, U.K.," *Wall Street Journal Europe*, July 12, 2001, pp. 1, 4.

(a)

(b)

Figure 4-3
Institutions of the Council of Europe: *(a)* the Palais de l'Europe and *(b)* the European Court and Commission for Human Rights.

In addition to these bodies, the European Union has adopted other common policies; among them are commercial policies, foreign and defense policies, and policies concerning immigration and the granting of asylum.

Other Para-Statal Institutions in Europe

The European Union is not the only para-statal institution in Western Europe. Other para-statal institutions have no affiliation to the European Union, and yet they are significant players in the life of this region. One such example is the Council of Europe, which is composed of forty European states that agree to accept the principle of the rule of law and guarantee of human rights and fundamental freedoms. The institution is involved in such areas as human rights; legal cooperation; cultural heritage; social, economic, and environmental planning; and local democracy. Two of its institutions are the Palais de l'Europe (see Figure 4-3*a*) and the European Court and Commission for Human Rights (see Figure 4-3*b*).

Chapter Summary

- **Provide an overview of the determinants of regional economic and political integration**

  A number of factors prompt countries to favor trade with other countries. They are sharing a common culture, language, traditions, a history of common economic and political dominance, regional proximity, a similar level of economic development, and the desire to relinquish part of a nation's national identity in favor of advancing other national priorities.

- **Examine the different levels of economic and political integration and identify, within each world region, economic and political agreements that have met with success**

  The first level of integration involves establishing bilateral and multilateral agreements; these agreements involve, to some extent, opening of markets and elimination of trade barriers. At the next level, a free trade agreement involves a reduction in, or even elimination of, customs duties and other trade barriers between member countries. Examples of free trade agreements are the European Free Trade Association, the Central European Free Trade Agreement, the Association of Southeast Asian Nations Free Trade Agreement, the North American Free Trade Agreement, the Southern African Development Community, and the Arab Maghreb Union. The Free Trade Area of the Americas is an ambitious plan to create a market of the democratic nations of North, Central, and South America. At the next level, a customs union is a free trade area that has eliminated or greatly reduced internal tariffs and that imposes common external tariffs. An example is the South African Customs Union. A common market is an agreement to eliminate all barriers to trade, to adopt external tariffs and to allow for the free movement of capital and labor in the region. Examples of common markets are the Latin American Integration Association, the Andean Community, the Southern Cone Common Market (MERCOSUR), the Central American Common Market, and the Common Market for Eastern and Southern Africa. The establishment of a monetary union involves the creation of a common central bank and the use of a single currency. Examples of monetary unions are the European Monetary Union, the West African Economic and Monetary Union, and the Economic Community of West African States. The only viable political unions that have survived to date are the European Union and the Commonwealth of Independent States.

- **Examine the functions of the different policy and governance bodies of the European Union**

  The different bodies of the European Union are the European Council, the highest policy-making body of the European Union, made up of heads of governments; the European Parliament, which debates policies and legislation of the European Union; the Council of Nations, which consists of representatives from parliaments of member states and acts as a constitutional council; the Council of Ministers, the decision-making body (the legislature) of the European Union that passes laws based on proposals of the European Commission; the European Commission, which is subordinated to the Council and initiates and supervises the execution of laws and policies; the European Central Bank, charged with enacting monetary policy for the twelve countries that share a common currency; and the European Court of Justice, an equivalent to the U.S. Supreme Court.

Discussion Questions

1. Identify the determinants of regional economic and political integration.
2. Describe the different stages of regional economic and political integration. What is the difference between a free trade association and a common market?
3. There are arguments that much of the groundwork for the Free Trade Area of the Americas already has been done by other free trade agreements in the region targeted for economic integration. Which free trade agreements are operating within this area?
4. Identify the different bodies of the European Union and describe their main function.

Cultural Influences on International Marketing

Key Terms

acculturation
adiaphoras
appearances
assimilation
chronemics
collectivism
culture
cultural variability
ecology
enculturation
ethnocentrism
exclusives
femininity
foreign consumer culture
    positioning
gender roles
gift giving

global consumer culture
    positioning
haptics
high-context cultures
ideology
imperatives
individualism
kinesics
language
local consumer culture
    positioning
low-context cultures
masculinity
materialism
monochronic time
national and regional character
nonverbal communication

norms
oculesics
olfactions
orientations
paralinguistics
polychronic time
postures
power distance
proxemics
religion
self-reference criterion
social structure
spoken/written language
status concern
time orientation
uncertainty avoidance
values

Outline

Learning Objectives
5-1 Culture Defined
5-2 Elements of Culture
    5-2a Language
    5-2b Religion
    5-2c Cultural Values
    *5-2d Cultural Norms:
        Imperatives, Exclusives,
        and Adiaphoras*
    *5-2e National/Regional
        Character*
5-3 Cultural Variability
    5-3a The Hofstede Dimensions
5-4 Cultural Change
    and Marketing
5-5 The Self-Reference Criterion
    and Ethnocentrism
5-6 The Global Consumer
    Culture
Chapter Summary
Discussion Questions

Learning Objectives

Learning Objectives

By the end of this chapter, you should be able to:

- Identify the elements of culture and examine how they affect marketing practices around the world
- Describe national and regional character based on dimensions such as time orientation, business practices, gift giving, socializing, gender roles, and materialism
- Discuss cultural variability in terms of the Hofstede dimensions with appropriate examples and address cultural change in a marketing context
- Address the self-reference criterion and ethnocentrism and describe how they impede mutual understanding and cooperation, with direct negative effects on marketing practices
- Describe the global consumer culture as it manifests itself around the world

You are in the middle of negotiations with a potential Turkish client in Istanbul, over lunch, at the Conrad Hilton Hotel. You go to the self-service buffet and pile on your plate some tasty pork chops from a plate clearly marked "pork." You ask the waiter to bring a bottle of wine and offer some to your potential Turkish client; he declines. Your products are known for their quality in Turkey and elsewhere in the world, and your client seems receptive to your price quote. After lunch, the potential client invites you to his home for coffee; you decline and state that you need to stay at the hotel to get some work done and bid him good-bye. You come back to the U.S. and find that you cannot reach your potential Turkish client. His secretary always claims he is not in, and he does not return your calls. What went wrong? You subsequently learn that, in Turkey, the dominant religion is Islam, and Islam bans the consumption of pork and alcohol. Could your lunch have turned off your client? Probably not too much because he still seemed receptive to your offer as you were eating the "dirty animal" in front of him. Could he have been offended by your not going to his house for Turkish coffee? Even though you refused, you did not tell him that you really hate the stuff and you were dreading spending even a few hours in 90-degree weather in a home that most likely was not air-conditioned. You were, after all, showing how dedicated you were to your job by staying home. Could the hotel staff have told him that you spent the evening next door, at another air-conditioned hotel, a former palace, having yet another bottle of wine?

This chapter will examine in depth the effect of different cultural influences on consumer behavior and on a company's international operations. It will examine national character and provide illustrations of behaviors in line with national character.

A full understanding of local culture in markets where one's firm is operating constitutes a minimal condition for successful global marketing operations. Although cultural understanding alone cannot guarantee a firm's success in a new international market, not fully understanding the local culture and engaging in marketing practices that may be discordant with the culture will guarantee failure.

Many companies find that their new foreign firm is about to collapse because they have failed to learn that country's "customs, cultures, and laws."[1]

One study conducted by Sami Abbasi and Kenneth W. Holman claims that two out of every three U.S. businessmen sent to Saudi Arabia are brought back home due to difficulties in adapting to the local culture, which obviously becomes very expensive for the companies involved.[2] (See Chapter 15, "International Personal Selling and Personnel Management," for illustrations of expenses involved in sending expatriates overseas.)

The wrong promotional strategies will quickly backfire for companies that do not fully research their target market. In the former Soviet Union, advertisements using the Marlboro Man did not produce much enthusiasm and did not initially enhance the adoption rate of the Marlboro brand; in spite of the popularity of Westerns, a cowboy was perceived as the U.S. equivalent of a peasant—an uncultured, poor individual with a low status in society. In general, advertisements that promise prosperity, higher status, and overall advancement tend to be more successful in this market.

When marketers are armed with knowledge about the local culture, they are in a better position to communicate effectively with the target consumer.

Culture is recognized as having a general influence on consumption; it is expressed in the consumption of numerous products and services, in homes, offices, stores and marketplace sites, with differences noted across various subcultures and nations.[3] Cultural factors also exert a profound influence on the firm's other stakeholders, such as government representatives, national and international consumer groups and interest groups, service providers, suppliers, channel members, and shareholders, among others. Culture is the key determinant of the manner in which individuals do business, or respond to a company's marketing strategy.

5-1 Culture Defined

Culture—a society's personality—is defined as a continuously changing totality of learned and shared meanings, rituals, norms, and traditions among the members of an organization or society.

Despite this definition, it should be noted that the notion of culture is relatively ambiguous and controversial among both practitioners and academics.[4] Some elements of culture, however, are thought to affect important aspects of marketing, and they are addressed in this chapter.

Culture The continuously evolving totality of learned and shared meanings, rituals, norms, and traditions among the members of an organization or society.

---

1. Alan L. Gilman, "Stay Afloat in Foreign Expansions," *Chain Store Executive*, May 1994, Vol. 70, No. 5, p.193.

2. Sami Abbasi and Kenneth W. Holman, "Business Success in the Middle East," *Management Decision*, 1993, Vol. 31, No. 1, pp. 55–59.

3. Lisa Penaloza and Mary C. Gilly, "Marketer Acculturation: The Changer and the Changed," *Journal of Marketing*, July 1999, Vol. 63, No. 3, pp. 84–104.

4. Raj Mehta and Russell W. Belk, "Artifacts, Identity and Transition: Favorite Possessions of Indians and Indian Immigrants to the United States," *Journal of Consumer Research*, March 1991, Vol. 17, pp. 398–411.

The pivotal constituents of culture are as follows:

- **Ecology**—The manner in which society adapts to its habitat, i.e., the distribution of resources within an industrialized country versus a developing country; the desire for efficiency, space-saving devices, or green products.
- **Social structure**—The organization of society.
- **Ideology**—The manner in which individuals relate to the environment and to others; this includes attitudes toward time, space, possessions, and referent others (peers).

These areas are complexly interrelated.[5] In Section 5-2, "Elements of Culture," we describe the elements of culture that are most relevant to international marketing managers.

5-2 Elements of Culture

5-2a Language

Language has a prominent role as an element of culture: The language one learns in the community where one is born and raised shapes and structures one's world view.[6] Some languages, such as the Bantu languages, are broad and do not differentiate, for instance, between the "here" and the "now."[7] Other languages are very precise, especially in domains such as agriculture; they may have several terms for an object, or a body part, depending on the current function of the object or respective body part. For example, for the word "tail," Batwa languages have a term that refers to its use by cattle as protection against flies, another term as an illustration of joy, yet another as an indicator of attention, and so on. The key to communicating in a particular culture is understanding all nuances and complexities of the language of the target market.

A number of points are relevant in this regard. At a primary level, language has two aspects: the spoken/written language and the nonverbal language.

Spoken/Written Language

Spoken/written language poses a number of concerns to marketers. First, in terms of translation, the diversity of languages creates numerous difficulties for marketers operating internationally. Even if the same language is shared by different countries, marketers should be aware of differences in meaning: Procter & Gamble sells "nappies" in the U.K., as opposed to "diapers"; the "boot" of the Ford automobile is actually its "trunk"; and housewives or househusbands who are "hoovering" in the U.K. may actually be "vacuuming" using an Electrolux vacuum cleaner.

Problems could arise in the process of translation: Firms have placed in jeopardy the viability of their brands by relying on primary translations and not ensuring that either the product name is appropriate in a given culture or that the communication actually conveys the intended message. Using procedures described in Chapter 6, "International Marketing Research: Practices and Challenges"—*back translation* (translation back into the original language) and *parallel translation* (translation by another translator for comparison purposes)—will diminish the likelihood that the company will commit blunders when communicating with the target market. Many companies have made translation blunders,

Ecology The manner in which society adapts to its habitat, i.e., the distribution of resources within an industrialized country versus a developing country; the desire for efficiency, space-saving devices, or green products.

Social structure The organization of relationships in a society.

Ideology The manner in which individuals relate to their environment and to others, including their attitudes toward time, space, possessions, and referent others.

Language The vehicle used for communication in a particular culture; includes spoken and written language and nonverbal communication.

Spoken/written language The language used in conversation/the language used in written communications.

---

5. Michael R. Solomon, *Consumer Behavior*, Fourth Edition, Prentice Hall, 1999.

6. Jean-Claude Usunier, *International Marketing—A Cultural Approach*, Prentice Hall, 1993.

7. Ibid.

and the marketing literature is replete with examples, from the chocolate and fruit product sold under the name *Zit* in English-speaking countries, to the *Fresca* soda pop sold in Mexico (where, in slang, it means lesbian).[8]

Translation is expensive, especially in markets where multiple languages are spoken. For example, in India, there are more than 300 minor languages and 3,000 dialects. Only 15 distinct languages are widely spoken, however; Hindi, the official language, is spoken by 30 percent of the population, and English is widely used in administrative, commercial, and political life. To effectively communicate with this very promising multicultural market of approximately one billion, a firm's decisions on which language to use are crucial.

Marketing practitioners using the same marketing strategy in a unified market experience a similar dilemma: deciding which language to use or whether to use multiple languages. The European Union presents an interesting case: When companies target this market, product information is typically provided in two to three languages. A product that has French, Dutch, and German labeling is probably sold in France, Belgium (where both French and Dutch are spoken), the Netherlands, Germany, Austria, Luxembourg, Liechtenstein, and in the German and French regions in Switzerland.

Finally, it is important to communicate in the appropriate language with the target market in areas where multiple languages are used. Marketers selling their products in the United Arab Emirates will find that a significant proportion of consumers there do not speak the national language, Arabic; guest workers in these countries are predominantly Indian, Pakistani, and Southeast Asian. In targeting these markets, firms would benefit from using English, which is widely understood, and the main language used in business, rather than Arabic.

Nonverbal Communication

Nonverbal communication includes body language, gestures, grimaces, eye contact, and even silence. Silent communications, especially gestures, have different meanings across cultures, and marketing managers must be aware of them in order to avoid embarrassing or costly mistakes. Among the more important nonverbal communication venues are the following:

- **Proxemics** refers to the relationship between physical space and the process of communication. One of the peculiarities of American culture that most foreigners find intriguing is the "bubble," the space around the individual, which, if one violates, one must apologize. In countries where standing in line means that the person behind another will periodically engage in a "poking exercise," pushing him or her lightly and hoping that he or she might advance somewhat, the bubble is unheard of. In these countries, even in polite society, it is not necessary to apologize for maneuvering too closely or cutting off another.

  In general, Greeks, Central and Eastern Europeans, Japanese, and South Americans feel more comfortable standing or sitting closer to strangers than do members of other nationalities.[9] Similarly, in the Middle East, even in the business world, men prefer standing close to people with whom they are conversing and take great offense if someone backs away from them.[10]

Nonverbal communication
All communication that is not written or spoken; includes body language, gestures, facial expressions, eye contact, and silence.

Proxemics   The amount of physical space individuals require to feel comfortable in the process of communication.

---

8. For this and many other examples of blunders of translation, see David A. Ricks, *Blunders in International Business,* Blackwell Publishers, 1993.

9. Ibid.

10. Abbasi and Holman, "Business Success in the Middle East," pp. 55–59.

Postures Individuals' physical postures during conversation.

Orientations Individuals' positioning relative to their counterparts during conversation.

Oculesics The use or avoidance of eye contact during communication.

- **Postures, orientations,** and **oculesics** refer to individuals' positioning relative to their counterpart and the use or avoidance of eye contact during communication. Individuals' approaches to greeting, for example, differ in different parts of the world. In the United States, when shaking hands, one is supposed to look his or her counterpart in the eye; this should make an impression of being forthright, as well as having a take-charge attitude. The handshake should be firm and brief. This same handshake, however, would be perceived as arrogant and aggressive by an Asian counterpart. In Asia, a soft handshake, a humble posture, and avoidance of eye contact convey an attitude of respect. In Eastern Europe, a woman expects to have her hand kissed (this also conveys respect for her as a representative of her gender), and men typically kiss each other on the cheeks. With an extensive Western presence in the countries mentioned, however, the expectation that foreigners should adhere to these patterns of behavior has diminished.

  Certain sitting positions may even get one in trouble; for example, a person should not cross his or her legs or show the sole of his or her shoe to another person in the Middle East because the gesture implies that the person is "worthy of being stepped on,"[11] or, according to other interpretations, "likened to a shoe sole."

Chronemics The timing of verbal exchanges.

- **Chronemics** refers to the timing of verbal exchanges. Americans expect prompt responses and are uncomfortable with a slow response or silence. They attempt to fill in the silence and to further probe into the issue at hand to ensure that their counterparts understand them. Other nationalities—the Japanese, for instance—prefer to use this "quiet time" as contemplation time, where they evaluate the message. Often, translation comes in handy in this situation, especially if the negotiating parties understand each others' languages. Simultaneous translation often provides the time necessary to digest and interpret messages, thus eliminating the need for the additional contemplation time. Often, the translator familiar with the Americans' discomfort with silence will intervene and explain that the time is being used for contemplating the deal.

Haptics The use of touch while conversing.

- **Haptics** refers to the use of touch while conversing. Again, this is rarely used by Anglo-Americans, who prefer to keep others at the periphery of their "bubble." Latinate cultures tend to make extensive use of touch in order to convey their messages. A woman could expect to have not just her shoulders, arms, and hands touched, but also her hair and face, all with good intentions.

Kinesics The movement of part of the body in order to communicate.

- **Kinesics** refers to the movement of part of the body in order to communicate. Compared with many cultures, Americans gesture very little while communicating. The French and Italians, however, use hand gestures frequently to express themselves. It is important to understand the meanings of these gestures to function efficiently in these cultures. At the same time, it is wise not to assume that the gestures used in one's home country are identical with those used in other countries. It is possible, for example, that those gestures may have no meaning in other cultures, or, worse yet, they may have meanings other than those one would like to convey. For example, the sign of "OK" commonly used in the U.S. signifies zero in France, is

---

11. Ibid.

a symbol for money in Japan, and is a vulgar gesture in parts of South America, as a company that had this sign printed quickly found out.[12]

One of the most difficult movements to interpret is head shakes. Western gestures such as shaking the head up and down to signify "yes" and from side to side to signify "no" have different equivalents in other cultures. In the Middle East, people raise their head in a haughty manner to say "no," while sometimes accompanying the gesture with a click of the tongue. "No" is conveyed with a wave of the hand in front of the face in parts of Asia, and with a shake of the finger from side to side in Ethiopia. On the other hand, the U.S. gesture to slit one's throat means "I love you" in Swaziland, folding one's arms conveys respect in Fiji and arrogance in Finland, and the list continues. . . .[13]

- **Paralinguistics** refers to nonverbal aspects of speech that include emotional intonation, accents, and quality of voice. Again, a louder, more aggressive intonation denoting self-assurance and strength in some cultures, such as that of the United States, may be perceived as threatening or insulting by other cultures, where softness is equated with politeness and respect. In the cultures of West Africa, laughter indicates embarrassment, discomfort, or surprise, whereas in some other cultures, laughter is discouraged altogether.[14]

  Although many people view North Americans as fairly loud and aggressive, the Spanish speak even louder, often shouting at each other to express enthusiasm.[15]

  Paralinguistics The nonverbal aspects of speech that include intonation, accents, and the quality of voice.

- **Appearances** refer to one's physical attire and overall grooming. Each culture has its own expectations and norms with regard to what is appropriate in different circumstances. For example, Western business attire for men consists of a well-tailored dark suit, complemented by a conservative shirt and tie and elegant shoes; Western business attire for women may also consist of a well-tailored suit or a conservative dress and high heels (European dress codes allow for a more casual look or a more personal style than North American dress codes). In the Middle East, depending on the country, men's business attire may consist of a *gallabeya* (a long, typically white garment) and a head cover, whereas women in business may have their hair covered, while wearing an equally long, conservative dress,[16] known as the *hijab*.

  Appearances An individual's physical attire and overall grooming.

  In South Asia (India, Pakistan, Bangladesh, Nepal, and others), appropriate business attire for women may be the traditional *sari*, typically an exquisitely embroidered or designed material that is wrapped using a specific pattern. In Africa, women wear a similarly colorful outfit, but taking the form of a gown with country-specific prints—a *bou-bou* (pronounced "boo-boo"); men wear a short-sleeve shirt with a political party pin attached and a pair of slacks, with the exception of the most formal circumstances, when a coat and tie are worn.

- **Olfactions** refer to the use of odors to convey messages. Typically, such messages have a religious meaning: Incense is frequently used to purify the

  Olfactions The use of odors to convey messages.

12. Ricks, *Blunders in International Business*, 1993.

13. Ibid.

14. Ibid.

15. Roger Colles, "Spain—A Hot Prospect," *Resident Abroad*, November 1993. pp. 16–20.

16. In countries where this type of dress is expected of women, those same women will be encountered only in a business environment that excludes the presence of males.

air of evil presence in both temples and churches, as well as in private homes. Finally, odors are evaluated differently in different cultures. For example, U.S. culture finds body odors and garlic breath as offensive, whereas East Asian cultures avoid consumption of dairy products believed to cause intolerably bad breath.

The Nonverbal Language and High- Versus Low-Context Cultures

Low-context cultures Cultures in which what is said is precisely what is meant so that the verbal message carries the full meaning of the sentence.

High-context cultures Cultures in which the context of a message—the message source, the source's standing in society or in a group, his or her expertise, tone of voice, and body language—are all meaningful parts of the message.

The high-low context continuum defines the extent to which a spoken statement conveys a full message.[17] In **low-context cultures,** what is said is precisely what is meant. For example, in the United States, Canada, Germany, and Switzerland, a verbal message carries the full meaning of the sentence. In this environment, business is typically done at arm's length and change is readily accepted.

In **high-context cultures,** such as those of East Asia, the Middle East, and North Africa, the context of the message—the message source, his or her standing in society or in the negotiating group, level of expertise, tone of voice, and body language—are all meaningful. Marketing managers must evaluate the nonverbal communication accompanying a message and interpret the full message accordingly. In low-context cultures, business is conducted via e-mail or on paper, in contract form, whereas in high-context cultures, it is more important to establish solid personal relationships and trust in the process of conducting business. In general, individuals are highly valued in high-context cultures, and, on the social side of commerce, trust is crucial: A handshake in the Middle East is as important and reliable as a paper contract.

5-2b Religion

Religion A society's relationship to the supernatural.

Religion defines a society's relationship to the supernatural and, as a result, determines dominant values and attitudes. Religious beliefs are important determinants of consumer behavior: Purchase motivation; consumption preferences and patterns; customs and business practices; attitudes toward authority, family, peers, and foreigners; as well as attitudes toward material possessions, cultural values, and norms, among others, can all be traced to religion.

Religion, then, can be linked to cultural behaviors that have an impact on economic development and marketing. For example,

- The Protestant religion stresses hard work and frugality and is linked to the development of capitalism and economic emancipation.
- Judaism, with its disdain for ignorance and sloth, stresses education and has led to industrial development.
- Islam dictates social etiquette and consumption and bans the use of interest rates, affecting, respectively, the relationship between men and women in society and in the workplace (as will be seen in the section "Religion and Gender Roles"); discouraging the consumption of pork products and alcohol; and requiring procedures to reconcile Islamic banking laws with Western banking practices—by, for example, charging periodic fees, rather than interest.
- The Hindu religion encourages a family orientation and dictates a nine-tier class structure and strict dietary constraints, affecting the workplace hierarchy and discouraging the consumption of animal products—beef, in particular.

---

17. E. T. Hall, *Beyond Culture,* Anchor Press, 1976.

- Buddhism stresses sufferance and avoidance of worldly desires, thus, in principle, rejecting most aspects of marketing.

Assuming that Buddhism has had a negative impact on marketing and economic development is erroneous, however, because a number of the more developed economies in Asia, for instance, are predominantly Buddhist. It is also erroneous to assume that Islamic law affects negatively all credit-granting activity or that, because of the restrictions imposed by gender isolation, marketing to women is impossible in Islamic societies—quite the contrary: These restrictions merely require the use of creative strategies and adaptation to local practices. For example, instead of selling on credit, businesses typically offer price discounts to individuals paying the full cash value, and no discount for those paying in installments. With regard to gender, women can use creative ways to interact (though not directly) with their male counterparts; more recently, the use of e-mail has greatly facilitated a timely interaction between genders at work, even in the most conservative societies.

Finally, the restrictions on consumption do not mean that the respective products are prohibited in a particular country. For example, alcohol is available at diplomatic and other expatriate shops even in one of the most strict of Islamic countries, Saudi Arabia; it is also readily available at regular supermarkets in expatriate enclaves. Pork and pork products are readily available in Islamic countries and in Israel, targeted to the Christian population, and beef is available in India for consumption by Muslim consumers. Even in India, however, fast-food chains having to choose between offending Hindu consumers, by offering beef, or Muslim consumers, by offering pork, have elected to offer chicken, lamb burgers, or vegetarian burgers instead.

Discussions of religions and their relationship to overall consumer/market behavior and, specifically, consumption are offered in the sections "Religion and Business Days," "Religion and Gender Roles," "Religion and Gift Giving," and "Religion and Marketing Practices."

Religion and Business Days

In terms of working days, in countries where Christianity predominates, it is customary to work full days Monday through Friday and a half day on Saturday. In Islamic countries, businesses are closed on Friday, the holy day of Islam. And, in Israel, the Shabbat (Saturday) is the day of worship when all businesses close.

In addition to noting business days, individuals doing business abroad must also note national holidays, when businesses are usually closed, and religious events/holidays. One religious observance that can substantially affect business operations is the month of Ramadan in the Islamic religion, when observers are not allowed to eat until sundown; this is typically not a productive time in the Near East and North Africa. In Israel, no business is conducted during the High Holidays (Rosh Hashanah and Yom Kippur).

During the regular work week, one should not be surprised if a Muslim with whom he is talking business abruptly ends the conversation by gathering his rug, kneeling on it, and then praying; Muslims are required to pray five times a day at specific times. In this situation, a businessman should just find a seat and wait quietly until the man is finished.[18]

---

18. Abbasi and Holman, "Business Success in the Middle East," pp. 55–59.

Religion and Gender Roles

In the most traditional Islamic countries, women's business activities are channeled toward interaction in a women-only environment. As such, a salesman cannot engage in door-to-door selling in Saudi Arabia, for instance, in an effort to appeal to the woman of the house. In this country, women depend on men in the family for simple activities, such as driving them to and from a destination; the law does not permit women to drive a car. Personal services can be performed only by individuals of the same gender. For example, women can bank only at women's banks, can have their hair done only by other women, etc. The genders typically do not interact in the very traditional Islamic countries except within the family. Even in the less traditional Islamic countries, women often are seated separately from men (in a separate dining room or area).

Although business is male-dominated in Islamic countries, it should, nevertheless, be noted that women have historically held prominent government positions in countries such as Turkey and Pakistan, for example.

Religion and Gift Giving

A more in-depth discussion of gift giving is offered in section 5-2e, "National/ Regional Character." This section will address religious holidays as important opportunities for sales. In countries where Christianity is predominant, holidays such as Christmas and Easter constitute important dates for product sales. In addition to these holidays, Saint Nicholas is celebrated on December 6, when gifts are offered to children, usually placed in their shoes which are nicely lined up under a window. During the time predating these holidays, promotional activity (advertising and sales promotion) is intense. In Eastern Orthodox countries, such as Greece, Bulgaria, Serbia, Romania, Russia, and the other European countries of the Commonwealth of Independent States, among others, name days (days of the Saints after whom one was named) are celebrated, and gift giving is a must. Days for common names such as Sts. John and Mary are also national holidays.

Diwali is an important Hindu holiday, when the believers engage in a Puja (prayer) and typically wear new clothing. This day also is an important marketing event. The Jewish holiday of Chanukah is also an occasion for exchanging gifts.

Religion and Marketing Practices

Firms often must adapt their offering to the local culture to address consumers' religious concerns. Fast-food restaurants operating in Israel find that they can better serve their Jewish consumers by offering ample choices of vegetarian food, which does not compromise consumer kosher requirements. Keeping kosher requires, among others, the separation of milk products and meat products and implements used to serve or process them; vegetarian products are pareve—neutral, with regard to kosher requirements.

With regard to advertising, substantial censoring occurs in many countries. In Saudi Arabia, women should not be portrayed in advertisements: It is appropriate to show the covered arms and wrists of a woman demonstrating product use. For magazines of Western provenance, censorship is enforced; for example, when such magazines are brought into the country by individuals, or when delivered by mail, any area of a woman's uncovered body and her face in photographs are blackened with a magic marker. In other Islamic countries, such as Malaysia, women should not be portrayed sleeveless, whereas in the streets of Turkey, one can actually see advertisements of women modeling bras.

Figure 5-1
Instrumental and terminal values.
Adapted from Milton J. Rokeach, *The Nature of Human Values* (New York: The Free Press, 1973).

5-2c Cultural Values

Values are enduring beliefs about a specific mode of conduct or desirable end-state; they guide the selection or evaluation of behavior, and are ordered by importance in relation to one another to form a system of value priorities.[19]

Values guide individuals' actions, attitudes, and judgments, which are derived from and continuously modified through personal, social, and cultural learning, ultimately affecting their product preferences and their perception of products. Cultures are set apart by their *value systems*—the relative importance or ranking of values. Western cultures (North American and Western European) place more stress on success, achievement, and competitiveness, whereas Eastern cultures are more likely to be concerned with social welfare.[20] Examples of universally held values are provided by Rokeach[21] (see Figure 5-1). According to this classification, values can be related to goals (*terminal values*) or to the processes whereby one can attain those goals (*instrumental values*).

Members of a culture share a system of meaning, a set of beliefs about what is right or wrong. Values are learned from those with whom individuals are in contact: family, friends, teachers, clergy, politicians, and the media. The process by which individuals learn the beliefs and behaviors endorsed by one's own culture is known as **enculturation.** Learning a new culture, which most managers must do when doing business abroad, is known as **acculturation.** Acculturation encompasses intercultural interaction and adaptation, and it includes the **assimilation** of a new culture, maintenance of the new culture, and resistance to both the new and old cultures. *Consumer acculturation* refers to contact with a new culture and the

Values Enduring beliefs about a specific mode of conduct or desirable end-state that guide the selection or evaluation of behavior.

Enculturation The process by which individuals learn the beliefs and behaviors endorsed by their own culture.

Acculturation The act of learning a new culture; encompasses intercultural interaction and adaptation.

Assimilation The act of abandoning all home-country traditions while learning a new culture.

19. See Milton J. Rokeach, *The Nature of Human Values*, The Free Press, 1973; and Jan-Benedict E. M. Steenkamp, Frenkel ter Hofstede, and Michel Wedel, "A Cross-Cultural Investigation into the Individual and National Cultural Antecedents of Consumer Innovativeness," *Journal of Consumer Research*, April 1999, Vol. 63, pp. 55–69.

20. Solomon, *Consumer Behavior*, 1999.

21. Rokeach, *The Nature of Human Values*, 1973.

resulting change for consumers in terms of their approach to consumption in the new environment, whereas *marketer acculturation* refers to contact with a new culture and the resulting change for the marketer.[22]

Acculturation does not necessarily mean abandoning all home country traditions; that is, it does not mean complete assimilation of the new culture. For example, recent Asian Indian immigrants to the United States are less likely to be assimilated in this culture because they maintain their original religious practices, language, food consumption, housing and friendship patterns, as well as contact with India.[23] Although Indian Americans are not easily assimilated, they are, nevertheless, acculturated in the U.S. culture: They consume fast food, shop at supermarkets, root for their favorite baseball team, and, overall, successfully integrate in the U.S. culture, without necessarily being assimilated. On the other hand, descendants of Japanese Americans tend to quickly acculturate to the U.S. culture, and, typically, by the third generation, they are likely to be fully assimilated.[24]

For the marketing practitioner, acculturation means adaptation to the new culture in a manner that would render him or her more readily capable of addressing the needs of the target market in that culture (see Figures 5-2 and 5-3).

5-2d Cultural Norms: Imperatives, Exclusives, and Adiaphoras

Norms are derived from values and are defined as rules that dictate what is right or wrong, acceptable or unacceptable. To be successful in the markets where the firm is currently operating or where it is planning a presence, marketers need to be capable of discerning between the following:

- What an outsider must or must not do (*cultural imperative*)
- What locals may do but an outsider cannot (*cultural exclusive*)
- What an outsider may or may not do (*cultural adiaphora*)[25]

Familiarity with the first two constitutes a minimum requirement for survival in a new country environment. Although most local employees are willing to accept that their foreign counterpart is not fully familiar with local practices, working for a firm that is planning a strong commitment to the respective market may render local representatives and clients less tolerant of ignorance of local customs.

Imperatives

Imperatives refer to what one must or must not do in a certain culture. Respecting rank and position, especially in more formal societies, is crucial in developing a lasting relationship. In Germany, for example, individuals in a close business relationship would address each other formally, by their last names, for decades. A representative of a U.S. firm working in this environment would need to be aware of this expectation (although this individual may be afforded some lenience, as a foreigner, if he or she did in fact address his or her counterpart by first name).

Also, obtaining the appropriate approval before conducting a transaction constitutes an important consideration in doing business abroad. To conduct business in many developing countries, a company needs to become acquainted with local officials at all levels of government and seek their expertise, as part of a close work-

Norms   Rules that dictate what is right or wrong, acceptable or unacceptable in a society.

Imperatives   The norms referring to what individuals must or must not do in a certain culture.

---

22. Penaloza and Gilly, "Marketer Acculturation," pp. 84–104.

23. Mehta and Belk, "Artifacts, Identity and Transition," pp. 398–411.

24. See Darrell Montero, "The Japanese Americans: Changing Patterns of Assimilation over Three Generations," *American Sociological Review,* December 1981, Vol. 46, pp. 829–839; and Mehta and Belk, "Artifacts, Identity and Transition," pp. 398–411.

25. Ricks, *Blunders in International Business,* 1993.

Figure 5-2
Exporting culture: Trends are quickly transferred from the United States. European stores carry a vast array of in-line skates and basketballs. Note Michael Jordan's dominance of the point-of-purchase basketball display.

Figure 5-3
Exporting culture: Music from the Andean region in downtown Prague. From Paris to Prague, folkloric groups from Latin America share their musical traditions and market their CDs to European consumers in metro stations, parks, and on the main downtown thoroughfares.

ing relationship. If a company does not, any operation of the firm in the country could come under scrutiny and could be subjected to complications and higher costs. Obtaining the appropriate permissions before building on company-owned grounds, before conducting marketing research, or before approaching potential distributors is crucial in many countries. Among outcomes of noncompliance would be costly delays, the use of expensive alternative middlemen or subcontractors, or even interdiction of operations.

Other examples of imperatives are provided by the special situation women in management positions face when dealing with clients in North Africa and the Middle East. For example, women are not allowed, by law, to drive or walk in public unaccompanied by a male in Saudi Arabia. They are not allowed in the streets, nor in shops by themselves. A female marketing manager sent to this country would have to make arrangements to be chauffeured to client firms, to be permanently in the company of a male in public. She also would have to wear clothing to cover her wrists, ankles, hair, and face. Finally, in many firms, males are not permitted to interact with females. For example, female accountants communicate with male colleagues by sending a tray back and forth through a wall that divides the two sexes.

Exclusives

Exclusives refer to activities that are appropriate only for locals and from which an individual from a foreign country is excluded. For example, whereas a citizen of Kenya is likely to show allegiance to the government of Daniel arap Moi by wearing a pin in his party's colors bearing his picture, a foreigner wearing such a pin would not only raise eyebrows, but he or she also may be perceived as attempting to interfere in the country's internal affairs.

Adiaphoras

Adiaphoras refer to customs that a foreign representative may engage in, but conformity in this respect is not required. Eating with chopsticks in East Asia, drinking banana beer in East Africa, greeting a woman by kissing her hand in Hungary or Romania are all examples of adiaphoras.

5-2e National/Regional Character

Each country is thought to have a distinct set of behavior and personality characteristics, characteristics that may be shared by a number of countries in a certain geographical region.[26] This section discusses some of the **national and regional characters** that are likely to influence international marketing operations.

Time Orientation

An aspect of time relevant to marketers is related to the manner in which tasks are approached. **Monochronic time** (m-time) is attributed to individuals who usually do one thing at a time, and in sequence. These individuals tend to be prompt and to adhere strictly to agendas; countries where individuals typically operate on monochronic time are Germany, Switzerland, Austria, the Scandinavian countries and the countries of Benelux, the United States, and Canada. **Polychronic time** (p-time) is attributed to individuals who tend to perform multiple tasks at once; for these individuals, time is not linear but, rather, fluid. They are less likely to adhere to schedules, and they consider business as an opportunity for socializing. Countries where individuals operate on polychronic time are Italy, France, Spain, the countries of North Africa and the Middle East, and Latin America. This aspect of **time orientation** explains some of the examples provided in this section, describing attitudes toward time in different parts of the world.

North Americans like to plan their activities or to expedite matters by setting deadlines. Arabs facing deadlines, on the other hand, may feel threatened and would back into a corner.[27] A saying translated as "God-willing tomorrow" means, loosely, "If I feel like it and I have the time, I will take care of it tomorrow or any day thereafter." At times, businessmen in the Middle East arrive late for a meeting or do not arrive at all; they believe that Allah (God) controls time, so punctuality is unimportant. One should not be surprised if a Middle Eastern businessman is not ready for an appointment. It is imperative that one does not criticize this lateness or absenteeism because the individual would most likely become offended and resentful.[28] It should be noted, however, that this behavior cannot be gener-

---

Exclusives The norms that refer to activities that are appropriate only for locals and from which individuals from a foreign country are excluded.

Adiaphoras The norms that refer to customs that a foreign national may engage in but is not necessarily expected to do so.

National and regional character A set of behavior and personality characteristics shared by individuals of a certain country.

Monochronic time The interpretation of time as linear, such that individuals do one thing at a time, and in sequence.

Polychronic time The interpretation of time as fluid, such that individuals can accomplish multiple tasks at once.

Time orientation The manner in which individuals view time in relation to accomplishing tasks.

---

26. Terry Clark, "International Marketing and National Character: A Review and Proposal for Integrative Theory," *Journal of Marketing*, October 1990, No. 54, pp. 66–79.

27. Ricks, *Blunders in International Business*, 1993.

28. Abbasi and Holman, "Business Success in the Middle East," pp. 55–59.

alized to all business conducted, especially in many of the larger cities or in international joint ventures operating in the region, where punctuality is mandatory and expected.

Further, this behavior is not limited to the Middle Eastern context. In many countries in Sub-Saharan Africa, Southern and Eastern Europe, and Latin America, delays are common. Greeks feel that setting time limits is not only constraining, but also insulting. Latinate cultures, such as those of Latin America and Southern Europe, do not put much premium on punctuality. When one is invited to a dinner party, arriving at the specified time indicates poor manners, suggesting that the person may be very hungry. Arriving half an hour after the indicated time is considered being on time, while arriving one hour late is still no reason to apologize, especially if one is socially prominent. In these same countries, however, for business meetings, it is safer to arrive within fifteen minutes of the agreed-upon time.

Business Hours, Business Days

The hours of doing business differ from country to country. The nine-to-five schedule prevalent in the United States is unusual in many countries. In countries where the climate is too hot to permit work at mid-day, businesses open early, at seven, and close for two to three hours at noon, to re-open again at two in the afternoon. This is also the case for businesses in Latin America and in many countries in Europe, where lunch time is spent at home having a large meal with the family, followed frequently by a nap.

In Spain, individuals and health experts have, for decades, argued for retaining the three-hour-long lunch period, despite changing standards attributed to regulations by the European Union. The long siesta time has been reduced to two hours (with the goal of further reducing it to one hour). At this time, stores are closed and no business is conducted. In Mexico, the federal government recently placed a new regulation into effect that brought a cultural revolution to this country: It required government workers to work from 9:00 A.M. to 6:00 P.M., with only one hour for lunch. In the past, as is still the case for most private businesses, employees had time for siesta, after which they had to return to work until later in the evening.[29]

In much of Europe, it is unusual to find someone at the office on Friday afternoons. In many European countries, there is a move toward shortening the work week. For example, the promise of 39 hours of pay for 35 hours of work was the campaign platform that catapulted Lionel Jospin's (Prime Minister of France) coalition to power in 1997.[30]

As mentioned in section 5-2b, "Religion," working days differ, depending on the dominant religion in the different countries. Where Christianity is dominant, Sunday is a rest day; in Islamic countries, businesses are closed on Fridays, and, in Israel, businesses are closed on Saturdays. In Islamic countries, during the month of Ramadan, observers are not allowed to eat until sundown, and, during the regular work week, Muslims are required to pray five times a day.

Finally, vacation time—designated in Europe as the latter part of July, the entire month of August, and the last two weeks in December—tends to be slow and not very productive for most business activity, with some exceptions. Such exceptions are sales, which often are offered nationally in different countries for two weeks during the latter part of the summer. During this time, retail activity is brisk.

---

29. Julia Preston, "A Downsized Lunch Unsettles a Mexican Rite," *The New York Times*, Sunday, October 17, 1999, p. 7.

30. Suzanne Daley, "A French Paradox at Work," *The New York Times*, November 11, 1999, Business Section, pp. 1, 27.

Gift Giving

Knowing what gifts are appropriate to give to one's hosts is very important. Some gifts are considered inappropriate in certain cultures, whereas others may be appropriate on certain occasions and inappropriate on others. In the United States, bringing a bottle of wine to one's host is perfectly appropriate; the same gesture would not be appropriate for a similar occasion in the Middle East, where Islamic religion prohibits alcohol. This rule holds true for any other gifts that may contain alcohol, such as chocolates. Also in the Middle East, bringing food or drink to the home of one's host could represent an insult, implying that the host's food is inadequate.[31]

Other inappropriate gifts are cutlery in Latin America, signifying cutting off a relationship,[32] or handkerchiefs in Latin America and in Southern and Eastern Europe, signifying a final, imposed separation, usually death; handkerchiefs and small hand towels are typically given as gifts at funerals of the Eastern Orthodox faith.

Although an even number of flowers (a dozen roses, etc.) constitutes the norm for **gift giving** in the United States, in Eastern Europe, odd numbers are expected, while even numbers of flowers and, especially, calla lilies, are offered only at funerals or religious commemorations. Giving one's host an even number of flowers or calla lilies could even trigger superstitious fears.

In developing countries, gifts of Western provenance such as good-quality pens or t-shirts with (preferably) English writing on them for children would probably meet with appreciation. So would some products that might be unimaginable as gifts in the United States, such as cigarettes, pantyhose, and hairspray. In fact, for more than two decades before the fall of communism, Kent cigarettes constituted the gift of choice in Romania, where they had the added value as commodity money.[33]

Even the manner in which gifts are given is very important. For example, in the Middle East, gifts should be presented publicly in order to avoid the appearance of bribery, whereas, in Asia, gifts of significance should be given privately, to avoid embarrassment.[34] Nevertheless, gifts such as pens with a company logo or insignia will be graciously accepted, regardless of timing.

Some rituals related to the giving and acceptance of gifts also should be noted. For instance, in many cultures, it is customary for the recipient to refuse the gift so vigorously that the gift giver may be tempted to withdraw it. Such a gesture, however, will meet with a noted disappointment; it is merely appropriate for the recipient to refuse the gift and then accept it reluctantly, but humbly and kindly. The ready, eager acceptance of a gift may be considered as a sign of bad manners or a confirmation of gift expectations.

In the Middle East, the mere admiration of any object in an individual's home will obligate the host to yield that object to the admirer. Although it may be appropriate to decline, such a gesture may be perceived, to a degree, as a rejection of the host's hospitality.

Gift giving The norms regarding the gifts that are appropriate to give to others.

31. Ricks, *Blunders in International Business*, 1993.

32. Ibid.

33. Guliz Ger, Russell W. Belk, and Dana-Nicoleta Lascu, "The Development of Consumer Desire in Marketizing and Developing Economies: The Case of Romania and Turkey," in L. McAllister (ed.), *Advances in Consumer Research*, Association for Consumer Research, 1993, Vol. 20, pp. 102–107.

34. Ricks, *Blunders in International Business*, 1993.

Socializing

If a marketing manager is planning on a working breakfast or a working lunch, or on discussing business over dinner, as is often done in the United States, it may be useful to first inquire about the extent to which such a practice is appropriate in the country where business is being conducted. Although many business partners may have been schooled in the United States and will, consequently, readily acquiesce to these types of working circumstances, other parties involved may feel uneasy if business is conducted during a meal.

In the countries of South America and in many countries in Europe, a meal is widely seen as an important occasion to personally get to know one's business counterpart; hence, the suggestion of a working lunch or dinner may indicate to the local representative a lack of interest in establishing a friendly basis for the future working relationship. For example, it is important not to plan a business meeting at first with a Mexican businessman because he usually prefers to become acquainted with his counterpart in a social atmosphere before doing business.[35]

Similarly, when first meeting a businessman in the Middle East, one should not begin right away with talk about the business at hand; instead, one should initiate "positive small talk." The first meeting in the Middle East is only to start developing a friendly relationship, not to secure business dealings.[36]

In countries such as China, knowing one's business partner socially is imperative, as the relationship is seen as a long-term engagement, rather than a short-term, transaction-related one.

Gender Roles

When one engages in business internationally, it is important to understand the role that women are expected to hold in the respective society. In the countries of East Africa and in parts of West Africa (Nigeria, for example), the role of women in business, and particularly in running a business and in sales, is crucial, and more important than the role of men. Men still hold an important decision-making role, however, when it comes to major sales or purchase decisions. In India and Pakistan, women share responsibility with men in business. It is noteworthy, however, that women play a more limited role politically, where only a few hold notable positions, despite the famous women leaders who have left important legacies in these countries.

A discussion of **gender roles** in Islamic societies, as well as their impact on marketing activity and consumer behavior, was provided in section 5-2b, "Religion."

Status Concern and Materialism

Related to one's background is one's concern with status, or **status concern**—maintaining it or acquiring it—and with material possessions, or **materialism.** Individuals' concern with status is related to the values placed on symbols of status and on the attainment of high status. Often, the products consumed convey messages about the consumer in the same way that language does.[37] Status—like

Gender roles The roles that women and men are expected to hold in a society.

Status concern The value placed on symbols of status and on the attainment of high status in a society.

Materialism Individuals' degree of concern with material possessions.

---

35. Perry A. Trunick, "Culture and Custom Combine with Logistics," *Transportation and Distribution,* January 1994, Vol. 35, No. 1, p. 38.

36. Abbasi and Holman, "Business Success in the Middle East," pp. 55–59.

37. David K. Tse, Russell W. Belk, and Nan Zhou, "Becoming a Consumer Society: A Longitudinal and Cross-Cultural Content Analysis of Print Ads from Hong Kong, the People's Republic of China, and Taiwan," *Journal of Consumer Research,* March 1989, Vol. 15, pp. 457–472.

social class, to which it is related—is easier to transcend in industrially developed countries than in developing countries. In the United States, the Protestant ethic of hard work has led to centuries of individual prosperity and, at the individual level, status advancement; in the U.S., it is not perceived as shameful for prominent politicians and business people to refer back to their humble beginnings.

In other countries, including Great Britain, Spain, and many developing countries, one's social class is rigid, and, consequently, one's status remains stable. Expatriates from these countries who have transcended their social class in the United States, for example, typically hide their lower-class origins. Those from developing countries might state, for instance, that they came from the capital city when, in fact, they did not, because of the high likelihood of low-class provenance associated with a village origin.

Due to the influence of 800 years of Moorish control, Spain still has a rigid class structure described as feudal and autocratic.[38] However, countries that historically have had a polarized class structure (for example, Mexico) are developing a middle class or merchant class in response to expanding capitalism.[39]

Within the context of highly hierarchical Asian societies, individuals are always conscious of their place in a group, institution, or society as a whole and of the appropriate behavior, dress, and speech corresponding to status. They also are extremely aware of the need to maintain their own dignity, and face, and that of others. Careful attention is given to purchasing products whose price, brand, and packaging match one's social standing. In terms of personal appearance, the color, material, and style of clothing should match an individual's status, which is defined by age, gender, occupation, and so on. In Japan, for example, a married woman's kimono is much more subdued in color than a single woman's.

One region of the world where status has undergone great changes and individuals have lost "status security" is Central and Eastern Europe. A study on status changes in Romania[40] notes that status, guaranteed during the communist regime by the degree of affiliation with the communist party, has undergone significant changes with the advent of democracy. In the past, nomenklatura members (top communist leaders) enjoyed the highest status and living standard, despite the communists' goal to abolish differences between social classes. In Russia, this same privileged class, before the fall of communism, could rent 100 square meters of living space for a ridiculous price; had the free use of a country home (dacha) in a prime vacation spot; and conspicuously consumed caviar, sturgeon, salmon, and other goods not available at regular shops—something that the average person could not aspire to. They drove foreign cars with low license plate numbers (indicative of high governmental position) at high speeds and without concern for traffic laws, dressed extravagantly, and conspicuously flaunted their Western possessions.[41]

With the transition to a market economy, former party members and intellectuals found that, in order to survive, they had to accept jobs below their former status, as taxi drivers, sales clerks, and street vendors. At the same time, individuals who had previously held a low status, such as gypsies and blue-collar workers

---

38. Cyndee Miller, "Going Overseas Requires Marketers to Learn More than a New Language," *Marketing News,* Vol. 28, No. 7, p. 8.

39. Trunick, "Culture and Custom Combine with Logistics," p. 38.

40. Dana-Nicoleta Lascu, Lalita A. Manrai, and Ajay K. Manrai, "Interpersonal Influences on Shopping Behavior: A Cross-Cultural Analysis of Polish and Romanian Consumers," in J. Bloemer, J. Lemmink, and H. Kasper (eds.), *European Marketing Academy Proceedings,* 1994, Vol. 3, pp. 1369–1371.

41. Ibid.

Figure 5-4
Other cultural and behavioral differences. In Bangladesh, buses with upper-level decks are a common means of transportation, whereas, in Holland, bicycles are very common and, as in many countries in Europe, they have their own paths that parallel most roads. Whereas, in the United States, most marketing strategies address a driving public, in other countries, marketers need to focus on the behavior of consumers using a different type of transportation.

Courtesy of Farheen Khurrum, with permission.

who started lucrative businesses, prospered and, as a consequence, engaged in consumption behavior previously reserved for the party nomenklatura.

Other Cultural and Behavioral Differences

Many other national and regional character differences also require companies to adapt their marketing practices. For example, as Figure 5-4 illustrates, people use different means of transportation to purchase products and get about in their daily lives. In the United States, most marketing strategies address a driving public, the shopper who can park at a strip mall and load the contents of an extra-large shopping cart into the family van. In much of the rest of the world, things are quite different. For example, Western Europeans might take their bicycles to the supermarket and use automobiles only to drive to out-of-town destinations. In Central Asia and Sub-Saharan Africa, buses with crowded upper-level decks, such as the one in the photograph, or trucks with protective bar grids are used for local and long-distance transportation. These consumers are likely to transport goods in crowded environments where they must also keep their balance. A typical fast-food drive-through is not likely to be the most efficient means for serving these consumers.

5-3 Cultural Variability

Cultural variability is the term used to identify differences between cultures using the Hofstede dimensions. All cultures can be classified based on a number of dimensions. Each dimension should be thought of as a continuum. Section 5-3a presents the Hofstede[42] dimensions: power distance, uncertainty avoidance, masculinity, and individualism.

5-3a The Hofstede Dimensions

Power Distance

Power distance refers to the manner in which interpersonal relationships are formed when differences in power are perceived. In some cultures, a vertical

Cultural variability The classification of cultures on a number of dimensions, or continuums; Hofstede classified cultures on the dimensions of collectivism, masculinity, power distance, and uncertainty avoidance.

Power distance The manner in which interpersonal relationships are formed when differences in power are perceived.

42. Geert Hofstede, *Culture's Consequences: International Differences in Work-Related Values*, Sage, 1984.

relationship is typical, whereas, in others, relationships are based on equality and informality. In the United States, for instance, individuals customarily address each other on a first-name basis, regardless of rank. Top managers often illustrate their solidarity with the lower ranks by engaging in work activities that they do, going to the plant floor or eating in the workers' cafeteria. In other countries (in Latin America, Eastern Europe, the Middle East, for example), it is a flagrant mistake to address a superior informally or for a superior to mingle with underlings. In these countries, most decisions are determined by the upper-level executives and only much later disseminated to individuals in the lower positions. This is one of the reasons why, in this environment, it is particularly important to address the senior management first, before addressing other individuals in the company.[43] When doing business in a country where relationships are of a vertical nature, it is important to find out who is one's counterpart in the partner firm, or the individual in the government responsible for regulating the activities of one's firm before one even approaches the business in question.

Uncertainty Avoidance

Uncertainty avoidance The extent to which individuals are threatened by uncertainty, risk, and ambiguous situations and thus adopt beliefs, behaviors, and institutions that help them to avoid the uncertainty.

Uncertainty avoidance refers to the extent to which individuals feel threatened by uncertainty, risk, and ambiguous situations and thus adopt beliefs, behaviors, and institutions that help them to avoid the uncertainty. In countries where uncertainty avoidance is high, there is a feeling that what is different is dangerous; consumers are resistant to change and focused on risk avoidance and reduction. In cultures low in uncertainty avoidance, there is a feeling that what is different, such as new products and services, is interesting and worth exploring.[44] In this regard, it is interesting to observe the changes taking place in the transition economies of China and Central and Eastern Europe. Traditionally, these cultures are high in uncertainty avoidance, primarily due to the communist system's assurances of work, a home, and a minimal standard of living. During the transition period, however, attitudes toward risk manifested themselves strongly, with some (especially the older generations) holding on to the status quo and rejecting privatization and all change, and with other, younger individuals taking unwarranted risks. Overall, most in this region continue to manifest symptoms of high uncertainty avoidance, electing (or supporting, in the case of China) conservative, welfare-oriented governments. Despite this trait, however, with regard to consumption, consumers here are eager to experience new products from different parts of the world and are open to new market offerings, such as food establishments and other services.

In another example, Belgian consumers, who are higher in uncertainty avoidance, prefer insurance that is higher in price but that does not have variable fees, whereas the Dutch, who are low on uncertainty avoidance, prefer lower-priced insurance with variable fees.[45]

Masculinity

Masculinity The degree to which a national culture is characterized by assertiveness, rather than nurturing.

Femininity The degree to which a national culture is characterized by nurturing, rather than assertive, values.

Masculinity is the degree to which a national culture is characterized by assertiveness, rather than nurturing. **Femininity** is the degree to which a national culture is characterized by nurturing, rather than by assertiveness. Masculine societies emphasize values such as wealth, material success, ambition, and

---

43. Abbasi and Holman, "Business Success in the Middle East," pp. 55–59.

44. Steenkamp, Hofstede, and Wedel, "A Cross-Cultural Investigation," pp. 55–69.

45. Ibid.

achievement; whereas, in feminine societies, benevolence, equality, caring for the weak, and preserving the environment are emphasized.[46] In masculine societies, such as those in Australia, Canada, Great Britain, and the United States, successful marketing strategies focus on consumers' achievement motivation: Marketing communications should stress personal accomplishment and have ego appeal. In feminine societies, such as in Asian cultures, marketing strategies should steer away from a materialist, acquisitive focus and, instead, appeal to consumers' sense of good will.

Individualism Versus Collectivism

Individualism refers to the degree to which people in a country prefer to act as individuals, in their self-interest, rather than as members of a group—which is a characteristic of collectivist societies. In individualist cultures, such as those of the United States, Great Britain, and Australia, the social fabric and group norms are much looser: People tend not to follow social norms but, rather, make decisions and initiate behaviors independently.[47] Such cultures stress the individuals' ability to achieve personal goals, make their way in life on their own, and, in the process, seek self-fulfillment and excitement. Collectivist cultures, such as those of Latin America, Asia, and the Middle East, stress subordination to the collectivity (group, business, family), and require acting in the interest of the group, rather than in one's self-interest. Cultures tend to evolve from collectivist to individualistic as countries become more industrialized,[48] and as individuals become less conformity oriented.

> **Individualism** The degree to which people in a country prefer to act as individuals, in their self-interest.

Although Asia, with 50 percent of the world's population, is culturally more heterogeneous than, for example, Europe, the emphasis on social harmony is an overriding and unifying belief across all societies. Asian societies are fundamentally collectivist. This is considered necessary in order not to disturb social harmony. Such thinking grounded in Confucianism, Buddhism, and Islam contrasts sharply with Western individualism. The difference is profound and has major implications for consumer behavior. Whereas Asians tend to identify themselves in terms of their social frame or relationships, Westerners define themselves in terms of personal attributes or achievements. Despite the fact that individualism has come to be considered a natural component of "modern" society, Asian cultures are now challenging this assumption. Japan, a "modern," industrialized nation by any standard, is still strongly collectivist. South Korea, Singapore, and Taiwan combine features of modern societies with a firmly entrenched **collectivism** orientation.[49]

> **Collectivism** The degree to which individuals prefer to act in the interest of the group, rather than in their own self-interest.

5-4 Cultural Change and Marketing

Being aware of the particulars of any culture may not be enough to succeed. Culture is undergoing continuous change all over the world as a result of external

---

46. See Hofstede, *Culture's Consequences*, 1984; and Steenkamp, Hofstede, and Wedel, "A Cross-Cultural Investigation," pp. 55–69.

47. Steenkamp, Hofstede, and Wedel, "A Cross-Cultural Investigation," pp. 55–69.

48. Harry C. Triandis, "The Self and Social Behavior in Differing Cultural Contexts," *Psychological Review*, July 1989, Vol. 96, pp. 506–520; and John A. McCarty and Patricia M. Hattwick, "Cultural Value Orientations: A Comparison of Magazine Advertisements from the United States and Mexico," *Advances in Consumer Research*, 1992, Vol. 19, pp. 34–38.

49. Hellmut Schutte, "Asian Culture and the Global Consumer," *Financial Times*, November 1998, Mastering Marketing, Part Two: Understanding Consumers, pp. 2–3.

influences. For example, a manager obtains a textbook training in business practices in a certain country. That textbook will probably not fully prepare the manager for all the changes in the cultural environment of the respective country that he or she can expect. Cultural training should involve immersion in the culture of the country, an understanding that goes beyond the world of business. Companies that are aware of the importance of such training go to great lengths to offer it: Consider, for instance, the case of Samsung, which spends $80,000 a year per person for employees to go abroad and literally goof off (go to malls, watch people, etc.), convinced that cultural immersion is likely to better help them understand what the customers of that country want.[50]

To appeal efficiently to a new market, marketers need to identify the symbolic elements and cultural meanings that are important to a market segment and use them effectively in creating the marketing mix. For example, the meaning of a fast-food joint in the United States is quite different from its meaning in other cultures. McDonald's and Pizza Hut are perceived in some cultures as trendy, fashionable places (see Figure 5-5). Marketers can use the following checklist[51] to integrate culture when designing a marketing strategy:

1. *Research* the present and possible symbolic elements and cultural meanings in consumers' lives.
2. *Identify* cultural meanings and physical properties of the product.
3. *Design* the product and packaging accordingly.
4. *Design* the marketing campaign using symbolic elements that carry cultural meanings.

5-5 The Self-Reference Criterion and Ethnocentrism

Self-reference criterion
Individuals' conscious and unconscious reference to their own national culture, to home-country norms and values, and to their knowledge and experience in the process of making decisions in the host country.

When interpreting cultural phenomena in other countries, marketers must avoid the unconscious reference to their own value systems, to their own way of doing things; that is, they should refrain from resorting to the **self-reference criterion,** as defined by Lee.[52] Instead, they should assess each culture as objectively as possible. Lee suggests a four-step correction mechanism to address individuals' tendency to resort to the self-reference criterion, which is herein adapted to a marketing context:

1. Define the marketing problem or goal in terms of one's home country's cultural traits, norms, and values.
2. Define the marketing problem or goal in terms of the host country's cultural traits, norms, and values.
3. Isolate the self-reference criterion influence and evaluate it to understand how it affects the marketing problem.
4. Redefine the marketing problem and, in the process, eliminate the self-reference criterion influence. Solve the marketing problem based solely on the unique conditions of the host country.

Negative outcomes of using the self-reference criterion are inflamed nationalist feelings or antiforeigner feelings targeting a particular company—even if the foreign company relies extensively on local suppliers and locally manufactures

---

50. *Wall Street Journal,* "Korea's Biggest Firm Teaches Junior Execs Strange Foreign Ways," December 31, 1991, p. 1.

51. Adapted from Grant McCracken, "Culture and Consumer Behavior: An Anthropological Perspective," *Journal of the Market Research Society,* January 1990, Vol. 32, No. 1, pp. 3–11.

52. James A. Lee, "Cultural Analysis in Overseas Operations," *Harvard Business Review,* March–April 1966, pp. 106–114.

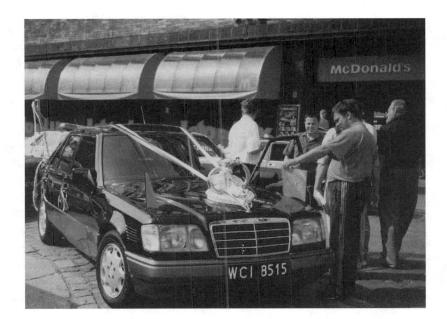

Figure 5-5
Get married at McDonald's! Did McDonald's marketing managers intend to market their fast-food restaurants as wedding reception destinations? Probably not. Yet this Polish couple rented a Mercedes Benz limousine and packed their wedding party into a McDonald's restaurant. The cultural meanings of McDonald's and Pizza Hut vary from country to country; in emerging and developing countries, they are not just fast-food joints: They are the hip place to take a girlfriend out on a date, the location where business is transacted, and where lifetime commitments are celebrated.

most products. The French frequently perceive Americans as imposing their way of life and their culture on the rest of the world without any sensitivity to the local culture. For the French, symbolizing these views are, among others, McDonald's, Coca-Cola, and Euro-Disney; Disney has often been referred to as an attempt to "McDonaldize France." Americans are successfully selling their fast food in a country where food preparation and serving constitute an art form, they are successfully selling mindless Hollywood action movies in a country that prizes high culture and art films, and, more recently, Americans have been arm-wrestling Europe, where natural foods are prized, into permitting the imports of hormone-treated beef. As expected, Gallic resentment and retaliation are omnipresent: Recently, 150 farmers in southwestern France (in Auch) occupied a McDonald's restaurant and slapped posters that said "No to the American dictatorship" and "No hormones in foie gras country." Similarly, a restaurant, Creperie Dominc, charges $8 per Coca-Cola bottle, instead of a little more than $1 (its regular price).[53]

Ethnocentrism is a belief related to the self-reference criterion, that a particular culture is superior to another and that strategies used in the home country (presumably a developed country) will work just as well abroad. Many examples illustrate the fallacy of this strategy in situations in which it is unwarranted. Attempting to sell clothes dryers in rapidly developing markets where the cost of electricity continues to remain high relative to a family's monthly income recently resulted in failure, as did television advertisements aired in a conservative country, depicting a woman who was describing in detail the use of a feminine hygiene product.

A related concept is *consumer ethnocentrism,* the belief that purchasing foreign products is wrong because it hurts the domestic economy, causes loss of jobs, and is plainly unpatriotic.[54] Although ethnocentric attitudes are, to a degree, related to the standard of living and economic performance in a country at a particular point in time, it is important to note that consumer ethnocentrist tendencies frequently affect foreign firms. The North American Free Trade Agreement was, to a

Ethnocentrism The belief that one's culture is superior to another and that strategies used in one's home country (presumably a developed country) will work just as well internationally.

53. Craig R. Whitney, "Food Fight: French Impose Own Tariffs," *The International Herald Tribune,* July 31–August 1, 1999, p. 9.

54. Terence A. Shimp and Subhash Sharma, "Consumer Ethnocentrism: Construction and Validation of the CETSCALE," *Journal of Marketing Research,* August 1987, Vol. 24, No. 3, pp. 280–289.

certain extent, diminished by ethnocentric feelings in the United States; similarly, in the 1990s, the potential of Japanese businesses in the United States did not entirely materialize due to strong ethnocentric feelings of U.S. consumers, many of whom felt that they had an obligation to buy American.

5-6 The Global Consumer Culture

Global consumer segments—consumers who associate similar meanings with certain places, people, and things—have developed worldwide and, with them, a global consumer culture. The global consumer culture is defined in terms of shared sets of consumption-related symbols, such as brands, and consumption activities that are meaningful to segment members. A global consumer culture is often attributed to the diffusion of entertainment from the United States to the rest of the world and to the dominance of English in both business and entertainment.[55] For example, MTV reaches 239 million viewers in 68 countries, and, among teens everywhere except for Africa, eight out of their top ten activities are media related. The direct outcome of this is a "global mall," whereby teens display the signs of this global culture by buying CDs, hamburgers, jeans, and running shoes—veritable emblems of the teen global culture.[56]

The global consumer culture has been identified as involving one or more of these trends:

- The proliferation of transnational firms and their brands worldwide and the related globalized capitalism
- Globalized consumerism and the desire for material possessions (the desire for fashionable or novel goods used to gain status and social acceptance)
- Global consumption homogenization, wherein consumers worldwide eat similar foods, desire similar brand names, and are exposed to the same entertainment

In addition to the described consumption behavior, certain gift-giving occasions have been adopted in many parts of the world where both traditions and religion are different from those in the industrialized Western world. Examples of such occasions are Christmas in Muslim countries where gifts are exchanged on New Year's Day, Valentine's Day in many countries of the world (including most of Western Europe) where it was not previously celebrated, and, increasingly, Halloween. Santa Claus (even in Buddhist, Muslim, and animist cultures), much like products such as Coca-Cola, represents the symbol of a consumer paradise widely imagined to exist in the United States.[57]

In response to an increasingly global consumer culture, marketers have devised marketing programs that appeal to individuals who would like to feel one with this culture. Among such messages are "United Colors of Benetton," "ADM, Supermarket to the World," and Philips' "Let's Make Things Better," which feature individuals and synopses from different countries. Such strategies are examples of **global consumer culture positioning** and identify a particular brand as a symbol

Global consumer culture positioning Marketing programs appealing to individuals who want to be part of a global consumer culture by purchasing a brand that is a symbol of that culture.

---

55. See Dana L. Alden, Jan-Benedict E. M. Steenkamp, and Rajeev Batra, "Brand Positioning Through Advertising in Asia, North America and Europe: The Role of Global Consumer Culture," *Journal of Marketing,* January 1999, Vol. 63, No. 1, pp. 75–87; and Guliz Ger and Russell W. Belk, "I'd Like to Buy the World a Coke: Consumptionscapes of the 'Less Affluent World,'" *Journal of Consumer Policy,* September 1996, Vol. 19, No. 3, pp. 371–404.

56. Chip Walker, "Can TV Save the Planet?" *American Demographics,* May 1996, Vol. 18, pp. 42–49; and Alden, Steenkamp, and Batra, "Brand Positioning Through Advertising," pp. 75–87.

57. See Ger and Belk, "I'd Like to Buy the World a Coke," pp. 371–404.

of a given global culture.[58] Such positioning is typically accompanied by the extensive use of English in environments where English is not widely spoken: As the primary language of international business, the mass media, and the Internet, English currently represents modernism and internationalism to many consumers. It is also accompanied by aesthetic styles, which are increasingly identified to belong to the global consumer culture: among others, the use of widely known spokespeople in advertising.[59] Examples of such endorsers are Michael Jordan for Nike, Roger Moore for Lark Cigarettes, and Michael Jackson for Pepsi.

According to Alden, et al., this strategy is different from **local consumer culture positioning,** which associates the brand with local cultural meanings, reflects the local culture, is portrayed as consumed by locals, and/or is depicted as locally produced for local people. For instance, Chevy trucks and Dr. Pepper have been positioned as part of the "American" way of life.

The strategy also differs from the **foreign consumer culture positioning,** whereby the brand is positioned as symbolic of a foreign culture. For example, Hermes in the United States is positioned as a desirable French product. Yoplait yogurt also emphasizes its French origin with the slogan "C'est si bon"— "it's so good"—(whereas, in France, its slogan is "La petite fleur"—"the little flower"). And men in lederhosen sing into the Alphorn with the Matterhorn mountain as the backdrop for the Swiss Ricola cough drops, while Juan Valdez stresses the quality of pure Colombian coffee. In Japan, Coca-Cola advertising shows young Japanese driving on American desert roads, stopping for a drink at a remote truck stop, and instantly gaining locals' acceptance by consuming Coke. All these examples illustrate successful foreign consumer culture positioning strategies, focusing on desirable countries of origin for the different product categories.

Local consumer culture positioning Positioning that associates the brand with local cultural meanings, reflecting the local culture, and portrayed as consumed by locals and/or depicted as locally produced for local people.

Foreign consumer culture positioning The positioning of a particular brand as symbolic of a desired foreign culture.

Chapter Summary

- **Identify the elements of culture and examine how they affect marketing practices around the world**

  Culture, a society's personality, represents a totality of shared meanings, rituals, norms, and traditions shared by members of society. Its elements are language (verbal, written, and nonverbal), religion, values, and norms. They have a significant impact on consumer behavior and marketing practices in general, delineating gender roles, rules for gift giving, and appropriate behaviors in a business setting; they also create rules for individual interaction. International marketing managers must be familiar with local culture, practices, and expectations and behave in accordance with those rules.

- **Describe national and regional character based on dimensions such as time orientation, business practices, gift giving, socializing, gender roles, and materialism**

  Traits such as time orientation, degree of status concern, and materialism at the societal level; rules for socializing; and gender roles are important to master in order to be able to perform optimally in a country's environment. Such knowledge should be used in determining the appropriate settings for transactions, the appropriate messages that should be used in advertising, and, in general, all interactions with local society.

---

58. Alden, Steenkamp, and Batra, "Brand Positioning Through Advertising," pp. 75–87.

59. Ibid.

- **Discuss cultural variability in terms of the Hofstede dimensions with appropriate examples and address cultural change in a marketing context**
Hofstede suggested four dimensions for classifying cultures that could benefit the marketing manager in deciding on the appropriate behavior. Those dimensions are power distance, which refers to interpersonal relationships when there are differences in power between the respective individuals; uncertainty avoidance, which refers to the extent to which individuals take risk in the respective culture; masculinity, which is the degree to which a culture is characterized by assertiveness; and individualism—the degree to which people prefer to act as individuals in their own self-interest—and collectivism—the degree to which people prefer to act as members of a group.

- **Address the self-reference criterion and ethnocentrism and describe how they impede mutual understanding and cooperation, with direct negative effects on marketing practices**
Two impediments to cross-cultural relationships are the self-reference criterion, which is the unconscious reference to one's own values and way of doing things, and ethnocentrism, the belief that one's culture is superior to others. Marketing managers must refrain from using self-reference or from adopting ethnocentric attitudes in the process of making decisions related to local operations.

- **Describe the global consumer culture as it manifests itself around the world**
The advent of a global consumer culture has created important opportunities for multinational firms: similar segments of consumers who share brand preferences; share a taste for similar consumer goods and services, such as fast food and entertainment; and respond similarly to a company's marketing strategies. Marketers are using three strategies to target consumers: global consumer culture positioning, which identifies brands as symbols of a particular global consumer culture; local consumer culture positioning, which targets the local consumer culture and portrays products as consumed by local consumers; and foreign consumer culture positioning, whereby the brand is positioned as symbolic of a foreign culture.

Discussion Questions

1. How does religion affect international marketing and international business operations in a target market?
2. What are the different cultural norms and values, and how do they differ around the world?
3. Margaret Hogan is an international marketing manager planning to accept an assignment representing her company interests in Saudi Arabia. What are some of the cultural elements that will have an impact on her performance? How can she best prepare for this assignment?
4. Many messages aimed at consumers in Central and Eastern Europe have a status message. Why? If you were assigned to work in this environment, would you, as a manager, show solidarity with the workers and symbolically work alongside them in the factory? Explain.
5. How do managers use the global consumer culture to position their goods in the local market?

International Marketing Strategy Decisions

Chapter 6
International Marketing
Research: Practices and
Challenges

Chapter 7
International Marketing
Segmentation, Targeting,
and Positioning

Chapter 8
The International Marketing
Plan and Entry Mode
Selection

International Marketing Research: Practices and Challenges

Key Terms

advertising effectiveness
   research
analogy method
back translation
brand awareness research
brand name generation
   and testing
buyer behavior research
causal research
channel performance
   and coverage studies
competitive pricing analyses
competitive product studies
concept development
   and testing studies
conceptual equivalence
consumer segmentation studies
content analysis
cost analyses
data collection instrument
decentering
decision support system
Delphi method
depth interview
descriptive research

emic instrument
etic instrument
experimental research
exploratory research
external secondary data
focus group interview
functional equivalence
import/export analyses
internal secondary data
international market potential
   studies
international marketing
   research
jury of expert opinion
media research
observational research
open-ended questions
parallel translation
plant/warehouse location
   studies
point-of-sale–based projections
price elasticity studies
primary data
product packaging design
   studies

product testing
profit analyses studies
purchase behavior studies
qualitative research
quantitative research
reliability
research approach
sales forecast
sales potential studies
salesforce compensation,
   quota, and territory studies
salesforce composite estimates
sample size
sampling frame
sampling procedure
sampling unit
secondary data
studies of premiums, coupons,
   and deals
survey research
test marketing
time series and econometric
   models
validity

Outline

Learning Objectives
6-1 The Need for International
   Marketing Research
6-2 Defining International
   Marketing Research
6-3 The Scope of International
   Marketing Research
   6-3a Research of Industry,
      Market Characteristics,
      and Market Trends
   6-3b Buyer Behavior Research
   6-3c Product Research
   6-3d Distribution Research
   6-3e Promotion Research
   6-3f Pricing Research
6-4 The International Marketing
   Research Process
   6-4a Defining the Research
      Problem and Research
      Objectives
   6-4b Developing the
      Research Plan
   6-4c Deciding on Information
      Sources
   6-4d Determining Research
      Approaches
   6-4e Designing the Data
      Collection Instrument
   6-4f Deciding on the
      Sampling Plan
   6-4g Collecting, Analyzing,
      and Interpreting
      the Information
6-5 Decision Support Systems
   for Global Marketing
   6-5a Sales Forecasting
Chapter Summary
Discussion Questions

Learning Objectives

Learning Objectives

By the end of this chapter, you should be able to:

- Define international marketing research and provide a description of its immense scope; offer examples of each type of research conducted in international marketing
- Describe the steps involved in the international marketing research

process while addressing, for each step, the international constraints involved
- Introduce the concept of decision support systems for international marketing and describe the sales forecasting process

International marketing managers operating in unfamiliar environments need to have a thorough understanding of their target market if their marketing efforts are to be successful. Numerous marketing plans fail due to an incomplete understanding of the market. Companies selling consumer products are especially prone to experiencing difficulties in foreign markets. Many such examples exist: An American manufacturer of cornflakes tried to introduce its product in Japan but failed; the Japanese were simply not interested at that time in the concept of breakfast cereals.[1] Also in Japan, Procter & Gamble did not take into consideration women's needs for a thinner diaper due to high frequency of changes and limited storage space, and their market share was quickly eroded by a local competitor who provided thinner diapers in line with market demands.[2]

Similarly, an ad for Procter & Gamble's Ariel detergent in Romania in the early 1990s portraying Dracula frightened at the sight of Ariel-cleaned white bedsheets assumed that Romanians were familiar with the Bram Stoker novel. TV viewers wondered at the count's reaction to a bedsheet, which had little to do with the story of Dracula as they knew it: Vlad the Impaler (Dracula) was a noble leader of the Romanian fight for independence from Ottoman dominance. Nowadays, the Bram Stoker version is widely known, and the P&G ad makes sense. One way to ensure that such blunders are averted is to engage in a thorough market investigation.

This chapter defines marketing research and examines its broad scope of marketing, across all components of the marketing mix (product, place, price, and promotion). The chapter addresses the international marketing research process and the complexities of the process in an international setting.

---

1. David Ricks, *Big Business Blunders*, Dow Jones, 1983.
2. Alecia Swasy, *Soap Opera: The Inside Story of Procter & Gamble*, Times Books, 1993.

6-1 The Need for International Marketing Research

Marketing managers need to constantly monitor the different forces affecting their international operations. Marketing information, which should constitute a basis for all executive action, must be taken into consideration to improve the chances of success in a complex global environment. Such information, though amply available in highly developed, industrialized nations, needs to be carefully evaluated and viewed in light of the purpose for which it was collected. In developing countries, relevant data may not be available at all, and, if available, it is often questionable in terms of both quality and integrity. For example, in the former Eastern Bloc countries, much of the production and sales data reported before 1990 was tainted by pressures of the communist governments on factories to exceed unrealistic five-year plans.

International marketing research is especially complex. International managers are likely to encounter not only the obstacles they have learned to master when conducting research in their own countries, but also obstacles laden with the specifics of the international market where they are conducting the research, specifics that may differ substantially from those of their national market. Consider, for instance, a male marketing researcher working for a haircare firm interested in launching its lines in the beauty salons of the Middle East. In the United States, it is perfectly appropriate for this individual to assess interest in the company's product line by collecting data in beauty salons. In most countries in the Middle East, however, women's beauty parlors cater exclusively to women (men's barber shops cater exclusively to men), and the presence of males in this environment would constitute a breach of Islamic law, which forbids males from seeing a woman's hair if they are not closely related.

Another aspect of the difficulty of engaging in research internationally is readily observable in Eastern Europe, where consumers remain suspicious of attempts by foreigners and locals to investigate local markets and related consumer behavior. Consumers are simply not accustomed to responding to opinion polls and regard such attempts as an intrusion or as suspect. And, since the transition to capitalism, prospective respondents are also likely to promptly demand payment for any time and effort demanded by the investigation.

These and many other environmental factors encountered in international marketing research complicate the task of marketing researchers, who should have not only an expertise in the most advanced techniques of scientific inquiry, but also a profound understanding of the markets under investigation.

6-2 Defining International Marketing Research

We define **international marketing research** as follows:

> International marketing research is the systematic design, collection, recording, analysis, interpretation, and reporting of information pertinent to a particular marketing decision facing a company operating internationally.

This definition of international marketing research contains a caveat also present in the general definition of marketing research: an acquired understanding of the market environment. In an international setting, the environment is particularly complex, and it displays obvious and important subtle differences in culture, religion, customs and business practices, and general market characteristics from the environment of the company's home country.

International marketing research
The systematic design, collection, recording, analysis, interpretation, and reporting of information pertinent to a particular marketing decision facing a company operating internationally.

Types of International Marketing Research

| Research of industry, market characteristics, and market trends |
| Buyer behavior research |
| Product research |
| Distribution research |
| Promotion research |
| Pricing research |

Figure 6-1
The scope of international marketing research.

6-3 The Scope of International Marketing Research

International marketing research has a broader scope than domestic research: Managers will need additional information to compensate for lack of familiarity with the foreign environment (see Figure 6-1). Sections 6-3a through 6-3f describe some general research categories).[3]

6-3a Research of Industry, Market Characteristics, and Market Trends

Studies of industry, market characteristics, and market trends, often in the form of acquisition, diversification, and market-share analyses, are conducted regularly by marketing research suppliers and shared with subscribers. This topic will be further addressed in the "Secondary Data" section. Export research is yet another type of research in this category; it is prompted by the shortening of the product life cycle and the intensity of international competition, as well as by the rapid technological change that increases the need to segment markets more frequently.[4] The research techniques range from formal methods, such as focus groups and concept testing,[5] to more informal approaches.

6-3b Buyer Behavior Research

Examining brand preferences and brand attitudes falls into the category of **buyer behavior research.** This type of research was recently conducted by DuPont, which, for six months performed qualitative and quantitative research in 20 countries with more than 85,000 respondents. In the process, the company found that 64 percent of the consumers interviewed perceived clothing made with DuPont Lycra to be of better quality, while 45 percent indicated that they wanted stretch in

Buyer behavior research
Research examining brand preferences and brand attitudes.

---

3. This section is organized based on a framework provided in a table in Thomas C. Kinnear and Ann R. Root, eds., *1988 Survey of Marketing Research: Organization, Functions, Budgeting, and Compensation,* American Marketing Association, 1989, p. 43.

4. See Rolf F. H. Seringhaur, "Comparative Marketing Behaviour of Canadian and Austrian High Tech Firms," *Management International Review,* Third Quarter 1993, Vol. 33, No. 3, p. 247; and James D. Hlavacek and B. C. Ames, "Segmenting Industrial and High-Tech Markets," Journal of Business Strategy, October 1986, Vol. 7, pp. 39–51.

5. William L. Shanklin and John K. Ryans, Jr., "Organizing for High-Tech Marketing," *Harvard Business Review,* 1984, Vol. 62, pp. 164–171; and Seringhaur, "Comparative Marketing Behaviour," p. 247.

their wardrobe, and a total of 30 percent actually asked for Lycra apparel.[6] As a result, DuPont launched its first global advertising campaign, created by Saatchi & Saatchi, to promote Lycra apparel to men and women ages 21–49 with a household income of more than $35,000, and to teenage girls ages 12–17 throughout the Americas, Europe, and Asia.[7]

In most Asian countries, uncertainty is strongly avoided, resulting in high brand consciousness, brand loyalty, greater insistence on quality, and consumers' active reliance on reference groups and opinion leaders. People tend to shop in groups, and they are slower to accept new products. Whereas consumers worldwide are concerned about monetary, functional, physical, psychological, and social risks, Asians tend to be more sensitive to social risk than Westerners.[8]

Brand awareness research and **purchase behavior studies** are frequently conducted by companies to assess their position in the market. For example, the International Research Institute on Social Change, a consultancy based in Switzerland and active in 17 markets, launched a study of luxury goods in the United States. A total of 3,000 respondents were interviewed in person at home and were asked, among others, about their familiarity, at least by name, with a set of 34 luxury brands. They were asked the following aided awareness question: "Here is a list of luxury brands. Please indicate which ones you know least by name." The researchers found that, in the United States, brands such as Daum, Christofle, and Bulgari were relative unknowns. Consequently, consumers were less likely to indicate an intention to purchase these brands: The study concluded that the consumers' desire for the brands is limited because awareness is low.[9] The respective marketers can address this problem by launching an awareness campaign for their brands.

Other useful studies that belong to this category are **consumer segmentation studies,** which are conducted to identify profiles of heavy product consumers, as well as occasions for consumption. Using the previous example of the problems faced by Procter & Gamble Japan when marketing Pampers to Japanese mothers, it is evident that the company might have benefited from a study of diaper use rate. Linking the heavy use of diapers (Japanese mothers change their children more frequently than mothers in other regions of the world), and the limited space available for storage in a typical Japanese home, the company could have easily identified the need for less bulky disposable diapers in this market.

6-3c Product Research

Concept development and testing studies are usually performed in developed countries by the firms' research and development departments. When going international, firms usually already have a successful product to bring to the marketplace; nevertheless, it is still important that they evaluate the product/service they offer and related marketing mix in light of the different target markets, regional and local.

Brand name generation and testing is used not only in the consumer goods industry, where its importance is obvious, but also in companies that have traditionally marketed their products regionally, such as agricultural goods companies.

Brand awareness research
Research investigating how consumers' knowledge and recognition of a brand name affect their purchasing behavior.

Purchase behavior studies
Research aimed at evaluating consumers' reaction to and interaction with a company's products.

Consumer segmentation studies
Research conducted to identify market segment profiles.

Concept development and testing studies Concept tests usually performed in developed countries evaluating the product/service offering and the related marketing mix in light of the different international target markets.

Brand name generation and testing The testing of brand names and logos, necessary when companies market their products internationally.

---

6. Kim Thuy Balin, "DuPont Lycra Goes Global," *Sporting Goods Business*, March 38, 1999, Vol. 32, No. 5, p. 16.

7. Ibid.

8. Hellmut Schutte, "Asian Culture and the Global Consumer," *Financial Times*, November 1998, Mastering Marketing, Part Two: Understanding Consumers, pp. 2–3.

9. Bernard Dubois and Claire Paternault, "Observations—Understanding the World of International Luxury Brands: The 'Dream' Formula," *Journal of Advertising Research*, July/August 1995, Vol. 35, No. 4, pp. 69–74.

These companies need to test brand names when they market their products internationally. For example, when American Cyanamid Company created a new global herbicide-tolerant crop production system, it used a research firm that started out with 600 possible names and then narrowed the list to 30 that were tested for linguistic appropriateness. After the company decided on the Clearfield brand, it then tested this brand and one other choice in seven different countries for six different crops. Testing showed the Clearfield name and logo to be meaningful, credible, appropriate, memorable, and likable.[10]

The annals of marketing are replete with examples illustrating the importance of testing a brand name in different countries. Rolls-Royce planned on marketing its Silver Mist in German-speaking countries only to find out before the launch that "mist" means "dung" in German.[11] Sunbeam Corporation, however, entered the German market without testing the name of its product, Mist-Stick, before introduction.[12] In other examples, a Finnish brewery introduced two new beverages in the United States, Siff beer and Koff beer, both unsuccessful.[13]

In the case of global products, it is important to research their meanings in different languages. Kodak, Exxon, Xerox, and Ajax are examples of product names selected only after extensive testing. Frequently, companies may have to come up with different names for products to ensure their acceptance in each region or country. As a result of brand-name-testing research, Maxwell House introduced its product under the name Maxwell Kaffee in Germany, Legal in France, and Monky in Spain.[14]

Product testing | Studies that estimate product preference and performance in a given market.

Product testing identifies the extent to which the product conforms to local tastes. For example, PepsiCo Foods International decided to undertake extensive product testing in China before introducing its Cheetos snack food brand. The outcome of the test was not favorable: Respondents indicated that they did not like the cheesy taste of the snack. As a result, PepsiCo's local joint-venture Guangzhou Frito-Lay decided to get rid of the cheese and replace it with cream and steak flavors. Sales increased dramatically.[15]

Competitive product studies | Studies that examine competitive product strategies in order to decide on the brand's product mix in the respective country.

Other types of studies that would be appropriate are **competitive product studies,** which are helpful in determining the overall product strategy for the product, the price that the market will bear for the respective product category, the promotion that is appropriate in light of the competition, etc.

Product packaging design studies | Studies that evaluate consumers' reaction to a package, the extent to which the package adequately communicates information to the consumer, and the distribution implications of the package.

As for **product packaging design studies,** firms need to take into consideration consumers' reaction to the package, the extent to which the package adequately communicates information to the consumer, and the distribution implications of the packaging decisions. For instance, in many emerging markets, packaging distinguishes between local products and international products. In Poland and Romania, many local dairy products are available in recyclable glass jars, have no brand name (just the product name, such as yogurt, kefir, etc.), and may contain only the dairy's address information. International products, on the other hand, come in colorful, sophisticated, disposable packaging. To the local consumers, however, simple packaging represents freshness and a lack of additives;

10. Erika Rasmusson, "Growing a Global Brand," *Sales and Marketing Management,* August 1999, Vol. 151, No. 8, p. 17.

11. Charlotte Clarke, "Language Classes," *Marketing Week,* July 24, 1997, Vol. 20, No. 17, pp. 35–39.

12. Ricks, *Big Business Blunders,* 1983.

13. Ibid.

14. Ibid.

15. Helen Johnstone, "'Little Emperors' Call the Shots," *Asian Business,* September 1996, Vol. 32, No. 9, pp. 67–68

after researching this phenomenon, a Romanian-German joint venture offered to the market dairy products in simple, recyclable glass packaging, rather than in sophisticated, disposable packaging.

The choice of package color is another important dimension that necessitates researching. One color could have different meanings in different countries: Green signifies abundance in North Africa and the Middle East, disease in the Amazon region, and healthful contents in North America.

In another example, Primus, a Belgian beer manufactured under license in Rwanda, is sold in one-liter bottles, rather than in the 33cl bottles that most other Western beers use in this market. In researching the Rwandan market, Primus found that the Rwandan consumer typically drinks beer at night, sharing with family and friends. Research also showed that beer is usually purchased and transported on foot for distances of one or two kilometers. Consequently, the bottles are typically sold in crates of 12 fitted such that they could be easily transported on one's head, allowing the individual to also carry other goods.

Test marketing is another important research procedure belonging to the product research category. In the late 1990s, Procter & Gamble test marketed Swiffer, a new disposable mop, in Cedar Rapids, Iowa, and Sens, France, among other disparate markets. The company hoped to craft an international new-product success with the goal of evaluating whether a consistent brand image could be achieved in a number of major markets.[16]

Test marketing Testing new-product performance in a limited area of a national or regional target market to estimate product performance in the respective country or region.

6-3d Distribution Research

The distribution function is particularly important in international marketing, where special attention should be given to import/export regulations and practices, and where companies are well advised to engage in comprehensive analyses. For example, **import/export analyses** aid companies in identifying the logistics companies most capable of handling the paperwork and getting products through customs in a timely and cost-effective manner. The Unites States government and state governments in the U.S. are often instrumental in helping with this type of research.

Import/export analysis Research that aids companies in identifying the necessary logistics that serve their needs in a timely and cost-effective manner.

Researching individual exporter and importer expertise and local influence is crucial to the success of the firm in a particular market. In a recent example, a small U.S. firm attempted to export older, high-quality Louis XV armchairs from Romania to the United States. In the process, the firm obtained the appropriate documentation from the State Patrimonium Commission, attesting to the fact that these armchairs were not antiques, nor important local historical artifacts; however, at customs, the firm through its local export company (a vestige of the former communist firm ROMTRANS) encountered obstacles that prevented it from exporting the armchairs. Only after contacting a different and much smaller firm, owned by a close relative of a top government official in the former communist regime, was the U.S. firm given clearance to export the armchairs. This same influential firm arranged for the chairs to be shipped via the Romanian airlines Tarom directly to New York at a fraction of the cost of the initial shipment that would have taken one month by truck to Hamburg and by ship to New York. Had the U.S. firm researched the local import/export service providers, it would have found that influence is crucial for the success of transactions. Of course, it should be noted that this type of influence often crosses the boundary of ethics and legality and could, potentially, cause problems for the company.

---

16. James I. Steinberg and Alan L. Klein, "Global Branding: Look Before You Leap," *Brandweek*, November 16, 1998, Vol. 39, No. 43, pp. 30–32.

Trade with Turkmenistan can serve as an example of the importance of researching specific requirements imposed on importers by the local government. The government of Turkmenistan tightly monitors all foreign trade through the State Commodity and Raw Materials Exchange. All import and export contracts must be registered with the exchange at a 0.3 percent commission. According to foreign companies, connections with someone holding a seat on the exchange facilitate registration. It is worth noting that the Turkmenistan president plays an integral role in the economy. He and a close circle of advisors centrally direct market activity, making all key decisions. To conclude, opportunity for a foreign company wishing to export to Turkmenistan is largely defined by the government's "priority projects."[17]

Consider another example. Kazakstan is a small but growing market for U.S. consumer goods. Distributing products in this large and sparsely populated country is a challenge. Geography and the inexperience of local wholesale distributors require exporters of consumer products to pay close attention to developing and maintaining a distributor network in this region—a task that is not easy to implement. Most of the population is located in two areas: the Southeast, around Almaty, and the North and Northeast, the republic's industrial and mining centers. Some existing infrastructure already supports distribution. An extensive railway network carries products within Kazakstan, to other newly independent states (NIS), and to Europe. On the other hand, poor roads and bad telecommunications, when combined with geography, make it virtually impossible to rely on just one regionally based distributor. Smaller foreign companies may wish to start with a small, regionally located distributor and gradually build a countrywide network from there. Larger firms may consider a larger up-front investment to establish their own infrastructure in Kazakstan.[18]

Channel performance and coverage studies Studies investigating whether existing channels are appropriate for communication, if channels exist at all, or whether they are appropriate for international marketing communications.

Another important type of study is that of **channel performance and coverage,** which may reveal either that channels need to be further developed at significant expense to the company, or that, in certain markets, particular channels dominate much of the activity in a particular area. Kraft, according to former Philip Morris U.S.A. (Kraft's former parent company) CEO William Campbell, had, for the longest time, delayed entering the Hong Kong market due to the high costs imposed by the dominant distribution companies. After many years and little progress in this market, however, Kraft decided, after all, to partner with the top distribution firm that has been instrumental to Kraft's success in Hong Kong.

Plant/warehouse location studies Studies that evaluate the appropriateness of plant or warehouse location to ensure that it is in accordance with the limitations of the national environment and with the needs of a company.

Finally, **plant/warehouse location studies** are important, as are evaluations of the transport infrastructure (roads, shipping, and warehousing infrastructure). In countries with an underdeveloped infrastructure and/or a mountainous terrain, warehousing is available only in the main cities, or just in the capital city. Consequently, distribution to a more remote location is complicated, and firms may elect to avoid it altogether. Research in this regard is important. For example, in the case of Ecuador, transportation between the capital city, Quito, and its second largest city, Cuenca, is facilitated by the well-developed highway system between the two cities, both of which are at a high altitude. Moving products from one location to another should not present problems because the transportation infrastructure is adequate and warehousing facilities exist in both cities. If, however, a firm is to transport goods to Guayaquill from the capital city, it is likely to

17. Irina Begjanova and Lisa Palluconi, "Trade with Turkmenistan," *BISNIS Bulletin,* September 1996, p. 5.

18. Kevin Lyons, "Distribution in Kazakstan," *BISNIS Bulletin,* November 1996, pp. 1, 5. This article was adapted from the *Country Commercial Guide* for Kazakstan, produced by the U.S. Commercial Service in Almaty.

encounter difficulties because the transportation infrastructure between these two locations is complicated by the terrain. Guayaquill is easily accessible by sea—the route taken by most imported goods and services aimed at the islands' tourist market. Goods from Quito are more likely to be transported by air than by truck.

6-3e Promotion Research

Promotion research is crucial for companies doing business internationally. By doing such research, the firm evaluates the extent to which it effectively communicates with the market, it ensures that certain promotional strategies are appropriate for that particular market, and, finally, it evaluates the extent to which the local media are appropriate for the intended message.

First, in terms of **studies of premiums, coupons, and deals,** it is important to identify the practices in each country where the specific promotion will run. When an agency has developed an idea to run in a number of countries, it first needs to check on the legality of premiums and coupons across those markets. For example, the sales promotion consultancy Black Cat has extensive experience in adapting pan-European strategies to different legislations in different countries. The agency has been running a promotion for 3M diskettes, data cartridges, mini cartridges, optical disks, and transparency film, offering millions of prizes. Whereas, in most European countries, this has taken the form of an "instant-win" promotion, with the game mechanism in the box, in some countries, such as Germany, the promotion has had to be adapted to include a "write-in-a-slogan" competition.[19] Similarly, giving away money-off vouchers is legal in the U.K., Ireland, and Spain but illegal in Germany, Norway, and Switzerland, whereas self-liquidating premiums are legal in the U.K., Germany, France, and many other countries but illegal in Luxembourg, Norway, and Switzerland. They may be allowed in the Netherlands, depending on exactly what form these premiums take.[20]

In addition to the legality of promotional practices, it is important to determine whether consumers are likely to respond to promotions as expected. According to sales promotions experts, the most difficult aspect about promoting in Eastern Europe is that consumers are just not accustomed to entering competitions and sending off coupons.[21] Alternatively, everyone may participate and overwhelm the postal system, as was the case when Pepsi offered a contest in which participants had to mail in bottle caps in Eastern Europe.

Advertising effectiveness research is frequently conducted to examine the effectiveness and appropriateness of advertisements aimed at individual markets. Frequently, ads that are initially developed for home-country markets and tested there are later used abroad; such ads are frequently dubbed and do not fit with the culture of the local environments where they are broadcast. One example is the Dracula Ariel advertisement previously discussed, but many other such examples exist. For example, Gitanes, a French cigarette maker, advertises its cigarettes on television in developing countries where the average monthly salary is less than $100 per month; the ad sells the good life by portraying a man driving a Porsche, with a beautiful, tall blonde on his arm (in a country where most women are petite and hardly ever natural blondes).

Media research also is important. First, in terms of media availability, developing countries pose the most problems. For example, in many countries in

Studies of premiums, coupons, and deals Studies that help identify the practices in each target country where a promotion is planned by investigating the practice and legality of premiums, coupons, and special deals.

Advertising effectiveness research Studies conducted to examine the effectiveness and appropriateness of advertisements aimed at individual markets.

Media research Studies that evaluate media availability and appropriateness of the medium for a company's message.

---

19. Martin Croft, "War of Independence," *Marketing Week,* March 3, 1995, Vol. 17, No. 49, pp. 47–48.

20. Ibid.

21. Ibid.

Central Africa, television is available only for a select few, via satellite. The majority of individuals have access to radio (local, or Deutsche Welle, the German broadcasting company) aimed at the individual countries in the region. The local radio station usually advertises only local service providers and only occasionally, whereas Deutsche Welle does not advertise at all. No advertising exists in locally available newspapers, nor in local magazines (Western publications, bought primarily by the expatriate community, have advertisements aimed only at the respective Western markets). Most advertising is limited to billboards on the main roads to the national airport in the capital city, and most are aimed at the business segment. Occasionally, one may see an ad advertising cigarettes, cola, or rum. In this type of environment, it would be difficult for a company to communicate with prospective customers using advertising; research would most likely indicate that the most effective communication would take place at the point of purchase.

In countries where various media venues are available, it is important to determine which channels, in the case of television, are likely to broadcast advertisements; frequently, the top television channel is government owned and does not carry advertisements (it receives revenues from private subscriptions). In many countries, advertising is broadcast only in between programs, rather than at ten-minute intervals, and consumers often use the advertising time to tend to different chores.

Finally, studies pertaining to personal selling activities, such as **salesforce compensation, quota, and territory studies,** are crucial in helping to determine the appropriate strategies for different markets. This material will be examined in greater detail in the personal selling section of Chapter 15, "International Personal Selling and Personnel Management."

6-3f Pricing Research

Internationally, pricing research is much more problematic than when it is performed locally, in a developed country. In addition to studies projecting demand, such as **international market potential, sales potential, sales forecasts, cost analyses, profit analyses, price elasticity studies,** and **competitive pricing analyses,** which are typical of most pricing research studies conducted by U.S. firms in the U.S., the firm also must look at issues regarding countertrade and currency issues, inflation rates, and a national tradition of bargaining for every transaction, all of which have implications for pricing decisions. These points will be further addressed in section 6-4e, "Designing the Data Collection Instrument," as well as in Chapter 16, "International Pricing Strategy."

At the retail level, pricing decisions could make or break a product. In countries where salespeople typically keep the change, it is important to price the product a few pennies/centimes below the amount that can be paid using larger currency denominations. For example, for a product costing $10.00, pricing it at $9.50 will give the salesperson a $.50 "tip" because customers would not demand change—an important consideration, especially in markets where salespeople have a considerable latitude as to which product they make available to the consumer.

Marketers of consumer goods in Kazakstan should research sales compensation practices. Potential distributors must be trained thoroughly in selling a given product. Many stores, although privatized, still have not grasped the concept of product marketing and often do not keep track of their inventories. As a result, it can be very difficult to build loyalty among retailers, who will often sell "whatever

---

Salesforce compensation, quota, and territory studies Different studies pertaining to personal selling activities; they are crucial in helping to determine the appropriate strategies for certain international markets.

International market potential studies Studies conducted to evaluate the potential that a particular country offers for a company.

Sales potential studies Studies forecasting optimal sales performance.

Sales forecast Projected sales for a particular territory.

Cost analyses Methods used for projecting the cost of research.

Profit analyses studies Studies that estimate product profit in specific international markets.

Price elasticity studies Studies examining the extent to which a particular market is price sensitive.

Competitive pricing analyses Pricing studies that determine the price the market will bear for the respective product category.

is available" at any given moment rather than try to establish a solid relationship with suppliers.[22]

Research in cost analysis would reveal that high product certification cost could significantly contribute to the price of a product and ultimately adversely affect its marketability. This is the case in Russia, where the lack of transparency connected with certifying products confronts both foreign and domestic companies. Although such companies are awaiting political solutions to these problems, marketers should be aware and plan ahead for certification. Often, the process may be cumbersome. Generally, there is some choice among the certification centers inside and outside Russia which are accredited to certify a given type of product or equipment. In some cases, however, the product itself may fall into several categories, and two certificates may be required.[23]

6-4 The International Marketing Research Process

Effective international research involves the steps shown here. Researchers attempting to obtain accurate and reliable information regarding a problem experienced in the firm's international operations are likely to encounter a number of difficulties, such as translation and cross-cultural comparison complications, which do not, as a rule, affect firms engaging only in domestic research. These difficulties will be addressed for each step in subsections titled "International Constraints."

6-4a Defining the Research Problem and Research Objectives

The first step in the international marketing research process requires international marketing manager and marketing researcher to define the research problem and jointly agree on the research objectives. The complexity of the environment of international operations does not afford marketing researchers the opportunity to have a very clear idea of the specifics that the research study should examine. Instead, they may need to engage in an **exploratory research** of the problem to define the relevant dimensions of the problem investigated. Exploratory investigations may help to further define the problem, suggest hypotheses, or even actually identify additional problems that need to be investigated. **Descriptive research,** on the other hand, portrays a situation—for instance, how frequently shoppers in Cairo shop for food items; whether they prefer to shop for meat products in state stores, which are cheaper but offer inferior-quality products, or in private stores, which are more expensive but offer a higher quality and assortment of meat products. Finally, **causal research** examines cause-and-effect relationships, such as the extent to which Sony's offer of financial incentives to electronics salespeople in Ahmedabad, India, is likely to increase sales of the Sony brand.

Managers must note that a fine line should be maintained between identifying the problem too broadly—"What are French consumers' entertainment needs?"—or too narrowly—"Will enough French consumers pay an additional 4 Euros to gain access to a specific American movie channel to make an investment in such a business worthwhile?" Better questions are: "What should be the price of this service in order to draw sufficient subscribers?" "What is the interest of French audiences in the movies carried by this channel?" "To what extent would the recently rekindled anti-American feelings affect subscriptions?"

Exploratory research Research conducted early in the research process that helps further define a problem or identify additional problems that need to be investigated.

Descriptive research All research methods observing or describing phenomena.

Causal research Research that examines cause-and-effect relationships.

---

22. Lyons, "Distribution in Kazakstan," p. 5.

23. Judith Robinson, "Product Certification in Russia," *BISNIS Bulletin,* August 1996, p. 6.

At this point, the researcher, in conjunction with the marketing manager, will set specific research objectives identifying

1. What is the interest of French audiences in the types of movies offered by the American movie channel?
2. How many subscribers will the company have if the subscription costs 4 Euros? 3 Euros? 2 Euros?
3. Will the channel gain customers in spite of the anti-American cultural-dominance feelings in France?

6-4b Developing the Research Plan

The research plan is a blueprint for the study, indicating all the decisions to be made with regard to information sources, research methods, data collection instruments, sampling procedures, data collection methods, data analysis, and, based on these decisions, the projected costs of the research.

6-4c Deciding on Information Sources

After the international manager and researcher define the problem and set the objectives, the researcher must determine the extent to which available information may shed further light on the problem at hand. The researcher will start by identifying information that may shed additional light on the problem and that has been collected either by the company itself (internal) or by some other firm or agency (external)—**secondary data.** The secondary data may, if needed, help the researcher to more clearly define the problem and set better objectives. It will also help the researcher pinpoint the type of information that needs to be gathered for the goals articulated in section 6-4a; the data collected in order to address the problem at hand is known as **primary data.**

Secondary data   Data collected to address a problem other than the problem at hand.

Primary data   Data collected for the purpose of addressing the problem at hand.

Conceptual equivalence   The extent to which meanings remain the same in different cultural environments.

International Constraints (for Both Secondary and Primary Data)

Conceptual Equivalence   Concepts have different meanings in different cultural environments. For example, the meaning of "household" in the United States is different from the meaning of "household" in many developing countries. In the United States, a household typically consists of a nuclear family, although this meaning is changing to include increasing numbers of single parents with children or of households with roommates. In developing countries, the household may include the extended family with distant relatives, as well as servants who have chosen to live with the respective families for the rest of their lives.

The urban versus rural distinction also varies from country to country. In the United States, rural areas typically benefit from excellent access to infrastructure; whereas, in many developing countries, rural areas have no electricity, they have poor roads, and the poverty level is very high. In other countries, little distinction exists between urban and rural areas. In a number of communist countries, governments decided to do away with villages so that they could build high-rise apartment buildings to replace quaint village homes. At the same time, some urban areas were (and remain) in a high state of disrepair, such that the newly built villages look much more developed than these urban areas.

Another issue that deserves mention is that many marketing applications in the United States are designed for the typical American who drives

Figure 6-2
What is a typical pastry shop? In downtown Bucharest, it is usually an elegant shop with comfortable seating.

a car, shops once a week at a supermarket, and, when the need arises, drives to the mall to purchase department-store goods. In most other countries of the world, however, the population is largely "pedestrian," consumers shop daily for food (they are unlikely to have refrigerators, or, if they do, the refrigerators are small, fitting under the countertop) and may have to make special and costly plans to take a long trip—using public transportation, rather than a personal car—to a larger city to shop for department-store items. How, then, should researchers study these markets differently than they study the U.S. market? Clearly, practices such as mall-intercept interviewing are not applicable. Imagine, for instance, conducting a research study at the Khan El Khalili bazaar in Cairo or at the "Russian markets" in the Ukraine or Poland where Russians sell their household goods. In both scenarios, even a study based solely on observation is logistically complicated, given the crowded, aggressive environment where consumers can barely keep their balance and get around, let alone respond to interviews.

Retailers and service providers differ greatly from one country to another. A drug store in much of the rest of the world outside the United States is known as a simple pharmacy. A pastry shop in the United States is usually a small Mom & Pop retailer selling warm pastries from behind the counter; elsewhere, it could offer an elegant environment much like that of a luxury restaurant that serves only desserts, as the one portrayed in Figure 6-2. Similarly, a mall in the United States typically describes one huge structure anchored by large department stores; in other countries, a mall could be a centrally located shopping avenue that may or may not be covered (see Figure 6-3).

Functional Equivalence Products themselves may be used for different purposes in different country environments. Whereas, in many countries, jewelry is used to advertise status and/or style and to reflect concern with appearance, in countries such as India and Pakistan, jewelry is used as a way to accumulate wealth.[24] Thus, a status scale containing the display of visible wealth such as jewelry will yield results that are not comparable across

Functional equivalence The difference in the purposes for which products may be used in different country environments.

24. This example is taken from Yusuf A. Choudhry, "Pitfalls in International Marketing Research: Are You Speaking French Like a Spanish Cow?" *Akron Business and Economic Review*, Winter 1986, Vol. 17, No. 4, pp. 18–28.

Figure 6-3
A mall is a popular retail establishment in the United States. In Eastern Europe, as in much of Europe, most popular are the central shopping avenues, some of which are covered, as in this photograph.

different environments. Also, if similar activities have different functions in different societies, they cannot be compared across the respective cultures. For example, refrigerators are used in some countries to store frozen food, whereas in others, they are used for chilling water and soft drinks. Warranties also have different meanings in different countries. In China, for example, firms are expected to support their products indefinitely, whereas in the United States, firms are much less generous. Finally, in many developing countries in Sub-Saharan Africa and in Eastern Europe, products cannot be returned, even if under warranty.

Problems are particularly frequent in the case of consumer products, where many companies have encountered difficulties in gaining market acceptance. For instance, an American company assuming that similar languages indicate similar tastes found out the hard way that British men saw no functional value in the use of aftershave, considering the use of scents as effeminate. Similarly, Chase and Sanborn, a British company, met with resistance when trying to market instant coffee in France. In France, coffee plays more of a ceremonial role than in Britain; the preparation of "real" coffee represents a touchstone in the life of a French housewife.[25]

Problems also are encountered when companies assume that, if individuals have a certain purchasing power, the market is ripe for time-saving devices that appeal to Western housewives. Standard of living is not necessarily an indicator of such needs, however, particularly in countries where a

25. Ricks, *Big Business Blunders*, 1983.

wide gap exists between the haves and the have-nots. In many middle-class and upper-class families worldwide, household work is done by hired workers, and there is little likelihood that much thought would be given to facilitating their work. Servants themselves perceive time-saving devices as a threat to their job security.

In fact, the immense popularity of Western luxury goods among high-income earners and teenagers in Asia is not necessarily proof that they have joined the rest of the world's Western consumers. They may try some goods, but for different reasons. Brand name goods such as Louis Vuitton bags may be bought more for "face" reasons and the importance of the regard of others than from an individual preference for the product. Remy Martin cognac and Lafitte red wine may not be consumed because consumers really prefer it over local liquor or beer but because of peer pressure. Strong market position can therefore be built on foundations different from those in the West and require different marketing activities—in other words, an approach especially geared toward globalization but more efficient in terms of creating value for the consumers, and, as a result, earning higher returns.[26]

Secondary Data

Researchers first must determine if information is available, and if so, and how much; doing so may aid in gaining insights into the problem at hand. Secondary data is defined as *data collected for a problem other than the problem at hand.*

Secondary data is typically examined first, and it offers the advantage of low cost and ready availability in many of the more-developed countries. The data that may be most relevant to the researcher's study, however, may not exist, or if it does, it may be dated or unreliable. For example, one company chose to cut costs and use research previously performed by a competitor on a specific Asian market. The study found that such investment had substantial support. After the firm built its plant, however, it noted that conditions had substantially changed since the study had been done. The company's use of an outdated feasibility study caused it to overestimate market potential.[27]

Secondary data can be categorized as *internal* (collected by the company to address a different problem, or collected by the company to address the same problem, but in a different country), or *external* (collected by an entity not affiliated with the company).

Internal Secondary Data

Assuming that Reynolds Aluminum Foil is available in Saudi Arabia, but not in Sudan, and assuming that the firm has no prior experience in Sudan, **internal secondary data** is useful only if the company has collected similar information from relevant respondents in a country with a similar environment (Saudi Arabia). For example, after considerable research, Reynolds' advertising in Saudi Arabia portrays the hands (with the wrists covered) of a woman preparing a sandwich for storage; an authoritative male voice describes the use of the foil and endorses its use. Because, from a religious perspective, the two countries are similar (although Sudan is less conservative), transferring this advertisement to Sudan will probably work. In this case, an analogy approach is appropriate.

Internal secondary data Data collected by a company to address a problem not related to the current research question.

---

26. Schutte, "Asian Culture and the Global Consumer," pp. 2–3.

27. Ibid.

If the environments of the countries are different, however, internal secondary data collected in one country is not useful in the second country. For example, Philip Morris advertises its Lark and Parliament brands in Japan using glamorous American images—scenes of the New York skyline at night, the Golden Gate Bridge, or movie-like clips of 007 in a subway chase or escaping whiskey-drinking bad guys. These advertisements were created as a result of extensive research in Japan, which revealed that Japanese consumers are admirers of many things American. In advertising to the Chinese, Philip Morris found that it cannot communicate using such advertisements: The Chinese are reticent to fully buy into U.S. values; moreover, China bans mass-media tobacco advertising. Thus, the only type of broadcast communication Philip Morris offers this market is an elaborate advertisement, glorifying Chinese culture, on the occasion of the Chinese New Year. Transferring research findings in the Japanese market to China is clearly not appropriate.

External Secondary Data

External secondary data   Data collected for purposes other than the problem at hand.

Marketing researchers in developed countries have ample access to different sources of **external secondary data.** They include government sources (provided by different government ministries/departments or bureaus—such as the Census Bureau), international agencies (such as the World Bank, the various United Nations agencies), professional associations, various magazine publications, and Internet sources.

Secondary Data Sources

The following are examples of publications that could offer information for researchers and national and international marketing associations that could be useful as external secondary sources:

Publications
Advertising Age
Adweek
American Demographics
Brand Marketing
Brandweek
Catalog Age
Chain Store Age
Discount Store News
Marketing
Marketing and Research Today
Marketing Management
Marketing News
Marketing Research
Mediaweek
Sales & Marketing Management
Target Marketing

Professional Organizations
Academy of International Business
Academy of Marketing (U.K.)
Academy of Marketing Science
Advertising Research Foundation
American Academy of Advertising
American Marketing Association
American Psychological Association

Asia Pacific Marketing Federation
Association Française du Marketing
Association for Consumer Research
Australia-New Zealand Marketing Academy
Center for Service Marketing
Chartered Institute of Marketing
Direct Marketing Association
European Direct Marketing Association
European Marketing Academy
Hong Kong Institute of Marketing
Institute for the Study of Business Markets
Institut fuer Qualitative Markt und Wirkungsanalysen, Germany
Interactive Marketing Institute
Japan Marketing Association
Market Research Society, U.K.
Marketing Research Association
Marketing Science Institute
Medical Marketing Association
Sales & Marketing Executives Association
Society for Marketing Advances

Research suppliers, such as A.C. Nielsen and others offer subscribers extensive information on different markets. Overall, secondary data collected by different research suppliers is quite useful. In the past, U.S. research suppliers dominated the market; nowadays, there are more and more international players. Among the top ten global marketing/ad/opinion research firms in the world are firms from the U.K., France, and Germany. The top firms are, in order of sales revenue: A.C. Nielsen Corp. (U.S.), Cognizant Corp. (U.S.), the Kantar Group Ltd. (U.K.), Information Resources Inc. (U.S.), GfK AG (Germany), SOFRES Group S.A.(France), Infratest Burke AG (Germany), IPSOS Group S.A. (France), the Arbitron Company (U.S.), and PMSI/Source Informatics (U.S.).[28]

The following are constraints researchers typically encounter in the process of gathering secondary data internationally.

International Constraints

Unlike the researcher's counterpart in the United States, in many international markets, information sources may be limited and inaccurate. Although information accuracy is usually closely linked to the level of country development, the data collected may have shortcomings attributed to factors other than development, such as translation, correspondence, etc. The following are some of the shortcomings of secondary data in international markets:

- *Availability*—In many markets, very little data is available. The detailed data readily available in developed countries may not exist in numerous regions in developing countries, where, for example, population censuses are frequently collected based on estimates made by village elders. If, for instance, demographic information—reliable and readily available in

---

28. *Marketing News*, "Top Global Marketing/Ad/Opinion Research Firms Profiled," August 18, 1997, Vol. 31, No. 17, pp. H2–H18.

developed countries—is deemed important to the project but is not available for the local market to be researched, the researcher may have to collect this type of data. Also, data on income and sales from tax returns can be inaccurate in countries where this information is not declared.[29] Finally, state-run research organizations are often reluctant to disclose the details of the data collection method and process used; no information may be available on response rates, questionnaire development, and the nature of the sample.[30]

Reliability The extent to which data is likely to be free from random error and yield consistent results.

Validity The extent to which data collected is free from bias.

- *Reliability and validity*—Governments in developing countries often exaggerate poverty figures to stimulate international aid. On the other hand, in many dictatorial environments where the government desires to project prosperity, figures attesting to the success of the economic policies may be inflated. Such was the case for many of the communist governments of Africa, Asia, and Eastern Europe, where figures demonstrating that workers were surpassing the five-year plans abounded, while, in fact, these same economies were experiencing severe shortages (typically attributed by government officials to consumer hoarding).

Errors also may be unintentional, attributed to lack of education or mere carelessness. Regardless, unless the researcher is convinced of the credentials of the research firm performing the study, it is best that the secondary data be regarded with skepticism.

Overall, the accuracy of government-published secondary data is questionable. Published statistics contain high margins of error, beyond the tolerance range of reliability.[31] In addition, published data may be fragmented or aggregated in inconsistent formats by different research organizations; researchers may pull the data for estimation, but, in most instances, they are likely to view the data with skepticism.[32]

Some reliable sources of data are those provided by the World Bank, the United Nations Development Program, and the Organization of Economic Cooperation and Development (OECD). Finally, even countries whose research reporting has been questionable for decades are presently revamping their data collection and reporting systems. For example, the Chinese government started to improve its marketing research infrastructure in the 1980s, introducing criteria for high-quality statistical service: accuracy, timeliness, relevance, diversity, and richness.[33] Overall, the State Statistics Bureau has expanded its role from data collection and compilation to a role similar to that of a business consultant.[34]

Regardless of the source, secondary data must be carefully scrutinized and interpreted. Researchers may construct a checklist to determine the extent to which the data is usable. This list may contain items such as

- Who collected the data and for what purpose? Was this actual research, or was it used to support a decision already taken (i.e., is it pseudo-research)?

29. William R. Dillon, Thomas J. Madden, and Neil H. Firtle, *Marketing Research in a Marketing Environment*, Second Edition, Irwin, 1993.

30. T. K. Sherriff Luk, "The Use of Secondary Information Published by the PRC Government," *Journal of the Market Research Society*, July 1999, Vol. 41, No. 3, pp. 355–365.

31. Naresh Malhotra and J. Agarwal, "Methodological Issues in Crosscultural Marketing Research: A State of the Art Review," *International Marketing Review*, 1996, Vol. 13, No. 5, pp. 7–43.

32. Luk, "The Use of Secondary Information," pp. 355–365.

33. Ibid.

34. Ibid.

- When was the data collected? What were the environmental country-conditions then?

- What stakes did the firm managers have in the study?

- What stakes did the researchers have in the study?

- Who else may have a stake in the findings of the study (government entities, businesses)?

- What methods were used?

- How consistently were the methods applied?

- Do the findings appear to be consistent with the findings of previous studies or with studies conducted in similar countries?

Primary Data

Primary research is used internationally far less than it should be. Cost-benefit analyses suggest that spending on research in remote markets of questionable value is unwise; consequently, the temptation is to use secondary data to serve all research functions.[35]

Yet many U.S. firms are interested in conducting research in the international markets where they operate. In a 1996 interview of 313 executives at major U.S. corporations who were responsible for conducting research and hiring outside research firms, 61 percent indicated that they would devote a larger percentage of their research budgets to international research over the following three years.[36]

Most international marketing research projects involve the collection of primary data, *information collected for a specific purpose, to address the problem at hand.* It requires substantial expertise in both instrument design and administration and, as a consequence, it is expensive and time consuming.

International Constraints

Lack of Marketing Infrastructure The costs of collecting primary data in foreign markets are likely to be much higher given the lack of a marketing infrastructure. Many markets do not have research firms or field-interviewing services; consequently, the sponsoring firm would have to invest in developing sampling frames and training interviewers.[37]

6-4d Determining Research Approaches

When collecting primary data, researchers may use *qualitative* and *quantitative* **research approaches.** Qualitative research methods typically have some of the following characteristics:

Research approach   The method used to collect data.

---

35. Michael R. Czinkota and Ilkka A. Ronkainen, "Market Research for Your Export Operations: Part II—Conducting Primary Market Research," *International Trade Forum*, 1995, Vol. 1, pp. 16–26.

36. Allison Lucas, "Market Researchers Study Abroad," *Sales and Marketing Management*, February 1996, Vol. 148, No. 2, p. 13.

37. Ibid.

- Fewer respondents belonging to a nonrandom sample
- Open-ended answer format
- Nonsystematic observation
- Researcher involvement as participant

Qualitative Research

Qualitative research Research
that uses nonsystematic processes,
such as nonrandom sampling and
open-ended data, as well as
involves the researcher as
participant.

Qualitative research has been particularly useful either as a first step in studying international marketing phenomena—when conducting exploratory research— or as one of the methods of exploring the problem at hand in a multiple-method approach. Focus group research and observation fit in this category. In certain countries, such as France and Italy, there is a preference for qualitative data as a complement to quantitative data, whereas in others, such as Germany, the U.S., and Scandinavian countries, quantitative data is deemed as most valuable.

Focus Group Interviews and Depth Interviews

Focus group interview
A qualitative research approach
investigating a research question
using a moderator to guide
discussion within a group of
subjects recruited to meet certain
characteristics.

Focus group interviews typically involve from 6 to 12 participants recruited to meet some previously decided characteristics—for instance, ethnic background, certain age group, social class, tribal allegiance, and use of certain products—and a moderator who guides the discussion based on a certain discussion agenda. Frequently, representatives from the sponsor observe the group's deliberations through a one-way mirror or on close-circuit television. A video camera or tape recorder may also be used to record the group's deliberations on a certain topic of interest to the sponsor. The participants are typically given a small financial reward for participating in the study, or products such as free beer and food, product samples, etc.

Depth interview A qualitative
research method involving
extensive interviews aimed at
discovering consumer
motivations, feelings, and
attitudes toward an issue of
concern to the sponsor using
unstructured interrogation.

Depth interviews are one-on-one attempts to discover consumer motivations, feelings, and attitudes toward an issue of concern to the sponsor using a very loose and unstructured question guide. They are typically used if the issue under study is a complex behavioral or decision-making consideration or an emotionally laden issue.

International Constraints

Focus groups, consumer panels, and depth interviews are frequently problematic to apply in international settings. In Eastern cultures, responses are likely to be affected by "acquiescence bias" or "good-subject role," whereby consumers agree in order to please the interviewer. When conducting international research using focus groups, researchers should be aware of the significance of culture in the dialogue because many societies do not condone open exchange and disagreement between individuals.[38] Also, topics such as domestic habits or sexual behavior are considered too private and embarrassing to discuss with strangers. In these environments, researchers would benefit more from using observational approaches.[39]

Observational research
A research approach used
frequently in international
markets, whereby subjects are
observed interacting with a
product and the related
components of the marketing
mix.

Observation

One type of **observational research** that is particularly useful in international research is naturalistic inquiry. Naturalistic inquiry requires the use of natural

---

38. Czinkota and Ronkainen, "Market Research for Your Export Operations," pp. 16–26.

39. Choudhry, "Pitfalls in International Marketing Research," pp. 18–28.

rather than contrived settings because behaviors take substantial meaning from their context.[40] The researcher is the data collection instrument, and part of the behavior—verbal and nonverbal. The analysis performed by the researcher is inductive, rather than deductive; that is, unlike in conventional research methods, the researcher does not rely on previous theory in the process of developing hypotheses, but, rather, theories are developed from data. Ethnography—the study of cultures—is largely based on naturalistic inquiry. Both academic researchers and practitioners have used this approach to better understand international consumers and consumer motivations. It is frequently used by researchers who attempt to increase the validity of their studies by acquiring an intimate knowledge of a culture's daily life through personal observation.[41]

Other observational methods—such as the study of garbage (garbology); physiological measurement methods that measure a respondent's nonvoluntary responses to stimuli; eye tracking, which is used in packaging research and in advertising; and response latency, measuring the time interval between the question and the response to that question—are used only to a limited extent in international research, usually in developed countries. They are very costly because they require sending expensive expertise to the research site abroad and obtaining data only on limited, usually nonrepresentative samples.

Information technology provides new sources for observation-based information, such as point-of-sale (POS) store scanner data, which can offer outlets high-quality, instant, as well as longitudinal, information on the movement of goods. Such resources are amply available in the U.S., Canada, and the countries of the European Union. Increasingly, they are available in Asia and in the emerging markets of Latin America. This information is used for tracking, as well as for managerial decision making. This topic will be addressed in section 6-5a, "Sales Forecasting." Other sources for observation-based information include people meters, used to identify television audience watching behavior; in the U.S., A.C. Nielsen also links this type of data with self-reported purchase behavior of consumers.

International Constraints

Observation can have a number of shortcomings. Individuals in different cultures may react differently if they note that their behavior is being observed. Also, the observer may need to be familiar with all the different languages spoken at the study site; this is especially the case in Europe, where store research is relatively novel.[42]

Quantitative Research

Quantitative research methods are more structured, involving either descriptive research approaches, such as survey research, or causal research approaches, such as experiments.

Quantitative research
A structured type of research that involves either descriptive research approaches, such as survey research, or causal research approaches, such as experiments.

---

40. See Yvonna S. Lincoln and Egon G. Guba, *Naturalistic Inquiry,* Sage Publications, 1985; Laura A. Hudson and Julie L. Ozanne "Alternative Ways of Seeking Knowledge in Consumer Research," *Journal of Consumer Research,* March 14, 1988, pp. 508–521.

41. Jerome Kirk and Marc L. Miller, *Reliability and Validity in Qualitative Research,* Sage Publications, 1986.

42. Czinkota and Ronkainen, "Market Research for Your Export Operations," pp. 16–26.

Content analysis   Method that assesses the content of advertisements in a medium with verbal and/or visual content.

Content Analysis

Content analysis, an example of descriptive research, is a quantitative analysis that entails counting the number of times preselected words, themes, symbols, or pictures appear in a given medium such as printed material or any medium with verbal and/or visual content. Content analysis is particularly useful in international marketing research, helping international marketing practitioners understand the complex multicultural environments in which they compete. At the same time, content analysis makes them aware of the subtle qualitative differences—such as taste, tradition, and symbolism among societies—that are especially useful in market segmentation.[43]

One area where content analysis is used extensively is advertising research, in an attempt to discover themes that are more popular in certain countries for particular product categories. One recent study[44] examined differences in the portrayal of women in magazines of different countries. Using U.S. and international male and female judges, the study found that, in general, North American and Western European magazines portrayed women displaying more positive emotions, compared to Latin American, East European, and African magazines. In addition, the women from Latin America appeared to be older, sexier, and more aggressive than their Western counterparts. Table 6-1 is a partial content analysis questionnaire used to gather this data.

Survey research   Descriptive research that involves the administration of personal, telephone, or mail questionnaires.

Survey Research

Survey research, another example of descriptive research, typically involves the administration of personal, telephone, or mail questionnaires. The use of the questionnaires assumes that respondents are both capable and willing to respond to the questions. The cheapest survey method is mail questionnaires; however, this method is fraught with obstacles in many developing countries. And, in most developing countries, there is a high level of illiteracy, which renders impossible the use of mail surveys. Nevertheless, this method is most popular in international marketing research, especially because it can be effectively used in cross-national comparisons.

International Constraints

Respondent Factors   In certain countries, researchers may not have access to certain household members. For example, a male researcher collecting data in Djeddah, Saudi Arabia, will not have access to female respondents; in fact, he may even get into trouble if he attempts to approach a woman in any environment. Companies are advised to hire local female interviewers for any study that may involve women and male interviewers for studies that involve male respondents. Procter & Gamble, for example, a Western company with a substantial presence in the Saudi market, conducted a study examining the consumer behavior of Saudi women. The marketing department invited the husbands and brothers of Saudi women to participate in a focus group study. In spite of its obvious limitations, the study produced use-

---

43. David R. Wheeler, "Content Analysis: An Analytical Technique for International Marketing Research," *International Marketing Review,* Winter 1988, Vol. 5, No. 4, pp. 34–40.

44. Dana-Nicoleta Lascu, "Women in Advertising: A Cross-Cultural Study of Emotion," in *Proceedings of the Annual Meeting of the Academy of International Business,* South-East 1997, pp. 19–32. Presented at the Academy of International Business Conference, South-East (Atlanta, Georgia), November 1997.

T A B L E **6-1** Partial Content Analysis Questionnaire

Women are frequently used in advertising. Advertisers portray them differently, depending on the mood/feeling they would like to convey. Please look at each ad and indicate to what extent you believe that THE WOMAN IN THE AD appears to have the following characteristics by circling the corresponding number, as follows:

> 1 = if the ad/woman DOES NOT AT ALL HAVE the respective characteristic
> 2 = if the ad/woman DOES NOT HAVE the respective characteristic
> 3 = if the ad/woman SEEMS TO HAVE the respective characteristic
> 4 = if the ad/woman HAS the respective characteristic
> 5 = if the ad/woman DEFINITELY HAS the respective characteristic

The woman in the ad appears to be ...

Soft	5	4	3	2	1
Cool	5	4	3	2	1
Seductive	5	4	3	2	1
Scornful	5	4	3	2	1
Kitten-like	5	4	3	2	1
Optimistic	5	4	3	2	1
Maternal	5	4	3	2	1
Loving	5	4	3	2	1
Practical	5	4	3	2	1
Proud	5	4	3	2	1
Comic	5	4	3	2	1
Calm	5	4	3	2	1
Superior	5	4	3	2	1
Elegant	5	4	3	2	1
Caucasian	5	4	3	2	1
AfroAmerican	5	4	3	2	1
Hispanic	5	4	3	2	1
East Asian	5	4	3	2	1
Asian Indian	5	4	3	2	

The woman is looking at...

People	5	4	3	2	1
An object	5	4	3	2	1
Nothing	5	4	3	2	1
The reader	5	4	3	2	1
Herself	5	4	3	2	1

The woman's age is approximately _____ years.

---

ful results that helped Proctor & Gamble develop appropriate strategies for this market.[45]

In Eastern Europe, on the other hand, there is considerable suspicion of any attempts to gain personal information. In fact, the word used for "research" is a variant of the Slavic *ankieta*, meaning inquiry (of the same type as that conducted by the former, feared secret police). Intercepting consumers in the marketplace typically meets with minimal response and with possible attempts to discredit the interviewer. A better method is "the apartment intercept," whereby the interviewer randomly chooses apartment buildings—typical mass structures found in most communist and formerly communist countries—located in representative neighborhoods and then attempts to interview every nth individual. The individuals approached may either live in the building, visit someone who lives there, or do business

45. Zafar U. Ahmed, Dana-Nicoleta Lascu, and D. Neil Ashworth, "International Management and Marketing Research in Developing Countries," in *Proceedings of the Sixth Annual Meeting of the American Society of Business and Behavioral Sciences*, February 1999, Vol. 10, pp. 9–14.

(shopping, renting videocassettes, etc.) in one of the apartments. An advantage of this method is the private environment protected from weather elements that may impede interaction.[46] Yet even this method does not yield a very high response rate because respondents may still suspect the interviewer's intentions. Moreover, Eastern European respondents believe that, in capitalism, people do not give something for nothing, and they almost always ask to be paid for their time.

In conclusion, it is crucial that researchers have a good understanding of the culture and local practices in order to obtain adequate response rates.

Infrastructure Factors   In many countries, the use of telephones will limit the data collection to a handful of individuals who have access to a telephone. This problem may disappear as the country develops; however, even more developed countries such as Poland, Spain, and India do not benefit from a very efficient telephone network. And, in many countries where mail is unreliable and slow, companies cannot rely on this type of data collection approach, leaving the personal interview, focus group, or observation as the only feasible research approaches. Even in India, which has one of the best home delivery mail systems in the entire developing world, mailing surveys to consumers' homes or offices has never been a part of the business culture of Indian society; similarly, in Saudi Arabia, which has one of the most efficient mail systems in the world using the most modern technologies, studies cannot be conducted through this venue because the system restricts the use of mail surveys.[47]

Another illustration of obstacles to the mail survey approach is offered by Nigeria: Attempts to collect data using mail surveys is restricted by literacy rates, which eliminate most potential respondents. Further, the mail delivery system is limited to the use of postal boxes, with home delivery being almost nonexistent; Nigerian roads/streets are not named and homes are not numbered.[48]

Finally, the sampling frames (mailing lists, telephone books, or other relevant databases) may not be available.

Experimental Research

Experimental research Research that examines cause-and-effect relationships; it has the highest validity and reliability of all types of research.

Experimental research has the highest validity and reliability of all types of research. This research looks at cause-and-effect relationships, eliminating or controlling other extraneous factors that may be responsible for the results, and eliminating competing explanations for the observed findings. It requires the use of matched groups of subjects who are subjected to different treatments, to ascertain whether the observed response differences are statistically significant.

Given the many constraints that this type of research imposes on the researcher, experimental research findings are difficult to transfer to other countries where the control factors behave differently. Given the fact that results are not easily generalizable to similar environments, and that this type of research can be very costly, experimental research is rarely used in international research.

---

46. Dana-Nicoleta Lascu, Lalita Manrai, and Ajay K. Manrai, "Marketing in Romania: The Challenges of the Transition from a Centrally-Planned Economy to a Consumer-Oriented Economy," *European Journal of Marketing*, 1993, Vol. 27, no. 11–12, pp. 102–120.

47. Ahmed, Lascu, and Ashworth, "International Management and Marketing Research in Developing Countries," pp. 9–14.

48. Ibid.

6-4e Designing the Data Collection Instrument

International marketing phenomena are particularly difficult to measure and require an intimate knowledge of the culture. Themes that are functionally and conceptually equivalent across nations, such as the universal concept of "affection," manifest themselves differently in different environments; for instance, kissing, a common manifestation in the West, is inappropriate in Eastern cultures and taboo in others.[49] Given these differences, phenomena specific to each culture are best measured by **emic instruments,** which are constructed for each nationality to measure the particular factor. The instrument employed must then conform to the specific characteristics of each culture.

International managers are frequently faced with problems related to the need for survey instruments that can be used across different cultures, especially for comparative evaluation of market characteristics such as response to an advertising campaign and other types of multi-country research. For this type of study, **etic instruments,** which are culture free and extremely difficult to develop, can be used to measure the same phenomenon in different cultures. For example, when one refers to the distance to the nearest supermarket in the United States, one uses the driving distance, whereas, in the rest of the world, the distance to the supermarket is measured in pedestrian terms. In fact, the word "supermarket" itself has different meanings in different countries. The type of store referred to as a "supermarket" in the United States is typically a large store belonging to a national or regional chain. A typical supermarket in Poland, such as a *Centrum,* is probably made up of different stores that carry an assortment of products that does not even come close to that of its U.S. equivalent, whereas a *Migros* in Switzerland, *Hertie* in Germany, and *Albert Heijn* in the Netherlands carry a larger variety of products, but not as wide an assortment of competing brands as their U.S. equivalents. Consequently, what would be the appropriate way to measure consumer shopping experience at these supermarkets? Surely, a forced-choice standardized questionnaire would not be appropriate for cross-national comparisons, unless it is properly modified to reflect these differences. And, should there be such modification, it is likely that the value of the direct comparison itself would be compromised.

When deciding on the **data collection instrument,** the researcher needs to come up with an appropriate format and to offer very precise instructions. Frequently, respondents may not answer entire sections of the questionnaire, unless advised that full completion is essential for the integrity of the study. A typical *semantic differential* scale, anchored by words with opposite meanings (good . . . bad, important . . . not important) could be confusing to respondents as well. Clear instructions, preferably with examples, would help respondents in filling out the questionnaire appropriately. A variant of the semantic-differential scale follows (note the detailed explanation of the numbers to be circled). The typical Likert scale anchored by "strongly disagree" and "strongly agree" is unfamiliar to respondents in many cultures. Explaining the procedure in detail, as well as the meaning of circling a particular response, is essential. See the questionnaire in Table 6-2 for a variant of the Likert scale.

An easier approach (from the point of view of the respondent, and certainly not from the perspective of the individual coding and analyzing the data) is to use **open-ended questions** that elicit the appropriate answer from the respondent. This format allows the interviewer to probe in depth into the issue at hand, and the respondent to fully address the points.

Emic instrument A data collection instrument constructed for each nationality to measure a particular factor; it is the best measure for culture-specific phenomena.

Etic instrument A culture-free data collection instrument that can be used to measure the same phenomenon in different cultures.

Data collection instrument The instrument used to collect data, such as a printed questionnaire, a paper-and-pencil measure, or an electronic measurement device.

Open-ended questions Questions with free-format responses that the respondent can address as he or she sees appropriate.

---

49. The material in this section is adapted from Choudhry, "Pitfalls in International Marketing Research," pp. 18–28.

T A B L E **6-2** **Sample Partial Consumer Research Questionnaire (Version Translated into Romanian, Bulgarian, and Hungarian)**

Please indicate the extent to which you agree or disagree with the statements below by circling 5 if you strongly agree, 4 if you agree, 3 if you neither agree nor disagree, 2 if you disagree, and 1 if you strongly disagree with the statement. Please answer *every* question; the questionnaire cannot be used unless you do so.

	Strongly Agree				Strongly Disagree
1. I don't care to find out about what types of brand names of appliances and gadgets my friends have.	5	4	3	2	1
2. I often read advertisements just out of curiosity.	5	4	3	2	1
3. I rarely read advertisements that just seem to contain a lot of information.	5	4	3	2	1
4. When I hear about a new store or restaurant, I take advantage of the first opportunity to find out more about it.	5	4	3	2	1
5. Companies are usually out to make money even if it means violating ethics and taking advantage of consumers.	5	4	3	2	1
6. Most durable products could be made to last much longer but are made to wear out quickly to necessitate repurchase.	5	4	3	2	1
7. If people really knew what businesses do to deceive and take advantage of consumers they would be up-in-arms.	5	4	3	2	1
8. Most Western products I buy are overpriced.	5	4	3	2	1
9. Most *LOCAL* products I buy are overpriced.	5	4	3	2	1
10. Businesses could charge lower prices and still be profitable.	5	4	3	2	1

International Constraints

Instrument Translation Instruments developed in one country require translation into the language of the country where they will be administered. Many concepts, however, are likely to lose some of their meaning when translated into another language. Idioms are particularly problematic, and their literal translation has led to numerous marketing blunders.

In cross-cultural research, all steps should be performed by individuals fluent in both the original language of the questionnaire and in the language of the country where it will be administered. First, a questionnaire is translated from the language in which it was originally written into the language in which it will be administered. There are two possible alternatives to further ensure that the instrument has been translated as intended. One is **back translation,** whereby the translated questionnaire is again translated into its initial language by a different individual. Another possibility is **parallel translation,** whereby the questionnaire is translated from its original language by two different individuals and the two versions are compared. The successive translation (by different translators) of the instrument between the original language and the language of administration with the purpose of obtaining an instrument that is closest in meaning to the original questionnaire is known as **decentering.**

The consumer research questionnaire in section 6-4e contains a number of scales developed in marketing in the United States, among which are attitudes toward business ethics, attitudes toward pricing practices, comparison shopping, dogmatism, fashion concern, dress conformity, and information searches. The translated scales performed well and were considered highly reliable when used in the different country environments.

Back translation The translation of translated text back into its original language, by a different individual, to ensure that the instrument has been translated as intended.

Parallel translation The process of translating the original instrument by different translators and comparing the translations.

Decentering The successive translation (by different translators) of an instrument between the original language and the language of administration with the purpose of obtaining an instrument that is closest in meaning to the original.

Instrument Reliability Even if the same scale is used in different cultures and has been subjected to decentering techniques, the same scale is likely to have different reliabilities (i.e., the extent to which the scale is likely to be free from random error and yield consistent results) when administered in different countries because respondents in one country might be more likely, for example, to give answers that would please the interviewer. This provides yet another argument against simple comparison of research results in international marketing.[50]

Other Instrument Issues In certain environments, such as the United States, respondents are unwilling to answer questions about income, whereas in others, such as France, respondents more readily volunteer such information. In other cultures, age is a taboo subject. It is important to take these differences into consideration when designing questionnaires. Creating categories of income, rather than asking the precise figure, tends to have a better success for data collected in the United States. Regardless, it is best if all demographic data is placed at the end of the questionnaire, to ensure response.

6-4f Deciding on the Sampling Plan

The sampling plan calls for the manager and researcher to jointly decide on the following issues:

- **Sampling unit**—Determining who will be included in the survey
- **Sample size**—Determining how many individuals will be surveyed (the larger the sample, the higher the study reliability)
- **Sampling procedure**—Determining how the sampling units will be selected (the most representative sample is a random probability sample)

Determining the sampling plan is likely to be affected by some of the same problems discussed previously. First, the sampling unit itself may have a different definition, depending on the country where the data is collected. In developed countries, for example, research examining family consumption patterns will typically survey a nuclear family, whereas in many developing countries, an extended family, including relatives living with the nuclear family, will be scrutinized. Similarly, as already mentioned, the concept of household varies across different countries.

The sampling procedure also presents a problem, as previously discussed, especially the **sampling frame** (the list from which sample units are selected). Mailing lists are inadequate, and telephones are available to only a small percentage of the population in many countries of the world.

6-4g Collecting, Analyzing, and Interpreting the Information

In the final stage of the marketing research process, the researcher or research team is ready to collect the primary data. This expensive undertaking can be eventful. Researchers are frequently faced with respondents who have never had any experience participating in surveys. *Nonresponse* (inability or, more frequently, refusal to participate in the study) can be a particularly serious problem, as previously seen. Even lateral processes that do not involve data collection per se, such as *briefing the field force* (training the interviewers) and *evaluating the fieldwork quality*, can be particularly difficult if the marketing researcher is not a national because communication may be encumbered by language and cultural differences.

Sampling unit The entity included in the study; it may be individuals or representatives belonging to particular groups.

Sample size The number of study participants necessary to obtain a high study reliability.

Sampling procedure A decision involving the selection of sampling units.

Sampling frame The list from which sample units are selected.

---

50. Ravi Parameswaran and Attila Yaprak, "A Cross-National Comparison of Consumer Research Measures," *Journal of International Business Studies*, Spring 1987, pp. 35–49.

Ideally, local researchers should be in charge of implementing the data collection process because they are aware of the particulars of the environment that may have an impact on the data collection.

Finally, it is important that marketing managers not base all their decisions on the data collected because even proper planning of the data collection effort does not exclude the possibility of shortcomings in the study. For example, after a market research firm indicated that there was a substantial market for a specific product, a Swiss pharmaceutical firm built an $8 million manufacturing firm in Southeast Asia. The researchers, however, overlooked an important aspect of that market: the black market controlled by government officials. The added competition of the black market led to lower earnings for the company.[51]

6-5 Decision Support Systems for Global Marketing

Decision support system
A coordinated collection of data, systems, tools, and techniques, complemented by supporting software and hardware designed for the gathering and interpretation of business and environmental data.

A **decision support system** is defined as "a coordinated collection of data, systems, tools, and techniques, complemented by supporting software and hardware designed for the gathering and interpretation of business and environmental data."[52] In a global environment, the environmental data takes into account home-country and host-country developments, as well as other developments in other global markets that may affect operations.

Ideally, a global marketing decision support system should be[53]

- *Computerized*—Having a computerized support system is now possible in the case of many global markets, including those of developing countries, due to the increase in the capability of personal computers to perform more and more complex tasks.
- *Interactive*—Managers can use on-line instructions to generate reports on the spot, without assistance from a programmer, who now may need to be present in the country of operations only periodically, for system updating and training. This, of course, reduces the number of expatriates necessary at the operations site and the overall costs to the company.
- *Flexible*—Managers can access and integrate data from a variety of sources and manipulate the data in a variety of ways (producing averages and totals, sorting the data, etc.). The system should allow managers to access information about firm operations in similar markets where the firm may be present and competitors' operations in the respective market where such information is available.
- *Discovery-oriented*—Such systems should produce diagnostics that reveal trends and identify problems.

In a global environment, there are different, country-specific information systems. Integrating the different approaches may lead to operational difficulties; managers must continuously take into consideration such differences as they interface with the system.

A number of areas lend themselves well to marketing decision support systems (MDSS). In section 6-5a, we discuss different possible applications for such systems.

---

51. Ricks, *Big Business Blunders,* 1983.

52. William R. Dillon, Thomas J. Madden, and Neil Firtle, *Marketing Research in a Marketing Environment,* Irwin 1993.

53. Ibid.

6-5a Sales Forecasting

Different approaches to sales forecasting are discussed in this section. The more complex these techniques are, the more their efficiency can be improved in an MDSS environment. Nevertheless, input obtained from using the simpler methods (salesforce composite estimates, jury of executive opinion, and the Delphi method) can be used to cross-validate the estimates given by the more sophisticated forecasting techniques (time series and econometric models).

Salesforce Composite Estimates

Forecasts from **salesforce composite estimates** are based on the personal observations and "hunches" of the local salesforce. These people are in the closest contact with the international consumer, and they are likely to find out about consumer desires and overall changing market trends. The salesforce is likely to be constituted of locals who have a good understanding of the market. They, in turn, report to the manager, who may or may not be an expatriate sent abroad by the home office. Ideally, the individual occupying this position is schooled under both home- and host-country systems; if not, it is recommended that this individual should undergo at least some training in host- or home-country approaches, respectively, to doing business. This training is important because this individual is typically responsible for interpreting the predictions of the salesforce.

Salesforce composite estimates Research studies wherein sales forecasts are based on the personal observations and forecasts of the local salesforce.

Jury of Expert Opinion

Forecasts from the **jury of expert opinion** are based on the opinions of different experts about future demand. The experts' opinions are then combined, and an aggregate demand estimation is offered. Because experts could come from both home and host country, as well as other countries where other companies, or the company in question, may face similar problems, obtaining a consensus perspective or aggregate forecast may be more difficult to achieve. At the same time, the awareness of the different possible outcomes or individual perspectives may prove invaluable in gaining insight on demand, particularly for a market new to the company.

Jury of expert opinion An approach to sales forecasting based on the opinion of different experts.

The Delphi Method

The **Delphi method** entails asking a number of experts to estimate market performance, aggregating the results, and sharing this information with the said experts. This process is repeated several times, until a consensus is reached. Clearly, such an approach would be most cumbersome when dealing with a global company. First, in addition to impositions on executives' time, the company also must incur expenses related to the logistics of bringing together experts from different countries. Second, should the company attempt to use the Delphi method by mailing the forecasting surveys, there is always the risk that international mail may impose, in addition to the high likelihood of noncompliance by executives, who may perceive such an exercise as an imposition on their time.

Delphi method A method of forecasting sales by asking a number of experts to estimate market performance, aggregating the results, and sharing this information with the said experts; the process is repeated several times, until a consensus is reached.

Time Series and Econometric Models

Time series models use data of past performance to predict future market demand. Typically, these models give more weight to more recent developments. These methods assume that the future will be similar to the past. Econometric models, on the other hand, take into account different deterministic factors that affect market demand—factors that may or may not depend on past performance trends.[54]

An example of an application of econometric models to global marketing is provided by the application of an autoregressive moving average (ARMAX) to predict consumer demand for beer in the Netherlands.[55] The variables used as predictors of the demand for beer were temperature, price, consumer expenditures, and company advertising expenditures. The study concluded that advertising expenditures are not good predictors for beer demand; the authors suspect that the reason is a saturated market where all competitors advertise extensively and where additional advertising efforts may go unnoticed.

Time series and econometric models are dependent on the availability of historical data, data that is mainly available in developed countries but not in developing countries. For these markets, then, it is appropriate to estimate demand *by analogy*, noting responses of markets with similar relevant characteristics, markets with similar levels of economic development, markets with similar cultural characteristics, etc.

Analogy Methods

The **analogy method** is an estimation method that relies on developments and findings in markets with similar levels of economic development, markets where the product is in the same development state, or markets with similar cultural characteristics, or it may be based on sales of a related product in the key market of study. For example,

- To estimate anticipated adoption rate of cellular phones in Latvia, it may be appropriate to identify the proportion of new adopters in a more advanced country in the Baltics—Estonia, which is more developed—where cellular phone service is widely available, but which shares a similar history and similar geopolitics with Latvia. This is an example of *country performance analogy.*
- To estimate the adoption rate of Internet service in Sri Lanka, it may be appropriate to evaluate the adoption rate of computers in this country. This is an example of *product performance analogy.*

Typically, in the country performance analogy, adjustments are made based on development level, cultural differences, trade barriers, competition, etc. In the product performance analogy, adjustments are made for consumer traits such as purchase power, consumer innovation rate, and competitive environment, among others.

Point-of-Sale–Based Projections

Point-of-sale–based projections are made with the help of store scanners, which are increasingly used by research suppliers, particularly in the U.S. (A.C. Nielsen and Information Resources, among others), to assess market share and other relevant market dimensions. Weekly or biweekly store audits reveal the movement of goods within the store and from warehouses. Internationally, although scanning technology is widely available, it is mainly used for inventory purposes, rather than for research purposes. For example, British retailer Marks & Spencer is using

Time series and econometric models Models that use the data of past performance to predict future market demand.

Analogy method A method for estimation that relies on developments and findings in similar markets or where the product is in the same life-cycle stage.

Point-of-sale–based projections Market share and other relevant market dimensions assessed by the use of store scanners in weekly and biweekly store audits.

---

54. Ibid.

55. Philip Hans Franses, "Primary Demand for Beer in the Netherlands: An Application of ARMAX Model Specification," *Journal of Marketing Research,* May 28, 1991, pp. 240–245.

bar code and wireless local area network (LAN) technology to improve operations in its stores. The company is installing a Symbol Technologies Spectrum24 wireless LAN, mobile computers, and bar code laser scanners to increase accuracy and efficiency and to improve customer service at its 323 European-based stores; the scanners will send data over the LAN, allowing Marks & Spencer to reconfigure point-of-sale stations or add and subtract stations based on need.[56] Overall, scan rates are lower in Europe when compared to the U.S., but higher than rates elsewhere around the world (with the exception of Canada); Europe, Great Britain, and France have 100 percent scanning for most food products.[57] Surprisingly, in the U.K., unlike the U.S., consumer data collection is dominated by face-to-face interviewing, which still accounts for more than 50 percent of U.K. research, whereas retail data collection is still dominated by the conventional retail audit. The use of scanners at POS and the difference in the level of development in the major store groups make it impossible to construct a nationally representative sample of scanner stores.[58]

Chapter Summary

- **Define international marketing research and provide a description of its immense scope; offer examples of each type of research conducted in international marketing**

  International marketing research involves gathering information for international marketing decisions. It is wide in scope, covering industry research, market traits and trends, buyer behavior, and the marketing mix. Examples of product research are product testing, product package studies, and competitive product analysis. Distribution research covers areas such as import/export analysis, international channel performance and coverage, as well as plant/warehouse location studies. Promotion research has the widest scope, with studies of premiums, coupons, and deals; advertising effectiveness; media research (which is especially important in highly industrialized countries); and salesforce analyses. Pricing research involves studies projecting demand, as well as international market potential studies, sales potential studies, cost analyses, and profit analyses, among others.

- **Describe the steps involved in the international marketing research process while addressing, for each step, the international constraints involved**

  The first step of the international research process involves defining the research problem and setting the research objectives; this is usually done in conjunction with a local team and international experts and consultants. The development of the research plan involves deciding on the information sources—primary and secondary (evaluating the validity and reliability of secondary data)—and determining the appropriate research approach. The research approach may involve collecting qualitative data, using focus groups or observation methods, or quantitative data, using descriptive (surveys, content analyses) or causal research methods (experimental research). They, in turn, determine the contact methods. The next step requires the researcher to design the data collection instrument and translate it into the local language(s). Next, the sampling plan must be determined: selecting the sampling procedure, sample size, frame, and unit. Finally, the researcher must collect, analyze, and interpret the information.

- **Introduce the concept of decision support systems for international marketing and describe the sales forecasting process**

  Decision support systems represent a coordinated approach to collecting and interpreting business and environmental data. International sales forecasting techniques can be improved in this environment. Methods used in international sales forecasting are international salesforce composite estimates, jury of expert opinion, the Delphi method, time series and econometric models, analogy method, and point-of-sale–based projections, all of which can be used in an international setting with various degrees of success.

---

56. *Automatic I.D. News*, "British Retailer Goes Wireless," October 1998, Vol. 14, No. 11.

57. Gerry Eskin, "POS Scanner Data: The State of the Art, in Europe and the World," *Marketing and Research Today*, May 1994, Vol. 22, No. 2, pp. 107–108.

58. Tim Bowles, "Data Collection in the United Kingdom," *Journal of the Market Research Society*, October 1989, Vol. 31, No. 4, pp. 467–477.

Discussion Questions

Discussion Questions

1. Describe the broad scope of marketing research with a focus on promotion-related research.

2. You have been hired to evaluate the purchase behavior of adolescents in Latvia. What types of research studies could you conduct?

3. What are some of the limitations of secondary data available to international marketing researchers?

4. Describe the challenges that researchers experience when designing and administering questionnaires in countries that are culturally dissimilar from their own.

5. Discuss the quantitative data collection methods that researchers can use in an international study and the problems they pose to the validity and reliability of the findings.

6. Describe the international sales forecasting methods that marketing managers can use to better monitor and more efficiently react to information in the local environment.

International Marketing Segmentation, Targeting, and Positioning

Key Terms

accessibility
actionability
applications positioning
attribute/benefit positioning
benefit segmentation
competitor positioning
concentrated targeting
demographic segmentation
differential response
differentiated targeting
geographic segmentation
global elite
global teenagers
measurability

price/quality positioning
product class positioning
product user positioning
psychographic segmentation
segmentation
stability over time
substantiality
target market
target marketing
undifferentiated targeting
usage segmentation
use positioning
user status segmentation

Outline

Learning Objectives
7-1 The Rationale for Target
   Marketing
7-2 International Market
   Segmentation
   *7-2a Requirements for
      International
      Segmentation*
   *7-2b Macro-Segmentation:
      Country Attractiveness
      Analysis*
   *7-2c Micro-Segmentation:
      Focusing on
      the Target Consumer*
7-3 Targeting International
   Consumers
   *7-3a Target Market Decisions:
      Country Screening
      and Selection*
   *7-3b Target Market Decisions:
      The Target Market
      Strategy*
7-4 Positioning the Brand
   *7-4a Attribute/Benefit
      Positioning*
   7-4b Price/Quality Positioning
   *7-4c Use or Applications
      Positioning*
   7-4d Product User Positioning
   7-4e Product Class Positioning
   7-4f Competitor Positioning
Chapter Summary
Discussion Questions

Learning Objectives

Learning Objectives

By the end of this chapter, you should be able to:

- Identify the rationale for adopting a target marketing strategy in international markets
- Identify the requirements necessary for effective international market segmentation
- Introduce the concept of country attractiveness analysis and offer a blueprint for conducting the analysis

- Identify the bases for consumer segmentation and offer company application examples
- Describe the three targeting strategies used by companies worldwide
- Describe the six positioning strategies that international companies can use to position their brands in the minds of target consumers

World Beat is a popular genre of music; it is a mix of techno and Latin beats, hip-hop, and African or Arab beats, with a synthesized ethnic melodic touch. This music is marketed effectively to the World Beat consumer segment worldwide. Jessica, a 22-year-old Swede of African ancestry and a World Beat star in her home country, first launched her CD internationally in the Asia-Pacific region before introducing it elsewhere—with rapid success: Her album went gold instantly in South Korea and is on its way to winning other markets around the world.[1]

World Beat (groups accessible at www.cdnow.com) ranges from more traditional Europop groups such as Enigma with its haunting, sinful, seductive French whispers and interjections of Greek Orthodox church choir; to Alabina, a group whose Arabic-Latin music is heard even in U.S. supermarkets; Disidenten, a German group playing Arabic songs; and Gypsy Kings, a French group playing French music with a Latin beat. The late Israeli singer Ofra Haza attempted to bridge Israeli and Arab culture with her album "Shaday"; her song "Im Nin Alu," based on a seventeenth century poem by Rabbi Shalom Shabazi, propelled her to international superstar status.

The market for World Beat is the world music consumer. This genre of music appeals across cultures and across age groups; in Europe and Africa, listeners range from teenagers to forty-somethings! The opportunities that this segment presents to entertainment companies are immense.

This chapter will introduce concepts and illustrate practices in international target marketing. The chapter covers tools for macro- and micro-segmentation and strategies for targeting international consumers; it also identifies the different product positioning strategies that companies use in world markets.

---

1. entertainment.iafrica.com, "Jessica: Europop with Substance," September 5, 2001.

7-1 The Rationale for Target Marketing

With the exception of very narrow markets, one single company, however large its resources and capacity, could not possibly serve all customers. Consumers worldwide are too numerous, and their needs and wants are too diverse. Companies must focus on those segments that they can serve most effectively and design products and services with these segments in mind; that is, they must engage in international **target marketing.**

International target marketing is used by companies to

- Identify countries and segments of international consumers that are similar with regard to key traits, who would respond well to a product and related marketing mix (international market segmentation)
- Select the countries and segments that the company can serve most efficiently and develop products tailored to each (international market targeting)
- Offer the products to the market, communicating, through the marketing mix, product traits and benefits that differentiate it in the consumer's mind (market positioning)

Target marketing The process of focusing on those segments that the company can serve most effectively and designing products, services, and marketing programs with these segments in mind.

7-2 International Market Segmentation

As mentioned in section 7-1, international market segmentation involves identifying countries and consumers that are similar with regard to key traits, such as product-related needs and wants, and that would respond well to a product and related marketing mix. International **segmentation,** thus, must be performed at the country level (macro-segmentation) and at the consumer level (micro-segmentation).

At the country level, segmentation analysis identifies countries that are similar in aspects relevant to the company. If a company produces luxury goods, for example, economic variables can help determine whether a sufficient number of consumers can afford to purchase the company products. At the consumer level, segmentation analysis identifies consumers who are looking for the same benefits in the product. While all consumers seek an efficient mode of transportation when they purchase an automobile, they also fulfill other desires. Consumers in rural Scotland may seek a small, versatile vehicle that can maneuver through tight single-lane roads, whereas executives in Muscat and Oman (one of the United Arab Emirates) may want a luxury automobile that exudes high status and elegance to navigate on the country's impeccable roads.

Segmentation The process of identifying consumers and/or international markets that are similar with regard to key traits, such as product-related needs and wants, and that would respond well to a product and related marketing mix.

7-2a Requirements for International Segmentation

Regardless of whether the segmentation analysis is performed at the country level or at the individual consumer level, several requirements must be met for market segmentation to be effective. The requirements, which apply equally to country and consumer segmentation, are shown in Figure 7-1.

Measurability

Individual market segments should be easy to identify and measure, thus ensuring **measurability.** International market segments pose numerous challenges in this regard. First, in many developing countries, reliable population statistics, including market size and economic development data, are difficult to come by. Even if the

Measurability The ability to estimate the size of a market segment.

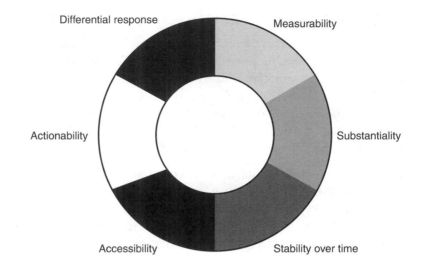

Figure 7-1
Requirements for effective international segmentation.

International Monetary Fund and other development organizations' data are reliable and valid, international companies still run into difficulties when evaluating culture-related dimensions, such as product preferences, especially food products, and benefits sought. Collecting data on such variables also presents many challenges.

For example, working backward, from product performance to segmentation, the Wonder Bra is selling very well in Islamic countries. What benefit could women seek when purchasing the Wonder Bra in an environment where many women are fully covered in thick clothing in public? Clearly, the product is not used to enhance one's attractiveness to the opposite sex. Research would find that women dress primarily to impress other women in many Islamic countries, in a friendly competitive way. To be able to reach such conclusions, the research study would have to explore motivations beyond basic product benefits. Furthermore, the subjects must be willing to share such information.

Substantiality

Substantiality The extent to which the market is large enough to warrant investment.

The segment should be large enough to warrant investment. Assuming that the segment can be measured, this step—determining **substantiality**—is relatively easy. Even if research determines that the local market segment is not large enough, it can be grouped together with an identical segment in another country and targeted jointly. Another dimension that must be evaluated is the segment's growth potential. Such data must be evaluated with surrogate statistics, such as economic development measures (i.e., as an increase in GDP per capita or income per capita), employment data, the level of foreign direct investment in the country, exports from the country, and trends in consumer spending. An important consideration here is also the intensity of competition directed at the same segment. All of these examples constitute important variables that must be evaluated to determine the market's viability in the future.

Stability over Time

Stability over time The extent to which preferences are stable, rather than changing, in a market segment.

In the past, stability of a segment over time was a primary consideration mainly for developed countries. Today, however, **stability over time** is an important consideration in a world environment where products are in different life-cycle stages and where preferences are continuously changing with the advent of the Internet and on-line ordering across borders from countries of all development levels. In a rapidly changing environment, it is important to constantly reevaluate this segment.

Accessibility

The ability to communicate with the **target market,** determining the market's **accessibility,** is essential as well. Internationally, the differences in language in individual countries may pose obstacles, greatly increasing the cost of advertising and other promotion. Marketing in large emerging markets, such as India and China, could present challenges for different reasons: Communicating with Indian consumers necessitates expensive translation into the local languages, whereas communicating with Chinese consumers may be difficult because the large rural population has only limited access to technology. The ability to serve the market is also essential. Companies should be able to freely access the market; the market must be open to international companies and reachable (its topography should permit access to the target market).

Actionability

The market should respond to the marketing strategies used; the segment should be actionable, assuming the company is targeting the market with the appropriate marketing mix. Consider, for example, the Colgate-Palmolive strategy for Latin America and the Balkans. In both markets, the company noted that its dishwashing liquid was not selling well. Research revealed, for this large market segment, a different approach to washing dishes—using soap slivers in a tub. As soon as the company developed a tub with dishwashing paste and promoted the product to the market, sales took off. The segment responded as intended to the strategy: The segment was **actionable.**

Differential Response

The segments should be easy to distinguish from each other and should respond differently from other market segments to marketing strategies; they should have a noticeable **differential response.** If consumers all over the world are similar and/or have identical preferences—and this is hardly the case—there is no need for international target marketing.

7-2b Macro-Segmentation: Country Attractiveness Analysis

Companies have different criteria that they consider essential for committing to a particular market. PepsiCo International did not consider profit as the main criterion when it approached the Former Soviet Union to establish a counter-trade agreement; rather, market size and the ultimate potential of the market were the company's primary concerns. As a first step in the segmentation process, companies engage in macro-segmentation, grouping countries based on such criteria as economic performance, evaluating the potential of a particular market; on their political, legal, and financial environment; on their marketing support infrastructure; on the company brand's standing or potential standing relative to existing competition; and on the degree of market fit with company resources, policies, and goals, among others. They, in turn, are used in the screening process to select and target the countries that present the highest potential to the company.

Target market Consumers and/or international markets that are similar in aspects relevant to the company.

Accessibility The ability to communicate with the international target market.

Actionability The extent to which the target market segment is responsive to the marketing strategies used.

Differential response The extent to which international market segments respond differently to marketing strategies.

The following are some criteria that firms could use to group countries, based on which they can select those countries that offer the most opportunity for the company and that should be targeted:

- Market potential
- The political, legal, and financial environment of the country
- The marketing support infrastructure in the country
- Brand/company franchise relative to competing products/companies
- Degree of market fit with company policies, goals, and resources

Market Potential

Countries can be grouped based on market potential. The potential of a market can be evaluated based on the rate of economic development, as expressed through validated, reliable market indicators, such as

- Gross Domestic Product (GDP) per capita
- Industrial and agricultural sectors statistics
- Market size and potential
- Consumer buying power
- International investment figures, such as foreign direct investment data and other trade statistics

Such indicators identify countries and markets where the company should invest important resources and engage in long-term commitment. Attractive big emerging markets, such as Brazil or China, have initially presented many challenges to international companies. Brazil in the 1970s and 1980s was plagued by runaway inflation and instability, whereas China was an unpredictable market closed to international scrutiny and influence.

With time, both countries have opened their markets to international investment, which has led to rapid economic development and prosperity. In the case of Brazil, statistics demonstrate an enormous growth. With a population of more than 160 million, of which almost half are under 20 years old, and with a GDP growing from US$800 billion in 1997 to more than US$5 trillion in the 2001, Brazil is performing very well. As a result, it has become a viable trade partner of the United States and the European Union, despite a few setbacks; Brazil was recently twice rescued by the International Monetary Fund.

Similar potential is now presented by the countries of the Former Soviet Union. These countries, despite being plagued by inflation and instability, all have a literate, educated workforce and excess of highly qualified labor on one hand and a consuming public that is eager to experience new products on the other. Among attractive markets of the Former Soviet Union are the Baltic Republics (Estonia, Latvia, and Lithuania), Russia, and Belarus, all of which are being actively targeted by multinationals. Of possible interest in the future are the Asian Republics of the Former Soviet Union, such as Armenia, Azerbaijan, Georgia, Kazakhstan, the Kyrgyz Republic, Turkmenistan, and Uzbekistan. A number of these countries have made important inroads on the path to economic development and prosperity: Kazakhstan and the Kyrgyz Republic are rapidly developing their banking systems and have both adopted pro-market structural reforms. Uzbekistan is not far behind, nor is oil-rich Turkmenistan.[2] Many companies that have initially only exported to these countries are now committing greater resources and embarking in some form of foreign direct investment.

---

2. *The Banker*, "Kyrgyzstan Leads the Banking Pack," March 2001, Vol. 151, No. 901, pp. 53–54.

The Political, Legal, and Financial Environment of the Country

Countries also can be grouped based on their political, legal, and financial environment. Some of the following criteria should be considered when evaluating a potential country for entry:

- Ethnic conflict in the region
- History of war engagement
- Antiforeigner rhetoric
- Recent nationalization activity
- Legal ambiguity—especially in business
- Trade barriers erected by government to protect local business
- Exchange rate controls

Companies are not likely to succeed in markets where there is high political risk. Sri Lanka, an attractive small country located southeast of the Indian subcontinent, is no longer even a viable export market. Tamil separatists have actively targeted Sri Lanka's airport and, consequently have practically demolished an economy that was already on the decline.

Even oil-rich countries could present a risk for companies considering entering these markets. Sudan, for example, discovered substantial oil reserves recently; however, its modest exports (primarily to Singapore) to date have only further fueled an ethnic civil war that has been raging for more than two decades. Although exporting to Sudan is still a viable entry-mode alternative, the country undoubtedly still represents risks for long-term investment.

Ambiguities in the legal system create an environment that renders companies vulnerable to competitive theft, lack of trademark protection, bribery pressures, and employee theft. In such an environment, where everything is perceived as allowed unless expressly forbidden, even exporting could pose difficulties. For example, it could force firms to incur bribery costs that cannot be justified to the headquarters, nor to the home-country government, for mere access to the market. Finally, exchange rate controls could restrict the types of products that can be exported to the target market and/or impede the repatriation of profits.

One related issue is whether the country is a member of the World Trade Organization or of a regional block, such as the European Union or the Southern Cone Common Market (MERCOSUR). Countries that adhere to regulations of the WTO and that have the supranational controls of regional integration are more likely to have a stable environment that promotes trade and investment.

The Marketing Support Infrastructure in the Country

The marketing support infrastructure of the target country is an important determinant of country attractiveness. Important to international firms are the availability and reliability of distribution and logistics providers in order to ensure that the product is delivered in a timely fashion at locations convenient to consumers.

Countries also can be grouped based on the availability of competent partners for firms contemplating international partnerships. A firm entering a new market should have access to capable local firms. In many developing countries, only few such firms may be available, and all other competitors will attempt to approach them. For instance, for large multinationals attempting to enter the Turkish market, Sabanci Holdings is in great demand and already boasts joint-venture and distribution partners in companies as varied as Carrefour supermarkets, Danone dairy products, Dresdner Bank, DuPont, IBM, Mitsubishi, Altria (formerly Philip Morris), and Toyota, to name a few.

The information technology available to members of the local distribution chain is an important consideration in that it maximizes supply chain efficiencies and minimizes warehousing and logistics costs to the company. The level of local telecommunications development is also essential in ensuring adequate data flow and access to suppliers, clients, and company headquarters. Countries also should be evaluated on the availability of adequate local advertising support, such as local advertising talent and open access to media for advertising and other communication purposes. Finally, the availability of other service providers, such as marketing research firms, financial firms, and management consulting firms, is also essential for company performance in the market.

Brand/Company Franchise Relative to Competing Products/Companies

Markets where a brand or company name is already established with local consumers, either by reputation, through advertising, or experience (for consumers who have bought the product abroad or have heard of the company) offer greater potential to the company.

This is especially true if the company has only few viable direct competitors. Markets can thus be segmented based on the reputation of the product and/or company in the market, and on the competitive density in the market for the company's products. Here, a related dimension is also useful: that of *lead country* (a country where products are first adopted) versus *lag country* (a country where products are last adopted). The lead/lag concept also is closely linked to the level of economic development and is particularly relevant to firms at the forefront of technology. These firms usually first introduce their products in lead countries.

Degree of Market Fit with Company Policies, Goals, and Resources

For companies that have the resources and the goal to saturate the world market, such as McDonald's and Coca-Cola, no market is too small. Other companies that have the resources but whose products cater only to the luxury market will most likely ignore countries with a limited number of elite consumers and focus on industrialized countries, or countries with substantial revenues from national resources, such as petrol and diamonds. Yet other companies have limited resources and can afford to target consumers in only one or a few countries. For these companies it is essential to select those markets that are perceived as the most appropriate for their goals and that provide the lowest level of risk.

7-2c Micro-Segmentation: Focusing on the Target Consumer

The purpose of micro-segmentation is to identify clusters of consumers that respond in a similar fashion to a company's marketing strategies. Identifying individual market segments will enable the company to produce products that meet the precise needs of target consumers with a marketing mix that is appropriately tailored for those segments. The international company typically conducts extensive marketing research to identify such segments.

Bases for Segmentation

In the process of analyzing consumer demand and identifying clusters of consumers that respond similarly to marketing strategies, firms must identify those bases for segmentation that are most relevant for its products or service offerings.

Demographic and Psychographic Segmentation

Demographics are statistics that describe the population, such as age, gender, race, income, education, occupation, social class, life-cycle stage, and household size. Demographics are easy to measure and to compare across countries; for this reason, they are widely used by international companies.

There are many differences between consumers worldwide with regard to **demographic segmentation** variables. The following few examples demonstrate how these differences have important implications for marketing:

- *Age*—Countries that have a rapidly aging population (the Scandinavian countries, for example) present different challenges and opportunities to international firms than countries with half of their population under the age of twenty (such as Brazil and most countries in Sub-Saharan Africa).
- *Urbanization and social class*—Industrialized countries, such as the United States, Japan, and the countries of Western Europe, are primarily urban and have a large middle class with substantial buying power. China's rural consumers are poor and have limited buying power; its urban consumers fall into four segments: "working poor" and "salaried class"—together accounting for 80 percent of the urban population; "the little rich," 15 percent of the urban population; and "yuppies," representing nearly 5 percent of the urban households.[3] Although multinationals such as Coca-Cola and Kodak actively target middle class consumers in the industrialized countries with their global brands, in China, they target their global brands primarily to yuppies; for the remaining 95 percent of the population, they have developed or acquired local brands in addition to their premium global brands.[4]
- *Education*—Most developed countries, countries that were formerly communist, and countries that are under a communist rule (China, for example) have a high literacy rate and heavily emphasize education. In contrast, countries in Sub-Saharan Africa have a lower literacy rate; here, education is a privilege. Companies that target these consumers have to adapt the marketing mix, describing pictorially product use in their communications. Countries where education is stressed will present opportunities for educational institutions intending to expand globally, to firms selling training technology and software, etc.

Demographics are closely linked to psychographics, which include lifestyles, values, attitudes, interests, and opinions. It is difficult to describe psychographics without demographics. Cultural variables such as religion, norms, and language influence consumer product preferences as well. As such, these variables can be used as bases for segmentation. For example, Hofstede's dimensions—described in Chapter 5, "Cultural Influences on International Marketing"—can be used to segment countries based on individualism/collectivism, masculinity/femininity, uncertainty/avoidance, and power/distance. A study conducted with consumers in Europe[5] found that consumers in the Scandinavian countries have a small

Demographic segmentation
The process of identifying market segments based on age, gender, race, income, education, occupation, social class, life-cycle stage, and household size.

3. Geng Cui and Qiming Liu, "Executive Insights: Emerging Market Segments in a Transitional Economy: A Study of Urban Consumers in China," *Journal of International Marketing*, Spring 2001, Vol. 9, No. 1, pp. 84–106.

4. Ibid.

5. Sudhir H. Kale, "Grouping Euroconsumers: A Culture-Based Clustering Approach," *Journal of International Marketing*, 1995, Vol. 3, No. 3, pp. 35–38.

power/distance (are more egalitarian), have a low uncertainty/avoidance (take more risks), rate high on individualism, and have a low level of masculinity (low ambition and competitiveness). These consumers share certain traits that marketers can stress: They seek variety and prefer environmentally friendly products.

Many management consulting firms have come up with systems for segmenting consumers, clustering them on different behavioral and psychological dimensions, or **psychographic segmentation.** In the United States, a popular classification system is Acorn (http://demographics.caci.com/products/life_seg. htm), which classifies individuals based on ZIP code. Another classification of lifestyles is provided by SRI Consulting Business Intelligence, which offers the VALS 2 (http:// future.sri. com/VALS/presurvey.shtml) psychographic consumer segmentation system. Upon completing a questionnaire containing lifestyle and demographic questions, individual respondents are categorized based on resources and on the extent to which they are action oriented. VALS also has a survey that is especially designed for the Japanese market.

Other approaches to psychographic segmentation have been used in Europe: The Anticipating Change in Europe program examined different types of European consumer segments. One large study conducted within this framework used a representative quota sample of 7,600 Europeans from the continent's five major luxury markets, attempting to identify the relationship between culture, trend following, income, and the acquisition of luxury goods.[6]

Consumers worldwide also share traits, presenting important opportunities for standardized marketing. Among the global psycho-demographic (a combination of psychographic and demographic segments) segments that have emerged are the following:

- **Global teenagers**—Psychographically, teenagers are described as astute consumers with precise desires for brand name clothing products and entertainment. They purchase Levi's and Diesel jeans, Nike shoes, and Ralph Lauren clothing. They listen to Madonna and World Beat music (introduced at the beginning of this chapter), go to discos, and see newly released movies. Marketers find this segment particularly attractive: Coca-Cola has successfully targeted global teenagers with messages that use local and international celebrity endorsers; Nike is continually producing new designs for them.
- **Global elite**—The global elite have the highest income of all consumers. From a psychographic perspective, they travel the globe, often have homes in more than one country, and spend money on luxury brands, such as Rolex, Prada, and Mercedes (E-Class and beyond). The marketing mix typically used to target this group focuses on status: exclusive distribution, high price, and status-oriented advertising messages.

An interesting segment is a combination of the two, a youth-driven Euroculture where national heritage has become less important for a multi-lingual, educated, and well-traveled cosmopolitan segment with commonalities based on continental values and lifestyles. For such consumers, European MTV can be used effectively to sell CDs and related products.[7] This Pan-European segment covers a broad spectrum of male and female consumers from ages 12 to 45.

Psychographic segmentation
The use of values, attitudes, interests, and other cultural variables to segment consumers.

Global teenagers
A psycho-demographic global group of teenagers considered to be astute consumers with precise desires for brand name clothing products and entertainment.

Global elite
A psycho-demographic group worldwide characterized by high income and desire for status brands and exclusive distribution.

---

6. Bernard Dubois and Patrick Duquesne, "The Market for Luxury Goods: Income Versus Culture, *European Journal of Marketing,* 1993, Vol. 27, No. 1, pp. 35–44.

7. Art Weinstein, "A Primer for Global Marketers," *Marketing News,* June 20, 1994, Vol. 28, No. 13, p. 4.

Benefit Segmentation

Benefit segmentation also is a very useful tool for identifying uniform consumer segments. Marketers who understand the motivation behind consumer purchases will be able to send the appropriate message to the relevant market segments. Internationally, important differences exist between the benefits sought from purchasing a particular product. Consumers in the United States purchase soft drinks such as Coke and Pepsi to quench their thirst on a regular basis. In Eastern Europe, these brands are purchased primarily as special-occasion drinks.

In other examples, the majority of consumers in developing countries are not as much interested in brand names as they are in product performance and value. Marketing strategies catering to these preferences have succeeded in China: Philips Electronics introduced a very popular combination video/CD player, which Chinese consumers perceived as good value for the money.[8] And, although consumers in the United States seek speedy service, quality food, and convenience in fast-food chains, consumers in emerging markets are particularly attracted to the clean environment, pleasant ambience, polite staff,[9] and air conditioning.

Usage and User Status Segmentation

Usage rate indicates the extent to which individuals are

- Nonusers
- Occasional users
- Medium users
- Heavy users

Consumers worldwide can be segmented based on these **usage segmentation** dimensions. Segments of consumers identified as heavy users of a product category would constitute prime target markets for new brands in the category. For example, French women are heavy users of perfume, have a refined understanding of scent, and use different brands (often of the same company) at different times of day and for different occasions. Similarly, German, Dutch, and Belgian consumers are heavy users of beer. In each country, hundreds of breweries carry specialty beers, and each country is also an exporter of global beer brands.

User status refers to the status as

- Users of competitors' products (nonuser)
- Ex-users
- Potential users
- First-time users
- Regular users

In terms of **user status segmentation,** the ideal consumer is the regular heavy user! Companies introducing a product for the first time to a market of nonusers face enormous and costly challenges, in that they have to educate consumers about the product and convince them to buy, but these companies also can reap huge rewards, especially if they are first in the market. The paper towel offering in Europe was rather limited before the introduction of the Procter & Gamble Bounty brand; consumers typically used cloth towels in the kitchen because the brands available locally did not have sufficient absorption capacity for cleaning jobs. Bounty introduced its quality, heavy-duty paper towels in the late 1990s,

Benefit segmentation
The process of identifying international market segments based on important differences between the benefits sought by the target market from purchasing a particular product.

Usage segmentation
The process of segmenting markets based on the extent to which consumers are nonusers, occasional users, medium users, and heavy users of a product.

User status segmentation
The process of determining the status as users of competitors' products, ex-users, potential users, first-time users, and regular users.

---

8. Cui and Liu, "Executive Insights," pp. 84–106.

9. Ibid.

accompanied by heavy promotion—particularly direct mail samples. The brand quickly took off, and now most households have an accessory previously nonexistent in European households: a paper towel holder.

Geographic Segmentation

Geographic segmentation can be performed at the macro-segmentation level—country analysis, membership in international trade forums, regional blocks, etc.—as well as within the country. Consumers differ within countries with regard to demographics and psychographics, such as ethnicity, religion, and language spoken. Even in small countries such as Switzerland, the marketing mix needs to be adapted for German Swiss, French Swiss, and Italian Swiss consumers; they constitute segments that differ not only linguistically, but also with regard to other aspects of culture, and consequently are likely to respond differently to marketing strategies. Belgium also is a case in point: A Flemish culture thrives in the north; in the French-speaking south, people view themselves as Wallonians rather than Europeans or Belgians; and a small German community exists in the southeast.[10]

Geographic segmentation
Market segmentation based on geographic location, such as country or region.

7-3 Targeting International Consumers

7-3a Target Market Decisions: Country Screening and Selection

Companies engage in processes that involve extensive evaluation of countries' attractiveness for the purpose of market entry. In this evaluative process, a company must ensure that it does not overlook countries with potential and that it does not target markets in countries that do not provide sufficient potential and/or that present a high risk. To ensure that markets that present the most promise to the company—based on the company's goals and resources—are selected, countries are submitted to a screening process. Most often, screening of potential markets follows a variant of these three stages:

- Assigning an importance score to country screening criteria
- Evaluating country performance on each of the screening criteria
- Calculating the country attractiveness score

Assigning an Importance Score to Country Screening Criteria

An international company would typically aggregate a selection of criteria—discussed in section 7-2b, "Macro-Segmentation: Country Attractiveness Analysis"—that the company deemed important. Among these criteria are market potential, determined using economic indicators; the degree of political and financial stability; the extent to which the legal system is transparent and predictable; the state of the marketing infrastructure in the country; the degree to which consumers have a preference for company brands; the extent of competitive intensity in the market; and the market fit with company goals, policies, and resources. The criteria deemed important are selected from brand managers in different international markets, salespeople, industry country specialists working for management consulting firms, and international suppliers and distributors, among others. Each criterion is then assigned an importance weight that denotes the extent to which the company considers a particular trait important in its decision to enter the market.

---

10. Weinstein, "A Primer for Global Marketers," p. 4.

Evaluating Country Performance on Each of the Screening Criteria

In the second stage of country screening and selection, potential target countries are rated on each of the criteria enumerated. The rating process may involve the same evaluators as in the first stage.

Calculating the Country Attractiveness Score

In the third stage of country screening and selection, the importance score is multiplied by the performance score for each of the screening variables. The total score for each country is then calculated by adding the resulting scores; this is the country attractiveness score that can be used to compare between potential target countries.

7-3b Target Market Decisions: The Target Market Strategy

Companies that have ample resources can, and often do, address the needs of all segments of consumers. Procter & Gamble, Henkel, and Kraft attempt to target all consumers with the products they sell, filling the supermarket and discount store shelf space with what seemingly are competing brands and saturating the media with their communication, meeting all related needs of the global consumer at a nice profit. Other companies with sufficient resources choose to focus on one well-established brand, improving it continuously, offering alternatives under the same umbrella brand name. Boeing uses such a strategy and, to date, it has only one true direct competitor—Airbus Industries. Not all international companies have the resources of the companies mentioned here. Frequently, small and medium-size businesses are quite successful internationally, as they are in the home-country market, by best addressing the needs of one segment, or a niche. One common trait of all these international companies is that they research very closely their consumers, and target and position their products accordingly.

Companies can use three main strategies to target their international markets: differentiated, concentrated, and undifferentiated (see Figure 7-2).

Differentiated Targeting Strategy

Companies that use a **differentiated targeting** strategy identify, or even create, market segments that want different benefits from a product and target them with different brands, using different marketing strategies. Some companies have the necessary resources to offer at least one product to every conceivable market segment. Procter & Gamble, for example, offers a variety of laundry detergents in North America: Bold, Cheer, Dreft, Era, Febreze Clean Wash, Gain, Ivory Snow, and Tide. To European consumers, the company offers Ace, Alfa, Ariel, Bold 2 in 1, Bonux Biomat, Dash, Daz, Dreft, Fairy, Moher, Tide, Tix, and Vizir.[11] Each of these laundry detergents appeals to a different market: consumers who want a detergent that has an excellent cleaning ability, consumers who need whitening, consumers who need fabric softening agents in the washing process, consumers who need a product for sensitive fabrics or for babies' sensitive skin, and consumers who may be allergic, to name a few.

Differentiated targeting
A targeting strategy identifying market segments with different preferences for a particular product category and targeting each segment with different brands and different marketing strategies.

Concentrated Targeting Strategy

Not all companies can afford to offer something for everyone. Not all companies want to meet the needs of all consumers. In fact, many companies select only one

---

11. See www.pg.com.

Figure 7-2
International targeting
strategies.

Concentrated targeting
The process of selecting only one
market segment and targeting it
with one single brand.

market, and segment and target it with one single brand, using a **concentrated targeting** strategy. Mont Blanc, a company manufacturing pens and fountain pens, offers a relatively limited product selection that it markets using the same theme worldwide—"the art of writing." The product is targeted at the professional class.

Companies that cannot afford to compete in a mature market with an oligopoly may choose to pursue a small segment—a niche. This option may be the only one available for the company's limited resources. Retailers often use a niching strategy—even international retailers, such as The Body Shop, catering to consumers who are environmentally concerned and who want to purchase natural products that have not been tested on animals. An Amsterdam retailer called de Witte Tanden-Winkel (the White Tooth Shop) shows how a small firm can compete successfully using niche marketing: It sells toothbrushes, floss, and dental products—and nothing more.[12]

Undifferentiated Targeting Strategies and Standardization

The existence of similar consumer needs worldwide presents opportunities for international firms. They can reap the benefits of standardization by achieving economies of scale in the manufacturing process, in distribution, and in promotion. Pure standardization can be described as an **undifferentiated targeting** strategy, where the product is aimed at the market using a single strategy regardless of the number of countries targeted, and regardless of the locations where it is marketed.

Yet even products that are created as pure global brands, such as Coke, are not marketed using a standardized, undifferentiated strategy. Coke is sold primarily in

Undifferentiated targeting
A targeting strategy aiming the
product at the market using a
single strategy, regardless of the
number of segments.

12. Weinstein, "A Primer for Global Marketers," p. 4.

recyclable glass and plastic bottles requiring a high deposit in Africa and Europe, whereas, in the United States, it is sold in disposable cans and plastic bottles. Its taste differs depending on the market. Diet Coke is sold as Coca-Cola Light elsewhere in the world. Heineken, the Dutch beer that bills itself as the world's most international brewery, uses a global positioning strategy of premium pricing and high quality, whereas, in Holland, the beer is positioned as a popular-priced product and usually costs no more than mineral water in most bars and restaurants.[13] The Nissan Sentra name was created by a U.S. research firm as a global brand to avoid language translation blunders; yet Sentra in Holland is called the Nissan Sunny and other Nissan brands include Bluebird, Cherry, and Micra.[14]

Certain products, such as food and culture-bound products, and most services do not lend themselves to a standardized strategy; they need to be customized to meet the specific needs and preferences of consumers. In general, it is advisable that firms standardize the marketing effort over similar worldwide segments and differentiate it across dissimilar worldwide segments.[15]

7-4 Positioning the Brand

Positioning entails placing the brand in the consumer's mind in relation to other competing products, based on product traits and benefits that are relevant to the consumer. Such a process entails identifying the international and local competitors, determining how the competitors are perceived and evaluated by local consumers, determining the competitors' positions in the consumers' mind, analyzing the customers, selecting the position, and monitoring it.[16]

Brands are positioned using a theme—a unique selling proposition. This theme could be unique to each market, for companies that customize their offering to local markets, or uniform, throughout the world. A third approach also is common: a uniform positioning strategy that still allows local offices freedom for adaptation, if necessary. Coca-Cola, for example, formulates its worldwide positioning at its Atlanta headquarters but enables its affiliates in different markets to alter the strategy as needed.

7-4a Attribute/Benefit Positioning

Procter & Gamble focuses on product attributes and benefits to position its products. An **attribute/benefit positioning strategy** uses product or service attributes and benefits to position it in the consumers' mind relative to competitors' products and services. The following are examples of product positioning by the company:[17]

- Bold is positioned as a powder laundry detergent with fabric softening and pill/fuzz removal.
- Cheer, in powder or liquid, with or without bleach, is positioned as protecting against fading, color transfer, and fabric wear.

Attribute/benefit positioning
Positioning that communicates product attributes and benefits, differentiating each brand from the other company brands and from those of competitors.

---

13. Ibid.

14. Ibid.

15. See Imad B. Baalbaki and Naresh K. Malhotra, "Marketing Management Bases for International Market Segmentation: An Alternate Look at the Standardization/Customization Debate," *International Marketing Review*, 1993, Vol. 10, No. 1, pp. 19–44; and, by the same authors, "Standardization Versus Customization in International Marketing: An Investigation Using Bridging Conjoint Analysis," *Journal of the Academy of Marketing Science*, 1995, Vol. 23, No. 3, pp. 182–194.

16. Adapted from David A. Aaker and Gary J. Shansby, "Positioning Your Product," *Business Horizons,* May/June 1982, Vol. 25, No. 3, pp. 56–62.

17. See www.pg.com.

- Dreft is positioned as a detergent that removes tough baby stains and protects garment colors.
- Gain, as a liquid and powder detergent, is positioned as having exceptional cleaning and whitening.
- P&G's premium product worldwide, Tide, in powder or liquid, with or without bleach, is positioned as a laundry detergent with exceptional cleaning, whitening, and stain removal.

Such precise positioning, which is reflected in the company's communication with its respective segments, clearly differentiates each brand from the other company brands and from those of competitors such as Unilever and Colgate-Palmolive.

7-4b Price/Quality Positioning

Price/quality positioning
A strategy whereby products and services are positioned as offering the best value for the money.

Products and services can be positioned as offering the best value for the money. The **price/quality positioning** strategy is especially useful for companies marketing in developing countries. Manufacturers such as Toyota, Daewoo, and Philips and retailers such as Wal-Mart and Sears emphasize the value aspect of their offerings.

Alternatively, products and services can be positioned at the other end of the price/quality continuum, as the best product that money can buy. In addition to stressing high price and high quality, such positioning also entails an exclusive distribution or access, an expert salesforce and service, and advertising in publications aimed at the global elite. Mercedes-Benz claims that, in a perfect world, everyone would drive a Mercedes. Kempinski Hotels and Resorts, an upscale German chain, "reflects the finest traditions of European hospitality, luxurious accommodation, superb cuisine and unrivalled facilities—complemented by impeccable service."[18]

7-4c Use or Applications Positioning

Use positioning The process of marketing a very precise product application that differentiates it in the consumers' minds from other products that have a more general use.

Applications positioning
The marketing of a very precise product application that is differentiated in the consumers' minds from other products that have a more general use.

Uses or applications are often used to position products in the **use positioning** or **applications positioning** strategies, respectively. Procter & Gamble's Era is positioned as a high-technology detergent that pre-treats and washes fabrics to suspend dirt. This very precise application differentiates it in the consumers' minds from other laundry detergents that have a more general use.

Sometimes the uses or applications differ from one market to another: A bicycle manufacturer would most likely position its offerings in Asia and Europe as efficient transportation machines, whereas, in the United States, it would position them as high-performance recreation instruments.

7-4d Product User Positioning

Product user positioning
A positioning strategy that focuses on the product user, rather than on the product.

The **product user positioning** strategy focuses on the product user, rather than on the product. The marketing mix for the Mont Blanc pen is targeted at the business executive anywhere in the world. The pen is usually pictured along with a quality business letterhead, with a passport, and/or with an attaché case. In this case, the product is understood to be among the highest quality pens around, so it receives only associative emphasis.

---

18. See www.kempinski.com

7-4e Product Class Positioning

Disney sells magic, not just entertainment. Harley sells excitement, not just motor-cycles. And Parliament sells glamorous, romantic America all over the world, not just cigarettes. Products using a **product class positioning** strategy differentiate themselves as leaders in a product category, as they define it.

7-4f Competitor Positioning

When a firm compares its brand with those of competitors, it uses a **competitor positioning** strategy. Some comparisons are direct, if the local legal environment allows it. Others are somewhat subtle. When Airbus asks readers of *The Financial Times* if they would be more comfortable with two or four engines when they are up in the air, it makes implicit reference to Boeing.

All positioning, ultimately, is relative to competition, only not always explic-itly so. Even symbols hint at competition: Merrill Lynch is bullish on the market (it is embodied by the bull); all other competitors are probably wimps. Quick, a local competitor of McDonald's in France, advertises cheaper prices: Its restau-rants are quick and they are cheaper than McDonald's—and they are right across the street. *The New York Times*' positioning as "all the news that's fit to print" ulti-mately states that, if it is not published there, it is not newsworthy. (This, of course, may be problematic because the paper is sold all over the world—even where the New York Metro section has minimal relevance to local readers.)

> **Product class positioning**
> A strategy used to differentiate a company as a leader in a product category, as defined by the respective company.
>
> **Competitor positioning**
> The process of comparing the firm's brand with those of competitors, directly or indirectly.

Chapter Summary

- **Identify the rationale for adopting a target marketing strategy in international markets**
  International target marketing is used to identify coun-tries and segments of international consumers that are similar with regard to key traits, who would respond to a particular marketing mix (i.e., to segment the market); to select the countries and segments that the company can serve most efficiently and develop products tailored to each (i.e., to target the market); and to offer the prod-ucts to the market, communicating, through the market-ing mix (i.e., positioning), product traits and benefits that differentiate it in the consumers' minds.

- **Identify the requirements necessary for effective international market segmentation**
  For segmentation to be effective, segments must be easy to measure, stable over time, accessible, actionable, and respond differentially from other segments to a com-pany's marketing strategy.

- **Introduce the concept of country attractiveness analysis and offer a blueprint for conducting the analysis**
  Country attractiveness can be assessed by measuring market potential using indicators such as GDP per

capita, industrial and agricultural sectors statistics, mar-ket size, and consumer buying power. It also can be assessed by evaluating international investment figures, such as foreign direct investment data and other trade statistics; the political, legal, and financial environment in the country; the existing marketing support infra-structure; the existing brand and/or company franchise for the product and/or company, and for competitors' products and/or companies; and the degree of market fit with company policies, objectives, and resources.

- **Identify the bases for consumer segmentation and offer company application examples**
  Consumers are segmented on demographics, psycho-graphics, geography, usage and user status, and benefits sought from purchasing the product or service. Interna-tional firms segment based on the criteria that are most appropriate for their product or service. The job of the international marketing manager is facilitated by the emergence of homogeneous demographic segments worldwide, such as global teenagers and the global elite.

- **Describe the three targeting strategies used by companies worldwide**
  These strategies are differentiated marketing, whereby companies address the needs of different segments by offering them different brands and using different marketing mix strategies; concentrated marketing, whereby companies address a single consumer segment that is large and stable enough to warrant the investment; and undifferentiated marketing, whereby a company can reap the benefits of standardization by using the same strategy to market to all consumers worldwide.

- **Describe the six positioning strategies that international companies can use to position their brands in the minds of target consumers**
  International companies can position products by focusing on product attributes or benefits; by positioning the brand as a high-price/high-quality product or as the best value for the money; by positioning the brand based on use or applications; by positioning the brand based on product users; or by positioning it as the best product in its class.

Discussion Questions

1. International marketing managers use a number of criteria to ensure that segments are useful. Describe the effective types of segmentation and offer examples for each.

2. Macro-segmentation refers to country-level segmentation, and micro-segmentation refers to consumer-level segmentation. What bases and strategies do marketing managers use for segmenting their international markets using macro- and micro-segmentation?

3. Describe the principal targeting strategies. Go to the Mercedes USA (www.mercedes.com) home page. What targeting strategy does the company use? Explain.

4. Go to the SRI VALS web page (http://www.sric-bi.com/VALS/types.shtml) and read the description of each population segment. Take the test to learn more about yourself (http://www.sric-bi.com/VALS/presurvey.shtml). Also go to the ACORN web page and take the test (http://demographics.caci.com/free_samples/zip_code_searches.htm). Based on VALS and ACORN, what segments would you ascribe to Mercedes users?

5. What are the six positioning strategies? What strategies does Mercedes USA use for its U.S. market? Does Mercedes use different strategies for its international market? (Go to the other English-language Mercedes sites to answer this question.)

The International Marketing Plan and Entry Mode Selection

Key Terms

consortia
contract manufacturing
cooperative exporting
direct exporting
distribution alliance
entry mode
franchisee
franchising
franchisor
greenfielding
indirect exporting

joint venture
licensee
licensing
licensor
manufacturing alliance
marketing alliance
mother henning
piggybacking
strategic alliance
wholly owned subsidiary

Outline

Learning Objectives
8-1 Developing an International
    Marketing Strategy
8-2 Developing an International
    Marketing Plan
8-3 Deciding on the
    International Entry Mode
  8-3a Indirect Exporting
  8-3b Direct Exporting
  8-3c Licensing
  8-3d Franchising
  8-3e Joint Ventures
  8-3f Consortia
  8-3g Wholly Owned
      Subsidiaries
  8-3h Branch Offices
  8-3i Strategic Alliances
Chapter Summary
Discussion Questions

Learning Objectives

Learning Objectives

By the end of this chapter, you should be able to:

- Develop a general understanding of international marketing strategy at the different levels of the international organization and provide some insights into the international marketing planning process of selected companies

- Offer an understanding of company entry mode selection and the risks involved at each level
- Describe different types of strategic alliances involving international companies

Many international companies use strategic alliances to broaden their market access and appeal and to take advantage of economies of scale. Airlines become instant world-class carriers by establishing strategic alliances. For example, Delta Airlines started new partnerships with Air France, AeroMexico, Air Jamaica, China Southern, Czech Airlines, Korean Air, Singapore Airlines, and South African Airlines, to name a few. These partnerships involve, in addition to mutual partner booking in areas not serviced by the airline, other types of advantages that ultimately benefit consumers, such as a frequent-flyer miles exchange. Other airlines actually share routes, with a flight bearing numbers of two airlines. Such sharing enables firms to have multiple flight options to a destination; it also lowers airport access fees. Examples of airlines sharing routes are United Airlines with German company Lufthansa, KLM Dutch Royal Airlines with Northwest (Northwest-KLM), and KLM with Alitalia.

As companies go into new territories to take advantage of opportunities worldwide, they find that the right marketing strategy will offer them a significant competitive advantage. After deciding which market to target, based on the macro- and micro-segmentation analyses and screening processes described in Chapter 7, "International Marketing Segmentation, Targeting, and Positioning," and selecting the product mix with which to target the respective market or markets, the company must develop an overall marketing plan and select the entry mode.

This chapter will offer an overview of international marketing strategy and provide insights into the international marketing planning process of selected companies. The chapter also will cover international entry mode selection and the control and risks that each entry mode choice will provide.

8-1 Developing an International Marketing Strategy

An international marketing strategy involves developing and maintaining a strategic fit between the international company's objectives, competencies, and resources and the challenges presented by its international market or markets. As such, the international strategic plan forges a link between the company's resources and its international goals and objectives in a complex, continuously changing international environment. Given the changing nature of the environment, the international company's strategic plan cannot afford a typical long-term focus (a five- or ten-year plan); rather, the planning process must be systematic and continuous, and it must re-evaluate objectives in light of new opportunities and potential threats.

Another dimension of international marketing strategy is linked to the company's commitment to its international markets. Some companies use international marketing only to test the waters or to unload overproduction. This approach to international marketing, although it might open long-term opportunities to the company, does not indicate a substantial commitment to internationalization and is not a premise for success in the long term in international markets. A long-term international commitment that entails substantial investment in terms of resources and personnel is likely to bring the company the greatest rewards in the long run. Such a strategy will make the company a stronger competitor in the world market, as well as at home.

International strategic planning takes place at different levels (see Figure 8-1):

- At the *corporate level,* the strategic plan allocates resources and establishes objectives for the whole enterprise, worldwide. The corporate plan has a long-term focus and involves the highest levels of management. PepsiCo Beverages headquarters (including its international headquarters) are located in Purchase, New York, USA. The company's corporate plan is developed here.

  Planning at this level involves international target market selection decisions: deciding which country or countries to target based on the screening criteria and processes described in Chapter 7.
- At the *division level,* the strategic plan allocates funds to each business unit based on division goals and objectives. In the PepsiCo example, its division for Eastern Europe is located in Vienna, Austria. From there, the company coordinates all local (country-level) operations. At this point, Pepsi may use various portfolio analysis tools to decide which brands to harvest, to invest in, or to divest, and plan its resources accordingly.
- At the *business unit level,* within each country, decisions are made regarding which consumer segments to target, using criteria described in Chapter 7. At this level, Pepsi develops a strategic plan.
- At the *product level* (line, brand), a marketing plan is developed for achieving objectives. PepsiCo's marketing plan for Poland, for example, might include increasing the consumption of Pepsi and Pepsi Light and launching Pepsi Max beyond the cities of Warsaw, Krakow, Wroclaw, and Poznan. The marketing plan is addressed in section 8-2, "Developing an International Marketing Plan."

8-2 Developing an International Marketing Plan

At this stage of the planning process, the international company develops a marketing plan. Assuming that the company has already analyzed its marketing opportunities and researched and selected the target market, it must now

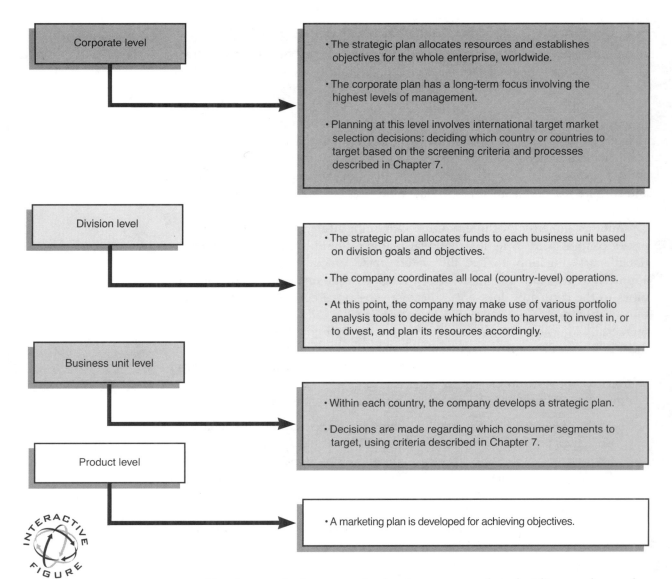

Figure 8-1
Planning activities in the international firm.

- Develop marketing strategies for the target market, deciding on the product mix for the local target market, as well as on the other components of the marketing mix—distribution, promotion, and pricing.
- Plan the international marketing programs.
- Manage (organize, implement, and control) the marketing effort.

The decision on which elements of the marketing mix to use in a particular target market is closely linked to the product's life cycle and to the market entry strategy selected: A product in the early stages of its life cycle, such as the Palm Pilot, will most likely be sold to consumers in highly industrialized countries for a high price, accompanied by heavy promotion. A product will most likely be manufactured in a developed country and exported to the rest of the world. Alternatively, a product in the later stages of its life cycle, such as a videocassette recorder, will be sold to consumers worldwide, regardless of country development level. The company selling the product will heavily compete on price and, thus, most likely manufacture the product in a developing country where labor is inexpensive, to sell all over the world. Most likely, the company will have at least one subsidiary located in the country of product manufacture.

Insights into the marketing strategies that companies use to target international markets reveal that marketing mix decisions are complex and based on extensive research. Kraft Foods (www.kraftfoods.com), for example, has made interesting product mix decisions: It sells coffee products and confectionery products that cover the spectrum of target consumers—and the brands often cannibalize!

Among the many brands of coffee Kraft Foods offers are

- *Jacobs coffee*—This product sells mainly in Central and Eastern Europe. Jacobs coffee is popularly known as a quality German brand. Because consumers in Central and Eastern Europe have traditionally had frequent interaction with German consumers and have acquired a taste and preference for German brands, marketing the Jacobs brand in this region was appropriate. Had Kraft brought the product to the United States, it would have had to challenge quality perceptions of bulk coffee associated with developing countries in Latin America (Colombia and Guatemala, in particular) and Africa (Kenya, especially) and value perceptions held by store brands and other low-priced national brands such as Folgers and Kraft's own Maxwell House.
- *Gevalia coffee*—This brand is aimed at the Scandinavian market and imported into the United States as a gourmet product sold exclusively by mail order.

Among the numerous confectionery products Kraft offers are the following:

- *Milka*—Kraft Foods is now importing its European Milka brand of chocolate into the United States, selling it primarily through chain stores such as Target. Mass-market consumers in the United States are increasingly replacing favorite local candy bars with products that are perceived as more sophisticated and that are available at competitive prices. Competitors such as Ferrero Rocher and Dove have had great success with the premium chocolates they sell in the U.S. market, and they are increasingly placing their products in the impulse-purchase section, by the cash register. Kraft's Milka is using a similar strategy, selling its basic milk chocolate with the picture of a Swiss cow in the Alps on the packaging at Target stores. Milka also is available in a wider selection at shops that specialize in foreign gourmet foods.
- *Suchard*—Kraft Foods is restricting the distribution of its premium chocolate Suchard to Western Europe. Suchard has been for decades the traditional competitor to Lindt in the premium chocolate market in Europe. The Suchard name has long been associated with French-speaking Switzerland, and most European consumers do not know that it is owned by an American company.
- *Toblerone*—Kraft is distributing its Toblerone chocolate brand extensively, all over the world.

Kraft also has numerous brands that are restricted to a few markets. Among them are Daim, aimed at Scandinavian consumers, and Bis, aimed at Argentina and Brazil.

Kraft Foods, a company based in the United States, has different mix strategies for each market. And it sells to the U.S. consumer only a fraction of its international offerings, some of which are positioned as premium European imports. It should be mentioned that companies with more limited resources will very likely be more restricted in their worldwide market coverage.

Companies entering more and more countries in search of new markets are likely to face increasing difficulty in continuously monitoring and controlling their international operations. These firms must monitor not only the constantly changing marketing environment, but also changes in competitive intensity, in competitor product/service quality strategies, in supply chains, and in consumer expectations.

8-3 Deciding on the International Entry Mode

Entry mode The approach to international expansion a company chooses based on desired control and on the risk it can afford.

The **entry mode** classifications offered in sections 8-3a to 8-3i follow a general model of low to high control and risk, respectively. That is, company control over operations and overall risk increase from the export mode to the wholly owned subsidiary entry mode. In general, companies tend to use the export mode in their first attempt to expand internationally and in environments that present substantial risk, and companies tend to approach markets that offer promise and lower risk by engaging in some form of foreign direct investment. There are, however, many exceptions to these statements: Companies that have been present for decades in attractive international markets, such as Airbus Industries and Caterpillar, continue to export to those markets, rather than manufacture abroad. Similarly, many new small businesses find that they can manufacture products cheaply abroad and distribute them in those markets without making a penny in their home country; this is increasingly becoming a possibility for companies selling on the World Wide Web.

8-3a Indirect Exporting

Indirect exporting An export entry mode whereby a company sells its products in the company's home country to intermediaries who, in turn, sell the product overseas.

Indirect exporting means that the company sells its products to intermediaries in the company's home country who, in turn, sell the product overseas. A company engaging in indirect exporting can use middlemen such as export management companies, trading companies, or agents/brokers (described in Chapter 11, "Managing International Distribution Operations and Logistics") to distribute its products overseas. Alternatively, the company can use **cooperative exporting,** also referred to as **"piggybacking"** or **"mother henning."** With cooperative exporting, companies use the distribution system of exporters with established systems of selling abroad who agree to handle the export function of a noncompeting (but not necessarily unrelated) company on a contractual basis. Such companies are paid on commission or are charged a discount price for the product; they are larger companies with extensive experience in and knowledge of the target international market.

Cooperative exporting/ Piggybacking/Mother henning Using the distribution system of exporters with established systems of selling abroad who agree to handle the export function of a noncompeting (but not necessarily unrelated) company on a contractual basis.

Using indirect exporting does not require market expertise, nor a long-term commitment to the international market. The company's risk also is minimal; at most, it can lose a product shipment. Among disadvantages are lack of control over the marketing of its products—which could ultimately lead to lost sales and a loss of good will that might ultimately affect the perception of the company and its brands in other markets where it has a greater commitment.

Some companies use indirect exporting as a first step toward a greater degree of involvement. After a sufficient consumer franchise is secured and the market is tested with the initial shipment, a company might commit resources for additional investment in the market. It should be mentioned, however, that indirect exporting in the long term does not necessarily mean that the company is not committed to the market; it simply means either that the company does not have the resources for greater involvement or that other markets are performing better and need more company resources. One of Europe's leading car makers, Germany's Volkswagen, operates through independent importers and distributors in Belgium, the Netherlands, Switzerland, and Austria, while in France, Germany, Italy, and Spain, which together account for 83 percent of European sales, it controls its wholesale operations directly.[1]

8-3b Direct Exporting

Companies engaging in **direct exporting** have their own in-house exporting expertise, usually in the form of an exporting department. Such companies have more control over the marketing mix in the target market: They can make sure that wholesalers and retailers observe the company's marketing policies, charging the suggested sale price, offering the appropriate promotions, and handling customer requests promptly and satisfactorily. More control, however, is expensive. Companies carry the cost of their export department staff, and the costs involved in selecting and monitoring the different middlemen involved in the distribution process—freight forwarders, shipping lines, insurers, merchant middlemen, and retailers—as well as other marketing service providers, such as consultants, marketing researchers, and advertising companies.

One venue that opens new opportunities for direct exporting is the Internet. With a well-developed web site, companies now can reach directly to customers overseas and process sales online. And many companies do: Catalog retailers and dot-com companies, such as Lands' End and Amazon, respectively, long ago made their first international incursions by exporting their products to consumers abroad and are rapidly expanding their international operations.

The challenges for companies using the Internet to export their products involve securing the appropriate credit in environments where credit cards and personal checks are uncommon and, finally, having sufficient sales to warrant staff expenditures needed to process and handle the international sales.

> **Direct exporting** An export entry mode whereby a firm handles its own exports, usually with the help of an in-house exporting department.

8-3c Licensing

A popular international entry mode, **licensing** presents more risks to the company but also offers it more control than exporting. Licensing involves a **licensor** and a **licensee**. The licensor offers know-how, shares technology, and often shares a brand name with the licensee. The licensee, in turn, pays royalties. The two approaches to licensing are licensing without the name and licensing with the name.

Licensing without the Name

A licensor is very selective when choosing a licensee, ensuring that products manufactured under license are of the highest quality. When quality cannot be guaranteed, either because the licensee does not allow the licensor sufficient control and scrutiny, or because the licensee cannot guarantee quality, it is preferable for the products produced under license not to carry the licensor's brand name. In the early 1970s, Italy's Fiat granted a license to AvtoVAZ, Russia's largest automobile manufacturer, to manufacture Lada, Russia's most popular automobile, and an important export to neighboring and other developing countries. Under a similar arrangement, France's Renault granted a license to build Dacia brand automobiles in Romania in the 1960s. Today, the automobile, which continues to sell under the Dacia name, is as popular as ever, and, in 1999, Renault acquired a 51 percent stake in the company.

> **Licensing** An international entry mode that involves a licensor, who shares the brand name, technology, and know-how with a licensee in return for royalties.
>
> **Licensor** The owner of a product license who agrees to share know-how, technology, and brand name with the licensee in return for royalties.
>
> **Licensee** The purchaser of the license who pays royalties to the licensor for the rights to use the licensor's technology, know-how, and brand name.

---

1. Frank Bradley and Michael Gannon, "Does the Firm's Technology and Marketing Profile Affect Foreign Market Entry?" *Journal of International Marketing*, 2000, Vol. 8, No. 4, pp. 12–36.

Licensing with the Name

Licensors can decide to adapt the names of their products when they have a greater confidence in the capability of the licensee's workforce. One example is Poland's Polski Fiat. Fiat was confident of the reliability of Polish manufacturing and did not require the use of a different name for the product. Today, Fiat no longer licenses the Fiat name to Polish manufacturers; it has set up a subsidiary with multiple operations, Fiat SpA, which manufactures many of the Fiats sold in Eastern Europe under the Fiat brand name (primarily lower-priced models, such as Fiat Punto and Seicento).

Licensing is a lower-risk entry mode that allows a company to manufacture a product all over the world for global distribution. Beverly Hills Polo Club, for example, conducts business in approximately 85 countries around the globe, producing apparel licensed under its own name, all licensed apparel for Harvard University, as well as Hype, Karl Kani, and Blanc Bleu—a line that sells in upscale European retailers.[2]

Licensing permits the company access to markets that may be closed or that may have high entry barriers. In the examples in the "Licensing without the Name" section, Lada, Dacia, and Polski Fiat were sold in the countries of manufacture at low prices, with few taxes, while automobile imports were charged tariffs at rates ranging from 50 to 100 percent.

Companies that engage in licensing agreements also limit their exposure to economic, financial, and political instability. In the event of a national disaster or a government takeover, the licensor licensing without the name incurs only the loss of royalties. The licensor that permits the use of the name may suffer a loss of reputation in the short term if the products are manufactured without licensor supervision and/or if they do not uphold the licensor's standard. In the latter case, the licensor has some control, at least in international markets. For example, it can bring to the attention of international trade bodies the sale of products that are illegally using its brand name, assuming the company has international trademark protection; in most markets, it also can sue the former licensee.

A downside of licensing is that it can produce a viable competitor in the licensee, who is well equipped to competently compete with the licensor. Simply training locals in company operations, particularly technology, can lead to the development of skills for future competitors.

8-3d Franchising

Franchising is a principal entry mode for the service industry, and it is the service industry's equivalent to licensing. The **franchisor** gives the **franchisee** the right to use its brand name and all related trademarks and its business know-how, such as secret recipes and customer interfacing techniques; the franchisor also may provide the franchisee with advertising and sales promotion support—all in return for royalties.

The popularity of U.S.-based franchises worldwide is undisputed: McDonald's Golden Arches decorate crowded Hong Kong streets, the picturesque Scottish countryside, elegant buildings in the downtown of centuries-old European cities, and strip malls in Holland (where one franchise commissioned a giant Michael Jackson sculpture); they also border the suks (bazaars) in the Middle East (see Figure 8-2). Among other fast-food franchises present all over the world are Pizza Hut, KFC, and Burger King. Many of these franchises are adapted to the local mar-

Franchising The main international entry mode for the service industry, whereby the franchisor gives the franchisee the right to use its brand name and all related trademarks in return for royalties.

Franchisor The owner of the franchise who gives the franchisee the right to use its brand name and all related trademarks and its business know-how, such as secret recipes and customer interfacing techniques, in return for royalties.

Franchisee The recipient party to a franchise who pays royalties in return for the right to use the franchisor's brand name and related trademarks.

---

2. Sherrie E. Zhan, "Choosing a Market Entry Strategy, *World Trade*, May 1999, Vol. 12, No. 5, pp. 40–46.

Figure 8-2
A most elegant McDonald's in elegant downtown Milan.

ket, serving spicy vegetarian dishes (and no beef) in India and Sri Lanka and beer and wine in Europe. Although some of the products might differ (as do the sizes of portions—gigantic in the U.S., minuscule in the rest of the world), the franchises look quite similar. They also offer the same courteous service, air conditioning, and toilets, and they run similar promotions.

Surprisingly, some franchises are successful even if the premise of the service's primary offering (hamburgers) runs counter to the local culture (religious ban on eating beef). When a company sets up franchises, however, it is especially important to evaluate the market's acceptance of the offering. For example, Starbucks is currently targeting Austria's coffee houses. Although Austria is a good market for coffee consumption, with an annual consumption of 56.8 gallons per person, Starbucks will encounter many challenges: It is unwilling to relax its global no-smoking policy, which is daring in a country with a high proportion of smokers. Also, the company's concept runs counter to an environment that perceives American coffee and the pace of life associated with American cafés as being different from the Austrian café business perfected over the course of 200 years[3]—the Kaffeehaus tradition.

The advantages and disadvantages of a franchise system are similar to those of licensing. The franchisor experiences less risk and a higher level of control over operations and offerings to the target market. Franchising also is a method that

---

3. *International Herald Tribune,* "Starbucks Targeting Austria's Coffeehouses," Frankfurt Edition, July 5, 2001, p. 12.

allows for very rapid market penetration, which is important especially when new markets open their doors to foreign firms. On the downside, franchising can create future competitors who know the ins and outs of the franchise's operations. In fact, one hears many stories of former employees from fast-food restaurants who offer a precise replica of the original franchise, while offering better prices. Ideas of franchises can also be copied (see Figure 8-3). As soon as Esso (Exxon) stations in Europe started offering a Tiger Mart (convenience store affiliated with the Esso franchise), local competitors immediately set up their own version that was even better adapted to local demands—selling, for example, potted flowers at discounted prices in affiliation with local growers.

8-3e Joint Ventures

Joint venture A corporate entity created with the participation of two companies that share equity, capital, and labor, among others.

Joint ventures involve a foreign company joining with a local company, sharing capital, equity, and labor, among others, to set up a new corporate entity. Joint ventures are a preferred international entry mode for emerging markets. In developing countries, joint ventures typically take place between an international firm and a state-owned enterprise; in this case, the company's partner is the local government. As such, the company is assured instant local access and preferential treatment.

Many developing countries welcome this type of investment as a way to encourage the development of local expertise, of the local market, and of the country's balance of trade—assuming the resultant production will be exported abroad. In most developing countries, the international firm will typically provide expertise, know-how, most of the capital, the brand name reputation, and a trademark that is internationally protected, among others. The local partner will provide the labor, the physical infrastructure (such as the factory and access to the factory), local market expertise and relationships, as well as connections to government decision-making bodies.

It is typical for the local government of the developing country to limit the joint-venture ownership of international firms to less than 50 percent. It is also typical for the local government to encourage the reinvestment of profits into the firm, rather than the repatriation of profits by the international firm. As such, the government, in effect, leads the international firm to engage in transfer pricing, a method whereby the parent company of the international joint-venture partner charges the joint venture for equipment and expertise, for instance, above cost.

Joint ventures could constitute a successful approach to a greater involvement in the market, which is likely to result in higher control, better performance, and higher profits for the company. Successful joint ventures abound. In one example, British Petroleum PLC established a joint venture in Russia, under the name Petrol Complex, with ST, a powerful local partner with close ties to the Moscow city government. The company owns 30 BP gas stations, each of which sells an average of 3.5 million gallons of gasoline a year, four times the average of a gas station in Europe.[4] BP offers Russian drivers good service (a rare commodity in this market), as well as minimarkets with espresso bars and a wide selection of wines; this is in stark contrast to the Russian gasoline stations where customers pay for gasoline by stuffing cash through a tinted window and where they communicate with the salesperson through a microphone.[5]

---

4. Sabrina Tavernise, "In Russia, BP Profits at the Pump," *International Herald Tribune*, Frankfurt Edition, July 5, 2001, p. 12.

5. Ibid.

(a)

(b)

Figure 8-3
Franchises often find that their concept is easily copied. McDonald's restaurants (a) in France often find a Quick copycat (b) setting up around the corner.

The joint-venture entry mode is not limited to developing countries. Numerous joint ventures are operating throughout Europe, and they are increasingly coming under the scrutiny of the European Commission, which assesses their impact on competition. Typically, the Commission appoints a taskforce to investigate the impact of the joint venture on competition and then issues a statement of objections within six to eight weeks, giving the companies involved a chance to respond and request a hearing before the Commission makes its final decision with regard to the joint venture; whenever no such statement is issued, the deal is assumed to be on its way for approval.[6] One joint venture that the European Commission has examined involves the diamond giant De Beers Centenary AG (the world's largest diamond-mining company) and the French luxury goods company LVMH Moët Hennessy Louis Vuitton SA (which owns, among others, Christian Dior, Moët & Chandon, Louis Vuitton, and Donna Karan); the company wants to produce De Beers-branded jewelry and open a network of exclusive shops all over the world.[7]

Overall, 70 percent of all joint ventures break up within 3.5 years, and international joint ventures have an even slimmer chance for success.[8] Companies can, to a certain extent, control their chances for success by carefully selecting the joint-venture partner; a poor choice can be very costly to the company. Other factors that will increase the success of the international joint venture are the firm's previous experience with international investment and the proximity between the culture of the international firm and that of the host country; a greater distance erodes the applicability of the parent's competencies.[9]

Reasons for the failure of joint ventures are numerous. The failure of a partner can lead to the failure of the joint venture—for example, the joint venture between a mid-size company, Bird Corp. of Dedham, Massachusetts, and conglomerate Sulzer Escher Wyss Inc., a subsidiary of Sulzer Brothers Ltd. of Switzerland. Although the joint venture performed well, Bird Corp. experienced serious problems, with unsteady revenues and slim profits, leading to the failure of the joint venture.[10] Even a natural disaster or the weather could lead to failure: Zapata, a $93 million Houston, Texas, company involved in natural gas exploration, took a 49 percent share in a joint venture with Mexican investors with the goal of fishing on Mexico's Pacific coast for anchovies, processing them, and selling them as cattle and poultry feed. The weather system El Niño caused the anchovies to vanish, leading to the failure of the joint venture.[11]

Like licensing and franchising, joint-venture partners can turn into viable competitors that know the firm's operations and competitive strategies. In this case, the local partner will undoubtedly become a formidable competitor locally, where the firm will be protected by the government. Internationally, however, the international firm has some capability to combat the new competitors through controls and agreements with the supply chain and distributors that will prevent access to equipment or to markets, for example.

---

6. Brandon Mitchener and Deborah Ball, "EU Clears De Beers-LVMH Venture," *Wall Street Journal Europe*, July 6–7, 2001, p. 3.

7. Ibid.

8. Dave Savona, "When Companies Divorce," *International Business*, November 1992, Vol. 5, No. 11, pp. 48–50.

9. Harry G. Barkema, Oded Shenkar, Freek Vermeulen, and John H. J. Bell, "Working Abroad, Working with Others: How Firms Learn to Operate International Joint Ventures," *Academy of Management Journal*, April 1997, Vol. 40, No. 2, pp. 426–442.

10. Savona, "When Companies Divorce," pp. 48–50.

11. Ibid.

8-3f Consortia

Consortia involve three or more companies. An example of a successful consortium that involves some companies with a substantial percentage of government ownership is Airbus Industries. Airbus is an international consortium involving France (Aerospatiale with a 37.9 percent ownership), the United Kingdom (British Aerospace, with a 20 percent ownership), Germany (DaimlerChrysler DASA subsidiary, with a 37.9 percent ownership), and Spain (Construcciones Aeronauticas, with a 4.2 percent ownership).

Most national governments and trade organizations are concerned with the monopoly effect that a consortium would create. In the case of Airbus, it was successfully argued that a single European country would not have the resources necessary to provide a challenge to Boeing, the U.S. manufacturer. In general, companies are allowed to set up consortia in the area of research and development, where they can share the cost of developing products that are at the forefront of technology.

8-3g Wholly Owned Subsidiaries

Companies can avoid some of the disadvantages posed by partnering with other firms by setting up wholly owned subsidiaries in the target markets. The assumptions behind a **wholly owned subsidiary** are that

- The company can afford the costs involved in setting up a wholly owned subsidiary.
- The company is willing to commit to the market in the long term.
- The local government allows foreign companies to set up wholly owned subsidiaries on its territory.

The company can develop its own subsidiary, referred to as **greenfielding,** which represents a costly proposition, or it can purchase an existing company through acquisitions or mergers. Many opportunities for acquisitions have recently emerged in developing and developed markets alike: Governments have been de-socializing services and industries, rapidly privatizing industries that were formerly government owned or operated. Opportunities have emerged in the area of telecommunications, health care, energy, and even the national mail service.

The most important advantage that a wholly owned subsidiary can provide is a relative control of all company operations in the target market. In particular, a subsidiary offers the company control over how to handle revenue and profits. Wholly owned subsidiaries also carry the greatest level of risk. A nationalization attempt on the part of the local government could leave the company with just a tax write-off.

Additional difficulties could arise when a company decides to acquire or merge with another. In the case of DaimlerChrysler, Daimler quickly found out that the former Chrysler was not performing up to par and quickly proceeded to restructure, weeding out former Chrysler employees. In general, the company acquiring another or building its wholly owned subsidiary will not be able to share risks with a local partner, nor will it benefit from a partner's connections; it must build its own.

Even selling the subsidiary can eventually haunt the company years later. Harrods Buenos Aires was originally set up as a subsidiary of Harrods London, but became an independent company in 1913 and changed hands several times. Today, Harrods Buenos Aires operates in Argentina and has no relationship whatsoever with Harrods London—which cannot address this issue successfully in the local courts in Argentina.

Consortia A company created with the participation of three or more companies; allowed in underserved markets or in domains where the government and/or the marketplace can control its monopolistic activity.

Wholly owned subsidiary The entry mode that affords the highest level of control and presents the highest level of risk to a company; it involves establishing a new company that is a citizen of the country where the subsidiary is established.

Greenfielding Developing a brand new subsidiary.

8-3h Branch Offices

The primary difference between subsidiaries and branch offices is that subsidiaries are separate entities, whereas branch offices are entities that are part of the international company. Companies that set up branch offices abroad often must engage in substantial investments. For example, Stihl, a German manufacturer of chainsaws, has a branch office in Bucharest, Romania, that handles all company operations in the country. In addition to overseeing product sales, Stihl also ensures that servicing contracts are appropriately honored and that the representatives have adequate training. In low-income countries in Sub-Saharan Africa, where Mercedes is a standard of luxury, but where few locals and a handful of expatriates can afford to purchase the brand, Mercedes must still incur substantial investment costs. At the very minimum, it must invest in a sales office that has substantial staffing requirements and in a showroom that displays a few models. The company also is likely to engage in the distribution of parts to service stations and in the training of mechanics in handling Mercedes parts.

Branch offices of service providers typically engage in a full spectrum of activity in the domain of their specialization: The Chase branch offices in different European capitals handle the banking needs and credit to corporate and individual clients, in effect serving these markets the same way they serve the home markets.

Branch offices, like subsidiaries, also offer companies a high level of control over operations and profits in international markets. In terms of risk, however, the company has invested much less in the market that can be lost in a government takeover attempt, compared to a subsidiary.

Companies also can have a presence in international markets in other formats that could be informal or more formalized. For example, the company could have a sales office (low risk, especially if the company does not carry any inventory in the country; some control). Alternatively, the company could be part of a strategic alliance, which will vary in the level of control it provides the international company, as well as in the level of risk to the company, depending on the type of alliance and resource commitments. Strategic alliances are described in section 8-3i.

8-3i Strategic Alliances

All joint ventures and licensing and franchising agreements are considered to be **strategic alliances** between companies attempting to reach joint corporate and market-related goals. This section addresses particular formats that tend to be more short term in nature and that do not entail the same level of commitment as the previous categories. Such alliances crop up frequently and have various forms and degrees of "alliance." They vary from a contract manufacturing agreement that requires the contracting firm to provide raw material and training to the contracting factory in return for production that could last for two years, to an exchange of loyalty points (hotel, frequent flyer) between companies. The following are some examples of alliances:

- Manufacturing alliances
- Marketing alliances
- Distribution alliances

Manufacturing Alliances

The category of **manufacturing alliances** covers many types of alliances, from **contract manufacturing** to technological, engineering, and research and development alliances. A typical example of a manufacturing alliance is that between the United States company Motorola, Inc., and Singapore's Flextronics International,

---

Strategic alliance Any type of relationship between one or more companies attempting to reach joint corporate and market-related goals; term used to refer to most nonequity alliances.

Manufacturing alliance A nonequity relationship between two firms, in which one firm handles the other's manufacturing or some aspect of the manufacturing process.

Contract manufacturing A relationship between two companies wherein one company contracts with another to manufacture products according to the contracting company's specifications and for a specified period of time.

Ltd., whereby the Singapore-based electronics manufacturer would make billions of dollars' worth of Motorola products. At present, Flextronics has manufacturing contracts for infrastructure and cell phones, among others.[12] In another example, Porsche has engaged in different types of technical alliances with Harley-Davidson, the U.S. motorcycle icon, primarily helping it develop low-noise, low-emissions motorcycles; most recently, Porsche is helping Harley-Davidson develop its water-cooled Revolution engine.[13]

Marketing Alliances

Some **marketing alliances** focus on all aspects of marketing. For example, Opel, the German subsidiary of U.S. auto manufacturer General Motors, signed a two-year contract to market its automobiles to 6.5 million America Online (AOL) subscribers in Germany by informing users about Opel and directing them to the Opel web site.[14] The two companies are also considering a marketing alliance involving mobile Internet: Opel will equip its automobiles with mobile Internet connections, and AOL will supply content for the mobile service. Other marketing alliances focus on sales; for example, U.S.-based Northwest Airlines is in charge of all sales in the United States for the KLM Royal Dutch Airlines. Yet other airline alliances focus on sales promotion. For example, Air France exchanges frequent-flyer mileage with Delta Airlines.

Marketing alliance A nonequity relationship between two firms, in which one firm handles the other's marketing or some aspect of the marketing process.

Distribution Alliances

Distribution alliances are common as well. Mitsui and Mitsubishi have set up distribution alliances with Coca-Cola in Japan, bottling and distributing all Coke products in this market.

Distribution alliance A nonequity relationship between two firms, in which one firm handles the other's distribution or some aspect of the distribution process.

Chapter Summary

- **Develop a general understanding of international marketing strategy at the different levels of the international organization and provide some insights into the international marketing planning process of selected companies**

  Planning takes place at different levels. At the corporate level, the strategic plan allocates resources and establishes objectives for the whole enterprise, worldwide. At the division level, the strategic plan allocates funds to each business unit based on division goals and objectives, whereas, at the business unit level, within each country, decisions are made on selecting target consumer segments. At the product level (line, brand), a marketing plan is developed for achieving objectives. An important decision is which product mix to use in the different countries where the company is present.

- **Offer an understanding of company entry mode selection and the risks involved at each level**

  A company can use different entry modes to enter a new market. Ranging from the lowest-risk mode and the mode that provides the least control, to the highest-risk/highest-control mode, they are indirect exporting, direct exporting, licensing, franchising, joint ventures, consortia, and wholly-owned subsidiaries/company branches.

- **Describe different types of strategic alliances involving international companies**

  A company can use various forms of strategic alliances (manufacturing, marketing, and distribution alliances) to enter a new market. Such alliances are industry-specific, and they have various degrees of stability over time.

12. *International Herald Tribune*, "Motorola Scales Back Flextronics Outsourcing Deal," Frankfurt Edition, July 4, 2001, p. 11.

13. Tim Burt, "Porsche Fires Revolution at Harley," *Financial Times*, July 14–15, 2001, p. 8.

14. Holger Schmidt, "Opel to Market Its Cars through AOL," *Frankfurter Allgemeine Zeitung*, July 4, 2001, No. 152/27, p. 5.

Discussion Questions

1. International planning involves planning activities at different levels of an organization. Describe the planning processes that take place at each level of an international company.

2. What is the difference between international franchising and international licensing? Explain.

3. Briefly describe each type of international entry mode, from exporting to wholly owned subsidiary, and address the risks and controls characterizing each entry mode.

4. There are many types of international alliances. Go to the home page of U.S. Air (http://usairways.com/dividendmiles/index.htm) and identify the company's alliances.

Part

Part 4

Managing the International Marketing Mix

Chapter 9
Products and Services:
Branding Decisions in
International Markets

Chapter 10
International Product
and Service Strategies

Chapter 11
Managing International
Distribution Operations
and Logistics

Chapter 12
International Retailing

Chapter 13
The International
Promotional Mix and
Advertising Strategies

Chapter 14
International Publicity,
Public Relations, and Sales
Promotion Strategies

Chapter 15
International Personal
Selling and Personnel
Management

Chapter 16
International Pricing
Strategy

Products and Services: Branding Decisions in International Markets

Outline

Learning Objectives
9-1 Standardization Versus
    Adaptation
    9-1a Global Standardization
    9-1b Regional Standardization
    9-1c Global Localization
    9-1d Mandatory Adaptation
    9-1e Local, Nonmandatory
       Adaptation
9-2 Private-Label (Retailer)
    Brands
9-3 Global Branding
    and Country-of-Origin
    Information
    9-3a Product-Country
       and Service-Country
       Stereotypes
    9-3b Country of Origin
       and Ethnocentrism
9-4 The Service Side: Tariff and
    Nontariff Barriers to Entry
9-5 Products, Services,
    and Culture
9-6 Protecting Brand Names
    9-6a Identifying Types
       of Counterfeiting
    9-6b Combating Counterfeiting
Chapter Summary
Discussion Questions

Key Terms

adaptation
brand name counterfeiting
core product strategy
country of manufacture
country of origin
design counterfeiting
ethnocentrism
global branding
global consumers
global localization

global standardization
glocalization
mandatory adaptation
modular adaptation
nonmandatory adaptation
private labels
product-country stereotypes
regional standardization
service barriers

Learning Objectives

Learning Objectives

By the end of this chapter, you should be able to:

- Describe drivers for international standardization and offer an overview of the international standardization–local adaptation continuum and respective company strategies
- Examine country-of-origin effects on brand evaluations in relation to product stereotypes and consumer ethnocentrism

- Examine challenges faced by service providers in international markets
- Address issues related to brand name protection and the reasons behind widespread international counterfeiting

---

The world has been gradually moving toward one large, global market place. As Chapter 4, "Regional Economic and Political Integration," illustrated, a fragmented Europe is merging into one large, unified market, as is South America; the Asian market also is gradually removing barriers and allowing more access to Western multinationals. A number of mature products—consumer electronics, for instance—have succeeded in addressing the needs of consumers worldwide in essentially the same format, with only minimal market modifications.[1] Sony (Japan), for example, is marketing the Trinitron television set using similar marketing strategies worldwide; Braun and Krups (Germany) sell kitchen appliances using the same marketing mix across continents with only minor mandatory adaptations (voltage, cycles, television systems).

Similarly, franchises such as the Tricon family (Kentucky Fried Chicken and Pizza Hut, in particular), McDonald's, and Burger King are only minimally altering their offerings to meet local demands, offering wine and beer in some European countries and miso soup in Japan. Mineral water distributors, such as Gerolsteiner (Germany), Evian and Volvic (France), and food manufacturers, such as the Altria (formerly Philip Morris) company Kraft Jacobs Suchard (Toblerone and Suchard chocolate, Jacobs coffee, among others), are only modifying their labels to conform to local requirements when selling their products across different continents.

Yet, for certain product categories that appeal to local preferences, international firms have had to adapt their offerings to effectively compete with local manufacturers and service providers and to more directly cater to the individual needs of local markets. Advertising agencies and numerous financial and legal service providers, for example, typically partner with local firms to create successful campaigns and strategies aimed at individual markets.

This chapter examines the driving forces behind the decision to standardize, or to partially or fully adapt the offerings to individual international markets. It also addresses barriers faced by brands from private-label offerings and by service providers from local government. The chapter addresses brand name protection issues and reasons behind the proliferation of counterfeiting activity worldwide.

---

1. Gary van Deursen, "The Globalization of Design," *Appliance Manufacturer*, March 1995, Vol. 43, No. 3, pp. 10–11.

Figure 9-1
The global
standardization–local
adaptation continuum.

9-1 Standardization Versus Adaptation

The topic of standardization versus **adaptation,** to a certain extent, parallels the concepts introduced in Chapter 1, "Scope, Concepts, and Drivers of International Marketing," addressing geocentric, regiocentric, and polycentric orientations—with global standardization reflecting a geocentric company orientation, regional standardization reflecting a regiocentric orientation, and local adaptation reflecting a polycentric orientation, respectively (see Figure 9-1). It must be noted, however, that multinational companies may adopt a combination strategy, depending on the particulars of individual markets. For instance, PepsiCo is a global company, with, most likely, a geocentric orientation; however, it has only recently moved from a localized strategy to a regional strategy in terms of its distribution and purchasing.

Adaptation   The strategy of altering a product to better meet the needs of a local market.

9-1a Global Standardization

Global standardization, frequently used interchangeably with the term "globalization," refers first to standardization of products across markets and, ultimately, to the standardization of the marketing mix worldwide. This latter definition will be used in this textbook.

Among the numerous arguments in favor of global standardization of the marketing mix are the following:[2]

Global standardization
The standardization of products across markets and, ultimately, the standardization of the marketing mix worldwide; more commonly called glocalization.

---

2. The three assumptions listed were initially stated by Theodore Levitt, "The Globalization of Markets," *Harvard Business Review,* May–June 1983, pp. 92–102.

- Global consumers
- International travel
- Consumer preference for higher quality and lower price

Global Consumers

Consumers' interests and product/service-related needs are becoming more and more homogeneous worldwide. As a consequence, product and, indeed, brand preferences are gaining a common definition across continents, leading to the emergence of **global consumers.** In-line skating constitutes a favorite pre-teen pastime in New York, Warsaw, and Delhi. Blonde, svelte Barbie dolls and Barbie-doll-look-alikes are on the wish-list of little girls in developed countries and developing countries. Little German viewers of the British *Teletubbies* television show watch Dipsy say "Winke-Winke" (bye-bye) and demand Teletubbies merchandise, as do toddlers in the United States. Professional loggers in the U.S. Northwest and those in the Scandinavian Peninsula perceive the German Stihl chainsaw as a high-quality product.

International Travel

As more and more consumers engage in international travel, they are confronted with advertisements for the same products that they have initially encountered in their home countries. Building brand awareness globally is simply easier, especially given the overlapping media in many countries and, consequently, the higher likelihood of exposure to the brand name.[3] Global brands also are more prestigious, signaling that the company has the resources necessary to back the respective brands.[4]

Consumer Preference for Higher Quality and Lower Price

Consumers worldwide are willing to sacrifice product-related features, function, and design to obtain higher quality at a lower price—achieved as companies acquire economies of scale in research and development, production, distribution, and promotion. To address uniform needs of consumers, Ford attempted a global product approach to vehicle design and production, building "world cars."[5] Its first such experiment was the launch of the Ford Contour/Mercury Mystique in the United States and the Mondeo in Europe in 1993.[6] This attempt was followed by the marketing of the Ford Focus, which is successful on both sides of the Atlantic.

The strategy used to address these needs is **global branding**. A global brand has the same name, logo, image, and positioning everywhere in the world. Main streets in most world capitals and malls worldwide advertise and sell brands such as Ralph Lauren, Escada, Donna Karan, while logos of Pepsi-Cola, Coca-Cola, and Camel and Kent cigarettes adorn umbrellas in many central squares. These are global brands, enjoying worldwide reputation and recognition, demanded by consumers in Beijing, Antananarivo, and Paris alike. These brands have a high awareness among consumers worldwide and are perceived to be of high quality.

Standardization is particularly important for product research and development. Economies of scale can be achieved if there is a concentration in research

---

Global consumers
The homogeneous consumer group worldwide sharing similar interests and product/brand preferences.

Global branding Approach to branding that uses the same name, logo, image, and positioning strategies everywhere in the world.

---

3. David A. Aaker, *Managing Brand Equity: Capitalizing on the Value of a Brand Name,* The Free Press, 1991.

4. Ibid.

5. van Deursen, "The Globalization of Design," pp. 10–11.

6. Ibid.

and development, and coordination also gives a firm flexibility in responding to competitors' R&D efforts.[7] Such coordination is expensive; moreover, governments may restrain the flow of information and people, which are required to coordinate research and development activities.[8]

With regard to the other components of the marketing mix, advertising savings can be achieved by having a uniform advertising strategy in each country. PepsiCo, for example, saved an estimated $10 million as a result of using the same film for television advertising in different international markets.[9] Similarly, the standardization of supply chains has resulted in cost reductions in transportation and distribution, with significant cost reductions and overall shorter transportation times; and, finally, research and development, purchasing, packaging, and customer service, among others, also have benefited from standardization.[10] These issues will be examined in Chapter 11, "Managing International Distribution Operations and Logistics," and Chapter 13, "The International Promotional Mix and Advertising Strategies."

9-1b Regional Standardization

A variation of global standardization, a **regional standardization** strategy refers to the use of a uniform marketing strategy within a particular region. This strategy is becoming more appealing to companies as regional market integration is gaining strength worldwide, with the European Union, MERCOSUR, and NAFTA in particular, gaining ground as veritable unified markets. Pan-European brands are becoming common, even for U.S. multinationals, such as Procter & Gamble (whose Ariel detergent was its first Pan-European product; today, the brand is available in most markets, with the exception of North America).

> **Regional standardization**
> The use of a uniform marketing strategy within a particular region.

In addition to regional branding strategies, companies also benefit from economies of scale by concentrating certain marketing activities regionally. PepsiCo, for example, centralized purchasing across all of its European businesses, thus achieving volume savings from sugar, cooking oil, flour, and packaging materials, for a total of $100 million per year.[11] In terms of distribution, Nike has traditionally utilized local warehousing to supply retailers; currently, the company is attempting to replace more than twenty national warehouses in Europe with one single distribution center located in Belgium, thus using a strategy similar to that used in the United States, where it has successfully centralized its American operations in Memphis.[12]

Mercedes-Benz (www.mercedes.com) is a brand that appears to have some degree of regional focus, targeting consumers in the United States differently than most other consumers. For example, its A-Class (a lower-priced series) is available everywhere except in the United States, where the company appears to have altogether a different strategy (see Figure 9-2). In the case of its compacts, the C-Class, for much of the rest of the world, Mercedes offers the Classic, the Elégance, and the Avantgarde models in the C-180, C-200, C-240, C-320, and the C-220 CDI versions, whereas for the U.S. markets, the C-Class is limited to C-240s and C-280s.

7. Shaoming Zou and Aysegul Ozsomer, "Global Product R&D and the Firm's Strategic Position," *Journal of International Marketing*, 1999, Vol. 7, No. 1, pp. 57–76.

8. Ibid.

9. Susan Segal-Horn, "The Limits of Global Strategy," *Strategy & Leadership*, November–December 1996, Vol. 24, No. 6, pp. 12–17.

10. Ibid.

11. Segal-Horn, "The Limits of Global Strategy," pp. 12–17.

12. Ibid.

Figure 9-2
The A-Class Mercedes is about as large as a Ford Focus; it even looks like one.

The different approach to the U.S. market is in large part attributable to the fact that Mercedes had to fight gray marketing channels until it instituted a strategy that made using alternate marketing channels a complicated proposition and took control of distribution under the Mercedes-USA umbrella organization.

A product often must be adapted to the demands of the local market because consumers might have certain specific preferences. Alternatively, adaptation might be dictated by the political and legal environment, by the technological environment, or by other particulars of the market (trade relationships, climate, etc.). The degree of economic development in a market also is a factor that determines the degree of product adaptation needed: The lower the level of economic and market development, the more the product needs to be changed to serve the needs and demands of the market.[13]

Host governments affect the globalization of products by imposing local content requirements, standards (technical, emission, etc.), and ownership restrictions and requirements on technology transfer; in the case of services, consumer participation in production may be affected by government barriers to global strategy.[14] Banking in the Middle East is gender-based; women's banks are separate from banks used by men, and cross-access is restricted. Government restrictions not only affect international banking: China, Singapore, and Saudi Arabia ban the private ownership of satellite dishes, and China is attempting to restrict citizen access to the Web.[15]

9-1c Global Localization

In general, few products and services can succeed through a purely global strategy; a degree of adaptation to local conditions is frequently imperative for company success. According to marketing experts, the idea of marketing a standardized product with a uniform marketing plan around the world remains purely theo-

---

13. John S. Hill and Richard R. Still, "Adapting Products to LDC Tastes," *Harvard Business Review*, March–April 1984, pp. 92–101.

14. Christopher Lovelock and George S. Yip, "Developing Global Strategies for Service Businesses," *California Management Review*, Vol. 38, No. 2, pp. 64–87.

15. Ibid.

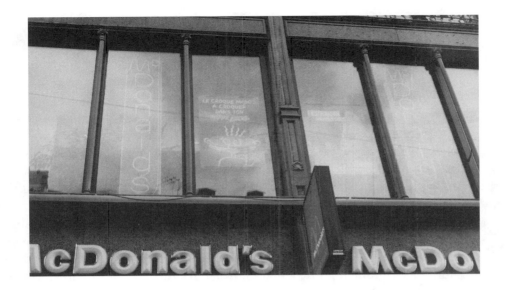

Figure 9-3
This McDonald's in France advertises its "Croque McDo, à croquer dans ton Happy Meal"—a melted cheese sandwich, to munch on in your Happy Meal. The name of the Croque McDo is a play on Croque Monsieur, the traditional French grilled cheese sandwich.

retical; although a product concept may be universal, it must still be adapted to differences in local culture, legislation, and even production capabilities.[16] The term **global localization,** or **glocalization,** is frequently used to describe the practice of global branding and localized marketing adaptation.

Product managers must decide on which aspects of a product they want to standardize across markets and which aspects of the product to localize. In this decision, they resort to two approaches: one involves offering parts (modules) that can be assembled worldwide in different configurations, depending on the needs of the market—**modular adaptation;** the other, standardizing the core product/service, but allowing for easy modification from market to market—**core product strategy.** In an instance of the latter, the core product is identical from one country to another, but certain aspects of the offering differ from market to market. To illustrate this concept, marketers with brands heralded as global icons often act using a local strategy: McDonald's Golden Arches are omnipresent throughout the world. Its offerings, however, are adapted to the local culture; at its restaurants in New Delhi, where Indian consumers consider cows sacred and don't eat beef, McDonald's offers the Maharaja Mac (two all-mutton patties, special sauce, lettuce, cheese, pickles, onions on a sesame-seed bun).[17] Similarly, Volvo, unlike Mercedes (as mentioned in section 9-1b, "Regional Standardization"), has a similar core product in every market; however, it offers air conditioning as a standard feature for the U.S. market.

Similarly, other fast-food restaurant services have adapted their offerings from market to market (see Figure 9-3). The Tricon companies (Pizza Hut and Kentucky Fried Chicken, in particular), Burger King, and McDonald's offer beer and wine in Europe, and most multinational fast-food companies offer miso soup in Japan. Along with this type of adaptation are other examples: McDonald's in the Netherlands offers its large Coca-Cola Light (Diet Coke)[18] in containers slightly smaller than the medium drink containers it serves in the United States. Pizza Hut in Germany sells cans of Pepsi from take-home windows—outside a café-restaurant on Leopoldstrasse, a street lined with cafés, in Munich, for instance. KFC found that, for its Japanese consumers, it needed to change its product's shape and size

Global localization   The practice of global branding and localized marketing adaptation to differences in local culture, legislation, and even production capabilities.

Glocalization
The standardization of products across markets and, ultimately, to the standardization of the marketing mix worldwide; also called global standardization.

Modular adaptation
The localization across markets of the product by offering parts (modules) that can be assembled worldwide in different configurations, depending on the needs of the market.

Core product strategy
The strategy of using the same standard core product/service worldwide, but varying certain aspects of the offering (product ingredients, advertising) from market to market.

---

16. Cyndee Miller, "Chasing the Global Dream," *Marketing News,* December 2, 1996, Vol. 30, No. 25, pp. 1–2.

17. Ibid.

18. This is yet another example of adaptation, this time by Coca-Cola, for consumers in Europe, to whom the term "diet" signifies medically imposed eating restrictions.

because they prefer morsel-sized food; similarly, Pampers disposable diapers were successful in Japan only after the size was adapted to accommodate smaller Japanese babies.[19]

9-1d Mandatory Adaptation

To render products usable, manufacturers of appliances adapt their products to local requirements. Such **mandatory adaptations** involve voltage—220 volts for Europe, whereas, in the U.S., the standard is 110. Other such adaptations involve cycles (50 versus 60), electricity and telephone jacks, and television/VCR systems (NTSC in the United States, PAL and SECAM I and SECAM II in the rest of the world).

In other examples, automobiles must be adapted to the left-hand driving requirements in the United Kingdom, Ireland, and Australia. The United States requires a conversion to local specifications (emissions and other standards) for any imported automobiles that were not manufactured according to U.S. standards; subsequent to conversion, the U.S. Department of Transportation must approve the conversion for the vehicle to be registered locally, which makes this, overall, a costly undertaking.

Other types of mandatory adaptation abound. For example, a number of Middle Eastern countries continue to restrict the import of products that have components manufactured in Israel. Food products, in particular, must be scrutinized: Alcohol content is prohibited from distribution without special and limited authorization in many countries in North Africa and the Middle East, and food products containing pork have very limited appeal and face inspections and other restrictions in this same region. Magazines are either marked with a black marker where a woman's body or face is evident or not allowed through altogether in Saudi Arabia. And the list continues.

9-1e Local, Nonmandatory Adaptation

Many global companies adapt their offerings to better meet the needs of the local market, thus performing a local, **nonmandatory adaptation.** Examples of multinational companies offering products aimed at local markets abound. In most instances, the products result from a buyout. Unilever and Procter & Gamble bought numerous brands in Central and Eastern Europe; for instance, Unilever bought Romania's Dero, a detergent that is now part of the company's product mix in this country.

Multinational companies also have developed new brands for individual local markets: Häagen-Dazs Japan offers its customers Royal Milk Tea ice cream, a full-bodied, creamy green ice tea; Weight Watchers offers consumers in France Mousse Legeres in two different four-pack combinations—Cherry/Green Tea, Pear/Jasmine, Apricot/Orange Flower, and Peach/Ginger; Nestlé offers in the United Kingdom a drinkable fruit yogurt named Squizzos, which sports Disney's *Jungle Book* characters.[20]

9-2 Private-Label (Retailer) Brands

Private-label (retailer) brands pose an increasing challenge to manufacturers' global or local brands. European food retailers, such as Sainsbury in the U.K. and

Mandatory adaptation
The adaptation of products to local requirements so that the products can legally and physically function in the specific country environment.

Nonmandatory adaptation
The strategy of adapting a product to better meet the needs of the local market, without being required to do so.

---

19. Segal-Horn, "The Limits of Global Strategy," pp. 12–17.

20. Donna Gorski Berry, "Global Dairy Food Trends," *Dairy Foods,* October 1998, Vol. 99, No. 10, pp. 32–37.

Albert Heijn in the Netherlands, as well as North American retailers, offer quality products with the "Sainsbury" and "ah" brands respectively, packaged impeccably and positioned on the shelves side-by-side with popular multinational/national brands. A European case study[21] found that, in general, retailers compete primarily on price with their private-label brands unless they are actually able to develop differentiated, high-quality store brands, thus creating consumer loyalty, which in turn translates to store loyalty.

In the United Kingdom, **private labels** are common. Sainsbury and Marks & Spencer have a century-long history of offering store brands perceived to be of high quality, whereas Tesco and Argyll have only recently started offering store brands. In contrast, in France, private-label brands were introduced only in the 1970s and positioned as cheap alternatives to national brands.[22] Later, French retailers such as Casino and Monoprix attempted to develop quality store brands but faced significant price competition from the national brands, leaving French consumers with the impression that store brands were inferior—a perception that was reinforced by the fact that French supermarkets, unlike their U.K. counterparts, were legally barred from using television advertising.[23]

In addition to offering quality premium store brands, retailers in developed countries also have attempted to be innovative and expand into new product categories.[24] Finally, private-label brands tend to be especially appealing to consumers during downturns in the economy, when they are more likely to make their brand selection based on price.[25] Generally, consumers worldwide have become more price conscious, demanding higher quality at lower prices. The private-label brand offering serves well this mindset, as does the proliferation of discounters such as Wal-Mart, Costco, and Toys "R" Us who are increasing price competition by offering their own dealer brands.

9-3 Global Branding and Country-of-Origin Information

Country of origin is defined as the country with which a particular product or service is associated. The country could be the **country of manufacture,** in the case of products, or the country where the company headquarters are located, for both products and services. The key to determining a product's perceived country of origin depends on which of the two (country of manufacture or home country of the company) elicits the stronger association (see Figure 9-4). For example, many of the appliances Philips sells are manufactured in Asia; however, the Philips' headquarters are in the Netherlands. The country of origin for Philips appliances, then, is not the particular country in Asia where they are manufactured, but the Netherlands. A new, unknown brand, however, will be associated more strongly with the country of manufacture.

In the absence of other product information, the country of origin of a product or service affects consumers' evaluations of that product or service. Country-of-origin information constitutes a product trait that is external to the product itself, acting as a surrogate for product quality, performance, reliability, prestige,

Private labels Brands sold under the brand name of a retailer or some other distributor.

Country of origin The country with which a particular product or service is associated.

Country of manufacture The country in which a particular product is manufactured.

21. Ryan Mathews, "A European Case Study," *Progressive Grocer,* Special Volume: *Branding the Store,* November 1995, pp. 8–9. This article discusses a study conducted by INSEAD on trends in the food industry in the U.K. and France.

22. Ibid.

23. Ibid.

24. John A. Quelch and David Harding, "Brands Versus Private Labels: Fighting to Win," *Harvard Business Review,* January–February 1996, Vol. 74, No. 1, pp. 99–109.

25. Mathews, "A European Case Study," pp. 8–9.

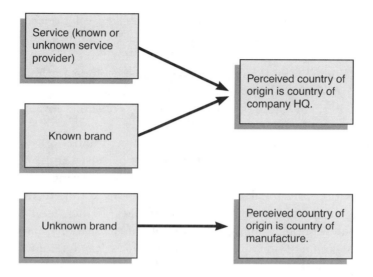

Figure 9-4
Country of origin effects.

and other product characteristics that cannot be directly evaluated.[26] In general, products manufactured in highly industrialized countries are perceived as being of higher quality and having greater prestige than those manufactured in developing countries. Consumers from highly developed countries tend, in general, to evaluate own-country products more favorably than products from other countries. The opposite is true for consumers in developing countries and newly marketizing economies[27] who evaluate own-country products as inferior to products from developed countries.

When consumers have additional product information, however, such as brand name, or if they purchase the product at a store known for its quality, and especially premium-quality, products, country-of-origin information is no longer a primary source consumers use for product quality evaluation. And, increasingly, with products manufactured using components made in various countries and assembled in yet other countries, determining the "true" country of origin of a product is difficult. For example, BMWs for the U.S. market are manufactured in South Carolina, rather than in Bavaria; Michelin tires are also manufactured in South Carolina; and many software products used by U.S. businesses are developed in India.

Finally, in some cases there may be a preference not to advertise the country of origin. Obviously, Poland would prefer not to be associated with the most infamous Nazi death camp; see Figure 9-5.

9-3a Product-Country and Service-Country Stereotypes

Kenyan or Colombian coffee, Chinese tea, German beer and electronics, French perfume, Italian fashion, Swiss chocolate, and Russian caviar are examples of strong **product-country stereotypes** of quality held by consumers in the United States. Among such stereotypes shared elsewhere in the world are Iranian pistachios and rugs, Polish vegetables, Israeli oranges, and Czech and Italian crystal, to name a few. Such stereotypes are product specific and do not apply usually to other products from that particular country.

Product-country stereotypes
Product-specific stereotypes that associate the country of origin as a certification of quality.

---

26. For a review of the country-of-origin effect literature, see Lalita A. Manrai, Dana-Nicoleta Lascu, and Ajay K. Manrai, "Interactive Effects of Country of Origin and Product Category on Product Evaluations," *International Business Review,* 1998, Vol. 7, pp. 591–615.

27. Ibid.

(a)

(b)

Figure 9-5
Destination nonmarketing: *(a)* Auschwitz, the largest concentration and death camp complex, is rarely associated with the country where it is located— Poland. Located close to the town of Oswiencim, on the Vistula River, the camp is, nevertheless, toured daily by international visitors. *(b)* Arbeit Macht Frei—Work Makes You Free—is the message reigning upon the entrance to the camp.

Advertisements often emphasize these stereotypes. In the United States, Colombian coffee is touted as a certification of quality. Petrossian in New York stresses its reputation as the authentic retailer of Russian Beluga and Sevruga caviar. Toblerone chocolate stresses its European origins, despite the fact that it is a Philip Morris (Kraft Jacobs Suchard) brand. Häagen-Dazs chocolate-dipped ice cream is really a product produced locally, in the United States; its name suggests an association with Europe, again affirming the quality association with European chocolate.

Services also are stereotyped. Eastern European cosmeticians, for example, are very popular in the West. Names such as Ilona of Hungary, Frederick Fekkai, and Erno Laszlo cosmetics are prominent on Madison and Fifth Avenues in New York.

Figure 9-6
Polish beauticians are world famous. Using dated equipment, fresh natural products, and impeccable dexterity, this beautician works wonders on tourists, as well as locals.

Figure 9-7
Waiter on the Champs Elysées, graciously and competently serving beer on a busy July 14 (a French national holiday).

Tourists going to Eastern Europe often use the services of local beauticians (see Figure 9-6) or even go for extended stays to spas specializing in mud baths and life-renewal therapies.

Unfortunate negative stereotypes also exist. French waiters have received unfair evaluations in the United States (see Figure 9-7). Their demeanor is merely a reflection of their competence and their elegance.

9-3b Country of Origin and Ethnocentrism

Ethnocentrism The belief that one's culture is superior to another and that strategies used in one's home country (presumably a developed country) will work just as well internationally.

We have learned about **ethnocentrism** as a company philosophy, as an approach to international marketing as an extension of domestic marketing with minimal adaptation to the needs of the international consumers and the peculiarities of the local market. This second definition of ethnocentrism, used in relation to country of origin, is related to consumers' beliefs that purchasing foreign products is morally wrong.[28] Ethnocentric consumers believe that purchasing imported products hurts the economy, causes loss of jobs, and is unpatriotic, and consumers purchasing foreign products are worthy of contempt.[29] This concept then translates into a preference for products from one's own country—i.e., "buy American"—and a rejection of products with a foreign country of origin. This attitude may exist at the individual consumer level or at the aggregate societal level.

Governments also frequently engage in practices in which they favor locally produced products, service providers, etc., in the performance of their tasks. In section 9-4, similar restrictions and related philosophies are explored in the area of services.

9-4 The Service Side: Tariff and Nontariff Barriers to Entry

This section examines challenges that service providers face in their international involvement. These challenges, or **service barriers,** in one form or another, represent a manifestation of ethnocentrism at the firm level, at the government level, or at the consumer level. Among such challenges are:[30]

> **Service barriers** Barriers encountered by services in different markets, such as requirements for local certification, local providers, and other requirements that favor local over international service providers.

- The requirement to use national services. This requirement is a form of protectionism: Company or government policies provide implicit or explicit preference for a domestic supplier, which makes it difficult for international service providers to survive.
- The prohibition against the employment of foreign nationals, or other barriers—for example, demanding a local certification such as Certified Public Accountant, which requires a degree in accounting from a U.S. institution as well as passing the CPA exam.
- Direct competition from government providers, such as a local government monopoly over natural gas and electricity.
- Restrictions on movement—for example, limiting access for tourists in a particular region or the number of flights allowed into the country.
- Tariffs imposed on international service providers.

Frequently, the challenges posed to international service providers can be attributed to the close cultural link between a society and services.[31] Section 9-5 addresses the relationship between products, services, and culture.

9-5 Products, Services, and Culture

Service encounters are primarily social encounters, and rules and expectations related to services vary from culture to culture.[32] Studies in marketing revealed that it is important for international service providers to understand the factors

---

28. Terrence A. Shimp and Subhash Sharma, "Consumer Ethnocentrism: Construction and Validation of the CETSCALE," *Journal of Marketing Research,* August 1987, Vol. 24, No. 3, pp. 280–289.

29. Ibid.

30. For an in-depth description of these and additional restrictions, see Lee D. Dahringer, "Marketing Services Internationally: Barriers and Management Strategies," *Journal of Services Marketing,* Summer 1991, Vol. 5, No. 3, pp. 5–17.

31. P. B. Kenen, *The International Economy,* 1989, Prentice Hall; and Ikechi Ekeledo and K. Sivakumar, "Foreign Market Entry Mode Choice of Service Firms: A Contingency Perspective," *Journal of the Academy of Marketing Science,* 1998, Vol. 26, No. 4, pp. 274–292.

32. John A. Czepiel, "Service Encounters and Service Relationships: Implications and Research," *Journal of Business Research,* Vol. 20, pp. 13–21; and Kathryn Frazier Winsted, "Evaluating Service Encounters: A Cross-Cultural and Cross-Industry Exploration," *Journal of Marketing Theory and Practice,* Spring 1999, Vol. 7, No. 2, pp. 106–123.

that affect customer considerations in service evaluations and to emphasize the various dimensions of service quality accordingly.[33] To illustrate, Japanese consumers do not expect special treatment in a medical environment. Medicine is perceived as a public good, and it would be selfish of anyone to expect special attention. Similarly, the Japanese also hold doctors in very high esteem, and customers expect and accept rudeness from doctors.[34] They also expect to be treated with a greater degree of formality by all service providers compared to consumers in the United States, whereas consumers in the United States prefer a greater degree of service personalization.[35]

Culture also influences the perception and evaluation of a brand in a particular country. Kent cigarettes continue to hold a high market share and are prominent in Romania due to the status they held as commodity money and a prestige product before the fall of communism.[36] Pepsi-Cola and Coca-Cola continue to market their diet brands as Pepsi Light and Coca-Cola Light in much of the rest of the world, where the word "diet" refers to a medically restricted diet. In Rwanda, Fanta Citron is a preferred mixer for most hard liquor. Housewives in the U.K. are "hoovering" when they are vacuuming (regardless of the brand of vacuum cleaner they are using), and they buy Jello in a semi-gelled, rather than powder, format.

Culture also determines the degree of brand loyalty. Consumers from more collectivist cultures, such as Latin American and Asian consumers, tend to prefer established brands and purchase them in the maturity stage. European consumers tend to be very brand name conscious and are especially loyal to top brands. In urban areas, high-priced designers such as Prada, Escada, Dolce & Gabbana, and Diesel jeans are common among middle- and upper-middle-class consumers who might otherwise live in small rental apartments.

Chapter 10, "International Product and Service Strategies," addresses strategies of manufacturers and service providers aimed at meeting the challenges imposed by culture.

9-6 Protecting Brand Names

Brand names are valuable assets to a company. Companies pay millions to protect their brand names from dilution, by registering them anywhere they are present and defending them in court, primarily because counterfeit merchandise harms the brand's reputation as well as company profits. The Uruguay round of the General Agreement on Tariffs and Trade (GATT) addressed standardizing global trademark legislation that is now incorporated under the World Trade Organization (WTO) umbrella. The question that remains is whether individual governments can and will enact this legislation. To illustrate, Yiwu, a city five hours from Shanghai, China, is one of the largest wholesale centers of China, where 200,000 distributors purchase up to 2,000 tons of goods daily; it also is China's counterfeit capital, where counterfeit products bearing established brand names—such as Procter & Gamble's Safeguard soap and Rejoice shampoo, Gillette razor blades,

---

33. Naresh K. Malhotra, Francis M. Ulgado, J. Agrawal, and I. B. Baalbaki, "International Services Marketing: A Comparative Evaluation of the Dimensions of Service Quality Between Developed and Developing Countries," *International Marketing Review,* Vol. 11, No. 2, p. 515.

34. Frazier Winsted, "Evaluating Service Encounters," pp. 106–123.

35. Ibid.

36. Guliz Ger, Russell W. Belk, and Dana-Nicoleta Lascu, "The Development in Consumer Desire in Marketizing and Developing Economies: The Cases of Romania and Turkey," in L. McAllister (ed.), *Advances in Consumer Research,* Association for Consumer Research, 1993, Vol. 20, pp. 102–107.

and other brands belonging to companies such as Philip Morris, Anheuser-Busch, Prada, Robert Bosch, Kimberly-Clark, and Nike—are sold at a fraction of their genuine counterparts' cost.[37] Counterfeiters in China range from manufacturers of shampoo and soap in back rooms to large state-owned enterprises and/or joint-venture partners making their profits selling knockoffs of soft drinks and beer, to factories producing car batteries, motorcycles, and even mobile CD factories with optical disk machines; these products are distributed all over the world, including the United States.[38]

9-6a Identifying Types of Counterfeiting

Examples of counterfeiting are design counterfeiting and brand name counterfeiting.

Design Counterfeiting

Copying designs or scents, known as **design counterfeiting,** is quite common and risk free. The polo-style shirt is replicated by many companies, with a design that approximates the polo rider. The design of women's Peugeot watches is close to that of the Rolex Oyster Perpetual. Unknown perfume manufacturers suggest that their brand is similar in scent to a particular brand of perfume, which they name in their product packaging and advertising.

Design counterfeiting Copying designs or scents of another company.

Brand Name Counterfeiting

At the next level is **brand name counterfeiting.** In Cairo, for about a dollar one can purchase simple, cotton shirts with the Christian Dior name on the label. In many capital cities, purses with names such as Prada, Fendi, and Louis Vuitton are sold practically on the steps of the actual retailer, as are fake Rolex watches. Bazaars in Istanbul and Cairo are known for their "quality" fakes. Hong Kong markets where counterfeit products are sold are very popular with tourists. Counterfeit products even make it to flea markets in the United States. In different countries, Pizza Huts and Domino's Pizza restaurants are quite different from the originals, and are not legitimate franchises.

Brand name counterfeiting Selling counterfeit products as brand name originals.

Multinational businesses need to address several factors that contribute to the counterfeiters' success:

- Consumer factors
- Technology factors
- Distribution factors
- Local-government factors

Consumer Factors

On the consumer side, there is a high willingness to purchase counterfeit goods. Studies have shown, for example, that a large proportion of consumers are likely to select a counterfeit apparel item over a genuine good when there is a price advantage, primarily because function risks are low for apparel, whereas prestige gains are high.[39] In this sense, products that are visible and/or consumed publicly

---

37. Dexter Roberts, Frederik Balfour, Paul Magnuson, Pete Engardio, and Jennifer Lee, "China's Pirates: It's Not Just Little Guys—State-Owned Factories Add to the Plague of Fakes," *Business Week,* June 5, 2000, Issue: 3684, pp. 26, 44.

38. Ibid.

39. Peter H. Bloch, Ronald F. Bush, and Leland Campbell, "Consumer 'Accomplices' in Product Counterfeiting," *Journal of Consumer Marketing,* 1993, Vol. 10, No. 4, pp. 27–36.

are more likely to be in demand than products that are less visible and/or consumed publicly.

Moreover, consumers in emerging markets are less likely to notice the difference between a prestige brand and a counterfeit brand.[40] In fact, retailers themselves, in these markets, might be unaware of any difference between prestige brands and counterfeits.

Technology Factors

The spread of advanced production technology (affordable, quality, color-copying machines), as well as production lines supplied by pirates or know-how stolen from joint-venture multinationals required to transfer technology to local partners, has made it possible for counterfeiters to make perfect replicas of the original products. Frequently, neither the manufacturer nor the consumers can tell fakes from the real product.[41]

Distribution Factors

Supply chains are not adequately controlled. Traders use Internet chat rooms and unauthorized dealership networks to sell the products and mix counterfeit products with legitimate products sold on the secondary gray market.[42]

Local-Government Factors

Governments in many developing countries are reluctant to crack down on counterfeiting, especially when state-owned enterprises are involved in the operations. In the case of China, for instance, local governments hesitate to crack down on product pirates because they create thousands of jobs and keep the local economy going; and, even when local authorities take action against counterfeiters (most of whom evade taxes), persuading them to close down the state-owned factories engaging in illegal production is impossible.[43]

Counterfeit products are openly available in many developing countries. Here, consumers, as well as customs representatives inspecting the counterfeit product shipments, are not familiar with many international brand names. Further, customs officials in many developing countries very often are not sufficiently trained in identifying illegal trade in mass-market products. And, as mentioned, counterfeit products are also widely available in developed countries; the prevailing reason is that in the industrialized countries, customs officers inspect the contents of only a small fraction of the goods that go through customs.

9-6b Combating Counterfeiting

Multinational companies have used a number of strategies to combat counterfeiting. Lobbying the U.S. government, as well as the governments involved, is a first step. This process involves filing appeals to the World Trade Organization and lobbying other governmental organizations in the United States and abroad regulating trade. The outcome is uncertain, however. For example, even though member countries of the World Trade Organization are expected to abide by the organization's antipiracy provisions, they are not entirely successful in combating the sales of counterfeit products.

---

40. Roberts, Balfour, Magnuson, Engardio, Jennifer Lee, "China's Pirates," pp. 26, 44.

41. Ibid.

42. Ibid.

43. Ibid.

Alternatives involve a concerted action on the part of companies to combat counterfeiting by changing a product's appearance to differentiate authentic products from fakes. Budweiser embedded in its beer bottles special images that appear only when the product is chilled, rendering them difficult to copy; Microsoft included holograms on its software boxes and inside user manuals, but pirates quickly learned the trick.[44]

The most successful attacks have been launched with the cooperation of local governments. In 2000 in China, a raid was launched by seven battery makers, including Gillette, Energizer, and Panasonic, with the help of 200 government agents, on twenty-one factories in a Southwestern city. As a result of the raid, a total of 150 pieces of manufacturing equipment and three million counterfeit batteries (with Russia as their destination) were confiscated.[45]

Chapter Summary

- **Describe drivers for international standardization and offer an overview of the international standardization–local adaptation continuum and respective company strategies**

  The emergence of uniform market segments, such as global consumers (global teenagers, the global elite), as seen in earlier chapters, increased international travel, and a general consumer preference for products of higher quality at a lower price led to opportunities for global standardization strategies. Such strategies offer numerous benefits, primarily the capability for a firm to market its goods at lower costs and higher profits. A purely global strategy, however, will invariably result in ignoring specific segment preferences and in targeting strategies that have a higher likelihood of failure. Some adaptation can be attempted using a global localization strategy, where the main module of the strategy is maintained, while making minor modifications from market to market. Sometimes, however, adaptation may be required (mandatory), or the adaptation is necessary to better meet the needs of the local market.

- **Examine country-of-origin effects on brand evaluations in relation to product stereotypes and consumer ethnocentrism**

  Country-of-origin information is used in making product evaluation inferences in situations in which very little other information (brand name, for instance) is available to evaluate the product. Country information also can be used to exclude products from the consideration set. For example, ethnocentric consumers, who believe that purchasing foreign products is morally wrong, will refuse to purchase products unless they are made in their own home country.

- **Examine challenges faced by service providers in international markets**

  Service providers face numerous barriers to entry in international markets. In addition to tariffs, international service providers may be prohibited from hiring international employees, or they may be required to have certain certifications that are difficult to obtain and can be obtained only locally. They might also face direct competition from government providers, such as a local government monopoly, or they could face restrictions on movement.

- **Address issues related to brand name protection and the reasons behind widespread international counterfeiting**

  Counterfeiting, ranging from direct copying to design counterfeiting, is flourishing due to improved technology, inadequate channel control, lax enforcement locally and worldwide (despite World Trade Organization involvement), and consumer demand.

---

44. Ibid.

45. Ibid.

Discussion Questions

Discussion Questions

1. Describe the global standardization–local adaptation debate. What are the drivers for globalization and for adaptation? Explain.

2. Give examples of mandatory and nonmandatory adaptations.

3. How do private-label (retailer) brands compete with international and local brands? Give examples.

4. Discuss the different barriers to entry that international service providers face worldwide.

5. What are the reasons behind counterfeiting, and what efforts are taking place to combat it? Are they successful?

International Product and Service Strategies

Key Terms

continuous innovation
controlled test marketing
decline stage
degree of product/service
    newness
designing and developing
    the product
developing and evaluating
    concepts
diffusion process
dynamically continuous
    innovation
early adopters
early majority
generating new product ideas
growth stage

innovation
innovators
international product
    life cycle (IPLC)
introduction stage
lag countries
laggards
late majority
launching the product
    internationally
lead countries
maturity stage
modification
new item in an existing
    product line
new line

new product to existing
    company
new product to existing market
performing a product business
    analysis
product consistency
product depth
product length
product line
product mix
product width
radical innovation
screening new product ideas
simulated test marketing
test marketing
trialability

Outline

Learning Objectives
10-1 The International Product
    Life Cycle (IPLC)
    *10-1a The Product Introduction
        Stage*
    10-1b The Growth Stage
    10-1c The Maturity Stage
    10-1d The Decline Stage
10-2 Managing the
    International Product
    and Service Mix
    10-2a Length
    10-2b Width
    10-2c Depth
10-3 New Product Development
    *10-3a Generating New
        Product Ideas*
    *10-3b Screening New
        Product Ideas*
    *10-3c Developing and
        Evaluating Concepts*
    *10-3d Performing a Product
        Business Analysis*
    *10-3e Designing and
        Developing the Product*
    10-3f Test Marketing
    *10-3g Launching the Product
        Internationally*
10-4 Degree of Product/Service
    Newness
10-5 Product Diffusion
    10-5a Product Factors
    *10-5b Country (Market)
        Factors*
    10-5c Consumer Adopters
Chapter Summary
Discussion Questions

Learning Objectives

Learning Objectives

By the end of this chapter, you should be able to:

- Evaluate the stages of the international product life cycle and identify locus of operations and target markets at each stage
- Identify the different dimensions of the international product mix with company illustrations

- Examine the new product development process and the activities involved at each stage in international markets
- Examine degrees of product newness and address international diffusion processes

Red Bull, an Austrian energy drink, has systematically taken over energy drink marketing around the world. The drink was adopted by consumers in the rest of Europe in the early 1990s and took the U.S. market by storm in 1997; today it is in nearly every retail shop in the U.S. (Tennessee and the Dakotas are among the few states without it). In less than three years, Red Bull single-handedly created and then propelled the energy drink category to $75 million in sales.[1]

The international marketing environment creates complex challenges for products and services. For example, during the product life cycle, firms must coordinate their marketing activities with international trade and investment decisions to remain price competitive in the face of increased competition from manufacturers in developing and developed countries alike. New product development decisions involve consumers in target markets that differ from home-country consumers in their attitudes, interests, and opinions; the challenges of new product/service launches are amplified by the complexities of the marketplace and the competition from both local and multinational firms. And managing the product mix and the product portfolio in line with company strategy and the demands of different consumers offers many dilemmas to brand managers. This chapter attempts to shed light on some of these challenges.

---

1. Kenneth Hein, "Bull's Market," *Brandweek*, May 28, 2001, Vol. 42, No. 22, pp. 21, 23.

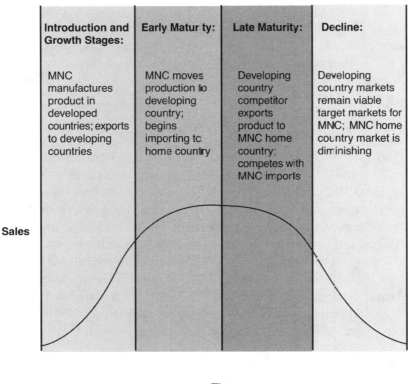

Introduction and Growth Stages:	Early Maturity:	Late Maturity:	Decline:
MNC manufactures product in developed countries; exports to developing countries	MNC moves production to developing country; begins importing to home country	Developing country competitor exports product to MNC home country; competes with MNC imports	Developing country markets remain viable target markets for MNC; MNC home country market is diminishing

Sales

Time

Figure 10-1
The international product life cycle (IPLC) and the multinational corporation (MNC).

10-1 The International Product Life Cycle (IPLC)

Products pass through distinct stages, during which profits may rise and fall, respectively; as a consequence, products require different marketing strategies in each stage. The **international product life cycle (IPLC)** involves a complex relationship between the product life cycle stage and international trade and investment. At a basic level, the premise of the IPLC is as follows: Firms from developed countries prefer to engage in domestic production in the early stage of the product life cycle primarily because product specifications and the manufacturing process are not yet stable. As the product advances to the maturity stage, product specifications and the manufacturing process stabilize. At this point, price competition becomes intense, and international markets emerge, prompting firms to move production abroad to benefit from lower manufacturing costs.[2]

The initial IPLC theory addressed three levels of country development: advanced (industrialized), developing, and less-developed. For the purpose of clarity, and in light of the lead/lag country differentiation (countries where the product or service is first introduced and adopted are referred to as *lead countries,* and countries where the product or service is adopted at a later life-cycle stage are known as *lag countries;* see also section 10-5, "Product Diffusion."), this section addresses the IPLC at two levels of development—industrialized/developed and developing. Figure 10-1 describes the international trade and investment activity of a multinational firm and of local competition during each stage of the international product life cycle (from the perspective of the multinational firm). During the introduction and growth stages, production takes place in the home country

International product life cycle (IPLC) A product life-cycle theory which states that firms from developed countries engage in domestic production in the early stage of the product life cycle, marketing the product to industrialized countries; as the product reaches maturity, product specifications and the manufacturing process stabilize, price competition becomes intense, and markets in developing countries become essential to the firm's success.

2. See Raymond Vernon, "International Investment and International Trade in the Product Cycle," *Quarterly Journal of Economics,* 1966, Vol. 80, No. 2, pp. 190–207, and another article by the same author, "The Product Cycle Hypothesis in a New International Environment," *Oxford Bulletin of Economics and Statistics,* 1979, Vol. 41, pp. 255–267.

or in another industrialized country, and the company exports the products to developing countries. At maturity, manufacturing moves abroad, and the product is imported to the home country and other industrialized countries. Local competitors then emerge; they compete with the multinational corporation in its home country or in other industrialized countries. During the decline stage, international sales keep the company afloat.

10-1a The Product Introduction Stage

Introduction stage The first stage of the international product life cycle when products are developed and marketed in industrialized countries.

During the **introduction stage,** products are developed in industrialized countries and supported by firms' substantial research and development budgets and by highly skilled product research teams. To quickly recover the high costs of product development and launching, a firm markets products in industrialized countries to consumers who can afford the high prices charged to recover the high costs, while it still has control of the market (it is the only manufacturer, or one of the few manufacturers of the product). According to the initial IPLC theory (see section 10-1), these products were first marketed in the products' country of origin. Assuming a reasonable adoption rate in highly industrialized countries, the product also becomes available in developing countries, where it is exported by the firm. Smart phones are currently in this stage.

10-1b The Growth Stage

Growth stage The stage of the international product life cycle characterized by increasing competition and rapid product adoption by the target market.

The **growth stage** is characterized by increasing competition, with new product variants offered to the market, as well as rapid product adoption by the target market. Toward the end of this stage, the focus is on developing economies of scale in the manufacturing process; price competition is increasing at this point and a standard is reached. Examples of products in the growth stage of the IPLC are DVD/CD players. At the end of the growth stage, the product is standardized; that is, a particular standard is reached, and products are manufactured to conform to this standard. In the case of VCRs, the VHS format became the standard. DVD/CD players were initially introduced as DVDs; at this point, the DVD/CD combination is standard. Production continues to take place in industrialized countries during this stage, and manufacturers in industrialized countries continue to export their products in developing countries.

10-1c The Maturity Stage

Maturity stage A stage of the international product life cycle characterized by a slowdown in sales growth as the product is adopted by most target consumers and by a leveling or decline in profits primarily due to intense price competition.

Usually the longest stage in the product life cycle, the **maturity stage** is characterized by a slowdown in sales growth as the product is adopted by most target consumers and by a leveling or decline in profits primarily due to intense price competition. At this point manufacturing moves to developing countries to save on labor costs. For example, the U.S. electronics company Motorola selected Krakow, Poland, as its first European software center and the location of a chip plant,[3] while Siemens AG, Macronix, and Intel Corp. are engaging in semiconductor manufacturing in Thailand, in a consortium with a local company.[4] Products manufactured abroad are then imported in the home country and other industrialized countries; these products successfully compete on price in the

---

3. Milton Keynes, "Motorola Chooses Poland for New Site," *Corporate Location,* European Edition, May/June 1998, p. 7.

4. Faith Hung, "Consortium Looks to Build Thailand Fab—Siemens, Intel and Macronix Want to Jumpstart Country's Semi Industry," *Electronic Buyers' News,* June 5, 2000, Issue 1214, p. 4.

respective developed countries. Examples of products in this category are television sets, hi-fi equipment, and video cameras, among others.

As companies establish strategic alliances with firms from developing countries or engage in local manufacturing under other forms, such as contract manufacturing, or through a wholly owned subsidiary, they train local talent and are likely to create local competition. Competitors from developing countries will then sell products in industrialized countries, competing directly with the multinational firm in its home market and in other developed countries. Examples of successful companies from developing countries exporting their products in developed countries abound. Shenzhen Electronics Group, a Chinese company, sells its television sets, hi-fi equipment, and quartz watches in the United States.[5] In other examples, "Made in India" is a sign of high-quality software; in this market, top software companies include subsidiaries of U.S. companies, such as Motorola India Electronics Ltd. and IBM Global Services India, as well as local companies such as Satyam Computer Services Ltd., Tata Consultancy Services, and Wipro Infotech.[6] India has a $5.5 billion software industry, growing at an annual rate of 50 percent, and it exports software primarily to the United States and Europe.[7]

10-1d The Decline Stage

Products in the **decline stage** are rapidly losing ground to new technologies or product alternatives. Sales and, consequently, profits are declining at this stage, and a firm might consider whether its presence in the market is warranted. However, having an international presence during the decline stage, particularly in developing countries, could be an advantage. One of the main benefits of going international and engaging in international marketing is the ability of a firm to extend the product life cycle. A product may be in the decline stage in the lead country, where it was developed, as well as in other industrial economies, and, at the same time, in a stable maturity stage in most developing countries.

Decline stage The stage of the international product life cycle in which products are rapidly losing ground to new technologies or product alternatives, causing a decrease in sales and profits.

10-2 Managing the International Product and Service Mix

The product portfolio of a firm is usually diversified into products that are in different stages of the product life cycle, such that profits from successful mature products can be used to invest in new products and products that have a lower market share. Most multinational corporations tend to have both local and global brands that they nurture through their life cycle. The international **product mix** is the complete assortment of the products that a company offers to its target international consumers, and has a number of important dimensions. An important dimension of the product mix is the **product line,** a number of related brands in the same product category. Companies use different line strategies to achieve market share and profitability goals; for example, companies engage in line extensions to target consumers who otherwise cannot afford a particular product. In the fashion realm, for example, numerous top-line designers target the masses with bridge offerings (secondary, more affordable lines): Escada with Laurel, Ann Klein with Ann Klein II, Donna Karan with DKNY, Armani with Emporio Armani, etc.

Product mix The complete assortment of products that a company offers to its target international consumers.

Product line All the brands the company offers in the same product category.

---

5. *Far Eastern Economic Review,* "Let 100 Firms Boom: China's Enterprise Groups Await Economic Reform," 1991, Vol. 153, No. 36, pp. 56–58.

6. Michael Cusumano, "'Made in India' a New Sign of Software Quality," *Computerworld,* February 28, 2000, Vol. 34, No. 9, p. 36.

7. Ibid.

Product consistency The extent to which a company's different product lines are related, use the same distribution channels, and have the same final consumers.

To illustrate the remaining product dimensions, we will use the example of Unilever (www.unilever.com), one of the largest consumer product companies in the world. Unilever is actually composed of two companies, Unilever NV and Unilever PLC, operating as one company linked by a series of agreements and common shareholders, and headquartered in London and Rotterdam, respectively.[8] Although Unilever is organized primarily into two divisions, the foods division and the personal care division, the company has a number of product lines that are addressed as separate strategic business units.

Another important dimension of the product mix is **product consistency;** this term refers to the extent to which the different product lines are related and use the same distribution channels and have the same final consumers. The Unilever brands are consistent within each of the company divisions, the foods division and the personal care division. DiverseyLever, the company's professional cleaning product (see Table 10-1), is probably the only product that might break this pattern of consistency.

The other dimensions of the product mix, as illustrated by the Unilever example in Table 10-1, are product length, width, and depth.

10-2a Length

Product length The total number of brands in the product mix.

The **product length** is the total number of brands in the product mix—all the brands sold by the company. Counting the Unilever brands in Table 10-1, the total product length is 37.

10-2b Width

Product width The total number of product lines that a company offers to its target international consumers.

The **product width** is the total number of product lines the company offers. Counting the different product lines in Table 10-1 (culinary products, frozen foods, ice cream, tea, margarine, household care products, detergents, deodorants, shampoos, personal care, oral care, fragrances, diagnostics, and professional cleaning products), the total product width is 14.

10-2c Depth

Product depth The number of different offerings for a particular brand.

The **product depth** refers to the number of different offerings for a product category. For example, Lipton tea comes in at least three variants: Lipton Yellow Label, Lipton Ice Tea, and Lipton Brisk. The depth of the tea category (the Lipton brand), therefore, is 3. Product depth for the tea line is thus calculated by adding all the variants under the Lipton brand.

Companies alter their product mix by purchasing existing international or local brands. For example, Unilever purchased the Ben & Jerry's Ice Cream brand. Companies also develop new brands and products that they can add to their portfolio. Section 10-3 discusses new product development.

10-3 New Product Development

To maintain their competitive advantage and to ensure survival and growth locally, regionally, or globally, companies must develop and introduce new products and services that meet the needs of their markets. International new product development is a costly process that involves the firm at all levels. If successful, product/service development is the key to a company's success and future.

8. Unilever is described in detail at www.Unilever.com, a source for some of the material in this section.

T A B L E **10-1** **Unilever Products**

Product Area	Brand Names
Culinary products	Ragu spaghetti sauces
	Calvé Whisky Cocktail
	Hellmann's Mayonnaise
	Knorr soups
Frozen foods	Findus 4 Salti in Padella
	Gordon's Tenders
Ice cream	Magnum
	Solero
	Bryers
	Ben & Jerry's
Margarine	I Can't Believe It's Not Butter
	Rama margarine
	Becel spreads
Tea	Lipton
Household care	Domestos
	Cif
Detergents	Omo
	Ala
	Snuggle
	Comfort
Deodorants	Rexona/Sure
	Axe
	Dove
Shampoos	SunSilk
	ThermaSilk
	Organics
Personal care	Lux
	Dove
	Vaseline Intensive Care
	Pond's
Oral care	Mentadent
	Signal
	Close-Up
Fragrances	Valentino
	Cerruti
	Calvin Klein
Diagnostics	Unipath fertility products
Professional cleaning	DiverseyLever

In general, new product development involves substantial risks and costs; the complex environment of the international marketplace adds considerably to both the risks and costs. Consider, for example, the case of Freeplay Energy, a company in Cape Town, South Africa, which developed wind-up, self-powered radios for the African market under the name Freeplay Energy. The product initially failed in Africa, where consumers preferred to purchase batteries, rather than incur a one-time expenditure of about $50 for such a radio; the company, however, remained in business primarily due to its success in the United States and Europe.[9] After refocusing on developed markets, Freeplay developed its products with a sophisticated, Western consumer in mind. With the initial product, the radio had to be wound 20 seconds to produce 30 minutes of radio time; a lighter, smaller version produced one hour of playing time. Subsequent to its success in Europe, the product started selling in developing countries as well. The product is marketed using

---

9. These examples are detailed in Harriet Marsh, "Adapting to Africa," *Marketing*, March 30, 2000, p. 39.

different strategies worldwide: In Japan and the U.S., the product is marketed as part of earthquake and tornado survival kits; in Germany, interest in the product is fueled by environmental concern; whereas in the U.K., consumers take pride in owning such an invention.

Interestingly, the same company is presently making a second attempt to fulfill the needs of the African market: Freeplay is in the process of developing a self-powered generator intended to enable consumers in developing countries to charge their satellite telephones. The entrepreneurs developing this product believe that most of the growth in cellular phones is in the developing world; however, most African countries cannot afford the infrastructure needed, leaving satellite communication fueled by either expensive disposable batteries or self-powered technology as the only options.

The two examples involving Freeplay's innovations illustrate some of the complexities involved in developing new products internationally. The following are examples of risks and difficulties companies face when developing new products:

- International and local competitors could appropriate the product/service idea and deliver the final product or service to the market more swiftly, economically, and with stronger company backing (brand reputation, financial support) than the initial product/service developer.
- International target consumers might not respond as anticipated to the offering (as in the case of Freeplay's wind-up radio) because it does not meet their needs, because they cannot afford it, or because they prefer to adopt a product later in the product life cycle stage.
- Local governments or the home-country government might impose restrictions on product testing procedures (in the case of pharmaceuticals, for example).
- The technological infrastructure of the market is substandard and cannot support the new product.

The steps that companies typically follow in the product development process are essentially the same as those involved in domestic product development. Figure 10-2 illustrates the international product development process. At each step, the process can be either terminated or restarted for each individual product idea; consequently, a product must go through each stage in order to reach the international product launching stage. Throughout the product development process, maintaining a strong market orientation is important: A thorough understanding of consumers' needs and wants and of the competitive situation and the nature of the market are critical to product success.[10]

10-3a Generating New Product Ideas

Generating new product ideas
Seeking ideas using different strategies as the first step in the new product development process.

The first step in the new product development process is **generating new product ideas.** Depending on the products provided and/or company philosophy, ideas will be sought using different strategies. Most product and service firms are driven by the marketing concept, and their product development decisions are based on identifying the needs, wants, and desires of consumers. For technology-driven firms, the focus is more likely to be on the product itself, and thus the research and development division is likely to be responsible for developing product ideas. Even in this second instance, however, products are developed with the needs of the consumer in mind. Freeplay Energy, with its wind-up radio, is an example of a

10. Robert G. Cooper, "New Products: What Distinguishes the Winners?" *Research Technology Management,* November/December 1990, Vol. 33, pp. 27–31.

Figure 10-2
Steps in the new product development process.

product-focused company. An inventor created the radio independent of the market, and a marketer identified a market for the product—consumers in Africa who do not have electricity, who use batteries for their radios and could benefit from using wind-up radios.

Companies use multiple sources for ideas. Among the most common are consumers; competitive analyses; and some additional sources such as channel members, company employees, and so on.

Consumers

The most obvious sources for ideas are consumers in the home-country market of the firm. Other sources of product ideas are consumers in the company's international markets. Although, traditionally, products of U.S. multinational firms were driven entirely by consumers in the United States, these companies are now increasingly drawing upon consumers around the world for new product or service ideas. A growing number of companies are developing products for one market and successfully marketing them in markets that are substantially different. Häagen-Dazs developed a caramel-flavored ice cream called Dulce de Leche for Argentina; the company brought this flavor to the United States, where, in stores that carry it, it is second only to vanilla, and to Europe, where it is moving from seasonal-flavor to year-round-flavor status.[11] In other examples, Nike found that a soccer boot designed and worn by Ronaldo, a player on the Brazilian soccer team, was very popular with consumers in the United States. Similarly, Levi Strauss, the quintessential all-American jeans manufacturer, offered a dark version

---

11. David Leonhardt, "It was a Hit in Buenos Aires—So Why Not Boise?" *Business Week*, September 7, 1998, Vol. 3594, pp. 56–57.

of denim jeans that has been very popular for a few years with consumers in Japan to U.S. consumers, who responded very favorably to it.[12]

Competitive Analyses

Competition represents an obvious source for product and service ideas. Products that are in the test market phase or that are just being launched are always vulnerable to having their ideas copied. For example, Kao, a Japanese detergent manufacturer, developed a super-absorbent diaper, causing Procter & Gamble's Pampers to lose its lead in the Japanese market; however, Procter & Gamble promptly developed its own super-absorbent version of Pampers, selling it aggressively worldwide.[13]

Additional Sources

Other sources of ideas are channel members, who are closer to consumers than the manufacturer; company employees, such as sales personnel, engineers, or even top management; and inventors; consultants; non-profit research laboratories; universities; and research firms, among others. Research conducted by the firm in the form of brainstorming sessions and qualitative research also may be used in the process of generating product ideas.[14]

10-3b Screening New Product Ideas

Screening new product ideas
Eliminating product ideas that do not fit with the target consumers and/or the overall mission of the organization.

In the process of **screening new product ideas,** it is best to consider both the extent to which the product fits with the target consumers as well as with the overall mission of the organization.[15] At this stage, a checklist is usually developed to screen out product ideas that do not meet these criteria.

In the screening process, the following should be taken into consideration:[16]

- The product to be developed should be superior, delivering unique benefits to users, rather than a "me-too" undifferentiated product. Such superiority is derived from design, features, attributes, specifications, and product positioning.
- The target market should be a large, attractive, growth market, where the product is perceived as important, where demand for it has been stable over time, and where customers are profitable and price-insensitive.
- There should be a fit between the new product requirements and the resources, skills, and experiences of the firm with regard to management capabilities, technical support, research and development, and manufacturing skills, as well as sales and distribution skills and resources in the company, or the firm's channel of distribution.

Factors that lead to a lower success rate normally are evaluated unfavorably in the screening process; these factors, however, are commonplace for firms targeting international markets. International involvement often takes the firm into unfamiliar territory: The company targets new customers, serves unfamiliar customer

---

12. Ibid.

13. C. Samuel Craig and Susan P. Douglas, "Configural Advantage in Global Markets," *Journal of International Marketing,* 2000, Vol. 8, No. 1, pp. 6–26.

14. Gordon A. Wyner, "Product Testing: Benefits and Risks," *Marketing Research,* Spring 1997, Vol. 9, No. 1, pp. 46–48.

15. Lisa Susanne Willsey, "Taking These 7 Steps Will Help You Launch a New Product," *Marketing News,* March 29, 1999, Vol. 33, No. 7, p. 17.

16. See Cooper, "New Products," pp. 27–31.

needs, uses new channels, and meets new servicing requirements. Success rates for such products are lower.[17]

10-3c Developing and Evaluating Concepts

The next stage, **developing and evaluating concepts,** is an important step for firms developing products for international markets. Key activities at this stage are to determine how the product will be viewed by consumers and how it will be used; this information can be determined by having the target consumers test the idea to gauge its usefulness.[18] Typically, the process involves developing a detailed description of the product and asking prospective consumers to evaluate it and to indicate their willingness to purchase the hypothetical product. Most often, this is done using a focus group of representative target consumers.

Even in cases in which firms are exporting products initially developed for the home-country market, it is essential that they engage in market research. The shortening of the product life cycle and the intensity of international competition increase pressure on exporters to evaluate and re-evaluate their market in light of rapid technological change and to conduct concept-testing research that ranges from formal methods, such as focus groups, to ad hoc information gathering.[19]

One method that is frequently used at this stage is conjoint analysis. In this method respondents receive descriptions of different hypothetical products with varying levels of the same attributes, which they are then asked to rank. Analysts can determine the ideal combination of attributes, ascertain the importance of each attribute, and, assuming the data was collected from a sufficiently large sample of the target population, estimate market share.

Developing and evaluating concepts Determining how consumers will perceive and use a new product; a step in the new product development process.

10-3d Performing a Product Business Analysis

Performing a product business analysis should include calculating projected project costs, return on investment, and cash flow and determining the fixed and variable costs for the long term.[20] However enthusiastic the target consumers queried, if these figures do not fit the company budget, the project will be high risk. For many product categories, product price is a critical characteristic; at this stage, it is important to identify the price level at which revenue or profit best fit the manufacturer's goals.[21]

Performing a product business analysis Calculating projected costs such as return on investment and cash flow, and determining the fixed and variable costs for the long term.

10-3e Designing and Developing the Product

At the next stage, **designing and developing the product,** product prototypes are developed. It is important that product prototypes precisely match the concept description developed in the concept development and evaluation stage; if the company strays from the initial description, it is crucial that the revised product description be tested.[22]

The product now acquires a name, a brand identity, and the marketing mix is developed. The cross-functional team developing the product—research and

Designing and developing the product Developing product prototypes and giving the product a name, a brand identity, and a marketing mix; a step in the new product development process.

---

17. Ibid.

18. Willsey, "Taking These 7 Steps," p. 17.

19. F. H. Rolf Seringhaus, "Comparative Marketing Behaviour of Canadian and Austrian High Tech Firms," *Management International Review,* 1993, Vol. 33, No. 3, pp. 247–270.

20. Willsey, "Taking These 7 Steps," p. 17.

21. Wyner, "Product Testing," pp. 46–48.

22. Robert S. Doscher, "How to Create New Products," *Target Marketing,* 1994, Vol. 17, No. 1, pp. 40–41.

development, engineering, operations, marketing, finance—must come together for this process.[23] This team must be focused on the project in such a way that a large percentage of team members' time is devoted to the project, rather than to other projects; it also is important that the team acts as a unit, focusing on project, rather than departmental, interests.[24]

For multinational companies, coordination takes place across subsidiaries, or in conjunction with international partners. Companies such as Boeing and Motorola coordinate research and development activities globally by establishing worldwide information systems to coordinate product and design development; for example, in developing the Boeing 777, the company used real-time computer-aided technology to design components jointly with Japanese partners.[25] Companies also tend to encourage communication among research and development facilities in different countries; Procter & Gamble and Unilever, for example, require extensive communication and information sharing among units.[26]

10-3f Test Marketing

Test marketing a product can provide good indication of how the product will be received when it is in the market, but this stage can also be expensive, time consuming, and open to competitive sabotage.[27] The following are test marketing options firms can choose to evaluate the reaction of the market to their product. At the lower involvement level is *simulated test marketing*, which is not as costly and does not give competition much information about the product. *Controlled test marketing* is limited to a few stores, is thus also less costly, and gives only limited exposure of the product to competition. *Actual test marketing* necessitates important strategic decisions and commitments that involve channel members, intensive promotion, and high promotional expenses; test marketing could create conditions for the product to be vulnerable to competitive reactions.

Simulated Test Marketing

Because eight out of ten products fail, simulated test markets are often used to reduce the risks a company would incur in terms of marketing, sales, and capital expenses, in terms of cannibalization of the parent brand through line extension and in terms of competitive reaction to the new product.[28] Among the **simulated test marketing** research systems used today are LITMUS, which is used especially for new packaged goods, consumer durables, and services; ASSESSOR, which is used for packaged goods; BASES, which is used primarily for food and health and beauty products; and ESP, which is used primarily for packaged goods.[29]

To illustrate, the LITMUS simulated test marketing study[30] recruits about 600 representative consumers who participate in a research study in a central facility in a number of markets. After responding to questions about their product-related

Test marketing Testing new-product performance in a limited area of a national or regional target market to estimate product performance in the respective country or region.

Simulated test marketing Test marketing simulating purchase environments where samples of target consumers are observed in their product-related decision-making process.

---

23. Willsey, "Taking These 7 Steps," p. 17.

24. Robert G. Cooper, "How to Launch a New Product Successfully," *CMA*, Vol. 69, 1995, No. 8, pp. 20–23.

25. Shaoming Zou and Aysegul Ozsomer, "Global Product R&D and the Firm's Strategic Position," *Journal of International Marketing*, 1999, Vol. 7, No. 1, pp. 57–76.

26. Ibid.

27. Willsey, "Taking These 7 Steps," p. 17.

28. Kevin J. Clancy and Robert S. Shulman, "It's Better to Fly a New Product Simulator than Crash the Real Thing," *Planning Review*, July/August 1992, Vol. 20, No. 4, pp. 10–16.

29. Ibid.

30. The LITMUS test is the creation of Kevin J. Clancy, who describes the procedure used in Clancy and Shulman, "It's Better to Fly a New Product Simulator," pp. 10–16.

attitudes and purchase behavior, they view advertising of the new brand and of competitive brands that are embedded in a television program. The respondents then comment on the television program and the advertising and then proceed to a simulated store stocking test brands and competitive brands where they can buy the products at a substantial discount. The proportion of individuals purchasing the test brand is then used to estimate product trialability.

Controlled Test Marketing

Usually conducted by a research firm in industrialized countries, **controlled test marketing** involves offering a new product to a group of stores and evaluating the market reaction to it (consumer reaction as well as competitive reaction). In the process, different aspects of the marketing mix are varied—price, in-store promotion, placement in the store, etc. A more informal controlled test marketing involves simply asking a number of stores to carry the product for a fee; depending on the outcome, the manufacturing firm may decide to produce the product on a larger scale, or not.

Controlled test marketing Test marketing that involves offering a new product to a group of stores and evaluating the market's reaction to it.

Actual Test Marketing

A number of important decisions are involved in full-blown test marketing. Companies at this stage must decide on the cities that are most appropriate for testing the product, based on the availability of retailers and other necessary distribution and logistics service providers, and on availability of the infrastructure needed to conduct the test market, such as the necessary media, research firms, direct mail providers, etc. Multinational companies do not limit test marketing nor product launching to their home countries. For example, Pepsi-Cola International test marketed its no-sugar Pepsi Max in Northern Italy and the United Kingdom.[31] The duration of the test market also may vary, from a few months to a year or more, depending on company goals and budget. In the case of Pepsi Max, the product was tested in the U.K. for one year.[32]

For companies selling financial products in industrialized countries and for companies that cannot afford large-scale testing in the marketplace, test marketing may be limited to direct mail. For example, MasterCard continuously tests new products in the Netherlands and Germany by using direct mail. This strategy also appeals to service providers from developing countries. For example, Mexican exporters often use direct mail to test a market in the United States or Canada; however, this approach is problematic because the national mail service can be unreliable, and ZIP codes are missing from database lists, etc.[33] Test marketing exclusively using direct mail works well when it is aimed at a narrow, well-defined target market; although this approach is possible in Europe, Canada, and the United States, where segmentation is a precise science based on refined methods of demographic and psychographic assessment, in developing countries, such well-defined databases are not always available.[34]

Although test marketing can provide valuable information for the manufacturer, anticipating product performance in the short run, its usefulness is often questioned given the high expense it necessitates. In a rapidly changing competitive environment, being first in the market constitutes an important competitive

31. Harriot Lane Fox, "Global Roll-Out for Pepsi Max," *Marketing*, April 7, 1994, p. 2.

32. Ibid.

33. Stacey Ramirez, "Hand Outs," *Business Mexico*, May 1996, Vol. 6, No. 5, pp. 12–16.

34. Ibid.

advantage addressed earlier—the first-mover advantage: As such, the company is the first to attract consumers and to commit channel members for its new product. A company is also vulnerable to competitive reaction during the test marketing stage. On one hand, competition could appropriate the product idea and be the first to offer the product to the market; on the other, competition could sabotage the new brand, cutting prices for all competitive offerings.

Test marketing, nevertheless, can be a reliable predictor of national market share, costs, and profitability and a tool to assess and compare between alternative product strategies; yet, surprisingly, this tool is frequently overlooked in international marketing.[35] Among errors to avoid in international test marketing are incorrect forecasts, unrealistic market conditions, incorrect media translations, and choice of the wrong test market.[36]

10-3g Launching the Product Internationally

Launching the product internationally   Introducing a new product to the international market as the last step in the new product development process.

Strategies for **launching the product internationally** have an impact on later product performance; products launched using a successful strategy have a higher rate of success and score high ratings on profitability, technical success, and positive impact on the company.[37] Goodness of launch is characterized by the following, in order of impact: high service quality, on-time shipment and adequate product availability, quality sales force and enough sales effort and support, quality of promotion, and sufficient promotional effort.[38]

Product Launch Decisions: Consumers and Countries

In international marketing, an important decision at the launching stage is what countries in which to launch the product. Whereas, in the recent past, most launching was aimed at consumers in the manufacturers' home countries, increasingly, multinationals launch products in countries that have the best consumer-product fit. In the case of Pepsi Max, Pepsi-Cola International launched the product in Australia, Ireland, and Holland, rapidly gaining market shares in these three countries between 3 percent and 4.8 percent.[39] The company aimed the brand at consumers who are health conscious but still looking for a caffeine kick.

Timing of Launch

Another important decision is the timing of the new product launch. Companies often attempt to gain the first-mover advantage by being the first to launch the new product. Alternatively, they could engage in later entry. The advantage of this approach is that the competitors would have to incur the costs of informing the market about the new product and its features; also, the company could market the product as a "me-too" product, reducing advertising costs significantly.

Marketing Mix Decisions

Other important decisions at the product-launching stage involve setting the price that the target consumer is willing to pay for the product. Prices might be higher

---

35. Tamer S. Cavusgil and Ugur Yavas, "Test Marketing: An Exposition," *Marketing Intelligence and Planning,* 1987, Vol. 5, No. 3, pp. 16–20.

36. Ibid.

37. Robert G. Cooper, "Debunking the Myths of New Product Development," *Research Technology Management,* July/August 1994, Vol. 37, No. 4, pp. 40–50.

38. Ibid.

39. Fox, "Global Roll-Out for Pepsi Max," p. 2.

Figure 10-3
In the United States, Mentos are available primarily in one flavor—mint. Jacobs Coffee, on the other hand, is not available here, even though it is a Kraft (U.S. company) product. In Europe, these two brands are very popular and are available in multiple varieties.

if the product is launched in industrialized countries with a wealthy consumer base—typically on par with competing products. For consumers in emerging markets, the product is usually launched at a lower price, to initiate trial. When Pepsi Max was first introduced in Romania, in 1995, the product was available at a relatively low price.

Firms typically choose to vary their product mix from one market to another. For example, in the United States, Mentos are available primarily in one flavor (mint). In the rest of the world, they are available in numerous flavors. On the other hand, Kraft's famous Jacobs Coffee is available only in Europe, in multiple flavors (see Figure 10-3).

Promotion—in the form of sales promotion, personal selling, and advertising—is crucial during the launching process. When Pepsi Max was launched in Romania, company representatives set up tables in front of the Academy of Economics, a premier business school located in the capital city, offering samples to consumers and offering cases of the product at a discounted price. Worldwide, Pepsi-Cola International backed the launch of Pepsi Max by more than $10 million in advertising, channeled through BBDO, a New York advertising agency.[40]

Finally, channel members constitute an important element of the marketing mix during the launching stage. Decisions such as shelf positioning, often contingent on the payment of slotting fees to retailers, as well as questions on inventory, trade allowances, and financing, among others, are addressed at this stage. As will be seen in Chapter 11, "Managing International Distribution Operations and Logistics," there are significant variations in the channels of distributions worldwide for individual product categories, with fragmented channels in markets such as Japan, concentrated channels in command economies, etc.; this factor adds to the complexity and expense of the product-launching effort.

10-4 Degree of Product/Service Newness

Innovation is thought of as the creation of a better product or process and may range from the substitution of a cheaper material in an existing product to a

---

40. Ibid.

Degree of product/service newness The extent to which a product is new to the market in general or to a group of consumers.

New product to existing market A product never before offered to the market.

New product to existing company A new product that the company offers to the market; the product competes with similar competitor offerings.

New line A new product category offered by the company.

New item in an existing product line A new brand that the company offers to the market in an existing product line.

Modification The alteration of an existing company product.

Innovation A product new to the world.

Radical innovation The creation of new industries or new standards of management, manufacturing, and servicing that represent fundamental changes for consumers, entailing departures from established consumption.

Dynamically continuous innovation Innovation that does not alter significantly consumer behavior but still entails a change in the consumption pattern.

Continuous innovation Product innovation where there is no disruption in consumption patterns; such innovations involve product alterations, such as new flavors or new products that are improvements over the old offerings.

better way of marketing, distributing, or supporting a product or service.[41] **Degree of product/service newness** refers to the extent to which a product or service is new to the market. Organizations that have a good record of innovation pursue innovation systematically, actively searching for change and supporting creative individuals who are internally driven.[42]

Innovation takes on many forms, and marketing literature uses various classifications for different categories of innovation. At a basic level, new products and services can be classified in one of five categories:[43]

- **New product to existing market, new product to existing company**—These categories account for 33.7 percent of products.
- **New line**—This category represents a new product or product line to a company, but for a company already operating in that market; it accounts for 16.8 percent of products.
- **New item in an existing product line** for the company—This category accounts for 11.9 percent of products; these products are likely to have the highest success rate (83 percent) and the greatest impact on company sales and profit.
- **Modification** of an existing company product—This category accounts for 18.8 percent of products.
- **Innovation**, new product to the world—This category accounts for about 18.8 percent of products.

Another popular classification organizes innovation into the *radical, dynamically continuous,* and *continuous* categories. **Radical innovations** (also known as discontinuous innovations) create new industries or new standards of management, manufacturing, and servicing, and they represent fundamental changes for consumers, entailing departures from established consumption.[44] Examples of relatively recent radical innovations are the Internet and endoscopy/endoscopic surgery. **Dynamically continuous innovations** do not alter significantly consumer behavior, but they represent a change in the consumption pattern; cellular telephones are an example of such innovation. **Continuous innovations** have no disruption on consumption patterns and involve only product alterations, such as new flavors, or a new product that is an improvement over the old offering. They usually are congruous, in the sense that they can be used alongside the existing systems; for example, a new Microsoft Windows version will work with computers that are only a few years old or older computers with enhanced capacity.

Most of the innovation taking place today is continuous. However, a relatively recent radical innovation, the Internet, has revolutionized all aspects of the marketing mix, with important implications for international marketing. As a distribution tool, it renders products accessible instantly worldwide, regardless of the firm's experience and size. It is an equal-opportunity distribution tool for companies from industrialized and developing countries alike, allowing for creative and innovative market penetration.

In one example demonstrating how the Internet can be used successfully in promoting developing country exports, the International Trade Center organized

---

41. Nicholas Valery, "Survey: Innovation in Industry: Industry Gets Religion," *The Economist,* February 20, 1999, Vol. 350, no. 8107, pp. S5–S6.

42. Ibid.

43. See Cooper, "Debunking the Myths," pp. 40–50.

44. See Michael-Jorg Oesterle, "Time-Span Until Internationalization: Foreign Market Entry as a Built-in-Mechanism of Innovations," *Management International Review,* 1997, Vol. 37, No. 2, pp. 125–149.

the world's first on-line coffee auction, selling Brazilian specialty coffee to bidders around the world via the Internet; the auction drew buyers around the world and generated high prices for Brazilian growers.[45] In another example, a small entrepreneur in rural Transylvania, Romania, used the Internet to identify retailers of custom-made hardwood borders (used in more elaborate wood flooring) in the United Sates. After requesting samples and prices via e-mail, the entrepreneur placed orders for similar hardwood borders with a local Transylvanian furniture manufacturer and, subsequently, approached the same U.S. retailers, offering them their products at considerably lower prices.

10-5 Product Diffusion[46]

Product diffusion refers to the manner in which a product is adopted by consumers worldwide—the speed of adoption by various groups. A number of factors influence the speed of product adoption in different countries; they are discussed in sections 10-5a through 10-5c.

10-5a Product Factors

In general, a number of attributes of an innovation are likely to accelerate the rate of adoption of a product or service.[47] First, the new product or service must offer a *relative advantage* compared to the other offerings available on the market and must be *compatible with the needs of consumers*. In addition, the product/service use must be *observable* (or communicable to others) and have a high **trialability** (for example, consumers can try the product on a limited basis, by renting it, for instance). Both product and country determinants of adoption rates are illustrated on Figure 10-4.

10-5b Country (Market) Factors

New products tend to be adopted at different rates in different international markets. Countries where the product or service is first introduced and adopted are referred to as **lead countries,** and countries where the product or service is adopted at a later stage are known as **lag countries.** This process is similar to the traditional two-step **diffusion process,** whereby products are first offered to

Trialability   The ability of the consumer to experience a product with minimal effort.

Lead countries   Countries where a product or service is first introduced and adopted.

Lag countries   Countries where a product or service is adopted after already being introduced in lead countries.

Diffusion process   The process by which a product is adopted by consumers worldwide.

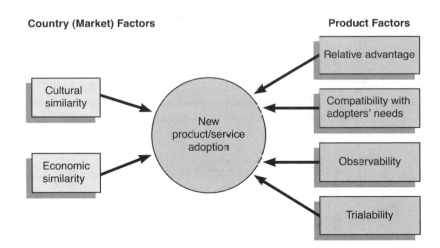

Country (Market) Factors

- Cultural similarity
- Economic similarity

New product/service adoption

Product Factors

- Relative advantage
- Compatibility with adopters' needs
- Observability
- Trialability

Figure 10-4
Determinants of new product/service adoption.

---

45. *International Trade Forum*, "World's First Internet Coffee Auction a Success," 2000, Issue 1, pp. 37–38.

46. The consumer adoption process is addressed in section 10-5c, "Consumer Adopters."

47. See Everett M. Rogers, *Diffusion of Innovations*, 3rd Edition, Free Press, 1983.

wealthy consumers and, subsequently, to the mass market. By analogy, consumers in wealthy, industrialized countries (lead countries) adopt the product first, whereas consumers in developing countries (lag countries) adopt the product later.

Generally, the diffusion rate tends to be faster in lag countries. Consumers in lag countries learn from the experiences of adopters in lead countries; for example, the dissemination of information on the benefits of retail scanners in the United States led to a very rapid diffusion of scanners in Europe, Japan, Australia, and Latin America.[48] The later the product or service is introduced in a lag country, the faster the adoption rate.[49] In addition, products and services are adopted at faster rates in lag countries that are culturally similar or that have similar economies.[50] And, although in the past geographic proximity was an important determinant of product diffusion in lag countries, international travel and media spillover across national borders are diminishing more and more the effect of geography on the product and service diffusion process.[51]

10-5c Consumer Adopters

Target consumers—national, regional, or worldwide—can be segmented based on the manner in which they adopt new products throughout the respective products' life cycle. The segments are

- **Innovators**—These few (2.5 percent of the total market) risk takers can afford to pay the higher purchase price charged by companies during the introduction stage of the product (to recoup investment costs). In developing countries, these consumers are the well-to-do business owners or leading government ministers, and their families.
- **Early adopters**—The next consumers to purchase the product tend to be opinion leaders in their communities who take risks, but with greater discernment than innovators. They constitute about 13.5 percent of the total population.
- **Early majority**—These consumers, who account for 34 percent of the total market, are more risk averse than individuals in the first categories but enjoy the status of being among the first in their peer group to buy what will be a popular product.
- **Late majority**—These consumers, who account for 34 percent of the total market, are individuals of limited means who are likely to adopt products only if the products are widely popular and the risk associated with buying them is minimal. The products themselves are much more affordable at this stage.
- **Laggards**—These consumers, who account for 16 percent of the total market, are the last to adopt new products and do so only in late maturity. In general, laggards are risk averse and very conservative in their spending.

Innovators   Risk takers who can afford to pay the higher purchase price charged by companies during the introduction stage of a product; they account for 2.5% of the total market.

Early adopters   Consumers who purchase a product early in its product life cycle and who tend to be opinion leaders in their communities who take risks, but with greater discernment than innovators; they account for 13.5% of the total market.

Early majority   Consumers who enjoy the status of being among the first in their peer group to purchase a popular product; they account for 34% of the total market.

Late majority   Individuals of limited means who are likely to adopt products only if the products are widely popular and the risk associated with buying them is minimal; they account for 34% of the total market.

Laggards   Consumers who are the last to adopt new products and do so only in late maturity because they are risk averse and very conservative in their spending; they account for 16% of the total market.

48. Jaishankar Ganesh and V. Kumar, "Capturing the Cross-National Learning Effect: An Analysis of an Industrial Technology Diffusion," *Journal of the Academy of Marketing Science,* 1996, Vol. 24, No. 4, pp. 328–337.

49. Hikorazu Takada and Dipak Jain, "Cross-National Analysis of Diffusion of Consumer Durable Goods in Pacific Rim Countries," *Journal of Marketing,* 1991, Vol. 55, No. 1, pp. 48–54.

50. Jaishankar Ganesh, V. Kumar, and Velavan Subramanian, "Learning Effect in Multinational Diffusion of Consumer Durables: An Exploratory Investigation," *Journal of the Academy of Marketing Science,* 1997, Vol. 25, No. 3, pp. 214–228.

51. Ibid.

The categories of adopters vary greatly in markets of different development levels. For example, all categories of consumers have significantly higher means in highly industrialized countries, compared to consumers in developing countries. Nevertheless, the segments are similar in terms of their risk proneness, their status in society, and their wealth relative to the rest of the consumers in the country where they live.

Chapter Summary

- **Evaluate the stages of the international product life cycle and identify locus of operations and target markets at each stage**

  Most products are introduced in developed countries, where consumers can afford the high costs charged by manufacturers to recoup product development costs. During growth, the multinational company faces increasing competition worldwide from products also produced in the developed country. At maturity, standardized products compete primarily on price; manufacturing moves overseas to take advantage of cheaper labor. The company has a sales focus on emerging markets. In a product's middle and late maturity stages, competitors from developing countries enter the company's world markets and compete for consumers. In the product's decline stage, the company seeks new markets in countries of lower development levels.

- **Identify the different dimensions of the international product mix with company illustrations**

  Companies use different product mix strategies for different markets. The product mix refers to the totality of brands the company offers to its target markets. A company such as Unilever offers products in many categories—for example, coffee, ice cream, detergent, and others—but does not offer many varieties of each. Unilever, thus, has low depth but high product width, and its product offering is not very consistent because it includes products for very different uses. Other companies may offer high depth in certain markets and have a very limited offering in yet other markets.

- **Examine the new product development process and the activities involved at each stage in international markets**

  The new product development process starts with idea generation, in and outside the company; the next step involves idea screening using predetermined criteria, followed by concept development and evaluation. Product business analysis determines the extent to which the product is likely to be viable. In the next stage, product design and development, product prototypes are developed and evaluated by target consumers. Test marketing involves great expense on the part of the company; it also leaves the company vulnerable to competitive idea theft. Often, companies use international markets as testing grounds for new products. The final stage, launching, requires significant commitment to the product and to the target market.

- **Examine degrees of product newness and address international diffusion processes**

  There are different types of new products: products that are new to an existing market or new to an existing company; new lines, i.e., new products or product lines to a company, but for a company already operating in that market; new items in an existing product line for the company; modifications to an existing company product; and innovations, i.e., products that are new to the world. New products are first diffused in lead countries, typically industrialized countries where consumers can afford the products; here, the diffusion rate is slow. The countries where the product is adopted last are known as lag countries; in lag countries, the diffusion rate is faster because consumers learn from the adoption experiences of consumers in lead countries.

Discussion Questions

1. Describe the international product life cycle and the activities involved in developed and developing countries.

2. What are the activities involved at each stage of the new product development process? Where are most new products developed?

3. Many products are advertised in the United States as "new and improved." What does this description mean in terms of new product classifications?

4. Describe the differences between lead and lag countries in terms of adoption status and adoption rate.

Managing International Distribution Operations and Logistics

Key Terms

brokers and agents
building channels
buying offices
complementary export agents
complementary export
  merchants
comprador
cooperative export
  arrangements
established channels
export management companies
export merchants
Export Trading Company Act
foreign-country middlemen
Foreign Sales Corporation (FSC)
home-country middlemen

import jobber
keiretsu
logistics alliances
managing agent
manufacturer's export agents
manufacturer's representative
merchant middlemen
mother henning
network marketing
Norazi agent
parallel imports
piggybacking
sogo shosha
trading companies
Webb-Pomerene Associations

Outline

Learning Objectives
11-1 Issues Related to
    International Distribution
  *11-1a Using Established
    Channels*
  11-1b Building Own Channels
11-2 Middlemen Involved in
    International Distribution
  *11-2a Home-Country
    Middlemen*
  *11-2b Foreign-Country
    Middlemen*
  *11-2c Alternative International
    Distribution Structures*
11-3 Facilitators of International
    Distribution and Logistics
  11-3a Distribution Centers
  11-3b Transportation Firms
  *11-3c Home-Country and
    Foreign-Country Freight
    Forwarders and Customs
    Brokers*
  11-3d Government Agencies
  *11-3e Nongovernmental
    Organizations*
  11-3f Other Service Providers
  11-3g Logistics Alliances
11-4 Challenges to International
    Distribution and Logistics
  *11-4a Challenges to
    Distribution in
    Developing Countries*
  11-4b Parallel Imports
Chapter Summary
Discussion Questions

Learning Objectives

By the end of this chapter, you should be able to:

- Describe the functions of home-country and host-country middlemen involved in international distribution
- Identify the different facilitators of international distribution and logistics and describe their involvement in the international distribution process
- Address the challenges encountered by distribution in countries of different development levels

---

International distribution channels link manufacturers and final international consumers. Internationally, distribution channels vary greatly from one region to another and from one market to another. For most markets, consumer product channels of distribution tend to be longer than industrial product channels. Beyond this general trait, however, channel characteristics differ worldwide. The following are examples of such differences:

- In Japan, there are many more levels of distributors for consumer products than in most other countries, whereas, for most industrial goods, large export trading or export management companies deal directly with retailers.

- In socialist countries, distributors are huge state-run enterprises that often carry unrelated products.

- In Central and Eastern Europe and other emerging markets, network marketing is rapidly becoming a very popular channel of distribution. Every network marketing company is active there, with Amway leading the way.

This chapter addresses all the aspects of managing international distribution, offering an overview of the different middlemen involved in the international distribution process, the facilitators involved in international distribution and logistics, and the challenges facing the distribution process.

11-1 Issues Related to International Distribution

Some international markets have an underdeveloped distribution system for many industrial sectors and, to a lesser extent, for consumer goods. Distribution to these markets may be opportunistic and not adequately organized, or distribution channels may not exist altogether. Alternatively, the complex structure of certain international channels may serve as a barrier to multinational company entry in an international market new to the company. The company first must determine whether it can use established channels or build its own.

11-1a Using Established Channels

Entering a new market can be problematic for companies. In most cases, competitors already have a hold on existing channels and are thus likely to *block* them for new entrants. In addition to competitors, there are other obstacles to using **established channels.** For example, the amount charged by distributors could be so high that the company may be unwilling to use them. This was the case for Philip Morris (now known as Altria) in its attempt to enter the Hong Kong market with its Kraft products. Distributors (keiretsu cross-investment structures that will be examined in "The Japanese Model") charged an exorbitant amount to distribute the brand. Philip Morris refused to pay the price but also faced barriers to entry on its own; a decade later, Philip Morris yielded, deciding to use the same overpriced distributors to sell its Kraft brand in Hong Kong and now China. The initial channel selection decision is very important: Once in a channel relationship, a company may be bound to that relationship and may not legally be allowed to change distributors.

Established channels
Distribution channels that already exist in a particular market.

11-1b Building Own Channels

Although **building channels** is very expensive, this strategy is especially necessary in situations in which no channels exist at all, or no channels conform to the needs of the company. The example of Coca-Cola in Eastern Europe after the fall of communism is a case in point. Although Pepsi had been present in the region since the late 1960s, Coke did not enter many of the countries until the 1990s. When Coca-Cola decided to enter this market, it found old state-enterprise channels that were selling Pepsi products, operating with low efficiency. Consequently, it decided to create its own channels of distribution that fit well with the market structure by, primarily, working with independent truck drivers who had some experience working with soft-drink retailers.

Building channels Creating new distribution channels, especially necessary in situations in which there are no channels at all, or there are no channels that conform to the needs of the company.

11-2 Middlemen Involved in International Distribution

Depending on company involvement in a particular market, a company can use home-country middlemen or host-country middlemen. A company that uses intermediaries in its own home country is likely not to be as involved in managing the marketing mix in the country where the target market is located. **Home-country middlemen** typically provide all marketing services for firms that do not wish to enter the foreign market and/or do not have the capability to do so. Companies relying on home-country middlemen relinquish their control of the marketing mix to their distributors in the target-market foreign country.

A company using intermediaries in the host country is likely to have a presence there, in the form of a sales office, at the lowest level of direct international involvement, or in the form of a wholly owned subsidiary, at the highest level of direct international involvement. The company, by using host-country middlemen, also seeks to have a greater degree of control of the marketing mix in the target-market foreign country.

Home-country middlemen
Intermediaries in the home country.

11-2a Home-Country Middlemen

Export Management Companies

Export management companies
Companies specializing in the export function for client companies in a particular industry.

Export management companies are highly specialized in certain industries, such as endoscopic surgery instruments or networking products, and typically represent smaller companies in a region of the country. Some of their activities include researching the international market, representing a company at trade shows and exhibitions, screening and selecting international distributors, shipping the company's product, and handling all the necessary export documentation, such as customs forms and export licensing. An example of such a firm is Amex, Inc., a company in Minneapolis, Minnesota, that offers export trading services for Midwest technology companies selling medical, networking, telecommunication, and data communication products. This type of firm works typically as a company's export department.

Trading Companies

The Japanese Model

Trading companies Large companies that specialize in providing intermediary services, risk reduction through extensive information channels, and significant financial assistance to manufacturing firms.

Japanese export **trading companies** have operations all around the world, ranging from finance to distribution, technology, mining, oil and gas exploration, and information. They act as intermediaries for half of Japan's exports and two-thirds of its imports. Currently, they are changing from pure traders to more financially sophisticated investment holding companies.[1]

Keiretsu A Japanese trading firm that consists of families of firms with interlocking stakes in one another.

The biggest and the best of the traders are members of **keiretsus,** which are families of firms with interlocking stakes in one another; here, the trading companies' role is to act as the eyes and ears of the whole group, spotting business trends, market gaps, and investment opportunities.[2]

Sogo shosha A large Japanese trading company that specializes in providing intermediary services, risk reduction through extensive information channels, and significant financial assistance to manufacturing firms.

Sogo shoshas, or general trading companies, offer their suppliers three primary services: specialization in providing intermediary services, risk reduction through extensive information channels, and significant financial assistance. Currently, a shift is occurring in sogo shosha activities to more third-country trade, increased participation in product areas requiring sophisticated distribution, and greater participation in high-risk overseas mega projects.[3] The top sogo shoshas are Itochu Corp., Sumitomo, Marubeni, Mitsui, and Mitsubishi.[4]

Japanese export trading companies are presently facing competition from Honda, Sony, and Toyota, which have set up their own direct export-sales networks; consequently, the trading companies are handling a decreasing proportion of Japan's exports.[5]

The U.S. Model

Export Trading Company Act
Legislation, passed in 1982, that encourages the formation of export trading companies by competing firms in order to promote U.S. exports without violating antitrust regulation.

In the United States, export trading companies are, in fact, consortia of smaller suppliers, service-oriented firms, multinational corporations, and quasi-public organizations or public entities.[6] In 1982, the U.S. Congress passed the **Export Trading Company Act** to encourage the formation of export trading companies to promote U.S. exports.

---

1. *The Economist,* "Japanese Trading Companies: The Giants That Refused to Die," June 1, 1991, Vol. 319, No. 7709, pp. 72–73.

2. Ibid.

3. Lyn S. Amine, Tamer S. Cavusgil, and Robert I. Weinstein, "Japanese Sogo Shosha and the U.S. Export Trading Companies," *Journal of the Academy of Marketing Science,* Fall 1986, Vol. 14, No. 3, pp. 21–32.

4. Ibid.

5. *The Economist,* "Japanese Trading Companies," pp. 72–73.

6. Amine, Cavusgil, and Weinstein, "Japanese Sogo Shosha," pp. 21–32.

Home-Country Brokers and Agents

Home-country **brokers and agents** bring international buyers and sellers together in the company's home country and do not carry title to the product. They can handle different export functions and specialize in certain product categories.

Alternatively, they may represent a certain manufacturer on a commission basis for a particular deal; they are known as **manufacturer's export agents.** Or they may be buyers located in the firm's home country, representing different firms located abroad; they are known as **buying offices.**

Cooperative Export Arrangements

Cooperative export arrangements, also referred to as **piggybacking** or **mother henning,** involve exporters agreeing to handle export functions for unrelated companies on a contractual basis. Generally, cooperative exporters are large multinationals with substantial in-house know-how and resources, as well as extensive knowledge of international markets. The piggybacked products are noncompetitive with the cooperative exporter's own products but may be, nevertheless, similar; an example is an auto manufacturer in the United States who agrees to market tires or seat covers for a much smaller company that is new to international marketing.[7]

Two types of firms are generally involved in cooperative export arrangements: **complementary export agents** and **complementary export merchants.** Complementary export agents export complementary products. This category includes individual firms exporting other firms' products that are complementary to their offerings (along with their own products). If these firms carry the other firms' products for a fee/commission, they act as complementary export agents. If, instead of operating on a fee/commission, the firms actually take title to the complementary products distributed and are compensated in the form of a discount in a buy-sell arrangement,[8] they act as complementary export merchants.

Webb-Pomerene Associations of Exporters

Webb-Pomerene Associations, established under the Webb-Pomerene Act, also are involved in cooperative exporting. Webb-Pomerene Associations are composed of competing companies that join resources and efforts to export internationally. The companies are granted immunity from antitrust prosecution, under the Webb-Pomerene Act, so that they can export products manufactured in the United States to compete effectively internationally, especially in world markets in which cartels are active.

Foreign Sales Corporation

The **Foreign Sales Corporation (FSC)** is a sales corporation that is set up overseas; establishing an FSC allows for a portion of a U.S. taxpaying firm's foreign-source income to be exempt from U.S. income tax. To qualify for tax exemption, the FSC must have a foreign presence; it must meet certain management requirements and certain economic process requirements with regard to both the extent and nature of the sales activities undertaken abroad; and it must incur abroad a minimum level of direct costs in sales activities, in areas such as marketing, advertising, and order processing.[9]

Brokers and agents Middlemen who bring international buyers and sellers together; they do not carry title to the product.

Manufacturer's export agents Agents in the firm's home country handling the exporting function of a certain manufacturer on a commission, per deal, basis.

Buying offices Buyers representing different firms located abroad.

Cooperative export arrangements/Piggybacking/ Mother henning Agreements that involve the use of a distribution system of exporters with established systems of selling abroad, who agree to handle the export function of a noncompeting (but not necessarily unrelated) company on a contractual basis.

Complementary export agents Firms that export other firms' products that are complementary to their offerings, along with their own products, for a fee/commission.

Complementary export merchants Distributors who take title to the complementary products distributed and are compensated in the form of a discount.

Webb-Pomerene Associations Associations of competing companies that are granted immunity from antitrust prosecution and that join resources and efforts to export internationally.

Foreign Sales Corporation (FSC) A sales corporation that is set up overseas; it allows for a portion of a U.S. tax-paying firm's foreign-source income to be exempt from U.S. income tax.

---

7. Ernest R. Larkins and Fenwisk Huss, "Establishing Trade Relations in Russia," *The CPA Journal,* August 1995, Vol. 65, No. 8, pp. 26–31.

8. Ibid.

9. Rob Lee, "Boeing in the Middle," *Airfinance Journal,* February 2001, Vol. 236, pp. 34–36.

Export Merchants

Export merchants are intermediaries who take title to and possession of the products they carry. They are responsible for shipping and marketing the products to the target market; in this sense, they have full control over the products' international marketing mix. Generally, they can carry competing brands. One type of export merchant is the *export jobber,* who carries primarily commodity goods but does not take physical possession of the products. Another type of export merchant is the **Norazi agent,** who deals in illegal and/or gray market products. See also section 11-4b, "Parallel Imports," at the end of this chapter.

11-2b Foreign-Country Middlemen

Foreign-country middlemen can be placed in two broad categories: merchant middlemen, who are intermediaries that take title to and possession of the products they carry, and agents and brokers, who bring buyers and sellers together but do not carry title to and take possession of the products they deal with.

Merchant Middlemen

Merchant middlemen are intermediaries who carry the manufacturer's product line in a particular country. They usually both carry title to and have physical possession of the products they distribute in the foreign target market. Companies often have close relationships with their international intermediaries; such relationships allow them to have control over their products' international marketing mix. Selecting one's middlemen carefully is important because, in many markets, the relationship with a distributor might be difficult or impossible to dissolve. A particular type of merchant middleman in a foreign country is an **import jobber,** who purchases usually commodity goods from the manufacturer to sell to the trade (wholesaler, retailer, business-to-business client) in the target market. In addition, wholesalers, retailers, and industrial consumers may import products directly for resale; as such, they act as merchant middlemen.

Agents and Brokers

A company can select from many different types of agents and brokers in its foreign target market. An agent can represent the manufacturer exclusively in this market, acting thus as a **manufacturer's representative.** This individual usually works practically as the company's sales representative and is paid on a commission basis. The **managing agent,** often called the **comprador,** has an exclusive arrangement with the company, representing its operations in a particular country; this individual does not take title to the goods and is usually paid as a percentage of sales of the company he or she manages.

11-2c Alternative International Distribution Structures

One type of alternative distribution structure is **network marketing,** a mode of distributing goods using acquaintance networks. Network marketing companies are gaining access to emerging markets all over the world, and many continue to find potential in developed countries. Because network marketing serves primarily a retailing function—all distributorships engage in selling to the final consumer—this topic will be addressed in Chapter 12, "International Retailing."

11-3 Facilitators of International Distribution and Logistics

The international distribution function is supported by a number of service providers. Among them are those described in sections 11-3a through 11-3g.

Export merchants
Intermediaries who take title to and possession of the products they carry; they are responsible for shipping and marketing the products to the target market.

Norazi agent   An export agent dealing in illegal and/or gray market products.

Foreign-country middlemen
Intermediaries who help distribute products in a target foreign market.

Merchant middlemen   Different intermediaries who carry the manufacturer's product line in a particular country; they both carry title to and have physical possession of the products they distribute.

Import jobber   A merchant middleman who purchases commodity goods from the manufacturer to sell to the trade (wholesaler, retailer, business-to-business client) in the target market.

Manufacturer's representative An agent who represents the manufacturer exclusively in the foreign target market.

Managing agent   A foreign agent who has an exclusive arrangement with a company, representing its operations in a particular country.

Comprador   A foreign agent with an exclusive arrangement with a company, representing its operations in a particular country; also referred to as a managing agent.

Network marketing
An alternative distribution structure using acquaintance networks for the purpose of distribution.

11-3a Distribution Centers

Distribution centers are designed to speed up warehousing and delivery, by channeling operations to one center (hub) that is particularly well equipped to handle the distribution of products to their destination. This function is becoming a popular choice of multinational firms that have to efficiently warehouse and distribute their goods in target markets situated thousands of miles from their home country. Certain locations have become important players as hubs to a number of multinational firms. For example, Singapore is a leading regional and international logistics hub and host to virtually every major logistics player; logistics account for about 7 percent of Singapore's Gross Domestic Product.[10]

11-3b Transportation Firms

Transportation firms are key players in international distribution, especially firms that can handle intermodal transportation, using two or more different transportation modes—truck, rail, ship (inland and sea/ocean shipping). Intermodal transportation has been greatly facilitated by containerization. For example, goods can be placed into containers at the factory, taken by truck to a train loading facility, transported to a port, and loaded aboard a ship; after crossing the ocean, the containers are loaded on a truck and transported to their final destination. All these maneuvers can be accomplished using the initial containers—thus providing a greater protection for the products, which do not have to be shifted individually from one vessel to another—at lower cost because loading the individual products from/into vehicles is more expensive than using containers.

11-3c Home-Country and Foreign-Country Freight Forwarders and Customs Brokers[11]

Freight forwarders and customs brokers arrange for transportation, customs clearance, and document filing for products exported abroad. Often, they specialize in geographic locations or other areas of expertise, such as commodities—for example, flowers, seafood, and other types of perishable products.

The Internet poses the greatest threat to freight forwarders and customs brokers, as it provides a venue for importers to use dot-com companies to arrange for transportation, customs clearance, document filing, and other activities. Moreover, the Department of Commerce, the U.S. Customs Service, and the World Trade Organization have rulings, forms, and other useful documentation posted on the Web.[12]

11-3d Government Agencies

In many countries, the governments are directly involved in the international distribution process. Often, private distributors are not permitted by law to engage in any type of direct international transaction. This is the case for many developing countries and/or countries where national currencies are under strict control. Government involvement in distribution and logistics processes is not limited to developing countries; in many developed countries, the governments are involved in the following processes:

---

10. David Biederman, "Intelligent Island Links the Globe," *Traffic World,* December 4, 2000, Vol. 264, No. 10, pp. 28–31.

11. Customs brokers are not discussed in section 11-3c primarily because they do not bring buyers and sellers together; rather, their function is strictly confined to customs-related paperwork.

12. Lara L. Sowinksi, "It's Sink or Swim for Freight Forwarders and Customs Brokers," *World Trade,* February 2001, Vol. 14, No. 2, pp. 54–56.

- As promoters of national security interests and national regulations
- As promoters of international involvement of firms, particularly of small and medium-size businesses
- As financing and insurance providers for higher-risk international ventures

In the United States, international distribution and logistics involvement are shared by a number of different government agencies—most of which are affiliated with the U.S. Department of Commerce:

- The International Trade Administration in the U.S. Department of Commerce offers export assistance to international firms and, in particular, to small to medium-size businesses. It offers trade education, mentoring programs for exporters (assistance from an experienced exporter), access to a market research database, country analysis information, economic data, as well as business counseling in the form of expert assistance from trade specialists. It also helps firms with export documentation (applications, licenses, declarations, etc.).
- The Bureau of Export Administration in the U.S. Department of Commerce advances U.S. national security, foreign policy, and economic interests by regulating exports of products and technologies that could affect those interests. This agency regulates exports of products such as high-platform computers and weapons, and imposes sanctions against certain countries (such as India, Pakistan, and Serbia in the recent past); it enforces compliance with those regulations and cooperates with other nations in monitoring the trade of sensitive goods.
- The U.S. Commercial Service promotes and protects small and medium-size U.S. business interests in key export markets. It operates Export Assistance Centers, which offer companies a range of export facilitation services.
- The Export-Import Bank of the United States (Ex-Im Bank) is an independent government agency that aids the financing of international sales of U.S. products and services. It guarantees loans and makes loans to international buyers of U.S. goods; it also insures many business ventures that international or local banks will not insure due to their high risk. The Ex-Im Bank does not compete with commercial lenders and insurance firms.
- The United States Trade and Development Agency creates jobs for Americans by helping U.S. companies pursue overseas business opportunities. Although not directly involved in distribution and logistics, this agency funds feasibility studies, training, business workshops, and technical assistance aimed at infrastructure and industrial projects in developing countries, covering the cost of logistics and distribution.

Equivalent structures exist in most other countries, typically housed under the Ministry of Foreign Trade (the equivalent of the Department of Commerce).

11-3e Nongovernmental Organizations

In addition to country-specific agencies, international bodies affect distribution and logistics. One example is the International Chamber of Commerce, a business organization that represents enterprises from all sectors in every part of the world engaging in international business. The ICC makes voluntary rules that govern the conduct of business across borders, and it provides important services, such as the ICC International Court of Arbitration, the world's leading arbitral institution.

11-3f Other Service Providers

Among other service providers are banks and insurance agencies financing and insuring international distribution transactions, marketing research firms providing information on the target markets and the trade, and various types of consultants that specialize in facilitating international distribution and logistics activities.

11-3g Logistics Alliances

In the process of setting up a firm's distribution activity in the target market, the firm will need to set up successful logistics relationships. Many **logistics alliances** in Europe have been very successful and are characterized by an atmosphere of openness between the customer and the provider, mutual trust, and a clear line of communication. Successful logistics alliances typically are formed using the following steps:[13]

1. Establish objectives and selection criteria. Because choosing a logistics provider is a long-term decision, it is important to choose a partner that is likely to be a good match.
2. Identify qualified providers, with the help of consultants.
3. Express needs and wants. Here, issues such as integrating computer systems with that of the partner and other information sharing needs should be expressed.
4. Evaluate bidders and select the partner, preferably after a site visit and interview.
5. Develop an integration plan. Because logistics involves many players, it is important to engage in systemwide integration.
6. Create a win-win relationship, based on continuous communication.
7. Measure and analyze performance.
8. Redefine goals and objectives.

> **Logistics alliances** Distribution alliances between two firms involving product transportation and warehousing.

11-4 Challenges to International Distribution and Logistics

Firms selling across borders encounter numerous challenges. The two most cited challenges are distribution in developing countries and parallel imports.

11-4a Challenges to Distribution in Developing Countries

One challenge faced by multinationals distributing their products in developing countries is the transportation infrastructure: Dirt roads are often impassable when wet, and, in tropical climates, cool temperatures must be maintained to ensure the quality of perishable goods such as pharmaceuticals. Containerization also poses problems: Most of the ports in West Africa have shallow drafts and cannot handle larger vessels. Furthermore, unloading the products from the container may take weeks, or the container may be held indefinitely for customs inspection.[14]

11-4b Parallel Imports

Parallel imports are products purchased in a low-price market and diverted to other markets by means of a distribution system not authorized by the

> **Parallel imports** A distribution system not authorized by the manufacturer whereby the products purchased in a low-price market are diverted to other markets; also called gray market.

13. Adapted from Prabir K. Bagchi and Helge Virum, "Logistical Alliances: Trends and Prospects in Integrated Europe," *Journal of Business Logistics*, 1998, Vol. 19, No. 1, pp. 191–213.

14. See Anthony Coia, "The Global Supply Chain Pill," *Traffic World*, September 27, 1999, Vol. 259, No. 13, p. 17.

manufacturer; this is also known as a *gray market.* A low-price market is one where the products can be purchased for a lower price either because the company is in a competitive situation in which it must lower the price or because local taxes do not significantly increase the price of the products. Most often, however, gray market goods come from authorized dealers who get rid of excess inventory, selling the products to discounters.[15]

The Netherlands, for example, is a low-price market for Similac, an infant formula manufactured by Abbott Laboratories; here, a 900-gram can of Similac sells for 13 guilders, or about $6. A can of Similac weighing 850 grams (50 grams less than the can sold in the Netherlands) sells for about $22 in the United States. The reasons Abbott Laboratories engages in the differential pricing of Similac may be numerous. First, it might be attempting to penetrate the market: Although the product is well known in the United States, it is not popular at all in Europe. Second, it is priced just less than the other, local, competing products: The company might be using a penetration-pricing strategy. Third, the Dutch government might have required the company to sell at a low price (unlikely, but possible). Consequently, the Netherlands constitutes a low-price market for Similac. If an entrepreneur decided to bring Similac from the Netherlands to sell it in the United States, he or she would be engaging in parallel imports and would have to sell the product on a gray market, not authorized by the manufacturer.

The illegal aspect of the transactions illustrated in this example clearly does not involve the product itself. Rather, what is in fact illegal is the distribution channel and the processes used to sell this product to consumers unintended by the company—U.S. consumers. When such products are available for sale in the unintended market, parallel imports then compete with the manufacturer's products intended for this very market, cutting into profits.

Examples of gray markets abound. In the 1970s, a thriving gray market for Mercedes-Benz automobiles existed in the United States. Automobiles manufactured for the European market were much cheaper than the ones sold through exclusive dealerships in the U.S. market. Entrepreneurs on both sides of the Atlantic took advantage of this discrepancy, transporting and converting the automobiles to U.S. specifications, obtaining the approval of the U.S. Department of Transportation, and selling the products openly to consumers in the United States.

In other examples, pharmaceutical manufacturers selling their products in the European Union find that products sold in low markets, such as Greece, Italy, France, Portugal, and Spain, are often distributed in countries where above-average prices are charged, such as Germany, Denmark, and the Netherlands.[16]

Gray markets also can harm a company's image. Cigarettes sold for the Chinese market are likely to have a higher nicotine content and to be more addictive. Diverting these cigarettes back to the United States can harm the company's brand image. The company needs to carefully control the distribution of such products.

Multinational corporations can choose from a number of alternative actions in the process of combating parallel imports (see Figure 11-1):

- *Charge similar prices worldwide*—If price differences are not substantial enough, there will not be a gray market. Although this strategy does not quite conform to the marketing concept, selling consumers products at prices they can afford and/or are willing to pay, it is, nevertheless, successful in preventing the success of a gray market for that particular brand.

---

15. Alexandra Alger, "'Gray' Watches," *Forbes*, August 11, 1997, Vol. 160, No. 3, p. 151.

16. Peggy E. Chaudry and Michael G. Walsh, "Gray Marketing of Pharmaceuticals," *Journal of Health Care Marketing*, Fall 1995, Vol. 15, No. 3, pp. 18–21.

Figure 11-1
Methods of combating parallel imports.

- *Create products for low markets that are not as attractive, or are not a perfect fit with an up-market*—Mercedes-Benz, after creating Mercedes USA, its subsidiary in the United States, attempted to create very different automobiles for the European and the U.S. market. To the European consumers, Mercedes offers the A-Class, which is not available in the United States, and lower-level models that are too small to meet U.S. consumers' demands for comfort. The same-level C-Class and E-Class are sold for comparable prices in the European and the U.S. markets.
- *Complicate the repair and servicing process for the gray market goods*— Individuals purchasing gray market Mercedes-Benz automobiles in the United States will find that, often, replacement parts for their automobiles must be ordered from Stuttgart, Germany, making the cost of maintenance prohibitive.
- *Inform consumers about the perils of buying gray market products*— Possible perils of gray market products might be that the product is new but technically outdated or that the product will not benefit from manufacturer warranties.
- *Litigate*—Unlike in the case of counterfeit products, litigating is often not possible in many of the integrated markets, such as the European Union, where the free movement of goods is guaranteed by law. Nevertheless, it is recommended that manufacturers keep up with the changing regulations to be able to take on unauthorized distribution when that is possible.[17] Frequently, loopholes in the national laws may allow parallel distribution, but states and localities may pass stringent gray market legislation; examples are Colorado, Michigan, and Georgia in the United States, which do not allow the importation of gray market cigarettes.[18]

---

17. Matthew B. Myers and David A. Griffith, "Strategies for Combating Gray Market Activity," *Business Horizons,* November/December 1999, Vol. 42, No. 6, pp. 2–8.

18. Marc Katz, "Gray Market Cigarettes," *NPN, National Petroleum News,* January 2000, Vol. 92, No. 1, p. 46.

Chapter Summary

- **Describe the functions of home-country and host-country middlemen involved in international distribution**

  Examples of home-country middlemen involved in international distribution are export management companies, which specialize in a particular industry; Japanese trading companies, whose operations range from distribution to manufacturing, mining, and, among others, technology, and U.S. trading companies, which are export consortia of small businesses; brokers and agents who do not carry titles and export merchants who carry titles to products; cooperative export arrangements, whereby exporters handle other firms' unrelated products on a contractual basis; Webb-Pomerene Associations, which allow competitors to join forces in exporting; and Foreign Sales Corporations, which allow for a portion of a firm's foreign income to be tax exempt. Foreign-country middlemen involved in logistics are merchant middlemen, who carry title to and have possession of products, and agents and brokers who do not.

- **Identify the different facilitators of international distribution and logistics and describe their involvement in the international distribution process**

  Among facilitators are distribution centers, which use a hub for efficient channeling of operations; transporta-

  tion companies; freight forwarders and customs brokers, both in the home and the host country, who arrange for transportation, customs clearance, and export documentation; governmental and nongovernmental organizations, such as the International Trade Administration, the Bureau of Export Administration, the Export-Import Bank, and the International Chamber of Commerce, which promote and facilitate international involvement of companies.

- **Address the challenges encountered by distribution in countries of different development levels**

  Multinationals operating in developing countries often must face challenges related to the transportation infrastructure, to containerization (ports with shallow drafts that cannot handle large vessels), and customs inspections. In both developed and developing countries, multinationals must deal with parallel imports (gray markets), from a low-price market to another market using distribution channels not authorized by the manufacturer. Increasingly, companies are combating such distribution by charging similar prices worldwide, creating products for low markets that are not attractive to the high market, complicating repair and service processes, informing consumers about buying such products, and litigating.

Discussion Questions

1. Companies either can build new channels or use existing channels in new markets they plan to serve.
2. What are the determinants of this choice? Explain.
3. Who are the different distributors available in your home country? Who can distribute your products abroad?
4. Who are the different distributors in your target market (host country)? Who can manage a company's distribution in the host country?
5. How does the U.S. government help companies in the process of distributing their goods internationally?
6. What types of distribution and logistics challenges do firms face in the process of going international?

International Retailing

Key Terms

all-purpose discount stores
catalog retailers
catalog showrooms
category killers
category specialists
combination stores
convenience stores
conventional supermarkets
cross-border shopping
department stores
direct mail retailing
direct selling
electronic retailing
food retailers

general merchandise discount
  stores
hypermarkets
interactive home shopping
Internet retailing
multilevel marketing
network marketing
off-price retailers
specialized markets
specialty stores
superstores
television home shopping
vending machines
warehouse clubs
wholesale clubs

Outline

Learning Objectives
12-1 International Expansion
  of Retailers
12-2 International Retailing
  Defined
12-3 Retail Formats: Variations
  in Different Markets
  *12-3a General Merchandise
    Retailing*
  12-3b Food Retailers
  12-3c Nonstore Retailing
12-4 Issues in International
  Retailing
  *12-4a Legislation and
    Regulation*
  *12-4b Taxation and Cross-
    Border Shopping*
  *12-4c Variation in Retail
    Practices: A Consumer
    Perspective*
  *12-4d Variation in Retail
    Practice: Salespeople
    and Management*
Chapter Summary
Discussion Questions

Learning Objectives

Learning Objectives

By the end of this chapter, you should be able to:

- Provide an overview and description of the general merchandise retailing category and offer examples and illustrations
- Provide an overview and description of the food retailing category and offer examples and illustrations

- Provide an overview and description of the nonstore retailing category and offer examples and illustrations
- Address issues related to legislation, taxation, and retailing practices around the world

Retailing is going through a process of rapid internationalization; the retailing environment worldwide is undergoing dynamic changes, with local retailers defensively countering competitive moves of mammoth international chains or successfully duplicating their strategies.

Major international retailers are no longer competing only for mature markets—and for consumers in highly industrialized countries. Retailers' competitive arena has expanded to all emerging markets, where they are responding to an increasing affluence of consumers and to their increasingly sophisticated consumption-related demands. Numerous successful global retailers and consumer-product-companies-cum-retailers such as Wal-Mart (United States), Promodes/Carrefour (France), Louis Vuitton Moët Henessy (France), and Royal Ahold (the Netherlands) are already present on four continents and have outlets in as many as twenty-five countries.[1]

This chapter offers insights into the internationalization efforts of retailers, describing different categories of retailers and their international involvement and expansion, and issues related to legislation and taxation that affect retailing operations. The chapter also illustrates retailing practices around the world.

---

1. *Chain Store Age*, "Global Retailing in the Connected Economy," December 1999, Vol. 5, No. 12, pp. 69–82.

12-1 International Expansion of Retailers

Retailers are rapidly expanding internationally to gain competitive advantage and to increase sales, profits, and overall firm performance. As they expand beyond their home-country borders, retailers also can take advantage of cost savings and learn from experiences in a way that could further enhance home-country operations. Tesco, the British retailer, for example, is using its stores in Central and Eastern Europe as a testing ground for ideas that are intended for application in the home market; the new Tesco Extra in Newcastle, U.K., is based on a Tesco hypermarket in Hungary.[2]

Retailers from the United States are expanding in Latin America, Asia, and Europe. Wal-Mart, for example, has adopted an aggressive strategy for international penetration: Its purchase of the Asda Group (United Kingdom) has boosted its international sales to $25 billion, which is only a fraction of its total sales figure of $165 billion. Its ambition is for its international operations to account for a third of sales growth by 2004, which would mean $72 billion in revenue from international operations. Although some of this growth can be attributed to its Latin American operations, Wal-Mart's primary focus remains on Europe.[3]

European retailers are rapidly gaining ground internationally as well. The top European grocery retailers are expected to command a 40 percent market share by 2005 in Europe; the five leading European retailers—Promodes/Carrefour, Metro, Intermarché, Rewe, and Auchan—presently control a 25.4 percent share of the European grocery market.[4] European retailers are prominent in the top 100 list of global retailers. In the list of top ten global retail companies alone, there are six European retailers. This list includes the following international retailers:

- Wal-Mart (U.S.), with sales of $137,634 million
- Metro AG (Germany), $52,131 million
- Sears Roebuck (U.S.), with sales of $36,704 million
- Rewe Gruppe (Germany), with sales of $36,212 million
- Edeka Gruppe (Germany), with sales of $32,573 million
- Aldi Gruppe (Germany), with sales of $32,403 million
- Dayton Hudson (U.S.), with sales of $30,951 million
- Carrefour (France), with sales of $30,489 million
- Tenzelmann Gruppe (Germany), with sales of $30,243 million[5]

In the process of internationalization, many retailers are subscribing to the current trend of consolidation in the food and general merchandise sectors. Examples of such consolidation are offered by Wal-Mart's acquisition of one of the largest United Kingdom grocery chains, the Asda Group; Royal Ahold's purchase of the Pathmark, Giant, and Stop & Shop chains in the United States; and the merger between two medium-sized French Wal-Mart lookalikes, Promodes and Carrefour.[6]

To understand the changes in the vibrant world of international retailing, one needs to gain some insight into the many categories of retailers (local and

2. Alexandra Jardine, "Retailers Go on International Shopping Trip," *Marketing,* January 20, 2000, p. 15.

3. Kerry Capell and Heidi Dawley, "Wal-Mart's Not-So-Secret British Weapon: It's Using Its Asda Unit for an All-Out Assault on Europe," *Business Week,* Industrial/Technology Edition, January 24, 2000, No. 3665, p. 132.

4. *Progressive Grocer,* "European Consolidation," January 2000, Vol. 79, No. 1, p. 22.

5. *Chain Store Age,* "Global Retailing," pp. 69–82.

6. For a discussion of these mergers, see Allyson L. Stewart Allen, "Ensure Success by Studying Europe's Lessons," *Marketing News,* February 14, 2000, Vol. 34, No. 4, p. 11; and *Chain Store Age,* "Global Retailing," pp. 69–82.

multinational) and their modus operandi in different parts of the world. It also is important to understand how international retailing differs from retailing as defined in marketing management texts. Both of these topics are addressed in sections 12-2 and 12-3.

12-2 International Retailing Defined

International retailing is defined as all the activities involved in selling products and services to final international consumers for their personal consumption.

International retailing differs from local retailing as defined in marketing management in that it addresses operations of international retailers beyond home-country borders, as well as operations of local retailers in different countries worldwide—in general and/or in response to the presence or entry of international retailers aiming for their target market. As such, an examination of international retail operations must include an evaluation of all global and local retailing formats, retail practices, and an overview of local retailing environments.

12-3 Retail Formats: Variations in Different Markets

There are three main retail formats: general merchandise retailing, food retailing, and nonstore retailing. Sections 12-3a through 12-3c describe the retailers in each category and address the different international variations for each retail format, with a focus on local markets.

12-3a General Merchandise Retailing

Specialty Stores

Specialty stores Retailers that offer a narrow product line and wide assortment.

Specialty stores offer a narrow product line and wide assortment. In this category are clothing stores (usually further specialized into women's, men's, or children's clothing stores), bookstores, toy stores, office supply stores, and consumer electronics stores, among others.

In many markets, specialty stores—chains in particular—are expanding at the expense of all forms of nonfood retailing. For example, specialty store chains are taking market share away from traditional department stores in the United Kingdom and France.[7] U.K. specialty retailers have made great strides in international expansion: Marks & Spencer is rapidly expanding in France, and retailers such as Virgin Records have already made substantial inroads into the U.S. market. In France, specialty stores appear to be particularly well suited to addressing the unique French lifestyle. Local players, as well as international firms such as The Gap, are very successful in this market.

For apparel retailing, many European companies are rapidly entering new markets: Mango, the Spanish retailer specializing in youth fashion, has 400 shops in 44 countries, including Israel, Eastern Europe, and South America.[8] Rival Spanish chain Zara, with its distinctive brushed-steel staircases, and Swedish chain Hennes & Mauritz are competing for these same consumers and are proving to be very successful in mature markets worldwide.

In most developing countries, specialty stores represent the main retail format. Although Western and local specialty chain stores are quite popular and have done well for decades, developing country markets are dominated by independent (usually family-owned) specialty stores, such as apparel stores, cosmetics stores,

---

7. Brenda Sternquist, *International Retailing*, Fairchild Publications, 1998.

8. *Marketing*, "Mango Hires BBJ to Boost Brand in UK Stores Launch," February 17, 2000, p. 4.

(a)

(b)

Figure 12-1
The Covered Bazaar in Istanbul, Turkey, is a prime example of a specialized market. It is divided into two main areas: *(a)* the gold bazaar and *(b)* the giftware bazaar.

and local arts and crafts stores aimed at the tourist market, as well as other traditional retail systems as exemplified by specialized markets.

Specialized Markets

Specialized markets contain specialty stores specializing in a particular product category. Examples of such markets exist worldwide, in both developed and developing countries. Examples of specialized markets are the Cairo Gold Market in the Khan El Khalili bazaar, the Jade Market in Hong Kong, and the Spice Market and Gold Market in the Covered Bazaar in Istanbul, Turkey (see Figure 12-1). Specialized markets may even cover entire cities. For example, the town of Otavalo, Ecuador, houses large and small retailers of leather goods.

Specialized markets Markets that contain specialty stores specializing in a particular product category.

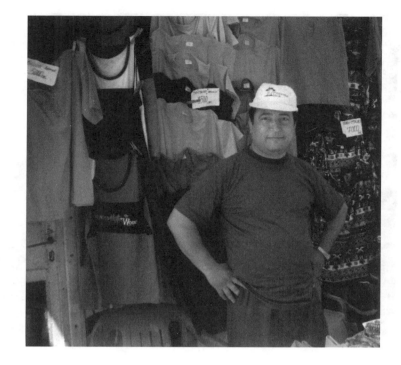

Figure 12-2
Specialized market, Gypsy (Roma) retailers. A clothing retail complex, located primarily outdoors in central Bucharest, Romania. All owners and salespeople belong to the Roma ethnicity.

In addition to these markets, local specialty stores affiliated with a project sponsored by governmental or nongovernmental organizations also are prevalent in many developing countries (see Figure 12-2). Examples may be a poultry shop partially owned by local investors selling poultry raised in a project funded by the World Bank and the United Nations Development Program aimed at helping a developing country become self-sufficient with regard to meat production, or a folk art outlet selling hand-made embroidery produced by young girls in a convent.

Department Stores

Department stores General retailers that offer a broad variety of goods and wide assortments.

Department stores offer a broad variety of goods and wide assortments. Among the products they carry are clothing for men, women, and children; household appliances and electronics; kitchenware; china; home furnishings; and toys and games. Outside the United States, department stores typically also have large supermarket sections, and some may even carry fresh produce.

In the United States and Canada, department stores have suffered substantial losses in the past decade, mostly attributed to the rise in discount stores, off-price retailers, and category killers. In an attempt to conquer new markets, however, a number of chains have been looking overseas for expansion: Sears Roebuck and JCPenney, in particular, have been looking at the Latin American market, with JCPenney recently opening a number of stores in Mexico and Chile.[9]

In Europe, department stores typically tend to address the needs of home markets, with efforts to expand mainly in the European Union. The United Kingdom has one of the oldest and best-established department stores in the world, accounting for 5 percent of total retail sales, and the four leading department store groups in this country control more than 65 percent of all department store trade.[10] The self-touted most famous shop in the world, Harrods department store in London (Knightsbridge), was established in 1849 and, by the end of the

9. See John S. Hill and Giles D'Souza, "Tapping the Emerging Americas Market," *The Journal of Business Strategy*, July/August 1998, Vol. 19, No. 4, pp. 8–11.

10. Sternquist, *International Retailing*, 1998.

Figure 12-3
Galeries Lafayette are present and successful in every large city in France; the company's international expansion attempts, however, have been problematic.

nineteenth century, was flourishing, selling airplanes and elephants, jewelry and pineapples, golf clubs and snuff boxes; today, it attracts an exclusive clientele to its 300 departments covering a million square feet of selling space and to its twenty-one restaurants.[11]

In the Netherlands, three department stores dominate: Vendex'Vroom & Dreesman, HEMA, and Bijenkorf. (The latter two belong to the KBB Group, which also owns a non-European specialty store, FAO Schwartz.) A similar concentration is encountered in Germany, where Karstadt (which also owns the Hertie department store chain) and Kaufhof dominate the market. French department stores are surviving despite the dominance of specialty shops and the increasing popularity of category killers and discount shops. Among the leading department stores in France are Printemps, Bon Marché, and Galeries Lafayette (see Figure 12-3). One, Galeries Lafayette, has made an unsuccessful attempt to enter the U.S. market by locating in the heart of Manhattan and has opened a new store in Old East Berlin—an architectural landmark in Germany's new capital. In Spain, the leading department store is El Corte Inglés, which dominates the Madrid retail scene.[12]

In Central and Eastern Europe, department stores abound; the former communist regimes found that large department stores offered economies of scale in terms of distribution and sales management. Consequently, department stores dominate the retailing environment of most large cities. With names such as Centrum or the Central Store in Central and Eastern Europe (see Figure 12-4a) and GUM in Russia, or bearing the name of the capital city or of socialist and nationalist symbols ("Victory," "Liberty," "Unity," etc.), these stores continue to thrive in a slightly different format: In addition to their merchandise, they also have a substantial presence of leased departments. The leased departments are noteworthy in that they carry merchandise that directly competes with the store's offerings and with that of other leased departments. For example, the Bucur Obor department store in Bucharest has at least three leased departments selling chandeliers (see Figure 12-4b). Alternatively, store space may be rented to retailers that are not

---

11. http://www.harrods.com

12. Dana-Nicoleta Lascu, Jose Fernandez-Olano, and Thomas D. Giese, "Holiday Shopping: A Cross-Cultural Examination of Spanish and American Consumers," in R. King (ed.), *Proceedings of the Fourth Triennial AMS/ACRA National Retailing Conference*, 1994, pp. 147–149.

Figure 12-4
(a) Centrum Store in Wroclaw, Poland, displays Legos and Barbie dolls. *(b)* Bucur Obor in Bucharest, Romania: Chandelier retailers compete in the store's leased department.
(c) Leased departments in Bucharest: Automobile retailers compete side-by-side with washing machines.

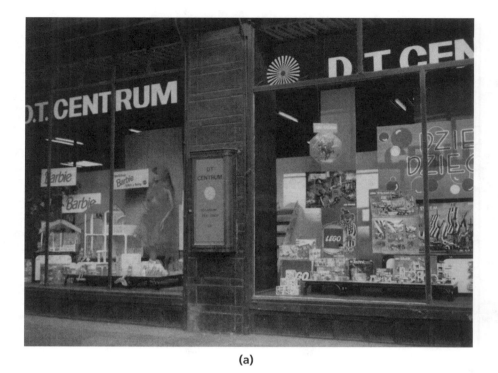

(a)

traditionally associated with department stores, such as automobile retailers (see Figure 12-4*c*).

In Asia, department stores have very different histories: Japanese department stores started out as kimono shops that originally sold textiles. At present, Japan's department store groups (Mitsukoshi, Daimaru, ADO, the Seibu stores and affiliates, and Takashimaya) are designed to be cradle-to-grave providers of goods and services. Japanese department stores have also expanded in China and Hong Kong, where they control 50 percent of the market. Finally, Taiwan's department stores have lagged behind; Da-Hsin and Ti-I department stores were the first to enter the market, followed by a number of newcomers, among them Far Eastern, Sesame, and Evergreen, most of which have sought affiliation with foreign (particularly Japanese) department store chains.[13]

Although department stores remain a dominant retail outlet in Asia, they are currently displaying symptoms of decline, such as oversupply, overduplication of merchandise, fierce competition, and declining profits. Shanghai alone witnessed the demise of five department stores in 1997. Existing department stores in this city have done well when changing their format, for example, specializing in European-style clothing and furnishings, or emulating the hypermarket environment by offering lower prices and maintaining a customer-friendly environment.[14]

General Merchandise Discount Stores

General merchandise discount stores sell high volumes of merchandise, offer limited service, and charge lower prices. Discount stores are divided into two categories: **all-purpose discount stores,** which offer a wide variety of merchandise and limited depth, and **category specialists (category killers),** which carry a narrow variety of merchandise and offer a wide assortment.

General merchandise discount stores Retailers that sell high volumes of merchandise, offer limited service, and charge lower prices.

All-purpose discount stores General merchandise discount stores that offer a wide variety of merchandise and limited depth.

Category specialists/Category killers Large general merchandise discount stores that carry a narrow variety of merchandise and a wide assortment.

---

13. Insights into developments in Asian department store retailing from Sternquist, *International Retailing,* 1998.

14. Andrew Ness, "Retail Space to Let," *The China Business Review,* May/June 1999, Vol. 26, No. 3, pp. 44–49; and *International Market Insight Reports,* "China: Shanghai Retail Sector in Transition," July 26, 1999, pp. 1–4.

(b)

(c)

The all-purpose category is dominated by stores such as Wal-Mart, Kmart, and Target in the United States. Internationally, this retailer category tends to draw a substantial portion of profits from its supermarket section; consequently, it will be addressed in section 12-3b, "Food Retailers." In the all-purpose category, Wal-Mart has more than 600 stores internationally (many of the international stores are hypermarkets); they are present in Canada, Mexico, Puerto Rico, Argentina, Brazil, Germany, and the United Kingdom. Wal-Mart also has a presence in China, through joint ventures, and two franchise locations in Indonesia. Its goals are to derive one-third of its earnings from international operations.[15]

---

15. Mike Troy, "Wal-Mart International Sets Goals at Vendor Conference," *Discount Store News,* March 23, 1998, Vol. 37, No. 6, pp. 3, 65.

Category specialists, also known as category killers or stores with category dominance, are large specialty stores that carry a narrow variety of merchandise and a wide assortment. Among examples of category specialists successful internationally are office supply stores, such as Staples, Office Max, and Office Depot; home improvement centers, such as Home Depot; bookstores, such as Borders, which are especially well received in East Asia; children's stores, such as Toys "R" Us, which leads sales in this product category from Scandinavia to South Africa; and furniture stores, such as Ikea, which dominates the modern, basic furniture market. Of the first category, office supply stores, Staples is present internationally in Europe, where it has seventy-nine stores—in Germany, the Netherlands, Portugal, and the United Kingdom. Office Max has stores in Mexico, Japan, and Brazil, while Office Depot operates seventy-six international units under joint-venture and licensing agreements.[16]

Many of the established international specialty retailers and numerous newcomers are attracting consumers with innovative approaches to merchandising. In the furniture business, Ikea has redefined furniture retailing for more than three decades with its impressive merchandising core competencies, its sourcing economies of scale, and the savings it passes on to consumers.

Off-Price Retailers

Off-price retailers Retailers who sell brand name and designer merchandise below regular retail.

Off-price retailers sell brand name and designer merchandise below regular retail; the products they sell may include overruns, irregular products, as well as products from previous seasons. Among examples of off-price retailers are factory outlet stores; close-out retailers, with broad, inconsistent assortments; and single-price retailers. Although this type of retailing is popular in the United States and Canada, in the rest of the world, there are only limited possibilities, other than store sales, for purchasing brand names at a discount. For example, Hugo Boss has an outlet store in Southern Germany, close to its factory, near Stuttgart, and Zurich has a famous designer outlet mall; Italy also has a few outlet stores for its famous designers. None of these examples come close in depth and variety to the North American off-price retailer presence, but that is about to change, as more and more international consumers demand similar deals as the ones offered in the United States.

Often, American companies must build their own outlet stores in environments where this type of retail format is unknown. In Japan, for instance, in the Tokyo suburb of Sagami-One, American Malls International opened an outlet mall for companies such as Guess! and Laura Ashley to sell discontinued merchandise at a discount.[17]

Catalog Showrooms

Catalog showrooms Showrooms displaying the products of catalog retailers, offering high-turnover, brand name goods at discount prices.

Catalog showrooms usually offer high-turnover, brand name goods at discount prices. A typical format for a catalog showroom is one in which customers order from a catalog in the showroom where the product is only displayed, and then pick up the merchandise at a designated location. Internationally, the goods sold in this retail format are not typically brand name goods, but, rather, they are goods that have not sold in season through a company's catalog. For example, Neckermann and Quelle, the well-known German catalog retailers, have catalog showrooms in

---

16. Mike Troy, "Staples Wins Race to 1,000th Office Store," *Discount Store News,* August 23, 1999, Vol. 38, No. 16, pp. 1, 38.

17. Peter Landers, "Stores and Stripes," *Far Eastern Economic Review,* December 24, 1998, Vol. 161, No. 52, pp. 48–50.

many of Germany's largest cities where they sell their catalog store brands. In addition, Ikea uses this strategy to sell to consumers worldwide: Customers receive a catalog, which is also available in the showroom; based on the offerings displayed in the catalog and in the showroom, they order in the store the product they would like to purchase and pick it up from a designated location in its unassembled state.

12-3b Food Retailers

Conventional Supermarkets

Food retailers include **conventional supermarkets,** which are self-service retailers with annual sales higher than $2 million and less than 20,000 square feet of store space. Such supermarkets abound worldwide, with local retailers and regional international retailers most prominent in this retail category.

Superstores

The **superstores** category includes **combination stores** (food and drug) and **hypermarkets** (which combine supermarket, discount, and warehouse retailing principles). In the United States, combination stores have been quite successful; all-purpose general discount stores, such as Wal-Mart and Kmart, are often transformed into superstores to facilitate one-stop shopping for consumers. In their new, enhanced formats, these stores are known as the Wal-Mart Superstore and Big K, respectively, and they carry an extensive food selection but have only limited refrigeration space.

These same stores have attempted, without success, to adopt a hypermarket format in the United States, by offering consumers an extensive supermarket section, with fresh produce and ample refrigeration space. However, such a format did not appeal to U.S. consumers. As previously mentioned, Wal-Mart's presence in retail in the rest of the world is mainly in the form of hypermarkets. With its advanced distribution logistics, Wal-Mart has changed the retail market worldwide, forcing local suppliers to grow with it at a fast pace and forcing competitors to match it in its everyday-low-pricing strategy.

Germany is a key target for Wal-Mart's international expansion. The company acquired the Wertkauf chain in 1997 and the Interspar hypermarket chain in 1998, adding almost 100 new hypermarkets.[18] In the United Kingdom, Wal-Mart purchased the Asda Group PLC, Britain's third-largest grocery chain; it also operates 13 stores in Argentina, 15 in Brazil, 154 in Canada, 425 in Mexico, 15 in Puerto Rico, and, under joint ventures, it also operates 6 hypermarkets in China and 4 in Korea.[19]

The shockwaves sent by Wal-Mart's extensive presence in Europe have led to substantial competitive and consolidation activity in the hypermarket category. The French hypermarket chain Carrefour merged with its former rival Promodes, competing for the position of the world's dominant retailer. Similarly, German retailer Metro AG strengthened its position by buying the Allkauf chain of eighty-six hypermarkets and the KriegbaumUnternemensgruppe chain of twenty-seven hypermarkets and sixteen supermarkets.[20] Tesco, the British supermarket chain, is rapidly expanding with its Tesco Extra hypermarkets in Central and Eastern

Food retailers Retailers selling primarily food products.

Conventional supermarkets Self-service food retailers with annual sales of more than $2 million and with an area less than 20,000 square feet.

Superstores Large retailers such as combination stores or hypermarkets that sell food, drugs, and other products.

Combination stores Medium-size retail stores that combine food and drug retailing.

Hypermarkets Very large retail stores that combine supermarket, discount, and warehouse retailing principles.

---

18. *Discount Store News,* "A Foothold in Europe's Heartland," October 1999, Supplement: "Wal-Mart: Retailer of the Century," pp. 77, 175.

19. *Home Textiles Today,* "Wal-Mart Buys Grocery Chain in the United Kingdom," June 21, 1999, Vol. 20, No. 42, p. 21.

20. *Discount Store News,* "A Foothold in Europe's Heartland," pp. 77, 175.

Europe—Poland, the Czech Republic, Hungary, Slovakia, and Latvia[21]—attempting to gain a first mover advantage in these markets.

Royal Ahold, the Dutch supermarket chain, is also planning to form a major alliance, presently eyeing both Safeway and Sainsbury in Great Britain.[22] Ahold owns, among others, a number of supermarket chains in the United States (BI-LO, Giant, Stop & Shop), as well as the Albert Heijn supermarkets and the Etos drugstores in the Netherlands. Ahold is also one of the most important international retailers in Asia; as one of the best food retailers in the world, with important capabilities in merchandising, inventory management, and management information systems, this chain is aggressively entering Southeast Asian markets through acquisitions and joint ventures.[23]

Also in Asia, hypermarkets Carrefour and Makro already have significant positions in Taiwan, Malaysia, Indonesia, and Thailand, and Tesco acquired a majority stake in the Lotus Supercenters in Thailand. In fact, Carrefour has more than 9,000 outlets around the world; employs 240,000 workers; and is the largest retailer in countries such as France, Belgium, Portugal, Spain, Brazil, Argentina, Taiwan, South Korea, and Indonesia. In France alone, the new Carrefour (including the recently acquired Promodes chain) represents an important employer—more than 600,000 people and generating a revenue equal to 15 percent of France's Gross Domestic Product.[24]

Warehouse Clubs or Wholesale Clubs

Warehouse clubs, also called **wholesale clubs,** require members to pay an annual fee and operate in low-overhead, warehouse-type facilities. They offer limited lines of brand name and dealer-brand groceries, apparel, appliances, and other goods at a substantial discount. They sell to final consumers who are affiliated with different institutions, as well as to businesses (in this capacity, they are wholesalers, rather than retailers). This retailing concept is presently pioneered worldwide by Sam's Club (part of Wal-Mart) and Price Club/Costco.

Sam's Club operates in forty-six international locations; its most important operations are in Mexico, where it has acquired its joint-venture partner, Cifra. Sam's Club entered Mexico in 1991 with an agreement to operate warehouse clubs patterned after Sam's Club, under the Club Aurerra name in Mexico City. It is also present in the Philippines, China, Panama, and Indonesia.[25] Price Club/Costco has units in Korea, Taiwan, Japan, Canada, the United Kingdom,[26] and Mexico, where it has a joint venture with the retail conglomerate Controladora Comercial Mexicana.[27] San Diego-based PriceSmart Inc. is presently forming joint ventures and licensing agreements with foreign partners to set up wholesale clubs in Latin America and Asia-Pacific countries.[28]

Warehouse clubs   Stores that require members to pay an annual fee operating in low-overhead, warehouse-type facilities, offering limited lines of brand name and dealer-brand groceries, apparel, appliances, and other goods at a substantial discount; also known as wholesale clubs.

Wholesale clubs   Stores that require members to pay an annual fee operating in low-overhead, warehouse-type facilities, offering limited lines of brand name and dealer-brand groceries, apparel, appliances, and other goods at a substantial discount; also known as warehouse clubs.

21. David Benady, "Continental Shift," *Marketing Week,* October 9, 1997, Vol. 20, No. 28, pp. 52–55.

22. Jardine, "Retailers Go on International Shopping Trip," p. 15.

23. Alan Treadgold, "The Outlook for Asian Retailing," *Discount Merchandiser,* May 1999, Vol. 39, No. 5, pp. 45–46.

24. *The Economist,* "Business: French Fusion," September 4, 1999, Vol. 352, No. 8135, pp. 61–62.

25. *Discount Store News,* "A Partnership for the Long Haul," October 1999, Supplement: "Wal-Mart: Retailer of the Century," pp. 85, 179.

26. *Discount Store News,* "Loyalty Helps Drive Club Sales Gains," August 9, 1999, Vol. 38, No. 15, p. 65; and *Discount Store News,* "Costco Expands into Korea," July 27, 1998, Vol. 37, No. 14, p. 54.

27. *Discount Store News,* "A Partnership," pp. 85, 179.

28. *Communications News,* "Rio-to-Manila-to-Jakarta," April 1998, Vol. 35, No. 4, p. 64.

(a)

(b)

Figure 12-5
The merchandise mix of convenience stores can vary greatly from one location to another. Here are two convenience stores. *(a)* This store is located in Warsaw, Poland, where Ariel laundry detergent (Procter & Gamble) dominates and where cleaning and hygiene products occupy more than half the store. *(b)* This store is located in Bucharest, Romania, where vice products and sweets dominate, although the owners also display a dairy case and some milk products.

Convenience Stores

Convenience stores are small retailers located in residential areas, convenient to consumers; they are open long hours, carry limited lines of higher-turnover necessities, and offer the possibility of a one-stop shopping experience. Formats of convenience stores vary worldwide (see Figure 12-5*a* and 12-5*b*)—from small independent retailers to chains such as 7-11 (owned by the Japanese company Ito Yokado); from large stores offering a one-stop shopping opportunity for convenience goods and fast food to kiosks selling food items and alcoholic beverages

Convenience stores Small retailers located in residential areas, open long hours, and carrying limited lines of high-turnover necessities.

obtained through both legal and illegal channels; from convenience stores-cum-pharmacies in a city's town square to seventh-floor apartments with a large opening in the front door selling milk, cheese, bread, and different types of chocolate. Convenience stores abound in both developing and developed countries, with many chains developing in conjunction with gas stations.

12-3c Nonstore Retailing

Internet Retailing

Interactive home shopping/Electronic retailing/Internet retailing A venue for selling through the Internet using web sites to increase market penetration and market diversification.

Also known as **interactive home shopping** or **electronic retailing,** selling through the Internet is quickly becoming an important retail format. In the **Internet retailing** category are both the new dot-com companies as well as traditional retailers. In this case, traditional retailers are attempting additional market penetration—making it convenient for loyal customers to purchase their products—as well as market diversification—expanding their market to consumers who otherwise would not normally shop in their particular retail establishment. With the Internet and the increase in the number of Internet users worldwide,[29] providing retailing services through a Web site that is accessible globally becomes much easier. Local retailers can easily become international retailers without making investments in store leases, aesthetics, atmospherics, etc.

Internet retailing provides opportunities for retail firms to define their market beyond their target regions. At the same time, it presents dilemmas with regard to customer service and control of the retail transactions (due to international and regional differences in mail reliability, and in customer orientation and skill of local service representatives, among others).

In developed countries, Internet purchasing is consumption-market–driven and not experience-driven: Consumers shop for needs and wants but do not view Internet surfing as a pleasure trip, as would consumers going to a mall or a store.[30] Consequently, shopping via the Internet for consumers in countries where attractive shopping alternatives are available, such as malls and stores with great merchandise assortment and variety, is quite different from shopping in many developing countries, where alternatives are very limited, and where both retailers and the products they sell are inferior. If it were not for the Internet and for catalog retailing, consumers in this second category would be able to purchase higher quality goods only if they went abroad.

One problem that consumers in developed countries might have to contend with are unethical retailers. Whereas brick-and-mortar retailers can be sued in a local court of law for nonperformance, Internet retailers are more elusive; the issue of the appropriate jurisdiction further complicates the situation.

Finally, it should also be mentioned that most catalog retailers selling worldwide, such Quelle and Neckermann from Germany and Ikea from Sweden, are now also selling through their own web pages.

Vending Machines

Vending machines Interactive modes of retailing convenience goods.

With the advent of the Smart Card, vending machine retailing has become more popular than ever (and, increasingly, more **vending machines** worldwide accept credit cards). Technology is now facilitating a more interactive consumer relationship, where videos illustrate product use and provide more information. The

---

29. Michael J. Mandel, "The Internet Economy: The World's Next Growth Engine," *Business Week,* Industrial/Technology Edition, October 4, 1999, No. 3649, pp. 72–77

30. *Chain Store Age,* "Sticking to the Web," July 1998, Vol. 74, No. 7, pp. 153–155.

extent to which vending machines are used as a retail venue varies from country to country. Vending machines are used most in Japan, where they sell just about anything one can think of, including beer, sausage, rice, life insurance, eggs, cameras, pantyhose,[31] and condoms. Coke alone has one million vending machines in Japan.[32] In fact, in central locations in Japan's major cities, there are so many vending machines that they interfere with pedestrian traffic.

Vending machines are encountered in different configurations around the world. In the Netherlands, for instance, one can enter an outfit known as an Automatiek and select sausages, meatballs, salads, and beverages from the different machines, all replenished frequently by a full-time employee. In Munich, Germany, a vending machine for fresh flowers is located in the center of town. In much of the rest of the world, with the exception of the United States and Canada, cigarettes are readily available in the streets at all times of the day. In Europe, condoms are sold in vending machines outside pharmacies.

Television Home Shopping

The **television home shopping** category includes cable channels selling to consumers in their homes, infomercials, and direct response advertising shown on broadcast and cable television. Television shopping networks, much like QVC and the Home Shopping Network in the United States, operate in many developed countries. Some offerings do not fit well in either category. For example, in a mid-1990s Romanian program, for one hour contestants had to perform different tasks, all of which involved Pepsi bottles or bottle caps. In another example, Britain's famous Harrods department store entered the home shopping business by selling its products on the TV-news channel CNBC Europe; a two-hour program called *Gold Card Television* offers shows about travel and fashion in addition to the opportunity to purchase products selected by Harrods.[33]

Western television shopping programs are also entering Asia; among the new entrants are Home Shopping Network Direct from Florida, International Shopping Network from San Diego, Interwood Marketing Group from Canada, London-based Regal Shop International and Quantum International, and Australia's International Media Management. They create or invest in television programs or ten- to thirty-minute infomercials that market products ranging from cosmetics to kitchen accessories. These programs are frequently prerecorded in their country of origin and later dubbed into Asian languages.[34]

Catalog Retailing and Direct Mail Retailing

Retailers of all categories are expanding internationally through catalog sales and **direct mail retailing.** Tiffany's is expanding its direct mail operations internationally; its international sales account for 42 percent of the company's total revenues. Marketers are using consistent marketing communications worldwide, coordinating their advertising with direct mail brochures and catalogs.[35] Traditional **catalog retailers** are expanding internationally as well. Germany's Quelle,

Television home shopping
Retailing through cable channels selling to consumers in their homes, through infomercials, and through direct response advertising shown on broadcast and cable television.

Direct mail retailing Retailing using catalogs and other direct mail, instead of brick-and-mortar stores.

Catalog retailers Retailers selling products through mail catalogs.

31. Haidee Allerton, "Vending Your Way," *Training & Development,* September 1996, Vol. 50, No. 9, p. 72.

32. Dean Foust, "Doug Daft Isn't Sugarcoating Things; He's Already Shaking Up Coke. But Can He Bring Back the Fizz?" *Business Week,* Industrial/Technology Edition, February 7, 2000, No. 3667, p. 36.

33. *Direct Marketing,* "Harrods to Start Home Shopping Business," November 1998, Vol. 61, No. 7, p. 16.

34. William J. McDonald, "The Ban in China: How Direct Marketing Is Affected," *Direct Marketing,* June 1998, Vol. 61, No. 2, pp. 16–19.

35. Sarah Lorge, "A Priceless Brand," *Sales and Marketing Management,* October 1998, Vol. 150, No. 11, pp. 102–111.

Neckermann, and Otto Versand are actively expanding their international operations; Otto Versand, for example, offers specialty goods to consumers in Europe, the United States, and Japan.

The potential for catalog sales remains high internationally and is greatly enhanced by the facilitations provided by the Internet. Germany, with 82 million people spending more than $27 billion a year on direct mail goods, is second only to the U.S. in mail order sales. Consequently, prominent U.S. catalog retailers are active in this market; among them are Eddie Bauer and Lands' End, and others, such as industrial supplies cataloger New Pig and Carol Wright Gifts, which targets older females in middle-to-lower-income households.[36]

Catalog sales provide challenges to businesses not familiar with local practices. For example, catalog and Internet retailers found that consumers in Japan expect to first receive the product and only then pay for it. The key to success of catalog retailing is adaptation to local market needs and practices. U.S. personal planner cataloger DayTimers mails its catalogs in North America, the U.K., Australia, New Zealand, Central Asia, and Germany; for its German calendars, which are translated into German, the company made Monday, rather than Sunday, the first day of the week and increased the size of the planners to accommodate Germany's larger paper sizes. Although Germans are accustomed to buying from catalogs, they are not used to the privileges considered standard in the U.S. catalog industry, such as 24-hour service, liberal return policies, or even life-time guarantees from apparel catalogers. Such guarantees were unheard of in Germany, and a group of German retailers took Lands' End to court, accusing it of "unfair" competition (and lost).[37]

In developing countries, however, many obstacles affect catalog retailing. First and foremost, the infrastructure must be sufficiently developed to warrant investment; for catalog companies, it means that telephone service and mail service must be reliable. In many countries—even in emerging markets—consumers must often purchase cellular phone service because standard telephone service is inadequate or is not available. In addition, the mailing system is lax and mail is often intercepted and opened, such that only a portion of a package's content may arrive at its destination. Finally, in many developing countries, average income is a fraction of the average income in developed countries; thus, products sold via catalog, such as clothing, appliances, housewares, etc., are prohibitively expensive.

Direct Selling

Direct selling Selling that involves a salesperson, typically an independent distributor, contacting a consumer at a convenient location—at his or her home or workplace, demonstrating product use and benefits, taking orders, and delivering the merchandise.

In the **direct selling** retail format, a salesperson, typically an independent distributor, contacts a consumer at a convenient location—at his or her home or workplace, demonstrates product use and benefits, takes orders, and delivers the merchandise. Direct selling is in the growth stage in most of the developing world; here, a number of impediments restrict firms' capability to successfully carry out their selling activity. Among these impediments are low per capita income, unreliable postal services, high levels of bureaucracy, lack of credit cards, few telephones, and a lack of mailing lists or access to mailing lists.

Direct selling firms are most active in growth markets, such as the emerging economies of China and Southeast Asia, Central and Eastern Europe, and Latin America. American direct selling firms, such as Avon Products, Nu Skin, and Mary Kay Cosmetics, are very active in these markets, as well as worldwide. Avon, for

---

36. Shannon Oberdorf, "U.S. Mailers Blitz Germany," *Catalog Age*, February 1998, Vol. 15, No. 2, p. 2.

37. Ibid.

example, earns more than half of its revenues from markets abroad, especially from developing countries.

In recent years, however, the negative publicity surrounding pyramid schemes has led to the development of legislation that does not favor this selling approach. China, for example, has a ban on direct selling. The ban does not apply to traditional forms of direct marketing such as direct mail, catalog marketing, telemarketing, or direct-response advertising. Rather, it reflects the Chinese government's concerns about the system of independent distributor networks, door-to-door sales, and motivational meetings, and the belief that criminals use these organizations to start secret societies, swindle consumers, seek exorbitant profits, sell smuggled or fake goods, and trick customers into buying unnecessary and expensive goods.[38]

It is unfortunate that this system of selling is closely associated with pyramid money schemes; this is especially the case with network marketing. Whereas pyramid schemes do nothing in terms of production and distribution, in network-based marketing, everyone is involved, bringing in the most profit to those who have created the distribution system.

Network Marketing

Network marketing, or **multilevel marketing,** is a variation on direct selling and an approach to selling at the same time. It involves signing up sales representatives to go into business for themselves with minimal start-up capital. Their task is to sell more "distributorships"—that is, to identify more sales representatives from their own personal network, to buy the product and to persuade others to buy the product. Network marketing is experiencing rapid growth, especially in emerging markets. In South Africa, for example, the poor transportation infrastructure that presents a challenge to many multinationals does not present a problem to network marketing; this and the fit with elements of traditional African culture make network marketing one of the most significant avenues for growth within the post-apartheid economy.[39] Among the most successful network marketing firms that have international operations are Amway, Herbalife International, and Equinox International.

Network marketing/Multilevel marketing Using acquaintance networks through an alternative distribution structure for the purpose of distribution.

12-4 Issues in International Retailing

12-4a Legislation and Regulation

Country regulations differ from one market to another, and legislation can have a profound impact on a firm's operations. In the case of China's ban on direct selling, leading international firms are forced to rethink their marketing strategies and offer their goods using alternative methods to direct selling. Further, in many markets (including China), retail legislation and rules differ from province to province, as well as at the national level.[40] For example, regulations allow foreign retail joint ventures to operate in more cities throughout China and to engage in wholesaling for the first time; however, most rural areas are off-limits to international retailers.[41]

---

38. McDonald, "The Ban in China," pp. 16–19.

39. Adrian Sargeant and P. Msweli, "Network Marketing in South Africa: An Exploratory Study of Consumer Perception," *Journal of International Consumer Marketing,* 1999, Vol. 11, No. 3, pp. 51–66.

40. *Chain Store Age,* "China: The Grandest Opening Ever," December 1997, Supplement: "Global Retailing," pp. 32–35.

41. *International Market Insight Reports,* "China: Shanghai Retail Sector in Transition," July 26, 1999, pp. 1–4.

Other types of regulations restrict expansion of superstores and hypermarkets (United Kingdom, France, and Belgium); limit the hours of operation to protect smaller stores (the Netherlands, Spain); require that stores locate in downtown areas (Germany); control disposal of packaging used for transportation (Germany); limit the use of promotional pricing (France, Germany);[42] and limit the period for sales to two weeks, twice a year (various countries in the European Union). French companies, for example, rarely offer an extra product for free because the amount companies are allowed to give away is limited to 7 percent of the total value. In Germany, it is illegal to offer three products for the price of two or other bundling offers, and cash discounts to the consumer are limited to 3 percent.

Legislation has also created stores that limit access of local consumers. In addition to shops created for the use of different categories of consumers, such as diplomatic shops or shops for the military, different countries have shops that are open to all consumers except nationals. This is the case in countries where locals are not allowed access to hard currency, which must be channeled through the Central Bank, and where all hard currency retail transactions are conducted only with expatriates. The only advantage these stores offer is that they might carry select merchandise that is not readily available in the market; however, overall, the quality of the merchandise is not necessarily above that of goods in the open market.

12-4b Taxation and Cross-Border Shopping

Cross-border shopping
Purchasing products from a neighboring country where the consumers may be charged lower duties.

In countries where consumers are not charged duties for products they purchase from a neighboring country (if the neighboring country belongs to the same free trade area, for example), **cross-border shopping** affects most retailers in the higher-tax countries. In the European Union, the U.K., the Irish Republic, and Denmark charge much higher taxes than the rest of the EU members. To avoid the large value-added tax on most products for personal consumption, consumers in these countries cross borders into countries where this tax is substantially lower. In this sense, consumers' purchase decisions are driven by tax differences rather than by underlying differences in producer prices, and cross-border shopping causes an inefficient allocation of resources, leading to significant reductions in sales by domestic retailers and manufacturers, reduced profits, and job losses.[43]

In other situations, retailers in neighboring countries suffer from the low taxes imposed by a tax haven nearby. Examples of consumer tax havens are Port Said in Egypt, and Bermuda or the Bahamas in North America, among others. In setting up retail operations overseas, a company must assess and seek the most favorable environment from the taxation perspective.

12-4c Variation in Retail Practices: A Consumer Perspective

Retail practices vary from one market to another. Consumers in the United States prefer to shop less frequently and purchase products in bulk, whereas consumers

---

42. See Sternquist, *International Retailing,* 1998; and David Reed, "Country Practice," *Marketing Week,* July 3, 1997, Vol. 20, No. 4, pp. 45–49.

43. Ian Crawford and Sarah Tanner, "Bringing It All Back Home: Alcohol Taxation and Cross-Border Shopping, *Fiscal Studies,* May 1995, Vol. 16, No. 2, pp. 94–115.

in Japan prefer to purchase products in smaller quantities, packaged individually. In Asia, store demonstrations are very popular, and, in Japan and Korea, Saturday is a major shopping day, when shopping and attending the respective demonstration are a family affair. Consumers in Asia and the United Kingdom prefer products of the highest quality and are willing to pay the price. In Argentina and Saudi Arabia, consumers prefer to purchase food products at mom-and-pop stores, rather than at the supermarket, whereas in Mexico consumers continue to go to farmers' markets for fresh produce. Even bugs on fruit are important to consumers in the Philippines; they indicate that the fruit is ripe. Finally, in the United Kingdom, store name is a better indicator of quality for food products than brand name; hence, private labels are thriving for very popular stores.[44]

12-4d Variation in Retail Practice: Salespeople and Management

Sales service differs greatly from one market to another. Whereas in the United States it is customary to have friendly salespeople waiting on customers, treating them with respect, in many other countries this is not always the case. In Eastern and Southeastern Europe, for example, salespeople tend to be curt, bordering on unfriendly. A Pizza Hut employee trained in customer service according to U.S. specifications sounds terribly out of place in Poland; in fact, the language used with customers appears to be unnatural. And a typical situation is one in which the telephone line of a Delta Airlines office in Bucharest sounds constantly busy; upon arriving at the respective office, one would note that two telephones are off the hook permanently, while the agents are drinking coffee with friends and neglecting consumers, who are casually waited on by one agent.

In other examples, in China, the sales staff tend to be overly correct: If a customer forgets to pick up the change after a sale is complete, the salesperson will most likely follow him or her into the street to return the change. In other countries, the situation is quite the contrary: Salespeople keep the change and sell only those products that are priced under an even price so that they can claim they do not have the change if a customer dares challenge them. In countries where there may be shortages of certain products, salespeople are bribed with money and other goods such as coffee, cigarettes, and perfume.

Finally, certain stores charge an admission price to ensure that individuals permitted to enter can actually afford the products sold there (an example is an antique store selling what locally would be considered masterpieces or national treasures). In these stores, it is also appropriate for customers to dress well so that they do not look "suspect." Similarly, not dressing well in environments considered upscale locally (despite the fact that, in most of the world, the respective retail environment would be perceived as average at best) could easily result in the denial of service.

---

44. Terry Hennessy, "International Flavors," *Progressive Grocer*, August 1999, Vol. 78, No. 8, pp. 67–73.

Chapter Summary

- **Provide an overview and description of the general merchandise retailing category and offer examples and illustrations**

In the general merchandise retailing category are a number of retailers. Specialty stores, offering narrow assortments and deep product lines, are rapidly increasing their presence internationally. From The Gap to Mango to Marks & Spencer, retailers find success well beyond their national borders. Specialized markets, specializing in one product category, are omnipresent worldwide. Department stores are experiencing a decline, with some exceptions. Innovative stores that position themselves creatively have more success; in Asia, the more successful department stores are those that position themselves as European retailers. General merchandise discount stores are rapidly expanding, with great success. Wal-Mart, in particular, has made great strides in conquering international markets. Category specialists, specializing in one product category, are also very successful in their international pursuits. Off-price stores, a staple of U.S. retailing offering brand name products at lower prices, are in great demand in other countries. Recently, however, such retailers have made more substantial inroads into markets in Asia and Europe. Catalog showrooms, selling high-turnover, brand name goods at discount prices, are also successful internationally, with many competing players. The Ikea "model" has been the most successful to date.

- **Provide an overview and description of the food retailing category and offer examples and illustrations**

Food retailers include conventional supermarkets, which are dominated by national and regional chains. Superstores can be combination stores (food and drug) or hypermarkets, which are very successful abroad but are slow to become mainstream retailers in the United States. Warehouse clubs are becoming very popular worldwide, and many U.S. retailers in this category are doing very well. Convenience stores abound in both developing and developed countries, with many chains developing in conjunction with gas stations.

- **Provide an overview and description of the nonstore retailing category and offer examples and illustrations**

Nonstore retailing is one of the areas with the highest growth and unlimited opportunities. Internet retailing has vastly expanded opportunities for small and medium-size retailers all over the world. Vending machines are increasing in sophistication and have different formats and capabilities in each market where they are available; the products they can carry also differ. Television home shopping is attracting more audiences, and today also offers opportunities to brick-and-mortar retailers to expand. Catalog retailers are still strong, expanding rapidly beyond their home-country borders. Direct selling and network marketing are gaining rapid ground, especially in developing countries.

- **Address issues related to legislation, taxation, and retailing practices around the world**

Retailers have many restrictions imposed on them, and those restrictions vary from one market to another. The restrictions cover hours of operation, sales activity, and pricing techniques; or the restrictions may limit access to local consumers. Retailing practices vary from one market to another: Salespeople may be more courteous and solicitous in some countries, and consumers may be more demanding in certain markets, shop more or less frequently, and may or may not rely on a product's brand name as an indication of quality.

Discussion Questions

1. What is the difference between a specialty store and a category specialist?
2. Describe the state of the department store around the globe. What strategies appear to be more successful for department stores?
3. Hypermarkets are a dominant retailing format in Europe but not in the United States. What are hypermarkets? Give examples of successful hypermarkets worldwide.
4. Direct selling and network marketing have found great success in emerging markets. What is the difference between the two categories of retailers, and how do they gain access to consumers?
5. What are some of the challenges that retailers face in international markets?

The International Promotional Mix and Advertising Strategies

Key Terms

adaptation of the advertising
  strategy
all-you-can-afford method
billboards
broadcast medium
channel of communication
competitive-parity method
decoding
encoding
executive-judgment method
feedback
historical method

infomercials
interactive medium
international communication
  process
international promotional mix
media availability
media infrastructure
media reliability
media restrictions
medium/media
noise
nonpersonal medium

objective-and-task method
percent-of-sales method
personal medium
print medium
product placement
receiver
sender
standardization of the
  advertising strategy
telemarketing
television shopping networks

Outline

Learning Objectives
13-1 The International
    Promotional Mix
13-2 The International
    Communication Process
13-3 Advertising
  13-3a The Media Infrastructure
  13-3b The Advertising
     Infrastructure
  13-3c The Advertising Strategy
Chapter Summary
Discussion Questions

Learning Objectives

Learning Objectives

By the end of this chapter, you should be able to:

- Describe the international promotional mix and the international communication process
- Explore the international advertising formats and practices around the world

- Describe the international advertising and media infrastructure and infrastructure-related challenges in different markets
- Describe advertising strategies and budgeting decisions and offer examples of international applications

---

"Kent, Camel, Marlboro, Gitanes, Gauloises, Cartier, Assos, Snagov, Carpati
Diminish memories of a deprived communist past.
Cancer peddlers pulse their glamour at half-hour intervals
On TV screens—now in full color!
To children shredding Red Youth Ties. . . .
Sleek cigarette posters adorn sidewalk cafés;
Freedom's effervescent conversation
Drowns in smoke, inhaling another summer day"[1]

Promotion and, as an element of promotion, advertising are omnipresent in all countries of the world. From billboards on national monuments in China to little lit boats advertising shoes on the Bosphorus, to Ronald McDonald hanging his two-floor-long legs in a town square or leading a local wedding ceremony in Poland, promotion today permeates life everywhere. It has become part of the world landscape, framing highways, lighting crowded downtowns, projecting glamour on walls of slums, and shading street cafés. It is the world's common mind-humming jingles and tag lines and echoing global brand themes. It reaches consumers on their doorsteps, in mail or e-mail, and via blasting stereos or drumbeats.

This chapter discusses the international promotional mix and the international communication process. Of the mix items, the chapter focuses on advertising and illustrates advertising formats, practices, and infrastructure-related issues around the world.

---

1. Dana Lascu, "Of Cigarettes," *Journal of Advertising*, September 1992, Vol. 21, No. 3, p. 56.

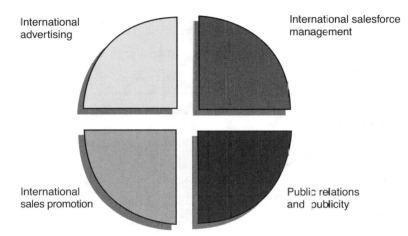

International
advertising

International salesforce
management

International
sales promotion

Public relations
and publicity

Figure 13-1
The international
promotional mix.

13-1 The International Promotional Mix

The components of the **international promotional mix** are international advertising, international salesforce management, international sales promotion, and public relations and publicity (see Figure 13-1). Companies use the promotional mix to communicate with international consumers about their products and services. In the process of expanding internationally, companies are faced with numerous challenges to their plans for communicating with the world's consumers. Many of the challenges are attributed to differences in culture. As described in Chapter 5, "Cultural Influences on International Marketing," understanding the norms, motivations, attitudes, interests, and opinions of the target market is crucial to company success in marketing to and communicating with different cultures around the globe. Companies also must be prepared to handle the challenges presented by the local media, by the local advertising infrastructure, and by the different layers of government regulating all aspects of communication with the target market.

Section 13-2, "The International Communication Process," describes the international communication process, and Section 13-3, "Advertising," presents the topic of international advertising. Chapters 14 and 15 will address the remaining elements of the international promotional mix: sales force management and the expatriate sales force, international sales promotion, international public relations, and international publicity, completing the topic of the international promotional mix.

13-2 The International Communication Process

The **international communication process** involves using the entire promotional mix to communicate with the final consumer (see Figure 13-2). Regardless of the elements of the promotional mix involved, the communication essentially has the same format. The international sponsor (**sender**), usually represented by an advertising agency, encodes a message into words and images. The message is then translated into the language of the target market and transmitted through a **channel of communication,** or **medium,** to the international consumer in the target market (**receiver**). The medium may be a **nonpersonal medium:**

- A **print medium,** such as a newspaper, magazine, billboard, pamphlet, a point-of-purchase display
- A **broadcast medium,** such as television and radio
- An **interactive medium,** such as a web page or a computer terminal on the retailer's premises

International promotional mix
The different modes of communication with international consumers about products and services, using international advertising, international salesforce management, international sales promotion, public relations, and publicity.

International communication process The communication process that takes place between the product sponsor and the international target market.

Sender The sponsor of an advertisement, usually represented by an advertising agency, who encodes the message into words and images and communicates it to the target market.

Channel of communication
The medium used to communicate a message about a product to the consumer.

Medium/media The channel(s) of communication that a company uses to send to the target consumer a message about its product or services.

Receiver The target market that receives the advertising message from a sender.

Nonpersonal medium
A channel of communication such as a print medium, a broadcast medium, or an interactive medium that does not involve contact between the seller and the consumer.

Print medium A nonpersonal channel of communication such as a newspaper, magazine, billboard, pamphlet, or point-of-purchase display.

The International Communication Process

Figure 13-2
The international
communication process.

Broadcast medium
A nonpersonal channel of
communication such as television
or radio.

Interactive medium
A nonpersonal channel of
communication such as a web
page or a computer terminal on
the retailer's premises.

Personal medium
A communication channel that
involves contact between the seller
and the consumer.

Telemarketing A personal
channel of communication that
involves a salesperson calling on
consumers.

Noise All the potential
interference in the
communication process.

Feedback Information regarding
the effectiveness of a company's
message.

Encoding The process whereby
the advertiser puts the company's
message about the product into
words and images that are aimed
at the target consumer.

Alternatively, the channel may be a **personal medium:**

- A salesperson calling on a supplier or a door-to-door salesperson calling on consumers
- A telemarketer calling on consumers (**telemarketing**)
- A trade show, where one can address questions to an individual who is knowledgeable about the product

The international consumer (receiver) receives the message and decodes it into meaning. Ideally, the meaning of the decoded message should be identical to the meaning of the encoded message. However, **noise**—all the potential interference in the communication process, particularly noise attributed to cultural differences—may impede communication. During the message transmission and delivery processes, noise may interfere with proper message reception. The sponsor (sender) collects and relies on information regarding the effectiveness of the message (**feedback**) to evaluate the success of the promotional campaign; such information may be provided by sales data or by advertising research evaluating message recall rates.

Each step of the international communication process presents challenges to the message sponsor beyond those encountered when marketing to home-country consumers. First, when **encoding** the message, the source determines whether the attitudes, interests, and motivations of consumers in the international target market are different from those in the home-country target market. Manufacturers of Peugeot bicycles in France selling their product in Germany and the United States need to be aware that consumer motivations behind the purchase differ. In Germany, the main purpose of using the Peugeot bicycle is transportation. Major cities have bicycle paths on the sidewalks, and pedestrians and automobiles are not allowed to block them; bicycle paths also have their own signals at intersections. In the countryside, paths, in parallel with the main roads or highways, are reserved for bicycles. A German consumer who purchases a Peugeot bicycle will want a product that is reliable and can perform optimally, regardless of weather. Communication about the product, then, should stress durability, reliability, and quality. In the United States, a Peugeot bicycle is used primarily for recreation. Communication about the product is more likely to be successful if it focuses on a weekend recreational activity and/or on performance.

Similarly, Pizza Hut in the United States and the United Kingdom is a staple family restaurant for busy families who do not have time to cook. Pizza Hut advertising focuses on deals for the entire family. In Poland, Pizza Hut is the in-place for a techno-music dinner before consumers descend to the downstairs disco in Wroclaw, and the place for a business lunch in Warsaw's prestigious Marriott building, located strategically between stores selling haute couture. Consequently, communication about Pizza Hut in Poland should not limit itself to a family focus.

When encoding the message, one must ensure that the message is appropriately translated. In the process of translating the message, one should note that language is closely related to advertising strategy. For example, English requires less space in print and less air time for broadcast advertising (this is one of the reasons it is widely used in advertising). Translated into German, the headline, body copy, and tag line will require more space for a print advertisement and more air time for a broadcast ad.

From product name to the entire marketing communication, all must be monitored to ensure that the meanings intended are the meanings conveyed. There is an explosion of naming consultancies, set up as offshoots of advertising agencies, which develop product names that are intended to work worldwide; because consumers travel everywhere, it is important that brand names are consistent in any country where they are sold.[2] From names such as Vauxhall's Nova automobile, meaning "no go" in Spanish, to airlines claiming that one will fly "naked" (as opposed to "on leather") in first class, companies have made many mistakes when communicating with international consumers.

Sending the message through the appropriate channel is frequently a challenge; the media infrastructure might be such that the most appropriate medium cannot be successfully used. In countries where mail is less reliable, such as India and Romania, it is advisable not to send direct mail containing samples. In other countries where the mailing system is reliable, such as Saudi Arabia, mail might not constitute a traditional medium for sending samples, and a direct mail package might be perceived as suspicious. In Rwanda and Burundi, the only broadcast medium available is the radio; however, international brands are rarely advertised on this medium. To reach the mass market in these two countries, the only appropriate communication medium is the billboard. Furthermore, it is preferable that the advertisement has few words and relies on pictorials to convey the message because many target consumers are illiterate.

All this competition, including other noise, such as audience inattention, from other channels of communication and from programming could negatively affect the **decoding** process, such that the target consumer does not fully comprehend the communication. To lessen the impact of these communication impediments, companies do the following:

Decoding The process whereby the target consumer receives the message from the advertiser and translates it into meaningful information.

- Hire research firms to evaluate the message in multiple international environments
- Evaluate the effectiveness of the communication in attracting target market attention, using recall tests and other memory-based procedures
- Evaluate the effectiveness of the communication in getting consumers to purchase the product

The company then uses this feedback in modifying or designing future communication strategies.

---

2. Sam Solley, "Developing a Name to Work Worldwide," *Marketing*, December 21, 2000, p. 27.

13-3 Advertising

International advertising is becoming increasingly complex; more and more local and international companies are competing for consumers who are increasingly sophisticated and demanding. International advertising is defined as *a nonpersonal communication by an identified sponsor across international borders, using broadcast, print, and/or interactive media.*

13-3a The Media Infrastructure

Media infrastructure The media vehicles and their structure in an international target market.

The **media infrastructure** provides different challenges in countries of different levels of economic development. And, even though the media structure is essentially the same in most industrialized countries, challenges still arise in terms of business practices: A medium might not be considered appropriate for advertising. For example, newspapers might not constitute the right medium for advertising a particular product in one country, whereas, in other countries, advertising a particular type of product or service might be restricted or prohibited in other media—for instance, television.

Some of the challenges firms encounter on the media front are availability, reliability, restrictions, and costs.

Media Challenges

Media Availability

Media availability The extent to which media are available to communicate with target consumers.

An important issue facing the international marketing manager is **media availability,** the extent to which the media needed for a particular communication exists locally, or if it does exist, how it can be used as intended for the company communication. Certain types of media simply might not be available in a company's target markets. In many countries in Sub-Saharan Africa, for example, there are no television stations. Alternatively, there may be one or two government-owned and/or government-controlled stations that do not permit advertising or that limit advertising to certain times. Although some television owners might have access to international satellite and cable television, especially in the emerging markets in Asia and Latin America, many more cannot afford a satellite dish or a subscription to cable television. Access to these consumers, then, is limited. And, even though more and more consumers have access to Internet advertising worldwide, such access primarily favors consumers from more developed countries, or wealthy consumers and government employees from developing countries.

Media Reliability

Media reliability The probability of the media to air advertising messages on time, at an acceptable quality, and with the agreed-upon frequency.

Media reliability, the extent to which the existing media reliably reach the target consumer in the intended format and within the intended time frame, is also an important consideration. In some cases, media may be unreliable. Magazine or newspaper issues might not be printed on time, or publishers might accept more advertisements than they can print. The quality of the medium itself may be questionable. Local newspapers might not be of a high enough quality to print advertising for a global brand. Television stations might go off the air indefinitely at inopportune times, when a company's advertisement is scheduled to air. This often happens to small television stations that compete with government stations for viewers' attention.

Media Restrictions

Media restrictions Legal or self-imposed restrictions on the types and the number of advertisements aired or published.

Media restrictions refer to the different limitations that existing media pose on the sponsor. For example, the media could limit the types and the number of advertisements aired or published. As mentioned in Chapter 5, advertising in a number of Islamic countries might not permit the portrayal of women, whereas in other countries (China, for instance) media does not readily encourage the advertising of feminine hygiene products. Air time might be limited; for example, the European Union allows only 12 minutes per hour for advertising on each television station.

Advertising also might be clustered and separated from editorial content, for newspapers or magazines, or from television programming. Many television stations in Europe, as well as in South America (Brazil, for instance), broadcast television advertising only between programs, in clusters. Consumers typically choose to engage in other activities in the home during that time. In these countries, a better venue for firms that need to send their message using visuals in broadcast media is movie advertising; cinema advertisements are typically shown before films to a captive audience. In many developing countries where the literacy rate is low, advertising is primarily limited to billboards that do not display words other than the company logo and brand name.

Media scheduling also constitutes a restriction. Lag times between the submission of the advertisement and printing could reach as much as one year for some publications, primarily due to space restrictions allotted to advertising. Also, a contract that requires a publication or a television station to print or air an advertisement on a particular date is not backed by guarantees in many countries.

Media Costs

Media costs differ greatly between countries, and even within a particular country. Factors that account for this difference range from income per capita of target market and competition for media by advertisers, to firm status (a local firm is charged less than an international firm in Eastern European countries, China, Cuba, and Vietnam).

Costs are high in countries where the advertising campaign must be translated into multiple languages. India is an interesting case in point. A campaign aimed at a more educated consumer can be communicated effectively in either Hindi or English. To reach the masses in Southern India and penetrate this target market, however, translating the advertisements into Malealam, Tamil, and Telegu would be important.

Media Formats, Features, and Trends around the World

Advertising Posters on Kiosks and Fences

The practice of using kiosks and fences for advertising posters takes place in the United States to a more limited extent than in much of the rest of the world. In the United States, some kiosks are used for neighborhood announcements, and construction fences in larger cities display advertisements for plays, concerts, and art exhibits. In much of the rest of the world, especially in developing countries, kiosks display advertisements for the international products they sell. Kiosks are valuable and relatively inexpensive communication venues for multinationals: They are typically required to have posters displayed in exchange for having the rights to carry particular brands. Fences and other display structures are omnipresent in international capitals and small towns alike (see Figure 13-3). In France, the *affichiste* movement of modern art, whose works are displayed in major museums worldwide, used layers of posters that had been displayed for decades and then torn off walls and placed on canvas.

(a)
(b)

Figure 13-3
Kiosks are omnipresent in downtown capital cities *(a)* and in remote village locations *(b)*. Often, they are rendered colorful by Coca-Cola and Marlboro posters.

Billboards Advertisements in public areas appearing on large posters or electronic panels.

Advertising on the Sides of Private Homes

Typically located in high traffic areas, homes from Bangladesh to Bulgaria display advertising for international brands. This advertising constitutes a substantial source of revenue for the homeowners.

Advertising on Plastic Shopping Bags

Although retailers and manufacturers often display their brand names on shopping bags, another phenomenon is quickly spreading in developing countries: the use of bags (that consumers actually have to pay for!) to advertise popular television programs. The individual portrayed in Figure 13-4 sells shopping bags with characters from the soap operas *Dynasty* and *Dallas,* among others, in a Bucharest market.

Advertising on Outdoor Umbrellas

In the United States, outdoor umbrellas, if they contain any information at all, typically display the name of the restaurant where they are located. In other locations worldwide, umbrellas display international brand names, such as Marlboro, Coca-Cola, Pepsi, and others (see Figure 13-5).

The Omnipresent Billboards

Although **billboards** are quite common in the United States, in other parts of the world they dominate the landscape. Elegant advertisements for Coca-Cola in Russia and for the same brand under the railway in Portugal, ads for Camel cigarettes on top of a building in Greece and in a pedestrian mall in Spain, and a Pepsi ad at a bus station urging "don't go without it"—all are examples of such advertising (see Figure 13-6). An especially interesting development is the fact that, increasingly, local ads are of comparable quality and compete effectively with ads of multinational firms. This new development is attributed to the proliferation of computer technology and lower technology costs.

The Dominance of Global Media

Late-night talk show host Jay Leno's jokes are a staple around the world, as are Conan O'Brian's. CNN and Bloomberg broadcast all over the world, including in Sub-Saharan Africa. CNN is a popular television station in Ethiopia for those who can afford a television set; in fact, Addis Ababa, its capital city, often has a more

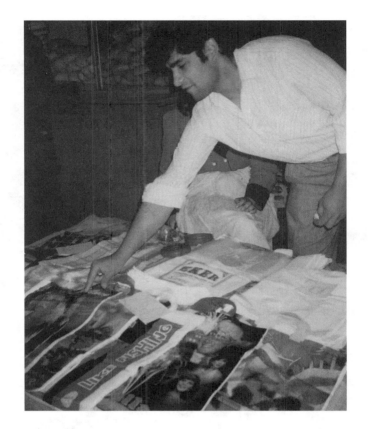

Figure 13-4
Sue Ellen and J. R. Ewing of the *Dallas* television series are popular in Eastern Europe, and shopping bags sporting their pictures are considered fashionable.

accurate forecast of the next day's weather in Hong Kong from the CNN satellite than for drought-prone regions in Ethiopia itself.[3] European television stations have competitors such as CNN Europe, Sky, and NBC. Asian stations compete with global companies such as CNN, MTV, NBC, Turner Broadcasting, Walt Disney/Capital Cities ABC, and the Cartoon Channel. ESPN Asia broadcasts American basketball in the Philippines and baseball in Taiwan, and millions of Chinese viewers watch badminton and U.S. National Basketball Association games.[4] Rupert Murdoch alone owns Star Plus, Star Plus Japan, Star Chinese Channel, and Star Movies in Asia, and has, among other media interests, resonant media companies such as Fox Broadcasting, 20th Century Fox, 20th Century Television, as well as investments in BskyB, Vox Channel, El Canal Fox, Australia's Channel 7, and 130 newspapers worldwide. All these stations can sell international brands to consumers all over the world.

Magazines such as *Glamour, Cosmopolitan,* and *Mademoiselle* are published in languages ranging from Mandarin to Italian to Polish to Japanese. These magazines are vehicles for global, regional, and local advertising campaigns of multinational companies.

Infomercials and Television Shopping Networks

Infomercials and **television shopping networks** once were a North American phenomenon. Currently, infomercials and television shopping channels exist in much of the industrialized world and in many emerging markets. Not only have QVC and the Home Shopping Network expanded in Europe, Latin America, and Asia, but also local competition is growing rapidly. Home Order Television in

Infomercials   Long television advertisements (one-half to one full hour in length) that are positioned as programming.

Television shopping networks   Cable channels that sell products to a television audience.

3. Anita Franklin, "Whose News? Control of the Media in Africa," *Review of African Political Economy,* December 1998, Vol. 25, No. 78, pp. 545–550.

4. Helen Johnstone, "Asian TV Companies Take Lead in Local Content," *Asian Business,* October 1996, Vol. 32, No. 10, pp. 26–33.

(a)

(b)

(c)

Figure 13-5
Outdoor umbrellas are
practical and prominent
modes of communication
with consumers worldwide.

Germany has created a strategic alliance with Quelle, the catalog store discussed in Chapter 12, "International Retailing," selling its products to television shoppers.

English in Local Advertising

Section 13-2, "The International Communication Process," stressed some of the benefits of using English for advertising. Other reasons for using English, particularly in advertising by local firms to local consumers, are to stress a cosmopolitan attitude and to endow a product or service with status. Words such as "very quick" are used in advertising for a tire inflation service (*vulcanizacion*) in Ecuador and "super wonderful" to describe the travel bags sold by a company in Poland. This is true also for product and service brand names—for example, the Romanian-American University, American Gold for a brand of gold-plated jewelry—when the products or services really have nothing to do with the United States, Canada, or Mexico. Figures 13-7 through 13-10 show some examples of advertisements using English in non-English-speaking countries, aimed at local consumers. Also, they show some examples of English names for retail establishments in non-English-speaking countries.

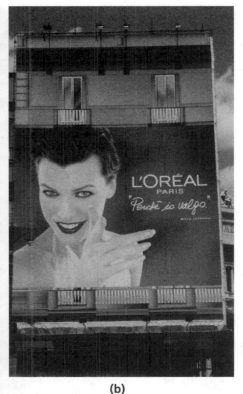

(b)

(a)

Figure 13-6
Billboards are omnipresent, appealing to consumers across economic strata, regardless of level of literacy. *(a)* Coca-Cola in Russia. *(b)* Loréal in Italy.
Courtesy of Christa Semka, with permission.

Product Placement

Product placement involves placing brands in movies with the purpose of promoting the products to viewers. Studies have found that product placement can produce a greater level of advertising recall than television advertising.[5] Year after year, films exported by the United States have swept the globe. In 1999, in spite of economic difficulties in Asia and Latin America, U.S. movies' box-office receipts were up by 17 percent, and, according to *Variety Magazine,* of 1998's most successful movies, U.S. films took the top 39 places.[6] As a result of the world dominance of Hollywood films, product placement is likely to be a venue providing high exposure for international brands.

Product placement The strategy of placing brands in movies with the purpose of promoting the products to viewers.

Advertising Regulations

Advertisers encounter numerous restrictions in their efforts to deliver communication to consumers worldwide. Most regulations are imposed by national

5. See Pola B.Gupta and Kenneth R. Lord, "Product Placement in Movies: The Effect of Prominence and Mode on Audience Recall," *Journal of Current Issues and Research in Advertising,* Spring 1998, Vol. 14, No. 1, pp. 47–59; and Steven J. Gould, Pola B. Gupta, and Sonja Grabner-Kräuter, "Product Placements in Movies: A Cross-Cultural Analysis of Austrian, French, and American Consumers' Attitudes Toward This Emerging International Promotional Medium," *Journal of Advertising,* Winter 2000, Vol. 29, No. 4, pp. 41–68.

6. *The Economist,* "Business: Worrying Statistix," February 6, 1999. Vol. 350, No. 8015, p. 68.

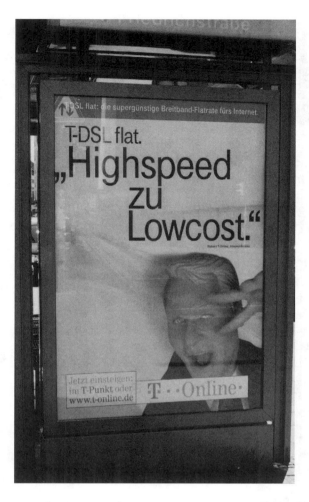

Figure 13-7
Use of English in Germany, appealing to the German consumers: "Highspeed zu Lowcost" Internet service.

(a)

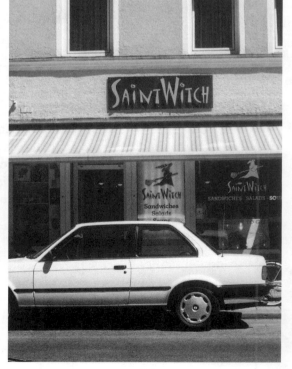

(b)

Figure 13-8
Sam's Salad & Sandwich *(a)* and Saint Witch *(b)* in Munich—all their point-of-purchase advertising and other communication is in English, even though they are appealing to German consumers.

Figure 13-9
German retailer, English communications.

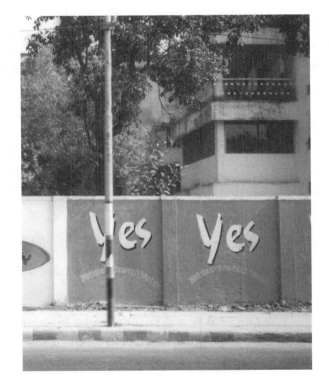

Figure 13-10
Yes Natural Mineral Water for Consumers in Bangladesh.
Courtesy of Farheen Khurrum, with permission.

(host-country) governments. Alternatively, local firms have established traditions and self-imposed regulations that must be observed by newcomers to the local advertising scene. Among advertising restrictions are the following:

- *Comparative advertising*—The United Kingdom and Ireland have rules that appear similar to those of the United States, allowing for truthful comparative advertising that is not confusing or falsely disparaging. By contrast, continental Europe condemns comparative advertising as denigration (comments, whether true or false, that are unduly negative), unfair competition, or unauthorized use of trademarks; therefore, for most of Europe, comparative advertising is unfair advertising.[7] In addition, the Benelux (Belgium, the Netherlands, and Luxembourg) Uniform

---

7. See Ross D. Petty, "Advertising Law in the United States and European Union," *Journal of Public Policy & Marketing*, Spring 1997, Vol. 16, No. 1, pp. 2-13.

Trademark Act forbids using another's trademark in advertising. Germany also prohibits denigrating advertising, such as Avis's "We try harder," but it allows truthful comparisons that are not negative ("as good as").[8]

- *Advertising to children*—The European Union Directive Concerning Television Broadcasting does not permit advertising that directly exhorts minors to buy a product or a service, that directly encourages minors to persuade their parents to purchase the goods advertised, that exploits the trust minors place in adults, or that show minors in dangerous situations. Local law restricts advertising to children further: French law limits the use of children as endorsers in advertising and prohibits the use of children's heroes as endorsers.[9]

- *Advertising vice products*—The European Union Directive Concerning Television Broadcasting prohibits television advertising for tobacco products and prescription drugs.[10]

- *Other regulations*—The French have regulations requiring advertisers (and all broadcasters) to keep the language pure, and not to use English terms or anglicized French terms (Franglais). Singapore does not permit advertising that is sexual in nature; the use of sex in advertising is also banned in most Islamic countries. Other challenges are posed by the need to copyright the advertising message in different languages in countries where multiple languages are spoken.

13-3b The Advertising Infrastructure

Advertising Agencies

The approach to advertising varies from one company to another, and the strategies used by different companies are numerous. Advertising decisions may be determined based on the product strategy. In one example, Henkel, a leading German manufacturer of household and cleaning products, uses a pan-European approach to advertising. The company attempts to achieve efficiency in advertising production and advertising impact by identifying how a particular product addresses target market needs (for consumers in Europe or a larger area); by assigning that specific need or benefit to one product with one brand name; by assigning that brand to one brand manager and to one advertising agency to develop and market; and by not permitting the use of that individual brand's benefit, name, or creative campaign for any other brand in the company.[11] This strategy results in the use of multiple advertising agencies, depending on the brand involved. Alternatively, the choice of the advertising agency in international markets may be based on a long-standing relationship with a particular agency in the home market; an advertising agency could follow a leading global brand anywhere in the world. This is the case of McCann Erickson, the advertising agency that has been handling the Coca-Cola account in 89 countries since 1942.[12]

A company can approach its international advertising strategy using one or more of the following options: developing local ads for the international markets in-house; developing ads using local advertising agencies, home-country agencies,

---

8. Ibid.

9. Ibid.

10. Ibid.

11. William Wells, John Burnett, and Sandra Moriarty, *Advertising Principles and Practice*, Fifth Edition, Prentice Hall, 2000.

12. Hillary Chura, "Coke Brands IPG as Global Ad Strategist," *Advertising Age*, December 4, 2000, Vol. 71, No. 50, p. 50.

or international advertising agencies with local offices; or using a combination strategy. The home-country agency and the in-house options by themselves are not likely to allow for local participation if they are located away from the target market.

The most common types of relationships between international corporations and the agencies providing advertising support are as follows:

- Hiring local advertising agencies
- Hiring international advertising agencies
- Hiring local advertising agencies to implement international agency messages

Hiring Local Advertising Agencies

A company that uses a localized strategy, targeting each individual market, is more likely to hire a local advertising agency. Hiring a local advertising agency is appropriate, especially when knowledge of the market is important. The Swedish furniture company Ikea, for example, engaged in a branding campaign aimed at the San Diego market. The company left it up to the San Diego Ikea franchise to hire a firm to build the Ikea brand in the San Diego market; it hired AM Advertising, a Los Angeles firm boasting top local talent.[13]

In a relatively uniform market, such as the Latin American market, advertisers often use Spanish and Portuguese to communicate with consumers. When advertising to the twenty-five countries of Latin America and the Caribbean, however, it is preferable to translate into each country's regional dialect to avoid presenting the company as an outsider.[14] A local agency could better design the campaign for each individual market. In addition to its knowledge of the local market, a local agency also offers the advantage of being capable of facilitating interaction with local media and government.

On the negative side, the quality of advertising is not at the level offered by a large international advertising agency. With the proliferation of technology, local companies, even in developing countries, are increasingly able to provide higher quality graphics, comparable to those produced by larger international advertisers. Nevertheless, if a company decides to hire local advertising agencies, it will not be able to coordinate a global, standardized advertising campaign.

Hiring International Advertising Agencies

In general, if a company uses a standardized (global) strategy for its products or services, it is more likely to use an international agency with local offices that can manage advertising in the respective markets. Most of the leading advertising agencies have branches in important international markets. In Eastern Europe, companies such as Saatchi & Saatchi, Leo Burnett, Young and Rubicam, and Ogilvy & Mather are represented in practically every capital city. Other companies select primarily markets of interest to their clients. For example, J. Walter Thompson is present as J. Walter Thompson/ARK Communications in Prague, the Czech Republic; as Partners J. Walter Thompson Budapest in Hungary; and as Scala JWT Advertising in Bucharest, Romania.

The five leading international advertising agencies or agency groups in terms of worldwide gross income are the Omnicom Group (U.S.), the Interpublic Group (U.S.), the WPP Group (U.K.), Dentsu, Inc. (Japan), and Young & Rubicam (U.S.).

13. David Lipin, "San Diego Ikea Hires a Local Ad Agency," *Adweek*, December 18, 2000, Vol. 50, No. 51, p. 4.

14. Peter Rosenwald, "Surveying the Latin American Landscape," *Catalog Age*, February 2001, Vol. 18, No. 2, p. 67.

In fact, more than half of the top fifty advertising agencies are from the United States.[15]

International advertising agencies benefit from access to the parent company's experience and talent, as well as technology and research capabilities. They also can take advantage of local representatives' expertise and relationships with the media and government. Increasingly, international advertising agencies are present with more than one type of agency in important markets. For example, Rapp Collins Worldwide, the third largest marketing services agency by non-U.S. revenue, opened an office of its interactive arm, Rapp Digital, in Brazil; because Latin America is advanced from the point of view of technology, the market has high potential for interactive services.[16] Grey Global Group is present in Europe with, among others, Grey Direct, its direct marketing arm; Grey Desire, a London-based customer relationship management consultancy for Europe;[17] Grey Interactive, GCI (one of the largest public relations firms in the world); and Grey Worldwide, the company's advertising arm.

Hiring Local Advertising Agencies to Implement International Agency Messages

Hiring an international advertising agency with local offices does not preclude the use of local advertising agencies. For example, although Coca-Cola uses the Interpublic Group (primarily McCann Erickson) to design its message for advertising worldwide, it also encourages each country office to appoint local agencies to implement the brand message devised by Interpublic; in fact, Interpublic is generating ideas at a global level, which are then translated by local marketers as part of Coke's "think global, act local" strategy.[18]

13-3c The Advertising Strategy

Standardization Versus Adaptation in Creating Message Strategies

One of the most important decisions of firms designing their international promotional mix is whether to standardize (globalize) their promotional strategy (**standardization of the advertising strategy**), to adapt their promotional mix to each country or market (**adaptation of the advertising strategy**), or to create local campaigns. Practitioners are divided on this issue. Sponsors, as well as advertising agencies, agree that using a standardized strategy worldwide presents substantial advantages. This is most obvious from a cost perspective: Costs will be reduced considerably if companies do not need to duplicate the creative effort and the resultant communication campaign in each market. In addition, as product life cycles shrink, companies are pressured to accelerate worldwide rollout of new products; developing communication strategies for each market would delay launch.[19] Moreover, world consumers are developing common product preferences and increasingly share similar frames of references with regard to products and consumption, as they are more and more exposed to the same sources of influence (broadcast and print media, in particular, as well as blockbuster films and tourists, among others).

Standardization of the advertising strategy The process of globalizing a company's promotional strategy so that it is uniform in all its target markets.

Adaptation of the advertising strategy The act of changing a company's promotional mix to each country or market, or creating local campaigns.

---

15. R. Craig Endicott, "Top 25 Global Advertising Organizations: Conglomerates Beef Up Through Mergers and Acquisitions," *Advertising Age,* April 19, 1999, Vol. 70, No. 17, pp. S18–S19.

16. Cara Beardi, "Grey's Global Desire," *Advertising Age,* November 20, 2000, Vol. 71, No. 48, pp. 22, 24.

17. Ibid.

18. Cordella Brabbs, "Can Coke and IPG Truly 'Think Local'?" *Marketing,* December 7, 2000, p. 7.

19. Anthony J. Rutgliano "The Debate Goes On: Global vs. Local Advertising," *Management Review,* June 1986, Vol. 75, No. 6, pp. 27–31.

Advertising executives often use a standardized communication approach due to pressure from clients, especially in cases in which the companies do not have a high degree of control over international operations, or where the quality and availability of local resources are in question.[20] Nevertheless, there are some country-specific preferences: Canadian firms have a predilection for standardization or, rather, transferring the campaign, whereas German and Japanese firms are more likely to adapt campaigns locally, and firms from the United States and the United Kingdom are more likely to develop campaigns locally.[21]

Differences exist between countries, however, which might render standardization a challenge, or even impossible. The following are barriers to advertising standardization:

- The communication infrastructure: A particular medium might be inappropriate or not available for advertising.
- International advertising agencies might not serve a particular market.
- Consumer literacy level: Consumers might not be able to read the body copy of the advertisement, so the information conveyed to the consumer should be visual.
- Legal restrictions and industry self-regulation might also impede standardization: Comparative advertising is not permitted in many countries, whereas, in others—Korea, for example—Confucianism forbids the public criticism of others.[22]
- Values and purchase motivations differ across countries and cultures, as illustrated in Chapter 5. Targeting consumers with a campaign that stresses the good life, exemplified by driving a luxury car and having a blonde on one's side, might be inappropriate in countries where consumers are living a subsistence existence and just as improper in highly developed, cultured environments. Consumers from collectivist cultures will also question the values suggested by such ads. The decision of whether to standardize is most often contingent on the degree of cultural similarity between the sponsor and the target market.[23] Standardization of communication is recommended when similarity exists between senders and receivers in the communication process.
- Attitudes toward the product or service country of origin; e.g., in environments where there is some level of hostility toward the United States and its economic and cultural dominance, it might be best to change an advertising campaign that stresses the product's country of origin.
- The elements of the promotional mix—particularly advertising[24]—are especially difficult to standardize because communication is language- and culture-specific.

Budgeting Decisions for International Advertising Campaigns

Companies use different approaches to advertising spending decisions.

20. Michel Laroche, V. H. Kirpalani, and Rene Darmon, "Determinants of the Control of International Advertising by Headquarters of Multinational Corporations," *Revue Canadienne de l'Administration,* December 1999, Vol. 16, No. 4, pp. 273–290.

21. Ibid.

22. Ibid.

23. Ibid.

24. Zahna Caillat and Barbara Mueller, "Observations: The Influence of Culture on American and British Advertising: An Exploratory Comparison of Beer Advertising," *Journal of Advertising Research,* May/June 1996, Vol. 36, No. 3, pp. 79–88.

Objective-and-Task Method

Objective-and-task method
An advertising budgeting method in which the company first identifies advertising goals, conducts research to determine the cost of achieving the respective goals, and allocates the necessary sum for the purpose.

Companies using the **objective-and-task method** first identify advertising goals in terms of communication goals such as target audience reach, awareness, comprehension, or even purchase. As a next step, research is conducted to determine the cost of achieving the respective goals. Finally, the necessary sum is allocated for the purpose.

This method is the most popular one used by multinational corporations in the process of deciding on their advertising budgets because it takes into consideration the firms' strategies. A comprehensive international study suggests that this method is more frequently used by firms from Canada and Singapore and less frequently by Swedish and Argentinean firms.[25]

Percent-of-Sales Method

Percent-of-sales method
An advertising budgeting method that determines the total budget allocated to advertising based on past or projected sales.

The **percent-of-sales method** determines the total budget allocated to advertising based on past or projected sales. This method is difficult to adopt for firms entering new markets, which are more likely to benefit from budgeting methods such as competitive parity or objective-and-task. The problem with this method is that it causes advertising expenditures to decline as sales decline; at this point, the company should increase advertising spending.

For firms that have been in a particular international market for some time, this method is used by almost half of the respondents in the study on transnational advertising practices. This study found that the percent-of-sales method is most popular in Brazil and Hong Kong, and less popular in Germany.[26]

Historical Method

Historical method An approach to budgeting that is based on past expenditures, usually giving more weight to more recent expenditures.

Firms using the **historical method** base their advertising budget on past expenditures, usually giving more weight to more recent expenditures. The percent-of-sales method utilizes the historical method as a first step, if the percentages allocated to advertising are based on past, rather than projected, sales. This method is not recommended for firms that operate in unstable economic, political, or competitive environments.

Competitive-Parity Method

Competitive-parity method
The strategy of using competitors' level of advertising spending as a benchmark for the company's own advertising expenditures.

The **competitive-parity method** uses competitors' level of advertising spending as benchmarks for a firm's own advertising expenditure. This approach is not recommended for a firm entering a new market and/or whose brands are not known locally. Moreover, this method suggests that a firm's goals and strategies are identical with those of competitors, which, most likely, is not the case.

Executive-Judgment Method

Executive-judgment method
A budgeting process that allocates the company's advertising budget based on the opinions of executives.

In the **executive-judgment method,** executive opinion is used in determining the advertising budget. A third of the responding firms queried in the study on transnational advertising practices reported relying on executive judgment.

All-You-Can-Afford Method

All-you-can-afford method
The process of allocating the maximum amount possible to advertising; this method is used by small and medium-size corporations.

Most small and medium-size enterprises entering a new market do not have the large budgets of multinational corporations. The **all-you-can-afford method** best suits the financial limitations of these firms. Unfortunately, this approach completely ignores strategic issues.

---

25. Nicolaos E. Synodinos, Charles F. Keown, and Lawrence W. Jacobs, "Transnational Advertising Practices: A Survey of Leading Brand Advertisers in Fifteen Countries," *Journal of Advertising Research,* April/May 1989, Vol. 29, No. 2, pp. 43–50.

26. Ibid.

Chapter Summary

- **Describe the international promotional mix and the international communication process**

  The components of the international promotional mix are international advertising, international salesforce management, international sales promotion, and public relations and publicity. The international communication process involves the sender encoding a message, sending it via a medium to the receiver, who then decodes the message; the goal is to have the message sent identical to the message received. In an international communications context, the process is complicated by interferences (noise) injected by cultural and language differences between the advertiser, sponsor, and the target audiences.

- **Explore the international advertising formats and practices around the world**

  International advertising—defined as a nonpersonal communication by an identified sponsor across international borders, using broadcast, print, and/or interactive media—faces many international challenges. The primary challenge is attributed to the lack of uniformity in media infrastructure, formats, and practices accepted in different markets. Among such challenges are media availability and reliability issues, such as media's inability to work with company deadlines and television going off the air frequently. The media could limit the types and the number of advertisements aired or published, or it might not permit the portrayal of women or advertising of certain products. It also might isolate advertising from programming or from editorial content. Media costs, formats, features, and trends may differ around the world.

- **Describe the international advertising and media infrastructure and infrastructure-related challenges in different markets**

  Advertising worldwide is dominated by U.S. advertising agencies; however, that fact is quickly changing. Firms from the U.K. and Japan are competing with large full-service agencies from the United States, and boutique advertising agencies worldwide are winning important accounts and awards for quality advertising. Multinationals today have more and more advertising agency choices. Depending on the availability of local talent and capability, companies advertising in international markets have a choice between advertising using a local agency, using an international agency, or using a local agency to advertise international agency messages.

- **Describe advertising strategies and budgeting decisions and offer examples of international applications**

  An important decision facing international firms is whether to use a standardized message worldwide or to adapt the message to local markets. Standardization would lead to great economies of scale and cost savings; in reality, standardization may not be possible because of variations in the advertising and media infrastructures due to differences in consumer literacy, motivations, or consumer interests, and due to differences in advertising legislation. Advertising budgeting may involve one of the following methods: objective-and-task, whereby marketing managers set objectives and then calculate the cost for reaching the objectives; percent-of-sales, whereby the advertising budget is set as a percent of sales; historical, whereby spending is based on past expenditures; competitive-parity, whereby spending is based on competitors' spending; executive-judgment, whereby the firm's executives make the decisions; and the all-you-can-afford method.

Discussion Questions

1. Describe the challenges involved in the international communication process and suggest how each challenge could be addressed by a firm's international marketing manager in conjunction with an advertising agency.
2. What are some important traits of the international media infrastructure that are likely to affect local advertising strategies?
3. Describe how media formats, features, and trends differ around the world.
4. What are the advertising agency choices that international companies have for communicating with local markets? Describe each choice, its advantages, and disadvantages.
5. Ideally, multinationals should standardize their message worldwide to benefit from economies of scale and other cost savings. What prevents companies from using a standardized message worldwide?
6. How do multinational firms determine their budget for advertising?

International Publicity, Public Relations, and Sales Promotion Strategies

Key Terms

advocacy advertising
company publications
corporate advertising
event sponsorship
global campaign
image advertising
local campaign
modular campaign

news releases
press releases
public appearances
public relations
publicity
sales promotion
trade shows and exhibitions

Outline

Learning Objectives
14-1 Publicity and
        Public Relations
    14-1a Publicity
    14-1b Public Relations
14-2 Consumer Sales Promotion
    14-2a Adaptation
            of Sales Promotion
    14-2b The Online Venue
            for Sales Promotion
    14-2c Legal and Ethical Issues
            in Consumer Sales
            Promotion
    14-2d The Future of Consumer
            Sales Promotion
14-3 International Trade
        Promotion (Trade Shows
        and Exhibitions)
Chapter Summary
Discussion Questions

Learning Objectives

Learning Objectives

By the end of this chapter, you should be able to:

- Provide an overview of international publicity and the different international public relations activities that can be used to influence it

- Describe the different approaches to international consumer sales promotion and the activities involved

- Describe the different approaches to international trade promotion and the different activities involved

---

In the past, multinational firms hired advertising agencies to be in charge of the advertising function of the promotional mix, and handled publicity and much of sales promotion in-house. Multinational companies today are attempting to coordinate all communication activities and typically hire international advertising agencies capable of coordinating their integrated marketing communications. Consequently, they are more likely to leave all public relations activities, local and international, to firms with public relations expertise. This fact is readily evident, especially in developed countries; the public relations machine stands ready to avert any negative doubts cast on multinationals. Whereas, in the past, it took Andrew Grove, CEO of Intel, several months before addressing a glitch in the company's microprocessors, today's firms stand ready to defend their reputations and assign blame elsewhere—as in the case of the Ford Explorer and Bridgestone/Firestone tires.

Sales promotion is quickly catching on worldwide. Companies such as McDonald's and Burger King believe they are as much in the fast-food business as in the toy business,[1] coming up with new promotions and generating excitement about the newest promotional event. The Butt-Ugly Martians' appearance on the U.S. Nickelodeon television network was preceded by an intense merchandising blitz that is certain to expand beyond U.S. borders into children's stores and fast-food restaurant promotions.

This chapter addresses the topics of international publicity, public relations, and sales promotion. It addresses the effect of competent international public relations activity on generating positive publicity for a firm; in the process, it discusses the different public relations tools that international marketing managers have at their disposal. The chapter also addresses the various international consumer sales promotion tools, the degree of sales promotion standardization worldwide, and the challenges presented by engaging in sales promotional activities in different countries. It also addresses international business-to-business sales promotion and offers examples of different international promotional activities of multinational companies.

---

1. cf. Doug Porter, Executive Vice President, Leo Burnett, in charge of the McDonald's account.

14-1 Publicity and Public Relations

The chapter addresses three of a total of five components of the promotional mix: publicity and public relations, which are closely related, and sales promotion. The other components of the promotional mix are advertising and personal selling, covered in Chapter 13, "The International Promotional Mix and Advertising Strategies," and Chapter 15, "International Personal Selling and Personnel Management." Figure 14-1 illustrates the communication vehicles used by each component of the promotional mix addressed in the chapter.

14-1a Publicity

Publicity is a communication about a company and/or the company's products that the company does not pay for. In this category falls any type of print article, broadcast message, or word-of-mouth communication about the company and/or its products; the message may be either positive or negative.

Multinational corporations, in particular, frequently experience negative publicity. In general, there is a negative perception of multinational firm dominance and globalization, as illustrated in the Seattle, Washington, revolts on the occasion of the 1999 World Trade Organization meetings. McDonald's experienced a classic example of negative publicity in France. In response to Europe's decision to ban hormone-treated beef, the U.S. government imposed high import tariffs on French Roquefort cheese, Dijon mustard, and foie gras. The French retaliated by, among others, vandalizing McDonald's restaurants; in their eyes, the company was

Publicity Any communication about a company and/or the company's products that the company does not pay for; may be positive or negative.

Figure 14-1
The publicity, public relations, and sales promotion components of the promotional mix.

a symbol of U.S. hegemony, globalization, multinationals, the power of the marketplace, and industrially produced food, at the expense of individuals' health and French peasants' livelihood.[2]

Positive publicity, although difficult to come by, is very valuable. Due to its independent nature, it is more credible than advertising. DaimlerChrysler received free positive publicity for its luxury Mercedes automobiles when a photograph of U.S. Secretary of State, General Colin Powell, appeared at the wheel of a Mercedes on the front page of *The New York Times,* with the caption "Do you mind if I drive?" The paper published a follow-up story on Powell driving Jordan's King Abdulla's Mercedes.[3] Although the impact of such publicity is difficult to measure in terms of dollars and cents, marketing executives in Stuttgart, the home of Mercedes-Benz, can rest assured that their brand received significant exposure and a credible endorsement in the U.S. market.

14-1b Public Relations

Public relations is defined as a concerted effort on the part of a company to generate goodwill among publics (community, government, consumers, employees, among others) that are essential to the company. Its main purpose is to generate positive publicity about the company.

Public relations efforts can fall into the following categories:

- News releases/letters, press releases, company publications
- Event sponsorship and presence
- Corporate advertising
- Image advertising
- Public appearances by company representatives

News Releases/Letters, Press Releases, Company Publications

Multinational firms must, on a regular basis, communicate with their different publics (home-country, local, and international customers; trade; stockholders; government; and community). When new products are introduced in local markets, company representatives are likely to offer **news releases, press releases,** or **company publications** touting the advantages of the new product or service.

Event Sponsorship and Presence

Event sponsorship is a growing venue for international marketing communication. Nearly every important international cultural or sports-related event has the backing of multinational corporations. Brands such as Adidas, MasterCard, Visa, Rolex, Coca-Cola, Pepsi, and Heineken sponsor events ranging from World Cup Soccer to World Cup Cricket to the Davis Cup for tennis. Across continents, cultural manifestations are supported by major international brands: Vodacom, a cellular network provider in Africa, sponsored Placido Domingo, Luciano Pavarotti, and Jose Carreras during their Bravo Africa concert;[4] Vodafone, NatWest, Air Emirates, and Pepsi sponsored World Cup Cricket;[5] and Gatorade was the official sports drink of the 2000 Olympic Games and has acquired affiliations with the

Public relations A concerted effort on the part of a company to generate goodwill among publics that are essential to the company; its main purpose is to generate positive publicity about the company.

News releases Statements issued to the public to introduce a new product, touting its advantages; any other information shared with the media.

Press releases Statements issued to the press to communicate news about a company and its products.

Company publications Public relations publications that describe the products of a company to potential customers and summarize financial achievements.

Event sponsorship The financial support of cultural or sports-related events; companies use these events to get positive publicity.

2. See Jon Henley, "Flip Flop," *The New Republic,* January 3, 2000, Vol. 222, No. 1, p. 24.

3. *The New York Times,* "How the General Put a Pedal to the Metal," February 26, 2001, p. A8.

4. *Finance Week—South Africa,* "Bravo Pretoria," January 22, 1999, p. 11.

5. Ian Darby, "Cricket World Cup L8m Short in Sponsorships," *Marketing,* March 25, 1999, p. 7.

National Hockey League, World Cup Soccer, and Tour de France, among others.[6] And the list continues.

International sponsorship is so prevalent that it has drawn the attention of artists. Near a bus stop in Kassel, Germany, a kiosk that would normally carry advertisements is actually a work by New York-based artist Hans Haacke displaying quotes from executives telling why they sponsor art shows. Hilmar Kopper, head of Deutsche Bank, says: "Whoever pays, controls." Alain Dominique Perrin, Cartier's head, says: "It is a tool for shaping public opinion."[7]

Corporate Advertising

Corporate advertising is used to promote the company behind the different brands. One particularly memorable advertisement of this kind was designed by Altria (formerly Philip Morris) for the Chinese market on the occasion of the Chinese New Year. This ad portrayed traditional Chinese dancers dancing on the Great Wall to the Marlboro theme song, which was still familiar to consumers despite the fact that Marlboro cigarettes are no longer advertised on television. At the end of the ad, the advertisement wished Chinese consumers a happy new year from the Altria companies.

Corporate advertising A type of advertising that is used to promote the company behind the different brands.

Image Advertising

Image advertising is used to enhance perceptions of a company in a given market. McDonald's used image advertising to combat the negative attitudes of consumers and farmers in France after the events described in section 14-1a, "Publicity." To address discontent with the restaurant and to dissipate the perceived link between McDonald's and the United States, the company created an advertising campaign that both made fun of Americans and stressed the fact that McDonald's avoided using genetically modified ingredients. It also stressed the French origins of McDonald's products; its slogan was "McDonald's. Born in the USA. Made in France."[8]

Image advertising An advertising campaign that enhances perceptions of a company in a given market by creating a positive impression on the target consumers.

Advocacy Advertising

Advocacy advertising is used by a company to stress a particular point of view. For example, one can assume that the Benetton (www.benetton.com) campaign portraying death-row inmates' perspectives on their lives, along with personal statistics that include the type and date of murder and related sentence, is in fact a statement against the death penalty. The ads portraying young people of all ages and races in colorful Benetton clothing could be perceived as welcoming the cultural diversity in our world. The ad for the French market showing a reporter interviewing an ethnic protester while he is being brutally arrested could be perceived as a protest against police brutality, and so on.

Advocacy advertising Advertising a particular position or point of view.

Public Appearances by Company Representatives

In addition to **public appearances** to speak on behalf of the international firm and its products, which are typical of this category, company representatives frequently

Public appearances Company representatives' public involvement, speaking on behalf of the international firm and its products.

---

6. Debbie Howell, "Gatorade vs. the Beverage Giants—Going Head-to-Head in Sports Drinks," *Discount Store News,* February 7, 2000, Vol. 39, No. 3, p. 58.

7. Thane Peterson and Sandra Dallas, "Tycoons on the Trail of the Next de Kooning," *Business Week,* August 25, 1997, Vol. 3541, p. 16E2.

8. Ibid.

attend important international events. One such event is *documenta,* an international contemporary art exhibit that takes place once every five years. At the last exhibit, prominent business representatives Ronald Lauder of Estee Lauder Cos. (also an art collector); Eli Broad of SunAmerica Corp.; Ronald Rosenzweig, CEO of Anadigics Inc., an electronics company; Charles Lazarus of Toys "R" Us Inc.; and Neuberger & Berman's Arthur Goldberg reflected on exhibits such as a dead mealworm in yellowish sand and a photo of an eviscerated rabbit. [9]

14-2 Consumer Sales Promotion

Sales promotion Sponsored communications to the target consumer or trade segment that stimulate purchases or improve relationships with middlemen.

Aside from advertising, personal selling, public relations, and publicity, all other sponsored communications offered to the end consumer or to the trade that stimulate purchases or improve relationships to middlemen and retailers in the short term fall in the category of **sales promotion.** Among examples of consumer sales promotion are point-of-purchase displays, free samples to initiate product trial or brand switching, other incentives (coupons, cents-off, gifts, product tie-ins) to initiate trial or brand switching, and sweepstakes and contests. Among examples of trade (business-to-business) promotion are trade discounts, sweepstakes and contests, and trade shows.

Sales promotion activities are often conducted in conjunction with advertising campaigns, as well as with personal selling and public relations efforts. Consequently, the sales promotion effort is frequently managed by the promotional arms of leading international advertising agencies—among them are WPP's OgilvyOne and Perspectives and Young and Rubicam's Wunderman Cato Johnson. In addition, new players are emerging, such as The Marketing Store Worldwide, which is quickly expanding in Europe, the United States, as well as in select markets in Latin America and Asia (Argentina, China, Taiwan).[10] However, even companies that have strong relationships with an advertising agency, such as Coke, which uses McCann Erickson for its advertising, frequently allow international subsidiaries to make their own sales promotion decisions. Coke Brazil has traditionally created all sales promotion in-house, for example.[11]

14-2a Adaptation of Sales Promotion

International sales promotion campaigns fall into one of three strategies, paralleling international advertising and international product marketing strategies: global campaigns, modular campaigns, and local campaigns.

Global Campaigns

Global campaign A worldwide standardized advertising campaign that is not adjusted to different target markets.

Global campaigns are rarely attempted in sales promotion; even a company such as IBM, which wants consistent strategies worldwide, requires a priori feedback from local markets to ensure that the central strategy can be implemented.[12]

Certain types of sales promotion, such as point-of-purchase displays, lend themselves to a more standardized campaign. They do not rely on words, so different language versions are not necessary; they speak an international language by reinforcing logos and emphasizing brand image visually.[13] Yet even point-of-

9. Ibid.

10. *Marketing,* "Pushing Back the Business Frontiers," October 1997, pp. 49–50.

11. James Curtis, "Coke's Brazilian Sales Pitch," *Marketing,* May 7, 1998, pp. 39–41.

12. *Marketing,* "Pushing Back," pp. 49–50.

13. Daney Parker, "Popular Choice," *Marketing Week,* May 31, 1996, Vol. 19, No. 10, pp. 39–40.

purchase displays need some adaptation. Smirnoff Vodka, a company that spends one-sixth of its advertising budget on such displays, finds that, in the townships of South Africa, posters bleach in the sun and rain, and metal advertising plates often disappear from the walls to be used as roofs.[14]

Occasionally, the target market itself may encourage the use of a global, standardized approach. For example, in markets where multiple languages are spoken, and where English is one of the unifying languages, as in the case of India, using English for sales promotion may be appropriate. Even in countries where English is not a language used nationally, such as in Switzerland, using English as the language of the promotion may be a benefit. For example, promotions aimed at Swiss consumers often use English, rather than French, German, or Italian because two groups of consumers would be offended if a campaign used only one of the three languages spoken in Switzerland.[15]

Modular Campaigns

Modular campaigns provide a template that can be varied from market to market. Even in the European market, different strategies are likely to be used in the U.K. than in continental Europe. For example, in continental Europe PepsiCo included *Star Wars* characters in its Walker and Lays chips, whereas, in the U.K., the same promotion offered consumers a chance to win a Jar Jar Binks toy through an in-pack scratch card.[16]

Multinational companies often launch a worldwide promotional campaign centered around one theme and then use advertising to customize the message for each individual market. For example, BBDO Mexico launched a worldwide campaign on behalf of Pizza Hut launching its promotion of the week, such as Pizza Pooch toys, coloring books, placemats, as well as product giveaways, such as skateboards; local agencies then provided voice-overs to produce local language spots.[17]

Local Campaigns

Local campaigns are tailored to local needs, and retailer cooperation is of particular importance in ensuring that such sales promotion campaigns are successful. In the Netherlands, Albert Heijn appears to be favored as a grocery store where multinationals offer their new products and attempt to initiate consumer trials. The store, part of the Royal Ahold retail conglomerate, offers quality products aimed at the middle and upper-middle class. It was there that Procter & Gamble first introduced Bounty paper towels to Dutch consumers. Albert Heijn displayed the product prominently using point-of-purchase displays located near the cash registers and also offered the product in the paper products section of the stores. Simultaneously, the company mailed samples of Bounty in individual sheets, with different designs, in plastic bags, to selected homes. In July 2000, Coca-Cola representatives offered free samples of Coke and Coke Light to consumers shopping at Albert Heijn. After sampling Coke in miniature cans, consumers were able to purchase the product with a two-for-the-price-of-one promotion.

Finally, local sales promotion campaigns gain significant importance in markets that are not reached by other media and where sales promotion constitutes a primary form of communicating with the final consumers.

Modular campaign
An advertising campaign that provides a template that is varied and customized from market to market.

Local campaign An advertising campaign that is tailored to local needs; especially used in markets that media cannot easily reach.

---

14. Ibid.

15. Rob Furber, "Centre Shop," *Marketing Week*, October 21, 1999, Vol. 22, No. 38, pp. 51–54.

16. *Marketing,* "Pushing Back," pp. 49–50.

17. Margaret McKegney, "Pizza Hut Casts Puppies in Global Kids Campaign," *Advertising Age*, August 7, 2000, Vol. 71, No. 33, p. 16.

14-2b The Online Venue for Sales Promotion

Online sales promotion is quickly becoming a pervasive mode of communication with prospective consumers. Whether the promotion involves sweepstakes, printed coupons, promotional pricing, or other strategies, companies find that consumers around the world respond well to aggressive online promotions. Most of the communications firms (the former traditional advertising firms) now serve their clients by providing to target consumers extensive interactive sales promotion that is in line with the company's other types of communications.

14-2c Legal and Ethical Issues in Consumer Sales Promotion

To a certain degree, adaptation to local markets is necessitated by legal requirements. Even in economically and politically integrated markets, such as the European Union, sales-promotion–related legislation differs from one country to another. In Germany, for example, "buy one, get one free" offers are illegal; in France, premiums are restricted to 7 percent of the product's value; and, in Belgium, retail sales can run for only a month and prices cannot be cut below one-third.[18] The European Commission has yet to decide on the process of harmonization of rules applying to sales promotion throughout the member countries.

Sweepstakes based on pure chance are deemed illegal in Holland,[19] Canada, Sweden, and Belgium,[20] whereas, elsewhere in the world, additional legal requirements for sales promotion strategies diverge. Puerto Rican law, for instance, requires rules for all promotions to be printed in both English and Spanish, and both versions should be printed in a general circulation newspaper at least once a week for the duration of the campaign. Quebec requires sponsors to provide French translations and to pay a duty based on the total value of the prize pool and to post a bond to run a promotion.[21] All paperwork regarding point-of-purchase displays must be legalized by going through embassies in the Middle East, while displays going to Eastern Europe must be marked as not being for resale to avoid additional customs duties.[22]

Often the companies themselves are responsible for creating a bad reputation for sales promotion. Sales promotions aimed at emerging markets over time have been questionable. For example, common in developing countries in Sub-Saharan Africa and Eastern Europe are local consumers wearing jackets and hats promoting luxury automobiles, investment funds, and airlines, whose products and services they could not possibly afford, and expensive cigarettes they should not spend their limited income on. In another example, in Eastern Europe in the early 1990s, a Pepsi Game was aired on prime-time television when consumers had little alternative programming to watch, occupying at least one hour of viewing time on Pepsi trivia. And umbrellas advertising cigarettes are often displayed in restaurants adjacent to elementary schools.

Historically, there are also examples of flagrant violations of businesses' ethical responsibilities in their management of sales promotion. A case in point is that of Nestlé, a multinational food-product company, which successfully lured new

18. Ken Gofton, "How Euro Rules Will Change SP," *Marketing,* October 5, 2000, pp. 60–61.

19. Furber, "Centre Shop," pp. 51–54.

20. Warner Bernhard, "Crossing the Border," *Brandweek,* December 16, 1996, Vol. 37, No. 48, pp. 37–38.

21. Maxine Lans Retsky, "Global Promotions Are Subject to Local Laws," *Marketing News,* May 12, 1997, Vol. 31, No. 10, p. 8.

22. Parker, "Popular Choice," pp. 39–40.

mothers in Sub-Saharan Africa to adopt the company's baby formula. Women dressed as nurses offered free samples to new mothers in maternities, urging them to feed formula to their infants as a replacement for breast milk. Lack of sanitary conditions for formula preparation, as well as the high cost of the product, ultimately led to the death of many infants. What is especially interesting in this case is the fact that the negative publicity for the company was generated abroad, where consumer groups brought this issue to international media attention, rather than on the African continent.

14-2d The Future of Consumer Sales Promotion

With time, it is becoming increasingly clear that sales promotion is emerging as an important component not only of a company's promotional strategy, but also of its brand strategy. Brand managers are noting that sales promotion tools can actually contribute to strengthening brand perceptions and attitudes; consequently, companies such as Ford, Kraft Jacobs Suchard (an Altria [formerly Philip Morris] company), and L'Oreal are involving sales promotion firms when deciding on brand strategies.[23] Important growth is anticipated especially in the area of point-of-purchase displays. As research suggests that European and U.S. consumers make more than 50 percent of their purchase decisions at the point of sale, point-of-purchase expenditures constitute an increasingly higher percentage of overall promotional expenditures worldwide.[24]

14-3 International Trade Promotion (Trade Shows and Exhibitions)

Most sales promotion addressed in section 14-2, "Consumer Sales Promotion," is primarily aimed at the final consumer—although sweepstakes and contests, as well as incentives such as price-off reductions, also may be aimed at the trade. **Trade shows and exhibitions** belong to the category of business-to-business promotion. They are also referred to as international trade promotion—sales promotion aimed at the trade. Trade shows and exhibitions are usually held annually in formats where companies purchase exhibit space to display and demonstrate their offerings to the target market. For U.S. industrial firms, trade shows and exhibitions account for one-fifth of the overall communication budget, and one-fourth for European industrial firms.[25] Trade shows and exhibits constitute a proven promotional tool capable of having a direct positive impact on sales.[26]

Trade shows and exhibitions offer potential buyers and sellers a chance to meet face-to-face, as they bring many decision makers to a single location for a limited time, enabling firms to get their message to a large number of people at one time.[27] In a typical promotional environment, the seller must pitch the product to the buyer; for trade shows and exhibits, however, the visitors are the ones who approach the seller, searching for new products and suppliers.[28] Finally, trade

Trade shows and exhibitions
Business-to-business promotions that usually are held annually in formats where companies purchase exhibit space to display and demonstrate their offerings to the target market.

23. Paul Gander, "Internal Examination," *Marketing Week,* June 24, 1999, Vol. 22, No. 21, pp. 57–60.

24. Robin Cobb, "POPAI Gets Right to the Point," *Marketing,* September 18, 1995, pp. 37–40.

25. D. Jacobson, "Marketers Say They'll Boost Spending," *Business Marketing,* March 1990, Vol. 75, pp. 31–32.

26. See C. M. Sashi and Jim Perretty, "Do Trade Shows Provide Value?" *Industrial Marketing Management,* 1992, Vol. 21, pp. 249–255; and Srinath Gopalakrishna and Gary L. Lilien, "A Three-Stage Model of Industrial Trade Show Performance," *Marketing Science,* Winter 1995, Vol. 14, No. 4, pp. 22–42.

27. Aviv Shoham, "Performance in Trade Shows and Exhibitions: A Synthesis and Directions for Future Research," *Journal of Global Marketing,* 1999, Vol. 12, No. 3, pp. 41–57.

28. Ibid.

Figure 14-2
Expo 2000, in Hanover, Germany, did not bring in the much-anticipated crowds.

shows and exhibits provide a neutral location for doing business and bring together managers from different departments in buyers' organizations, thus increasing the probability of meeting every decision maker who will influence the buying decision.[29]

Country and state governments are often involved in ensuring that national/local companies are represented at important fairs. In the United States, the Department of Commerce is actively involved in promoting U.S. companies abroad using trade shows as venues. Usually, the U.S. government shares the cost of the exhibits by sponsoring a national pavilion at the different fairs.

As mentioned, trade shows and exhibitions are organized annually or at set intervals, and tend to be specialized in one domain. The Frankfurt Book Fair, for example, draws publishers and authors on all topics from around the world every fall to the city of Frankfurt, Germany. The *documenta*, mentioned in section 14-1a, takes place every five years, and the Venice Biennale takes place biannually; both exhibits show art works of contemporary artists. In other examples, DRUPA is an annual trade exhibition for the graphic arts industry, and Interkama is an international trade fair for industrial communication, automation, measurement, and analytics. Messe Dusseldorf, in Dusseldorf, Germany, for example, specializes in international trade shows for machinery, as well as for the medical, fashion, and services industries.

The World Exposition (the World Fair) cuts across domains and is one of the most important venues for exhibiting new ideas, technology, and art in an environment where numerous countries are represented. The city of Hanover, Germany, hosted the most recent World Fair, Expo 2000, an exhibition of art, science, and culture (see Figure 14-2). The theme of the fair was "Humankind—Nature—Technology: A New World Arising" and its aim was to focus on creating guiding principles for living in the twenty-first century. Projects stemming from the Expo are taking place around the world, emphasizing the use of environmentally friendly technology.

More than 170 countries were represented at Expo 2000, and more than 50 countries built their own pavilions. Businesses were prominently represented at

---

29. Ibid.

the fair. Among those present with impressive pavilions were appliance manufacturer Bosch, the German telephone company Deutsche Telekom, the automobile manufacturer DaimlerChrysler, and German publisher Bertelsmann. Countries worldwide also were represented: Uzbekistan and Turkmenistan displayed artisanal work and music, the Romanian pavilion displayed wine and clothing from a Transylvanian village, and the Colombian pavilion offered quality coffee to visitors. The Netherlands pavilion was one of the most important attractions at the fair; it consisted of a stacked landscape, with flowing water and trees on the highest floor.[30] Among the millions of visitors at the Expo were heads of state (Chancellor Gerhard Schröder of Germany visited the Expo numerous times) and royalty (Queen Beatrix of the Netherlands, Queen Margrethe of Denmark, Prince Rainier of Monaco, and Prince Phillippe of Belgium, among others).

Chapter Summary

- **Provide an overview of international publicity and the different international public relations activities that can be used to influence it**
  Publicity is a promotional tool that companies do not pay for; rather, publicity is a result of companies' performance and/or perception in world markets. For companies conducting business internationally, publicity in one country may have important repercussions on company perception in all the markets where the companies are present. Publicity can be positively influenced by using appropriate public relations tools, such as releasing relevant company publications, press releases, news releases; engaging in appropriate public appearances; and hiring agencies to design image advertising and corporate advertising that reflects company philosophies and strategies.

- **Describe the different approaches to international consumer sales promotion and the activities involved**
  International consumer promotions are becoming very popular worldwide. Such activities include point-of-purchase displays, free samples to initiate product trial or brand switching, and other incentives (coupons, cents-off, gifts, product tie-ins) designed with the purpose to initiate trial or brand switching. Promotional activities can be global in nature; modular, with some adaptation in select markets; and local, designed with local consumers in mind.

- **Describe the different approaches to international trade promotion and the different activities involved**
  International trade promotion, aimed at the business-to-business market, can involve trade shows and exhibitions, as well as trade discounts, sweepstakes, and contests. Trade shows provide a neutral environment where buyer and seller can meet face-to-face, in a low pressure situation in which the buyer is most likely to approach the seller, rather than vice versa.

Discussion Questions

1. Describe the relationship between international public relations activities and international publicity.
2. What are the different public relations tools that an international firm can use to fend off negative publicity?
3. Describe some of the international consumer promotion activities that international firms currently engage in, while addressing ethical issues and international standards involved.
4. How does international business-to-business sales promotion (trade promotion) benefit international companies and target consumers?

---

30. The United States was not represented at the World Fair, primarily because U.S. companies did not want to create their own pavilion and did not want to be in a U.S. pavilion; they claimed that they were international companies.

International Personal Selling and Personnel Management

Key Terms

cost-of-living adjustment
culture shock
education allowance
expatriate
home-country national
home-leave allowance
host-country national
housing allowance
international buyer-seller
    relationship

moving allowance
national character
organizational culture and
    personality
post adjustment
repatriation
repatriation allowance
reverse culture shock
third-country national

Outline

Learning Objectives
15-1 International Presence and
Personnel Issues
    15-1a Expatriates
    15-1b Host-Country Nationals
        (Locals)
    15-1c A Recent Alternative:
        Long-Distance
        International Selling
15-2 Managing International
    Employees
    15-2a Managing Relationships
    15-2b Understanding the
        International Buyer-
        Seller Relationship
    15-2c Understanding Cultural
        Values and the
        Relationship between
        Buyer and Seller
15-3 Successfully Managing
    Expatriates
    15-3a Recruiting Expatriates
    15-3b Attenuating Culture
        Shock
    15-3c Training for
        International
        Assignments
    15-3d Motivating Expatriates
    15-3e Obstacles to the
        International Sales
        Mission
    15-3f Repatriation Issues
Chapter Summary
Discussion Questions

Learning Objectives

Learning Objectives

By the end of this chapter, you should be able to:

- Examine companies' expatriate management strategies
- Describe the different types of employees suited for a company's international operations

- Address issues related to expatriate management, such as motivating international employees and ensuring successful assignment performance and repatriation

International sales representatives are often the frontline personnel in a firm's relationship with an international target market. Their expertise, ability, demeanor, and appearance all convey information that is integral to the firm's product or service offering and will help shape the firm's relationship with the target market, distributors, suppliers, and local government agencies overseeing the firm's operations. Frequently, sales representatives are expatriates, crossing cultural divides and bridging cultures on behalf of the firm, often in unfamiliar settings, where the culture and marketing practices differ from those in the sales representatives' home country. Expatriate sales representatives must survive the challenges posed by the new environment, continuously adapt to its changing demands, and play by the host-country rules while representing the company and selling its products and services in a foreign market.

Local sales representatives also have challenges as the company's frontline personnel. Although, as nationals of the host country, they understand the market and its intricacies, as representatives of the company, they also need to understand the company's home-country and organizational culture, as well as its marketing practices.

This chapter addresses issues related to managing expatriate employees, motivating them for optimal performance, and ensuring their successful repatriation to the home country.

15-1 International Presence and Personnel Issues

From a company perspective, hiring expatriates or locals is a function of the company's involvement in the market. The company's presence in the market—entry mode—and its commitment to the market are important considerations in determining a) the size of the sales team and b) the types of sales representatives the company employs. Companies primarily involved in exporting are likely to engage in only minimal international sales activity. An example of such an activity might be sending representatives to an international trade show, to exhibit the firm's products.

Companies using a home-country middleman, such as an export trading company or an export management company, rely on the salesforce of the intermediary for international sales and limit sales activity to the domestic market. The situation is similar if host-country middlemen such as foreign-country brokers or agents are used. However, when using all the other types of host-country middlemen, such as manufacturers' representatives and distributors, the company directly engages in some level of personal selling. When using host-country distributors, the respective company hires sales representatives who call on the distributors.

A firm that has manufacturers' representatives in a particular market typically has a substantial overall presence in that market. This presence may range from having a local sales office in the respective market, operated by local and/or international sales representatives, to operating a wholly owned subsidiary and controlling every aspect of the marketing function, including the distribution function. In these two examples, the foreign salesforce of the multinational corporation could include *expatriates* (home-country nationals and third-country nationals) and *host-country nationals.*

15-1a Expatriates

Expatriates working in a particular foreign country belong to two categories: One category is the *home-country national,* successful as a sales representative in the home country, assigned overseas. An example would be an Altria (formerly Philip Morris) U.S. employee engaging in sales in the company's Hong Kong operations. Representing the second category is the *third-country national,* a truly international salesperson, the expatriate who works in numerous countries. An example would be a Latin American salesperson who previously worked in sales in Italy and Spain calling on Colgate-Palmolive's trade accounts in Bulgaria.

Expatriate An employee working in a foreign country.

Home-Country Nationals

Home-country nationals—known also as *parent-company nationals*—are preferred by companies whose products are at the forefront of technology, and when the selling function relies on extensive training and highly specialized information. In general, in situations in which a greater interdependence exists between an overseas unit and corporate headquarters, firms are more likely to dispatch home-country nationals; this is also true for situations in which complex operations are involved, there is a greater political risk, and there is a greater level of competition.[1]

A disadvantage of hiring home-country nationals for international operations is the high costs involved; in addition to the regular salary and commission the

Home-country national An expatriate from the company's home country working in a foreign country.

---

1. Nakiye Boyacigiller, "The Role of Expatriates in the Management of Interdependence, Complexity and Risk in Multinational Corporations," *Journal of International Business Studies,* Third Quarter 1991, Vol. 22, No. 3, pp. 357–381.

employee would have received in the home country, numerous incentives are considered standard for international assignment. A cost-of-living allowance, a housing allowance that often permits hiring household help, and a substantial education allowance for children, which pays for education at expensive international private schools, are standard. Other standard perks are an annual or biannual home-leave for the entire family, or an annual visit from immediate family members living in the home country. In addition, the firm also is expected to pay for the costs of selling the employee's home in the home country, for furniture storage, and/or for moving household goods overseas, making it very expensive for the firm to send the employee overseas.

Even sending an employee overseas for five months can be costly to the company. In one example, a Motorola employee working for a Siemens-Motorola joint venture in Dresden, Germany, was housed in a hotel for his entire stay, rented an automobile, and had a living allowance that even included a phone card to keep in touch with family in the U.S. In addition, the company paid for two business-class round-trip leave tickets back to the U.S., team-building exercises, and trips to London and Prague, among others. These costs were covered in addition to salary, bringing the overall company costs to more than $100,000 for the five months.

Among other disadvantages of hiring home-country nationals are

- The numerous cultural barriers faced by the home-country nationals in the country of assignment
- The expenses involved in training the home-country nationals in the culture (and, often, language) of the country of assignment
- The lack of local personal connections to the important decision makers in the government and the local trade
- The difficulty of finding quality employees willing to take on international assignments because they are reluctant to uproot their families, or because they fear that they will lose visibility and status at the head office (international companies offer many incentives to overcome this impediment)

Third-Country Nationals

Third-country national
An employee working in the country of assignment who is not a national of that country nor of the country in which the corporate headquarters of the company he or she works for are located.

Third-country nationals are employees working temporarily in an assignment country, who are not nationals of that country, nor of the country in which the corporate headquarters of the company they work for are located.[2]

Third-country nationals are "professional expatriates." They are accustomed to constantly adapting to new environments. They speak numerous languages, are familiar with customs and business practices in different environments, and have learned, through their vast international experience, to adopt optimally for international assignments. In certain countries, third-country nationals are more likely than home-country nationals and locals to be on international corporations' payrolls. Examples of such countries are the United Arab Emirates and Saudi Arabia, where international companies hire highly skilled employees from India, Pakistan, Egypt, and the Philippines. A recent study found that expatriates working in Saudi Arabia typically save for future consumption and gear most of their purchases toward home-country consumption.[3]

---

2. Calvin Reynolds, "Strategic Employment of Third-Country Nationals," *HR: Human Resource Planning,* 1997, Vol. 20, No. 1, pp. 33–93.

3. Dana-Nicoleta Lascu, Lalita A. Manrai, and Sugandha Kamalapuri, "Purchase Behavior of Expatriate Consumers in Saudi Arabia: An Exploratory Study," in W. D. Herrington and R. Taylor (eds.), *Marketing Advances in Theory, Practice, and Education,* 1998, pp. 128–134.

Often, third-country nationals are competent company employees transferred from a subsidiary of the company operating in another country. Usually, third-country nationals cost less than home-country nationals (but more than locals) because they are not as likely to forgo the high salaries of the company's home country and expatriate allowances typical for home-country employees. And they are less likely to be a costly early return for the company, due to difficulty in adaptation to the local environment.

In the case of both home-country nationals and third-country nationals, it should be noted that many governments, primarily in developing countries, dictate the number (usually, percentage) of foreign nationals that a foreign firm operating in the respective country is permitted to hire. In the case of third-country nationals, it is not uncommon for local governments to delay visas or otherwise complicate the hiring process. In all these situations, firms are forced to rely heavily on host-country nationals (locals) and may tap into international sales talent and expertise only to a limited extent.

15-1b Host-Country Nationals (Locals)

The local salesperson who works in his or her home country for an international corporation is a **host-country national.** An example would be the Hungarian brand manager schooled in a university in the United States, working for Procter & Gamble (www.pg.com) in Hungary. This individual understands the U.S. business environment, is well trained technically at an accredited U.S. institution, and is willing to return to his home country to work for a U.S. multinational firm.

Host-country national A local employee who works in his or her home country for the international corporation.

Increasingly, international firms appear to prefer local employees to expatriates. Cost is only one consideration. Frequently, locals with similar levels of education and training are available for employment at a fraction of the cost of expatriates. Host-country nationals also speak the local language and often have a well-developed network within the local industry and government. And, as mentioned in section 15-1a, host governments restrict the number of foreign nationals working in the country; thus, host-country nationals also fit with the country's employment policies.

Many international firms compete for the types of individuals described here. Although the multinational company will deem it appropriate to remunerate host-country nationals below the level of expatriates, not offering them the appropriate motivation to remain with the company will increase their risk of flight to a competitor.

15-1c A Recent Alternative: Long-Distance International Selling

Selling via the Internet or mail is likely to become an important venue in approaching new customers overseas in the near future. Costs of distance selling are lower—companies do not have to dispatch salespeople abroad and spend on cross-cultural training—allowing for greater market coverage. For the moment, however, distance selling is difficult to coordinate internationally, often largely due to cultural differences. For example, a financial salesperson seeking new customers in the Netherlands would have a difficult time penetrating the market, primarily due to the fact that sales have traditionally been exclusively handled by local agents and brokers at local branch offices.[4] This difficulty is presently being addressed in the area of financial sales. The European Commission is advancing regulation that

---

4. *International Insurance Monitor,* "EC Proposed Legislation No Guarantee for Distance Selling," 1991, Vol. 52, No. 1, p. 2.

promotes pan-European consistency and fosters trade in the region; among other things, the regulation covers consumers' right to reflection on the offer and contract for 14 days, as well as consumers' right for withdrawal without any penalty if they were subjected to unfair pressure or were not aware of all the conditions of the sale.[5]

15-2 Managing International Employees

15-2a Managing Relationships

Managing internationals—expatriates and host-country nationals—is no easy task for multinational corporations. Companies that attempt to transplant personnel policies proven successful in the home country will run against obstacles in different international environments. Establishing quotas, assigning management responsibilities to employees within the firm, or even simply addressing employees by first names could prove to be challenges for the firm. Issues related to culture, such as national character, could come into play: Rolling up one's sleeves and working on the assembly line will result in an instant loss of status for the manager in Southeast Asia, Eastern Europe, and South America. Problems related to social class or caste will bring additional challenges: Placing a pariah (untouchable) in charge of a Brahman in India may be problematic, as would be placing someone of peasant origins in charge of someone from the intellectual class in Eastern Europe (even if training and education justify such an assignment).

15-2b Understanding the International Buyer-Seller Relationship

International buyer-seller relationship The distribution between the buyer and the individual involved in personal selling.

In a personal selling environment, challenges also arise in the **international buyer-seller relationship.** Certain approaches to selling work better than others. For example, a hard sell is not likely to be successful in most Asian countries, where modesty, a humble attitude, and respect are seen as valuable traits. Looking one's counterpart directly in the eye—a sign of honesty in the United States—is likely to be perceived as an aggressive stance in Asia. In one's first encounter with a Chinese counterpart, it is advised that business cards are exchanged; when one takes the Chinese manager's business card, one should do so with both hands and read it, as a sign of respect. The U.S. manager is advised to have business cards written in English and Chinese when dealing with the Chinese.

In other examples, Italians typically enjoy engaging in the negotiation process and want to feel that they are special customers. They want to have a special deal; offering them a bottom-line price at first is a strategy that will most likely meet with failure.[6] The strategy of focusing on closing the deal and aiming toward the next sale is unlikely to work in Latin America, where individuals prefer to take time to build a relationship with suppliers.[7] In this environment, it is best to first socialize, to build a relationship of friendship and trust, preferably involving the family. In the Middle East, this approach also works well, although it most often does not involve the family.

---

5. Ibid.

6. Cynthia Kemper, "Global Sales Success Depends on Cultural Insight," *World Trade*, May 1998, Vol. 11, No. 5, pp. S2–S4.

7. Erika Rasmusson, "Can Your Reps Sell Overseas?" *Sales and Marketing Management*, February 1998, Vol. 150, No. 2, p. 110.

15-2c Understanding Cultural Values and the Relationship between Buyer and Seller

National Character, Organizational Culture, and Personality

The level of psychological overlap in communication between buyer and seller will vary across three dimensions: **national character, organizational culture and personality,** and individual personality.[8] A personal selling situation involves *content* and *style*. Content includes substantive aspects of the interaction, such as suggesting, offering, or negotiating product-specific utilities and expectations, whereas style refers to rituals, format, mannerisms, and ground rules of the buyer and seller during the course of their interaction.[9] An interaction between buyer and seller is satisfactory if the two parties are compatible on these two dimensions.[10] In cross-cultural sales interactions, content and style are shaped by national character, organizational culture, and the personality of the individuals involved in the interaction.[11]

Chapter 5, "Cultural Influences on International Marketing," described national character in terms of personality traits shared at the national level. The dimensions identified as constituting national character are individualism, power distance, uncertainty avoidance, and masculinity/femininity.[12] Organizational culture refers to shared norms and values that guide collective behavior in organizations.

Personality refers to enduring traits that characterize individuals, motivating them to act or react to external stimuli in a particular manner. Congruency within the three dimensions between the buyer and seller is likely to result in the most successful transaction, whereas discrepancy is likely to result in a low chance for success.[13] To have a higher chance for success in international markets, a company could select a target market with a national character similar to that of its own home country, target companies with similar organizational culture, and hire international salespeople with the appropriate personality traits, as will be described in section 15-3a, "Recruiting Expatriates."[14]

Low- and High-Context Cultures

As mentioned in Chapter 5, individuals from cultures with a low context of communication use formal, direct communication that is verbally expressed, whereas individuals from cultures with a high context of communication use less verbal information to convey the message, relying instead on cues such as gestures and facial expressions. In the latter case, status of the speaker, individual background, values, associations, and so on are very important in completing the message conveyed, thus linking the message to the context in which it was delivered.[15]

National character A set of behavior and personality characteristics shared by individuals of a certain country.

Organizational culture and personality The shared norms and values that guide collective behavior in organizations, and enduring traits that characterize individuals, motivating them to act or react to stimuli in the organization and in the environment in a particular manner.

---

8. Sudhir H. Kale and John Barnes, "Understanding the Domain of Cross-National Buyer-Seller Interactions," *Journal of International Business Studies*, First Quarter 1992, Vol. 23, No. 1, pp. 101–131.

9. Jagdish N. Sheth, "Cross-Cultural Influences on the Buyer-Seller Interaction/Negotiation Process," *Asia Pacific Journal of Management*, 1983, Vol. 1, No. 1, pp. 46–55.

10. See Rosann L. Spiro and Barton A. Weitz, "Adaptive Selling: Conceptualization, Measurement, and Nomological Validity," *Journal of Marketing Research*, August 1990, Vol. 16, No. 3, pp. 355–369; and Kale and Barnes, "Understanding the Domain," pp. 101–131.

11. Kale and Barnes, "Understanding the Domain," pp. 101–131.

12. Geert Hofstede, *Culture's Consequences: International Differences in Work-Related Values*, Sage Publications, 1980.

13. Kale and Barnes, "Understanding the Domain," pp. 101–131.

14. Ibid.

15. Alma Mintu-Wimsatt and Julie B. Gassenheimer, "The Moderating Effect of Cultural Context in Buyer-Seller Negotiation," *Journal of Personal Selling Sales Management*, Winter 1999, Vol. 20, No. 1, pp. 1–9.

Negotiators from high-context cultures, such as those of Latin America and Asia, are less programmatic and less rigid, especially in time management, contract signing, and closing deals, whereas negotiators from low-context cultures follow Western logic, with the negotiation terminating when an agreement is formally reached and in writing.[16] Furthermore, individuals from high-context cultures are less confrontational and place greater emphasis on interpersonal interaction than individuals from low-context cultures.[17]

15-3 Successfully Managing Expatriates

International management experts estimate that the cost of a failed expatriate assignment is in the millions of dollars and that more than 50 percent of expatriate assignments fail.[18] The direct costs associated with each expatriate turnover are estimated to be between $55,000 and $150,000; and indirect costs, such as reduced productivity and efficiency, lost sales, reduced market share, diminished competitive position, unstable corporate image, and tarnished corporate reputation are even greater.[19]

Firms could attempt to minimize their early return rate by engaging in the appropriate training and development strategies for expatriates. Such strategies should involve the use of effective selection and screening criteria for recruiting expatriates, training them and preparing them for the international assignment, motivating them for peak performance, and ensuring their successful **repatriation** (see Figure 15-1).

Repatriation The return of the expatriate employee to the home country.

15-3a Recruiting Expatriates

In the process of recruiting expatriates, companies should select those individuals who have traits such as

- An openness and sensitivity to others, cultural sensitivity and awareness, awareness to relate across cultures, awareness of their own cultural values[20]
- The ability to change their usual behavior in cross-national settings[21]
- A high level of resiliency,[22] as ascertained from the individuals' performance histories
- Extensive international knowledge and/or willingness to gain it[23]
- A desire to go overseas[24]

Typically, potential recruits for international assignments—from within or outside the company—are given batteries of personality tests and are subjected to

---

16. Ibid.

17. See Edward Hall, *Beyond Culture,* Anchor Press/Double Day, 1976; and Mintu-Wimsatt and Gassenheimer, "The Moderating Effect ," pp. 1–9.

18. Rasmusson, "Can Your Reps," p. 110.

19. Earl Naumann, "A Conceptual Model of Expatriate Turnover," *Journal of International Business Studies,* Third Quarter 1992, Vol. 23, No. 3, pp. 499–531.

20. David M. Noer, *Multinational People Management,* Bureau of National Affairs, 1975.

21. Nancy J. Adler and John L. Graham, "Cross-Cultural Interaction: The International Comparison Fallacy?" *Journal of International Business Studies,* Third Quarter 1989, Vol. 20, No. 3, pp. 515–537.

22. Noer, *Multinational People Management,* 1975.

23. Stephen J. Simurda, "Finding an International Sales Manager," *Northeast International Business,* Vol. 1, No. 3, pp. 15–16.

24. Rasmusson, "Can Your Reps," p. 110.

Recruiting the Right Expatriates—Preferred Traits:

- An openness and sensitivity to others, cultural sensitivity and awareness, awareness of one's own cultural values

- The ability to change one's usual behavior in cross-national settings

- A high level of resiliency, as ascertained from the individual's performance history

- Extensive international knowledge and/or willingness to gain it

- A desire to go overseas

Attenuating Culture Shock:

- Culture shock (anxiety resulting from being in an unfamiliar culture, which often results in failure) can be reduced by familiarizing the expatriate and his or her family with the new environment and creating realistic expectations.

Training for International Assignments:

Strategies range from short courses in cross-cultural communications to extensive cultural immersions, including study of

- Language

- Cultural customs

- Business protocol

Motivating Expatriates:

- Allowances

- Incentives

- Financial adjustments

Figure 15-1
Successful expatriate management.

interviews to determine their motivation for an international assignment. Those prospects who are primarily interested in completing the assignments to earn promotions are not likely to be as successful as those who are eager to experience different environments.

15-3b Attenuating Culture Shock

Culture shock, which frequently accounts for early repatriation, is defined as a pervasive feeling of anxiety resulting from one's presence in a new, unfamiliar culture. Culture shock could result in feelings of inadequacy, reluctance to experience the environment, and fear of failure, among others. Cross-cultural communication experts advise companies that culture shock can be diminished when employees know what to expect in their new environment. Companies need to provide some familiarity with the physical and social environment (local customs, in particular) to the prospective expatriates to attenuate culture shock.

The family, in particular, must be prepared for the international assignment. While the expatriate employee interacts within the company and has a company culture around him/her, the spouse and children often find themselves isolated, lacking support.

Culture shock A pervasive feeling of anxiety resulting from one's presence in a new, unfamiliar culture.

15-3c Training for International Assignments

Companies use different strategies in training their employees for international assignments. The strategies range from short courses in cross-cultural communications to extensive cultural immersions. For example, Procter & Gamble, Motorola, Microsoft, and Hewlett-Packard require extensive cross-cultural training courses for their international salespeople, whereas other companies require employees to read books and other materials on the cultures before departure for the sales mission.[25] When the Abril Group, a diversified media company, sends its salespeople to Brazil, a country where it does much of its business, it requires them to participate in a ten-day Portuguese immersion program, studying the country's language, culture, and customs.[26]

15-3d Motivating Expatriates

The success of an international assignment is predicated on a high degree of motivation. The intrinsic (internal) aspects of motivation for an international assignment are addressed in the recruiting process, which ensures that only those candidates who have the appropriate traits (see section 15-3a) are deployed. The company controls the extrinsic aspects of motivation, such as compensation, leave and family policies, career incentives, etc.

In terms of compensation, certain companies attempt to use uniform policies worldwide. For instance, IBM uses a sales compensation plan that links 140,000 salespeople from North America, Latin America, Europe, and the Asia Pacific region, allowing sales managers to act locally and think globally. Their compensation is derived from team performance in a regional or industry group (20 percent), personal contribution to customer solutions and use of business partners (60 percent), and challenges and contests (20 percent).[27]

Other companies offer numerous compensation incentives above those used for assignments in the home country, thus making the international assignment very attractive. Among such incentives are those shown in Figure 15-2.

Cost-of-Living Adjustment/ Post Adjustment

For many companies, the **cost-of-living adjustment** is above and beyond that justified by the local conditions. This type of compensation, also referred to as **post adjustment,** includes payment for household help, such as maids, cooks, gardeners, night watchmen, etc.

Housing Allowance

Often, companies will cover part or the entire cost of housing for the expatriate employees while abroad. Even if the **housing allowance** does not cover permanent housing, it will most likely cover the cost of staying at a quality hotel until housing becomes available.

Education Allowance

The **education allowance** covers the cost of children's education at an international private school. U.S. companies pay the education allowance for their employees primarily so that they will be on par with employees working for Euro-

Cost-of-living adjustment/ Post adjustment   A compensation incentive whereby the company adjusts expatriate salaries to reflect the cost of living in the new environment at standards in the expatriate's home country.

Housing allowance
A compensation incentive whereby the company covers part or the entire cost of housing for the expatriate employee while abroad.

Education allowance
A compensation incentive whereby the company agrees to cover the cost of children's education at an international private school in the country of assignment or at a boarding school in the expatriate's home country.

---

25. Kemper, "Global Sales Success," pp. S2–S4.

26. Rasmusson, "Can Your Reps," p. 110.

27. Michele Marchetti, "Global Gamble," *Sales and Marketing Management,* July 1996, Vol. 148, No. 7, pp. 64–65.

Figure 15-2
Motivating expatriates. Ensuring a successful assignment is expensive. Aside from assurances of job advancement upon the successful completion of the international assignment, expatriates receive generous allowances for moving expenses, liberal vacations at home and abroad, educational allowances for expensive private schools, and even allowances for full-time household staff.

pean multinationals. Many European firms pay for high-quality education for their employees' children, regardless of whether they are in their home country or overseas, and for as long as they are attending school.

Home-Leave Allowance

The **home-leave allowance** pays for the family abroad to vacation in the home country. The company also may pay for the children remaining in the home country to attend school to visit the family member or members posted abroad.

Moving Allowance

Household moving expenses to the country of assignment are usually covered. The **moving allowance** also may cover storage in the home country. Some companies also arrange for the sale of the expatriate's home, often incurring losses if the housing market is in a slump.

Repatriation Allowance

The **repatriation allowance** covers expenses for moving to the home country. In addition, the repatriation allowance may consist of a considerable sum paid to the expatriate simply for returning from the international assignment.

Other Types of Allowances

Expatriates also can benefit from other types of allowances. Such allowances may, for example, cover family membership in a social and/or health club designed primarily for expatriates and for well-to-do locals.

Noncompensation incentives are very important. Multinational corporations frequently offer as incentive to the expatriate a guaranteed promotion in the company ranks upon his or her successful return from the country of assignment. Companies also must address career-related concerns of the accompanying spouse. In an effort to recruit the best candidates for international posting,

Home-leave allowance
A compensation incentive that pays for the expatriate and his or her family to vacation in the home country.

Moving allowance
A compensation incentive whereby the company pays for the household moving expenses to the country of assignment and, at the end of the assignment, back to the home country.

Repatriation allowance
A compensation incentive whereby the company covers expenses involved in moving back to the home country, as well as, frequently, a large sum paid for successfully completing the international assignment.

companies often offer spouses positions in the companies congruent with their talents and objectives to ensure the continuity of their careers.

15-3e Obstacles to the International Sales Mission

Once in the country of assignment, expatriates must learn the culture quickly and not gravitate toward home-country expatriates.[28] When they are living in the expatriate community, however, this may not be avoidable. First, if the expatriates are assigned to a country where restrictions are imposed on interactions with foreigners, such as Saudi Arabia, China, and Cuba, the expatriate community is likely to be the only forum for social interaction.

Expatriates may be drawn toward their home-country expatriate community in other countries as well. For example, for U.S. expatriates, many home-country offices and representatives play an important part. Among them are the United States Embassy, the various other offices present in a particular country in conjunction with the embassy (the Unites States Information Agency, the United States Agency for International Development, the Fulbright Office, and other agencies), as well as others associated with the embassy—the cultural, the military, and the commercial attaché. One responsibility of U.S. officers within these respective positions and structures is to organize activities that involve the participation of U.S. expatriates. Expatriates are invited to various functions, activities, and celebrations to participate and to represent the United States. Often, there are even American schools for expatriates' children and American clubs. The Marine House, which houses the marines stationed at the embassy, periodically shows American movies, accompanied by receptions. Most often, a recreation center is open to American expatriates so that they can play pool, watch American football games, and reminisce about life in America.

At the very least, there is a web site that unites expatriates in a particular region. Expatforum.com is such an example, helping individuals cope with their foreign assignments, compare benefits and other company practices, as well as costs. Although the forum is open to any participants, most are U.S. expatriates. Another site, expatries-france.com, is aimed at French expatriates, and helps them, according to its slogan, to live abroad as they would in France (*vivre à la française à l'étranger*).

All these factors have the potential to impede expatriates' immersion in the local culture. An extreme outcome would be the expatriate who is isolated and lives primarily for his or her return to the home country; the only motivation for this individual's international presence is strictly monetary, or is linked to the international assignment as a precondition for promotion. Individuals in this predicament are more likely to fail than those who actively participate in the life and culture of the host country.

Yet another extreme is the expatriate who has "gone native." In extreme cases, this individual may refuse to return to the home country, insisting on remaining abroad in the company's service, and in some situations even serving locals to the detriment of the company.

15-3f Repatriation Issues

Upon repatriation, expatriates often find themselves working in a company that has changed drastically during their absence. They find that their corner offices are

---

28. Rasmusson, "Can Your Reps," p. 110.

occupied by their former underlings or by professionals new to the company, and that they do not quite fit in their new work environment. They also suffer a loss of status in their home environment. Whereas, during their international assignment, expatriates and their families were involved in a close, elite social environment that was reserved for the local international community, upon return, they often find themselves to be no more than average dwellers in nondescript suburbia. At this point, they may experience **reverse culture shock,** a feeling of anxiety associated with a longing for the international environment left behind, or fear of not adapting in the new environment and/or losing one's job due to lack of fit.

Companies often try to soften the reverse culture shock experienced by expatriates—especially professional expatriates, who are often reluctant to return to their home country. Strategies used by companies to better prepare the expatriates for repatriation involve, among others, offering a substantial incentive package, such as a raise upon return; guaranteeing a promotion; and/or providing a repatriation grant.

One of the most important actions of the company may be to keep the expatriates "in the loop" for the duration of their assignments.[29] This can be accomplished by flying them back to headquarters on a regular basis, preferably for extended stays, and keeping them on a regular mailing list for intra-office and intra-company communication. Expatforum.com recommends ongoing communication to avoid the renegade syndrome and the "out-of-sight, out-of-mind" mindset, and arranging for a mentor in upper management.

Reverse culture shock Anxiety experienced after returning to the home country, associated with a longing for the international environment left behind and with the difficulty of readjusting to the home country and to corporate life at one's firm.

Chapter Summary

- **Examine companies' expatriate management strategies**
Managing international employees requires using appropriate personnel management policies—a process complicated by obstacles presented by the international environment. Decisions such as assigning management responsibilities to employees, establishing quotas, or even simply addressing employees by their first names could prove to be a challenge. To further complicate matters, local culture and national character will affect relationships between management at each tier of the organization, as will social class or caste.

- **Describe the different types of employees suited for a company's international operations**
A company will hire three types of employees for its international operations. Expatriates are home-country nationals groomed from within the firm's national operations. These employees are familiar with firm policy, operations, goals, and objectives and are likely to best represent company interests. Third-country nationals are professional expatriates who adapt easily regardless of the environment to which they were assigned. On the downside, they need to learn both about the local envi-

ronment and the company's culture, procedures, and goals. Locals (host-country nationals) are familiar with the host-country operating environment and have relationships already established with the national government and other important agency representatives. They also are the employees most likely to sell out the company by creating a local competitor.

- **Address issues related to expatriate management, such as motivating international employees and ensuring successful assignment performance and repatriation**
To ensure top performance, expatriates need to be appropriately trained and motivated. Training in the local language, however superficial, may benefit the expatriates, as will cultural training; all will minimize culture shock. Appropriate motivation will also improve performance. Some typical perks for expatriates are a housing allowance, moving allowance, education allowance, post-adjustment pay, and home-leave pay. In addition, the employees should be prepared for re-entry in the firm and home country at the end of the assignment, to minimize reverse culture shock.

---

29. Lambeth Hochwald, "Luring Execs Overseas," *Sales and Marketing Management,* February 2000, Vol. 152, No. 2, p. 101.

Discussion Questions

Discussion Questions

1. Describe the three types of employees a company is likely to send to a foreign post. What are their strengths and weaknesses?

2. Discuss some of the management and culture-related challenges involved in international salesforce management. How do companies address those challenges?

3. How do international companies select and train employees for international assignments?

4. What are some of the methods that international firms use to motivate employees for international assignments, and how do these companies ensure that employees face minimal culture shock upon repatriation?

International Pricing Strategy

Key Terms

aggressive export pricing
antidumping duties
barter
buyback agreements
clearing account
clearing currency
compensation
cost-based transfer pricing
counterpurchase
countertrade
countervailing duties
dumping
dynamic incremental pricing
gray market

hard currency
infant-industry argument
local pricing
market-based transfer pricing
offset purchase
parallel barter
parallel imports
penetration pricing
skimming strategy
soft currency
standardized pricing
swing credits
switch trading
transfer pricing

Outline

Learning Objectives
16-1 Pricing Decisions and
    Internal Challenges
    of Multinational Firms
    16-1a Production Facilities
    16-1b Ability to Keep Track
    of Costs
16-2 Environment-Related
    Challenges and Pricing
    Decisions
    16-2a The Competitive
    Environment
    16-2b The Political and Legal
    Environment
    16-2c The Economic and
    Financial Environment
16-3 International Pricing
    Decisions
    16-3a Price Setting
    16-3b Aggressive Export Pricing
    16-3c Standardized Pricing
    Versus Local Pricing
    16-3d Penetration Pricing and
    Skimming Strategies
Chapter Summary
Discussion Questions

Learning Objectives

Learning Objectives

By the end of this chapter, you should be able to:

- Identify pricing-related internal challenges facing international firms
- Identify pricing-related challenges imposed by competition on international firms
- Identify pricing-related challenges imposed by the political and legal environment on international firms
- Identify pricing-related challenges imposed by the economic and financial environment on international firms
- Address international pricing decisions of international firms

Pricing is especially important in international marketing strategy decisions, due to its effect on product positioning, market segmentation, demand management, and market share dynamics.[1] The international pricing decision is complex: Numerous internal and external variables, such as the nature of the product, the location of production plants, the type of distribution system used, and the economic climate, must all be evaluated before determining the final price of products and services.[2] Pricing decisions are further affected by currency fluctuations and by exchange rate controls in individual markets.

This chapter addresses challenges that international firms face internally when setting prices. It also addresses the impact of the international competitive, political and legal, and economic and financial environment on firm pricing decisions. Finally, it evaluates pricing policies of firms for different international markets.

1. Terry Clark, Masaaki Kotabe, and Dan Rajaratnam, "Exchange Rate Pass-Through and International Pricing Strategy: A Conceptual Framework and Research Propositions," *Journal of International Business Studies,* Second Quarter 1999, Vol. 30, No. 2, pp. 249–268.

2. Virginia Citrano, "The Right Price," *CFO,* May 1992, Vol. 8, No. 5, pp. 71–72.

16-1 Pricing Decisions and Internal Challenges of Multinational Firms

16-1a Production Facilities

The location of production facilities determines the extent to which companies can control costs and price their products competitively. Multinationals usually can afford to shift production to take advantage of lower costs and exchange rates, whereas small to medium-size firms are often limited to exporting as the only venue for product distribution.[3] Companies can and often do price themselves out of the market in certain countries, especially if they do not shift production to a low-labor-cost, low-tax country. As an example, Marc Controls, in order to lower the price of its products, purchases raw materials in Korea, China, and India and ships them to the United States for manufacturing; its products are competitively priced when sold on the German market, but they are considered overpriced in most of Asia.[4]

16-1b Ability to Keep Track of Costs

Product components often are manufactured in different countries. Often, the final products are assembled in a particular country—which is frequently not the company's home country—and then sold all over the world. It is consequently difficult for financial officers to keep track of product costs.[5]

16-2 Environment-Related Challenges and Pricing Decisions

Pricing decisions are affected by all the external elements in a company's international environment. An international company must react effectively to changes in the competitive environment, in the political and legal environment, and in the economic and financial environment. Figure 16-1 addresses examples of different challenges in the international firm's environment that affects the firm's pricing decisions.

The Competitive Environment	• Gray market/parallel imports as a competitive threat • Dumping as a competitive threat
The Political and Legal Environment	• Transfer pricing • The price of protectionism
The Economic and Financial Environment	• Inflationary pressures on price • Fluctuating exchange rates • Shortage of hard currency and countertrade

Figure 16-1
Environmental factors affecting pricing decisions.

---

3. Ibid.

4. Ibid.

5. Ibid.

16-2a The Competitive Environment

Competition

International and local competition often pose serious concerns to multinational firms. If competition can keep product prices low by manufacturing in a low-labor-cost country, firms must meet this challenge and maintain a low price, potentially at a loss. At a retail level, and especially in service environments, companies often are challenged by local competitors offering legal copycat products at a much lower price. For example, Pizza Hut is challenged in every market in Poland by a local pizza chain that offers almost identical products, such as Neapolitan pizza, at a fraction of Pizza Hut's offering.

Frequently, challenges at the retail level may be difficult to identify. Here's an example of such a challenge: Firms operating in markets where retailers are likely to keep the change price their products under the even number of the banknote that would normally be used in purchasing those products. For example, in Egypt, Romania, and Turkey, among others, retailers are unlikely to give back small change, or even any change at all, to customers. In such an environment, a company using an even-pricing strategy will be at a disadvantage because retailers will choose to sell competitors' products. This is the case even if the company's prices are below competitors' prices.

Gray Market/Parallel Imports as a Competitive Threat

Parallel imports/Gray market A distribution system not authorized by the manufacturer whereby the products purchased in a low-price market are diverted to other markets.

A firm engaging in a differential pricing strategy could be vulnerable to competition from unauthorized channels. In fact, differential pricing (price discrimination) by the manufacturer has been identified as a main cause of parallel importing—diverting products purchased in a low-price market to other markets (**parallel imports**) by means of a distribution system not authorized by the manufacturer, otherwise known as a **gray market.**[6] A manufacturer may charge different prices in different markets for the same product

- To meet the needs of target consumers who have a limited purchasing power
- To keep the product price competitive in markets that are actively targeted by competition
- Due to changes in the exchange rate in countries where the products are sold; the product is likely to be cheaper in the countries with the weakest currency
- Due to the fact that it offers discounts to wholesalers buying higher quantities
- Due to differences in wholesale prices in different markets; for example, wholesale prices for luxury goods are relatively high in the United States, compared to wholesale prices in the rest of the world

Dumping as a Competitive Threat

Dumping Selling products below cost to get rid of excess inventory and/or to undermine competition.

Firms also can face challenges from companies **dumping** products in their target market. Dumping is an important factor affecting pricing decisions. A typical example of dumping involves a foreign company that enjoys high prices and high profits at home as a result of trade barriers against imports; the company uses those profits to sell at much lower prices in foreign markets to build market share and suppress the profitability of competitors with open home markets.[7] According to the World Trade Organization, dumping should be condemned if it threat-

---

6. For an extended discussion on parallel imports, see Chapter 11, "Managing International Distribution Options and Logistics."

7. Greg Mastel, "The U.S. Steel Industry and Antidumping Law," *Challenge*, May/June 1999, Vol. 42, No. 3, pp. 84–94.

ens to cause injury to an established industry in a particular market and/or if it delays the establishment of a viable domestic industry.[8]

Antidumping policies differ somewhat from country to country. China, according to its Antidumping and Anti-Subsidy Regulations set forth by the State Council, defines dumping as the subsidization of exports resulting in substantial injury, or the threat of substantial injury, to an established domestic industry, or substantially impeding the establishment of a comparable domestic industry.[9] According to the Chinese, dumping is involved if a product is sold at a price below its normal value, where normal value may be based on production costs plus reasonable expenses and profit, or on the comparable price in the exporting country for an identical or like product; if there is no comparable price for the product in the exporting country, reference is made to the price at which the exporter sells a similar product in a third country.[10]

Similarly, the United States Department of Commerce, the government branch responsible for determining whether products are dumped on the U.S. market, considers that dumping takes place if products are priced only minimally above cost, or at prices below those charged in the producing country. The European Commission, in charge of antidumping regulation in the European Union, requires a vote of the Council of Ministers for action against dumping activity and other unfair trade practices.

Dumping challenges and charges abound. China, Japan, and South Korea have often been challenged for dumping products in the United States and Europe. China is currently fighting back, enforcing its antidumping legislation to protect local industry from international competition; one target of Chinese scrutiny is U.S. newsprint.[11] Another point of contention centers on calculating product prices in nonmarket and transition economies, such as those of China and Russia. There is a strong disagreement on exactly how to determine product costs in a state-owned or directed economy; the U.S. Department of Commerce is attempting to address this unknown by making reference to tangible measures, such as product price in the product's home country, or in other markets.[12]

As established by the World Trade Organization, after determining that price discrimination did indeed occur and that a particular local industry was injured by the dumping activity, governments are entitled to impose **antidumping duties** on the merchandise. Similar to these are **countervailing duties,** which are imposed on subsidized products imported into the country. Such subsidizing could, for example, take the form of government aid in the processes of production and/or distribution.

Enforcement of antidumping regulation is particularly intense when the economy is not faring well and when price competition is intense. In the recent past, the United States Department of Commerce and the International Trade Commission scrutinized numerous importers' pricing practices, using strict criteria to determine whether the importer had committed price discrimination and, if so, if it resulted in injury to a particular local industry. Electronics, textiles, and steel, among others, originating in countries from Japan to Russia to Mexico, have been at the center of antidumping action in the past few decades.

Antidumping duties Duties that must be paid by firms as a punishment for engaging in unfair price competition.

Countervailing duties Duties imposed on subsidized products imported into a country.

---

8. Ibid.

9. Lester Ross and Susan Ning, "Modern Protectionism: China's Own Antidumping Regulations," *The China Business Review,* May/June 2000, Vol. 27, No. 3, pp. 30–33.

10. Ibid.

11. Ibid.

12. Ibid.

In spite of a more strict enforcement, companies continue to be affected by pricing actions of importers taking advantage of loopholes in the antidumping legislation. To avoid price discrimination charges, the importers modify their products slightly so as not to permit them to be directly compared with products sold in other countries at higher prices.

16-2b The Political and Legal Environment

Governments regulate prices charged by multinational firms. Regulations and restrictions exist with regard to many pricing decisions, ranging from dumping to setting limits on wholesalers' gross margins and on the product's retail price. As mentioned in Chapter 12, "International Retailing," Wal-Mart has been challenged in the European Union for charging prices that are too low (just above cost) and that drive competition out of business. Price promotions are severely restricted, limiting the manufacturers' ability to boost sales in the short term and to help retailers renew their inventories.

Multinational companies also are affected by local government subsidies to local manufacturers, in particular, to producers of agricultural products and to exporting firms. Subsidies lower the price charged in international markets for products and challenge the competitive position of firms operating in the same industry. Finally, governments can also impose tariffs and other duties on products in certain industries, especially if those industries are in infancy in the respective countries. Governments defend such action under the **infant-industry argument,** which permits setting high tariffs on imports that challenge emerging local producers.

In general, governments use numerous strategies in their attempts to restrict the repatriation of profits by multinationals and to tax and/or to encourage the reinvestment of profits. One way that companies can bypass such restrictions is through the use of transfer pricing.

Transfer Pricing

Transfer pricing is a pricing strategy used in intra-firm sales: The pricing of products in the process of conducting transactions between units of the same corporation, within or beyond the national borders of the parent company, is known as transfer pricing and regarded as a legitimate business opportunity by transnational corporations.[13] Developing countries often bring the issue of transfer pricing to the attention of international trade bodies as a strategy that could help a multinational company under-report profits and decrease its tax burden in countries where it has foreign direct investment, thus evading taxation. Instead of pricing products at cost, products can be priced *at market level,* known as **market-based transfer pricing,** where the price reflects the price products sell for in a particular market; *at cost,* known as **cost-based transfer pricing,** where the cost reflects not the cost incurred by the company, but the estimated opportunity cost of the product; or products can be priced using a combination of the two strategies.

The Price of Protectionism

Protectionism adds to the final price paid by consumers. In spite of the Uruguay round of trade liberalization and the strides made by the World Trade Organization, protectionist actions continue to increase the costs of goods, and hence the

Infant-industry argument
A protectionist strategy aimed at protecting a national industry in its infancy from powerful international competitors.

Transfer pricing A pricing strategy used in intra-firm sales for commercial transactions between units of the same corporation, within or beyond the national borders of the parent company.

Market-based transfer pricing
A pricing strategy used in intra-firm sales for commercial transactions between units of the same corporation, within or beyond the national borders of the parent company, whereby products are priced at market cost, rather than at the cost incurred by the company.

Cost-based transfer pricing
A pricing strategy used in intra-firm sales for commercial transactions between units of the same corporation, within or beyond the national borders of the parent company, where the costs reflect not the costs incurred by the company, but the estimated opportunity costs of the product.

---

13. Messaoud Mehafdi, "The Ethics of International Transfer Pricing," *Journal of Business Ethics,* December 2000, Vol. 28, No. 4, pp. 365–381.

price for the final consumer. Europe's economy, for example, is almost as protected as it was ten years ago, and its costs are as high as 7 percent of the Gross Domestic Product of the European Union—some $600 billion.[14] To illustrate, the EU's banana-import restrictions cost European consumers up to $2 billion a year or about 55 cents per kilogram of bananas. And since the United States has retaliated with punitive tariffs on $191 million of European imports, the cost of the EU's banana regime is even higher.[15] In other examples, European beef farmers receive large subsidies, while tariffs of up to 125 percent are imposed on beef imports; in addition, the EU has a ban on hormone-treated beef from the U.S. The costs incurred by European beef consumers for subsidies, tariffs, and other restrictions amount to $14.6 billion a year in the form of higher prices and taxes, or around $1.60 per kilogram of beef.[16]

These figures are high in the United States as well, especially in service industries such as shipping and banking.[17] And it is difficult to ascertain the impact of the three years of tariffs, ranging from 8 percent to 30 percent, imposed by the United States on a variety of imported steel products.

16-2c The Economic and Financial Environment

Inflationary Pressures on Price

An inflationary environment places strong pressures on companies to lower prices; often, pricing competitively may mean that companies are not producing a profit. During inflationary periods, firms often find that they must decide between maintaining a competitive presence in a market and weathering the downside of the economic cycle or abandoning the market, which is a high-cost, high-risk proposition. Companies operating in Latin America in the 1980s and early 1990s often faced challenges posed by inflation.

Fluctuating Exchange Rates

Fluctuating exchange rates provide both challenges and opportunities to firms trading on the global arena. Companies that do not pay attention to fluctuations in exchange rates could find that their profits are greatly eroded during the time lapsed between contract negotiations and the actual product delivery. Including a percentage that covers exchange rate fluctuations when specifying the product price is one strategy companies use to address the unpredictability of such fluctuations.

Traditionally, firms specified all transactions in a strong, stable, hard currency, usually the dollar. Since the dollar's ups and downs in the 1970s and 1980s, however, other currencies have emerged as standards for exchanges. Increasingly, pricing decisions are facilitated by the advent of successful venues for regional integration, such as the European Union and MERCOSUR (the Southern Cone Common Market). Member countries are adopting a single currency, in the case of the European Union, or, in the case of MERCOSUR, they are attempting to peg the currency of member countries relative to each other. The advent of the Euro in the European Union has greatly facilitated transactions in the region. Currently, all prices throughout the European Union are listed both in the national currency and in Euros.

---

14. *The Economist*, "Finance and Economics: Europe's Burden," May 22, 1999, Vol. 351, No. 8120, p. 84.

15. Ibid.

16. Ibid.

17. Ibid.

Hard currency   Currency that is accepted for payment by any international seller.

Soft currency   Currency that is kept at a high artificial exchange rate, overvalued, and controlled by the national central bank.

Countertrade   A form of trade whereby a company sells a product to a buyer and agrees to accept, in return for payment, products from the buyer's firm or from the trade agency/institution of the buyer.

Shortage of Hard Currency and Countertrade

Developing countries face a significant shortage of hard currency reserves. **Hard currency** is currency that is accepted for payment by any international seller; **soft currency** is currency that is kept at a high artificial exchange rate, overvalued, and controlled by the national government. This situation, compounded by the inability to borrow from international banks or other sources such as the International Monetary Fund, has led developing countries to resort to **countertrade** in order to remain active in international trade and to address the needs of local consumers. Moreover, as global markets are growing competitive, increasingly, the balance of power is shifting from sellers to buyers; in the process, buyers require sellers to engage in reciprocal purchases, known as countertrade.[18]

Countertrade involves selling a product to a buyer and agreeing to accept, in return for payment, products from the buyer's firm or from the trade agency/institution of the buyer. Countertrade has been traditionally associated with companies from countries in the former Soviet Bloc and from other countries with a tightly controlled soft currency. The classic countertrade example is the one initiated by PepsiCo with the former Soviet Union. In the late 1960s, Nikita Khruschev, then president of the Soviet Union, was impressed by the taste of Pepsi and agreed to an exchange of Pepsi syrup and bottling equipment in return for Stolichnaya vodka. This exchange was an example of successful countertrade conducted over decades.

Countertrade is on the increase worldwide; it is estimated that the percentage of the total world trade financed through countertrade transactions is just more than 20 percent.[19] Many developing countries rely heavily on countertrade in their international trade activity; for example, as much as 70 percent of Russian industrial activity involves barter.[20]

A typical countertrade exchange today would involve a seller from a developed, industrialized country and a buyer from a developing country where hard currency is scarce and tightly controlled by national institutions, such as the Central Bank and the Ministry of Foreign Trade. Usually, firms in the developing country are unable to secure bank loans that would finance imports of products deemed to be unessential, such as consumer products. In many developing countries (even in countries with a greater access to hard currency—primarily due to the export of natural reserves, such as oil and diamonds), governments actually mandate countertrade as a form of payment for firms purchasing imported goods.

The Position of the U.S. Government on Countertrade

The United States, in line with the mandates of the General Agreement on Tariffs and Trade (GATT) and the World Trade Organization (WTO), has a policy that opposes government-mandated countertrade. The U.S. government interferes only in the case of firms that operate with U.S.-government financing or firms that have contracts with the U.S. government. In this case, the U.S. government could compromise the competitive position of U.S. firms, which are at a disadvantage in developing countries compared to their Japanese and European competitors.[21]

18. Dorothy A. Paun, Larry D. Compeau, and Dhruv Grewal, "A Model of the Influence of Marketing Objectives on Pricing Strategies in International Countertrade," *Journal of Public Policy & Marketing*, Spring 1997, Vol. 16, No. 1, pp. 69–82.

19. Sam C. Okoroafo, "Determinants of LDC-Mandated Countertrade," *International Marketing Review*, Winter 1988, Vol. 5, pp. 16–24.

20. David Woodruff, *Money Unmade: Barter and the Fate of Russian Capitalism*, Cornell University Press, 1999.

21. Paun, Compeau, and Grewal, "A Model of the Influence of Marketing Objectives," pp. 69–82.

However, the U.S. government does not deter firms from engaging in countertrade with private parties. Furthermore, the U.S. government supports countertrade for the sale of weapons and aircraft (countertrade constitutes the key form of trade internationally for defense equipment) and for agricultural surplus.[22]

Countertrade Brokers

Often, countertrade is conducted with the help of countertrade brokers because it is rare that a perfect match can exist for product exchanges and because the exchanges themselves are complex. Exchanges could range from paying sausages to rock stars for their performances, and bringing French high fashion to Russian consumers by selling quality Russian crystal to Saudi merchants. In the second example, the barter of French high fashion for Russian crystal is mediated by Saudi parties, who pay cash for the product to the French couturiers.

Numerous companies specialize in brokering barter deals. Located in many financial centers, such as London and New York, as well as in countries that have traditions of brokering barter agreements, such as Sweden, these brokers can put together intricate exchanges. Among the major U.S. corporate barter firms doing a large-volume business are the New York firms of Atwood Richards, Inc.; Active International; Global Marketing Resources; Media Resources International; and Tradewell, Inc.[23] These barter agents or brokers, known in the trade as commercial trade exchanges, number approximately 400 in the United States and typically utilize extensive computerized databases to locate and match demand and supply.[24]

Advantages of Countertrade

Countertrade offers substantial advantages to the involved parties. Countertrade allows firms from industrialized countries to sell their products in markets in the developing world that otherwise would not be accessible. Many countries that have a shortage of hard currency and that otherwise cannot secure bank loans to finance imports restrict the import of products considered nonessential by using foreign exchange controls and/or other barriers. Countertrade can help an exporting company bypass such restrictions.

In addition to offering an opportunity to many developing countries to participate in trade, countertrade also offers individuals from developing countries access to consumer products. Ministries of Foreign Trade in many developing countries tend to favor *heavy* industry imports and to restrict *light* industry imports, especially imports of soft consumer goods. For example, countertrade makes it possible for consumers in developing countries to have access to brand name clothing and small appliances and to attend concerts of popular rock stars.

Disadvantages of Countertrade

Among the disadvantages of countertrade are the following:[25]

- Companies countertrading with an indebted nation may find that foreign lenders have prior claim on goods offered as part of the countertrading agreement.

22. Ibid.

23. Janet Aschkenasy, "Give and Take," *International Business*, September 1996, Vol. 9, No. 8, pp. 10–12.

24. Richard E. Plank, David A. Reid, and Frank Bates, "Barter: An Alternative to Traditional Methods of Purchasing," *International Journal of Purchasing and Materials Management*, Spring 1994, Vol. 30, No. 2, p. 52.

25. Nabil A. Ibrahim and John P. Angelidis, "Countertrading with Eastern Europe: A Comparative Analysis of the Benefits and Pitfalls," *International Journal of Commerce & Management*, 1996, Vol. 6, pp. 22–40.

- Countertrade arrangements frequently restrict profit margins and, often, during negotiations, price setting is difficult because not all cost factors are known in advance.
- Countertrade practices encourage economic inefficiency and are a cumbersome and time-consuming way of doing business.
- Prices are distorted as deliveries, which could take place over time, are made without reference to changes in technology, taste, quality, market structure, or competing products.
- Companies may receive inferior quality products as payment, as rigorous quality control may not be a practice in the trading partner's enterprise.
- Exchange partners can, in the long term, become competitors.
- Countertrade agreements often require long and expensive negotiations.

Often, the goods firms receive as payment are unrelated to the products they sell, and the firms have no expertise in marketing these products; for example, Caterpillar Tractor received Algerian wine in exchange for its products but was unable to sell it in the U.S. market.

Types of Countertrade

The different types of countertrade usually involve monetary exchange to a certain degree. Barter is the only type of exchange that does not involve monetary exchange. At the next level are clearing agreements and switch trading, which involve the transfer of currency, usually a mutually-agreed-upon hard currency. All other types of countertrade are based on direct monetary exchange.

Barter   **Barter** can be traced for centuries as a form of exchange. It involves a simple, nonmonetized exchange of goods and/or services between two parties. Although no money is involved in the exchange, the parties calculate the value of the goods in a particular currency and attempt to achieve value parity for the exchanged goods.

Clearing agreement   A clearing agreement, also known as a **clearing account,** is a somewhat complex form of countertrade. Under this form of countertrade, a third party, usually a barter agent or some other type of broker, creates clearing accounts that represent trade credits for the respective parties, and companies trade in and out as necessary.[26] Under a clearing agreement, countries are likely to trade products up to a certain amount stated in a particular, mutually-agreed-upon hard currency, and within a given time frame. When an imbalance occurs and one country owes money to the other, **swing credits** are paid in an agreed-upon hard currency, known as the **clearing currency.**

Switch trading   **Switch trading** involves buying a party's position in a countertrade in exchange for hard currency and selling it to another customer.[27] Professional switch trading firms purchase products that are not accepted by the seller as payment for products and, for a commission, sell them on the market at a discount.

Compensation   **Compensation** involves payment in products and in cash, usually in a mutually-agreed-upon convertible currency. The firm compensated using this system is at lesser risk—especially if the proportion of cash is high—than the

Barter   A simple, nonmonetized exchange of goods and/or services between two parties.

Clearing account   A complex form of countertrade whereby countries trade products up to a certain amount stated in a particular, mutually-agreed-upon hard currency and within a given time frame, and, when an imbalance occurs and one country owes money to the other, swing credits are paid in an agreed-upon hard currency, known as the clearing currency; also called a clearing agreement.

Swing credits   Amounts paid within the framework of a clearing agreement by the country that owes money to the other when an imbalance occurs.

Clearing currency   The agreed-upon currency used to pay swing credits in a clearing account or agreement.

Switch trading   The process of buying a party's position in a countertrade in exchange for hard currency and selling it to another customer.

Compensation   The payment in products and in cash, usually in a mutually-agreed-upon convertible currency.

---

26. Plank, Reid, and Bates, "Barter: An Alternative," p. 52.

27. Jean F. Hennart, "Some Empirical Dimensions of Countertrade," *Journal of International Business Studies,"* Second Quarter 1990, Vol. 21, No. 2, pp. 243–270.

firm that is entirely dependent on the sale of the products it receives from the trading partner.

Counterpurchase   **Counterpurchase** involves two exchanges that are paid for in cash; as such, counterpurchase involves two parallel contracts—hence its name of **parallel barter.** The seller agrees to purchase products that usually are unrelated to its business from the buyer and sell them on international markets. The purchase could be for the total sum of the products sold or for a fraction thereof. The exporter agrees to buy goods from a shopping list provided by the importer; the list typically consists of light manufactures and consumer goods. In one example, Volkswagen sold 10,000 cars to the former East Germany and agreed to purchase, over a period of two years, goods for the value of the automobiles, from a list of goods provided by the East German government.[28] Another illustration of counterpurchase is the classic countertrade example whereby PepsiCo sold its syrup to Russia in the late 1960s; the export agreement stated that PepsiCo would subsequently import Stolichnaya vodka to be sold in the United States.[29]

The advantage of counterpurchase is that, typically, the seller is paid up front, in cash; the seller also has a specified, limited period (usually no more than a year) to sell the goods obtained through the exchange. Many governments of developing countries mandate counterpurchase as a requirement for firms exporting products to them. For example, Indonesia used to require 100 percent counterpurchase on state contracts higher than $500,000, except where aid funds were involved; however, due to pressure from GATT and governments of industrialized countries, this policy has changed.[30]

Offset purchase   **Offset purchases** involve large hard currency purchases, such as the purchase of defense equipment, airplanes, telecommunications networks, railway or road building, and other expensive civil engineering projects, by a developing country. The seller agrees, in return for the sale of its offering, to purchase products that are valued at a certain percentage of the sale, ranging from 20 percent, which is quite typical, to as much as 100 percent for highly competitive deals. China, for example, often imposes offsets for its purchases. Other examples of offset purchases may involve sourcing some of the production locally, transferring technology to the importing country, or marketing different products sourced in the purchasing country.[31]

An example of an offset agreement is the sale of DC-9s by McDonnell Douglas to the former Yugoslavia in the 1960s; to secure the order, McDonnell Douglas agreed to help sell products sourced in the Yugoslavia to buyers in the United States to generate capital to help finance the purchase of the passenger planes.[32]

Buyback agreements   In a **buyback agreement,** the seller builds and provides a turnkey plant, as well as the manufacturing know-how, the necessary equipment, patents, and licenses necessary for production and distribution of the product. The seller is paid up front part of the cost of the plant in an agreed-upon convertible currency, which is typically obtained by borrowing from international banks or the International Monetary Fund. The seller agrees to purchase specific quantities of the plant's output over an extended period of time. An advantage of

Counterpurchase/Parallel barter
A form of trade that involves two exchanges paid for in cash; it involves two parallel contracts whereby the seller agrees to purchase products that are usually unrelated to its business from the buyer and sell them on international markets.

Offset purchase   A large, hard-currency purchase, such as the purchase of defense equipment, airplanes, telecommunications networks, railway or road building and other expensive civil engineering projects, whereby the seller agrees, in return, to purchase products that are valued at a certain percentage of the sale.

Buyback agreements
Agreements whereby the seller builds and provides a turnkey plant and is paid up front part of the cost of the plant in an agreed-upon convertible currency; in return, the seller agrees to purchase specific quantities of the plant's output over an extended period of time.

28. Ibid.

29. Aschkenasy, "Give and Take," *International Business,* pp. 10–12.

30. *Project Trade and Finance,* "Indonesia to Reform Countertrade Policy," January 1996, No. 153, p. 15.

31. Hennart, "Some Empirical Dimensions," pp. 243–270.

32. Aschkenasy, "Give and Take," pp. 10–12.

this type of countertrade to the seller is that it has the know-how in terms of marketing and distributing the products because the company operates in a similar business.

An example of a buyback is that of two British firms, ICI and Davy Powergas, which in 1977 sold a methanol plant to the Soviet Union for $250 million and agreed to purchase 20 percent of the plant's output in the years 1981 to 1991, for a total of $350 million.[33]

16-3 International Pricing Decisions

16-3a Price Setting

Setting prices internationally tends to be intuition- and experience-driven and highly decentralized. The skill in pricing lies in exploiting differences in consumers' willingness to pay; consequently, it is important for marketing managers to be familiar with the price elasticities of their products in a particular international market.[34]

Prices Higher in the Home Market

Setting prices higher in the home market than in the international market is justified by, among others, one or a combination of the following:

- A lower labor or raw material cost in the international market
- Strong local competition in the international market
- A lower buying power of host-country consumers relative to consumers in the company's home market
- A firm goal to increase market share by using a penetration pricing strategy in the international market, as is most likely in the example offered in Figure 16-2.

Prices Lower in the Home Country

Setting prices lower in the home country, compared to company prices in the international market, is justified, among others, by one or a combination of the following:

- There may be no cost advantages to producing overseas, such as economies of scale and labor to justify a lower price.
- There may be few or no challenges from competition in the international market.
- The market potential might be limited.
- Buyers in the international market can afford the higher price.

One strategy used by multinational firms to penetrate an attractive international market is aggressive export pricing.

16-3b Aggressive Export Pricing

To gain market share and/or to remain competitive in international markets, companies often engage in **aggressive export pricing.** One example of aggressive export pricing is **dynamic incremental pricing,** whereby a company assumes that it will have certain fixed costs whether or not it exports its products overseas; as such, the company does not factor in its international price marketing and pro-

---

Aggressive export pricing
A pricing strategy that prices products below market price in order to penetrate new markets.

Dynamic incremental pricing
A pricing strategy whereby a company assumes that it will have certain fixed costs whether or not it exports its products overseas and does not factor in its international price marketing and promotion costs for domestic distribution, nor its full overhead.

---

33. Hennart, "Some Empirical Dimensions," pp. 243–270.

34. Simon Herman, "Pricing in a Global Setting," *Marketing News,* October 9, 1995, Vol. 29, No. 21, pp. 21–22.

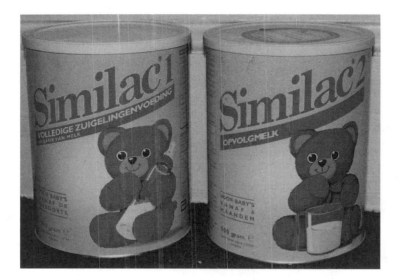

Figure 16-2
In the Netherlands, Similac is made by Abbott Laboratories, where it is sold for about $6, while U.S. consumers of Similac pay more than $22. Why? Only Abbott knows, and the company is not telling. It's no wonder that savvy parents who travel to Holland bring back Dutch Similac for their children rather than pay the U.S. prices.

motion costs for domestic distribution, nor its full overhead.[35] The company allows for the product cost to reflect only the *variable cost* of taking the product abroad (thus using variable-cost pricing), rather than the *full cost* of the product (that is, full-cost pricing). Companies from Japan, Taiwan, and South Korea exporting semiconductor chips to the United States gained high market share rankings using aggressive export pricing.[36]

Exports priced well below fair market value, however, might place the company at risk for dumping challenges. The U.S. Department of Commerce challenged a Japanese company selling active matrix computer screens at 63 percent less than fair value.[37]

16-3c Standardized Pricing Versus Local Pricing

Enormous price differentials exist between countries. Companies charge different prices for their products to meet the needs of consumers and to fit their purchase power and to account for differences in distribution systems, market position, and tax systems; this type of pricing is known as **local pricing**.[38] Even in unified markets such as the European Union, price differentials exist: If a person living in France purchases a car elsewhere, he or she can save 24.3 percent on a Citroën (a French automobile), 18.2 percent on a Peugeot (another French automobile), or 33 percent on a Volkswagen Jetta (a German automobile).[39]

In spite of the obvious advantages of tailoring the price to the budget of the consumer, many companies selling high-end technology products opt for using a **standardized pricing** strategy. IBM, Toshiba, Hewlett-Packard, and Compaq all use a regionally standardized pricing plan.[40] In addition to the cost benefits of standardized pricing, this strategy is also a deterrent to gray market activity; by charging a uniform price worldwide, manufacturers no longer have to deal with parallel imports from a market where the company charges a lower price.

Local pricing A pricing strategy in which different prices are charged in different markets, reflecting differences in consumer purchase power, distribution costs, tax systems, or other market traits.

Standardized pricing A pricing strategy in which the same price is charged for a product regardless of local market conditions.

35. Citrano, "The Right Price," pp. 71–72.

36. Ibid.

37. Ibid.

38. Herman, "Pricing in a Global Setting," pp. 21–22.

39. Ibid.

40. Jack Sweeney, "PC Vendors Bend Pricing for Overseas Customers," *Computer Reseller News,* January 23, 1995, No. 614, p. 3.

Penetration pricing A pricing strategy in which a product is first priced below the price of competitors' products in order to quickly penetrate the market at the competitors' expense and then raised to target levels.

Skimming strategy A pricing strategy in which a product is priced above that of competitors' products, when competition is minimal, to quickly recoup investments; consumers responding to skimming strategies are more concerned with quality, uniqueness, and status, rather than price.

16-3d Penetration Pricing and Skimming Strategies

Multinationals that have sales-based objectives, attempting to gain a high sales volume, are likely to use **penetration pricing.** Firms using this strategy price the product at first below the price of competitors to quickly penetrate the market at competitors' expense. Compaq was able to quickly capture the European market by using this strategy. In the Netherlands, for example, Compaq offered deals unmatched by any brand name competitor and coupled this pricing strategy with excellent warranties and support.

Alternatively, firms may have pricing objectives that are centered on generating a high profit and recovering the costs of product development quickly. Companies thus use a **skimming strategy,** pricing the product above that of competitors, when competition is minimal. In general, consumers responding to skimming strategies are more concerned with quality, uniqueness, and status, rather than price.

Chapter Summary

- **Identify pricing-related internal challenges facing international firms**
Product pricing is partially determined by the location of the production facilities; companies that do not move production to take advantage of low-cost labor are likely to price themselves out of the market. Because products are manufactured in one country, assembled in another, and then modified in yet another country, keeping track of product costs is difficult. Companies need to keep track of costs and ensure that the maximum profitability is achieved.

- **Identify pricing-related challenges imposed by competition on international firms**
Products can face challenges from legitimate competitors; from gray markets, whereby a company's products from a low-priced market are sold through unauthorized channels in a high-priced market, competing with authorized distributors; and from dumping activities of competitors who price their products below cost to gain competitive advantage.

- **Identify pricing-related challenges imposed by the political and legal environment on international firms**
Governments often regulate prices charged by multinationals, thus setting limits on wholesalers' gross margins and on the product's retail price and restricting price promotions. Governments can impose tariffs and other duties, thereby increasing the prices charged by the international firm.

- **Identify pricing-related challenges imposed by the economic and financial environment on international firms**
Multinational companies are facing many challenges; among them are inflationary pressures on price, fluctuating exchange rates, and even the inability of governments to guarantee payment in hard currency. For the latter, a viable solution is countertrade, whereby a company accepts payment in kind, in product output of a company, or in some other format, in return for the products it sells or for setting up operational factories in the respective country.

- **Address international pricing decisions of international firms.**
International firms use different pricing strategies in different markets. They may set prices higher in the home country if they want to penetrate new international markets or if the international markets cannot afford high prices. Or prices may be higher in international markets if those markets can afford it and pricing is in line with competitors' pricing, or if the international markets are not perceived as offering viable long-term opportunities. Companies need to make decisions such as determining whether aggressive export pricing is an appropriate strategy or whether they should use standardized prices throughout or local prices in their target markets.

Discussion Questions

1. What are gray markets? How do distributors using parallel imports affect a multinational firm's operations in the target market?

2. What is dumping? Why do international companies use dumping strategies in select target markets?

3. Countertrade helps a company do business in markets that otherwise would be inaccessible. What are the different approaches to countertrade that a manufacturer of telecommunications equipment could use in order to penetrate such markets?

4. What are the different motivations behind a company setting prices higher or lower in the home country?

International Marketing Strategy: Implementation

Chapter 17
Organizing and Controlling
International Marketing
Operations and Developing
an International Marketing
Plan

Organizing and Controlling International Marketing Operations and Developing an International Marketing Plan

Key Terms

formal controls
informal controls
international division structure
matrix structure
organizational design

organizational structure
performance standards
product division structure
worldwide regional division
   structure

Outline

Learning Objectives
17-1 Organizing for
   International Marketing
   Operations
   17-1a Factors in the Firm's
     Environment
   17-1b Factors within the Firm
17-2 Examining International
   Organizational Designs
   17-2a The International
     Division Structure
   17-2b The Worldwide Regional
     Division Structure
   17-2c The Product Division
     Structure
   17-2d The Matrix Structure
17-3 Controlling International
   Marketing Operations
   17-3a Formal Controls
   17-3b Informal Controls
17-4 Devising the International
   Marketing Plan
   17-4a Company and Country
     Background
   17-4b Environmental Analysis
   17-4c International Marketing
     Mix Decisions
   17-4d Establishing Methods for
     Control of the
     International Operation
Chapter Summary
Discussion Questions

Learning Objectives

Learning Objectives

By the end of this chapter, you should be able to:

- Identify the factors in a firm's external and internal environment that determine the organizational design best suited for international operations

- Describe different organizational designs and offer examples of designs that different international firms have adopted

- Identify formal and informal controls necessary to ensure that company operations are in line with company goals and objectives as stated in the strategic plan

- Provide a blueprint for a company's country-specific marketing plan

---

Multinational companies today are confronted with aggressive competition for markets worldwide. To meet the challenges of intensifying competition, multinationals have been forced to alter their organizational structures and to adapt their standards to the new environment, aligning executive compensation with the companies' new goals.

Ford, responding to rapid changes in the global economy, implemented a major reorganization, ending competing regional fiefdoms by consolidating engineering, design, and development within new global divisions. Motorola, faced with aggressive Asian competitors and falling profits, adopted a similar plan, replacing decentralized and competing businesses with three distinct global groups focusing on retail customers such as cell-phone users, telecommunications companies, and government and industrial clients. Procter & Gamble initiated the broadest overhaul in its industry, transforming four business units based on geographic regions into seven global entities based on product lines such as Baby Care or Food & Beverage.[1]

This chapter addresses the process of organizing for international marketing and controlling international operations, offering examples of organizational structures of firms worldwide. It also provides a blueprint for a country-specific international plan.

---

1. Jeffrey E. Garten, "Cutting Fat Won't Be Enough to Survive This Crisis," *Business Week,* November 9, 1998, No. 3603, p. 26.

17-1 Organizing for International Marketing Operations

Firms need to consider organizational designs that fit with their external environment and with company characteristics and goals. Organizational design is determined by numerous factors in the firms' operating environments, as described in sections 17-1a and 17-1b.

17-1a Factors in the Firm's Environment

Competitive Environment

In environments characterized by intense competition, where decisions must be made quickly to counter competitive moves, a decentralized organization would allow for the most immediate reaction.

Environmental Stability

Countries characterized by unstable political environments or countries where government policies are unstable, countries that are characterized by high inflation and high unemployment, and countries with unstable currency require companies to adapt quickly to the changing environment. Such companies need to be able to take immediate action to adapt to the new environments and need an **organizational structure** that allows them to react quickly.

Organizational structure
The outcome of the organization of reporting and coordination within a company.

Environmental Similarity with the Home Country

Companies operating in countries that are similar to their home country are likely to use similar strategies; these companies would opt for an organization that integrates operations between the home and host countries.

Common Regional Traits and/or Regional Integration

Companies can organize their operations with a regional focus in countries that share language, religion, or other cultural similarities; countries that share a border; or countries that are members of a regional alliance.

Availability of Local Qualified Labor

Companies operating in countries that have ample educated and qualified labor will delegate more control to local operations and have organizational structures that allow for more local control.

17-1b Factors within the Firm

Organizational design also is determined by company traits. A firm that considers internationalization a priority is likely to have an organizational structure with regional divisions in charge of particular countries. Other organizations involved in international business might have only an international division that oversees international operations. Companies that are only minimally involved in international business might have only a small international department.

Companies are likely to maintain their organizational structure when they go international. An organization that is hierarchical and centralized is likely to have a centralized international organization. An organization structured based on product lines is also likely to maintain this structure for its international operations.

17-2 Examining International Organizational Designs

Multinational companies use four types of formal structures in their international **organizational designs:** international divisions, worldwide regional divisions, product divisions, and the matrix structure.

Organizational design
The organization of reporting and coordination within a company.

17-2a The International Division Structure

Firms with an **international division structure** have two main divisions: the domestic division and the international division. When firms become involved in international business by exporting products overseas, they typically assign responsibility for all international operations to an export department. As their international involvement increases, they will most likely have an international division in charge of all their international operations. These firms are still primarily focused on domestic operations, but their international operations have an important standing, at the same level with all other divisions. In an international division structure, all foreign subsidiaries report directly to a single division responsible for international operations, which is separate from domestic operations.

International division structure
An organizational structure whereby firms have separate domestic and international divisions.

17-2b The Worldwide Regional Division Structure

A worldwide regional division structures operations either by geographical region or by country. Under this model, subsidiaries report directly to the single division responsible for operations in the country or geographic region. Although this structure allows for some duplication of activities and thus might increase costs, managers consider this organization to be very effective in creating competitive advantage for the firms.[2] A particular advantage of the **worldwide regional division structure** is that it is better equipped to immediately process and respond to country-specific information and conditions than other formal structures—at some cost to product-related information—because of its strong regional focus.[3]

Frito-Lay, one of the three companies of the PepsiCo family, has a worldwide regional division structure. The Frito-Lay Company, headquartered in the United States, oversees all the functional areas, i.e., marketing, manufacturing, research and development, finance, etc. The regional divisions—Frito-Lay North America, headquartered in the United States; Frito-Lay Europe/Africa/Middle East, headquartered in Geneva, Switzerland; and Frito-Lay Latin America/Asia Pacific/Australia—oversee all regional operations, country subsidiaries, and offices (see Figure 17-1).

This type of structure is helpful for firms that have similar congruent product lines, such as Frito-Lay, or for services. The Guggenheim museum also has this type of structure, with the Guggenheim New York (the main museum and Guggenheim Soho), Guggenheim Venice (Italy), Guggenheim Bilbao (Spain), Guggenheim Berlin (Germany), and the Guggenheim Virtual Museum, an on-line museum for virtual exhibitions and artists' projects.

Worldwide regional division structure An organizational structure whereby operations are organized by region or by country, and where subsidiaries report directly to the single division responsible for operations in the country or geographic region.

17-2c The Product Division Structure

In a regional or worldwide **product division structure,** subsidiaries report to the product division (strategic business unit) with responsibility for the particular

Product division structure
An organizational structure whereby subsidiaries report to the product division (strategic business unit) with responsibility for the particular products.

2. Allen J. Morrison, David A. Ricks, and Kendall Roth, "Globalization Versus Regionalization: Which Way for the Multinational?" *Organizational Dynamics*, Winter 1991, Vol. 19, No. 3, pp. 17–29.

3. Bruce T. Lamont, V. Sambamurthy, Kimberly M. Ellis, and Paul G. Simmonds, "The Influence of Organizational Structure on the Information Received by Corporate Strategists of Multinational Enterprises," *Management International Review*, Third Quarter 2000, Vol. 40, No. 3, pp. 231–252.

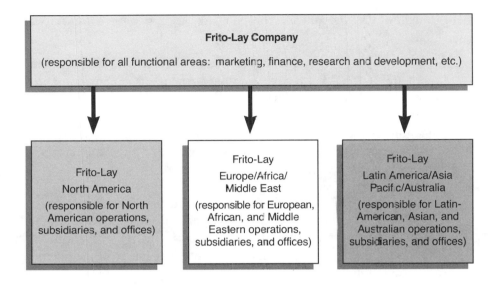

Figure 17-1
Worldwide regional division structure: Frito-Lay.

products. In the past, this structure was common for high-tech companies or multinational companies with diversified portfolios. However, increasingly, this format is replaced by the matrix structure. Even companies that once were identified as typical examples of the product division structure, such as Sun Microsystems and Whirlpool, have adopted a matrix structure.

17-2d The Matrix Structure

The **matrix structure** takes into account the multiple dimensions involved in doing business internationally—functional areas, product, and region/country. In a matrix structure, two dimensions are integrated such that each operational unit reports to both region/country managers and product managers.

Many large multinationals have had a matrix structure for decades—among them Philips Electronics, Unilever, Electrolux, IBM, Texas Instruments, and Procter & Gamble. And, in recent years, many more multinationals have adopted this organizational structure—among them, BASF, Disney, and Rockwell International. This type of format works especially well for firms that have global brands as well as local brands; such companies need to coordinate marketing activities worldwide involving the global brands and need to focus on the local market for the local brands.

Unilever's matrix structure is organized based on products (Home and Personal Care Products and Bestfoods products) and on regions around the world. Its divisions are Home & Personal Care, Africa, Middle East & Turkey; Home & Personal Care, Asia; Home & Personal Care, Europe; Home & Personal Care, North America/Latin America; Unilever Bestfoods Africa, Middle East & Turkey; Foodservice; Ice Cream and Frozen Foods; Latin America & Slim.fast worldwide; Unilever Bestfoods, Asia; Unilever Bestfoods, Europe; and Unilever Bestfoods, North America.[4]

Matrix structure
An organizational structure whereby each operational unit reports to both region/country managers and product managers.

17-3 Controlling International Marketing Operations

Controls are necessary to ensure that international company operations are in line with company goals and objectives, as stated in the company's strategic plan. Yet, controlling international operations and ensuring that performance standards are

4. www.Unilever.com

met throughout the company is a complex task. Adding to the complexity are the following:

- Local units and a regional focus often add intermediate levels of management and staffing that further complicate the management, communication, and evaluation processes.
- Multinational companies are likely to have subsidiaries and branch offices in countries where the external environment is changing at different rates, having a different impact on company operations; thus, standards and measures instituted for evaluation purposes are often not comparable across countries.
- Given the distance of subsidiaries from headquarters, there is a tendency to resist influence in both directions, such that subsidiaries often fight to retain autonomy in decision making and performance evaluation, while the headquarters may resist input from the subsidiaries in the planning and evaluation process.

Difficulties imposed by the complexity of the international management context can, to a certain extent, be offset by instituting the appropriate formal and informal controls.

17-3a Formal Controls

Instituting **formal controls** involves the following process:

- Establishing performance standards
- Measuring performance
- Addressing discrepancies

Establishing Performance Standards

The first step in establishing formal controls involves establishing **performance standards** in light of the company's projected market potential. Parameters must be developed in the strategic plan for evaluating dimensions of the external environment for the purpose of setting standards based on that potential. The evaluation must include a continuous assessment of competitive intensity (local and international competitors in the market), political stability, developments in the economy, regional and local trade, and other developments that directly affect company performance. In many emerging economies, currencies have fluctuated widely over the past few years, and many of these economies have seen major political overhauls; hence, it is difficult to accurately measure outcomes and evaluate managerial performance. Moreover, postprivatization restructuring may take a long time to complete and may produce soft outcomes, so outcome measurability becomes problematic, thereby complicating management evaluation.[5]

Measuring Performance

Actual performance is measured based on established standards. At this point, measures such as sales, profit, and market share are assessed for the target market in a particular country or region and measured against previous performance and/or against competitors. These assessments are compared with company goals and objectives for the target market as expressed in the company plan.

Formal controls Systematic controls, such as performance standards and measurement, used in international marketing to ensure that international company operations are in line with company goals and objectives.

Performance standards A priori measures against which firm performance is evaluated.

---

5. Ravi Dharwadkar, Gerard George, and Pamela Brandes, "Privatization in Emerging Economies: An Agency Theory Perspective," *Academy of Management: The Academy of Management Review,* July 2000, Vol. 25, No. 3, pp. 650–669.

Addressing Discrepancies

At the final stage of this process, discrepancies between standards and performance are corrected. If the standards were unreasonable or were not reached due to unanticipated changes in the external environment, they will be adjusted accordingly for the next assessment period. Lessons from the company's experience in other parts of the world and lessons learned from other companies' experiences are useful at this stage. For example, studies have found that the performance of European and Japanese multinationals is positively correlated with corporate policies emphasizing innovation and globally standard product designs with local adaptation.[6] A company that may be very keen on a standardized international product strategy may benefit from adapting its offer to suit local preferences. The company may also need to offer more innovative products to the target market. Both the local adaptation strategy and the focus on innovation need to be coordinated with the headquarters; in fact, for many firms, innovation takes place at the company's national headquarters—although, for example, companies such as Procter & Gamble have multiple (18) innovation centers around the world.[7]

17-3b Informal Controls

In addition to the formal controls described in section 17-3a, companies also can use **informal controls** to ensure that there is a fit between the standards and actual performance. The following are examples of informal controls a company can use:

Informal controls Systematic controls, such as dialogue between the headquarters and the international field operations, used in international marketing to ensure that international company operations are in line with company goals and objectives.

- Establishing frequent contact between the home-country headquarters and the regional and/or local office. Such contact serves as a means to better coordinate activities and ensure clear communication of expectations in both directions.
- Rotating managers to different assignments to obtain the maximum benefit from international experience. One often-used strategy is to hire third-country managers (from a country other than the home or the host country) to oversee new or problematic operations; these individuals have the flexibility and experience but not the biases that association with the home or host country of the company would create. In general, moving expatriates from one subsidiary to another will offer valuable exchange in information to be used as input into the control function.
- Training the employees and inculcating a management culture that is consistent with company goals and objectives. Management development training can be used to share the mission and objectives of the company expressed in the relevant performance terms. For example, a company can focus on company growth or profitability objectives, on innovation, on the relationship with the target customer, or on any other dimension that the company deems important.

17-4 Devising the International Marketing Plan

When the decisions regarding controls are in place, the company can place the international marketing strategy and the marketing plan, described in Chapter 8, "The International Marketing Plan and Entry Mode Selection," in motion. Whereas Chapter 8 focused on the activities involved in international market planning in general, sections 17-4a through 17-4d will provide a blueprint for the

---

6. Masaaki Kotabe, *Global Sourcing Strategy: R&D, Manufacturing, and Marketing,* Quorom Books, 1992.

7. *Annual Report, Procter & Gamble,* 2000.

plan, outlining the activities involved at each step. The points outlined in this blueprint are general and should be adapted based on the information available and based on the industry and on country conditions. The steps involved in developing a country-specific marketing plan also are illustrated in Figure 17-2.

17-4a Company and Country Background

As a first step, the marketing plan should include a brief company background, with a focus on the product that will be marketed internationally and the country where the product will be introduced. (See further details on this step in Figure 17-2.)

17-4b Environmental Analysis

In the second step, the local and regional environment must be assessed to evaluate the country and target market attractiveness. At this stage, the local economy and the trade, political, and legal infrastructures will be evaluated to determine the extent to which investing in the country constitutes a sound decision. The social-cultural environment also will be assessed to identify the most viable marketing strategy to use in the respective country. Finally, the competitive environment will be examined; here, the competitive intensity (local and international) and the existing and potential barriers to entry imposed by the competition will be evaluated to determine the resources needed for market penetration. (See further details about the economic and trade analysis, political and legal analysis, socio-cultural analysis, and target market and competitive analysis in Figure 17-2.)

17-4c International Marketing Mix Decisions

In the third step, international marketing mix decisions will address product, price, promotion, and distribution strategies that will be used for entering the international target market and the controls needed to evaluate marketing performance. These decisions will make up the overall marketing plan, which is further described in Figure 17-2.

17-4d Establishing Methods for Control of the International Operation

At the final step, the company will set performance standards and related controls to ensure that performance is in line with market potential given the country-specific operating environment. (Read about the implementation and control step in Figure 17-2.)

Step 1: Company and Country Background

- Brief profile of the company
- Brief product profile
- Brief country background
- Rationale for introducing the product in the respective country

Step 2: Environmental Analysis (A)

A. Economic and Trade Analysis

- Population statistics and relevance of demographics to company plans
- Economic development statistics (GNP, GDP, economic growth) and relevance to company plans
- Overview of industrial and agricultural sectors, national resources, and labor
- Analysis of transportation and telecommunication infrastructure
- General analysis of the marketing support infrastructure:
  - ° distribution and logistics
  - ° promotion infrastructure
  - ° marketing research suppliers
- Trade trends
  - ° membership in regional and international trade organizations
  - ° trade patterns (imports, exports, foreign direct investment) and rate of growth
  - ° barriers to trade

Step 2: Environmental Analysis (B)

B. Political and Legal Analysis

- Political stability
  - ° legitimacy of political elite
  - ° diversity of ethnic groups with divergent interests
  - ° degree of political repression
  - ° nationalism
  - ° stability of government policies
- Type of legal system (code law, common law, Islamic law)
- Transparency of the legal system
- Degree of ambiguity of commercial laws
- Degree to which laws are followed and enforced

Step 2: Environmental Analysis (C)

C. Socio-Cultural Analysis

- Languages and dialects and implications for marketing
- Social institutions and implications for the company
  - ° family
  - ° social class
  - ° social status
  - ° groups and group dynamics
- Religion, norms, and value systems and marketing implications

Step 2: Environmental Analysis (D)

D. Target Market and Competitive Analysis

- Target consumer analysis (product use, shopping behavior)
- Existing distribution patterns for product category and availability of local distributors (wholesalers, retailers, logistics companies)
- Existing promotion patterns for product category and availability of local promotion talent and media
- Degree of competitive intensity
- Competitor marketing strategies
- Competitive barriers

Step 3: The Marketing Plan

- Set marketing objectives (express objectives in terms of sales, profit, and market share) based on corporate goals and objectives and market potential
- Product decisions
  - ° decisions on standardization vs. adaptation
  - ° product mix decisions (short and long term) for the target market
- Promotion decisions
  - ° advertising objectives
  - ° media decisions
  - ° message decisions
- Distribution decisions
  - ° use existing channels or build own distribution
  - ° decisions on wholesalers, retailers, warehousing, logistics firms
  - ° logistics decisions (intermodal transportation, freight forwarders, customs brokers, insurance agents, other facilitators)
- Pricing decisions
  - ° Identify local market traits and needs and product cost
  - ° Develop international marketing budget based on cost
  - ° Identify human and capital resources needed for local operations

Step 4: Implementation and Control

- Establish standards for operation in light of market potential
- Measure performance in light of standards
- Address discrepancies

Figure 17-2
The international marketing plan.

Chapter Summary

- **Identify the factors in a firm's external and internal environment that determine the organizational design best suited for international operations**

  Organizational design is determined externally by the competitive environment: Intense competition requires a company to react quickly, and it can do so effectively if it has a decentralized structure. Companies operating in environments plagued by high inflation, unemployment, and political instability must be organized to be able to react quickly to changes. Multinational companies are likely to have similar operating structures to those in their home country if the countries where they operate are culturally similar to their own country. Companies that have competent, educated, local employees are likely to delegate more control to local operations. Companies that operate in a region with common traits, or within a regional bloc, will most likely organize the company with a regional focus. Firm traits such as degree of focus on international operations or its organization in the home country also have an impact on organizational structure.

- **Describe different organizational designs and offer examples of designs that different international firms have adopted**

  There are four organizational designs for international operations: the international division structure, for firms with limited international involvement that are likely to have an export department; firms with a worldwide regional division structure, which operate either by region or by country; firms with a product division structure, where subsidiaries report to the product division with responsibility for the respective product; and firms with a matrix structure, which combine functional areas, product, and region in their organization.

- **Identify formal and informal controls necessary to ensure that company operations are in line with company goals and objectives as stated in the strategic plan**

  Formal controls involve establishing performance standards, measuring performance, and addressing discrepancies by either changing the standards to correct for differences in market traits, or changing executive compensation to reflect firm priorities. Informal controls involve maintaining contact between headquarters and international operations, rotating managers to share experience with new operations, and appropriately indoctrinating new employees in the company's culture.

- **Provide a blueprint for a company's country-specific marketing plan**

  A blueprint is provided in section 17-4 as a guide for setting up international operations.

Discussion Questions

1. List the factors that influence organizational design. Describe how each factor influences the design.
2. Compare the international division structure and the regional division structure. What would make a company move from an international division structure to a regional division structure?
3. How does the matrix structure differ from the other three organizational structures? Explain.
4. Discuss the formal and informal controls used to ensure that international marketing operations are in line with company goals and objectives.

Appendix

Appendix

The eight cases within this Appendix were developed to provide illustrations of international marketing practice for the course material. A number of the cases were first outlined by students in conjunction with the textbook author and, subsequently, the author went to the different businesses to interview company representatives. The textbook author interviewed company representatives and former employees at Munich Re and Siemens, in Germany; at Campina and Philips, in the Netherlands; and at the Hilton Sorrento Palace, in Italy. She also visited Disneyland Paris, in France, in order to prepare the case.

Each case illustrates one particular aspect of international marketing: international portfolio decisions and entry modes (Siemens), marketing mix decisions in times of political uncertainty (Munich Re), international product mix strategies (Campina and BMW), competitive strategies in the face of growing international competition (AvtoVAZ), and strategies aimed at changing target markets (Hilton Sorrento Palace). At the end of each case are suggestions that will guide students in their analyses.

Munich Re

Jodie Applegate, Kristin DeYonker, Andrea Fuller,
Dana Lascu, Brian Stroop, Elise Woodling

Case Outline

A-1 Background
A-2 The Reinsurance Industry
A-3 Munich Re
A-4 The Munich Re Product
A-5 The September 11 Terrorist
     Attacks
A-6 Changing the Marketing
     Mix at Munich Re
Analysis Suggestions
Notes

A-1 Background

On September 11, 2001, apocalyptic images from the World Trade Center and the Pentagon inundated broadcast and print media around the world. The events of 9/11 marked the beginning of new levels of vulnerability for businesses, for national and local governments, for the airlines, and for individuals. The insurance and reinsurance industries experienced the largest aggregate losses ever as a result of the attacks. Half a world away, in Munich, Germany, the world's largest reinsurance company, Munich Re (in German, Münchener Rück), suffered a loss of $1.84 billion as a result of the terrorist attacks on U.S. soil.[1] In an effort to adapt to the new, post-September 11, business environment and its new challenges, the insurance and reinsurance firms were forced to change their entire marketing mix. One company that is undergoing a complete overhaul of its marketing strategy is Munich Re.

A-2 The Reinsurance Industry

Insurance firms rely on reinsurance firms to minimize losses, allowing for costs attributed to insurance losses to be distributed among multiple companies; the reinsurance industry makes it possible for insurance companies to take risks that they would not otherwise,[2] creating new opportunities for increased revenue and market share. The amount of risk assumed by reinsurers varies with the market. When the market is optimistic, reinsurers are more likely to assume greater risks; more capital is available, so the companies are capable of underwriting additional risk.[3] In 2001, the faltering state of markets worldwide depleted the reinsurance companies' capital; reinsurance companies were further confronted by the implications of the September 11, 2001, terrorist attacks. As a result, the reinsurance industry is exploring the different ways in which it can alter the mix of products offered to insurance firms all over the world and their pricing strategies to most effectively operate in the present volatile environment.

A-3 Munich Re

Munich Re was founded in 1880 by Carl Thieme, who, with a vision far ahead of his time, created the reinsurance business: He convinced investors of the insurance companies' need for reinsurance as a means for redistributing risk (and loss) among insurance firms, thus allowing them to take advantage of opportunities that otherwise they could not afford to consider.[4] Munich Re is headquartered in downtown Munich, Germany, where it covers a couple of square blocks with impressive older and contemporary architecture. In front of its newest building, the tall figure of the Walking Man, by American artist Jonathan Borofsky, appears to leave the complex in a hurry (see photograph).

Inside the Munich Re complex, a Japanese garden offers an environment of meditation. Underground, all the buildings are connected with active corridors where color and light set a theatric stage; here, a second "downtown"—the downtown of Munich Re employees—exists in parallel to the bustling street, Leopoldstrasse. The environment projects a strong spirit of innovation, the very theme of Munich Re's corporate culture.[5] In addition to its quest for product innovation, Munich Re was the first German company to introduce English working hours in the nineteenth century, requiring shorter days from its employees and granting them greater leisure time; the company is also among a few in Germany that provide benefits such as access to a holiday home in the Alps and an on-site daycare—the Munich Re Giants Childcare Center.[6]

The Munich Re
Headquarters
in Munich, Germany.

A-4 The Munich Re Product

With a dependable brand, international presence, and diversified product offering and forty-two offices around the world, Munich Re has attracted customers and investors alike, and today it remains the largest reinsurance company in the world. The company offers several different types of insurance services, such as Alternative Risk-Financing and Risk-Transfer Solutions (ART), Agricultural Insurance, Managed Care Services, and Life Insurance. ART, including Finite Risk Reinsurance and Integrated Risk Management, supplements conventional reinsurance as a means of maximizing risk retention and discovering additional financial resources. This is an area that Munich Re has pioneered and that is especially in great demand today, after the September 11 events. Finite Risk Reinsurance allows the company to undertake more risk by using innovative financing techniques, rather than simply by transferring risk from the insured to the insurer.

Integrated Risk Management merges insurance risks with the risks involved in financial markets—for example, in currency fluctuation and in fluctuating interest rates. The objective of Integrated Risk Management is to achieve both the reinsurer's goals of the lowest possible risk and the client's goals of highest possible security and support.

Munich Re provides a number of other insurance services, covering all aspects of the economy. For example, Agricultural Insurance is a service that Munich Re has developed to protect commercial farmers in times of catastrophe and natural disaster. Its Managed Care Services, part of the Munich Re Health Division, are involved in evaluating each potential medical procedure that it insures to determine if, in fact, the procedure is essential. Finally, the company's Life Insurance services give the company access to final consumers—a different market than its traditional business-to-business market segments (its organizational consumers).

A-5 The September 11 Terrorist Attacks

Munich Re, much like other reinsurance companies, has had numerous challenges, many dealing with medical advances and genetics decoding, and others with natural disasters. More recently, Munich Re had to absorb the costs involved in the recall of Lipobay, a cholesterol-reducing drug that was linked to death among users; a large typhoon in Taiwan; and a chemical plant explosion in France.[7] Yet these losses were dwarfed by the September 11, 2001, terrorist attacks, when terrorists crashed passenger airplanes demolishing the World Trade Center in New York and severely damaging the Pentagon in Washington, D.C. Total estimates for damages were between $10 and $12 billion; in addition to property costs and life insurance coverage, the insurance industry had to bear the costs for clean-up, replacement of items lost, and an array of other losses.[8] Original estimates were low, but by mid-September the major players of the reinsurance industry alone were expecting claims to total more than $3 billion for the disaster.[9] Munich Re's claims totaled $1.84 billion.[10]

Before September 11, 2001, terrorist attacks of this magnitude were inconceivable and were not considered in the calculations of premiums and the like. According to P. J. Crowley of the Insurance Institute of America, "There has never been a premium dollar collected to cover terrorism."[11] Reinsurance firms had to reconsider their stance on what coverage they would offer in the event of future terrorist attacks. For now, many insurance and reinsurance companies have included clauses in their policies that exclude the coverage of losses from any type of terrorism. Munich Re "was hit by the claims from September 11th more than other members of the reinsurance industry and thus it will have to make careful decisions concerning what to do about providing protection against terrorist claims in the future."[12]

Reinsurance companies consider four primary criteria of general risk insurability:

- Assessibility; most of the reinsurance companies have been lax in the past about ensuring that insurance companies have a clear (transparent) assessment of potential risk.
- Randomness
- Mutuality
- Economic feasibility

After evaluating these risks, only a handful of companies have opted to provide terrorism risk coverage; however, if national governments agree to subsidize the industry, it is likely that more will join. These companies are

- **General Cologne Reinsurance** (General Re); the company owns General Reinsurance Corporation, the market leader in the United States. General Re alone lost $1.7 billion from the September 11 attacks, but, for now, it continues to cover terrorist actions (although this might change in the future).
- **Swiss Re,** a challenger to Munich Re as the number-one reinsurance firm worldwide, has also experienced substantial losses.
- **Copenhagen Re,** once a large and active player in the reinsurance business and a major competitor of Munich Re, has ceased underwriting for two years as a consequence of the attacks and, as a result, has lost consumer confidence.

A-6 Changing the Marketing Mix at Munich Re

Compared to competition, Munich Re has handled the aftermath of September 11 well. After the attacks, insurance and reinsurance companies were reevaluated by A.M. Best and Standard & Poor's to assess the appropriateness of rating that had been determined before September 11. Both raters agreed that their ratings of A++ and AAA/Stable, respectively, were still appropriate for Munich Re, based on the company's performance by the end of 2001.[13] Although the company had considerable losses, Munich Re reported an increase in premium income by 20 percent from the year 2000. Also, in the wake of claims payout from the terrorist attacks, Munich Re found itself with less competition in the reinsurance industry as a number of smaller reinsurers had losses attributed to the September 11 attacks that caused them to leave the industry altogether.[14]

No reinsurance company had ever considered terrorist actions of such magnitude when calculating Probable Maximum Loss (PML) for the properties insured. Insurance companies had to cover losses of more than 1,200 corporations housed in the World Trade Center complex, damage to the operating areas, loss of experienced employees, and destruction of business data and business income. More than fifty buildings were affected in addition to the World Trade Center and 150,000 people were out of work permanently or temporarily.[15] These extreme circumstances led the reinsurance companies to change their marketing mix—especially the reinsurance product and its price.

According to Nicholas Roenneberg, senior executive manager, corporate underwriting/global clients division at Munich Re, if such a catastrophe were to happen, it did so at an opportune time for the company—when the company was renewing its policies for the year 2002 (most policies start at the beginning of the calendar year). At that point, the company placed all policy negotiations on hold so that it could reconfigure its marketing mix.

For the short term, Munich Re determined that terrorism was no longer insurable, given the high risks especially in high property concentrations. In these environments, it is impossible to estimate the frequency of such attacks and their total impact, thus presenting a situation in which an important criterion of general risk insurability, assessibility, cannot be met. In the long term, however, there may be some custom options for insurance for properties evaluated at more than 50 million Euros (less than $50 million), on a case-by-case basis. Ultimately, all types of insurance options may be subject to negotiation. No terrorism exclusion, however, is imposed on life and personal accident insurance.

After the events of September 11, companies doing business with Munich Re were required to document all risks—many companies had not diligently met this requirement in the past. Transparency has become a most important criterion of insurability for Munich Re clients.

In terms of price, the company raised rates for aviation insurance by 80 percent; coincidentally, and to the advantage of Munich Re, aviation renewals were due on October 1, 2001, just after the September terrorist attacks. For property insurance, rates have gone up by 20 to 40 percent across the board.

With regard to promotion, the company has not changed its strategy substantially: It offers no advertising, no sponsorship. One of its main venues for communicating beyond its customer base is its web site, which is comprehensive and well updated. Just after the September 11 attacks, the company undertook a tremendous public relations effort to inform shareholders about the impact of the attacks on the company's bottom line. The company increased the frequency of communication, particularly with large institutional investors; a preferred venue for such communication was telephone conferencing.

According to Christian Lahnstein, a specialist in genetic engineering law and liability law with Munich Re, there is an interest in the industry to learn from the experience of the September 11, 2001, events about the intervention of government in bailing out industries affected by disaster and about issues related to the equity of distribution of funds from the government and charitable sources. These findings may have an impact on the marketing mix of the company in the future.

Analysis Suggestions

1. Before analyzing the Munich Re case, address the political risk signals that brought about the September 11, 2001, terrorist actions. How can companies reduce their likelihood of becoming victims of terrorism?

2. As you conduct your case analysis, address the strategic changes to each element of the marketing mix at Munich Re as a result of the September 11 terrorist attacks.

Notes

1. "Munich Re Costs $1.1B Loss," CNN.com Europe, http://europe.cnn.com/, November 29, 2001, p. 1 (web); February 21, 2002.
2. "What Exactly Does a Reinsurer Do?" *Jobs and Career,* Munich Re, http://www.munichre.com/index.html, February 25, 2002, p. 1 (web).
3. "Finance and Economics: Premium Rates; Reinsurance," *The Economist,* February 9, 2002. p. 79.
4. "Profit Through Pioneering Spirit," *History,* Munich Re, http://www.munichre.com/index.html, February 24, 2002, p. 1 (web).
5. "Corporate Responsibility," *120 Years of Innovation,* Munich Re, http://www.munichre.com/index.html, February 24, 2002, p. 1 (web).
6. Ibid.
7. "Reinsurer Munich Re Posts US $1.06B Loss, Keeps Damage Estimates from Attacks," *Canoe Money,* http://www.canoe.ca/MoneyEarnings/nov29_munichre-ap.html, November 29, 2001, pp. 1–2 (web); February 21, 2002.
8. "11th September 2001," *Munchener Ruckversicherungs-Gesellschaft,* 2001, p. 9.
9. "Reinsurers Double Terrorist Claims," *CNN Money,* http://money.cnn.com/2001/09/20/europe/insurance/index.htm, September 20, 2001, p. 1 (web); February 21, 2002.
10. "Munich Re Posts $1.1B Loss," http://europe.cnn.com/.
11. Dan Ackman, "Insurers Make a Claim on Taxpayers," Forbes.com, http://www.forbes.com/, October 22, 2001, p. 1 (web); February 21, 2002.
12. Deborah Orr, "Risk Buster," Forbes.com, http://www.forbes.com/, January 21, 2002, pp. 1–2 (web); February 21, 2002.
13. "After the Terrorist Attacks: US Rating Agencies Affirm their Top Rating for Munich Re," *Munich American News,* http://www.marclife.com/news01/mr100501.htm, October 5, 2001, p. 1 (web); February 21, 2002.
14. "Reinsurer Munich Re Posts US $1.06B Loss, Keeps Damage Estimate from Attacks," p. 2 (web).
15. "11th September 2001: The Attack on the World Trade Center in New York from an Insurance Point of View," p. 2 (web).

Bavarian Motor Works: Diversifying a Prestige Brand

Matt Crumley, Dana Lascu, Lisa Myers, Pascal Ontijd, Taylor Roberts, Kerrie Robinson, Sean Wygovsky

Case Outline

B-1 The Automobile Industry

B-2 The Company

B-3 Communicating Excellence at BMW

B-4 The BMW Driver

B-5 All Things BMW

B-6 Competition within the Luxury Automobile Segment

B-7 Targeting to Lower-Price Segments: The MINI and the Certified Pre-Owned BMWs

Analysis Suggestions

Notes

B avarian Motor Works (BMW) is a leading global manufacturer of luxury automobiles. A high-priced, high-performance automobile, the BMW has long been a status product for consumers worldwide. The "Beemer" for consumers in the United States, the "BMW" (pronounced *Beh Em Veh*) for most consumers in continental Europe, this automobile is a legend of style and class. One of BMW's greatest challenges is retaining its leadership position in the luxury automobile market—a challenge that has been recently compounded by the company's decision to diversify into the lower-priced automobile market. Recently, in one of its most daring moves, BMW successfully launched the MINI—a very non–BMW-like automobile, the progeny of BMW's ill-fated relationship with the British Rover group, known as the most beloved British car.

B-1 The Automobile Industry

The boom in the global economy in the late 1990s, coupled with increased consumer confidence, led to high growth in the automobile industry. Vehicle manufacturers were under pressure as never before to increase production, and the globalization of the industry posed further challenges with long-term structural changes for the industry:

1. Mergers and other strategic alliances led to a diminishing pool of independent manufacturers left in the industry.[1] Ford and DaimlerChrysler are likely to acquire additional companies, leading to the projection that by 2005, there will be fewer than ten international players in the automobile market.[2]

2. The Internet is also changing many aspects of the automobile industry. Consumers increasingly use it to research features, specifications, styles, and designs of numerous makes and models. Most importantly, consumers can use independent sources to precisely assess dealer profit and bargain successfully on price, adding to the downward pressure on price the industry is experiencing. In addition, many web sites offer detailed information about specific models, and it is predicted that consumers will be able to circumvent dealerships and order automobiles from manufacturers via the Internet.[3] According to J.D. Power and Associates, 62 percent of new automobile buyers surveyed in 2001 in the United States logged on to the Internet for information on their prospective purchases.[4]

3. Another structural change in the industry is attributed to the evolving technology. The industry has seen substantial growth in "telematics"—the technologies that keep drivers connected to electronic networks.[5]

4. Finally, there is a rising trend of automakers establishing a niche in the marketplace. These automakers are relying on new categories of vehicles that will expand the overall market. Chrysler's new design, the PT Cruiser sedan, has proven to be especially popular, with demand exceeding supply.[6]

In the United States alone, sales of new cars and light trucks reached a record level of 17.4 million units in 2000—an increase of 500,000 units over the previous year's sales of 16.9 million automobiles.[7] The U.S. automobile market is the largest in the world for passenger vehicles.[8] However, with the downturn of the economy in 2001, sales volume fell 2.5 percent, to 16.92 million vehicles.[9] Globally, sales of new vehicles worldwide have also been projected to grow from 50.6 million units in 1998 to 57.2 million in 2005.[10] In Europe, automobile sales for 2001 surpassed the 14.7 million units recorded in 2000.[11]

BMW Headquarters
in Munich.

B-2 The Company

Karl Rapp created BMW in 1913 as an aircraft engine design shop just outside Munich, the capital of the state of Bavaria, Germany. The name of the shop was Bayerische Motoren Werke (Bavarian Motor Works). At the end of World War I, German aircraft production declined drastically, and the company began producing railway brakes. BMW made its first motorcycle in 1923, and the company began making automobiles in 1928 after purchasing a small automobile manufacturing company. Larger automobiles were added to the product line in 1933 and, in 1941, the company stopped automobile production to produce aircraft for the German air force. Following World War II, the production of automobiles and motorcycles resumed. Over the remainder of the decade, the company expanded through acquisitions and, in 1986, it began producing luxury vehicles. Sales rose and, in 1992, BMW outsold Mercedes in Europe for the first time ever.[12]

Currently, the BMW headquarters constitute a Munich landmark, reigning in its imposing three-cylinder building just outside the Middle Ring (the Middle Beltway) as the city's tallest structure. See photograph.

BMW Group products are currently in greater demand worldwide than ever before. The fiscal year for 2000 held the record for deliveries, sales, and profits, with net income recorded at $966.1 million.[13] BMW pursues a premium brand strategy and concentrates on markets with above-average growth potential and high margins; with this strategy, BMW sales rose an additional 7 percent in 2001, and sales are expected to grow at a faster pace than the overall market because consumers who typically purchase luxury cars are not affected as much by recession.[14]

B-3 Communicating Excellence at BMW

BMW developed the Herbert Quandt Foundation to promote the company's social involvement. The Herbert Quandt Foundation fosters national and international dialogue and mutual understanding between business, politics, and society. In addition, the foundation organizes a range of important events to bring together the leaders of industry and society. BMW focuses on environmental sustainability, understanding that oil is a limited resource and other forms of energy need to be explored. BMW is currently introducing a new 7 Series powered by hydrogen, and uses much research and development to explore solar-powered alternatives. But BMW's social consciousness goes beyond the environment. In addition to just traffic safety, BMW focuses on social development issues such as intercultural learning, sponsorship of gifted students, and other educational programs.[15]

In addition to its foundation, BMW spreads the word of its excellence in other forums. It is present at the North American International Auto Show in Detroit and the Frankfurt Auto Show. It also sponsors the BMW International Open, one of the most important golf tournaments; the BMW Golf Cup International; and it is present in the Formula 1 Racing circuit.

BMW has national web sites in Austria, Belgium, Czech Republic, Denmark, Ireland, Estonia, Finland, France, Germany, Greece, Great Britain, Hungary, Italy, Lithuania, Netherlands, Norway, Portugal, Russia, Sweden, Switzerland, Spain, and the Ukraine. Also, it covers nineteen countries in the Americas, three in the Middle East, nine in Asia, and in South Africa, Australia, and New Zealand. Its web site offers insights into its long-standing tradition of innovation and quality. Its site, www.bmwfilms.com, offers a display of quality in the form of five different short films with action-packed mini plots. Its automobiles are placed in James Bond movies, and its "Ultimate Driving" message is widely known.

BMW offers zero-percent financing and reasonable leasing structures to penetrate the lower income market. Also, it prides itself on continuous customer service with credit, personal banking, credit cards, and insurance.[16] BMW also offers a protection plan, certification, and roadside assistance on all new and used BMW automobiles for most consumers in developed countries. Finally, BMW facilitates buying by offering a program that allows the buyer to customize his or her own car on the web site and have it delivered without even leaving home.

B-4 The BMW Driver

Although BMW has many different types of consumers, a certain type tends to purchase its vehicles: upper middle class and upper class professional males. BMW has recently seen an increase in its female customers.[17] Baby boomers are the primary consumers, as they tend to have the most money to spend. In fact, consumers in this group aged 35–44 account for more new vehicle sales dollars than any other group.[18] Over the years, BMW has sought to target young professionals who are well-educated, college graduates.[19] Recently, however, BMW has widened its target market. It now caters to single, male executives, to families with children, and to older couples.[20] Also, with the addition of the 3 Series, it is attempting to attract the "20-something" generation.

BMW's superior design and quality attract consumers who are very safety conscious, but who are also seeking the status of owning a BMW. BMW's sleek styling also attracts consumers who are style conscious. With the introduction of the 3 Series, a more affordable automobile, BMW has seen a decrease in the average age of its consumers.[21]

The company offers a full line of automobiles for a large variety of luxury market segments: It produces sports cars, family cars, performance machines, and a variety of non-car products. BMW's introductory automobile is a BMW 3 Series. The company has a 5 Series targeted at the mid-luxury market and offers a 7 Series for the high-end luxury automobile buyer. BMW also offers sports cars, SUVs, and other vehicles.

The 3 Series BMW, its introductory automobile, is offered as a sedan, coupe, convertible, touring car, and a compact, with 4–8 cylinders and a choice of gas or diesel. Safety is also a key concern in any BMW car, and the 3 Series BMWs have a variety of safety features: special headlight adjustments, multiple airbags, and special braking systems.[22] Manufacturer's Suggested Retail Price (MSRP) for these cars ranges from $27,100 to $42,400.[23] A typical 3 Series BMW could be considered a 325 Series four-door vehicle. The price tag of this car usually runs $27,100. The BMW has as standard features a 2.5L, 6-cylinder, and 184-horsepower engine with a 5-speed transmission, ABS brakes, front and rear antiroll bars, a multilink suspension, rack and pinion steering, front- and rear-vented brakes, sixteen-inch alloy rims, and a full-size spare. Standard safety features include side impact bars, driving lights, a full gauge panel, multiple airbags, and a security system.[24]

The BMW 5 Series is its mid-price offering. A sedan and a touring car are the options available in the 5 Series. These vehicles are also offered in a 4-cylinder engine with a choice of fuel consumption. Safety and design are enhanced for this series. The sophisticated safety system includes crumple zones, airbags, and tire pressure controls, among others.[25] MSRP ranges from $35,950 to $39,450.[26]

The top of the line BMW is the 7 Series. This high-end vehicle is available in an 8-cylinder, 6-speed transmission. Safety and the ultimate in luxury are the key components in this vehicle. The car comes with a very sophisticated safety system that utilizes fourteen sensors to maintain safety and comfort.[27] MSRP for this automobile ranges from $67,850 to $71,850.[28]

BMW also offers a variety of additional vehicles such as sports cars and sports utility vehicles (SUVs). The BMW Z3 is its sports car. The automobile is available in a coupe or roadster with a 4- or 6-cylinder engine. Safety features include impact safety absorbers, electronic ignition immobilizer, and smart airbags.[29] MSRP ranges from $31,300 to $37,900 for this BMW.[30] The X5 is the BMW performance SUV, available in the normal X5 and the X5 4.6is. The normal X5 comes with a 6-cylinder engine, while the X5 4.6 is available with a powerful 8-cylinder engine. Safety features include a high-impact body shell, head and side airbags, and a sophisticated braking system.[31] The MSRP ranges from $38,900 to $66,200.[32] The BMW Z8 is the ultimate in driving performance, offering the highest quality and performance of any of BMW's products. The car comes with an electronic-start 8-cylinder engine that is completely electronically controlled. This BMW is a high-performance computer-run car.[33] The MSRP for this car is around $130,000.[34]

BMW also produces M Series stock vehicles with "muscle" as the main function. These high-performance machines are made especially for those individuals searching for very high performance, safety, and design. Suspension, wheels, brakes, exhaust, and engine components are all modified to increase performance to its highest level. The M series is available as an M3 coupe, M3 convertible, M5 sedan, M coupe, or an M roadster.[35] MSRP for these driving machines range from $44,900 to $69,990.[36]

B-5 All Things BMW

BMW also has an array of other products in an attempt to decrease the cyclical aspect of automobile retailing and increase diversification. BMW offers eleven different types of motorcycles that are used for a variety of purposes: touring, racing, street, and off-road use. Prices range from $8,000 upward to $30,000. BMW also offers a full line of motorcycle and car apparel and accessories. Clothes, bikes, and other similar products are all offered by the company.[37]

The automobile manufacturer also offers financial services, BMW driver training, BMW international Direct and Corporate Sales, BMW ASSIST, and sponsorships. The company makes information available such as split-screen maps, digital road maps, and drivers' assistance programs. BMW also produces a C1, similar to a covered motorcycle, which is used in crowded cities to move in tight places. It is also involved in the comeback of the MINI as it reaches for world markets.[38]

B-6 Competition within the Luxury Automobile Segment

According to numerous web sites quoting *Consumer Reports*,[39] a comparison between luxury automobiles with prices between $40,000 to $60,000 reveals that the BMW 5 Series lives up to the slogan "the ultimate driving machine," and it is spacious, comfortable, responsive, powerful, and safe, yet its options are very expensive. In comparison, the Mercedes E class is more fuel efficient than the BMW; it is large, comfortable, among the safest in the automobile industry; and it handles well but not in snow. The Lexus GS is also more fuel efficient than the BMW; it is comfortable, reliable, and quite luxurious; and it fits its slogan "Passionate pursuit of perfection." It has rear-wheel drive, which needs getting used to, and its options are also expensive.

For automobiles with a price range from $30,000 to $40,000, the BMW 3 Series is very responsive; it accelerates quickly and breaks well, has smooth steering, but also has rear-wheel drive, which may pose a challenge; and it is quite loud. The Mercedes C class is less fuel efficient, but it provides a safe and quiet ride. The Lexus ES has a firm front-wheel drive; it is luxurious, spacious, and reliable, but its extra options are expensive.

In terms of market performance, BMW's sales rose 15 percent through November 2001, vaulting it into second place among luxury automobiles in the United States. BMW sales jumped over Mercedes-Benz, which now holds the third spot. Mercedes-Benz has been slumping since 1998, when the company completed its merger with Chrysler, forming DaimlerChrysler. Toyota Motor Corporation's Lexus currently holds the number-one slot in the U.S. market.[40] There is fierce competition among the luxury automobile makers, and focusing on such factors as customer service, price, and new product innovations will help BMW outperform its competitors.

B-7 Targeting to Lower-Price Segments: The MINI and the Certified Pre-Owned BMWs

B-7a A Truly Unique Car: "The MINI puts a smile on your face."

With the March 2002 introduction of the MINI to the United States, BMW hopes to gain a share of the small and compact car market. Targeting a high-tech and high-style consumer, the MINI features heated mirrors, a computer navigation system, an air-conditioned glove box, rain-sensing windshield wipers, and an eight-speaker premium stereo.[41] The very "Euro-looking" MINI also features bright, flashy colors and a hard top that is of a different color. The wide range of colors and options gives each owner the opportunity to personalize it.

The BMW Group's 2000 Annual Report states, "Through the MINI brand, the BMW Group will further enhance its appeal to young and modern customers. With its emotional character, the MINI is tailored precisely to these target groups and meets the growing demand for premium offers also in the small car segment."[42] The MINI has fared well in Europe. The drivers, typically young, urban, and trendy, find the MINI easy to drive and park in congested cities and appreciate the high kilometer to gasoline liter ratio.[43] The MINI is quite small, under 12 feet long, and 4 feet 7 inches tall; with its doors open, it is wider than it is long.[44] BMW hopes to lure the same segment that Volkswagen did so successfully with its new Beetle.[45]

BMW hopes not only to woo new customers, but also to bring back current owners of the larger BMW cars. "The MINI will give BMW Group an excellent position in the small car segment in the future, especially as a MINI is the ideal second or third car for the BMW driver and other customers in existing BMW segments."[46] The price is right for many consumers at $16,850 to $19,850, less than half the price of a BMW.[47]

BMW sells the MINI through MINI franchises, which do not carry the BMW name; any dealers that are approved to carry the MINI have to provide separate facilities for the automobiles.[48] In addition, the car itself will not show the BMW logo but will have a separate MINI logo.

B-7b Problems with the MINI

In an effort to reach bargain-conscious consumers, BMW provides the MINI at an exceptionally low price. Serious concerns have been raised about the quality of the MINI and the fact that it is associated with the BMW name. Brand name dilution may be a serious future concern. BMW owners typically desire luxury and status; however, with the MINI being so price competitive, it is possible that many who cannot afford to purchase a BMW will purchase a MINI to be a part of the BMW family of cars. On the other hand, "as a luxury brand, if you lower your price range, it gets more risky," says Wendelin Wiedeking, president and chief executive of Porsche AG. "Exclusivity is very much related to price."[49]

More problems with the MINI have arisen in the company's international markets. A recall of 500 MINIs took place after workers noticed sparks while fueling vehicles.[50] More than 6,500 vehicles were retrofitted in order to correct the problem, costing BMW more than $508,000.[51] These types of setbacks have the potential to inflict damage to a prestigious brand name. "People are watching the MINI launch very carefully," said John Lawson, an analyst at Schroder Salomon Smith Barney. "They need to be convinced that the MINI will be a high-quality product and will be sensitive to anything that suggests it is not."[52]

B-7c The Certified Pre-Owned BMWs

BMW has focused its advertising efforts on its Certified Pre-Owned vehicles in 2002. The Certified Pre-Owned BMW is given a warranty and a series of checks in order to be classified as Certified. With this new push toward selling used cars, BMW might again be risking a dilution of brand image with luxury-conscious consumers. Making the BMW name a more affordable prospect to more segments of the population may reduce the prestige and luxury appeal of a BMW. In addition, continuous advertising of a pre-owned vehicle can lessen the brand name in the eyes of prestige-conscious consumers.

Analysis Suggestions

1. As you analyze this case, focus on segmentation and the targeting strategy used by BMW in marketing the MINI and the Certified Pre-Owned BMW.
2. How is the BMW positioned in the consumer's mind? Describe the typical BMW driver, using psychographic and demographic variables for the description. What

leisure activities does this driver engage in? What are the driver's hobbies? What magazines does the driver subscribe to?
3. What strategy suggestions would you offer to BMW to ensure that the MINI and the Certified Pre-Owned BMW do not dilute the BMW brand?

Notes

1. "Worldwide Automotive Database and Forecasts," *Motor Business International,* London, Second Quarter 2000, pp. 165–271.
2. "Passenger Cars, ATVs, RVs and Pick-ups in the USA (July 2001)," www.euromonitor.com.
3. Ibid.
4. "Autos & Auto Parts Industry Survey," *Standard & Poor's,* December 27, 2001.
5. Ibid.
6. Ibid.
7. "Passenger Cars, ATVs, RVs and Pick-ups in the USA (July 2001)," www.euromonitor.com.
8. "Autos & Auto Parts Industry Survey," *Standard & Poor's,* December 27, 2001.
9. Ibid.
10. "World Vehicle Industry Prospects to 2005," *Motor Business International,* London, Third Quarter 1999, pp. 88–100.
11. Michael Robinet, "The Mixed Scene in Europe," *Automotive Design & Production,* Cincinnati, February 2002, Vol. 114, No. 2, pp. 24–25.
12. www.hoovers.com
13. Ibid.
14. Beth Reigber, "Companies: BMW Says Sales…" *The Wall Street Journal Europe,* January 29, 2002.
15. More information about the Herbert Quandt Foundation can be found at www.herbertquandtstiftung.com.
16. A complete list of financial services can be found at http://www.bmw-financialservices.com/international/index.html.
17. "Passenger Cars, ATVs, RVs and Pick-ups in the USA (July 2001)," www.euromonitor.com.
18. Ibid.
19. "BMW" Encyclopedia of Major Marketing Campaigns.
20. Ibid.
21. "Passenger Cars, ATVs, RVs and Pick-ups in the USA (July 2001)" www.euromonitor.com.
22. www.carsDirect.com, Research Center, February 25, 2002.
23. www.bmw.com, Products, February 25, 2002.
24. www.carsDirect.com, Compare Vehicles, February 25,2002.
25. www.bmw.com, Products, February 25, 2002.
26. www.carsDirect.com, Research Center, February 25, 2002.
27. www.bmw.com, Products, February 25, 2002.
28. www.carsDirect.com, Research Center, February 25, 2002.
29. www.bmw.com, Products, February 25, 2002.
30. www.carsDirect.com, Research Center, February 25, 2002.
31. www.bmw.com, Products, February 25, 2002.
32. www.carsDirect.com, Research Center, February 25, 2002.
33. www.bmw.com, Products, February 25, 2002.
34. www.carsDirect.com, Research Center, February 25, 2002.
35. www.bmw.com, Products, February 25, 2002.
36. www.carsDirect.com, Research Center, February 25, 2002.
37. www.bmw.com, Products, February 25, 2002.
38. Ibid.
39. Information is taken from the following web pages: www.epinions.com; www.caranddriver.com; www.newcartestdrive.com; www.auto.com; www.edmunds.com and www.autoweb.com.
40. Bill Koenig and Jeff Green, "High-end Cars…," *National Post,* December 11, 2001.
41. Gregory White, "High Style in a Tiny Package…," *The Wall Street Journal,* October 17, 2001.
42. BMW Group AG, 2000 Annual Report
43. White, "High Style in a Tiny Package…," October 17, 2001.
44. Ibid.
45. Terry Box, "Got Your Eye on a MINI?…" *The Dallas Morning News,* January 26, 2002.
46. BMW Group AG, 2000 Annual Report
47. Box, "Got Your Eye on a MINI?…" January 26, 2002.
48. Ibid.
49. White, "High Style in a Tiny Package…," October 17, 2001.
50. Suzanne Kapner, "BMW Faces Setback with Its Entry into Small Car Market," *The New York Times,* September 4, 2001.
51. Ibid.
52. Ibid.

Campina, Naturally[1]

Dana Lascu

Case Outline

C-1 Industry Trends
C-2 Meeting Competitive
    Challenges at Campina:
    Adopting a Market
    Orientation
C-3 International Expansion at
    Campina
Analysis Suggestions
Notes

C ampina is one of the leading dairy companies in the world and one of the few that produces only dairy products. A European company that remains close to its Dutch roots, Campina's image evokes picturesque Dutch cow pastures and healthy lifestyles. The company's history can be traced to Southern Holland, in the Eindhoven area; a dairy cooperative with the name "De Kempen" was created in 1947 and used the brand name "Campina." In 1964 the cooperative merged with another cooperative in the Weert region in Holland and formed Campina (named after a regional moor—its meaning is "from the land"). After several consecutive mergers—more recently, with Melkunie Holland—Campina Melkunie (or Campina, as it is informally known) became the largest dairy cooperative in the Netherlands.

In the Netherlands alone, Campina boasts 7,500 member dairy farmers. The farmers own the cooperative: Campina must buy all the milk the farmers produce, while the farmers must finance the cooperative and, in return, they obtain a yield of the products sold. Campina itself is a nonprofit organization. Member farmers receive all the company profits. They have voting rights in the company that are proportional to the amount of milk they deliver, and they are represented by the Members' Council, the highest managerial body of the cooperative.

The separation between Campina, the operating company, and its cooperatives is evident: Campina is headquartered in Zaltbommel, in an industrial park in Southern Holland, while the dairies are located close to the consumers they serve, in different areas of the country.

C-1 Industry Trends

Among the main trends in the international dairy industry are the following:

Consolidation is a dominant trend of the dairy industry. The number of dairy companies is falling, and the production capacity of those that remain is increasing and becoming more efficient.[2] Yet there are still companies that exist successfully in the $100 million to $200 million range of sales, surviving through a mix of ingenuity and innovation.[3]

The European Union remains the world's top dairy producer, manufacturer, and trader of dairy products; because the EU is a mature dairy market, the emphasis is on value growth and processing milk into products with high added value.[4] As such, Campina's strategy and general mission, "adding value to milk," fits well with this trend. Of the world's top twenty-five dairy organizations, fourteen have their headquarters in Europe.[5]

The degree of concentration varies significantly, however, from region to region. In Scandinavia and the Netherlands, a handful of major cooperatives dominate. In Greece, there are more than 1,000 dairy businesses, of which more than 700 make cheese. In Germany, the industry has changed from numerous small, localized firms to most milk processors either collapsing or merging. In France, the top five control 55 percent of milk production. And in Scandinavia, the major players wield even more control: in Denmark, MD Foods and Klover Maelk control 95 percent of milk production, and in Sweden, Arla handles 80 percent.[6]

Another important trend is the focus on convenience (a packaging issue) and on value-added nutrition for functional foods (a product ingredient issue). Changes include creating new packaging and unique containers for innovative products. For example, German-based Schwalbchen Molkerei has debuted Go!

Campina truck in Eindhoven.

Banana, the first milk-energy drink made from fresh milk and real, pureed bananas, packaged in 330 ml Tetra Prisma cartons with fluted sides. Spain's Pascual Dairy offers milk-based energy drink Bio Frutas in two flavors: Tropical and Mediterranean. German milk processor Immergut has introduced Drinkfit Choco Plus, a vitamin-fortified, chocolate-flavored milk, in the same carton. The United Kingdom company Miller offers dual-compartment, side-by-side containers of refrigerated yogurt, while a new drinkable fruit yogurt from Nestle SA debuted in the United Kingdom under the name Squizzos, sporting Disney Jungle Book characters in a triangular-shaped package that is easy to tear, squeeze, and drink.[7]

Cheese is also presented in innovative packaging. Baars, a subsidiary of the BolsWessanen Group, a United Kingdom Dutch company, launched a smooth, flavorful medium/mature cheddar cheese, named Maidwell, that does not crumble; it is sold in an attractive, innovative, clear-plastic, resealable pack. Rumblers, a convenient all-in-one breakfast product manufactured by Ennis Foods Ltd., United Kingdom, is also available in an innovative package that holds cereal and fresh, semiskimmed milk separately, all in one pack.[8]

Functional ingredients (health foods or ingredients that enhance the nutritional value of products) represent yet another important trend in the dairy industry: Dairy products represent the most important sector, accounting for 65 percent of sales in a sector that is very buoyant given the consumer interest in health and diet.[9] The leading companies in Europe in this domain are Campina Melkunie (Netherlands), Nestle (Switzerland), and Danone (France).[10] Worldwide, Japan leads in the functional foods trend and is the only country with a regulatory policy on such foods: FOSHU (Foods for Specified Health Use).[11] There is a tradition of lactic acid bacteria culture drinks and yogurts in Japan, and many of these fermented drinks and yogurts contain other functional ingredients, such as oligofructose, calcium, and DHA, which is a polyunsaturated fatty acid derived from fish oil that is said to improve learning, lower blood pressure, help prevent cancer, and lower serum cholesterol.[12] And from Dairy Gold, Australia, comes Vaalia Passionfruit Smoothie, a low-fat milk-based drink containing 25 percent fruit juice, acidophilus and bifidus cultures, and insulin.[13]

C-2 Meeting Competitive Challenges at Campina: Adopting a Market Orientation

Historically, milk production has been supply driven, and excess milk was used to produce cheese and powder milk; this strategy led to excess cheese/commodities on the market and the need for subsidies. Campina initiated a change in this practice. In the past fifteen years, the company has been demand driven: Farmers are assigned production quotas that they are not allowed to exceed.

In other attempts to adopt a market orientation, Campina decided to eliminate all milk powder production because milk powder is a low-margin commodity. Instead, the company is focusing on building the brand to ensure recognition by consumers as a value offering and as a quality brand name.

According to R. J. Steetskamp, Director of Strategic Business Development at Campina, the company examines consumer behavior to determine where to fit Campina products in consumers' lives. As such, Campina offers four categories of products:

1. **Indulgence products.** This category constitutes an important growth area for the company. Campina produces numerous milk-based desserts, with the exception of ice cream—primarily due to the product's seasonality and the logistics strategies involved in the transportation and storage of ice cream, which differ from those for the rest of the company's offerings.

2. **Daily essentials.** This category includes Campina products that shoppers purchase routinely, such as milk, buttermilk, yogurt, coffee cream, butter, cheese, and others. Campina, using a strategy employed by all its competitors, also sells daily essentials under dealer (store) brands, rather than under its own brand name. For example, in Holland, it sells milk, plain yogurt, butter, Gouda cheese, and vla (chocolate or vanilla custard) under the Albert Heijn brand name. Albert Heijn is a dominant, quality supermarket chain in Holland that is owned by Royal Ahold—a large conglomerate that also owns supermarket chains in the United States (BI-LO, Giant, and Stop & Shop). The company also sells daily essentials under dealer brands in Germany.

3. **Functional products.** According to Mr. Steetskamp, this product category needs to be further explored and defined by the company. In this category are health foods and other milk-based nutritional supplements sold to consumers. DMV International is a Campina division that is present all over the

Indulgence products.

Campina daily essentials. In the Netherlands, a vla dessert is a daily essential.

world; it produces pharmaceutical products, food ingredients, and ingredients used to enhance the nutrition of consumers and their pets, such as proteins and powders with different functions. All these products are milk-based, and many of them are well known. For example, Lactoval is a popular calcium supplement.

4. **Ingredients (food and pharmaceutical ingredients).** This product category is targeted at other food product manufacturers, rather than at the individual consumers. The primary purpose of the food and pharmaceutical ingredients is to enhance the quality, taste, texture, and/or nutritive content of the products manufactured by Campina's clients. The company's Creamy Creation unit specializes in blending dairy and alcohol to make various cream liqueurs, leading to both healthy and indulgent drinks. In this category fall meal replacement drinks and high protein drinks as well. With this category, Campina becomes a supplier to other manufacturers, rather than a product manufacturer distributing to supermarkets.

C-3 International Expansion at Campina

One of the most important undertakings at Campina in the last decade was to expand beyond the Netherlands. In its first expansion effort, the company bought Belgium's Comelco, another dairy cooperative. In Belgium, the company boasts the Joyvalle dairy products and milk brand and the Passendale, Père Joseph, and Wynendale cheese brands, all marketed under the Campina umbrella brand.

Campina expanded into Germany, purchasing a number of cooperatives: Sudmilch (Southern Germany), Tuffi (Western Germany), and Emzett (Berlin). In Germany, its primary brand is Landliebe; here, the company sells Landliebe milk, cream, yogurts (seasonal, fruit, plain, and in different types of containers); different types of puddings including rice pudding, ice cream, cheese, and qwark (a traditional creamy cheese) plain or with fruit; yogurt drinks (with fruit flavors such as banana, cherry, lemon, peach, and orange); and different milk drinks with flavors such as vanilla and chocolate. The company also offers products such as coffee machines, cups, spoons, and others for purchase online at its site, www.landliebe-online.de. According to R. J. Steetskamp, the Campina name will

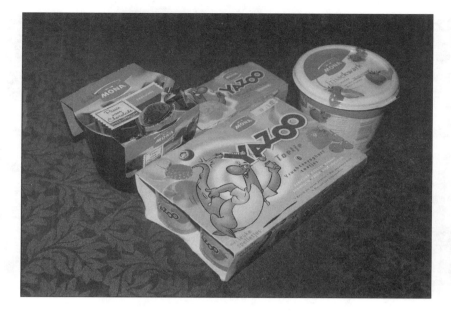

Offerings under the Mona umbrella brand.

be used as the umbrella brand for all the company products; the name comes from the Latin "from the land," and it is easily pronounced in all the different languages in Europe, the brand's target market. The only brands that will not be brought under the Campina umbrella brands, according to Mr. Steetskamp, are the Mona brand in the Netherlands and the Landliebe brand in Germany because both have high brand franchise with consumers in their respective countries. Interestingly, the Landliebe brand name is close in meaning to Campina, both making reference to the land.

As a result of these acquisitions and mergers, according to Mr. Steetskamp, Campina is the market leader in Holland, Germany, and Belgium—as the company web site states, "Campina is a household name in the Netherlands, Belgium and Germany."[14]

Campina has further expanded, with its own subsidiaries in the United Kingdom, Spain, Poland, and Russia, where it ultimately plans to use the Campina brand name (the Campina Fruttis brand is one of the most popular fruit yogurt brands in Russia).

Analysis Suggestions

1. Perform a product mix analysis for Campina. Calculate product length, width, and line depth and evaluate product consistency across the different lines. Refer to www.campina-melkunie.nl for additional brand information.

2. Attempt a comparison with U.S. dairy strategies: Go to your local grocery store chain and note the different brands of milk. Are indulgence products offered by the same company? (Most likely they are not.) Can you find one dairy cooperative that offers milk, butter, cream cheese, and sour cream? Explain the differences between Campina strategies and U.S. dairy cooperatives' strategies.

Notes

1. Case designed with input from Anne Carson, Todd Fowler, Kim Hribar, Liz Manera, and Brian Thoms.
2. Sarah McRitchie, "Europe Shrinks to Expand," *Dairy Foods*, January 1999, Vol. 100, No. 1, pp. 75–79.
3. Gerry Clark and Dave Fusaro, "Survival of the Smallest," *Dairy Foods*, August 1999, Vol. 100, no. 8, pp. 48–55.
4. Ibid.
5. Ibid.
6. McRitchie, "Europe Shrinks to Expand," pp. 75–79.
7. Ibid.
8. Ibid.
9. Ibid.
10. Ibid.
11. Donna Gorski Berry, "Global Dairy Food Trends," *Dairy Foods*, October 1998, Vol. 99, No. 10, pp. 32–37.
12. Ibid.
13. Ibid.
14. www.campina-melkunie.nl

D

Royal Philips Electronics

Christianne Goldman, Ryan Ganley, Dana Lascu,
Leslie Ramich, Akshay Patil

Case Outline

D-1 Background
D-2 Philips' Offerings
D-3 The Competition
D-4 Philips' Brand Image
Analysis Suggestions
Notes

D-1 Background

Royal Philips is the world's third-largest consumer electronics firm, following market leaders Matsushita and Sony. The Philips brands include Philips, Norelco, Marantz, and Magnavox. The company was established in 1891 in Eindhoven, in the Southern region of the Netherlands, primarily as a manufacturer of incandescent lamps and other electrical products. The company first produced carbon-filament lamps and, by the turn of the century, it had become one of the largest producers in Europe. Later, the company diversified into many other areas, such as electronics, small appliances, lighting, semiconductors, medical systems, and domestic care products, among others. The company headquarters moved to Amsterdam in the 1980s, but its lighting division continues to occupy the center of Eindhoven (see photograph).

Around the early 1900s, Philips started to diversify its offerings to radio valves and X-ray equipment, and later to television. Later in the century, Philips developed the electric shaver and invented the rotary heads, which led to the development of the Philipshave electric shaver. Philips also made major contributions in the development of television pictures, its research work leading to the development of the Plumbicon television camera tube, which offered a better picture quality. It introduced the compact audiocassette in 1963 and produced its first integrated circuits in 1965. In the 1970s, its research in lighting contributed to the development of the PL and SL energy-saving lamps. More recent Philips innovations are the LaserVision optical disc, the compact disc, and optical telecommunication systems.[1]

Philips expanded in the 1970s and 1980s, acquiring Magnavox (1974) and Signetics (1975), the television business of GTE Sylvania (1981), and the lamps division of Westinghouse (1983). Currently, Philips operates in more than sixty countries, with more than 186,000 employees, and is market leader in many regions for a number of product categories—for example, lighting, shavers, and LCD displays.[2]

In the 1990s, Philips carried out a major restructuring program and changed from highly localized production to globalized production; this change translated into a more efficient concentration of manufacturing—from more than 100 manufacturing sites to 36, and to 14 sites for production: Juarez and Manaus in

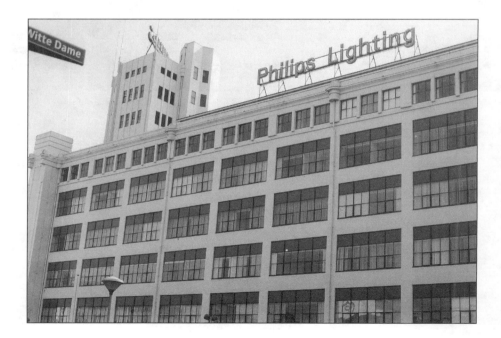

Philips Lighting reigns in downtown Eindhoven. "The White Lady"—Witte Dame in Dutch.

Latin America; Bruges, Dreux, and Hasselt in Western Europe; Kwidzyn, Szekesfehervar, and Szombathelv in Eastern Europe; and Beijing, Suhzou, Shenzen, and Chungli (all in China) in Asia.

Another important change was the appointment of Gerard Kleisterlee as president of Philips and chairman of the Board of Management in 2001. Kleisterlee has been seen as a Philips man, following a traditional Philips career path that had been embraced by company employees until the 1980s. He was trained locally, at the Eindhoven Technical University, in electronic engineering, and he has worked with the company for three decades. According to Martien Groenewegen, former research and development engineer with Philips, Kleisterlee is perceived by present and former employees as taking the company back to its original path to success. In fact, in a recent interview, Kleisterlee mentioned that the company is presently concentrating on its initial core activities with a focus on its key areas of profitability; this is a different type of restructuring from earlier attempts, when the company pursued "wrong activities."[3] Mr. Groenewegen contends that the perception among employees and the industry is that Philips, under Kleisterlee's leadership, will have a strong product orientation and that it would support an environment in which product innovation will constitute a primary focus of the company. That has been, historically, Philips' proven path to success.

Philips offers consumer products, such as communications products (cordless phones, mobile phones, fax machines), electronics (Flat TV, Real Flat TV, digital TV, projection TV, professional TV, DVD players and recorders, Super Audio CD, VCRs, satellite receivers, CD recorders/players, home theater systems, Internet audio players, shelf systems, portable radios, clock radios, PC monitors, multimedia projectors, PC cameras, PC audio, CD rewriteable drives, DVD drives, among others); home and body care products (vacuum cleaners, irons, kitchen appliances, shavers, oral healthcare products), and lighting products. Its professional products include connectivity, lighting, medical systems (such as magnetic resonance imaging, ultrasound equipment, X-rays), semiconductors, and other products, such as security systems, manufacturing technologies, automotive products, broadband networks, and so on.

D-2 Philips' Offerings

Among Philips' competitors are Matsushita, Sony, Hitachi, and Thomson. Matsushita Electric Industrial is the world's number-one consumer electronics firm. In North America, Matsushita makes consumer, commercial, and industrial electronics (from jukeboxes to flat-screen TVs) under the Panasonic, Technics, and Quasar brands. Matsushita sells consumer products (which account for 40 percent of sales) such as VCRs, CD and DVD players, TVs, and home appliances. It also sells computers, telephones, industrial equipment (welding and vending machines, medical equipment, car navigation equipment), and components such as batteries, semiconductors, and electric motors. The Matsushita group includes about 320 operating units in more than forty-five countries. Its products are sold worldwide, but Asia accounts for more than 70 percent of sales.[4]

Sony is another competitor whose PlayStation home video game systems account for nearly 10 percent of the company's electronics and entertainment sales. Sony, the world's second-largest consumer electronics firm after Matsushita, also makes several other products, including semiconductors, DVD players, batteries, cameras, MiniDisc and Walkman stereo systems, computer monitors, and flat-screen TVs. The company's TVs, VCRs, stereos, and other consumer electronics account for more than 65 percent of sales. Sony's entertainment assets include

D-3 The Competition

Columbia TriStar (movies and television shows) and record labels Columbia and Epic. The company also operates insurance and finance businesses.[5]

Hitachi, another large player in the consumer electronics industry, is a leading manufacturer of both electronics components and industrial equipment. The company manufactures mainframes, semiconductors, workstations, elevators and escalators, power plant equipment, and also metals, wire, and cable. Hitachi produces consumer goods, such as audio and video equipment, refrigerators, and washing machines. Similarly to Philips, Hitachi is focusing on developing Internet-related businesses and expanding its information technology units, which account for more than 30 percent of sales.[6]

Finally, Thomson Multimedia is another major competitor and leading manufacturer of consumer electronics (which account for nearly 80 percent of sales), including TVs, video cameras, telephones, audio products, DVD players, and professional video equipment. Thomson Multimedia also produces displays and TV components. Its products, which are sold in more than 100 countries, include brands such as RCA in the United States and Thomson in Europe. Almost 60 percent of the company's sales are in the U.S.[7]

D-4 Philips' Brand Image

Philips' primary mission is to "continually enhance people's lives through technology and innovation."[8] This philosophy is also reflected in its tagline "Let's make things better," launched in 1995.[9] Philips focuses on the multisensory impact of its products and their power to create memories and spur emotions to touch people's lives on a very personal level; Philips also aspires to be the world's leading eco-efficient company in electronics and lighting.[10]

While Philips is a household name in European markets, the company continues to struggle to spread brand awareness in the United States. As recently as 1996, the Philips brand was virtually unknown in the United States, compared with competitors Sony and RCA; the brand was associated with milk of magnesia, petroleum, or screwdrivers.[11] After spending millions to build brand awareness, Philips has successfully achieved recognition among consumers in the U.S. as a brand that makes exciting products that improve people's lives. In 1998, for example, Philips spent $100 million in advertising, sponsorships, movie tie-ins, and retail promotions worldwide to boost brand awareness.[12] In the same year, Philips embarked on its Star campaign in an attempt to create a more human, imaginative, and seductive brand image. Using dynamic state-of-the-art products, the Philips campaign was able to reach consumers on a very personal level, thus gaining their trust, loyalty, and brand preference. The campaign resonated very well with its target market: well-educated, independent, and carefree consumers.[13]

Another venue for communicating with its target market is Philips' five-year sponsorship of the U.S. Soccer Federation as of June 2001. This sponsorship is also expected to help Philips reach more of its young target consumers and more female consumers. Philips thus has 30-second air spots on ABC and ESPN during soccer broadcasts, as well as a presence on stadium billboards, and logo visibility on all training kits; and the Philips' branded goal cameras are highly visible.[14]

Apart from the need to generate awareness in the U.S. markets, Philips also recognizes the need for consolidation and consistency across all of its marketing communications worldwide. To this end, Philips awarded its $600 million account in media buying and planning to the Aegis Group's Carat International.[15] With Carat's help, Philips is attempting to

- Create a consistent brand experience that will give all products a shared look and feel and will demonstrate a deep understanding of the customer[16]
- Become more consumer-focused and more brand-centric in its marketing efforts, expanding beyond its traditional television and print communications to direct marketing and more unconventional media
- Create a total marketing package, which will resonate well with the U.S. consumer and therefore lead to increased U.S. sales[17]
- Engage in extensive direct marketing and Internet marketing; this is especially possible given Philips' alliance with AOL Time Warner[18]

Analysis Suggestions

1. Use the standardization versus adaptation arguments to support Philips' strategies worldwide. What are some of the advantages of its new standardization strategy?

2. Some may argue that Philips is a Pan-European brand that is trying to make inroads into the United States. Find support for and against this argument.

3. Offer suggestions to Philips regarding the strategies that it can use to create a unified, resonant global brand.

Notes

1. Material available at www.philips.com.
2. www.philips.com
3. Bill Griffeth, *Philips Electronics—CHM & CEO—Interview*, Dow Jones Business Video, January 9, 2002, p. 1.
4. Hoover's Online, www.hoover.com, February 19, 2002.
5. Ibid.
6. Ibid.
7. Ibid.
8. Jennifer B. Simes, "Philippines a Key Hub, Says Philips," *Computerworld Philippines*, Dow Jones Interactive, December 10, 2001, p. 1.
9. "Brand Building," www.philips.com, p. 1.
10. "A Serious Responsibility," www.philips.com, p. 1.
11. Michael McCarthy, "Philips Can't Lose with Puppies, Beatles," *USA Today*, www.usatoday.com, January 15, 2001, p. 2.
12. Tobi Elkin, "Building a Brand," *Vision Magazine*, www.ce.org/, July/August 1999, pp. 1–2.
13. See "Owning the Right Image," www.news.philips.com, p. 1, for a more extensive analysis of the Philips communication strategy.
14. Tobi Elkin, "Philips to Sponsor U.S. Soccer Games," Adage.com, www.adage.com, June 19, 2001, p. 1.
15. Tobi Elkin and Richard Linnett, "Media Moves Up," *Advertising Age*, ABI Inform, July 9, 2001, p. 2.
16. Message from the President, Annual Report 2001, www.philips.com, p. 2.
17. Elkin and Linnett, "Media Moves Up," p. 3.
18. Philips Mainstream Consumer Electronics Powerpoint presentation, www.philips.com.

Hilton Sorrento Palace:
Changing Targeting Strategies

Dana-Nicoleta Lascu

Case Outline

E-1 The Hotel Offerings
E-2 Marketing Strategies
Analysis Suggestions
Notes

Two hours south of Rome, to Naples, by the Eurostar, the Italian high-speed train, and an additional hour west along the Bay of Naples via the Circumvesuviana regional railway is the town of Sorrento. The Hilton Sorrento Palace reigns high on the hills of Sorrento, overlooking Mount Vesuvius, the now dormant volcano (since 1944), which buried the towns of Pompeii and Herculaneum in the year 79 A.D.

The Hilton Sorrento Palace reigns high on the hill above the Bay of Naples.

Sorrento is a small resort town, known well throughout Europe, an ideal vacation destination for its picturesque location and mild weather. A favorite of British travelers, the town of Sorrento has 10,000 beds according to Mr. Ziad Tantawi, director of business development at the Hilton Sorrento Palace. The Hilton Sorrento Palace is the largest of all hotels in the small resort town, with 383 rooms. Owned by the Sorrento Palace Gruppo, its owner since its year of construction (1981), the hotel became part of the Hilton chain in May 2001, and is now under Hilton management. One of the few hotels open in the winter, the Sorrento Palace boasts an average occupancy rate of 60 percent, with an average occupancy of 30 percent from November to March and more than 85 percent from May to October.[1]

The Hilton Sorrento Palace faces competition from three categories of competitors. Bed and breakfast, family-run lodging is very popular. The bed and breakfasts are competitively priced at or below the room rates of leading hotels in the area. Most bed and breakfast accommodations are open year round. Sorrento is also a popular destination for cruise lines during the summer months. For cruise ship passengers, Sorrento offers easy access to the ruins of Pompeii, Mount Vesuvius, and the Isle of Capri. Overall, prices for cruise ships are higher than that of hotels, but they include meals and entertainment, as well as airfare to Italy.

Other local hotels compete directly with the Sorrento Hilton. The historic Europa Palace Grand Hotel, for example, offers close views of the Bay of Naples and the cliffs of Sorrento.

E-1 The Hotel Offerings

The four-star Hilton Sorrento Palace is situated on a hill overlooking the town and the Bay of Naples, a short walk from downtown's busy tourist markets. Surrounded by residences and lemon and orange groves, the hotel is modern and elegant. Its restaurant L'Argumento is situated amidst blooming cannas and orange and lemon trees. Le Ginestre has frescoes and elegant columns, and an indoor pool with a lush painted background. Its other four restaurants abound in blooming bougainvillea and oleander and have a splendid view of the Bay of Naples and Mount Vesuvius.

The L'Argumento restaurant, among orange and lemon trees.

The indoor lounge has excellent performers scheduled every evening and boasts a view of the city and the Bay.

The lounge—offering a stylish open indoor space.

The executive lounge is situated on the top floor of the hotel and has a splendid view of the Gulf and town. It also boasts a swimming pool at the highest altitude in the region. The lounge serves complimentary food and drinks to executive guests and to gold- and diamond-level Hilton Honors members.

The executive lounge—an elegant indoor lounge with a Bang & Olufsen stereo system.

The executive lounge swimming pool perched high above the city, with a Bay view.

The view from the executive lounge.

The hotel has a total of six outdoor swimming pools of different depths, flowing into each other, a tennis court, and a relatively well-equipped fitness center. Among the services offered at the hotel pool are the Hilton Kids Club: Every day, from 10 to 12 and from 2 to 4 in the afternoon, the Hilton kids can enjoy entertainment by the pool (uno spazio giochi per bambini).

A partial view of the swimming pool.

Perspective from the swimming pool area.

The hotel's targeting strategies focus primarily on meetings: Its meeting space is one of the largest in Europe. The Centro Congressi (congress center) has a full range of rooms for conferences and conventions of any type or size, from the 1,700-seat auditorium to smaller rooms, a 2,300-square meter exhibition space, a banquet facility that can accommodate 1,000 people, and parking facility that can accommodate 300 automobiles. In addition, the Centro also offers conference interpreting systems (six conference interpreting booths) and audiovisual presentation equipment, including a megascreen, making it an ideal venue for international events. About 65 percent of all hotel guests are conference participants.

E-2 Marketing Strategies

Hilton's sales offices in Italy (Milan) and overseas (in Germany, the United Kingdom, France, Sweden, and the Emirate of Dubai) are responsible for conference sales.

Tour operators constitute a second target group, accounting for 25 percent of the hotel's business. Their demand is highest in the months of July and August, when demand exceeds supply—Sorrento's location on the Bay and up a steep hill does not allow for space that could accommodate additional hotels. Only 10 percent of the hotel's business comes from individual bookings, Internet, and telephone.

Sorrento Palace's main target market is Italy. In addition, the hotel also actively targets groups from the United Kingdom, Germany, Belgium, France, and Japan—in that order, according to Mr. Tantawi. Visitors from the United States constituted an important presence at the hotel, particularly in the summer, in organized tours; however, after the terrorist attacks of September 11, 2001, demand has fallen sharply.

Mr. Tantawi would like to direct the hotel's marketing strategies to the United States. In particular, he would like to increase conference attendance at the hotel, as well as the number of tour groups and individual tourists in the off-season (November to March). At present, the hotel draws guests primarily from Italy and the United Kingdom. However, because European economies tend to follow a similar cycle, it is preferable for the hotel to diversify to other markets. Recently, the hotel has made extensive marketing attempts aimed at Japanese tour groups, with great success. Mr. Tantawi would like to find a way to bring in more tourists from the United States—especially conferences and tour groups.

Analysis Suggestions

1. How should Hilton Sorrento Palace market more effectively to the U.S. market? Design marketing communication strategies aimed at consumers in the United States promoting the differentiating characteristics of the hotel—views, restaurants, pools, etc. Share your solutions in class and e-mail them to dbd_sorrento@hilton.com.

2. An important difference between the Hilton Sorrento Palace and other Hilton and competing hospitality properties is the reliance on the conference segment. How should the hotel market more effectively to other market segments—in particular, individual guests and their families?

Notes

1. Interview with Mr. Ziad Tantawi, Director of Business Development.

AvtoVAZ: Maintaining Local Competitive Advantage

Dana Lascu, Maria Vornovitsky,
and Ramil Zeliatdinov

Case Outline

F-1 AvtoVAZ in the Soviet Era
F-2 Post-Soviet AvtoVAZ
F-3 AvtoVAZ Today
F-4 VAZ Competitors
F-5 The AvtoVAZ-GM
      Joint Venture
Analysis Suggestions
Notes

AvtoVAZ, or Automobile Factory of the Volga Region, also known as VAZ, was created in 1966 by the Soviet government. The government had as a goal to create a venue for the mass production of affordable automobiles for the Soviet consumer. The company was built by transplanting a defunct Fiat assembly plant from Italy to Togliatti, a small industrial town on the Volga River shores.

F-1 AvtoVAZ in the Soviet Era

AvtoVAZ's first car, the Zhiguli (better known in the West as Lada), was built based on Fiat 124, an automobile produced in Italy twenty years earlier. This first Lada was produced on April 19, 1970, and quickly became Russia's most popular passenger automobile.[1] Its first model was VAZ 2101, which was endearingly called "kopeika" (the penny). It was considered to be of very high quality, and many of these models can still be seen on the road today. Russians were so infatuated with this automobile that there was a movie made titled *Kopeika,* dedicated to this automobile, illustrating the life of the car and its owners.

Over the years, the factory began to gain popularity as it strove to "supply Russian citizens with cars especially made for the tough Russian climate and harsh road conditions."[2] During the Soviet era, AvtoVAZ quickly grew and expanded its production of the Lada. It later introduced Niva, a new model, in 1977, and Samara, in the 1980s. These efforts allowed the company to move ahead of other Soviet automobile manufacturers AZLK, producer of Moskvich, a higher-end automobile, and AvtoGAZ, producer of the Volga, an automobile used primarily for government officials and functions.

F-2 Post-Soviet AvtoVAZ

After 1989, the end of Communism brought drastic changes to the political and economic environment. In addition to the breakup of the Soviet Union, the drive toward a new market economy placed substantial pressure on the old state-owned enterprises. AvtoVAZ needed to implement important changes in order to continue to compete in the new transition economy and to operate successfully in an unstable economic environment. The company privatized immediately after the fall of Communism—it was the first automobile company in Post-Soviet Russia to adapt to a market environment[3]—and promptly lost its former government protection. It also became a target of corruption and mismanagement. At first, the Yeltsin government turned a blind eye to conflicts of interest and theft by corporate managers to win support for policies such as privatization. Today, Russia and AvtoVAZ are paying the price: Companies are held hostage by networks that rob the government of tax revenues, soak up cash needed for industrial modernization, and fuel organized crime.[4]

In 1989, Boris A. Berezovsky, a management-systems consultant to AvtoVAZ, organized a nationwide car-dealership chain that would later bring him vast wealth; he persuaded AvtoVAZ Chief Executive Vladimir Kadannikov to supply him with automobiles without up-front payment. As hyperinflation raged in the early 1990s, Berezovsky earned billions of rubles, partly by delaying payments for AvtoVAZ cars.[5] When the company privatized, in 1993,[6] Kadannikov and Berezovsky set up a company, called the All-Russian Automobile Alliance, which gradually amassed a 34 percent stake in AvtoVAZ. Other AvtoVAZ managers and employees own 35 percent of the company, and Automotive Finance Corp., an affiliate headed by Kadannikov, holds an estimated 19 percent.[7]

Subsequently, trading companies mushroomed around AvtoVAZ, taking advantage of its need for parts and its poor distribution network. The companies swapped components for cars—straight from the factory—at prices as much as 30 percent below market value. Many traders took cars without prepaying, often waiting months before settling. By late 1996, some 300 trading companies were operating with AvtoVAZ. While they raked in millions of dollars in profits, they also owed AvtoVAZ $1.2 billion, about 35 percent of annual sales, for cars delivered to dealers.[8] Furthermore, organized crime became involved in AvtoVAZ, requiring payments equivalent to $100 per automobile to ensure safe delivery. The late 1990s, however, announced a new period for AvtoVAZ, one in which the company was forced to address these irregularities. These changes, along with a slowdown in rampant inflation, have helped the company turn around and have enabled it to explore new growth options through joint ventures.

F-3 AvtoVAZ Today

Currently, AvtoVAZ has a substantial part of the Russian automobile market. A high percentage of automobiles on Russian roads (70.31 percent, or 960,000 automobiles) are produced by AvtoVAZ, while only 13.02 percent are produced by its largest Russian competitor, AvtoGAZ. In provincial Russia, there are primarily just two makes of automobiles: the Zhiguli, by AvtoVAZ, which has about 60 percent of the market share, and the Volga, by AvtoGAZ.[9] AvtoVAZ exports more than 98,000 automobiles yearly.[10]

Even though AvtoVAZ operates less efficiently than its foreign competitors (it builds an automobile in 320 hours, whereas it takes an average of 28 hours to build an automobile at a European plant[11]), it is a perfect fit with the budget and aptitudes of the Russian consumer. AvtoVAZ touts itself as "optimal for the Russian market relationship between price and quality."[12]

Indeed, Russian automobile buyers spend an average price of $5,000 to $6,000 for a new Lada and have an interesting relationship to the automobile. For example, VAZ owners hardly ever use official dealer automobile services; instead, they prefer to use private garages, with self-taught mechanics. Russian automobile buyers are practical: They do not expect the automobile to function perfectly right off the assembly line; the automobile's performance problems are addressed by the private garages at a reasonable fee. Russians expect their brand new Ladas to have some sort of defect; it is recommended to take the car for tuning as soon as it is bought. The tuning typically consists of a complete change of transmission, some modification of the battery, and a complete change of brakes and tires.[13]

Russian buyers are not too concerned about design—their main consideration is price. Russians also make practical choices when it comes to automobile options: They prefer metallic color, which lasts longer; metal protection for the bottom against winter damage; and rubber mats so that they do not vacuum the automobile often. Russian drivers value Ladas for their simplicity, which allows them to fix the automobile themselves; for their durability in withstanding tough climate and road conditions; and for their small size, which makes driving and parking in cities easier.[14]

AvtoVAZ is also planning to introduce a new model, the Kalina, a cheaper car than the Lada; it will sell for about $4,000. However, the company has had difficulty raising the funds to develop the new car.[15]

F-4 VAZ Competitors

In spite of the popularity of its Lada model, AvtoVAZ is rapidly losing market share to foreign competitors. Used automobiles from Europe, especially from Germany, compete directly with the VAZ automobiles, and especially with its latest models—2110, 2111, 2112; German automobiles continue to function without needing any repairs after four years of operation. In fact, without duties on imports of up to 100 percent, Russian automakers would be out of business. Even with the duties, more than 400,000 automobiles are imported yearly.[16] But important drawbacks for imported foreign cars are parts, which are expensive, and service; moreover, neither exists outside Moscow and St. Petersburg.[17]

Competitors such as Daewoo Corporation (Korea) and Skoda (Czech Republic) are also assembling cars in Russia,[18] creating additional competition for AvtoVAZ. General Motors and Ford are trying to set up assembly operations: GM to make 50,000 Chevy Blazers a year in Tatarstan, 700 miles from Moscow, and Ford to assemble 6,000 cars and vans near Minsk.[19]

Among Russian competitors, the worst of the local carmakers, AZLK (making the Moskvich) and truckmaker ZIL, are practically shut down. The viable Russian competitors, truckmaker Kamaz and GAZ, have seen production pick up in the past few years. The GAZ (Gorky Auto Works) factory complex was built in Gorky—known today as Nizhny Novgorod—in the 1930s, with help from Henry Ford. GAZ has a huge plant, with a capacity for 400,000-plus vehicles, including 300,000 medium-size trucks targeted to the military, agriculture, and industrial markets. GAZ has also created a light truck, the Gazelle, targeted toward Russia's new small businesses. The GAZ passenger car is the Volga, targeted initially for government use, which maintains its 1970s looks.[20] As the company is changing its focus from production to profits as its principle, the price of the Volga has been raised, which ultimately has hurt sales (its price is now close to that of many foreign automobiles); consequently, spare capacity was switched to making the more profitable light trucks and minibuses.[21]

Soviet planners decided to build the largest truck factory in the world: They built the Kamaz plant along the Kama River in Tatarstan, near the Urals. Kamaz covers 50 square kilometers with foundries, an engine plant, and an assembly line theoretically capable of producing 150,000 big trucks a year. (For comparison, the U.S. heavy truck market is about 150,000 in a normal year.) The fall of Communism led to a plummeting production, and the company was ripe for restructuring; costs were cut so that Kamaz would produce just 25,000 to 35,000 units a year, and the firm Deloitte & Touche was hired to keep the books and suggest improvements. The firm Kohlberg Kravis Roberts agreed to raise $3.5 billion over six years in exchange for 49 percent of Kamaz; the money was used to develop a new 25-ton truck for the oil and timber industries—a tractor trailer capable of competing with the best from abroad, with a diesel engine from Cummins (of the U.S.), a transmission from ZF (of Germany), and a cab from DAF (of the Netherlands)—and a light truck to challenge the Gazelle. Kamaz is also moving into passenger cars, with a microcar, the 30hp Oka, which sells for $3,500. Kamaz loses $1,000 or so per automobile, but its goal is to be profitable at 50,000 units.[22]

The last of the still-healthy Russian carmakers is UAZ. It makes off-road utility vehicles and small buses, for a total of 93,000 yearly. Its designs date back to the 1970s. The company has limited working capital.[23]

F-5 The AvtoVAZ–GM Joint Venture

General Motors and the European Bank for Reconstruction and Development, whose mission is to finance economic development projects in Eastern Europe, have created a new opportunity for AvtoVAZ: a $340 million joint venture to manufacture off-road vehicles in Togliatti. GM owns a 41.5 percent stake in the joint venture and invested $100 million; EBRD has a 17 percent stake, with $40 million, lending an additional $100 million; and AvtoVAZ contributed manufacturing facilities and intellectual property valued at $100 million, for a 41.5 percent stake. The new company produces the new GM-branded Niva, aiming for a maximum yearly output of 75,000 vehicles, of which more than half are built for export.[24] The new Niva is sold in Western Europe and to markets in Africa, Asia, Latin America, and the Middle East, where the old Niva was popular.[25] In Germany, the Niva will be equipped with engines from Adam Opel.[26]

The joint venture is attempting to maintain the price of the new cars below $10,000 (still beyond the reach of most Russian automobile buyers), but this requires dependence on domestic components; and lack of these in sufficient volumes and at required quality levels have previously set back plans by Ford (U.S.) and Fiat (Italy) to produce for the Russian market.[27]

The Niva sport-utility vehicle looks very attractive and has an impressive design. However, Russian consumers, in addition to balking at its price, still perceive it as being of lower quality: The automobile is assembled on the VAZ platform by VAZ workers. Also, the automobile body is produced at VAZ facilities—not at new GM facilities—so the Niva buyers do not expect the automobile finishing to be superior and last longer than that of the Niva ancestor, VAZ 21213.

Analysis Suggestions

1. Discuss the positioning strategies of the different competitors in the Russian market. Are the competitors competing for the same segments? Explain.

2. Address the potential contribution of the GM–AvtoVAZ joint venture to creating competitive advantage for the AvtoVAZ.

Notes

1. www.vaz.ru
2. www.vaz.ru
3. www.vaz.ru
4. Carol Matlack, "Anatomy of a Russian Wreck," *Business Week*, September 7, 1998, No. 3594, p. 86b.
5. Ibid.
6. www.vaz.ru
7. Matlack, "Anatomy of a Russian Wreck," p. 86b.
8. Ibid.
9. Ben Aris, "A Tale of Two Car Companies," *Euromoney*, January 2002, Vol. 393, pp. 24–25.
10. *Manufacturing Engineering*, "GM's Russian Partner," February 2001, Volume 126, No. 2, pp. 20–22.
11. Matlack, "Anatomy of a Russian Wreck," p. 86b.
12. www.vaz.ru
13. www.avtoreview.ru
14. www.avtoreview.ru
15. Aris, "A Tale of Two Car Companies," pp. 24–25.
16. Jerry Flint and Paul Klebnikov, "Would You Want to Drive a Lada?" *Forbes*, August 26, 1996, Vol. 158, No. 5, p. 66.
17. Ibid.
18. Matlack, "Anatomy of a Russian Wreck," p. 86b.
19. Flint and Klebnikov, "Would You Want to Drive a Lada?" p. 66.
20. Ibid.
21. Aris, "A Tale of Two Car Companies," pp. 24–25.
22. Flint and Klebnikov, "Would You Want to Drive a Lada?" p. 66.
23. Ibid.
24. *Country Monitor*, "GM Seals AvtoVAZ Deal," July 16, 2001, Vol. 9, No. 27, p. 8.
25. *Manufacturing Engineering*, "GM's Russian Partner," February 2001, Vol. 126, No. 2, pp. 20–22.
26. *Country Monitor*, "GM Seals AvtoVAZ Deal," p. 8.
27. ———, "Auto Investment," February 19, 2001, Vol. 9, No. 6, p. 2.

Disneyland Resort Paris: Reinventing the Mouse for the European Market

Dana Lascu and Jessica DiTommaso

Case Outline

Analysis Suggestions
Notes

Disneyland Resort Paris was known as Euro Disney in its first incarnation on the European continent. After its launch in April 1992, many name changes were made with the purpose of distancing the company from bad publicity.[1] After four different name revisions, the Disney Corporation has settled on Disneyland Resort Paris.

The idea of expanding the Disney magic to Europe proved to be a project that involved more attention to marketing than even this advertising giant could handle. Many Europeans did not want the American dreamland to distract their children, economy, and country from their own home-grown successful entertainment. David Koenig, author of *Mouse Tales: A Behind-the-Ears Look at Disneyland*, commented, "To the Parisian intellectuals, Disneyland was a symbol of everything contemptible about America: artificial, unstimulating, crass, crude, for the masses. Yet here was a 5,000-acre Disneyland springing up half an hour from the Louvre."[2]

From the very beginning, the Disney Corporation had the best of intentions for its European operation. After a successful opening of Disneyland Tokyo, the company was ready for its next international challenge. The company believed that locating the theme park in close proximity to Paris, France, would both ensure growth for Disney and offer an opportunity for it to incorporate different European cultures. It envisioned a Discoveryland that incorporated the histories of European countries through its fairytales: Italy for Pinocchio, England for Alice in Wonderland, and France for Sleeping Beauty's chateau.[3]

As Euro Disney, the company failed in many aspects of its marketing strategy:

- Euro Disney failed to target the many different tastes and preferences of a new continent of more than 300 million people; addressing the needs for visitors from dissimilar countries, such as Norway, Denmark, Germany, on one hand, and Spain, Italy, and France, on the other, was a challenge.
- Disney's high admission costs were 30 percent higher than a Disney World ticket in the United States, and the company refused to offer discounts for winter admissions.
- Euro Disney ignored travel lifestyles of Europeans: Europeans are accustomed to taking a few long vacations, rather than short trips, which would fit with the Disney model.[4] The company also neglected to consider national holidays and traditional breaks when Europeans are more likely to travel.
- Its restaurants did not appeal to visitors. Morris Nathanson Design in Rhode Island was responsible for designing the restaurants for Euro Disney. The company designed classic American-style restaurants— American-style restaurants are considered by most Europeans as exotic and unusual; unfortunately, the Europeans did not respond well to this format.[5]
- Euro Disney assumed that all Europeans wanted gourmet meals, which is not the case. While French consumers tend to live a more lavish lifestyle and spend larger amounts for gourmet meals, many other consumers in Europe do not—especially when they have to also spend large amounts on air travel, resorts, and park entrance fees. Meal scheduling was also problematic: the French, for example, are accustomed to having all businesses close down at 12:30 for meal times, but the park's restaurants were not made to accommodate such larger influxes for meals, leading to long lines

and frustrated visitors.[6] Finally, Euro Disney initially had an alcohol-free policy, which did not fit with local traditions, where wine is an important part of the culture.

Disney's failed marketing strategy for Euro Disney led to below-average attendance levels and product sales; the park was on the edge of bankruptcy in 1994, with a loss per year of more than a billion dollars.[7] Changing strategies—as well as its name, to Disneyland Resort Paris—has recently led to increased revenues of more than 4 percent, with operating revenues increasing by $32 million to $789 million.[8] Net losses have also decreased from $35.4 million to $27.6 million.[9]

With a full-scale change in the company's marketing direction, Disneyland Resort Paris has been successful in attracting visitors from many countries. Access was a priority for Disney. The company worked on access to the park via the fast train—the TGV; it also worked deals with the EuroStar and Le Shuttle train companies.[10] Disney has worked deals with trains and airlines to reduce prices—a move that ultimately benefited all; the price for transportation to Disney has dropped by 22 percent since the park's opening.[11] In 1992, the Walt Disney Company negotiated with Air France to make Air France the "official" Euro Disney carrier. [12] For visitors from the United Kingdom, British Airways is the preferred carrier of Disneyland Resort, and British Airways Holidays, its tour subsidiary, is the preferred travel partner.[13]

Disney also adapted targeting strategies to individual markets to address the interests and values of different segments of European consumers. It placed representatives around the world with the task of researching specific groups of consumers and creating the best package deals for potential visitors; the new Disney offices were established in London, Frankfurt, Milan, Brussels, Amsterdam, and Madrid.[14] Research results led to the tailoring of package deals that were in line with vacation lifestyles of the different European segments. In addition to the package deals, Disney offered discounts for the winter months and half-price discounts for individuals going to the park after 5:00 P.M.

To better accommodate its guests, Disneyland Paris revised its stringent no-alcohol policy, allowing wine and beer to be served at its restaurants. The resort hotels also lowered their room rates and offered less expensive menu choices in their restaurants.[15] The restaurants created more suitable food options, catering to different regional European tastes, but continued to offer large American-size portions.[16] Crepes and waffles are on the menu of almost every street stand in the park.

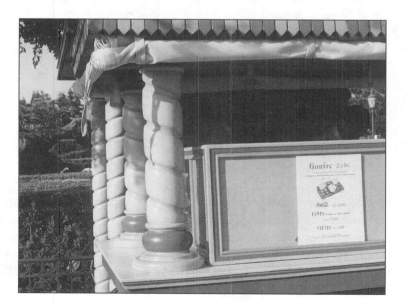

This stand sells waffles for 2.45 Euros (waffles are primarily a dessert in Europe), Vittel water, Fanta, and Coca-Cola.

Mickey Mouse and Donald Duck have French accents, and many rides were renamed to appeal to French visitors: in Adventureland, Le Ventre de la Terre (Galleries under the tree), l'Ile au Tresor (Treasure Island), La Cabane des Robinson (Robinsons' Cabin); in Fantasyland, Le Chateau de la Belle au Bois Dormant (Sleeping Beauty's Castle, rather than Cinderella's Castle at Disney World, United States), Blanche-Neige et les Sept Nains (Snow White and the Seven Dwarfs), Le Carrousel de Lancelot, Le Pays des Contes des Fee (the Country of Fairytales); and in Discoveryland, L'Arcade des Visionnaires, Le Visionarium (a time-travel adventure with Jules Verne), Les Mysteres du Nautilus (Nautilus's Mysteries).

Le Chateau de la Belle au Bois Dormant (Sleeping Beauty's Castle) in the background.

Le Carousel de Lancelot.

The French-named attractions exist alongside attractions such as Main Street U.S.A. (see photograph), with its Main Street Station, vehicles and horse-drawn streetcars, and Frontierland, with Thunder Mesa River Boat Landing, Legends of the Wild West, Rustler Roundup Shootin' Gallery, and other similar themes. The hotels also have more traditional American themes—New York, Newport Bay, and Sequoia Lodge.

Main Street, U.S.A.
Disneyland Railroad Main
Street Station.

The park also has numerous attractions that appeal to European guests in general, such as Pinocchio's Fantastic Journey, and Cinemas Gaumont, which feature live concerts with performers from around the world.

Pinocchio's Fantastic
Journey.

Along with creating an environment of greater appeal to European visitors, Disney changed the name of its resort to Disneyland Resort Paris. In its advertising strategy, the company decided to focus its efforts on brand building, initially targeting consumers with a new communication strategy implemented by Ogilvy & Mather Direct.[17] Disney charged its advertising, aiming its message at Europeans who did not grow up with Mickey Mouse; in the park's new commercials, parents and grandparents are shown delighting in the happiness of their children and grandchildren. The advertisements feature "children impatient to depart for and thrilled to arrive at the Magic Kingdom or a grandfather delighted by his grand-daughter's excitement at the prospect of seeing Mickey; or grown-ups sitting tensely before riding on the Space Mountain."[18]

The park is also working with Red Cell, a leading Paris-based advertising agency, for all its television campaigns for the park's new attractions.[19]

Disney is capitalizing on its recent European success by offering yet another grand theme park adjacent to Disneyland—the Walt Disney Studios. Disney is attempting to promote Walt Disney Studios in a manner that would not cannibalize attendance at Disneyland Paris.[20] Among its attractions are a Rock'N'Roller Coaster Starring Aerosmith, capitalizing on the U.S. band's success in Europe; Animagique; and Cinemagique. The park is dedicated to the art of cinema, animation, and television, and it focuses on the efforts of many Europeans who made it all possible to bring fantasy to reality.

Analysis Suggestions

1. How do the values and lifestyles of European consumers differ from those of consumers in the United States? Discuss the Disney failure to address European consumers' preferences based on the respective values and lifestyles.

2. A large proportion of the park's visitors come from Spain and Latin America. How can Disneyland Resort Paris appeal more effectively to this market? Design a new target marketing strategy aimed at the Spanish and Latin American market.

Notes

1. Harriet Marsh, "Variations on a Theme Park," *Marketing*, London. May 2, 1996.
2. David Koenig, *Mouse Tales: A Behind-the-Ears Look at Disneyland.* Irvine: Bonaventure Press, 1994.
3. Ibid.
4. "Euro Disneyland SCA," International Directory of Company Histories, Vol. 20, p. 209–212.
5. Gail Ghetia, "As American as French fries: Euro Disneyland, when it opens, will feature typically American restaurants," *Restaurant Hospitality*, August 1990.
6. "Euro Disneyland SCA," p. 209–212.
7. "The Kingdom inside a Republic," *The Economist*, April 13, 1996.
8. Juliana Koranteng, "Euro Disney revenues rise," *Amusement Business*. August 6, 2001.
9. ———, "Future may be bright for Euro Disney," *Amusement Business*, May 21, 2001.
10. "Euro Disneyland SCA," p. 209–212.
11. Marsh, "Variations on a Theme Park."
12. Ibid.
13. Barbara J. Mays, "French park still negotiating for airline partnership," *Travel Weekly*, April 20, 1992.
14. "The Kingdom inside a Republic," *The Economist.*
15. Barbara Rudolph, "Monsieur Mickey: Euro Disneyland is on schedule, but with a distinct French accent," *Time*, March 25, 1991.
16. Ibid.
17. Marsh, "Variations on a Theme Park."
18. "The Kingdom inside a Republic," *The Economist.*
19. Juliana Koranteng, "Taking it to the tube: Parc Asterix to unleash national TV campaign," *Amusement Business*, February 11, 2002.
20. Koranteng, "Euro Disney revenues rise."

Siemens: International Entry Modes and the Siemens Umbrella Brand

Tiffany Allen, Jessica DiTommaso, Kate Hopkins, Dana Lascu, Paula Munafo, and Amber Summers

Case Outline

H-1 Siemens and the Medical Equipment Industry
H-2 Siemens and the Lighting Industry
H-3 Siemens and the Automation and Control Industry
H-4 Siemens and the Power Industry
H-5 Siemens and the Financial Services Industry
H-6 Siemens Transportation
H-7 Siemens and the Information Technology Industry
Analysis Suggestions
Notes

Siemens, a German company whose business portfolio comprises industries such as information and communications, automation and control, power, transportation, medical, and lighting, has spearheaded innovation in many domains: It linked the first long-distance telegraph system in Europe in 1848; it completed a 6,600-mile telegraph line from London, United Kingdom, to Calcutta, India, in 1870; and it created the first electrified railway and one of the first elevators.[1] Today, Siemens offers 54 different products, 48 types of services, and a total of 60 brand names. The company is headquartered in Munich, Germany, and is a multinational corporation with a presence in 190 countries, employing 480,000 people. Formally, its operating groups include Automation and Drives, Power Generation, Transportation Systems, Medical Solutions, Financing and Real Estate, Information and Communication Networks, Information and Communication Mobile, and Siemens Business Services. Despite the weakening economy, most of these sectors returned positive earnings in recent years.[2]

H-1 Siemens and the Medical Equipment Industry

The medical equipment industry consists of different products, services, and solutions for integrated health care; in this category are makers and distributors of medical supplies, instruments, and equipment. Siemens ranks fifth in sales among manufacturers of medical equipment, behind GE Medical Solutions, Baxter, Tyco Healthcare, and Medtronic.[3] Siemens focuses on innovative technologies for accurate diagnoses and therapies, and it offers services that optimize processes and efficiency in hospitals and offices.[4] Siemens is also the world's largest application service provider for the health-care industry, in areas such as anesthesia systems, angiography, computed tomography, fluoroscopy, hearing aids, intensive care systems, magnetic resonance systems, mammography, nuclear medicine, oncology care, radiography, surgery, ultrasound, and urology.[5]

Siemens has recently entered into a partnership with HealthSouth Corporation in the United States to create the world's first all-digital and automated hospital: Siemens will serve as the primary technology provider and support the hospital in health-care information technology applications and infrastructure, medical equipment, telecommunications, and "smart" building techniques.[6] The hospital offers such services as an Internet connection to every bed for videoconferencing and a wireless wellness monitor to evaluate the health status and indicate the exact location of each patient.[7]

H-2 Siemens and the Lighting Industry

In the lighting area, Siemens specializes in lighting sources and the associated electronic control gear, offering products such as general lighting solutions, automotive lighting (an industry in which the company is ranked first), photo-optic lamps, and display lighting. In this sector, it competes with GE Lighting, Matsushita Electric Works, and Philips Electronics.[8] Siemens' focus in this industry is on innovative products, such as e-business, and expansion into Asia and Eastern Europe. Its latest joint venture in opto-semiconductors with Osram Sylvania has helped the company during difficult economic conditions: Its sales grew 5 percent in fiscal 2001, mostly attributed to Osram.[9]

H-3 Siemens and the Automation and Control Industry

Siemens is the world's largest supplier of products, systems, solutions, and services in the industrial and building technology sector: Its four major automation markets consist of manufacturing, process, building, and logistics automation. Siemens Automation and Control is divided into four subgroups: Automation and

Drives, Industrial Solutions and Services, Siemens Dematic, and Siemens Building Technologies.[10] Its major products include industrial networks, human/machine interfaces, power controls and supplies, industrial components, AC/DC drives, motion-control products, analyzers, scales, motors and pumps, circuit breakers, transformers, and residential electric products such as surge protectors and meters. The company's products range from airport logistics to consumer daily life: Its Smart Homes have electronic butlers who greet homeowners at the door, lock up when commanded, and answer the telephone, while their fire detectors can differentiate between the smoke from a cigar or a fire.[11] Top competitors in this segment of the business include Emerson, GE Industrial Products and Systems, and Schneider.[12]

Siemens Power Generation (PG) is an important player in the global power plant development business, focusing on the design and construction of fossil-fueled plants, which account for about 75 percent of sales.[13] Siemens PG manufactures gas and steam turbines, compressors, catalysts, and other electrical products and builds nuclear, hydroelectric, biomass, and combined heat and power plants.[14] A division of the power segment, the Siemens Power Transmission and Distribution department, which constructs and installs electrical transmission and distribution systems, including high- and medium-voltage power lines, transformers, and switching equipment, accounts for 5 percent of its parent company sales.[15] Siemens has recently contracted to build the world's largest diesel power plant in Africa.[16] Siemens' competitors in the power industry include companies such as ALSTOM, GE Power Systems, HOCHTIEF, Schneider, ABB, and Fluor.[17]

H-4 Siemens and the Power Industry

In the financial services sector, Siemens specializes in innovative corporate financing and related risk management. Siemens offers financial services such as leasing, factoring, asset securitization, pension advisory, insurance, investment management, treasury and financing services, equity investment, project and export financing, and e-financing. Siemens Financial Services focuses on sales and corporate financing. Siemens specializes in balance sheet and liquidity management for large international companies and develops products and services for each client, involving the client, business partners, and, when necessary, public agencies and other service providers such as banks. The Siemens Financial Services ventures in India and the United States have been especially profitable.

H-5 Siemens and the Financial Services Industry

The transportation sector of Siemens is divided into two groups: Transportation Systems and Siemens VDO Automotive AG. Through these two different groups, Siemens offers transportation solutions and systems, such as modular vehicles for light rail and mainline systems, technology for driverless subways and computer-controlled electronic interlockings, and optical sensor systems and GPS-based service and diagnostic concepts, among others.

H-6 Siemens Transportation

The products offered by the transportation sector of Siemens are mass transit, regional passenger rail, main line and high-speed traffic, turnkey systems, and a service sector that includes service on infrastructure and telecommunications equipment. Siemens partners with the automotive industry to create innovative solutions and systems integration. Its goal is to grow faster than the overall market, expanding its position in Europe, Asia, and the Americas to become the number-one supplier for automotive electronics and to increase the number of patents and industrial rights to more than 25,000 in four years.[18]

H-7 Siemens and the Information Technology Industry

Siemens' information technology division, which accounts for approximately 37 percent of Siemens' total sales,[19] is organized into three groups: Information and Communications Networks, Information and Communication Mobile, and Siemens Business Services. Information and Communication Networks provides products such as broadband access gear, e-business systems, network management systems, professional consulting services, security systems, switches, and telephone systems.[20] The Information and Communication Mobile group specializes in core network equipment, intelligence network equipment, mobile networking systems, and wireless modules. Siemens Business Services specializes in business and enterprises services, consumer services, public sector services, and service provider and network operator services; and e-business Solutions and Services address five core areas: supply chain management, enterprise resource management, business information management, customer relationship management, and electronic commerce.[21]

Siemens recently bought Efficient Networks, a United States firm specializing in digital subscriber line (DSL) technology—which allows Internet transmission and voice calls to take place at the same time. In January 2001, Siemens also introduced its first cellular phone into the United States; Siemens is the third biggest producer of handsets in Europe.[22]

A recent Siemens initiative is the SURPASS program, which will enable it to increase the services that it provides to its customers in the packet-based network area. The company will use SURPASS technology and combine it with applications delivered by outside vendors (Broadsoft, Comverse, Iperia, LongBoard, Pactolus, Tornado Development, and Ubiquity).[23] According to Roland Koch, CEO of Siemens' Information and Communication Networks, there are great opportunities in the mobile arena and the business is just in its beginning stages.[24]

In this sector, Siemens competes with Alcatel, Ericsson, and Nokia in offering communications products for public networks, homes, and businesses. Alcatel, a French company, has a contract with Deutsche Telecom and is one of Siemens' major competitors in Germany.[25] Ericsson, a Swedish telecommunications giant, sells equipment for communication networks and mobile telephones. Ericsson and Sony have formed a joint venture to produce mobile phones, which may give it an edge over mobile phone rivals Nokia and Motorola.[26] Nokia is the number-one seller of wireless phones and offers mobile phones and networks. Siemens is the most profitable of all its major competitors and consistently reports high profits.[27]

Technology firms have been affected by the technology slump that started in the second half of the year 2000, at a time when computer prices began to decline. Technology firms had over-invested and are consequently struggling as a result, with large fixed costs and excess computing and network capacity.[28] The Siemens Information and Communications Network, which makes telecom equipment, issued a profit warning and was forced to cut 5,500 jobs.[29] However, despite the slowing market and the technology slump, the division's sales are increasing at a rate of more than 50 percent yearly—a turnaround attributed to the leadership of the new head of this unit, Thomas Ganswindt.[30]

The Siemens Business Services Group, a leading supplier of solutions and services in the information and communication sector, with 35,900 employees and a revenue of 6 billion Euros, has recently undergone important changes as well. Paul Stodden was appointed president in December 2001. Internally, his appointment was hailed by employees as a significant move in turning around a stagnating business. Stodden has turned around other Siemens businesses and gained the respect and allegiance of employees in the process. Among them are Fujitsu Siemens, where he was president and CEO and where he restructured the company and developed it into a provider for Mobility and Business Critical Computing Solutions without firing and/or alienating employees in the process. More recently, as the CEO of Siemens IT Services, he turned this business into a top-performing Siemens unit.

Analysis Suggestions

1. Perform an analysis of the Siemens product portfolio. Comment on the Siemens branding strategy. Refer to www.siemens.com for additional information.

2. Siemens has expanded internationally using different entry modes. Identify and classify some of the entry mode relationships that Siemens has established with companies worldwide.

3. Siemens' diverse product portfolio is centered on one theme: innovation. Comment on product and service innovation at Siemens.

Notes

1. www.siemens.com.
2. Hoover's, Siemens AG-industry conglomerates, www.hoovers.com.
3. Hoover's, Medical Equipment Snapshot, www.hoovers.com.
4. Welcome to Siemens, Health Care, www.usa.siemens.com.
5. Hoover's, Siemens Medical Solutions, www.hoovers.com.
6. www.siemens.com.
7. Welcome to Siemens, www.usa.siemens.com.
8. Hoover's, OSRAM GmbH, Company Capsule, www.hoovers.com.
9. Management's Discussion and Analysis, www.siemens.com.
10. Automation and Control, www.siemens.com.
11. Ibid.
12. "Siemens Automation," Hoover's Database, www.hoovers.com, February 12, 2002.
13. "Power," Siemens Business Segments, www.siemens.com, January 23, 2002.
14. Ibid.
15. Ibid.
16. "Press Releases," Siemens Business Segments, www.siemens.com, February 12, 2002.
17. "Siemens Power," Hoover's Database, www.hoovers.com, February 12, 2002.
18. Transportation, www.siemens.com.
19. Hoover's Online, "Siemens AG—Information and Communications, www.hoovers.com.
20. Ibid.
21. Siemens web site, "Siemens Business Services," www.siemens.com.
22. Hoover's Online, "Siemens Buys DSL Company to Spur Internet-Related Growth," www.hoovers.com, February 18, 2002.
23. Hoover's Online, "Siemens Debuts Program to Build Revenue-Generating Applications for Next Generation Converged Network Solution," www.hoovers.com, February 18, 2002.
24. Responsive Database, "Roland Koch: Company Man," Baines Stewart, *Communications International*, www.rdsweb1.rdsinc.com, July 2000, pp. 42–44.
25. Hoover's Online, "Alcatel Background," www.hoovers.com, February 18, 2002.
26. Hoover's Online. "Ericsson Background." www.hoovers.com, February 18, 2002.
27. Hoover's Online, "Competitive Landscape," www.hoovers.com.
28. Alster, Norm, "What Recession?" *Electronic Business*, January 2002. Volume 28, pp. 64–68.
29. Greimel, Hans, "Siemens weighs slashing more jobs," *Toronto Star Newspapers, LTD*, August 4, 2001, p. C09.
30. Ibid.

Glossary

A

accessibility The ability to communicate with the international target market.

acculturation The act of learning a new culture; encompasses intercultural interaction and adaptation.

actionability The extent to which the target market segment is responsive to the marketing strategies used.

adaptation The strategy of altering a product to better meet the needs of a local market.

adaptation of the advertising strategy The act of changing a company's promotional mix to each country or market, or creating local campaigns.

adiaphoras The norms that refer to customs that a foreign national may engage in but is not necessarily expected to do so.

advertising effectiveness studies Studies conducted to examine the effectiveness and appropriateness of advertisements aimed at individual markets.

advocacy advertising Advertising a particular position or point of view.

African Development Bank A bank, headquartered in Abidjan, Ivory Coast, that has as a primary goal poverty reduction in Africa, providing support and expertise in agriculture, human resources, and health services, with an emphasis on small business. (See www.afdb.org.)

aggressive export pricing A pricing strategy that prices products below market price in order to penetrate new markets.

all-purpose discount stores General merchandise discount stores that offer a wide variety of merchandise and limited depth.

all-you-can-afford method The process of allocating the maximum amount possible to advertising; this method is used by small and medium-size corporations.

analogy method A method for estimation that relies on developments and findings in similar markets or where the product is in the same life-cycle stage.

Andean Common Market (AnCom) A trade group of the Andean countries that aspires to become a common market; it is currently in the process of agreeing upon common external tariffs. (See www.comunidadandina.org.)

antidumping Legislation designed to counter unfair price competition; lengthy antidumping investigations can also serve as an impediment to trade.

antidumping duties Duties that must be paid by firms as a punishment for engaging in unfair price competition.

antitrust laws Laws designed to prevent anticompetitive activities, such as the creation of monopolies and cartels.

appearances An individual's physical attire and overall grooming.

applications positioning The marketing of a very precise product application that is differentiated in the consumers' minds from other products that have a more general use.

Arab Maghreb Union (AMU) An attempt, in the early 1980s, at creating a free trade area in the Southern Mediterranean area; it was not successful due to conflict.

arbitration Binding procedure for conflict resolution involving an independent third party; a faster and less costly procedure than a lawsuit.

ASEAN Free Trade Area (AFTA) A free trade agreement signed by members of the Association of Southeast Asian Nations (ASEAN). (See www.asean.or.id.)

Asian Development Bank   A bank, headquartered in Manila, the Philippines, that focuses on the private sector in Asia, sponsoring projects aimed at increasing access to technology and improving the functioning of government in the region. (See www.adb.org.)

Asia-Pacific Economic Cooperation (APEC)   A trade group including all major economies of the Asia-Pacific region, it is a forum for economic cooperation and has as its goal the gradual reduction of barriers to trade and investment between member countries. (See www.apecsec.org.sg.)

assimilation   The act of abandoning all home-country traditions while learning a new culture.

Association of Southeast Asian Nations (ASEAN)   A successful example of integration in Asia, creating an environment that promotes mutual involvement in industrial development in the region and a free trade area composed of Brunei, Cambodia, Indonesia, Laos, Malaysia, Myanmar, the Philippines, Singapore, Thailand, and Vietnam. (See www.asean.or.id.)

attribute/benefit positioning   Positioning that communicates product attributes and benefits, differentiating each brand from the other company brands and from those of competitors.

automatic import license   A license granted freely to importing companies but may be used by government for the purpose of import surveillance, thus discouraging import surges, imposing administrative and financial burdens on importers, and delaying shipment.

B

back translation   The translation of translated text back into its original language, by a different individual, to ensure that the instrument has been translated as intended.

barter   A simple, nonmonetized exchange of goods and/or services between two parties.

benefit segmentation   The process of identifying international market segments based on important differences between the benefits sought by the target market from purchasing a particular product.

big emerging markets (BEMs)   Large markets characterized by rapid economic development and high potential; big emerging markets set the pace for the economy in their geographic region.

bilateral agreement   Regional trade cooperation between two countries aimed at reducing or eliminating trade barriers for all or for selected products.

billboards   Advertisements in public areas appearing on large posters or electronic panels.

blocked currency   A strategy that does not allow importers to exchange local currency for the seller's currency or a currency that the seller is willing to accept as payment (hard currency).

bourgeoisie   A dominant social class, which, according to Marxist-Leninist theory, establishes lucrative means of production and achieves high productivity at the expense of exploited workers.

boycott   An action calling for a ban on consumption of all goods associated with a particular company and/or country.

brand awareness research   Research investigating how consumers' knowledge and recognition of a brand name affect their purchasing behavior.

brand name counterfeiting   Selling counterfeit products as brand name originals.

brand name generation and testing   The testing of brand names and logos, necessary when companies market their products internationally.

broadcast medium   A nonpersonal channel of communication such as television or radio.

brokers and agents   Middlemen who bring international buyers and sellers together; they do not carry title to the product.

building channels   Creating new distribution channels, especially necessary in situations where there are no channels at all, or there are no channels that conform to the needs of the company.

buyback agreements   Agreements whereby the seller builds and provides a turnkey plant and is paid up front part of the cost of the plant in an agreed-upon convertible currency; in return, the seller agrees to purchase specific quantities of the plant's output over an extended period of time.

buyer behavior research   Research examining brand preferences and brand attitudes.

buying offices   Buyers representing different firms located abroad.

C

capitalism   A stage of economic and political development, which, according to Marxist-Leninist theory, is characterized, in its early stages, by an emerging bourgeoisie, the shift of production from the agrarian sector to the industrial sector, and, in its later stages, by imperialism, where capital loses its national identity by crossing borders and establishing monopolies.

catalog retailers   Retailers selling products through mail catalogs.

catalog showrooms   Showrooms displaying the products of catalog retailers, offering high-turnover, brand name goods at discount prices.

category killers   Large general merchandise discount stores that carry a narrow variety of merchandise and a wide assortment; also called category specialists or stores with category dominance.

category specialists   Large general merchandise discount stores that carry a narrow variety of merchandise and a wide assortment; also called category killers.

causal research   Research that examines cause-and-effect relationships.

Central American Common Market (CACM)   An economic agreement between Central American countries; this agreement includes plans for forming a regional economic union similar to the European Union, and to advance regional and international trade.

Central European Free Trade Agreement (CEFTA)   An economic alliance between the most developed of former Soviet Bloc countries attempting to reduce all duties and nontariff barriers on goods; member countries are adopting policies that will facilitate their adherence to the European Union. (See www.cefta.org.)

channel of communication   The medium used to communicate a message about a product to the consumer.

channel performance and coverage studies   Studies investigating whether existing channels are appropriate for communication, if channels exist at all, or whether they are appropriate for international marketing communications.

chronemics   The timing of verbal exchanges.

clearing account   A complex form of countertrade whereby countries trade products up to a certain amount stated in a particular, mutually-agreed-upon hard currency and within a given time frame, and, when an imbalance occurs and one country owes money to the other, swing credits are paid in an agreed-upon hard currency, known as the clearing currency; also called a clearing agreement.

clearing currency   The agreed-upon currency used to pay swing credits in a clearing account or agreement.

code law   Comprehensive written laws that specify what constitutes legal behavior.

collectivism   The degree to which individuals prefer to act in the interest of the group, rather than in their own self-interest.

combination stores   Medium-size retail stores that combine food and drug retailing.

common law   Laws that are based on prior court rulings (legal precedents).

common market   A market composed of member countries, characterized by the unrestricted movement of goods, labor, and capital.

Common Market for Eastern and Southern Africa (COMESA)   An agreement between twenty member countries aimed at achieving economic integration; COMESA is currently eliminating all tariff and nontariff barriers to trade and is in the process of adopting common external tariffs. (See www.comesa.int.)

Commonwealth of Independent States (CIS)   A political agreement between the twelve non-Baltic countries of the former Soviet Union. (See www.cis.minsk.by.)

communism   A stage in economic and political development, which, according to Marxist-Leninist theory, is characterized by state and cooperative ownership of all means of production and property.

company publications   Public relations publications that describe the products of a company to potential customers and summarize financial achievements.

compensation   The payment in products and in cash, usually in a mutually-agreed-upon convertible currency.

competitive pricing analyses   Pricing studies that determine the price the market will bear for the respective product category.

competitive-parity method   The strategy of using competitors' level of advertising spending as a benchmark for the company's own advertising expenditures.

competitive product studies   Studies that examine competitive product strategies in order to decide on the brand's product mix in the respective country.

competitor positioning   The process of comparing the firm's brand with those of competitors, directly or indirectly.

complementary export agents   Firms that export other firms' products that are complementary to their offerings, along with their own products, for a fee/commission.

complementary export merchants   Distributors who take title to the complementary products distributed and are compensated in the form of a discount.

comprador   A foreign agent with an exclusive arrangement with a company, representing its operations in a particular country; also referred to as a managing agent.

concentrated targeting   The process of selecting only one market segment and targeting it with one single brand.

concept development and testing studies   Concept tests usually performed in developed countries evaluating the product/service offering and the related marketing mix in light of the different international target markets.

conceptual equivalence   The extent to which meanings remain the same in different cultural environments.

confiscation   The foreign government seizure of company assets and/or investors' assets without any compensation.

consortia   A company created with the participation of three or more companies; allowed in underserved markets or in domains where the government and/or the marketplace can control its monopolistic activity.

consumer segmentation studies   Research conducted to identify market segment profiles.

content analysis   Method that assesses the content of advertisements in a medium with verbal and/or visual content.

continuous innovation   Product innovation where there is no disruption in consumption patterns; such innovations involve product alterations such as new flavors or new products that are improvements over the old offerings.

contract manufacturing   A relationship between two companies wherein one company contracts with another to manufacture products according to the contracting company's specifications and for a specified period of time.

controlled test marketing   Test marketing that involves offering a new product to a group of stores and evaluating the market's reaction to it.

convenience stores   Small retailers located in residential areas, open long hours, and carrying limited lines of high-turnover necessities.

conventional supermarkets   Self-service food retailers with annual sales of more than $2 million and with an area less than 20,000 square feet.

cooperative export arrangements   Agreements that involve the use of a distribution system of exporters with established systems of selling abroad, who agree to handle the export function of a noncompeting (but not necessarily unrelated) company on a contractual basis; also called mother henning or piggybacking.

cooperative exporting   Using the distribution system of exporters with established systems of selling abroad who agree to handle the export function of a noncompeting (but not necessarily unrelated) company on a contractual basis; also called mother henning and piggybacking.

copyright   The rights to an original work of art (literature, music, film, design, and other works), enabling the owner to reproduce, sell, perform, or film the work.

core product strategy   The strategy of using the same standard core product/service worldwide, but varying certain aspects of the offering (product ingredients, advertising) from market to market.

corporate advertising   A type of advertising that is used to promote the company behind the different brands.

corruption laws   Laws designed to prevent multinational corporations from using unethical means to obtain competitive advantage in a particular market.

cost analyses   Methods used for projecting the cost of research.

cost-based transfer pricing   A pricing strategy used in intra-firm sales for commercial transactions between units of the same corporation, within or beyond the national borders of the parent company, where the costs reflect not the costs incurred by the company, but the estimated opportunity costs of the product.

cost-of-living adjustment   A compensation incentive whereby the company adjusts expatriate salaries to reflect the cost of living in the new environment at standards in the expatriate's home country; also called post adjustment.

Council of Ministers   The decision-making body (the legislature) of the European Union, composed of one minister from each member country.

Council of Mutual Economic Assistance (CMEA)   A trade agreement between the countries of the Soviet Bloc that disintegrated after the fall of communism. CMEA was an economic body similar in nature to a free trade area, and approached what would be considered a political union.

Council of Nations   The constitutional council of the European Union consisting of representatives from parliaments of EU member states. (See www.europa.eu.int.)

counterpurchase   A form of trade that involves two exchanges paid for in cash; it involves two parallel contracts whereby the seller agrees to purchase products that are usually unrelated to its business from the buyer and sell them on international markets; also called parallel barter.

countertrade   A form of trade whereby a company sells a product to a buyer and agrees to accept, in return for payment, products from the buyer's firm or from the trade agency/institution of the buyer.

countervailing duties   Duties imposed on subsidized products imported into a country.

countervailing duty actions   Investigations initiated to determine whether imports are sold below fair prices as a result of foreign subsidies and the subsequent establishment of measures to offset subsidies.

country of manufacture   The country in which a particular product is manufactured.

country of origin   The country with which a particular product or service is associated.

creeping expropriation   A situation characterized by bureaucratic red tape and corruption, an unreliable judicial system, and shifting regulations, where foreign government actions discourage foreign investment, especially investment in nonessential sectors.

cross-border shopping   Purchasing products from a neighboring country where the consumers may be charged lower duties.

cultural variability   The classification of cultures on a number of dimensions, or continuums; Hofstede classified cultures on the dimensions of collectivism, masculinity, power distance, and uncertainty avoidance.

culture   The continuously evolving totality of learned and shared meanings, rituals, norms, and traditions among the members of an organization or society.

culture shock   A pervasive feeling of anxiety resulting from one's presence in a new, unfamiliar culture.

currency and capital flow controls   All protectionist activities involving the control of capital and hard currency flows in and out of a particular country.

customs union   A market composed of member countries imposing identical import duties and sharing import regulations.

D

data collection instrument   The instrument used to collect data, such as a printed questionnaire, a paper-and-pencil measure, or an electronic measurement device.

decentering   The successive translation (by different translators) of an instrument between the original language and the language of administration with the purpose of obtaining an instrument that is closest in meaning to the original.

decision support system   A coordinated collection of data, systems, tools, and techniques, complemented by supporting software and hardware designed for the gathering and interpretation of business and environmental data.

decline stage   The stage of the international product life cycle in which products are rapidly losing ground to new technologies or product alternatives, causing a decrease in sales and profits.

decoding   The process whereby the target consumer receives the message from the advertiser and translates it into meaningful information.

degree of product/service newness   The extent to which a product is new to the market in general or to a group of consumers.

Delphi method   A method of forecasting sales by asking a number of experts to estimate market performance, aggregating the results, and sharing this information with the said experts; the process is repeated several times, until a consensus is reached.

demographic segmentation   The process of identifying market segments based on age, gender, race, income, education, occupation, social class, life-cycle stage, and household size.

department stores   General retailers that offer a broad variety of goods and wide assortments.

depth interview   A qualitative research method involving extensive interviews aimed at discovering consumer motivations, feelings, and attitudes toward an issue of concern to the sponsor using unstructured interrogation.

descriptive research   All research methods observing or describing phenomena.

design counterfeiting   Copying designs or scents of another company.

designing and developing the product   Developing product prototypes and giving the product a name, a brand identity, and a marketing mix; a step in the new product development process.

developed countries   Highly industrialized countries with well-developed service sectors, mature markets, and intense competition; they are characterized by the World Bank as high-income, with a GNP per capita of US$9,266 and above.

developing and evaluating concepts   Determining how consumers will perceive and use a new product; a step in the new product development process .

developing countries   Countries that are primarily agrarian, often neglected or under-served by large multinationals, and characterized by the World Bank as low-income countries, with a GNP per capita of less than US$755.

differential exchange rate   The rate imposed by the local government to promote imports of desirable and necessary goods; it also can be the difference between the black market exchange rate and the official government rate.

differential response   The extent to which international market segments respond differently to marketing strategies.

differentiated targeting   A targeting strategy identifying market segments with different preferences for a particular product category and targeting each segment with different brands and different marketing strategies.

diffusion process   The process by which a product is adopted by consumers worldwide.

direct exporting   An export entry mode whereby a firm handles its own exports, usually with the help of an in-house exporting department.

direct mail retailing   Retailing using catalogs and other direct mail, instead of brick-and-mortar stores.

direct selling   Selling that involves a salesperson, typically an independent distributor, contacting a consumer at a convenient location—at his or her home or workplace, demonstrating product use and benefits, taking orders, and delivering the merchandise.

distribution alliance   A nonequity relationship between two firms, in which one firm handles the other's distribution or some aspect of the distribution process.

domestic marketing   Marketing that is focused solely on domestic consumers and on the home-country environment.

domestication   The process initiated by a foreign government leading to the gradual transfer of ownership and management to locals.

drive to maturity   A stage in economic development, described by Rostow, as characterized by the technological and entrepreneurial skill to produce anything society chooses to produce.

driver of internationalization   A driver in the environment—such as competition, technology, or labor costs—or within the firm—such as product life cycle—that causes the firm to go international.

drivers in the business environment   Elements in the business environment, such as competition, technology, and labor costs, causing the firm to become involved internationally.

dumping   Selling products below cost to get rid of excess inventory and/or to undermine competition.

dynamic incremental pricing   A pricing strategy whereby a company assumes that it will have certain fixed costs whether or not it exports its products overseas and does not factor in its international price marketing and promotion costs for domestic distribution, nor its full overhead.

dynamically continuous innovation   Innovation that does not alter significantly consumer behavior but still entails a change in the consumption pattern.

E

early adopters   Consumers who purchase a product early in its product life cycle and who tend to be opinion leaders in their communities who take risks, but with greater discernment than innovators; they account for 13.5% of the total market.

early majority   Consumers who enjoy the status of being among the first in their peer group to purchase a popular product; they account for 34% of the total market.

ecology   The manner in which society adapts to its habitat, i.e., the distribution of resources within an industrialized country versus a developing country; the desire for efficiency, space-saving devices, or green products.

Economic Community of West African States (ECOWAS)   A free trade agreement that strives to achieve economic integration in West Africa; domination by Nigeria, civil unrest, and regional conflict have served as impediments in the group's success. (See www.ecowas.int.)

education allowance   A compensation incentive whereby the company agrees to cover the cost of children's education at an international private school in the country of assignment or at a boarding school in the expatriate's home country.

electronic retailing   Selling through the Internet using web sites to increase market penetration and market diversification; also called interactive home shopping and Internet retailing.

embargo   The prohibition of all business deals with the country that is the target of the embargo, endorsed or initiated by the company's home country.

emerging markets   Countries that are developing rapidly and have great economic potential; the World Bank characterizes them as middle-income countries, with a GNP per capita of US$766 to US$9,265.

emic instrument   A data collection instrument constructed for each nationality to measure a particular factor; it is the best measure for culture-specific phenomena.

employment protection   Protection of local employment by not granting import licenses for products competing with similar, locally produced, goods.

encoding   The process whereby the advertiser puts the company's message about the product into words and images that are aimed at the target consumer.

enculturation   The process by which individuals learn the beliefs and behaviors endorsed by their own culture.

entry mode   The approach to international expansion a company chooses based on desired control and on the risk it can afford.

established channels   Distribution channels that already exist in a particular market.

ethnocentric orientation   Company strategies consistent with the belief that domestic strategies, techniques, and personnel are superior to foreign ones and therefore provide the most effective framework for the company's overseas involvement; companies adopting this perspective view international operations and customers as secondary to domestic operations and customers.

ethnocentrism   The belief that one's culture is superior to another and that strategies used in one's home country (presumably a developed country) will work just as well internationally.

etic instrument   A culture-free data collection instrument that can be used to measure the same phenomenon in different cultures.

Euroland   The nickname of the European Monetary Union. (See www.europa.eu.int.)

European Atomic Energy Community   A precursor to the European Union, it addressed issues related to the use and control of atomic energy.

European Bank for Reconstruction and Development   A bank headquartered in London, United Kingdom, which has as main goals reforming and strengthening markets in the transition economies of Central and Eastern Europe. (See www.ebrd.com.)

European Central Bank   The bank of the European Union charged with enacting monetary policy for the twelve countries that share a common currency, the Euro. (See www.europa.eu.int.)

European Coal and Steel Community   An agreement that represents an early attempt at tariff reduction between members of the European Union.

European Commission   The body of the European Union in charge of initiating and supervising the execution of laws and policies. (See www.europa.eu.int.)

European Council   The highest policy-making body of the European Union. (See www.europa.eu.int.)

European Court of Justice   The Supreme Court–equivalent of the European Union. (See www.europa.eu.int.)

European Exchange Rate Mechanism (ERM)   A precursor of the Euro, a float that included the Euro, the then-theoretical currency of the European Union; the float allowed for variability in each currency.

European Free Trade Association (EFTA)   A free trade agreement between Iceland, Liechtenstein, Norway, and Switzerland; previously, Sweden, Austria, and Finland were also members, but they have since joined the European Union. (See www.efta.int.)

European Monetary Union (EMU)   A union composed of the members of the European Union who adhere to the joint monetary policy enacted by the European Central Bank and who have adopted the Euro as the single currency. (See www.europa.eu.int.)

European Parliament   The Parliament of the European Union, composed of members elected every five years by direct universal suffrage; seats in the Parliament are allocated among member states based on their population. (See www.europa.eu.int.)

European Union   An economic union consisting of most of the Western European countries; it is the only agreement that has achieved full economic integration and is now pursuing political integration. (See www.europa.eu.int.)

event sponsorship   The financial support of cultural or sports-related events; companies use these events to get positive publicity.

exclusives   The norms that refer to activities that are appropriate only for locals and from which individuals from a foreign country are excluded.

executive judgment method   A budgeting process that allocates the company's advertising budget based on the opinions of executives.

expatriate   An employee working in a foreign country.

experimental research   Research that examines cause-and-effect relationships; it has the highest validity and reliability of all types of research.

exploratory research   Research conducted early in the research process that helps further define a problem or identify additional problems that need to be investigated.

export management companies   Companies specializing in the export function for client companies in a particular industry.

export marketing   Involvement in international marketing limited to the exporting function; although the firm actively seeks international clients, it considers the international market an extension of the domestic market and does not give it special consideration.

export merchants   Intermediaries who take title to and possession of the products they carry; they are responsible for shipping and marketing the products to the target market.

Export Trading Company Act   Legislation, passed in 1982, that encourages the formation of export trading companies by competing firms in order to promote U.S. exports without violating antitrust regulation.

expropriation   The foreign government seizure of company assets with partial reimbursement, usually not at market value.

external secondary data   Data collected for purposes other than the problem at hand.

F

feedback   Information regarding the effectiveness of a company's message.

femininity   The degree to which a national culture is characterized by nurturing, rather than assertive, values.

feudalism   A stage in economic and political development, which, according to Marxist-Leninist theory, is characterized by the dominance of feudal lords, who own the land and its dwellers.

firm-specific drivers   Elements specific to the firm, such as product life cycle, causing the firm to become involved internationally.

focus group interview   A qualitative research approach investigating a research question using a moderator to guide discussion within a group of subjects recruited to meet certain characteristics.

food retailers   Retailers selling primarily food products.

foreign consumer culture positioning   The positioning of a particular brand as symbolic of a desired foreign culture.

Foreign Corrupt Practices Act   Legislation that makes it illegal for companies and their representatives to bribe government officials and other politicians or candidates to political office, either directly or through third parties.

foreign exchange permit   A permit that is generally provided by a country's Central Bank in conjunction with the Department of Trade (Ministry of Foreign Trade) and that gives priority to imports of goods considered to be in the national interest.

Foreign Sales Corporation (FSC)   A sales corporation that is set up overseas; it allows for a portion of a U.S. tax-paying firm's foreign-source income to be exempt from U.S. income tax.

foreign trade zones   Tax-free areas in a country that are not considered part of the respective country in terms of import regulations and restrictions.

foreign-country middlemen   Intermediaries who help distribute products in a target foreign market.

formal controls   Systematic controls, such as performance standards and measurement, used in international marketing to ensure that international company operations are in line with company goals and objectives.

franchisee   The recipient party to a franchise who pays royalties in return for the right to use the franchisor's brand name and related trademarks.

franchising   The main international entry mode for the service industry, whereby the franchisor gives the franchisee the right to use its brand name and all related trademarks in return for royalties.

franchisor   The owner of the franchise who gives the franchisee the right to use its brand name and all related trademarks and its business know-how, such as secret recipes and customer interfacing techniques, in return for royalties.

free trade agreement   An agreement whose goal is the reduction in, or even elimination of, customs duties and other trade barriers on all goods and services traded between member countries.

Free Trade Area of the Americas (FTAA)   A plan to create a free trade association by 2005 that would comprise all member countries of the thirty-four democratic nations of North, Central, and South America. (See www.ftaa-alca.org.)

functional equivalence   The difference in the purposes for which products may be used in different country environments.

G

gender roles   The roles that women and men are expected to hold in a society.

General Agreement on Tariffs and Trade (GATT)   The international trade agreement promoting trade and eliminating trade barriers, opening markets to international business, and creating a forum for resolving trade disputes; GATT issues are now addressed by the World Trade Organization. (See www.wto.org.)

general merchandise discount stores   Retailers that sell high volumes of merchandise, offer limited service, and charge lower prices.

generating new product ideas   Seeking ideas using different strategies as the first step in the new product development process.

geocentric orientation   Company strategies that are consistent with the belief that the entire world, without national and regional distinctions, constitutes a potential market with identifiable, homogeneous segments that need to be addressed differentially.

geographic segmentation   Market segmentation based on geographic location, such as country or region.

gift giving   The norms regarding the gifts that are appropriate to give to others.

global branding   Approach to branding that uses the same name, logo, image, and positioning strategies everywhere in the world.

global campaign   A worldwide standardized advertising campaign that is not adjusted to different target markets.

global consumer culture positioning   Marketing programs appealing to individuals who want to be part of a global consumer culture by purchasing a brand that is a symbol of that culture.

global consumers   The homogeneous consumer group worldwide sharing similar interests and product/brand preferences.

global elite   A psycho-demographic group worldwide characterized by high income and desire for status brands and exclusive distribution.

global localization   The practice of global branding and localized marketing adaptation to differences in local culture, legislation, and even production capabilities.

global marketing   International marketing activities that do not have a country or region focus and that are possible due to the emergence of global consumer segments and efficient global allocation of company talent and resources.

global standardization   The standardization of products across markets and, ultimately, to the standardization of the marketing mix worldwide; more commonly called glocalization.

global teenagers   A psycho-demographic global group of teenagers considered to be astute consumers with precise desires for brand name clothing products and entertainment.

glocalization   The standardization of products across markets and, ultimately, to the standardization of the marketing mix worldwide; also called global standardization.

gray market   A distribution system not authorized by the manufacturer whereby the products purchased in a low-price market are diverted to other markets; also called parallel imports.

greenfielding   Developing a brand new subsidiary.

Group of Eight (G8)   A group of the eight most industrialized countries: Canada, France, Germany, Italy, Japan, the United Kingdom, the United States, and Russia; the group addresses issues such as biotechnology and food safety, economic development, arms control and nonproliferation, organized crime, drug trafficking, terrorism, environmental issues, digital opportunities, microeconomic issues, and trade. (See www.g7.utoronto.ca.)

growth stage   The stage of the international product life cycle characterized by increasing competition and rapid product adoption by the target market.

H

haptics   The use of touch while conversing.

hard currency   Currency that is accepted for payment by any international seller.

high mass consumption   A stage in economic development, described by Rostow, as characterized by leading sectors shifting toward durable goods.

high-context cultures   Cultures in which the context of a message—the message source, the source's standing in society or in a group, his or her expertise, tone of voice, and body language—are all meaningful parts of the message.

historical method   An approach to budgeting that is based on past expenditures, usually giving more weight to more recent expenditures.

home-country laws   Laws of a company's home country that follow the international company all over the world.

home-country middlemen   Intermediaries in the home country.

home-leave allowance   A compensation incentive that pays for the expatriate and his or her family to vacation in the home country.

host-country laws   Local laws; laws of the different countries where a company operates.

host-country national   A local employee who works in his or her home country for the international corporation.

housing allowance   A compensation incentive whereby the company covers part, or the entire cost, of housing for the expatriate employee while abroad.

hypermarkets   Very large retail stores that combine supermarket, discount, and warehouse retailing principles.

I

ideology   The manner in which individuals relate to their environment and to others, including their attitudes toward time, space, possessions, and referent others.

image advertising   An advertising campaign that enhances perceptions of a company in a given market by creating a positive impression on the target consumers.

imperatives   The norms referring to what individuals must or must not do in a certain culture.

imperialism   A stage of economic and political development, in which, according to Marxist-Leninist theory, capital loses its national identity by crossing borders.

import jobber   A merchant middleman who purchases commodity goods from the manufacturer to sell to the trade (wholesaler, retailer, business-to-business client) in the target market.

import quota   The maximum quantity (unit limit) or value of a product that may be imported during a specified period.

import/export analysis   Research that aids companies in identifying the necessary logistics that serve their needs in a timely and cost-effective manner.

indirect exporting   An export entry mode whereby a company sells its products in the company's home country to intermediaries who, in turn, sell the product overseas.

individualism   The degree to which people in a country prefer to act as individuals, in their self-interest.

infant-industry argument   A protectionist strategy aimed at protecting a national industry in its infancy from powerful international competitors.

infomercials   Long television advertisements (one-half to one full hour in length) that are positioned as programming.

informal controls   Systematic controls, such as dialogue between the headquarters and the international field operations, used in international marketing to ensure that international company operations are in line with company goals and objectives.

innovation   A product new to the world.

innovators   Risk takers who can afford to pay the higher purchase price charged by companies during the introduction stage of a product; they account for 2.5% of the total market.

intellectual property rights   Laws protecting the rights of the inventor or of the firm employing the inventor to use and sell an invention for a specified period of time.

interactive home shopping   A venue for selling through the Internet using web sites to increase market penetration and market diversification; also called electronic retailing and Internet retailing.

interactive medium   A nonpersonal channel of communication such as a web page or a computer terminal on the retailer's premises.

Inter-American Development Bank   A bank headquartered in Washington, D.C., aiding companies in the Americas that do not ordinarily deal with the large development banks; this bank is involved in funding private sector projects, modernizing governments, strengthening institutions, and eliminating technology barriers. (See www.iadb.org.)

internal secondary data   Data collected by a company to address a problem not related to the current research question.

international buyer-seller relationship   The distribution between the buyer and the individual involved in personal selling.

international communication process   The communication process that takes place between the product sponsor and the international target market.

international division structure   An organizational structure whereby firms have separate domestic and international divisions.

international laws   Rules and regulations that countries agree to abide by, addressing agreements among countries with regard to trade, protection of property, and other issues in the political and economic sphere.

international market potential studies   Studies conducted to evaluate the potential that a particular country offers for a company.

international marketing   The processes involved in the creation, production, distribution, promotion, and pricing of products, services, ideas, and experiences for international markets; these processes require a substantial focus on international consumers in a particular country or countries.

international marketing research   The systematic design, collection, recording, analysis, interpretation, and reporting of information pertinent to a particular marketing decision facing a company operating internationally.

International Monetary Fund (IMF)   Traditionally the lender of last resort; the IMF also has assumed the position of mediator between debtors and creditors, imposing stabilization programs; debt-reduction guidelines; ceilings for bank credit, budget deficit, borrowing, and international reserves; and development programs for borrowing countries. (See www.imf.org.)

international product life cycle (IPLC)   A product life-cycle theory which states that firms from developed countries engage in domestic production in the early stage of the product life cycle, marketing the product to industrialized countries; as the product reaches maturity, product specifications and the manufacturing process stabilize, price competition becomes intense, and markets in developing countries become essential to the firm's success.

international promotional mix   The different modes of communication with international consumers about products and services, using international advertising, international salesforce management, international sales promotion, public relations, and publicity.

Internet retailing   Selling through the Internet using web sites to increase market penetration and market diversification; also called interactive home shopping and electronic retailing.

introduction stage   The first stage of the international product life cycle when products are developed and marketed in industrialized countries.

Islamic law   A system of law based on the interpretation of the Koran, Islam's holy book, and on interpretations of the practices and sayings of the prophet Muhammad.

J

joint venture   A corporate entity created with the participation of two companies that share equity, capital, and labor, among others.

jurisdiction   The country and/or legal body where a particular dispute should be adjudicated, according to the country's law, or according to the legal body's principles, respectively.

jury of expert opinion   An approach to sales forecasting based on the opinion of different experts.

K

keiretsu   A Japanese trading firm that consists of families of firms with interlocking stakes in one another.

kinesics   The movement of part of the body in order to communicate.

L

lag countries   Countries where a product or service is adopted after already being introduced in lead countries.

laggards   Consumers who are the last to adopt new products and do so only in late maturity because they are risk averse and very conservative in their spending; they account for 16% of the total market.

language   The vehicle used for communication in a particular culture; includes spoken and written language and nonverbal communication.

late majority   Individuals of limited means who are likely to adopt products only if the products are widely popular and the risk associated with buying them is minimal; they account for 34% of the total market.

Latin American Free Trade Association (LAFTA)   An attempt by Latin American countries to establish a free trade association; its demise is attributed to the economic disparity between member countries and to protectionist policies.

Latin American Integration Association (LAIA)   Latin America's largest trade agreement striving to establish bilateral and multilateral agreements aimed at reducing tariff and nontariff barriers.

launching the product internationally   Introducing a new product to the international market as the last step in the new product development process.

lead countries   Countries where a product or service is first introduced and adopted.

licensee   The purchaser of the license who pays royalties to the licensor for the rights to use the licensor's technology, know-how, and brand name.

licensing   An international entry mode that involves a licensor, who shares the brand name, technology, and know-how with a licensee in return for royalties.

licensor   The owner of a product license who agrees to share know-how, technology, and brand name with the licensee in return for royalties.

local campaign   An advertising campaign that is tailored to local needs; especially used in markets that media cannot easily reach.

local consumer culture positioning   Positioning that associates the brand with local cultural meanings, reflecting the local culture, and portrayed as consumed by locals and/or depicted as locally produced for local people.

local content requirement   A protectionist measure requiring that a certain percentage of the products imported are locally produced.

local pricing   A pricing strategy in which different prices are charged in different markets, reflecting differences in consumer purchase power, distribution costs, tax systems, or other market traits.

logistics alliances   Distribution alliances between two firms involving product transportation and warehousing.

low-context cultures   Cultures in which what is said is precisely what is meant so that the verbal message carries the full meaning of the sentence.

M

Maastricht Treaty   The treaty credited with establishing the European Union, eliminating all tariffs; establishing common external tariffs; allowing for the free movement of capital and labor within its territory; and setting regulations involving common trade policies, common agricultural and industrial policies, and common monetary and fiscal policies between member countries. (See www.europa.eu.int.)

managing agent   A foreign agent who has an exclusive arrangement with a company, representing its operations in a particular country.

mandatory adaptation   The adaptation of products to local requirements so that the products can legally and physically function in the specific country environment.

manufacturer's export agents   Agents in the firm's home country handling the exporting function of a certain manufacturer on a commission, per deal, basis.

manufacturer's representative   An agent who represents the manufacturer exclusively in the foreign target market.

manufacturing alliance   A nonequity relationship between two firms, in which one firm handles the other's manufacturing or some aspect of the manufacturing process.

maquiladora   Customs-privileged contract manufacturing facilities in Mexico that take advantage of low-cost labor.

market-based transfer pricing   A pricing strategy used in intra-firm sales for commercial transactions between units of the same corporation, within or beyond the national borders of the parent company, whereby products are priced at market cost, rather than at the cost incurred by the company.

marketing alliance   A nonequity relationship between two firms, in which one firm handles the other's marketing or some aspect of the marketing process.

Marxist-Leninist development model   A development model attributed to Karl Marx and Vladimir Lenin which maps the development of society from an agrarian, traditional society to a society characterized by shared ownership of the means and outcomes of production and an equitable resource allocation; advancement from one stage to another is based on class struggle and transfer of ownership from one class to another and, ultimately, to the state.

masculinity   The degree to which a national culture is characterized by assertiveness, rather than nurturing.

materialism   Individuals' degree of concern with material possessions.

matrix structure   An organizational structure whereby each operational unit reports to both region/country managers and product managers.

maturity stage   A stage of the international product life cycle characterized by a slowdown in sales growth as the product is adopted by most target consumers and by a leveling or decline in profits primarily due to intense price competition.

measurability   The ability to estimate the size of a market segment.

media availability   The extent to which media are available to communicate with target consumers.

media infrastructure   The media vehicles and their structure in an international target market.

media reliability   The probability of the media to air advertising messages on time, at an acceptable quality, and with the agreed-upon frequency.

media research   Studies that evaluate media availability and appropriateness of the medium for a company's message.

media restrictions   Legal or self-imposed restrictions on the types and the number of advertisements aired or published.

mediation   Nonbinding procedure for conflict resolution involving an independent third party.

medium/media   The channel(s) of communication that a company uses to send to the target consumer a message about its product or services.

merchant middlemen   Different intermediaries who carry the manufacturer's product line in a particular country; they both carry title to and have physical possession of the products they distribute.

Ministry of Foreign Affairs   The international institutional equivalent of the State Department; it coordinates a country's involvement in international relations.

Ministry of Trade   The international institutional equivalent of the Department of Commerce; it coordinates a country's international trade relations.

modification   The alteration of an existing company product.

modular adaptation   The localization across markets of the product by offering parts (modules) that can be assembled worldwide in different configurations, depending on the needs of the market.

modular campaign   An advertising campaign that provides a template that is varied and customized from market to market.

monetary union   A form of economic integration characterized by the establishment of a common central bank enacting monetary policy for the group.

monochronic time   The interpretation of time as linear, such that individuals do one thing at a time, and in sequence.

monopolistic capitalism   A stage of economic and political development, in which, according to Marxist-Leninist theory, multinational companies establish monopolies and expand internationally with the goal of subjugating developing countries.

Most-Favored-Nation Status   Favored trade status granted by Congress for imported products from selected countries, which are not party to a preferential trade agreement with the United States.

mother henning   Using the distribution system of exporters with established systems of selling abroad who agree to handle the export function of a noncompeting (but not necessarily unrelated) company on a contractual basis; also called piggybacking and cooperative exporting.

moving allowance   A compensation incentive whereby the company pays for the household moving expenses to the country of assignment and, at the end of the assignment, back to the home country.

multilateral forums and agreements   Agreements that involve multiple countries, have an informal structure, and/or do not necessarily have regional integration as their goal.

multilevel marketing   Using acquaintance networks through an alternative distribution structure for the purpose of distribution; also called network marketing.

multinational marketing   Marketing in different countries without coordinating across operations.

N

national and regional character   A set of behavior and personality characteristics shared by individuals of a certain country or region.

nationalism   An expression of fierce nationalist sentiment in a country where a company is operating, which poses an implicit threat to the company and its operations.

nationalization   The takeover of company assets by a foreign government with the aim of creating a government-run industry.

network marketing   Using acquaintance networks through an alternative distribution structure for the purpose of distribution; also called multilevel marketing.

new item in an existing product line   A new brand that the company offers to the market in an existing product line.

new line   A new product category offered by the company.

new product to existing company   A new product that the company offers to the market; the product competes with similar competitor offerings.

new product to existing market   A product never before offered to the market.

news releases   Statements issued to the public to introduce a new product, touting its advantages; any other information shared with the media.

noise   All the potential interference in the communication process.

nonautomatic import license   A license issued on a discretionary basis to restrict imports of a given product and/or from a particular country.

nonmandatory adaptation   The strategy of adapting a product to better meet the needs of the local market, without being required to do so.

nonpersonal medium   A channel of communication such as a print medium, a broadcast medium, or an interactive medium that does not involve contact between the seller and the consumer.

nontariff barriers   All measures, other than traditional tariffs, used to distort trade flows, used to increase prices of imports, and thus favor domestic over foreign products.

nonverbal communication   All communication that is not written or spoken; includes body language, gestures, facial expressions, eye contact, and silence.

Norazi agent   An export agent dealing in illegal and/or gray market products.

norms   Rules that dictate what is right or wrong, acceptable or unacceptable in a society.

North American Free Trade Agreement (NAFTA)   An agreement between the United States, Canada, and Mexico, aiming to eliminate tariff and nontariff barriers between the countries. (See www.nafta-customs.org.)

North Atlantic Treaty Organization (NATO)   A military agreement between countries that were, initially, not part of the Soviet Bloc. (See www.nato.int.)

O

objective-and-task method   An advertising budgeting method in which the company first identifies advertising goals, conducts research to determine the cost of achieving the respective goals, and allocates the necessary sum for the purpose.

observational research   A research approach used frequently in international markets, whereby subjects are observed interacting with a product and the related components of the marketing mix.

obstacles to internationalization   Impediments that the firm may encounter in the process of internationalizing.

oculesics   The use or avoidance of eye contact during communication.

off-price retailers   Retailers who sell brand name products and designer merchandise below regular retail prices.

offset purchase   A large, hard-currency purchase, such as the purchase of defense equipment, airplanes, telecommunications networks, railway or road building and other expensive civil engineering projects whereby the seller agrees, in return to purchase products that are valued at a certain percentage of the sale.

off-shore assembly plants   Plants located in customs-privileged bonded areas in countries with low labor costs, where products are manipulated and re-exported.

olfactions   The use of odors to convey messages.

open-ended questions   Questions with free-format responses that the respondent can address as he or she sees appropriate.

orderly market arrangements   Protectionist measures involving intricate processes for establishing quotas in the textile and apparel industries.

Organization for Economic Co-operation and Development (OECD)   An economic multilateral agreement. (See www.oecdobserver.org.)

Organization of the Petroleum Exporting Countries (OPEC)   Industry-specific (oil) multilateral agreement aimed at managing the output and price of oil. (See www.opec.com.)

organizational culture and personality   The shared norms and values that guide collective behavior in organizations, and enduring traits that characterize individuals, motivating them to act or react to stimuli in the organization and in the environment in a particular manner.

organizational design   The organization of reporting and coordination within a company.

organizational structure   The outcome of the organization of reporting and coordination within a company.

orientations   Individuals' positioning relative to their counterparts during conversation.

Overseas Private Investment Corporation (OPIC)   U.S. government corporation that provides loans, guarantees and insurance to U.S. corporations investing in countries that present high political risk.

P

paralinguistics   The nonverbal aspects of speech that include intonation, accents, and the quality of voice.

parallel barter   A form of trade that involves two exchanges that are paid for in cash; it involves two parallel contracts whereby the seller agrees to purchase products that are usually unrelated to its business from the buyer and sell them on international markets; also called counterpurchase.

parallel imports   A distribution system not authorized by the manufacturer whereby the products purchased in a low-price market are diverted to other markets; also called gray market.

parallel translation   The process of translating the original instrument by different translators and comparing the translations.

paratariff measures   Additional, nontariff fees that increase the costs of imports in a manner similar to tariffs.

patent   Protection of the rights of the inventor or of the firm employing the inventor to use and sell an invention for a specified period of time.

penetration pricing   A pricing strategy in which a product is first priced below the price of competitors' products in order to quickly penetrate the market at the competitors' expense and then raised to target levels.

percent-of-sales method   An advertising budgeting method that determines the total budget allocated to advertising based on past or projected sales.

performance standards   A priori measures against which firm performance is evaluated.

performing a product business analysis   Calculating projected costs such as return on investment and cash flow, and determining the fixed and variable costs for the long term.

personal medium   A communication channel that involves contact between the seller and the consumer.

piggybacking   Using the distribution system of exporters with established systems of selling abroad who agree to handle the export function of a noncompeting (but not necessarily unrelated) company on a contractual basis; also called mother henning and cooperative exporting.

plant/warehouse location studies   Studies that evaluate the appropriateness of plant or warehouse location to ensure that it is in accordance with the limitations of the national environment and with the needs of a company.

point-of-sale–based projections   Market share and other relevant market dimensions assessed by the use of store scanners in weekly and biweekly store audits.

political risk   The risk associated with actions of local, regional, and/or parastatal governing bodies affecting the international company, and with the overall economic and political stability within a particular country.

political union   The highest level of regional integration; it assumes a viable economic integration and involves the establishment of viable common governing bodies, legislative bodies, and enforcement powers.

polycentric orientation   Company strategies predicated on the assumption that each country's market is unique and should be addressed individually, with a country-specific marketing mix.

polychronic time   The interpretation of time as fluid, such that individuals can accomplish multiple tasks at once.

post adjustment   A compensation incentive whereby the company adjusts expatriate salaries to reflect the cost of living in the new environment at standards in the expatriate's home country; also called cost-of-living adjustment.

postures   Individuals' physical postures during conversation.

power distance   The manner in which interpersonal relationships are formed when differences in power are perceived.

press releases   Statements issued to the press to communicate news about a company and its products.

price controls   Strategies requiring a product to sell for a particular price in the local market; price control strategies are typically used to increase the prices of imports to match the minimum prices of local competition.

price elasticity studies   Studies examining the extent to which a particular market is price sensitive.

price/quality positioning   A strategy whereby products and services are positioned as offering the best value for the money.

primary data   Data collected for the purpose of addressing the problem at hand.

primitive society   The first stage of economic and political development, characterized, according to Marxist-Leninist theory, by the joint tribal ownership of primitive means of production centered on agricultural tasks.

print medium   A nonpersonal channel of communication such as a newspaper, magazine, billboard, pamphlet, or point-of-purchase display.

private labels   Brands sold under the brand name of a retailer or some other distributor.

product class positioning   A strategy used to differentiate a company as a leader in a product category, as defined by the respective company.

product consistency   The extent to which a company's different product lines are related, use the same distribution channels, and have the same final consumers.

product depth   The number of different offerings for a particular brand.

product division structure   An organizational structure whereby subsidiaries report to the product division (strategic business unit) with responsibility for the particular products.

product length   The total number of brands in the product mix.

product line   All the brands the company offers in the same product category.

product mix   The complete assortment of products that a company offers to its target international consumers.

product packaging design studies   Studies that evaluate consumers' reaction to a package, the extent to which the package adequately communicates information to the consumer, and the distribution implications of the package.

product placement   The strategy of placing brands in movies with the purpose of promoting the products to viewers.

product testing   Studies that estimate product preference and performance in a given market.

product user positioning   A positioning strategy that focuses on the product user, rather than on the product.

product width   The total number of product lines that a company offers to its target international consumers.

product-country stereotypes   Product-specific stereotypes that associate the country of origin as a certification of quality.

profit analyses studies   Studies that estimate product profit in specific international markets.

protection of markets with excess labor   The erection of barriers to imports of products competing with local offerings in an effort to protect local jobs.

protection of markets with excess productive capacity   A protectionist measure used to prevent foreign buyouts, invoking the protection of local labor.

protectionism   All actions by national and local governments aimed at protecting local markets from foreign competitors.

proxemics   The amount of physical space individuals require to feel comfortable in the process of communication.

psychographic segmentation   The use of values, attitudes, interests, and other cultural variables to segment consumers.

public appearances   Company representatives' public involvement, speaking on behalf of the international firm and its products.

public relations   A concerted effort on the part of a company to generate goodwill among publics that are essential to the company; its main purpose is to generate positive publicity about the company.

publicity   Any communication about a company and/or the company's products that the company does not pay for; may be positive or negative.

purchase behavior studies   Research aimed at evaluating consumers' reaction to and interaction with a company's products.

Q

qualitative research   Research that uses nonsystematic processes, such as nonrandom sampling and open-ended data, as well as involves the researcher as participant.

quantitative research   A structured type of research that involves either descriptive research approaches, such as survey research, or causal research approaches, such as experiments.

R

radical innovation   The creation of new industries or new standards of management, manufacturing, and servicing that represent fundamental changes for consumers, entailing departures from established consumption.

receiver   The target market that receives the advertising message from a sender.

regiocentric orientation   Company strategies that view world regions as distinct markets that share economic, political, and/or cultural traits that will respond to a regionwide marketing approach.

regional standardization   The use of a uniform marketing strategy within a particular region.

reliability   The extent to which data is likely to be free from random error and yield consistent results.

religion   A society's relationship to the supernatural.

repatriation   The return of the expatriate employee to the home country.

repatriation allowance   A compensation incentive whereby the company covers expenses involved in moving back to the home country, as well as, frequently, a large sum paid for successfully completing the international assignment.

research approach   The method used to collect data.

reverse culture shock   Anxiety experienced after returning to the home country, associated with a longing for the international environment left behind and with the difficulty of readjusting to the home country and to corporate life at one's firm.

Rostow modernization model   An economic development model attributed to Rostow, according to which each stage of economic advance is a function of productivity, economic exchange, technological improvements, and income.

S

sales forecast   Projected sales for a particular territory.

sales potential studies   Studies forecasting optimal sales performance.

sales promotion   Sponsored communications to the target consumer or trade segment that stimulate purchases or improve relationships with middlemen.

salesforce compensation, quota, and territory studies   Different studies pertaining to personal selling activities; they are crucial in helping to determine the appropriate strategies for certain international markets.

salesforce composite estimates   Research studies wherein sales forecasts are based on the personal observations and forecasts of the local salesforce.

sample size   The number of study participants necessary to obtain a high study reliability.

sampling frame   The list from which sample units are selected.

sampling procedure   A decision involving the selection of sampling units.

sampling unit   The entity included in the study; it may be individuals or representatives belonging to particular groups.

sanctions   Punitive trade restrictions applied by a country or a group of countries against another country for noncompliance.

screening new product ideas   Eliminating product ideas that do not fit with the target consumers and/or the overall mission of the organization.

secondary data   Data collected to address a problem other than the problem at hand.

segmentation   The process of identifying consumers and/or international markets that are similar with regard to key traits, such as product-related needs and wants, and that would respond well to a product and related marketing mix.

self-reference criterion   Individuals' conscious and unconscious reference to their own national culture, to home-country norms and values, and to their knowledge and experience in the process of making decisions in the host country.

sender   The sponsor of an advertisement, usually represented by an advertising agency, who encodes the message into words and images and communicates it to the target market.

service barriers   Barriers encountered by services in different markets, such as requirements for local certification, local providers, and other requirements that favor local over international service providers.

simulated test marketing   Test marketing simulating purchase environments where samples of target consumers are observed in their product-related decision-making process.

skimming strategy   A pricing strategy in which a product is priced above that of competitors' products, when competition is minimal, to quickly recoup investments; consumers responding to skimming strategies are more concerned with quality, uniqueness, and status, rather than price.

slavery-based society   A stage of economic and political development, which, according to Marxist-Leninist theory, emerges as a result of tribes' dominance over other tribes: Dominant tribes claim ownership of conquered tribes and their property.

social structure   The organization of relationships in a society.

socialism   A transition stage of economic and political development, characterized, according to Marxist-Leninist theory, by the disappearance of private property and its replacement with collective, state property.

soft currency   Currency that is kept at a high artificial exchange rate, overvalued, and controlled by the national central bank.

sogo shosha   A large Japanese trading company that specializes in providing intermediary services, risk reduction through extensive information channels, and significant financial assistance to manufacturing firms.

South African Customs Union (SACU)   A customs union that includes Botswana, Swaziland, Lesotho, and Namibia. The group's main trading partner is South Africa, and member countries have partially or entirely tied their currencies to the South African rand.

Southern African Development Community (SADC)   A free trade organization that promotes economic cooperation among a coalition of fourteen of Africa's more affluent and developed nations, designed to foster increased economic and governmental stability through the use of collective peace-keeping forces.

Southern Cone Common Market (MERCOSUR)   A free trade agreement in South America that has met with considerable success; MERCOSUR is presently in the process of becoming a viable customs union. (See www.mercosur.org.)

special economic zones   Customs-privileged manufacturing facilities in China where multinational companies can take advantage of low-cost labor.

specialized markets   Markets that contain specialty stores specializing in a particular product category.

specialty stores   Retailers that offer a narrow product line and wide assortment.

spoken/written language   The language used in conversation/the language used in written communications.

stability over time   The extent to which preferences are stable, rather than changing, in a market segment.

standardization of the advertising strategy   The process of globalizing a company's promotional strategy so that it is uniform in all its target markets.

standardized pricing   A pricing strategy in which the same price is charged for a product regardless of local market conditions.

standards as barriers to trade   Trade barriers imposing performance, environmental, or other requirements that are primarily aimed at imports.

status concern   The value placed on symbols of status and on the attainment of high status in a society.

strategic alliance   Any type of relationship between one or more companies attempting to reach joint corporate and market-related goals; term used to refer to most nonequity alliances.

studies of premiums, coupons, and deals   Studies that help identify the practices in each target country where a promotion is planned by investigating the practice and legality of premiums, coupons, and special deals.

substantiality   The extent to which the market is large enough to warrant investment.

superstores   Large retailers such as combination stores or hypermarkets that sell food, drugs, and other products.

survey research   Descriptive research that involves the administration of personal, telephone, or mail questionnaires.

swing credits   Amounts paid within the framework of a clearing agreement by the country that owes money to the other when an imbalance occurs.

switch trading   The process of buying a party's position in a countertrade in exchange for hard currency and selling it to another customer.

T

take-off   A stage in economic development described by Rostow as one in which economic growth becomes the norm and improvements in production lead to the emergence of leading sectors.

target market   Consumers and/or international markets that are similar in aspects relevant to the company.

target marketing   The process of focusing on those segments that the company can serve most effectively and designing products, services, and marketing programs with these segments in mind.

tariffs   Taxes imposed on goods entering a country.

telemarketing   A personal channel of communication that involves a salesperson calling on consumers.

television home shopping   Retailing through cable channels selling to consumers in their homes, through infomercials, and through direct response advertising shown on broadcast and cable television.

television shopping networks   Cable channels that sell products to a television audience.

test marketing   Testing new-product performance in a limited area of a national or regional target market to estimate product performance in the respective country or region.

third-country national   An employee working in the country of assignment who is not a national of that country nor of the country in which the corporate headquarters of the company he or she works for are located.

time orientation   The manner in which individuals view time in relation to accomplishing tasks.

time series and econometric models   Models that use the data of past performance to predict future market demand.

trade secrets   Intellectual property such as know-how, formulas, special blends, and other elements that are not registered, and are thus not protected by law.

trade shows and exhibitions   Business-to-business promotions that usually are held annually in formats where companies purchase exhibit space to display and demonstrate their offerings to the target market.

trademark   A brand name, mark, symbol, motto, or slogan that identifies a particular manufacturer's brand and distinguishes it from the competitors' brands in the same product category.

Trade-Related Aspects of Intellectual-Property Rights (TRIPS)   An international agreement, under the World Trade Organization, that sets out minimum standards for the legal protection of intellectual property. (See www.wto.org.)

trading companies   Large companies that specialize in providing intermediary services, risk reduction through extensive information channels, and significant financial assistance to manufacturing firms.

traditional society   A stage in economic development defined by Rostow as one in which the economy is dominated by agriculture and relatively few exchange transactions occur.

transfer pricing   A pricing strategy used in intra-firm sales for commercial transactions between units of the same corporation, within or beyond the national borders of the parent company.

transitional society   A stage in the economic development process described by Rostow as characterized by increased productivity in agriculture and by the emergence of modern manufacturing.

trialability   The ability of the consumer to experience a product with minimal effort.

U

uncertainty avoidance   The extent to which individuals are threatened by uncertainty, risk, and ambiguous situations and thus adopt beliefs, behaviors, and institutions that help them to avoid the uncertainty.

undifferentiated targeting   A targeting strategy aiming the product at the market using a single strategy, regardless of the number of segments.

United Nations organizations   The totality of United Nations bodies created to maintain international peace and security; to develop relations among nations; to achieve international cooperation in solving international economic, social, cultural, or humanitarian problems; and to encourage respect for human rights and fundamental freedoms using the venues offered by the different UN organizations. (See www.un.org.)

United States Agency for International Development (USAID)   An independent agency of the federal government that supports the economic development of and trade with developing countries aligned politically with the United States. (See www.usaid.gov.)

United States Department of Commerce   The U.S. governmental agency that oversees and promotes trade, offering export assistance and counseling to U.S. businesses involved in international trade, providing country information and country specialists, and bringing buyers and sellers together.

United States State Department The foreign affairs arm of the United States government, in charge of promoting relations with other governments. (See www.state.gov.)

usage segmentation The process of segmenting markets based on the extent to which consumers are nonusers, occasional users, medium users, and heavy users of a product.

use positioning The process of marketing a very precise product application that differentiates it in the consumers' minds from other products that have a more general use.

user status segmentation The process of determining the status as users of competitors' products, ex-users, potential users, first-time users, and regular users.

V

validity The extent to which data collected is free from bias.

values Enduring beliefs about a specific mode of conduct or desirable end-state that guide the selection or evaluation of behavior.

vending machines Interactive modes of retailing convenience goods.

voluntary export restraints A government's self-imposed export quotas to a particular country that are established to avoid more severe protectionist action by the respective importing country.

voluntary import expansion A government's response to protectionist threats from another country whereby it agrees to open markets to imports and/or to increase foreign access to a domestic market to avoid more severe protectionist action.

W

warehouse clubs Stores that require members to pay an annual fee operating in low-overhead, warehouse-type facilities, offering limited lines of brand name and dealer-brand groceries, apparel, appliances, and other goods at a substantial discount; also known as wholesale clubs.

Webb-Pomerene Associations Associations of competing companies that are granted immunity from antitrust prosecution and that join resources and efforts to export internationally.

West African Economic and Monetary Union (WAEMU) One of the first attempts at economic integration in Africa. Although it is successful as a monetary union that has adopted a single currency, trade is quite modest within the WAEMU. (See www.dakarcom.com/EconReports/econ_waemu.htm.)

wholesale clubs Stores that require members to pay an annual fee operating in low-overhead, warehouse-type facilities, offering limited lines of brand name and dealer-brand groceries, apparel, appliances, and other goods at a substantial discount; also known as warehouse clubs.

wholly owned subsidiary The entry mode that affords the highest level of control and presents the highest level of risk to a company; it involves establishing a new company that is a citizen of the country where the subsidiary is established.

World Bank The World Bank Group, headquartered in Washington, D.C., that is one of the largest sources of funds for development assistance aimed at the poorest countries worldwide. (See www.worldbank.org.)

World Trade Organization (WTO) The largest and most influential international trade organization whose primary goal is ensure the free flow of trade; WTO's agreements (negotiated and signed by member countries, ratified in their parliaments) represent trade rules and regulations and act as contracts guaranteeing countries trade rights and binding governments to trade policies. (See www.wto.org.)

worldwide regional division structure An organizational structure whereby operations are organized by region or by country, and where subsidiaries report directly to the single division responsible for operations in the country or geographic region.

Index

Note: Page numbers in italics identify an illustration. An italic *t* next to a page number (e.g., 177*t*) identifies information that appears in a table.

A

Accessibility of market segments, 149
Acculturation, 95–96
Acorn, 154
Acquiescence bias, 132
Actionability of market segments, 149
Actual test marketing, 210, 211–212
Adaptation
    of advertising, 266
    of products, 183–188
    of sales promotions, 276–277
Adiaphoras, cultural, 96, 98
Admission fees, 249
Adoption determinants, *215*, 216
Advertising
    advertising infrastructure, 264–266
    corporate, 275
    global strategies, 185
    media infrastructure issues, 256–264
    regions with limited media, 122
    religious rules, 94
    strategy development, 266–268
Advertising agencies, 264–266, 276
Advertising effectiveness research, 121, 134, 135*t*
Advocacy advertising, 275
African Development Bank, 59
Age, segmentation by, 153
Agency for International Development
        (USAID), 60–61
Agents, 223, 224
Aggressive export pricing, 308–309
Airbus, 175
Air Emirates, 274
Airlines
    competitor positioning, 161
    consortia and alliances, 164, 175, 177
Air travel, internationalization and, 10
Alabina, 146
Albert Heijn, 277
Alcohol prohibitions, 86, 93
Allowances for expatriates, 292–294
All-purpose discount stores, 238–239
All-you-can-afford method, 268
Altria, 275. *See also* Kraft Foods; Philip Morris
American Cynamid Company, 118
America Online (AOL), 177
Amex, Inc., 222

Analogy methods, 142
Andean Common Market (AnCom), 77
Anticipating Change in Europe program, 154
Antidumping duties, 301
Antidumping policies, 50, 301
Antitrust laws, 35, 40
Apartment intercepts, 135–136
Appearances, cultural differences, 91
Applications positioning, 160
Arab Maghreb Union, 76
Arbitration, 37
Argentina, IMF bailout, 58
Ariel detergent, 114, 185
Asda Group, 233
ASEAN Free Trade Area, 74
Asian Development Bank, 59
Asian retailing, 238, 242
Asian Tigers, 26
Asia-Pacific Economic Cooperation (APEC), 72
ASSESSOR, 210
Assimilation of culture, 95, 96
Association of Southeast Asian Nations, 74
Asros, 14–15
Attribute/benefit positioning strategies, 159–160
Auschwitz, *191*
Auto industry
    licensing in, 169–170
    mandatory adaptations for different
        markets, 188
    world cars, 184
Automatic import licenses, 49
Autoregressive moving average, 142
Availability of media, 256
Avon Products, 246–247
AvtoVAZ, 169
Axion paste, 12–13

B

Back translation, 88, 138
Banks, development, 57–59
Bar code data, 133, 142–143
Barriers to entry. *See* Trade barriers
Barter, 305, 306
BASES, 210
Batwa languages, 88
Belgium, geographic segmentation, 156
Benefit segmentation, 155

Benelux Uniform Trademark Act, 263
Benetton, 275
Berne Convention, 39
Beverly Hills Polo Club, 170
Big emerging markets, 26, 28
Bilateral agreements, 71–73
Billboards, 258, *261*
Bird Corp., 174
Black Cat, 121
Black markets, 53
Blocked currency strategies, 53
Bou-bous, 91
Bounty promotion in Europe, 155–156, 277
Bourgeoisie, 23
Boycotts, 34, 52
Branch offices, 176
Brand awareness research, 117
Brand name generation and testing, 117–118
Brands
    cultural views of, 194
    global, 11–12, 184, 189–193
    loyalty, 117, 194
    positioning, 159–161
    private-label, 188–189
    product placement of, 261
    protecting, 37–39, 194–197
    recognition levels, 152
    testing, 117–118
Brazil, market potential, 150
Bretton Woods Agreement, 57
Bribery, 40
Bridge offerings, 203
British Petroleum, 172
Broadcast media, 253, 254
Brokers
    countertrade, 305
    customs, 225
    international product distribution, 223, 224
"Bubble," 89, 90
Bucur Obor, 237, *238, 239*
Buddhism, 93
Budgeting approaches, 267–268
Budweiser, 197
Building channels of distribution, 221
Bulk orders, in free trade zones, 63
Bureau for the International Registration
        of Trademarks, 39

Bureau of Export Administration, 226
Business attire, 91
Business days, 93, 99
Business publications, 29, 128
Business-to-business promotion, 279–281
Business unit–level strategies, 165, *166*
Butt-Ugly Martians, 272
Buyback agreements, 307–308
Buyer behavior research, 116–117
Buyer-seller relationships, elements of, 288–290
Buying offices, 223

C

Capitalism, Marxist-Leninist view, 23–24
Carrefour, 241
Catalog retailing, 245–246
Catalog showrooms, 240–241
Category specialists (category killers), 238, 240
Causal research, 123
Cellular phones, marketing to developing
          countries, 206
Censorship, 94
Central American Common Market, 78
Central Europe
     department stores in, 237
     network marketing, 220
     Pepsi versus Coca-Cola, 4
     social class changes, 102–103
     transition to market economies, 11
Central European Free Trade Agreement, 74
Centrum, *238*
Certification of products, 123
Certified Public Accountants, 193
Channel performance and coverage, 120
Channels of communication, 253, 255
Chase Bank branch offices, 176
Cheetos, 118
Children, advertising to, 264
China
     antidumping policies, 301
     cigarette advertising in, 128
     consumer segmentation in, 153
     counterfeiting in, 194–195
     direct selling ban, 247
     local content requirements, 51
     marketing research in, 130
     market potential, 150
     requirements for WTO membership, 55
Chocolate, 167
Christianity, 92, 94
Chronemics, 90
Cigarettes
     as gifts, 100
     gray market activities, 228
     product life cycle, 12
     promoting abroad, 121, 128
Cigna International, 35
Civil law, 35–36
Class structures, 101–103, 153
Clearfield brand, 118
Clearing accounts, 306
Clearing currency, 306
CNN, 258–259
Coca-Cola
     advertising strategy, 266
     boycotts of, 52

distribution channels in Eastern Europe, 221
foreign consumer culture positioning, 109
Pepsi's challenges in Eastern Europe, 4, 34
sales promotions, 277
targeting strategies, 158–159
Code law, 35–36
Coffee
     cultural differences, 126
     Kraft's marketing mix, 167
     on-line auction, 214–215
Collectivism, 105
Colonialism, 69
Combination stores, 241
Commerce Department (U.S.)
     antidumping policies, 301
     export assistance, 226
     major functions, 61
     trade show support, 280
Commercial trade exchanges, 305
Commitment to international markets, 165
Common law, 35
Common Market for Eastern and Southern
          Africa, 78
Common markets, 76–78. *See also* Regional
          trade agreements
Commonwealth of Independent States
          (CIS), 72, 150
Communication
     low- versus high-context, 92, 289–290
     nonverbal, 89–92, 133, 288
     process overview, 253–255
Communism
     class structures, 102–103
     excess production under, 46
     in Marxist-Leninist model, 24
Company goals, 152
Company publications, 274
Compaq, 310
Comparative advertising rules, 263–264
Compensation
     in countertrade, 306–307
     of expatriates, 292–294
Competition
     assessing, *323*
     effects on internationalization, 9, 14–15
     influence on organizational design, 317
     influence on pricing, 300–302
     new product ideas from, 208
Competitive-parity method, 268
Competitive pricing analyses, 122
Competitive product studies, 118
Competitor positioning, 161
Complementary export agents
          and merchants, 223
Compradors, 224
Concentrated targeting strategies, 157–158
Concept development and evaluation, 209
Concept development and testing studies, 117
Conceptual equivalence, 124–125
Confiscation, 32
Conjoint analysis, 209
Consistency, product, 204
Consortia, 175
Consumer acculturation, 95–96
Consumer demand, 11–12
Consumer ethnocentrism, 31, 107–108

Consumer protection, 47
Consumers
     categories of, 216–217
     demand for counterfeit products, 195–196
     global, 108–109, 184
     product ideas from, 207–208
Consumer sales promotions, 276–279
Consumer segmentation studies, 117
Container shipping, 10, 225
Content analysis, 134, 135*t*
Continuous innovations, 214
Contract manufacturing, 176
Controlled test marketing, 210, 211
Controls, for international marketing
          operations, 319–321
Convenience stores, 243–244
Conventional supermarkets, 241
Cooperative exporting, 168, 223
Copyright, 37–38
Core product strategy, 187
Corporate advertising, 275
Corporate-level strategies, 165, *166*
Corruption, 40, 45
Cost analyses, 122
Cost-based transfer pricing, 302
Cost-of-living adjustments, 292
Council of Europe, 83
Council of Ministers, 80
Council of Mutual Economic Assistance, 80
Council of Nations, 80
Counterfeiting
     brand name, 38, 195–196
     efforts against, 196–197
Counterpurchase, 307
Countertrade, 304–308
Countervailing duties, 301
Countervailing duty actions, 50
Country attractiveness analysis, 149–152,
          156–157
Country of manufacture, 189
Country-of-origin information, 189–193
Country performance analogy, 142
Country risk, 29, 30. *See also* Political
          environment
Country-specific plans, 322
Coupons, 121
Covered Bazaar, *235*
Creeping expropriation, 33
Cross-border shopping, 248
Cross-cultural training, 292
Cross-functional teams, 209–210
Cuba, 32, 52
Cultural adiaphora, 96, 98
Cultural exclusives, 96, 98
Cultural imperatives, 96–98
Cultural sensitivity, 14
Cultural variability, 103
Culture
     assessing, *323*
     conceptual equivalence, 124–125
     defined, 87–88
     failure to transcend one's own, 106–108
     global consumer, 108–109, 184
     importance to regional integration, 69
     influence on buyer-seller
          relationships, 288–290

influence on services and products, 193–194
intellectual property rights violations
and, 38
language, 88–92
monitoring changes, 105–106
national or regional character, 98–103
norms, 96–98
religion, 92–94
training salespeople in, 292
values, 95–96
variability, 103–105
Culture shock, 291
Currency and capital flow controls, 52–54
Customer services, 249
Customs brokers, 225
Customs offices, decline in EU, 68
Customs unions, 76

D

Dacia automobiles, 169
DaimlerChrysler, 175
Data
analysis and interpretation, 139–140
collection approaches, 131–136
collection instruments, 137–139
reliability, 115, 147–148
sources, 124–131
Davy Powergas, 308
DayTimers, 246
Deadlines, culture and, 98
De Beers Centenary AG, 174
Decentering, 138
Decentralization, 7
Decision support systems, 140–143
Decline stage, 203
Decoding, 255
Degree of product/service newness, 213–215
Delphi method, 141
Demographic data, 129–130
Demographic segmentation, 153–154
Department stores, 236–238
Depth interviews, 132
Depth of product mix, 204
Descriptive research, 123
Design copying, 38, 195
Design counterfeiting, 195
Designing new products, 209–210
Developed countries, defined, 26
Developing and evaluating concepts, 209
Developing countries
catalog retailing obstacles, 246
cellular phone marketing, 206
defined, 26–27
distribution challenges, 227
protectionism in, 45, 46
specialty retailing in, 234–235
Development banks, 57–59
Development levels, 26–28
Development philosophies, 22–26
de Witte Tanden-Winkel, 158
DHL, 4
Differential exchange rates, 53
Differential pricing, 300
Differential response, 149

Differentiated targeting strategies, 157
Diffusion, product, 215–217
Digital Millenium Copyright Act, 39
Direct exporting, 169
Direct mail retailing, 245–246
Direct mail test marketing, 211
Direct selling, 246–247
Discounts, legal restrictions, 248
Discount stores, 238–240
Discrepancies, standards versus
performance, 321
Disidenten, 146
Disney, 107
Dispute Settlement Body, 56
Distance selling, 287–288
Distribution
challenges to, 227–229
methods for international markets, 168–177,
221–224
middlemen, 221–224
researching, 119–121
service providers for, 224–227
variation among channels, 220
Distribution alliances, 177
Distribution centers, 225
Division-level strategies, 165, *166*
Diwali, 94
Documenta, 276, 280
Domestication, 33–34
Domestic marketing, 5, 6–7
Drivers in the business environment, 8, 9–12
Drivers of internationalization, 9
Drive-to-maturity stage, 22
DRUPA, 280
Dubai, 63–64
Dulce de Leche, 207
Dumping, 50, 300–301, 309
DuPont, 116–117
Duties, 10, 301. *See also* Trade barriers
DVD/CD players, 202
Dynamically continuous innovations, 214
Dynamic incremental pricing, 308–309

E

Early adopters, 216
Early majority, 216
Eastern Europe
bribery in, 40
department stores in, 237
market research obstacles, 115, 135–136
network marketing, 220
Pepsi versus Coca-Cola, 4, 34
promotions in, 121
social class changes, 102–103
transition to market economies, 11
Ecology, 88
Econometric models, 141–142
Economic and trade analysis, *323*
Economic Community of West African
States, 79–80
Economic development
disparity in world, 21, *27*
importance to regional integration, 70
levels of, 26–28

organizations supporting, 54–62
perspectives, 22–26
Economic growth, 11
Economic performance, political risk
and, 29–30
Economic policies, potential risks, 32
Economies of scale, 12
Ecuador, 120–121
Education, segmentation by, 153
Education allowances, 292–293
El Corte InglÇs, 237
Electronic retailing, 244
Eli Lilly, 6
Elite consumers, 154
Embargoes, 52. *See also* Trade barriers
Embassies, 294
Emerging markets, 26, 27–28
Emic instruments, 137
Employment, protecting, 46
Encoding, 254
Enculturation, 95
Energy drinks, 200
English language
in international advertising, 260, *262, 263*
role in global consumer culture, 109
for sales promotions, 277
Enigma, 146
Enola beans, 39
Entry modes, 168–177
Environmental analysis, 322, *323*
Environmental protection, 45, 46–47
EPRG framework, 6–8
ESP, 210
Esso, 52, 172
Established channels of distribution, 221
Ethnic diversity, 30–31
Ethnocentric orientation
of companies, 6–7
by consumers, 31, 107–108, 192–193
as obstacle to overseas marketing, 107–108
Etic instruments, 137
Euro
creation, 76–77, 79
effect on transactions, 303
Euroland, 79
European Atomic Energy Community, 71
European Bank for Reconstruction
and Development, 57, 59
European Central Bank, 82
European Coal and Steel Community, 71
European Commission
antidumping policies, 301
antitrust enforcement, 40
overview, 81–82
review of joint ventures, 174
European Council, 80
European Court and Commission
for Human Rights, 83
European Court of Justice, 36, 82
European Economic Area, 73
European Economic Community, 76
European Exchange Rate Mechanism, 76–77
European Free Trade Association, 73–74
European Monetary Union, 79. *See also* Euro
European Parliament, 80

European Union
advantages promoting integration, 69–70
creation, 76–77
imported beef ban, 47
languages for marketing to, 89
nickname, 44
as political union, 80–83
price differences within, 309
relations with EFTA, 73–74
trade growth within, 68
European Union Directive Concerning
Television Broadcasting, 264
Even-pricing strategies, 300
Event sponsorship, 274–275
Excess labor, protecting, 46
Excess productive capacity, protecting, 46
Exchange rates, 53, 303
Exclusives, cultural, 96, 98
Executive-judgment method, 268
Exhibitions, 279–281
Expatforum.com, 294
Expatriates
managing, 290–295
moving between assignments, 321
types, 285–287
Expatries-france.com, 294
Experience transfers, 12–13
Experimental research, 136
Expert opinions, 141
Exploratory research, 123
Expo 2000, 280–281
Export-Import Bank, 61, 226
Exporting methods, 168–169
Export management companies, 222
Export marketing, 5
Export merchants, 224
Export research, 116
Export Trading Company Act, 40, 222
Expropriation, 32–33
External secondary data, 128
Eye contact, 90, 288

F

Fast-food chains
differing perceptions, 106, *107*, 155
franchising success, 170–171
local adaptations, 187
Federal Express, 4
Feedback, 254
Femininity, 104–105
Fences, advertising on, 257
Feudalism, 23
Fiat, 169, 170
Films, product placement in, 261
Financial environments, segmentation by, 151
Firm-specific drivers, 8, 12–13
First-mover advantage, 212
First World, 26
Flextronics International, 176–177
Flowers, 100
Fluctuating exchange rates, 303
Focus group interviews, 132, 209
Food and Agriculture Organization, 60
Food prohibitions, 86, 92, 93
Food retailers, 241–244
Ford Focus, 184

Ford Motor Co. reorganization, 316
Forecasting sales, 122, 141–143
Foreign consumer culture positioning, 109
Foreign Corrupt Practices Act, 40
Foreign-country middlemen, 224
Foreign exchange permits, 54
Foreign ownership restrictions, 51
Foreign Sales Corporations, 223
Foreign trade zones, 62–64
Formal controls, 320–321
Fortress Europe, 44
France
leading department stores, 237
private-label brands in, 189
resistance to American culture, 107
specialty retailing in, 234
Franchising, 170–172
Frankfurt Book Fair, 280
Freeplay Energy, 205–206
Free trade agreements, 73–76. *See also* Regional
trade agreements
Free Trade Area of the Americas, 75
Free trade zones, 62–64
Freight forwarders, 225
Frito-Lay, 318, *319*
Full-cost pricing, 309
Functional equivalence, 125–127

G

Galeries Lafayette, *237*
Gallabeyas, 91
Gatorade, 274–275
GATT. *See* General Agreement on Tariffs
and Trade (GATT)
Gender roles, 94, 97–98, 101
General Agreement on Tariffs and Trade
(GATT), 55
General Agreement on Trade in Services
(GATS), 56
General Electric, 40, 81–82
General merchandise discount stores, 238–240
Generating ideas, 206–208
Geocentric orientation, 8
Geographic segmentation, 156
Germany, retailing in, 237, 246
Gestures, 90–91
Gevalia coffee, 167
Gift giving, 94, 100, 108
Gitanes, 121
Global branding, 184, 189–193
Global campaigns, 276–277
Global consumer culture, 108–109, 184
Global elite, 154
Global localization, 186–188
Global marketing, 6, 182
Global Risk Advisors, 33
Global standardization, 183–185
Global teenagers, 154
Glocalization, 186–188
Good-subject role, 132
Governments
advertising regulations, 261–264
approval of business transactions, 96–97
countertrade policies, 304–305
as data sources, 130
development organizations, 60–62

influence on counterfeiting, 196
influence on globalization, 14, 186
intellectual property rights protection by, 39
involvement in product
distribution, 225–226
potential threats to foreign businesses, 32–34
pricing laws, 301–303
restrictions on foreign nationals, 287
role in joint ventures, 172
stability, 29–31
Gray markets, 228–229, 300, 309
Greenfielding, 175
Greetings, cultural differences, 90
Grey Global Group, 266
Grocery retailers, 233, 241–244
Gross national product, *27*
Group of Eight (G8), 56–57
Growth stage, 202
Guest workers, marketing to, 89
Guggenheim Museum, 318
GUUAM grouping, 72
Gypsy Kings, 146
Gypsy retailers, *236*

H

Häagen-Dazs
new product ideas, 207
regional brands, 188
stereotyping in ads, 191
Handshaking, 90
Haptics, 90
Hard currency, 304
Harley-Davidson, 177
Harrods Buenos Aires, 175
Harrods London, 236–237
Head shaking, 91
Heineken, 159
Henkel, 264–266
Hennes & Mauritz, 234
High-context cultures, 92, 289–290
High Holidays, 93
High mass consumption stage, 22
Hijabs, 91
Hinduism, 92, 94
Historical method of budgeting, 268
History of dominance, 69
Hofstede dimensions, 103–105
Holidays, 93, 94
Home-country laws, 35, 40
Home-country middlemen, 221, 222–224
Home-country nationals, in sales force, 285–286
Home-leave allowances, 293
Home markets, pricing in, 308
Homes, advertising posters on, 258
Honeywell, 40, 81–82
Host-country laws, 35
Host-country middlemen, 221, 224
Host-country nationals, in sales force, 287
Hostile takeovers, European Parliament
restriction, 80
Housing allowances, 292
Hypermarkets, 241

I

IBM, 292
ICI, 308

Idea generation, 206–208
Ideology, 88
Ikea
    advertising agency approach, 265
    catalog sales, 241
    as category killer, 240
Image advertising, 275
Imperatives, cultural, 96–98
Imperialism, 23–24
Importance scoring, 156
Import/export analyses, 119–120
Import jobbers, 224
Import licenses, 49
Import quotas, 48
Incentives for expatriates, 292–294
Income, research questions about, 139
Incongruent interests, 30–31
India, software industry, 203
Indirect exporting, 168–169
Individualism, 105
Individual personality, 289
Indonesia, auto industry protectionism, 51
Industrialization, protectionism and, 45
Infant formula, 228, 278–279
Infant industry argument, 45, 46, 302
Inflation, effect on prices, 303
Infomercials, 259–260
Informal controls, 321
Information sources, 124–131
Infrastructures
    advertising media, 256–264
    catalog retailing, 246
    importance to regional integration, 69–70
    for marketing research, 131, 136
    marketing support, 151–152
    transportation and telecommunication, 10,
        103, 120–121
Innovation, 213–214, 321
Innovators, 216
Instrumental values, 95
Insurance, 33–34, 35
Intellectual property rights, 37–39, 56
Intelligence on country risk, 29
Interactive home shopping, 244
Interactive media, 253, 254
Inter-American Development Bank, 59
Interkama, 280
Intermodal transportation, 225
Internal secondary data, 127–128
International advertising agencies, 265–266
International buyer-seller relationship, 288
International Chamber of Commerce, 226
International communication process, 253
International conventions, 39
International Court of Justice, 36
International division structure, 318
International entry modes, 168–177
International Intellectual Property Alliance
        (IIPA), 37–38
International laws, 35. *See also* Legal
        environments
International marketing
    basic orientations, 6–8
    defined, 5
    development levels and, 26–28
    forces driving, 8–13

legal environment, 35–40 (*see also* Legal
        environments)
    levels of involvement, 5–6
    obstacles, 13–15
    operational controls, 319–321
    organizational design for, 317–319
    organizations supporting, 54–64
    overview of economic environment, 21
    plans, 165–168, 321–322, *323*
    political environment, 28–35 (*see also*
        Political environment)
    purposes, 4, 5
    research (*see* International marketing
        research)
International marketing research
    approaches, 131–136
    data analysis and interpretation, 139–140
    data collection, 137–139
    decision support systems, 140–143
    defined, 115
    defining problems and creating plans,
        123–124
    importance, 115, 209
    information sources, 124–131
    sampling, 139
    scope, 116–123
International marketing strategies, 165, *166*
International market potential studies, 122
International Monetary Fund (IMF), 57–59
International product life cycle, 201–203
International promotional mix, 253
International retailing, 234. *See also* Retailing
International Trade Administration, 61, 226
International Trade Center, 214–215
International trade organizations, 54–64
International travel, 184
Internet
    APEC and, 72
    as direct exporting tool, 169
    freight forwarding and customs
        clearance, 225
    innovation and, 214–215
    marketing alliances using, 177
    on-site salespeople versus, 287–288
    restrictions on, 47
    retailing formats, 244
    sales promotions, 278
Introduction stage, 202
Iran, 32
Islam, 36, 92

J

Jacobs coffee, 167, *213*
Japan
    cigarette advertising in, 128
    export trading companies, 222
    industry leaders from, 5
    leading department stores, 238
    marketing failures in, 114, 117
    price controls, 50
    vending machines, 245
JCPenney, 236
Jebel Ali Free Zone, 63–64
Joint ventures, 172–174, 242
Judaism, 92, 93, 94
Jurisdictions, 36–37

Jury of expert opinion, 141
J. Walter Thompson, 265

K

Kaffeehaus tradition, 171
Kazakstan, 120
Keiretsus, 222
KFC, 187–188
Kia Motors, 33
Kinesics, 90–91
Kiosks, 257, *258*
KMart, 241
Kosher requirements, 94
Kraft Foods
    Hong Kong distribution challenges, 120, 221
    marketing mix decisions, 167

L

Labor, protecting, 46
Labor costs, 12
Labor groups, 34
Lada automobiles, 169
Lag countries, 152, 201, 215–216
Laggards, 216
Land's End, 246
Language
    defined, 88
    as element of culture, 88–92
    English in ads, 260, *262, 263*
    importance to regional integration, 69
    for sales promotions, 277
Late majority, 216
Latin American Free Trade Association, 77
Latin American Integration Association, 77
Latin American norms, 99, 100, 101
Launching new products, 212–213
Lead countries, 152, 201, 215–216
Leased departments, 237, *238, 239*
Legal environments
    of advertising, 261–264, 267
    assessing, *323*
    effects on pricing, 301–303
    for retailing, 247–249
    for sales promotions, 278–279
    segmentation by, 151
    worldwide variability, 35–40
Length of product mix, 204
Levi Strauss, 207–208
Licensing, 49, 169–170
Likert scales, 137
Lipton tea, 204
Literacy, effects on marketing, 153, 267
LITMUS, 210–211
Local advertising agencies, 265, 266
Local campaigns, 277
Local consumer culture positioning, 109
Local content requirements, 51, 63
Local government development organizations,
        61–62. *See also* Governments
Local pricing, 309
Logistics alliances, 227
Low-context cultures, 92, 289–290
Low-income countries, 27
Low-price markets, 227–228
Lycra, 116–117

M

Maastricht Treaty, 76, 79
Macro-segmentation, 149–152
Madrid Arrangement, 39
Magazines, 259
Mail surveys, 136
Malls, 125, *126*, 240
Management
    of international marketing
        operations, 319–321
    personnel, 288–295
Managing agents, 224
Mandatory adaptations, 188
Mango, 234
Manufacturer's export agents, 223
Manufacturer's representatives, 224
Manufacturing alliances, 176–177
Maquiladoras, 64
Marc Controls, 299
Marine House, 294
Market-based transfer pricing, 302
Market economies, 11
Marketer acculturation, 96
Marketing alliances, 177
Marketing decision support systems, 140–143
Marketing mix decisions
    in international marketing plans, 166–167
    planning, 322
    at product launch, 212–213
Marketing plans, 165–168, 321–322, *323*
Market potential, segmentation by, 150
Marks & Spencer, 142–143
Marlboro, 14–15, 87
Marxist-Leninist economic model, 22, 23–25.
    See also Communism
Masculinity, 104–105
Mass consumption, 22
Materialism, cultural differences, 101–103
Matrix structure, 319
Maturity stage, 202–203
McCann Erickson, 9, 264
McDonald's
    boycotts of, 52
    domestication by, 33
    franchising success, 170
    geocentric orientation, 8
    image advertising, 275
    local adaptations, 187
    overseas image, 106, *107*, 273–274
McDonnell Douglas, 307
MCI Worldcom, 40, 82
Meals, business discussions during, 101
Measurability
    of market segments, 147–148
    of performance, 320
Media
    defined, 253
    infrastructures, 121–122, 256–264
    researching, 121–122
Media restrictions, 256–257
Mediation, 36–37
Mentos, *213*
Mercedes-Benz
    branch offices, 176
    gray market activities against, 228, 229

marketing mix, 185–186
    positive publicity, 274
Merchant middlemen, 224
MERCOSUR, 70, 71, 78
Mergers, 40, 81–82
Messe Dusseldorf, 280
Metro AG, 241
Micro-segmentation, 152–156
Microsoft, 197
Middle Eastern norms, 98–99, 100, 101
Middlemen, 221–224
Milka, 167
Ministry of Foreign Affairs, 60
Ministry of Trade, 60
Modular adaptation, 187
Modular campaigns, 277
Monetary union
    defined, 78
    examples, 76–77, 79–80, 303
Monochronic time, 98
Monopolistic capitalism, 24
Mont Blanc pens, 158, 160
Most-Favored-Nation status, 64
Mother henning, 168, 223
Motivation of expatriates, 292–294
Motorola
    home-country salesperson example, 286
    manufacturing alliances, 176–177
    reorganization, 316
Movies, product placement in, 261
Moving allowances, 293
Multidomestic market concept, 7
Multifiber Arrangement, 48–49
Multilateral agreements, 71–73
Multilevel marketing, 247
Multinational firms, imperialism and, 23–24
Multinational marketing, 5
Murdoch, Rupert, 259

N

NAFTA, 74–75
Name days, 94
Naming consultancies, 255
National character, 98–103, 289
National defense, trade barriers for, 47
Nationalism, 31
Nationalization, 33
National sovereignty, 28–29
NATO. *See* North Atlantic Treaty Organization
    (NATO)
Naturalistic inquiry, 132–133
Natural resources. *See* Environmental
    protection
NatWest, 274
Neckermann and Quelle, 240–241
NestlÇ, 278–279
Netherlands
    industry leaders from, 5
    leading department stores, 237
    as low-price market for Similac, 228, *309*
Network marketing, 220, 224, 247
Newness, degree of, 213–215
New product classification, 214
New product development. *See* Product
    development

News releases, 274
The New York Times, 161
Niche marketing, 158
Nigeria, mail survey obstacles, 136
Nike
    distribution savings, 185
    new product ideas, 207
    product development costs, 12
Noise, 254
Nomenklatura, 102–103
Nonautomatic import licenses, 49
Nongovernmental organizations, 226
Nonmandatory adaptations, 188
Nonpersonal media, 253
Nonstore retailing, 244–247
Nontariff barriers, 48–54
Nonverbal communication
    in buyer-seller relationships, 288
    elements of, 89–92
    marketing research on, 133
Norazi agents, 224
Norms, 96–98
North American Free Trade Agreement
    (NAFTA), 74–75
North Atlantic Treaty Organization (NATO), 72

O

Objective-and-task method, 267–268
Observational research, 132–133
Obstacles to internationalization, 13–15
Oculesics, 90
Odors, cultural differences, 91–92
Office Depot, 240
Office Max, 240
Office supply stores, 240
Off-price retailers, 240
Offset purchases, 307
Off-shore assembly plants, 64
Ofra Haza, 146
Oil industry, 21
Olfactions, 91–92
Online sales promotions, 278
OPEC, 72
Opel, 177
Open-ended questions, 137
OPIC, 34
Orderly market arrangements, 48–49
Organizational culture, 289
Organizational designs, 317–319
Organizational structures, 317
Organization for Economic Cooperation
    and Development, 72
Organization of Petroleum Exporting Countries
    (OPEC), 72
Orientations, 90
Otto Versand, 246
Outdoor umbrellas, 258, *260*
Outlet stores, 240
Overseas Private Investment Corporation
    (OPIC), 34
Ownership restrictions, 51

P

Packaging design research, 118–119
Palais de l'Europe, 83

Paper towels, 155–156
Paralinguistics, 91
Parallel barter, 307
Parallel imports, 227–229, 300
Parallel translation, 88, 138
Para-statal institutions, 80–83
Paratariff measures, 50
Parent-company nationals, 285–286
Paris Convention, 39
Pastry shops, 125
Patent and Trademark Office, 39
Patents, 37, 39
Penetration pricing, 310
People meters, 133
People's republics, 24
PepsiCo
    centralized purchasing, 185
    countertrade with U.S.S.R., 304, 307
    entry into Eastern European markets, 4, 34
    event sponsorships, 274
    modular sales promotions, 277
    new product launches, 211, 212, 213
    overseas product testing, 118
    questionable promotions, 278
    regiocentric orientation, 8
    strategic planning, 165
Pepsi Max, 211, 212, 213
Percent-of-sales method, 268
Performance measurement, 320
Performance standards, 320
Personality, 289
Personal media, 254
Personal selling, elements of, 288–290
Personal space, 89
Personnel
    managing, 288–295
    selecting, 285–288
Petrol Complex, 172
Peugeot bicycles, 254
Philip Morris, 120, 128, 221
Piggybacking, 168, 223
Pizza Hut
    local adaptations, 13, 187
    sales promotions, 255, 277
Plant/warehouse location studies, 120–121
Point-of-purchase displays, 276–277
Point-of-sale–based projections, 133, 142–143
Political environment
    assessing, 29–31, *323*
    effects on pricing, 302–303
    overview, 28–29
    risk management, 32–35
    segmentation by, 151
Political integration, 70–71
Political risk, 28. *See also* Political environment
Political union, 80–83
Polski Fiat, 170
Polycentric orientation, 7
Polychronic time, 98
Population, GNP distribution and, *27*
Porsche, 177
POS data, 133, 142–143
Positioning, 108–109, 159–161
Post adjustment, 292
Posters, 257

Postures, 90
Power distance, 103–104
Prayer, 93
Premiums, 121. *See also* Promotions
Press releases, 274
Price Club/Costco, 242
Price controls, 50
Price elasticity studies, 122
Price/quality positioning, 160
PriceSmart Inc., 242
Pricing
    to combat gray markets, 228
    environmental factors, 299–303
    production locations and, 299
    research, 122–123, 209
    retail variations, 248–249
    setting internationally, 308–310
Primary data, 124, 131
Primitive society stage, 23
Primus beer, 119
Print media, 253. *See also* Media
Private-label brands, 188–189
Proctor & Gamble
    Bounty promotion in Europe, 155–156
    differentiated targeting strategy, 157
    marketing challenges in Japan, 114, 117, 208
    positioning strategy, 159–160
    reorganization, 316
    research methods in Saudi Arabia, 134–135
    test marketing, 119
Product business analyses, 209
Product certification, 123
Product class positioning, 161
Product consistency, 204
Product-country stereotypes, 190–192
Product depth, 204
Product development
    concept evaluation and business
        analysis, 209
    costs as driver of internationalization, 12
    design, 209–210
    idea generation and screening, 205–209
    launch, 212–213
    overview, 204–206, *207*
    test marketing, 210–212
Product diffusion, 215–217
Product division structure, 318–319
Product length, 204
Product-level strategies, 165, *166*
Product life cycles
    as driver of internationalization, 12
    effect on marketing plans, 166
    stages, 201–203
Product line, 203
Product mix, 203–204
Product packaging design studies, 118–119
Product performance analogy, 142
Product placement, 261
Product research, 117–119
Product testing, 118
Product user positioning, 160
Product width, 204
Professional organizations, data from, 128–129
Profit analyses studies, 122
Promotion research, 121–122

Promotions. *See also* Advertising
    consumer sales, 276–279
    mix defined, 253
    process overview, 253–255
    publicity and public relations, 273–276
    trade shows and exhibitions, 279–281
Protectionism. *See also* Trade barriers
    arguments for, 45–47
    defined, 45
    effect on prices, 302–303
    tools, 47–54
Protestant religion, 92, 102
Prototypes, 209–210
Proxemics, 89
Psychographic segmentation, 154
Public appearances, 275–276
Publications, 29, 128
Publicity, 273–274
Public relations, 274–276
Punctuality, 98–99
Purchase behavior studies, 117
Pyramid schemes, 247

Q

Qualitative research, 131–133
Quality, country of origin and, 190
Quantitative research, 133–136
Questionnaires, 134–139
Quick restaurants, 161, *173*
Quotas, 48, 49–50

R

Radical innovations, 214
Ramadan, 36, 93
Rapp Collins Worldwide, 266
Receivers, 253
Recruiting expatriates, 290–291
Red Bull, 200
Regiocentric orientation, 7–8
Regional character, 98–103
Regional Economic Commissions, 60
Regional integration
    determinants, 69–71
    levels of, 71–83
Regional standardization, 185–186
Regional trade agreements. *See also* European
        Union; MERCOSUR; NAFTA
    determinants, 69–71
    as driver of internationalization, 9–10
    intellectual property rights protection, 38–39
    membership as risk factor, 151
    tariffs and, 14
Regulation
    of advertising, 261–264, 267
    of pricing, 301–303
    of retailing, 247–248
    of sales promotions, 278–279
Reliability
    of advertising media, 256
    of research instruments, 138–139
    of secondary data, 130, 147–148
Religion, 92–94
Renault, 169
Repatriation, 290, 294–295

Repatriation allowances, 293
Repressive regimes, 30
Research. *See* International marketing research
Research approaches, 131
Research problems and objectives, 123–124
Retailer brands, 188–189
Retailing
current issues, 247–249
food, 233, 241–244
general merchandise, 234–241
nonstore, 244–247
overview of internationalization, 233–234
Reverse culture shock, 295
Rice price controls, 50
Risk
new product adoption and, 216
political, 28, 29–31 (*see also* Political environment)
uncertainty avoidance and, 104
Rolls Royce, 118
Roma, *236*
Romania
exporting products from, 119
marketing failures in, 114
Pepsi Max launch, 213
Roma retailers, *236*
Rostow modernization model, 22, *25*
Rotating managers, 321
Royal Ahold, 242
RUNDT's World Business Intelligence, 29
Russia, 56–57, 123

S
Sabanci Holdings, 151
Salesforce compensation, quota, and territory studies, 122
Salesforce composite estimates, 141
Sales forecasting, 122, 141–143
Salespeople
managing, 288–295
researching, 122
selecting, 285–288, 290–291
variability, 249
Sales potential studies, 122
Sales promotions, 276–279
Sample sizes, 139
Sampling frames, 139
Sampling plans, 139
Sampling procedures, 139
Sampling units, 139
Sam's Club, 242
Samsung, 106
Sanctions, 52. *See also* Trade barriers
Santa Claus, 108
Saris, 91
Saudi Arabia, 87, 134–135
Scanner data, 133, 142–143
Screening new product ideas, 208–209
Secondary data, 124, 127–131
Second World, 26
Segmentation
basic requirements, 147–149
defined, 147
macro level, 149–152
micro level, 152–156
Self-reference criterion, 13–14, 106–107

Semantic differential scales, 137
Senders, 253
September 11 attacks, 34–35
Service barriers, 193
Service markets, WTO role, 56
Service mix, managing, 203–204
Service stereotypes, 191–192
Sex in advertising, 264
Sha' ria, 36
Shenzhen Electronics Group, 203
Shipping containers, 10
Shopping bags, advertising on, 258, *259*
Shopping malls, 125, *126*
Shopping practices, 248–249
Siestas, 99
Similac, 228, *309*
Simulated test marketing, 210–211
Skimming strategies, 310
Slavery-based societies, 23
"Smart sanctions," 52
Smirnoff Vodka, 277
Social class, 101–103, 153
Socialism, 24, 25, 36
Socialist republics, 24
Socializing, cultural differences, 101, 288
Social structure, 88
Soft currency, 304
Sogo shoshas, 222
South African Customs Union, 76
South Carolina, 61–62
Southern African Development Community, 75
Southern Cone Common Market (MERCOSUR), 70, 71, 78
Sovereignty, 28–29
Soviet Union (former). *See* Commonwealth of Independent States (CIS)
Spain
class structures, 102
leading department stores, 237
siestas, 99
Special economic zones, 64
Specialized markets, 235–236
Specialty stores, 234–235
Spoken/written language, 88–89
Sprint, 40, 82
SRI Consulting Business Intelligence, 154
Sri Lanka, 151
Stability
of market segments over time, 148–149
political, 29–31 (*see also* Political environment)
Standardization
of advertising, 266–267
of pricing, 309
of products, 183–188
Standards, 12, 51
Staples, 240
Starbucks, 171
State Department, 61
State government development organizations, 61–62
Status concern, 101–103
Steel industry, 21, 50
Stihl, 176
Stolichnaya vodka, 304, 307
Strategic alliances, 164, 176–177

Strategies, 165, *166*
Structural adjustments, 58
Studies of premiums, coupons, and deals, 121
Subsidiaries
autonomy of, 320
avoidance of duties with, 10
in polycentric orientation, 7
Substantiality, 148
Suchard, 167
Sudan, 151
Sunbeam Corporation, 118
Supermarkets, 137, 241
Superstores, 241–242
Survey research, 134–136
Sweepstakes, 278
Swing credits, 306
Switch trading, 306
Switzerland, 74, 156

T
Taiwan, 238
Take-off stage, 22
Target marketing. *See also* Segmentation
defined, 147, 149
screening, selection, and strategies, 156–159
Tariffs. *See also* Trade barriers
basic features, 47–48
free trade zones and, 63
as obstacle to internationalization, 14
Taxation, 248
Technology
as driver of internationalization, 10
influence on counterfeiting, 196
market segmentation by, 151–152
Telecommunication infrastructures, 10, 256–257
Telemarketing, 254
Television home shopping, 245, 259–260
Television programming
internationalization, 10, 258–259
restrictions on, 47
Terminal values, 95
Terrorism, 34–35
Tesco, 233, 241–242
Test marketing, 119, 210–212
Themes for positioning, 159
Third-country nationals, 286–287
"Third freedom" rights, 51
Third World, 26. *See also* Developing countries
Tiffany's, 245–246
Tiger Mart, 172
Time orientation, 98–99
Time-saving devices, 126–127
Time series models, 141–142
Timing of new product launch, 212
Toblerone, 167
Touch, in communication, 90
Trade barriers
avoidance with subsidiaries, 10
effect on prices, 302–303
as obstacle to internationalization, 14
for services, 193
tools, 32, 47–54
WTO efforts against, 56
Trademarks, 38, 39
Trade policies, 32

Trade-Related Aspects of Intellectual Property Rights (TRIPS), 39
Trade secrets, 38
Trade shows, 279–281
Trading companies, 222
Traditional society stage, 22
Training expatriates, 292
Transfer pricing, 302
Transitional society stage, 22
Translation
    challenges, 88–89
    of local advertising, 265
    of promotional messages, 255
    required for sales promotions, 278
    of research instruments, 138
Transportation firms, 225
Transportation infrastructures
    distribution challenges, 227
    as driver of internationalization, 10
    effects on marketing messages, 103
    plant/warehouse location and, 120–121
Travel, global standardization and, 184
Treaty of Rome, 76
Trialability, 215
Tricon companies, 187
Turkmenistan, 120

U

Umbrellas, advertising on, 258, *260*
Uncertainty avoidance, 104
Undifferentiated targeting, 158–159
Unemployment, protecting against, 46
Unilever
    matrix structure, 319
    product dimensions, 204, 205*t*
Union of Four, 72
United Kingdom, private-label brands in, 189
United Nations Conference on Trade and Development, 60
United Nations development organizations, 59–60
United Nations Development Program, 59

United Nations Industrial Development Organization, 60
United States
    Commerce Department activities, 61, 226, 280, 301
    development agencies, 60–62, 226
    embassies, 294
    export trading company model, 222
    Patent and Trademark Office, 39
    role in world economy, 21
    State Department, 61
United States Trade and Development Agency, 226
Urban-rural distinctions, 124, 153
Uruguay Round, 55
Usage segmentation, 155
U.S. Commercial Service, 226
Use positioning, 160
User positioning, 160
User status segmentation, 155–156

V

Vacation times, 99
Validity of secondary data, 130
VALS 2, 154
Values, 95–96, 267
Variable-cost pricing, 309
Vending machines, 244–245
Venice Biennale, 280
Vodacom, 274
Vodafone, 274
Volkswagen, 168–169
Voluntary export restraints, 49–50
Voluntary import expansions, 49
Volvo, 187

W

Wal-Mart
    international presence, 233, 239, 241
    pricing challenged, 302
    superstores, 241

Warehouse clubs, 242
Warsaw Pact, 80
Webb-Pomerene Associations, 223
Weight Watchers products, 188
West African Economic and Monetary Union, 79
Wholesale clubs, 242
Wholly owned subsidiaries, 175
Width of product mix, 204
Wind-up radios, 205–206
Women's roles
    cultural norms, 97–98, 101
    depictions in advertising, 134, 135*t*
    religion and, 94
Wonder Bra, 148
World Bank, 26–27, 57–59
World Beat, 146
World Expositions, 280–281
World market interdependence, 21
World Trade Center attack, 34–35
World Trade Organization
    free trade role, 44
    import license requirements, 49
    intellectual property rights protection, 37, 38–39
    major functions, 55–56
Worldwide regional division structure, 318
World Wide Web. *See* Internet

Y

Yoplait, 109

Z

Zapata, 174
Zara, 234